Questions & Answers
Copyright Law

CAROLINA ACADEMIC PRESS
QUESTIONS & ANSWERS SERIES

Questions & Answers: Administrative Law,
Third Edition
Linda D. Jellum, Karen A. Jordan

Questions & Answers: Antitrust
Shubha Ghosh

Questions & Answers: Bankruptcy
Second Edition
Mary Jo Wiggins

Questions & Answers: Business Associations,
Second Edition
Douglas M. Branson

Questions & Answers: Civil Procedure,
Fourth Edition
William V. Dorsaneo, III, Elizabeth Thornburg

Questions & Answers: Constitutional Law,
Third Edition
Paul E. McGreal, Linda S. Eads, Charles W. Rhodes

Questions & Answers: Contracts,
Second Edition
Scott J. Burnham

Questions & Answers: Copyright Law,
Second Edition
Dave Fagundes, Robert C. Lind

Questions & Answers: Criminal Law, Third Edition
Emily Levine, Paul Marcus

Questions & Answers: Criminal Procedure —
Police Investigation, Third Edition
Neil P. Cohen, Michael J. Benza, Wayne A. Logan

Questions & Answers: Criminal Procedure —
Prosecution and Adjudication, Third Edition
Neil P. Cohen, Michael J. Benza, Wayne A. Logan

Questions & Answers: Environmental Law
Dru Stevenson

Questions & Answers: Evidence, Fourth Edition
David P. Leonard, Paul Giannelli

Questions & Answers: Family Law, Second Edition
Mark Strasser

Questions & Answers: Federal Estate & Gift
Taxation, Second Edition
Elaine Gagliardi

Questions & Answers: Federal Income Tax
David L. Cameron

Questions & Answers: The First Amendment,
Third Edition
Russell L. Weaver, William D. Araiza

Questions & Answers: Intellectual Property,
Second Edition
Gary Myers, Lee Ann W. Lockridge

Questions & Answers: International Law
Rebecca Bratspies

Questions & Answers: Patent Law
Cynthia Ho

Questions & Answers: Payment Systems,
Second Edition
Timothy R. Zinnecker

Questions & Answers: Professional Responsibility,
Fourth Edition
Patrick Emery Longan

Questions & Answers: Property, Second Edition
John Nagle

Questions & Answers: Remedies
Rachel Janutis, Tracy Thomas

Questions & Answers: Secured Transactions,
Third Edition
Bruce A. Markell, Timothy R. Zinnecker

Questions & Answers: Taxation of Business Entities
Kristofer Neslund, Nancy Neslund

Questions & Answers: Torts, Fourth Edition
Anita Bernstein

Questions & Answers: Trademark and
Unfair Competition
Vince Chiappetta

Questions & Answers: Wills, Trusts, and Estates,
Third Edition
Thomas Featherston

Questions & Answers
Copyright Law

SECOND EDITION

Dave Fagundes
Robert C. Lind

CAROLINA ACADEMIC PRESS
Durham, North Carolina

ISBN: 978-1-63281-548-4
eBook ISBN: 978-1-63281-549-1
LCCN: 2018939783

Carolina Academic Press, LLC
700 Kent Street
Durham, North Carolina 27701
Telephone (919) 489-7486
Fax (919) 493-5668
www.cap-press.com

Printed in the United States of America

Dedication

To JLR and LJF—DF

To Larry Sullivan, a professor who enjoyed copyright law, and those who study it.
And to Joseph De Marco, my best copyright student.—R.C.L.

Contents

Questions

Requirements for Copyright Protection

1.   Musician has recently created a musical jingle she hopes to license to a greeting card company for its television advertising campaign. Musician has memorized the lyrics and music that make up the musical composition and has often sung the jingle from memory for a large number of friends at parties. Musician has not written down the lyrics or music, nor has she recorded the musical composition. Is the jingle protected by a federal copyright?

     (A)   No, because Musician has not fixed the jingle in a tangible medium.

     (B)   No, because Musician publicly performed the jingle prior to its registration with the Copyright Office.

     (C)   Yes, because copyright law protects a work upon its creation.

     (D)   Yes, because the musical composition clearly constitutes original expression.

2.   Musician has recently composed an original musical composition that she recorded by singing the composition herself, and recording her singing it on her personal digital audio recorder. She has not performed the composition for anyone, nor has she shared the recording with anyone. She has not placed a copyright notice on the digital recording. Is the musical composition protected by a federal copyright?

     (A)   Yes, because the musical composition is sufficiently fixed in a copy.

     (B)   Yes, because the musical composition is sufficiently fixed in a phonorecord.

     (C)   No, because the recording is not accompanied by a proper copyright notice.

     (D)   No, because no one can see the musical composition in the digital recording.

3.   Poet wrote a poem honoring the first butterfly of the season. After writing the poem by hand in a notebook, Poet placed it in a desk drawer. A month later, Poet recited the poem to members of his local literary society who unanimously commented that the poem was poorly crafted. That evening, in a fit of embarrassment, Poet ripped the page containing the poem from the notebook and burned the page in his fireplace. After Poet burned the poem, is there still a valid federal copyright protection in the poem?

     (A)   No, because the poem was poorly crafted.

     (B)   No, because the poem is no longer fixed in a tangible medium of expression.

(C) Yes, because the poem had been fixed in a tangible medium of expression.

(D) Yes, because Poet believed the poem had literary merit at the time he wrote it.

4.   Songwriter is performing a live concert in an auditorium. During the concert, she sings a new musical composition she has composed, but not yet recorded or written down. Unbeknownst to Songwriter, Audience Member is sitting in the back of the auditorium recording the performance. Is Songwriter's musical composition protected by federal law?

5.   One recent evening in Los Angeles, Comedian included in her act at a comedy club a 10-minute extemporaneous original comedy routine concerning the recent firing of a government official. The content of the routine was created on the spur of the moment. Comedian had not written out the material, nor did she record the routine when she presented the material at the comedy club. Is Comedian's extemporaneous comedy routine protected?

(A) The routine is protected by federal copyright because a 10-minute comedy routine undoubtedly includes expression as well as ideas.

(B) The routine is protected by federal copyright because it is a literary work.

(C) The routine is protected by state common-law copyright because it was merely a performance.

(D) The routine is protected by state common-law copyright because a 10-minute comedy routine undoubtedly includes original expression as well as ideas.

6.   Currently, Novelist A lives in San Francisco where he wrote *The Great West Coast Novel*. One year later, Novelist B, who is based in New York City, wrote and published *The Great East Coast Novel*. Novelist A subsequently registered the copyright in *The Great West Coast Novel*, which remains in manuscript form, with the Copyright Office. The contents of both novels are creative and are identical. Neither Novelist knows the other and neither has seen the other's work. Who owns the copyright in the expression of the novels?

(A) Both Novelist A and Novelist B own the copyrights in their respective literary works.

(B) Novelist A, because *The Great West Coast Novel* was created first.

(C) Novelist B, because *The Great East Coast Novel* was published first.

(D) Novelist A, because *The Great West Coast Novel* was registered first.

7.   Artist has created a new work. It is a five-pointed star cut out of cardboard. Artist has cut a square out of the middle of the star, permitting the insertion of a small photograph. Is Artist's creation protected by copyright?

(A) No, because the square cut-out renders the star an unprotected useful article.

(B) No, because the star is a common shape.

(C) Yes, because the material used to create a work does not affect its copyrightability.

(D) Yes, because it is a sculptural work.

8. Videographer happened upon the scene of a very recent car crash involving a well-known television star, who was obviously inebriated. Videographer filmed the scene with the video function of her cell phone. The video was two minutes in length. The quality of the video's audio and images was poor. Videographer uploaded the video onto a website that permits the public to view submitted videos of celebrities in candid, often embarrassing, moments. The best argument for denying copyright protection for the video is:

(A) The audiovisual work was of poor quality.

(B) The length of the audiovisual work is too short for copyright protection.

(C) The audiovisual work lacks sufficient originality.

(D) Uploading the video onto such a public website constitutes an abandonment of copyright.

9. A motion picture was recently released for general exhibition that depicted a used guitar store on the moon after the people of Earth had colonized it. Two years later, a dramatic television series that depicted a small alien civilization engaged in intergalactic space travel included a stop on the moon where one of the aliens purchased a guitar from a used guitar store. The signage, size, and contents of the stores differed substantially, as did the store's proprietor and customers. Has the television series infringed on the copyright of the motion picture?

(A) Yes, because it is the similarities between the two works that are at issue, not the dissimilarities.

(B) Yes, because the idea of a used guitar store on the moon is novel.

(C) No, because television is a different medium from motion pictures.

(D) No, because once the motion picture was released to the public, anyone has the right to use ideas found in the motion picture.

10. Museum Services Corporation markets and services the Atmospheric Recordation Device (ARD). The device provides a continuous daily measurement of room temperature and humidity needed by museums to conserve their collections. ARD provides continuous markings on a specially designed roll of graph paper on which the device prints time measurements as well as temperature and humidity levels. A competitor, Collections Management, Inc., markets rolls of paper suitable for use with the ARD that has an identical design to the paper marketed by Museum Services Corporation. Can Museum Services Corporation enforce a claim of copyright infringement in the graph paper against Collections Management, Inc.?

11. In 1975, Artist created a painting of Elvis Presley on velvet. After receiving numerous compliments on her artistic achievement, Artist offered it for sale at a local arts and craft

show. What actions could Artist have taken to vest federal copyright protection in the painting?

12. A work has been fixed in a physical disc. Has it been fixed in a copy or a phonorecord?

    (A) Copy.

    (B) Phonorecord.

    (C) Neither a copy nor a phonorecord.

    (D) It depends.

13. Sarah, a professional poker player, dreamed of writing a book about her life in the high-stakes world of professional gambling. She often told Fred, her boyfriend of two years, the details of how she would structure the book and the anecdotes she would include. After Sarah's recent unexpected death, Fred wrote a book about Sarah's life in the gambling world, based entirely on his memories of his conversations with Sarah. Because Fred has an outstanding memory, his book nearly verbatim reflects the content that Sarah related to him during their conversations about her prospective book.

    Sarah's mother, her only surviving relative, is now suing Fred for copyright infringement. Assuming Sarah's mother has standing to sue, what is the mother's likelihood of success?

14. Artist has created a digital artwork that appears on a large high definition plasma screen installed in a local public museum. The screen features a random combination of images sent to it by 10 computers, each with a different bank of images contained on its hard drive. Photographer has taken unauthorized photographs of the images appearing on the plasma screen and sells them in his art gallery. Artist sues Photographer for copyright infringement. Artist's lawsuit will be:

    (A) Unsuccessful, because the images comprising the digital artwork are not fixed in a single object or device.

    (B) Unsuccessful, because the work has been dedicated to the public domain.

    (C) Successful, because each image is capable of being reproduced.

    (D) Successful, because the photographs taken by Photographer have fixed the images in a tangible medium.

15. Pursuant to an exclusive license, Television Station broadcasts a day baseball game live from the local ballpark. The live broadcast is comprised of images from several television cameras located in the ballpark from which the director of the television program selects the images to be included in the broadcast signal. It is not simultaneously recorded. Bar Owner makes a digital video recording of the game and plays it at night for his customers. Has Bar Owner infringed the federal copyright in Television Station's audiovisual work?

(A) Yes, because the director's camera location and image selection are sufficiently original.

(B) No, because the Television Station did not record the broadcast at the same time it transmitted the game to its viewers.

(C) Yes, but only if the broadcast contains a sufficient amount of commentary by an announcer.

(D) Yes, but only if the bar is larger than 3,700 square feet.

16. Law Student is enrolled in a copyright law course and sends numerous emails to her professor asking substantive questions about the course. Professor responds to each email, but does not print a copy of his answers. The following year, Law Student compiles Professor's answers and sells printed copies of them without Professor's permission. Are Professor's email responses sufficiently fixed for federal copyright protection?

17. Arranger has been hired to provide piano accompaniment to Singer on her upcoming concert tour. Singer has had difficulty reaching the high notes of the opening musical composition. Arranger made the musical composition easier to sing by transposing it from the key of C into the key of A. The transposition of the composition from the key of C to the key of A is easily accomplished by applying a simple, familiar formula that renders the transposition with mathematical precision. Does the transposition of the musical composition into the key of A create a derivative work that is protected by copyright?

(A) No, because transposing a musical composition from one key to another is a mechanical exercise that is not protected by copyright.

(B) No, because the lyrics remain the same.

(C) Yes, because the notes of the resulting musical work are different from the original musical work.

(D) Yes, because only a person knowledgeable in music would have the ability to transpose a musical composition from one key to another.

18. In 1980, Verso conceives and writes the haiku *Leaves of Autumn* on rice paper in ink. Verso deems the work inadequate and puts it in his desk drawer. One day, Verso's friend Poetaster snoops around in Verso's office and runs across *Leaves of Autumn*. Poetaster copies the work verbatim onto a piece of note paper, and later publishes it under his own name in *Poetry* magazine. Verso is incensed that Poetaster has copied his haiku, and sues Poetaster for copyright infringement. Poetaster responds by showing that in 1979, a poet named Quarto wrote a haiku titled *Rainbow Leaves* that is identical to Verso's haiku. Verso admits that the 1979 and 1980 haikus are identical, but truthfully avers that when he wrote *Leaves of Autumn* in 1980, he had never seen or heard of Quarto's *Rainbow Leaves*. Who will prevail in the infringement suit, Verso or Poetaster?

(A) Verso will prevail because *Leaves of Autumn* possesses the necessary degree of creativity sufficient to meet the standard of originality.

(B) Verso will prevail because *Leaves of Autumn* possessed the necessary degree of creativity sufficient to meet the standard of originality, and that creativity originated with Verso.

(C) Poetaster will prevail because Verso's haiku was identical to a previously created haiku.

(D) Poetaster will prevail because Verso will not be able to prove that Poetaster copied Verso's *Leaves of Autumn*, as opposed to Quarto's *Rainbow Leaves*.

19. A basic rule of copyright law is that ideas cannot be protected, only the expression of ideas may be protected. Are any legal protections available for ideas or the use of ideas?

20. French Novelist has written a lengthy murder mystery novel in French. French Novelist has assigned the English translation rights to Translator, who has yet to translate the novel. French Novelist retained all other rights. Without authorization, Publisher, an American, has translated the French novel into English and has published the English version of the novel. Publisher has entered into a settlement with French Novelist, but has refused to settle with Translator. Publisher claims that its translation was a merely mechanical process and does not constitute an actionable adaptation of the French novel. If Translator sues Publisher for copyright infringement, in the majority of jurisdictions the lawsuit will be:

(A) Successful, because there is necessarily sufficient originality in Publisher's translation of the French novel into English to constitute an unauthorized derivative work.

(B) Successful, because Publisher's translation of the French novel and its publication of the English translation necessarily constitute an unauthorized reproduction.

(C) Unsuccessful, because the selection of an English word or phrase automatically follows from the French word or phrase being translated.

(D) Unsuccessful, because Translator has yet to create an English translation and, therefore, does not have standing to sue Publisher for copyright infringement.

21. Writer is writing an article about the discrimination suffered by female police officers within the police department. In the course of that work, Writer interviewed Police Detective. Writer asked Police Detective questions regarding his activities as a police officer and his attitude toward female officers. Police Detective's comments included racial epithets and derogatory remarks about women. Writer openly tape-recorded the interview, using a cassette recorder that she had purchased for interviewing purposes. The recorder had a built-in microphone. Writer supplied the cassette tapes used to tape the interviews, positioned the recorder in front of Police Detective, turned the recorder on and off, and operated its recording volume. Writer has assigned the print publishing rights to the interview to Publisher. Writer's tape-recording of the interview was subsequently stolen by Audio Company, which then sold copies of the interview on the Internet without permission. Can Writer successfully sue Audio Company for infringing her copyright in the interview?

22.   Record Company created an analog sound recording of a musical composition titled *Megaron* in 1965. Recently, Record Company released a digital version of the sound recording of *Megaron*. The digital sound recording was created with the aid of a computerized mastering machine that converted the 1965 analog recording into a digital recording. An employee of Record Company "equalized" the digital recording by listening to it and adjusting the volume, tones, and acoustics of the sounds captured in the digital recording. The employee raised the level of the bass guitar and reduced the level of the snare drum. No other adjustments were made to the digital recording. Once the digital recording had been equalized, it was saved to a separate computer file, then sold in .mp3 format on Record Company's website. Pirate.com has begun to offer this digital version of the *Megaron* recording as a free download without the authorization of Record Company. If Record Company sues Pirate.com for federal copyright infringement, will it succeed?

23.   Composer is the author of a musical play titled *Flash, Trash & Cash*. The musical play is based on the true story of an aspiring singer who tragically dies in an avalanche. Composer is concerned that *Flash, Trash & Cash* is also the title of an earlier published fictional novel, protected by copyright, that is based in the milieu of the exotic dance clubs that populate the east coast of the United States. Should Composer be concerned about a possible claim of copyright infringement resulting from her choice of title for her musical play?

       (A)   No, the subject matter of the two works is not substantially similar.

       (B)   No, titles of books are not protected by copyright.

       (C)   Yes, the titles are identical.

       (D)   Yes, the book's title was used prior to the title's use in the musical play.

24.   Book Publisher has published a cookbook that contains 50 recipes featuring the use of beets. Each recipe lists the necessary ingredients for the dish as well as directions for preparation and nutritional information, without any creative narrative. Newspaper has included in its food section recipes for three of the dishes found in the cookbook. Although there are slight differences in the listing of ingredients, the recipes published by Newspaper will produce substantially the same final products as those described in the cookbook. Does Book Publisher have a valid basis for bringing a copyright infringement action against Newspaper?

       (A)   No, because the recipes are not protected by copyright.

       (B)   No, because the recipes constitute useful articles.

       (C)   Yes, because the final products are substantially the same.

       (D)   Yes, because the recipes are substantially similar.

25.   *Space Station* is a video game in which a spaceship maneuvers through obstacles such as alien space vehicles, space creatures, black holes, gravitational fields, and meteors to return to its space station. *Hangar* is a video game in which a World War I biplane maneuvers through obstacles such as anti-aircraft shells, dirigibles, telegraph lines, tall trees,

and flocks of birds to return to its hangar. For each and every game element in the *Space Station* game there is a corresponding game element in *Hangar*. The relationship of the game elements in *Hangar* is identical to the relationship of game elements in *Space Station*. The rules for *Space Station* printed on the screen are: "Use joystick to move spaceship up, down, forwards and backwards. The game will end after the destruction of the third spaceship. An additional spaceship is acquired after 30,000 points are accumulated." The rules for *Hangar* are: "Use the joystick to move the biplane up, down, forwards and backwards. The game will end after the third biplane is lost. An additional biplane is won after 25,000 points." The manufacturer of *Hangar* has admitted to playing *Space Station*, but has had no access to the game's computer program. What is the likely outcome if the copyright owner of *Space Station* sues the manufacturer of *Hangar* for the copyright infringement?

26.   Hunter creates realistic turkey decoys for a living. He has recently noticed that the turkey decoys sold by Competitor are substantially similar, although not exactly identical, to his decoys. Will Hunter be successful if he brings a copyright infringement action against Competitor and can show that Competitor had access to Hunter's decoys?

(A) Yes, because sculptural works are copyrightable subject matter.

(B) Yes, because the reproduction right protects against copies that are substantially similar.

(C) No, because anyone can copy items found in nature.

(D) No, because depictions of natural objects have limited copyright protection.

27.   *All Fall Down* is a best-selling novel written and published by Novelist in 2015. The novel tells the story of the discovery of an experimental plastic material that is used by a leading architectural firm to construct the world's tallest building in Los Angeles. In the novel, shortly after its completion, the building suddenly melts on the hottest day of the year, smothering thousands of people and shutting down the city for months. In 2017, Studio released *The Collapsible Tower*, a motion picture about the discovery of an experimental plastic material that is used to construct a Presidential Library in Washington, D.C. In the film, one of the team of scientists who made the discovery is a member of a spy network. The spy has also discovered a solvent that causes the plastic material to immediately liquefy. During the dedication of the Library, the spy applies the solvent to its structural supports, causing the building to melt, smothering the President and her cabinet. Does Novelist have a viable claim that the film infringed the copyright in his novel?

(A) No, because only unprotected elements were used in the film.

(B) No, because the defendant's work is in a different medium.

(C) Yes, because the idea of a melting plastic building was taken from the novel.

(D) Yes, because Studio is presumed to have had access to the plaintiff's novel.

28.   Young Attorney was asked by a client to draft a copyright mortgage agreement, something Young Attorney had never encountered in her short legal career. Young Attorney went to the nearest law library to look for a form book that contained such an agreement. She found a copy of the *Entertainment Law Form Book* that was published by Publisher. Young Attorney photocopied the pages containing the copyright mortgage agreement, brought them back to her office, inputted the language of the form agreement into her computer verbatim and filled in her client's information. Publisher recently registered the *Entertainment Law Form Book* with the Copyright Office. Is Young Attorney liable for infringing the copyright in the *Entertainment Law Form Book*?

(A)   Yes, because Young Attorney reproduced protected material without the permission of the copyright owner.

(B)   No, because under the "use doctrine" enunciated by the Supreme Court in *Baker v. Selden*, the use of such a work in the manner intended by the copyright owner does not constitute a copyright infringement.

(C)   Yes, because Young Attorney did not own the copy of the *Entertainment Law Form Book* that was used to make the copies of the form agreement.

(D)   No, because such form contracts are not protected by copyright.

29.   Author wrote *Shadow Land*, a biographical literary work about the life of Frances Farmer, an independent, free-spirited actress who fought against the conventions of her time. In *Shadow Land*, Author described how Farmer was institutionalized by her mother, underwent a lobotomy, and emerged from the psychiatric facility with her spirit broken. *Shadow Land* was marketed as the "true story" of Frances Farmer. After *Shadow Land* was published, Producer produced *The Farmer Story*, a motion picture based on the life of Francis Farmer. The motion picture presented a dramatization of Farmer's lobotomy and its aftermath that closely resembled the description of those events in the literary work. Author has now sued for copyright infringement. Producer is defending the lawsuit on the basis that she only used the relevant facts that were published in the literary work. Author argues that the lobotomy and its aftermath were not facts, but fictional elements that Author had created. Will Author be successful with his copyright infringement claim?

(A)   No, because facts are not protectable by copyright.

(B)   Yes, because fictional elements are protectable by copyright.

(C)   No, because fictional elements that are presented by the copyright owner as fact will be treated as though they were facts.

(D)   Yes, because the elements at issue were important plot points in the literary work.

30.   Telecom sells various ringtones that are downloaded to the customer's cell phone at the time of purchase. One of the ringtones offered by Telecom consists of one line of recorded dialogue from the motion picture *Scarface* spoken by actor Al Pacino, who portrayed the character Tony Montana in that film: "Say hello to my little friend!" Telecom made an audio

recording of the dialogue, converted it into a ringtone, and offered it for sale in .mp3 form on their website. Telecom did all this without the permission of Universal Pictures, the owner of the copyright in the motion picture. If Universal Pictures sues Telecom for copyright infringement, Universal Pictures will likely be:

(A) Unsuccessful, because motion pictures have no public performance rights.

(B) Successful, because the recorded dialogue is the most memorable line of dialogue from *Scarface*.

(C) Successful, because the motion picture *Scarface* is protected by copyright.

(D) Unsuccessful, because the line of dialogue is not protected by copyright.

31. Uncle Unique lives in Pleasant Valley, Wisconsin, and is the town's unofficial greeter. He spends his days walking in the tourist section of town, saying hello to visitors and providing directions while offering advice and opinions. Every day the bearded Uncle Unique wears his long hair in a braid and the same clothes: a floppy weathered hat, a poncho, large boots, and paisley pants. He always carries a copy of *In Watermelon Sugar*, a novel written by famed Wisconsin novelist Richard Brautigan, and quotes from it throughout the day.

Recently, Network aired a new cable series titled *Pleasant Valley* that depicts a fictional town in Oregon with an ensemble of interesting characters. One of the main characters, Uncle Natural, looks exactly like Uncle Unique and carries a copy of *Trout Fishing in America*, another novel written by Richard Brautigan. It turns out that one of *Pleasant Valley*'s producers had earlier vacationed in the real Pleasant Valley, had met Uncle Unique and had taken a photograph of him with his permission. Later, when the *Pleasant Valley* project was in development, the producer shared his photograph of Uncle Unique with the series' writers and instructed them to make the lovable character Uncle Natural look like the person in the photograph. Does Uncle Unique have a copyright infringement claim against Network?

32. Two years ago, Millennium Studios released its motion picture *FangTastic!*. The film deals with a modern day vampire who lives in a trailer park and details her efforts to have a romantic relationship with a human. Her lifestyle is chronicled throughout the motion picture: sleeping in a coffin during the day, inability to withstand sunlight, living off the blood drained from the necks of humans with her long fangs, superior physical strength, aversion to silver, garlic and crosses, and the threat of death via stake through the heart.

Recently, De Marco Studios has produced *Casket Capers*, a motion picture that deals with a successful married mortician who is a modern-day vampire and uses his fangs to drain the blood from the bodies entrusted to his care. The extremely strong mortician must sleep in his coffin during the day, cannot attend funerals during the day due to his inability to withstand sunlight. He has an aversion to silver, garlic and crosses. The only way the mortician can die is if someone drives a stake through his heart.

Millennium Studios has filed a lawsuit against De Marco Studios for copyright infringement. Will the lawsuit succeed?

(A) No, because De Marco Studios has taken only ideas from the plaintiff's motion picture.

(B) Yes, because the elements at issue are nearly identical.

(C) No, because both motion pictures are part of the vampire genre.

(D) Yes, because the plaintiff's *FangTastic!* used the elements at issue before they were used by defendant's *Casket Capers.*

33. Programmer has created a device she calls Picabrandt, which creates drawings on its own. Picabrandt was built by Programmer to use ink and paper to make drawings. Programmer programmed Picabrandt to follow certain basic protocols, such as "no more than two eyes" and "mouth must be below nose." Apart from the protocols, Picabrandt has no limitations on what or how it draws. Some of Picabrandt's drawings have sold for $15,000.

Are the drawings by Picabrandt protected by copyright?

34. *Style Over Substance* is a black-and-white motion picture, produced by Studio, that is no longer protected by copyright. Network has invested the necessary funds to colorize the motion picture without Studio's permission. Each pixel of each frame of the motion picture was colored from a palette of 16 million colors. Network has issued a press release stating that any broadcast or cable television channel or station that transmits *Style Over Substance* without Network's permission will be liable to Network for copyright infringement. Is Network's claim accurate?

(A) Yes, because the colorized version of *Style Over Substance* contains all of the elements of the original motion picture.

(B) Yes, because Network has a copyright in the colorized version of *Style Over Substance.*

(C) No, because *Style Over Substance* is in the public domain.

(D) No, because the original version of *Style Over Substance* may be used without Network's permission.

35. Novelist has published a romantic novel concerning the detailed planning and operation of a dinosaur zoo. The novel begins with the selection of a remote island on which to build the zoo, the creation of a dinosaur nursery, the use of uniformed guards and tall electric fences for security, and the design of automated tours for those attending the zoo.

Subsequent to the publication of Novelist's work, Publisher releases a children's book about an adventure park that contains dinosaurs. The adventure park in the children's book is set on a prehistoric island far from the mainland where the dinosaurs are hatched in a nursery. At the park, children ride on automated vehicles alongside tall electric fences that corral the dinosaurs. Throughout the story, uniformed guards accompany the children.

Novelist claims that Publisher's children's story infringes the copyright in her romantic novel. Will Novelist's infringement action be successful?

(A) Yes, because strikingly similar elements appear in both works.

(B) No, because the elements that have been identified by Novelist constitute *scènes à faire*.

(C) Yes, because the children's story is infringing even if the details of the elements in question differ between the two works.

(D) No, because the two works are directed at different audiences.

36.   B-Loko is a popular energy drink made and owned by B-Loko, Inc., that contains very high doses of both caffeine and sugar. Every can of B-Loko contains the following warning:

> "This beverage contains an amount of caffeine that significantly exceeds the Food and Drug Administration's Recommended Daily Allowance (RDA) of caffeine. You may experience some adverse symptoms upon drinking this beverage, such as sweating, redness in the face and neck, and an elevated heartbeat. Limiting your caffeine intake will help to ameliorate these symptoms."

Recently, a competitor of B-Loko, produced and owned by a company called B-Krazy, Inc., entered the market. This beverage, called B-Krazy, also contains very high levels of both caffeine and sugar, though it also adds a supplement called tuanine that has been said to increase energy. Cans of B-Krazy feature a warning label that uses the exact same language as the B-Loko warning.

B-Loko, Inc. sues B-Krazy, Inc., arguing that their B-Krazy, Inc.'s unauthorized use of the warning from cans of B-Loko infringes B-Loko, Inc.'s copyright in that material. B-Krazy, Inc. admits that they copied the warning verbatim, but argues that they cannot be held liable for copyright infringement because the warning is not copyrightable.

Who will prevail on this argument?

(A) B-Loko, because B-Krazy's use of a very similar name and its admission that it used the warning without authorization show that it had clear intent to infringe.

(B) B-Loko, because the warning met the very low standard for copyright originality.

(C) B-Krazy, because while the warning did possess some spark of creativity, it was insufficient to meet the high standard for copyright originality.

(D) B-Krazy, because the warning lacked any creativity or originality, and thus did not qualify for copyright protection.

37.   Beth pitches her idea for a television series to BCS Studios in the offices of their Los Angeles corporate headquarters. She describes her idea to the executives of a reality TV show called "Cat Fanciers" about the obsessive, highly competitive cat owners who enter their pets in cat shows. Beth's presentation is only verbal; she does not share any written or electronic

materials describing the show with the executives. The executives respond very favorably to Beth's presentation, but a week later she is surprised when she learns that they pass on the project.

Then, a year later, Beth is incensed to find that BCS Studios is producing a show called "The Fanciest Cat," which features the foibles of the obsessive, highly competitive cat owners who enter their pets in cat shows. Beth, who lives in Los Angeles, wants to sue BCS Studios for using her idea without her permission. Assuming that BCS Studios did use Beth's idea, what if any options does she have for legal relief against them?

38. Grant Jones robbed several banks in the 1990s before disappearing. He was recently captured when a tourist taking a quick, informal family picture with her cellphone in Times Square happened to accidentally capture a clear image of Jones standing on a street corner. The FBI used the tourist's picture, with her permission, to feature Jones in its Ten Most Wanted List, and this led to Jones' capture in Brooklyn within a month.

Soon after, a major film and television production studio, came out with "Most Wanted: On the Trail of Grant Jones," a made-for-TV movie that chronicled the pursuit and capture of Jones. In making "Most Wanted," the studio created a highly accurate recreation of the now-famous image of Jones incidentally captured by the tourist. To re-create the tourist's photo, the studio had the actor portraying Jones in its film stand on the same street corner in New York City at the same time of day, and hired other actors who posed in the same position as the individuals featured in the tourist's photograph. The result was a photograph that looked very much like, though was identifiably different from, the tourist's photograph.

The tourist sued the studio, arguing that its unauthorized recreation of the photograph infringed her copyright in the work. Who will prevail?

(A) The tourist, because courts have repeatedly held that photographs are copyrightable subject matter.

(B) The tourist, because the studio intentionally sought to create a photograph that was as close to the tourist's photograph as possible.

(C) The studio, because it copied only unprotected facts from the photograph, not copyright-protected expression.

(D) The studio, because it did not make a verbatim copy of the tourist's photograph.

39. Blooey is a famous circus clown known for his outrageous and distinctive face makeup. In 1990, Blooey came up with the highly creative design for his face makeup, which he applies to his face without assistance before each of his performances. Blooey typically performs for about an hour, and his makeup—which is composed of durable grease paint—lasts unchanged throughout his performances. Following each performance, Blooey removes his makeup, which takes him about five minutes.

Recently, Blooey noticed that a clown performing under the name Reddo was using the exact same face design as Blooey. Blooey sent Reddo a polite email asking Reddo to stop using Blooey's face design, and Reddo responded by admitting that he copied his face design from Blooey but insisting that he would continue to use it. Blooey responded by telling Reddo that Blooey's face design was copyright protected, and Reddo replied that Blooey could not have an enforceable copyright in his face design.

Who is right, Blooey or Reddo?

(A) Blooey, because his makeup comprises an original creative work of authorship fixed in a tangible medium of expression.

(B) Blooey, because courts have consistently held performers' makeup designs to be copyrightable works of authorship.

(C) Reddo, because Blooey's work was unfixed.

(D) Reddo, because face makeup does not fall into one of the Copyright Act's enumerated categories of works of authorship.

Copyrightable Subject Matter

40. Historian has written a short history of the City of San Angeles. He obtained the facts contained in the short history from public records and newspaper articles published by the *San Angeles Bee*, as well as from Historian's personal knowledge. Historian has not received the permission of the *San Angeles Bee* to use any of its articles. The short history of the City of San Angeles is:

   (A) Not copyrightable because it is a factual work.

   (B) Not copyrightable because it is an unauthorized derivative work.

   (C) Copyrightable, but only if the short history was written prior to 1978.

   (D) Copyrightable, though the copyright protection it receives may be more limited than the copyright protection given to a work of fiction.

41. Musical Group recently performed six musical works in a nightclub, pursuant to a public performance license obtained by Club Owner. Club Owner filmed the performance with a digital camera with the permission of Musical Group, which also agreed to its release on DVD. Musical Group has entered into a contract with Record Company, under which Record Company is assigned the copyright in all sound recordings created by Musical Group. After the release of Musical Group's performance on DVD, Record Company seeks compensation for the unauthorized distribution of its sound recordings on the DVD. Record Company's claim will be:

   (A) Successful, because Record Company owns the copyrights in the sound recordings contained in the DVD release.

   (B) Successful, because Club Owner's public performance license only addresses the performance of musical compositions, not the creation of sound recordings.

   (C) Unsuccessful, because there is no privity of contract between Club Owner and Record Company.

   (D) Unsuccessful, because the DVD release contains an audiovisual work, not a sound recording.

42. Compare the rights enjoyed by the owner of a copyright in a sound recording to the rights enjoyed by the owner of a copyright in a musical work.

43.   After submitting her latest manuscript for publication, Author decides that she wants to change the ending. She writes a letter to Publisher outlining the ending and asking that Publisher not send the book to press until she revises the manuscript. Under pressure to get the book out, Publisher releases the manuscript in its original form, but includes Author's letter verbatim as an epilogue. Author, who never gave permission for Publisher to publish anything but the manuscript, is angry and sues Publisher for infringing her exclusive rights in the letter. Will she prevail?

(A)   No, because letters are expository, and thus do not count as "literary works" as defined by the Copyright Act.

(B)   No, because by sending the letter to Publisher, Author granted an implied license to publish its contents.

(C)   Yes, because the publication of the letter violates her exclusive rights in a copyrightable work of authorship.

(D)   Yes, because the final chapter included in the letter is literature, and this makes the letter sufficient to meet the definition of "literary works" in the Copyright Act.

44.   Consider question 43. Assume that Author demanded that Publisher send back the letter she sent. Publisher refuses, saying that the letter is his property to keep. Who is right, and why?

45.   Author, a noted writer of mysteries who has worked with Agent for years, trusts Agent implicitly. One day, Author sends Agent an email that reads, "I want to stop writing mysteries, and instead write an historical romance set in the Middle Ages. In this story, an earnest commoner seeks to woo a princess. The twist is that the royal family wants the princess to wed a prince, and stands in the way of their union. The princess and commoner truly love each other, so they run away, but misfortune befalls them and they die tragically. What do you think?" Agent tells Author that he should stick to mysteries, but the email inspires Agent to pen her own novel following the rough outline and plot points that Author sent her. When Agent's novel is published, Author sues Agent for copyright infringement. Will he prevail?

(A)   Yes, because Agent copied the plot points that Author included in the email.

(B)   Yes, because the material in the email was the sweat of Author's brow, and Agent's conduct amounted to wrongful misappropriation.

(C)   No, because Agent's copying of the material in the email was not verbatim.

(D)   No, because what Agent copied, the general outline of a plot in Author's email, amounted only to unprotected ideas.

46.   Employee was recently fired from Company, and is none too happy about it. Late one night, he sneaks into Company's headquarters with revenge on his mind. He rifles through Company's files and finds several documents: a brochure containing information about

Company's secret new product line that it is planning to release in two months; internal memos discussing Company's strategy to bilk employees out of health care; and a video from a Christmas party, produced by a professional videographer as a work made for hire, that shows Company executives sloppily drunk. Employee posts all this material on his website, and a scandal ensues. Company sues Employee for, among other things, copyright infringement, and seeks an injunction ordering Employee to take the offending material offline. Will Company succeed, and if so, with respect to which documents?

(A) Company will succeed, but only with respect to the brochure and the video, because the memo is not copyrightable subject matter.

(B) Company will succeed, but only with respect to the brochure and the memo, because the video is not copyrightable subject matter.

(C) Company will succeed with respect to the brochure, the memo, and the video, because all of them are copyrightable subject matter.

(D) Company will not succeed with respect to any of the documents because none of them amount to copyrightable subject matter.

47.   Student is a sophomore at the University of Spoiled Children, where he is a member of the biggest fraternity on campus. One night, as a gag, Student takes the University's campus directory (which includes names, phone numbers, and campus addresses of all 2,500 of the students currently enrolled at the University, arranged by year and address), and publishes "Student's Guide to the Most Popular People on Campus" in a printed leaflet. The guide takes 50 of the listings from the campus directory verbatim, reflecting the individuals who Student deems to be the most popular on campus, and lists them in alphabetical order. The University claims to own the copyright in the campus directory, and, not amused by the gag, sues Student for infringing its copyright in the directory. Will the University succeed?

(A) Yes, the University will succeed because Student copied its protectable expression verbatim.

(B) Yes, the University will succeed because its copyright extends to all student directories for its enrollees, regardless of how they are arranged.

(C) No, the University will not succeed because directories are in no way copyrightable.

(D) No, the University will not succeed because Student copied only unprotectable elements of the directory (information) and nothing that could be copyrighted (such as selection or arrangement).

48.   Consider question 47. Assume instead that the University loved the gag and did not sue Student, and further assume that Student's friend Compatriot also loved the Guide and put a PDF copy of it on his personal website without asking Student's permission. Under

such circumstances, if Student sued Compatriot for copyright infringement, would he prevail? Why or why not?

49. Professor has been chosen to give the keynote address at his university's commencement. He crafts various written drafts of the address for weeks before the event. When he finally produces a written draft he is satisfied with, Professor spends days committing it to memory. By the time commencement rolls around, Professor knows the address word for word, and he delivers the address at commencement entirely from memory, reciting every word precisely as he had written it down. Student is a big fan of Professor, and digitally records, without permission, the address as Professor gives it, then transcribes the digital audio file into a Microsoft Word file and posts the text on his personal website. Professor learns of this and sues Student for copyright infringement. Will Professor prevail?

   (A) Yes, Professor will prevail because non-extemporaneous speeches that are composed in a written form prior to their delivery are generally considered copyrightable.

   (B) Yes, Professor will prevail because his memorization of the text amounts to fixation in a tangible medium of expression.

   (C) No, Professor will not prevail because spoken word performances do not amount to copyrightable fixations.

   (D) No, Professor will not prevail because speeches are a form of conversation, which is never copyrightable.

50. Consider question 49. Assume that, after commencement, Student met Professor at a cocktail party, where they struck up a conversation. Student surreptitiously recorded Professor's conversation as he bantered casually about the stormy weather that day. Assume further that Student transcribed this recording and put it online as well, and that Professor sued Student for infringing the copyright in Professor's cocktail party chat. Could Student be held liable for recording, transcribing, and posting this material on the Internet? Why or why not?

51. Archaeologist publishes a blockbuster article in which he reveals that he has discovered a new store of Mayan artifacts deep in the Yucatan, and argues persuasively that this discovery supports the theory that Mayan civilization began several centuries earlier than previously believed. The article draws a host of strong reactions. For example, Amateur runs a website devoted to archaeology as a hobby, in which he publishes a brief news item entitled *Big Discovery in the Yucatan*. Amateur's feature recounts the details of Archaeologist's discovery, listing where it happened, what techniques were used in the excavation, and what was uncovered. Subsequently, Archaeologist's longtime academic rival, Nemesis, publishes an article in which he describes Archaeologist's theory about the dawn of Mayan civilization, using Nemesis' own words, and then explains why he thinks the theory is bunk. Archaeologist is incensed at both Amateur and Nemesis, and sues each of them for infringing the copyright in his original article. Will Archaeologist prevail?

(A) Yes, Archaeologist will prevail, but only against Amateur, because Nemesis did not copy any protectable subject matter.

(B) Yes, Archaeologist will prevail, but only against Nemesis, because Amateur did not copy any protectable subject matter.

(C) Yes, Archaeologist will prevail against both Amateur and Nemesis, because both of them copied protectable subject matter.

(D) No, Archaeologist will not prevail against either Amateur or Nemesis, because neither of them copied protectable subject matter.

52. Cartoonist creates a series of comic books based on a character he calls "SuperCop," who is a bumbling, feckless policeman by day, but morphs into a crime fighter with super powers by night. SuperCop lives in present-day Urbania, a city modeled on Detroit, and typically fights familiar, realistic enemies such as drug kingpins and serial murderers. After the series has become very successful, Cartoonist learns of the recent publication of a comic book series titled *SuperCop in Outer Space,* which portrays a graphically identical Super-Cop character living on a futuristic space station and fighting strange creatures from outer space. Cartoonist contacts Publisher, the company that publishes *SuperCop in Outer Space*, and complains about its unauthorized use of his character. Publisher responds, "Sure, it's the same character, but it's not infringement because we didn't copy any of your stories, and in our series SuperCop is in a completely different setting." Unconvinced, Cartoonist sues Publisher for copyright infringement. Will he prevail?

(A) Yes, Cartoonist will prevail because his original creation of the SuperCop character gives him the right to control all subsequent literary or pictorial representations of police performing extraordinary feats.

(B) Yes, Cartoonist will prevail because Publisher's use of SuperCop is a verbatim copy of the attributes of Cartoonist's character that comprises an original work of authorship.

(C) No, Cartoonist will not prevail because Publisher's use of SuperCop sufficiently decontextualized the character from its original setting to such a degree that the taking does not appropriate any protected expression.

(D) No, Cartoonist will not prevail because graphic characters are not copyrightable.

53. Consider question 52. Assume that another comic book comes along featuring a main character called "PooperCop." This comic is about a bumbling policeman, albeit one without any super powers. "PooperCop" is an antic, not a heroic, tale and its main character gets laughs by continually screwing up, rather than earning admiration for saving the day. Still, Cartoonist notices several similarities between PooperCop and SuperCop, such as the fact that each are policeman, each of them are bumbling at least some of the time, and that they have similar sounding names. Republisher, the company that publishes the PooperCop series, admits to Cartoonist that it got the idea for PooperCop after reading

material that included, but was not limited to, SuperCop. Cartoonist decides to sue Republisher for infringement of copyright in his SuperCop character. Will Cartoonist succeed? Why or why not?

54. Author pens a best-selling series of mystery novels that feature a central character named Judy McGee. Judy McGee is a lovable amateur sleuth who always manages to stumble onto a big case—and solve it. Her visual appearance is distinctive: she wears blue checked gingham dresses, carries an absurdly oversized, pink-handled magnifying glass to look for clues, and whenever praised, blushes modestly and utters the phrase, "Aw, jeez Louise." Author's novels become famous and the Judy McGee character becomes an admired and well-recognized cult figure. One day, Studio, a film production studio based in Manhattan, announces that it is going to develop and release a film version of a new Judy McGee story that is based on a plot written by a Studio employee, not by Author. The movie will, though, feature a Judy McGee character that faithfully includes all of her distinctive dress, magnifying glass, speech, and characteristics as described in Author's novels. Author, who has not licensed the rights to the Judy McGee character to Studio, is incensed and files for an injunction to prevent Studio from developing the movie, arguing that the use of her character amounts to copyright infringement. Assuming that the case is brought in the Southern District of New York, will Author prevail?

   (A) Yes, Author will prevail, because literary characters are always copyrightable as subsets of the literary works in which they appear.

   (B) Yes, Author will prevail because Judy McGee is sufficiently fleshed out with distinctive physical and personality traits to merit copyright protection.

   (C) No, Author will not prevail, because Judy McGee is merely a plot device and does not constitute the story being told.

   (D) No, Author will not prevail, because literary characters, unlike characters depicted in graphic form, are not copyrightable.

55. Consider question 54. Assume that NoveltyCo releases an oversized, pink-handled magnifying glass just like the one that Judy McGee carries throughout her adventures in Author's novels. In fact, NoveltyCo concedes that it designed the magnifying glass based on the description of McGee's magnifying glass in several of Author's novels. Author contacts NoveltyCo, which did not request permission to create and market the novelty, and demands that it pay her royalties for its use of her creation. NoveltyCo refuses, and Author sues for copyright infringement. Who will prevail?

   (A) Author. Her copyright in the distinctive Judy McGee character extends also to identifying features of the character's persona, such as the oversized, pink-handled magnifying glass that Judy McGee uses all the time.

   (B) Author. Her copyright in the distinctive Judy McGee character extends also to anything associated with that character in any context.

(C) NoveltyCo. Extending copyright protection to the idea of magnifying glasses would grant Author control over uncopyrightable ideas.

(D) NoveltyCo. The magnifying glass is a useful article that cannot be protected by copyright.

56. Consider question 54. Explain how a court within the Ninth Circuit would approach this issue differently.

57. Animator created the *Mice-a-Roni* comic strip in the mid-twentieth century. *Mice-a-Roni* featured Mikey the Mouse, a lovable anthropomorphic mouse, as its main character. Assume for the purposes of this question that the Mikey character is clearly copyrightable. Animator's *Mice-a-Roni* comic strip enjoyed some success and ran in newspapers for about 20 years, when it fell out of popularity and Animator ceased to produce it. Animator did not include a copyright notice on his comic strip during the first few years that he produced *Mice-a-Roni*, but as the series began to enjoy some popularity, he started to include the necessary formalities. As a result, the earliest five years of the *Mice-a-Roni* comics have fallen into the public domain. The subsequent 15 years of the comic strip have contained a copyright notice. One day, Animator learns that Publisher has released a book titled *Classic Comix of the 50s Re-imagined* in which he portrays various old comic characters, including Mikey the Mouse, in a modern setting. Publisher did not seek permission to use the Mikey character. Animator sues Publisher for copyright infringement. What result?

(A) Animator will prevail. As long as a single episode of *Mice-a-Roni* is protected by copyright, the Mikey character is protected by copyright as well.

(B) Animator will prevail. The copyright protection period for graphic characters is limitless.

(C) Animator will not prevail. Characters fall into the public domain when the work of authorship in which they initially appeared falls into the public domain.

(D) Animator will not prevail. A court would regard Animator's failure to comply with copyright formalities during the early years of *Mice-a-Roni* as a form of laches, which means Animator forfeits any right to enforce his copyright in Mikey the Mouse later on.

58. Programmer writes and registers the source code for *MacroSoft Bird*, a program that allows birdwatchers to catalog their avian sightings. The program is a big success, and soon after its release, a rogue programmer named Pirate releases a similar program. Pirate's program, titled *Birds in Flight*, allows birdwatchers to catalog their avian sightings, but also provides information that enables birdwatchers to identify different species as well as connect with birdwatchers around the globe. Programmer learns that Pirate created *Birds in Flight* by cutting and pasting the entirety of the source code for *MacroSoft Bird* into a file, and then appending additional portions of original source code that enable the other features of the

program. Programmer wants to sue Pirate for infringement of the *MacroSoft Bird* source code as well as the program's bird-cataloging feature. What will the result be?

(A) Programmer will prevail with respect to both the source code and the cataloging feature.

(B) Programmer will prevail with respect to the source code only.

(C) Programmer will prevail with respect to the cataloging feature only.

(D) Programmer will fail with respect to both aspects of his infringement suit.

59. Techie created a new computer chip in 1990, and he then died in 1995. When will the period of federally enforceable exclusive rights in the structure of the computer chip expire?

(A) 2000

(B) 2010

(C) 2065

(D) Computer chips are not considered copyrightable subject matter, so no federal protection is available.

60. User is the owner of an authorized copy of *DethKlok 2000*, a popular new video game, and proceeds to play it on his home computer. Any time User activates the game, his computer automatically copies several of the files, written in object code (machine language), that comprise *DethKlok 2000* into its Random Access Memory (RAM). Does this duplication of the object code that comprises *DethKlok 2000* amount to copyright infringement?

(A) Yes. The unauthorized duplication of any literary work, including a computer program written in object code, infringes the copyright in that work.

(B) No. While computer source code may be copyrightable, a computer program written in object code is not, so this copying is not actionable.

(C) No. This kind of copying appears to be prima facie infringement, but the Copyright Act includes an exception to permit it.

(D) No. Because User did not intend for any copying to take place, there can be no infringement.

61. Consider the facts of question 60. User buys a new laptop computer and is disappointed to discover that the version of *DethKlok 2000* he purchased is no longer compatible with the operating system on his new computer. User searches the Internet and finds that by making a few modifications to the source code of the *DethKlok 2000* program he can render the application compatible with his new laptop. User modifies the source code and the alteration successfully renders *DethKlok 2000* compatible with his new computer. Does User's alteration of the *DethKlok 2000* program amount to copyright infringement?

(A) Yes. User's alteration of the source code that comprises *DethKlok 2000* amounts to an unauthorized derivative work, violating the copyright owner's exclusive right of adaptation.

(B) Yes. User's creation of what is essentially a new version of *DethKlok 2000* violates the copyright owner's exclusive right of reproduction.

(C) No. User's ownership of the *DethKlok 2000* program entitles him to alter the source code that comprises that program in any way he sees fit.

(D) No. While User's alteration of the source code that comprises the *DethKlok 2000* program is an unauthorized adaptation of a copyrighted work of authorship, owners of computer programs are entitled to make such alterations in order to make applications compatible with new hardware.

62. Printer owns a printing shop. One day, he invents a new typeface script called Lucinda that allows for more characters to appear on a page without sacrificing readability. Printer does a brisk business formatting documents with his new typeface, and refuses to license Lucinda to other printers or to makers of word processing software so he can capture all the value associated with the font. Printer discovers that an exact copy of Lucinda has been added to the latest edition of a word processing program produced and marketed by the software company MacroSoft. Printer wants to sue MacroSoft for its unauthorized appropriation of his lucrative original font. Will he succeed?

(A) Yes. Fonts are protectable as pictorial or graphical works.

(B) Yes. Fonts are protectable as literary works.

(C) No. Fonts cannot possess the requisite degree of originality to merit copyright protection.

(D) No. Regardless of their originality, fonts or typefaces cannot be protected by federal copyright.

63. Polly Math is a multitalented artist who writes the melody and lyrics to a tune titled *Only Me* and then records an *a cappella* version of the tune using her home recording studio. What copyrights does she own, and in what categories of works of authorship are they included?

(A) Polly owns copyrights in the melody and lyrics of *Only Me*, which comprise a single musical work.

(B) Polly owns the copyright in the melody and lyrics of *Only Me*, which comprise a single musical work; and the copyright in the recording of her performance of *Only Me*, which comprises a sound recording.

(C) Polly owns the copyrights in the lyrics of *Only Me* as a musical work, and the copyright in the melody and her performance of *Only Me*, which comprise a single sound recording.

(D) Polly owns the copyrights in the melody, lyrics, and performance of *Only Me*, which comprise three separate musical works.

64. Dancer is known for her powerful live dance performances, during which she performs impromptu ecstatic free-form modern dance routines, accompanied by performances of public domain classical music. Every one of her dance performances is unique, and none is planned or scripted in any way. Last year, Dancer performed her greatest work to date at Carnegie Hall. The performance was recorded with Dancer's authorization, and copies of the video were released as a DVD titled *Dancer at Carnegie Hall—Live!* The DVD sold well for a few months, then sales fell off because a much cheaper DVD began to circulate. Titled *Carnegie Hall Hosts Dancer, Live!*, the second DVD was based on an unauthorized recording of the same event. Dancer sues the makers of the second DVD for infringing her federal copyright in the choreographic work she performed at Carnegie Hall. Will she prevail?

   (A) Yes. Dancer will prevail because the second DVD infringes her federal copyright in the dance she performed at Carnegie Hall.

   (B) Yes. Dancer will prevail because the content of the second DVD infringes the audio-visual work fixed in the original DVD authorized by Dancer.

   (C) No. Dancer will not prevail because her dance was not fixed in a tangible medium of expression.

   (D) No. Dancer will not prevail because choreographic works that do not communicate a story are not copyrightable.

65. Photog takes a photograph of a wet kitten in a sink and prints it on shirts that he sells via the Internet. The sales of the shirts are a great success. Soon, Knockoff starts a website from where he sells an identical shirt, including its unique button holes and an exact copy of Photog's kitten photograph, for a fraction of the price charged by Photog. Photog sues Knockoff for copyright infringement. Will he succeed?

   (A) Yes. Photog will succeed because by appending an original photograph to a functional object like a shirt, he acquires exclusive rights over the entire shirt as well as what is depicted on it.

   (B) Yes. Photog will succeed, but only with respect to Knockoff's reproduction and distribution of the photograph contained on the shirt.

   (C) No. Photog will not succeed because clothing is not copyrightable.

   (D) No. Photog will not succeed because by appending a copyrightable image to a non-copyrightable useful object, he forfeits copyright protection in the former.

66. GamerCo designs, creates and distributes a video game called *A-Maze-ment*. The game features a two-dimensional display in which players navigate a maze while fighting off monsters. *A-Maze-ment* consists of 20 different levels of increasing difficulty, each with

its own distinctively designed maze accompanied by music that has been composed and recorded for the video game. GamerCo seeks to register the video game with the Copyright Office. How will the Copyright Office categorize the video game?

(A) The game screens are pictorial works, and the accompanying music is a sound recording.

(B) The game screens are pictorial works, and the accompanying music is a musical work.

(C) The video game and all of its components constitute an audiovisual work.

(D) The music may be registered as both a musical work and a sound recording, but the video game screens depicting the distinct levels are not copyrightable because they are not fixed in a tangible medium of expression.

67. Studio releases its big summer blockbuster, *Frantic Man*, which includes a hip-hop soundtrack created by the popular rap artist Poppa Bigg as a work made for hire. Studio registers *Frantic Man* with the Copyright Office as an audiovisual work, but does not separately apply for registration of the motion picture's accompanying soundtrack. Soon after, up-and-coming rapper Sonny Smallz releases a recording that incorporates wholesale a full minute from the *Frantic Man* soundtrack. Studio, which owns all rights in the music soundtrack, sues Sonny Smallz for infringement. Among Sonny's responses to Studio's complaint is that the music soundtrack was never validly registered with the Copyright Office. Is this argument valid?

(A) Yes. Studio's failure to separately register its copyright in the music soundtrack when it registered its copyright in the motion picture means Studio forfeited any opportunity to register the former.

(B) Yes. Studio failed to separately register the copyright in the music soundtrack, but this does not prevent it from registering it at a later time.

(C) No. Studio did not separately register the music soundtrack, but this was not necessary because a motion picture's music soundtrack is protected under the motion picture copyright.

(D) No. Although Studio did not separately register the music soundtrack, this is irrelevant because the Copyright Act's registration provisions do not apply to sound recordings.

68. Musician composes a concerto for piano, then performs the concerto himself and records the performance using his own recording equipment. Musician releases the recording as *Musician's Concerto Live* and it becomes a hit in the classical music world. Pianoman is a devoted amateur pianist. He buys a copy of *Musician's Concerto Live* and listens to it so often that he memorizes the whole composition and, without ever having seen the sheet music, can play it by heart. In fact, as an homage to Musician, Pianoman videotapes himself performing Musician's concerto and posts it on the Internet. Musician does not appreciate Pianoman's

doing this and sues him for infringing both the musical work that comprises the concerto as well as the sound recording *Musician's Concerto Live*. Will Musician prevail?

(A) Yes. Musician will prevail because Pianoman infringed both the musical work and the sound recording.

(B) Yes. Musician will prevail because Pianoman infringed the sound recording.

(C) Yes. Musician will prevail because Pianoman infringed the musical work.

(D) No. Musician will prevail because Pianoman did not infringe either the musical work or the sound recording.

69. In 1967, Donny Dank penned the melody and lyrics to *Sir Surfs-a-Lot*. Two years later, the band Big Waves, with Dank's permission, recorded *Sir Surfs-a-Lot* in its own studio and released it that same year to great success. Assuming that the creators of each work of authorship have retained the rights to them, what are the various federal copyright owner-ship interests in *Sir Surfs-a-Lot* in 1969?

(A) Dank owns the copyright in the musical work that comprises *Sir Surfs-a-Lot*, but the Big Waves recording is not protected by federal copyright.

(B) Dank owns the copyright in the musical work that comprises *Sir Surfs-a-Lot*, and Big Waves owns the federal copyright in the sound recording.

(C) Dank owns the copyright in the musical work that comprises *Sir Surfs-a-Lot* and in the sound recording that resulted from Big Waves' recording of it.

(D) Dank owns the copyright in the musical work that comprises *Sir Surfs-a-Lot*. Dank and Big Waves are joint owners of the sound recording.

70. In 1991, Architect drafts the blueprints for Jones Manor, which is then built to his speci-fications. Architect's design for Jones Manor consists not only of the original exterior structure of the house, but also of a distinctive interior spiral staircase. Architect has reserved the rights in any and all works of authorship generated by his efforts with respect to Jones Manor. Which of the following statements most accurately characterizes Architect's copyright ownership interests?

(A) Architect owns copyrights in the blueprints as both pictorial and architectural works, as well as the exterior structure of the house and the interior staircase as an architec-tural work.

(B) Architect owns the copyright in the exterior structure of the house as well as the inte-rior staircase as an architectural work.

(C) Architect owns copyrights in the blueprints as a pictorial work, and in the exterior structure and interior staircase as an architectural work.

(D) Architect owns copyrights in the blueprints as a pictorial work, and in the exterior structure as an architectural work.

71. Fed and Statie are artists who were recently employed by the federal government and the state of Grace, respectively. They are working on a joint federal/state project to commemorate Grace's bicentennial. Fed's contribution is an original painting depicting the first meeting between explorers and Grace's native inhabitants. Statie produces an original poem that gives narrative context for the events portrayed in the painting. These works of authorship hang in the Grace statehouse next to each other. One day, Copyist releases a pamphlet giving his own, unofficial version of the history of Grace's founding, and includes in it a photo reproduction of Fed's painting and Statie's poem, without having obtained permission to do so. Accused of copyright infringement, Copyist argues that as works created by government employees, neither the painting nor the poem is copyrightable. Is Copyist correct?

   (A) Yes, Copyist is correct. Neither work of authorship is copyrightable.

   (B) Yes and no. Statie's poem is not copyrightable, but Fed's painting is.

   (C) Yes and no. Fed's painting is not copyrightable, but Statie's poem is.

   (D) No, Copyist is wrong. Both works of authorship are copyrightable.

72. Novelist's book *Nonesuch* is rumored to be his finest work yet, but few can confirm that rumor because Novelist wrote *Nonesuch* in Cornish, a Celtic language spoken by less than 1,000 people. Novelist is committed to the revival of the Cornish language, and thus he refuses to license translations of *Nonesuch*. Novelist also takes care to register his copyright in nations around the world, including the United States. Critic has spent his career studying Novelist's work, and is so anxious to read *Nonesuch* that he learns Cornish and creates his own translation of the novel, which he then posts on his password-protected website to limit access to the translation. However, Publisher breaks the code, makes a copy of the translation, releases an English-language version of *Nonesuch*, and sells many copies. Both Novelist and Critic are incensed, and each sues Publisher for copyright infringement in federal district court. Who will likely prevail?

   (A) Novelist will prevail, but Critic will not.

   (B) Critic will prevail, but Novelist will not.

   (C) Novelist and Critic will both prevail.

   (D) Neither Novelist nor Critic will prevail.

73. *PoundSigne* is a popular French comic strip featuring an original and distinctive main character, Le Mec. *PoundSigne*'s creator has registered all of his comics with the United States Copyright Office, and has licensed Publisher to create an English translation of the comic strip. Publisher does so, with his work consisting only of translating the French-language text in the *PoundSigne* comics into English, while leaving the graphics untouched. Publisher's

translated versions of *PoundSigne* become very popular in the United States. Eventually, Fan, an overly enthusiastic reader of Publisher's translations, creates a website on which he presents *Le Mec's New Adventures*, a comic featuring an exact copy of the Le Mec character in new contexts. *PoundSigne*'s creator and Publisher each sue Fan for copyright infringement. Who will prevail?

(A) Neither *PoundSigne*'s creator nor Publisher will prevail.

(B) *PoundSigne*'s creator will prevail, but Publisher will not.

(C) Publisher will prevail, but *PoundSigne*'s creator will not.

(D) *PoundSigne*'s creator and Publisher will both prevail.

74. In 1995, Photog took a picture of a lion during an African safari. He then licensed *Adventure* magazine to use the photograph on the front cover of the January 1996 issue, but retained all other rights in the photograph. Recently, *Adventure* released a DVD titled *50 Years of Adventure* that is a digital archive containing an exact copy of each issue of the magazine. The back issues are presented just as they appeared on the newsstand, allowing users to scroll through them page-by-page and see all the material as it was presented in the original print versions. *Adventure* did not seek Photog's permission to re-use his photo in the context of the DVD. Photog now sues *Adventure* for infringing his copyright in the lion photograph. Will Photog prevail?

(A) Yes. Photog will prevail because this is a violation of his right to reproduce and distribute his copyrighted work.

(B) Yes. Photog will prevail because the Copyright Act requires users to seek express written permission for any use of a previously licensed analog work in a digital context.

(C) No. Photog will not prevail, because even though *Adventure* reproduced and distributed his copyrighted photograph in the DVD, that use is protected by the section 201(c) privilege for collective works.

(D) No. Photog will not prevail, because a license to use a work of authorship in one context necessarily implies a license to use that same work in any reasonably related context.

75. Webcaster streams digital recordings of music over its website. Webcaster has obtained no licenses. Music Publisher owns the copyrights in several musical compositions that have been streamed by Webcaster. If Music Publisher sues Webcaster for copyright infringement, the claimed primary infringement will be:

(A) The adaptation right of section 106(2).

(B) The public performance right of section 106(4).

(C) The public display right of section 106(5).

(D) The digital transmission right of section 106(6).

76.   Webcaster streams recordings of music over its website. Webcaster has obtained no licenses. Record Company owns the copyrights in several sound recordings that have been streamed by Webcaster. If Record Company sues Webcaster for copyright infringement, the claimed primary infringement will be:

(A) The adaptation right of section 106(2).

(B) The public performance right of section 106(4).

(C) The public display right of section 106(5).

(D) The digital transmission right of section 106(6).

77.   Pipes International (PI) has been making high-end, very expensive tobacco pipes for smoking enthusiasts for centuries. In the 1950s, they developed their best-selling model, called "The Curve." While most pipes have a straight stem, The Curve has an S-shaped stem. Pipe connoisseurs prize The Curve because the S-shaped stem has great aesthetic appeal, and also because the precise shaping of the curved stem imparts a richer, smoother taste to smoking tobacco. As PI's advertisements truthfully state, "Even the slightest change in the smooth shape of The Curve, and the distinctive flavor it creates would be lost." PI registered The Curve with the Copyright Office as a sculptural work in 1958 and properly renewed the copyright.

Recently, a rival pipe maker, Smokers International (SI), introduced a pipe called "The S," which has precisely the same S-shaped stem as The Curve. As a result, The S has the same visual appearance and functional qualities as The Curve, though SI charges a much lower price for its product. PI sues SI, arguing that The S infringes the copyright in The Curve. SI counters by conceding that it copied the PI's pipe, but arguing that The Curve is uncopyrightable.

Who will win this argument?

(A) PI, because the shape of The Curve possesses aesthetic appeal.

(B) PI, because the Copyright Office implicitly affirmed the copyrightability of The Curve when it registered the work in 1958.

(C) SI, because the aesthetic elements are inseparable from its function.

(D) SI, because the shape of The Curve performs a utilitarian function.

78.   RG Construction is a builder of suburban tract homes. RG's homes have often been derided by critics as "McMansions" because they are largely indistinguishable from one another. In fact, RG offers several different floor plans, though its homes do share a number of common features. One such feature is what RG calls the "master down, 3 up" configuration in which a house has a master bedroom on the ground floor and three bedrooms on the upper floors. RG has extolled the virtues of its plan, saying "The 'master down, 3 up' configuration allows parents to have a separate oasis all to themselves while kids can be as rambunctious as they want upstairs."

Recently, one of RG's main competitors in building tract housing, Alvernaz Homes, constructed a number of homes that use the same basic configuration as RG's "master down, 3 up" model. RG files suit, alleging that Alvernaz's construction of the "master down, 3 up" homes infringed RG's copyright in that design.

Will RG's lawsuit against Alvernaz succeed?

(A) Yes, because Alvernaz's status as a direct competitor to RG suggests it was trying to free-ride off RG's creation of a novel home design.

(B) Yes, because the "master down, 3 up" model contained sufficient creative expression to merit copyright protection.

(C) No, because the "master down, 3 up" model was primarily functional, not aesthetic.

(D) No, because Alvernaz constructed homes based on RG's plans; it did not copy the plans themselves.

79.   Extra has been trying to make it big in Hollywood as an actor for more than 10 years. Recently, he was excited to get a very brief speaking part in a film that he was told would be a lighthearted family movie about a troupe of clowns that travels around entertaining kids. Extra's scene in the film involved him in full clown makeup on the eve of a big trip saying, "I'm excited, here we go!" Extra worked very hard to read this line convincingly, and the director commended him on his delivery. When the film was ultimately released, though, Extra was shocked and angered to find that it was actually a horror movie about a group of clowns who traveled around murdering people. Extra's one line had been overdubbed to read, "I'm excited, off with their heads!"

Before he worked on the film, Extra signed a release stating that he "transferred and assigned any and all copyright interest in the film to Producer." Extra nevertheless sues Producer for copyright infringement, claiming that Extra has an independent copyright interest in his performance that is separate from Producer's copyright in the film itself. Extra argues that he alone infused his performance of the original line with creativity, that such creativity amounts to an independent dramatic work that Extra owns alone, and that Producer infringed it by overdubbing his line and creating an unauthorized adaptation.

Will Extra win his copyright infringement suit against Producer?

(A) Yes, because Producer failed to obtain a sufficient waiver of Extra's rights to his performance copyright.

(B) Yes, because Extra's delivery of his line was unusually convincing and therefore merited copyright protection.

(C) No, because courts have construed agreements disclaiming copyright interest in film copyrights to apply to performance copyrights as well.

(D) No, because actors' performances are not copyrightable works of authorship.

80. "Jumpin' Jack" was a contemporary television children's series about a youthful crime-fighting superhero named Jack that ran from 1992 through 1997. Jack was never seen without his pogo stick, Lightning. Lightning has a distinctive colorful design featuring a racing stripe and tail fins, and a face that allows him to communicate with Jack and speak his famous catch phrase, "Let's get the jump on crime!"

BizMo, Inc. is a company that makes updated versions of items from vintage television shows. Last year, it released "Lightning 2017," which it indicated was an updated version of the "Lightning" pogo stick from the "Jumpin' Jack" series. Lightning 2017 featured the same basic color design and features as the original version from the television show, though they were all changed slightly in an effort to make them, in the words of BizMo's PR department, "more up-to-date." And Lightning 2017 also included a button that, when pressed, would utter the famous catch-phrase "Let's get the jump on crime!" in a voice that sounded very close to the actor who voiced the original Lightning (the original actor refused to sign on to BizMo's project out of a sense of loyalty to the original show).

BizMo never got permission to create Lightning 2017 from the owner of the rights in the "Jumpin' Jack" series, Producer. Producer has sued BizMo for infringing its copyright in the Lightning character. Will producer's infringement suit succeed?

(A) Yes, because Lightning is copyrightable as a sculptural work.

(B) Yes, because Lightning is copyrightable as a non-human character.

(C) No, because only humans are subject to character copyrights.

(D) No, because BizMo did not copyright the Lightning character verbatim.

81. Boomer is a famous bodybuilder who released a very popular and profitable workout video titled "The Boom Method" in 2005. The video guides viewers through a series of 20 standard weight-based exercises like squats, arm curls, and shoulder presses, all in a particular sequence that Boomer claims is specifically designed to maximize muscle growth. "The Boom Method" video is very spare and technical, simply showing Boomer working through the sequence while explaining each exercise and giving the viewers encouragement and tips. "This isn't entertainment, it's a workout," Boomer famously tells viewers during the video.

Last year, an up-and-coming trainer named Betty released a workout video titled "Get Pumped!" The video takes viewers through the exact same 20 exercises that are featured in "The Boom Method" in the exact same sequence they appear in that video. Betty's presentation of the exercises, though, is very different. "Get Pumped!" features high production values, plays energetic music, and takes place in a variety of exciting outdoor settings. As Betty tells her viewers, "If you're having this much fun, you forget you're exercising!"

Boomer sues Betty for copyright infringement, alleging that "Get Pumped!" infringes his copyright in "The Boom Method." Will Boomer prevail?

82.   Jane is a talented topiary artist whose specialty is creating whimsical figures by trimming bushes into creative shapes. In the past year, she has earned particular renown for creating in topiary form the character "Larry the Lion." Jane's topiaries of "Larry the Lion" feature the lion Larry's face, framed by its mane, with a toothy grin. Blave is a local photographer who has taken several photographs of Jane's "Larry the Lion" topiaries and is selling photo prints of them as well as displaying them on his professional website — all without Jane's permission.

Jane sues Blave for copyright infringement. Who will prevail?

(A)   Jane, because her "Larry the Lion" topiaries are highly original and fixed in a tangible medium of expression.

(B)   Jane, because her "Larry the Lion" topiaries feature a high degree of originality that makes up for the fact that the work is not fixed in a tangible medium of expression.

(C)   Blave, because the "Larry the Lion" topiaries are not fixed in a tangible medium of expression.

(D)   Blave, because the "Larry the Lion" topiaries are not original, but rather depictions of naturally occurring wildlife.

Ownership of Copyright

83.   Recently, Florist hired Programmer, an independent contractor, to create a computer program to assist in the operation of Florist's flower shop. Florist described the operation of his business to Programmer, who subsequently delivered a completed computer program to Florist. Who is the owner of the copyright in the computer program?

(A) Florist.

(B) Florist, but only if Florist and Programmer signed a written work made for hire agreement.

(C) Programmer.

(D) Programmer, but only if Florist and Programmer had not signed a written work made for hire agreement.

84.   Author's new novel *Mysterious Friendship* is due to come out on Friday, and Frontera Bookstore is planning a big event to celebrate the book's release. Author's sworn enemy, Envy, breaks into Frontera Bookstore on Thursday night, absconds with all the copies of Author's novel that the bookstore was planning to sell at the event, and then publishes the last chapter of the book online in order to ruin the novel's surprise ending. Frontera and Author both sue Envy for copyright infringement. Will they prevail?

(A) Yes, both will prevail.

(B) Frontera Bookstore will prevail, but Author will not.

(C) Author will prevail, but Frontera Bookstore will not.

(D) No, neither Frontera Bookstore nor Author will prevail.

85.   Painter recently finished his latest masterwork, a series of oil on canvas paintings, which he painted by himself. Based only on this information, which of the following statements accurately describes Painter's copyright ownership status with respect to the work?

(A) Painter is the creator, owner, and author of the work.

(B) Painter is the creator and author of the work, but may not be its owner.

(C) Painter is the creator and owner of the work, but may not be its author.

(D) Painter is the creator of the work, but may not be its owner or author.

86.   Recently Sculptor, as an employee of Left Coast Studios, made a crystal sculpture of a large bird for Left Coast's classic motion picture, *The Maltese Condor*. Upon the completion of the motion picture, in which the sculpture was used, Museum purchased the sculpture. What status, i.e., creator, author, and owner, do the parties have with respect to the sculpture on this set of facts?

87.   In 1950, tycoon Fritzlinger hired Poet as an independent contractor to compose an epic poem lionizing Fritzlinger's vast fortune. Fritzlinger told Poet that he wanted the poem to comment on Fritzlinger's rise from poverty to wealth, and to compare Fritzlinger's fortune favorably to that of other tycoons. Poet worked on the poem for a month, then showed it to Fritzlinger, who made substantial suggestions for changes, which Poet incorporated in their entirety. Upon completion of the work, Fritzlinger paid Poet for his time and the two parted ways, never to see each other again. Assuming that no written agreement memorialized the relationship between Fritzlinger and Poet, who is considered the author of the copyright in the poem?

   (A) Fritzlinger, because Poet was an independent contractor.

   (B) Fritzlinger, because he initiated Poet's work and paid him for it.

   (C) Poet, because he exercised more creative control over the final version than did Fritzlinger.

   (D) Poet, because he was an independent contractor.

88.   Consider question 87. Assume that Poet was not an independent contractor, but a regular employee of Fritzlinger. How, if at all, does this affect the authorship of the poem?

89.   Worker has served as a product safety inspector for Manufacturer for the past 20 years. During that time, she has taken very little time off for vacation, and last year her boss agreed to let her take all her six months of accumulated vacation time at once. Worker spent those months fulfilling her lifetime dream of writing a novel about a boy and his dog in turn-of-the-century Albania.

   Recently, Worker's published her novel to great critical and commercial success. Manufacturer wants to cash in on Worker's windfall, and claims that Manufacturer is the novel's author because the novel is a work made for hire. Worker, of course, claims that she is in fact the novel's true author. In the absence of any written agreement addressing the issue, which assertion about authorship is correct?

   (A) Worker is the novel's author because her creation of the novel occurred outside the scope of her employment.

   (B) Worker is the novel's author because she was effectively functioning as an independent contractor for Manufacturer while she was on her six months' paid vacation.

   (C) Manufacturer is the novel's author because Worker was an employee of Manufacturer at the time she wrote the novel.

(D) Manufacturer is the novel's author because in the absence of a written agreement, any work of authorship created by an individual in the employ of a corporation is assumed to belong to the corporation.

90. Big Press hires Polly Glot to translate a successful Spanish-language novel into English. Polly works on the translation from her home office, refuses to accept any comments from Big Press's editorial staff, and is paid a one-time lump sum fee for her work, without benefits or tax withholdings. She has signed a contract with Big Press, also signed by the President of Big Press, containing a provision that Big Press, not Polly Glot, will be the "author of the work." A few months after completing the English translation, Polly noticed that Big Press has used large segments of her translation in its corporate promotional materials. This upsets Polly, and she sues for infringement, but Big Press responds that it is the owner of the translation and can do what it wants with it. Who will prevail?

(A) Polly will prevail because she clearly worked as an independent contractor when creating the English translation, and any agreements to the contrary are void under federal law.

(B) Polly will prevail because she, not Big Press, authored the translation.

(C) Big Press will prevail because, although Polly worked as an independent contractor, her claim of copyright in the English translation was overcome by the agreement defining Big Press as the author of one of the nine categories of works for which such agreements are enforceable.

(D) Big Press will prevail because Polly created the translation as an employee acting within the scope of her employment.

91. Lucy is the CEO of DynaCorp. After a poor earnings report came out, the DynaCorp board of directors demanded that Lucy produce a memorandum identifying the parties responsible for the corporation's declining profits. Lucy went home and penned a long, detailed memo in which she placed blame on the board for DynaCorp's poor recent earnings. Shortly thereafter, Lucy was fired as the CEO of DynaCorp. To get revenge, Lucy posted the memo on her personal web page. The DynaCorp board was embarrassed by Lucy's revelations and filed for an injunction to have Lucy take the memo off her web page. DynaCorp's counsel argues that Lucy's conduct amounts to copyright infringement because DynaCorp is the author of the memo and did not authorize its reproduction or display. Will DynaCorp prevail?

(A) Yes, DynaCorp will prevail because anything Lucy writes during her employ by DynaCorp is considered a work made for hire.

(B) Yes, DynaCorp will prevail because the work product of corporate officers is considered a work made for hire of which the corporation is the author.

(C) No, DynaCorp will not prevail because CEOs are effectively independent contractors and their work product is not work made for hire.

(D) No, DynaCorp will not prevail because business-related memos are insufficiently creative to merit copyright protection.

92.   Consider question 91. Assume that the DynaCorp board hires an outside consulting firm, ConsultCo, to investigate the problems associated with a bad earnings report and provide an impartial report. The consulting agreement includes no mention of copyright or ownership of the report. ConsultCo creates the requested report, and receives a one-time payment for its work from DynaCorp. Some time later, ConsultCo posts its report about DynaCorp on the ConsultCo company website to show an example of its work. DynaCorp is displeased that ConsultCo posted the sensitive material without its permission and sues for an injunction to remove the material from the ConsultCo webpage, arguing that the unauthorized posting infringes DynaCorp's copyright. ConsultCo argues that it is the author of the report and is thus entitled to post it. Who will prevail, and why?

93.   GiantCo recently hired Fuchsia, a well-known muralist, to paint a mural on the interior of its corporate headquarters' lobby, pursuant to an oral agreement. Fuchsia paints the mural using her own design, though she uses materials provided by GiantCo. Fuchsia sticks to her artistic vision, frequently rejecting editorial suggestions from GiantCo as to how the mural should look. When Fuchsia finishes the mural, GiantCo is pleased with the final product and pays her a one-time lump sum, without any tax withholdings. This project is the only time Fuchsia does any work for GiantCo. Who is the author of the mural?

(A) Fuchsia is the author. More of the relevant factors that determine her employment status weigh in favor of Fuchsia being an independent contractor rather than an employee.

(B) Fuchsia is the author. She used her own design, which is dispositive of her status as an independent contractor.

(C) GiantCo is the author. At least one of the relevant factors, whose materials were used in making the mural, weighs against Fuchsia, and this is enough to negate her status as an independent contractor.

(D) It is not possible to say unless we know whether GiantCo provided Fuchsia with health insurance benefits.

94.   Writer recently completed two collaborative projects. One project was called *Spring*, a series of essays about the eponymous season. Writer co-wrote *Spring* with Author. In creating *Spring*, Writer came up with an outline for each essay, then sent it to Author, who fleshed out the text a bit more. Through successive iterations of this process, including a few meetings at which they discussed particular details of the project, Writer and Author eventually arrived at a final version of *Spring* with which they were both pleased.

For his second project, Writer worked with Musician to create lyrics for a composition called *Autumn* that Musician had already written. Musician is a bit of a recluse, and he simply sent Writer the sheet music and a sound recording of *Autumn*. Writer read the sheet music and listened to the recording, and penned lyrics to accompany the musical composition. Writer wrote the lyrics without any comments, suggestions, or input from Musician. When Writer sent the lyrics to Musician, Musician did not even look at them, instead simply sending both the musical composition and lyrics to his publisher, which published them as a single integrated work. According to the definition of the Copyright Act, which of these compositions are joint works?

(A) *Spring.*

(B) *Autumn.*

(C) *Spring* and *Autumn.*

(D) Neither *Spring* nor *Autumn.*

95. Producer wants to produce a CD that will merge East Coast and West Coast hip-hop styles. His only problem is that there is currently an East Coast/West Coast conflict afoot, and all the rappers from the respective camps hate each other and refuse to work together. So Producer approaches West Coast DJ W.C. and asks him to provide the music track for a hip-hop recording. Producer tells W.C. that a big name rapper is attached to provide the lyrics, but that he cannot tell W.C. who it is. W.C. produces the music track, and Producer promptly invites East Coast rapper E.C. to create and perform lyrics to accompany it, but does not tell E.C. who created the music track. Producer then combines the two tracks using an automated digital process, and releases the resulting work to great success. A dispute erupts between W.C. and E.C. regarding ownership of the musical composition embodied in the sound recording. Who owns this work of authorship?

(A) W.C. owns it, because he began the project.

(B) E.C. owns it, because he completed the project.

(C) Producer still owns it in the absence of a written agreement that secures him the rights, because he was the creative force behind the making of the work.

(D) W.C. and E.C. own the work as joint authors.

96. Screenwriter recently penned a script about two star-crossed lovers that is set in the Australian outback. In order to make the motion picture as authentic as possible, Screenwriter hires his Aussie friend Haul Pogen to advise him on the details of life in the outback. After Screenwriter finishes a nearly final draft of the script, he sends it to Haul, who returns extensive comments about how to make the settings, scene details, and characters' dialogue consistent with life in the Australian outback. Screenwriter looks at the revisions and says, "Haul, this is great, but I'm swamped. Tell you what: I'll double your fee if you just put these in yourself." Haul does as requested, and makes substantial revisions to the script, even including a new two-page scene. Screenwriter approves the changes, pays Haul double his one-time lump sum fee, and says, "Thanks, buddy, I'll make sure you're listed as a consultant in the credits." Haul responds, "That sounds great. It was my pleasure to chip in a bit." Screenwriter sells the completed script to Studio, which produces a

successful motion picture based on the script. Haul soon after decides that he is entitled to half of the fee Screenwriter received for the script, claiming that he is joint author of the script. Is Haul correct?

(A) No. Haul is not a joint author because there is no written agreement with Screenwriter identifying him as one.

(B) No. Haul is not a joint author because at the time of his collaboration with Screenwriter, neither he nor Screenwriter intended that he would be a joint author.

(C) Yes. Haul is a joint author because he contributed substantial creative material to the final version of the screenplay.

(D) Yes. Haul is a joint author because at the time he created material for the script, both he and Screenwriter intended the material to be added to the script.

97.   Consider question 96. Assume instead that when Screenwriter asked Haul for help on the screenplay, he said, "The outback scenes in this thing don't ring true. Fix it and I'll give you a piece of the action." Assume further that Screenwriter gave Haul complete control over the revisions, and that Haul's revisions included revising the title page to read "Screenplay by Screenwriter and Haul Pogen," which remained part of the script when it was sold to Studio. How would these facts affect Haul's claim to joint authorship, and why?

98.   Author works on a novel for six months and then comes down with a case of writer's block. He gives his half-completed manuscript to his friend Advisor and says, "I need some fresh ideas to get going. Can you help me out?" Author tells his agent that he has recently given the manuscript to Advisor for comments, and that if Advisor comes up with any good thoughts, he will include Advisor in the acknowledgments page of the final draft. Advisor, however, tells other friends that he is now "collaborating as a co-author" with Author on the novel. Eventually, Advisor reads the manuscript, meets with Author, and shares some fruitful suggestions that spur Author to finish the novel, which Author then publishes with great success. However, when the novel is released, Advisor is shocked to see that he is not credited as a co-author, but merely received an acknowledgment from Author. As a result, Advisor now sues Author for 50 percent of the royalties resulting from the exploitation of the novel. Advisor believes he is entitled to the royalties as a joint author. Is he correct?

(A) Yes. Advisor is a joint author because his creative contribution was critical to completion of the project.

(B) Yes. Advisor is a joint author because the conversation with his friend reveals his subjective expectation that he was in a co-authorial relationship at the time of the contribution.

(C) No. Advisor is not a joint author because his contribution to the novel was objectively less significant than Author's.

(D) No. Advisor is not a joint author because Author clearly did not regard him as a co-author at any point during their collaboration.

99. Worker and Slacker decide to co-author a screenplay. They sign a contract beforehand stating that the product of their collective labor will be regarded as a joint work of authorship for the purposes of copyright analysis. The agreement does not specify how any proceeds from the potential sale of the script will be divided. Worker slaves away on the screenplay for six months, and during that time produces 44 scenes. By contrast, Slacker works hardly at all and ends up contributing only a single original three-page scene to the final product, which is a screenplay consisting of 45 scenes. Producer reads the script, loves it, and offers to buy it from Worker and Slacker for $1 million. Worker and Slacker then dispute the appropriate split of the fee in court. Worker claims that he should get almost all of the money because he did almost all of the work. Slacker responds that the contract requires that as joint authors, Worker must split the proceeds equally. How will a court rule in this dispute?

(A) Slacker will prevail. Judges regard any contribution by a co-author as deserving an equal distribution of profits realized from the use or licensing of the screenplay as a matter of law.

(B) Slacker will prevail. As a contractually defined joint author of the work of authorship, he owns the work as a tenant in common with Worker, and this entitles him to an equal share.

(C) Worker will prevail because he did significantly more work than Slacker.

(D) Worker will prevail because courts have ruled that profits from jointly authored works should be split in proportion to the amount of work each author invested in them.

100. Composer has been working on a musical composition for the past several weeks. She has completed the music and most of the lyrics, but has been stuck on finding a single rhyme that will allow her to complete the last verse. Neighbor visits Composer and notices that Composer is toiling at her piano and is in a frustrated state of mind. Composer tells Neighbor that she has been deeply frustrated because she cannot find a word to rhyme with "orange." Neighbor suggests that she try "door hinge," a suggestion that fits the composition nicely and that Composer uses to complete the composition. Is Neighbor entitled to joint authorship status in light of this contribution?

101. Author loves his spouse, Wife, very much, and wants her to be a co-owner of his forthcoming nonfiction literary work on the history of copyright law. Which of the following statements most accurately describes the means by which Author can extend co-owner status to Wife?

(A) Author can assign a 50 percent interest in the copyright of the literary work to Wife while reserving a 50 percent interest for himself.

(B) Author can create a partnership with Wife and make the copyright of the literary work one of the assets of the partnership.

(C) Author can write an introductory note stating, "While she may not have written a line of this work, Wife is an author in spirit because she has always been my biggest supporter."

(D) (A) and (B) are both valid means of making Wife a co-owner of the copyright in the literary work; (C) is not.

102. Biggie and Smalls co-write a musical work titled *Young and High-Strung*. Smalls then performs and records the musical work on his own, and the resulting track becomes a big success in digital download sales. Which of the following statements accurately reflects the copyright ownership rights of Biggie and Smalls in the musical work and the sound recording of *Young and High-Strung*?

(A) Biggie and Smalls each own an undivided interest in the copyrights in both the musical work and sound recording.

(B) Biggie and Smalls each own an undivided interest in the whole of the copyright in the musical work, while Smalls owns the copyright in the sound recording.

(C) Biggie owns 100% of the copyright in the musical work, while Smalls owns 100% of the copyright in the sound recording.

(D) Biggie and Smalls each own an undivided interest in the copyright in *Young and High-Strung* and share equally in profits from its exploitation.

103. The Midnights are a three-piece rock band consisting of Vocalist, Guitarist, and Drummer. The three members of The Midnights co-author the melody, harmony, and lyrics for a musical work entitled *Fighty Aphrodite*. They then record the musical work and the resulting track becomes a big hit. A year later, Pianist approaches Guitarist and says she wants to record a version of *Fighty Aphrodite* on piano, and offers a licensing fee of $1,000 for the nonexclusive right to re-arrange the musical work, and to perform, record, and release a piano version of the new arrangement. Guitarist agrees and signs an agreement with Pianist granting her the license. Vocalist and Drummer, however, are opposed to the deal because they know and despise Pianist's work. Vocalist and Drummer file suit to enjoin Pianist from going forward with her project. Will they prevail?

(A) No. Co-owners of a work can nonexclusively license derivative works, but they owe their co-owners accounting for any profits generated by the license.

(B) No. Co-owners of a work can nonexclusively license derivative works, and the licensor is entitled to keep all the profits generated by the license.

(C) Yes. Nonexclusive licensing of a co-owned work requires the assent of more than 50 percent of the owners; one co-owner of three is insufficient.

(D) Yes. Nonexclusive licensing of a co-owned work requires the assent of all owners; one co-owner out of three is insufficient.

104. Consider question 103. Assume that Guitarist granted Pianist an exclusive rather than a nonexclusive license. How would this change the analysis, and why?

105. Composer and Lyricist co-write the musical work *Temptations*, and then they mutually agree to exclusively license Singer to record her own version of the musical work, and to publicly perform *Temptations* as well. The resulting sound recording of *Temptations* becomes a big hit, but while Composer likes it, Lyricist thinks it is awful and wants to rescind Singer's license. Over Composer's strong objection, Lyricist's lawyer sends Singer a letter saying that the license is rescinded, and that Singer is no longer permitted to publicly perform *Temptations*. Singer, on advice of counsel, continues to publicly perform the musical work, and Lyricist sues to enjoin Singer from doing so. Will Lyricist prevail?

(A) No. Lyricist will not prevail, because once an exclusive license to perform or otherwise use a copyrighted work of authorship has been granted, it can never be rescinded.

(B) No. Lyricist will not prevail, because an exclusive license to perform or otherwise use a copyrighted work of authorship can be rescinded only by unanimous consent of all its owners.

(C) Yes. Lyricist will prevail, because an exclusive license to perform or otherwise use a copyrighted work of authorship can be rescinded by any one of its owners.

(D) Yes. Lyricist will prevail because one co-owner's desire to rescind an exclusive license is sufficient evidence from which the desire for rescission by all owners may be inferred.

106. Consider question 105. Assume that once Singer's licensed recording of *Temptations* was released to the public as a digital download, Record Company decided to have one of its recording artists record *Temptations* without any authorization by Composer and Lyricist. Record Company has now released its recording in digital form and is offering it for purchase and download from its website. Composer and Lyricist threaten to sue Record Company for copyright infringement. This lawsuit will likely be:

(A) Successful, because Record Company is making unauthorized reproductions of the *Temptations* musical composition.

(B) Successful, because Record Company has no privity of contract with Composer and Lyricist's exclusive license with Singer.

(C) Unsuccessful, because the compulsory mechanical license provisions of section 115 of the Copyright Act obviate any liability for Record Company's unauthorized reproduction of the musical composition.

(D) Unsuccessful, so long as Record Company takes advantage of the compulsory mechanical license provisions of section 115 of the Copyright Act.

107. Clark and Michael recently co-wrote a novel that remains unpublished. Clark thinks the novel could be the basis for a great movie. Michael, however, does not trust the entertainment industry, fearing that a film production studio would ruin the story and characters developed in the novel. Clark nevertheless decides to write a screenplay based on the novel. He shows the completed screenplay to Studio, which loves it. Clark enters into an agreement with Studio pursuant to which Clark assigns to Studio his copyright interest in the novel for $100,000, as well as all right, title, and interest in the copyright of the screenplay for $250,000. In addition, Studio hires Clark to write two sets of revisions of the script for $50,000. Studio ultimately makes a motion picture based on Clark's revised script that makes a profit of $10 million. Nothing has been paid to Michael, who now sues Studio and Clark for copyright infringement and, in the alternative, an accounting. Analyze the possibility of Michael's success with this lawsuit.

108. Studio owns the copyright in *Tiger Woman*, a recently produced motion picture. Studio licenses Distributor, a film distribution company, to release the film, but under very limited circumstances. Studio grants to Distributor the exclusive right to exhibit *Tiger Woman* only in theaters that seat 50 or more patrons, only in states bordering the Atlantic Ocean, and only for two months. Distributor agrees to the terms of the license, but one day its in-house counsel advises that the agreement is unenforceable. Is Distributor's lawyer correct, and if so, why?

(A) Distributor's lawyer is correct because a copyright owner cannot limit via license the venues in which their work is shown, and this license limited showings of *Tiger Woman* to larger theaters.

(B) Distributor's lawyer is correct because a copyright owner cannot limit via license the geographical area in which a work is exploited, and this license limited the exhibition of *Tiger Woman* to states bordering the Atlantic Ocean.

(C) Distributor's lawyer is correct because a copyright owner cannot limit via license the time during which a licensee may exploit a work, and this license limits the time of Distributor's exploitation of *Tiger Woman* to two months.

(D) Distributor's lawyer is wrong; the license is valid.

109. Writer pens a novel that Speculator thinks is excellent, and Speculator wants to acquire its copyright. Writer and Speculator orally agree that Writer will sell Speculator the copyright in the novel for $500. After Speculator has paid the $500 to Writer, he learns that Writer subsequently licensed the rights to make a screenplay based on the novel to Studio. Speculator contacts Writer and says, "You can't do that, I own the copyright now." Is Speculator correct?

(A) No. Speculator is wrong, because when a creator sells a copyrighted work of authorship, he reserves the right to nonexclusively license uses of that work.

(B) No. Speculator is wrong; his agreement with Writer was invalid because it was not memorialized in writing.

(C) Yes. Speculator is correct, because the transfer of copyright ownership from Writer means that Writer retains no enforceable rights in the novel.

(D) Yes. Speculator is correct, because Writer's conduct was in bad faith.

110. Consider question 109. Assume that instead of an oral agreement, the parties had executed a written agreement that said "Writer hereby agrees to transfer the copyright in his novel to Speculator in exchange for a fee of $500" and was signed by Speculator. How would this change the outcome, and why?

111. Publisher admires Artist's most recent sculpture, and offers to purchase the copyright in the sculpture. Publisher and Artist orally agree that Artist will transfer to Publisher the copyright in the sculpture for $1,000. Publisher makes out a check to Artist in the amount of $1,000. In the memorandum area of the check, Publisher writes "Fee for purchase of copyright in Artist's sculpture." Artist receives the check signed by Publisher, endorses the back of it, and writes her initials next to Publisher's note in the memorandum area of the check. Is this transfer enforceable?

(A) Yes. The transfer is enforceable because it is in writing and signed by the transferee, Publisher.

(B) Yes. The transfer is enforceable because it is in writing and signed by the transferor, Artist.

(C) No. The transfer is not enforceable because a check is too informal to count as the kind of written memorandum required by the Copyright Act.

(D) No. The transfer is not enforceable because the memorandum was written by the transferee, Publisher, rather than the transferor, Artist.

112. In 1958, Screenwriter completes a script. Screenwriter does not publish the script or register it with the Copyright Office, but does begin talking the script up around Hollywood, and gets some significant buzz going. In 1959, Executive calls Screenwriter and tells him that Executive's company, Studio, wants to purchase all the rights to Screenwriter's script. Screenwriter is thrilled with the offer. He drives over to Studio, enters Executive's office with a copy of the screenplay, places it on Executive's desk, and says, "Here you go. I can't wait to see this baby on the silver screen!" Executive shakes Screenwriter's hand and gives him a check for the full amount of the agreed-upon fee. At no point during the exchange is any written agreement reflecting transfer of the copyright in the screenplay executed. Is the agreement enforceable?

(A) Yes. The agreement is enforceable because prior to 1978, transfers of unpublished and unregistered works of authorship could be effectuated by oral agreements and implied by courses of conduct.

(B) Yes. The agreement is enforceable because under the 1909 Act, no writing was required to transfer ownership of a copyright.

(C) No. The agreement is not enforceable because it was never memorialized in a writing signed by the transferor copyright owner, Screenwriter.

(D) No. The agreement is not enforceable because the parties never discussed the copyright in the work.

113. ShoeCo recently hired Designer to create a logo for its new line of running shoes. Designer created a distinctive logo design that met the approval of ShoeCo. Thereafter, the two parties executed a valid written agreement assigning all of Designer's rights in the logo to ShoeCo, including all copyrights, in exchange for valuable consideration. Soon, BigCorp decided it wanted the logo for use in connection with its multinational enterprise. Big-Corp offered ShoeCo a substantial fee in exchange for an assignment of all rights in the logo. ShoeCo accepted the offer and the two parties signed a written agreement assigning the copyright in the logo to BigCorp. BigCorp started to use the logo in connection with its products. This new use came to the attention of Designer, who is a staunch opponent of multinational companies such as BigCorp. Designer became incensed and now seeks an injunction preventing BigCorp from using the logo. Will Designer prevail?

(A) Yes. Designer will prevail because an assignment of copyright does not include the right to assign the copyright to other parties.

(B) Yes. Designer will prevail because, although copyright assignees can assign those copyrights to other parties, they retain a right of first refusal with respect to those third-party assignments.

(C) No. Designer will not prevail because ShoeCo, as the assignee of all rights in the logo, is free to assign its copyright to whomever it chooses.

(D) No. Designer will not prevail because the assignment from ShoeCo to BigCorp was invalid.

114. Consider question 113. Assume that rather than an assignment of copyright ownership, Designer granted to ShoeCo an exclusive license to use the logo in connection with any product, and that ShoeCo subsequently granted BigCorp an exclusive license to use the logo on its products. Would this variation change the outcome of the case and, if so, why?

115. AdAgency recently contracted with Musician to deliver a dozen short musical compositions to be used in television commercials for a storage company. AdAgency agreed, in a handshake deal, to pay Musician $600 for his services and an additional $500 for each musical composition used for a commercial on a buy-out basis, under which AdAgency would be given all of the rights, including copyright, in the composition it used in the commercial. Musician delivered to AdAgency 12 musical compositions that he had created a year earlier and AdAgency paid him the agreed-upon $600. After reviewing the

compositions, AdAgency selected one for use in the storage company commercial. Musician was paid an additional $500 for that musical composition.

Six months later, AdAgency used the same musical composition in a radio commercial for a local bank. Musician has demanded an additional $500 payment from AdAgency for the use of the musical composition in the bank commercial. AdAgency has refused payment on the ground that it "owns the rights to the composition."

If AdAgency claims that its rights to the musical composition are based on the fact that the composition was a work made for hire, AdAgency will likely be:

(A) Successful, because it obtained the musical composition via an agreement entered into by both parties and the composition was used for a television commercial that falls within the statutory category of audiovisual work.

(B) Unsuccessful, because the musical composition was not created pursuant to the agreement.

(C) Successful, because Musician was paid for creating and delivering the musical compositions.

(D) Unsuccessful, because the composition does not fall within any of the work made for hire statutory categories.

116.   Consider question 115. Assume that Musician decides not to sue AdAgency for breach of contract and instead opts to sue for copyright infringement of the musical composition. Musician will likely be:

(A) Unsuccessful, because AdAgency acquired the copyright to the musical composition through a valid assignment.

(B) Successful, because AdAgency never acquired a lawful right to use the composition.

(C) Unsuccessful, because Musician's course of conduct with AdAgency evidences the grant of a nonexclusive license from Musician to AdAgency to use the musical composition.

(D) Successful, because even if an implied nonexclusive license was created, it encompassed only the use of the musical composition in a television commercial for a storage company, not a radio commercial for a bank.

117.   Crafty McGee owns the copyright in a poem that she wrote. Crafty executes a written agreement to transfer ownership of the copyright in the poem to Publisher for $500. Publisher does not record the transfer with the Copyright Office. Crafty then offers to execute another written agreement transferring ownership of the copyright in the poem to Collector. Collector is aware of the original agreement between Crafty and Publisher, but enters into the agreement anyway, paying $700 to Crafty in exchange for the transfer of copyright

ownership. Six months later, Publisher releases an anthology of poems that includes the one penned by Crafty, and Collector sues Publisher for infringement. Will Collector prevail?

(A) Yes. The initial transfer of ownership to Publisher was invalid because Publisher failed to record it.

(B) Yes. As the first party to record a transfer of ownership of the copyright in the poem from Crafty, Collector has rights superior to all other purported transferees, including Publisher.

(C) No. Because Crafty transferred the copyright in the poem to Publisher before he transferred it to Collector, Publisher's rights are superior to Collector's.

(D) No. Because Collector was not a good faith transferee, her recordation of the transfer cannot create superior rights, and the initial transfer to Publisher remains valid.

118. In 1950, Novelist signed a publishing agreement with Publisher. The agreement stated that Novelist licensed the copyright in his novel, *Holidaze*, for the purpose of publishing it "in hardcover, paperback, or other printed form" for the life of the copyright. The agreement contained a clause explicitly reserving in Novelist the right to license the rights in *Holidaze* for "any other uses." Recently, Publisher partnered with a company that produces eBooks. Publisher provided CompuCo with the text of its most profitable 500 works, including *Holidaze*, so that CompuCo could reduce them to digital form so that they could then be marketed as eBooks. Novelist was incensed that Publisher did so without seeking a license, and sued Publisher for copyright infringement. Publisher responded that the 1950 agreement allowed it to publish or facilitate the publication of *Holidaze* in any book form possible, including digital media. Who will prevail?

(A) Novelist. The grant of a license to publish a work in analog format never implies a right to publish that same work in digital format.

(B) Novelist. This particular grant was narrowly worded to apply only to "printed form," which excludes digital media.

(C) Publisher. The grant of a license to publish a work in analog format always implies a right to publish that same work in digital format.

(D) Publisher. This particular grant did not exclude digital media, so it should be construed in favor of the licensee.

119. It is 1970 and the artist Avant has a studio from which he sells his artwork and accepts commissions to create paintings. Collector visits the studio and finds a painting, *Sunrise Over Shatto*, to her liking and pays the asking price of $5,000. Avant takes the canvas down from the wall and hands it to Collector, who walks out of the studio to her apartment, where she hangs the painting in her living room. Which of the following is correct?

(A) Avant is the creator and author, and Collector is the owner of the copyright in *Sunrise Over Shatto*.

(B) Avant is the creator, and Collector is the author and owner of the copyright in *Sunrise Over Shatto.*

(C) Avant is the creator, author, and owner of the copyright in *Sunrise Over Shatto.*

(D) Collector is the creator, author, and owner of the copyright in *Sunrise Over Shatto.*

120. It is 1970 and the artist Avant has a studio from which he sells his artwork and accepts commissions to create paintings. Collector visits the studio, but does not find a painting to her liking. Collector pays Avant $5,000 to paint *Sunrise Over Palms*, a painting that depicts the rising sun through the leaves of several palm trees. When Collector arrives at the studio a month later to pick up the painting, Avant takes the canvas down from the wall and hands it to Collector, who walks out of the studio to her apartment, where she hangs the painting in her living room. Which of the following is correct?

(A) Avant is the creator and author, and Collector is the owner of the copyright in *Sunrise Over Palms.*

(B) Avant is the creator, and Collector is the author and owner of the copyright in *Sunrise Over Palms.*

(C) Avant is the creator, author, and owner of the copyright in *Sunrise Over Palms.*

(D) Collector is the creator, author, and owner of the copyright in *Sunrise Over Palms.*

121. It is 2018 and the artist Avant Jr. has a studio from which he sells his artwork and accepts commissions to create paintings. Collector visits the studio and finds a painting, *Moonlight Over the Bay*, to her liking and pays the asking price of $5,000. Avant Jr. takes the canvas down from the wall and hands it to Collector, who walks out of the studio to her apartment, where she hangs the painting in her living room. Which of the following is correct?

(A) Avant Jr. is the creator and author, and Collector is the owner of the copyright in *Moonlight Over the Bay.*

(B) Avant Jr. is the creator, and Collector is the author and owner of the copyright in *Moonlight Over the Bay.*

(C) Avant Jr. is the creator, author, and owner of the copyright in *Moonlight Over the Bay.*

(D) Collector is the creator, author, and owner of the copyright in *Moonlight Over the Bay.*

122. It is 2018 and the artist Avant Jr. has a studio from which he sells his artwork and accepts commissions to create paintings. Collector visits the studio, but does not find a painting to her liking. Collector pays Avant Jr. $5,000 to paint *Sunset Boulevard*, a painting that depicts the setting sun as it illuminates a major urban thoroughfare. When Collector arrives at the studio a month later to pick up the painting, Avant Jr. takes the canvas down from the wall

and hands it to Collector, who walks out of the studio to her apartment, where she hangs the painting in her living room. Which of the following is correct?

(A) Avant Jr. is the creator and author, and Collector is the owner of the copyright in *Sunset Boulevard*.

(B) Avant Jr. is the creator, and Collector is the author and owner of the copyright in *Sunset Boulevard*.

(C) Avant Jr. is the creator, author, and owner of the copyright in *Sunset Boulevard*.

(D) Collector is the creator, author, and owner of the copyright in *Sunset Boulevard*.

123.   Vanessa is a talented video game developer. GreatGames is a video game developer that sometimes retains Vanessa's services as an independent contractor to work on projects they are developing. Recently, one of GreatGames' employees, Angie, tells Vanessa that Great-Games has tasked her with developing a game "that is set in a futuristic wasteland with players competing to survive." Vanessa is intrigued by the idea, and she and Angie begin working on the game. They agree that the game will be called *Dirt Wars*, and that its premise will feature players competing to survive in a post-apocalyptic setting. Vanessa composes about 75% of the code for the game, while Angie composes the rest. Throughout the creative process, Angie and Vanessa discuss the game's development, each making substantive contributions to it.

GreatGames is very pleased with the result, and they decide to release and promote *Dirt Wars* as part of the GreatGames catalogue. *Dirt Wars* is a huge success, and earns $10 million in profits. GreatGames tells Vanessa about this in an email, and says "Thanks for helping us out. We want to compensate you fairly, so here is a check for $500,000; this is the same amount we paid Angie for her contribution. This represents the entirety of your compensation for your contribution to *Dirt Wars*."

Vanessa feels she has been undercompensated for her contribution to *Dirt Wars*, and asks you what she was entitled to earn for the success of the game under copyright law. What should you tell her?

(A) Vanessa should receive three times what GreatGames paid Angie because Vanessa wrote three times as much code as Angie.

(B) Vanessa should receive half the profits generated by *Dirt Wars* because she is a joint author of the game along with Angie.

(C) Vanessa should receive half the profits generated by *Dirt Wars* because she is a joint author of the game along with GreatGames.

(D) Vanessa's compensation is whatever GreatGames wants to pay her, since she created the game as a work made for hire for GreatGames, which alone owns the copyright in the game.

124. Consider question 123. Assume that, after creating *Dirt Wars*, Vanessa validly assigns her full copyright interest in the game to GreatGames for $3 million. Which of the following statements correctly describes the state of title in the copyright to *Dirt Wars*?

   (A) Vanessa remains a joint owner of the copyright in *Dirt Wars*, but GreatGames now owns a 75 percent ownership share in the copyright, while she owns only 25 percent of the copyright.

   (B) Vanessa remains a joint author of *Dirt Wars*, but GreatGames owns the entirety of the copyright in that work.

   (C) Vanessa remains a joint owner of the copyright in *Dirt Wars*, but GreatGames is now the sole author of that work.

   (D) GreatGames is now the sole author and sole owner of the copyright in *Dirt Wars*.

125. Consider question 123. Assume two additional facts. First, assume that when the game is released, Vanessa is not credited as a co-creator of *Dirt Wars* on the game's web page or anywhere else, and that in the game's credit roll, she is listed as a "contributing programmer" along with several other programmers who made marginal technical contributions to the code base of *Dirt Wars*. Second, assume further that Jane Paz, founder and CEO of GreatGames, had never heard of Vanessa until Angie told Jane of Vanessa's substantial contribution to the *Dirt Wars* after the game had enjoyed great commercial success.

   Would these facts undermine Vanessa's claim to being a co-author of *Dirt Wars*?

126. In 2015, Ed and Sesilia jointly authored a screenplay. They shopped it around to numerous film production studios without success, eventually becoming discouraged, giving up, and moving on to other projects. Recently, Sesilia's friend Jeremy got a job as the assistant to the vice president for development at Tantamount Studios. Jeremy offered to show his boss the screenplay. Sesilia mentioned the opportunity to Ed, who said "Sure, go ahead. I mean, no one wants our stupid screenplay anyway, and I've stopped caring about it since I'm working on some other really cool projects."

   Sesilia then gives the screenplay to Jeremy, who shows it to his boss, who loves it. Tantamount offers to pay $1 million for a one-year non-exclusive option to produce the screenplay. Jeremy did not tell Tantamount that the screenplay was co-authored, though, so Sesilia alone signs the development deal and cashes the check from the studio. Eventually, Ed hears about the deal through the grapevine and becomes incensed. He calls Sesilia and tells her, "You better give me my half of that cash, or I'll sue."

   Sesilia contacts you and asks whether Ed is legally entitled to half the money she received for transferring the development option to Tantamount. What should you tell her?

   (A) Ed has a federal cause of action for accounting to compel Sesilia to split the money with him.

(B) Ed has a state cause of action for accounting to compel Sesilia to split the money with him.

(C) Sesilia does not have to split the option fee with Ed because he gave her an implied license to do the deal on her own.

(D) Sesilia does not have to split the option fee with Ed because he abandoned his interest in the copyright.

127. Consider Question 126. Assume that, instead of demanding his share of the option fee from Tantamount, Ed wants to prevent the studio from developing the screenplay into a film. He hires a lawyer, who sends Tantamount a letter indicating that he does not give the studio permission to use the screenplay in film development, and threatening to sue for injunctive relief preventing them from doing so. Will a court grant Ed's motion for injunctive relief against Tantamount?

(A) Yes, because only Sesilia, not Ed, signed the option agreement.

(B) Yes, because Ed formally notified Tantamount that they did not have his permission to use the screenplay in film development.

(C) No, because Sesilia asked Ed for permission to let Jeremy share the screenplay with Tantamount.

(D) No, because as a co-owner of the work, Sesilia has a right to use it however she wishes and to non-exclusively license it, subject only to a right to account to Ed for half of any profits earned by such uses and licenses.

Protection of Exclusive Rights

128. Animator is working on an animated feature film for Studio. He creates several animation cels. Studio owns the copyrights in all these works as works made for hire. The cels
feature fanciful anthropomorphic animals in a medieval setting with castles and quaint
villages. None of Animator's cels are ultimately used in the final version of Studio's film,
though, and Animator takes them home. Animator subsequently creates his own project,
an animated short film featuring cartoon human characters that is also set in the Middle
Ages. Almost all of Animator's short film consists of his own work, but in a few scenes,
he copies and uses background images of a castle and segments of the cels he created for
the feature film to fill out the background of some of the cels for his short film. While Animator never screens his short film publicly, an executive of Studio hears that some features
of Animator's short film are the same as the ones Animator created for Studio. Studio
sues Animator for copyright infringement. Will Studio prevail?

(A) Yes. Studio will prevail, because by copying some features of the animated cels owned
by Studio, Animator violated Studio's right of reproduction in those works of
authorship.

(B) Yes. Studio will prevail, because by copying some features of the animated cels owned
by Studio, Animator violated Studio's right of public display in those works of
authorship.

(C) No. Studio will not prevail, because the animation cels that Animator created for Studio never appeared in the ultimate work of authorship for which they were originally
intended.

(D) No. Studio will not prevail, because Animator used only segments of the original cels
in his short film.

129. Joe buys a copy of the popular video game Bonestorm to play on his personal computer.
Joe's roommate, Bo, who also enjoys video games, notices Joe's CD-ROM copy of Bonestorm
lying around their shared apartment. One day when Joe is out, Bo takes the Bonestorm
CD-ROM, places it on his own personal computer, and plays a few games. Although Bo
does not install the application onto his hard drive, during his game play, a copy of the
object code of the Bonestorm program is made in the RAM of his computer. Joe later finds
out what Bo did, and reports him to SoftCo, owner of the copyright in the Bonestorm object
code. SoftCo then brings a copyright infringement suit against Bo. Will SoftCo prevail?

(A)   No. SoftCo will not prevail because the object code placed in RAM is temporary and evanescent, and thus does not count as a copy.

(B)   No. SoftCo will not prevail because the Digital Millennium Copyright Act held that RAM copies of object code can never violate a copyright owner's exclusive right of reproduction.

(C)   Yes. SoftCo will prevail because Bo's reproduction of the object code in the RAM of his computer violates SoftCo's reproduction right in that object code.

(D)   Yes. SoftCo will prevail because Bo's reproduction of the object code in the RAM of his computer violates SoftCo's adaptation right in that object code.

130.   Consider question 129. Assume that rather than surreptitiously taking and using Joe's Bonestorm CD-ROM for the purpose of playing the game, Bo took and used the CD-ROM only because his personal computer was malfunctioning, and he needed to use it in order to diagnose and fix the problem. Would this change the result, and if so, why?

131.   Synchro is choosing the music for the soundtrack for the new motion picture to be released by his employer, Studio. Synchro finds a great track titled *Speed Demon* that he uses as the background music for a chase scene, but does not secure the rights because he understands that the musical work that comprises *Speed Demon* is in the public domain. However, when the motion picture is released, the owner of the copyright in the sound recording version of *Speed Demon* featured in the soundtrack sues Studio for infringement. What exclusive right does Synchro's unauthorized use of the *Speed Demon* track violate prior to the exhibition of the motion picture in theaters?

(A)   Public distribution.

(B)   Public display.

(C)   Reproduction.

(D)   Public performance.

132.   Groupie is a big fan of Band, and goes to one of its concerts with a hidden recording device. Groupie records Band's live performance of public domain musical compositions and later listens to the recording on his portable music player. Does Groupie's conduct subject him to any liability?

(A)   Yes. Groupie is liable for infringing Band's exclusive right of reproduction.

(B)   Yes. Groupie is liable for violating federal anti-bootlegging provisions.

(C)   No. Groupie cannot be held liable because Band's live performance was unfixed and thus uncopyrightable.

(D)   No. Groupie cannot be held liable because he never sold or distributed the copy he made of Band's performance.

133. San Begonio Public Library (SBPL) is a municipal institution that is open to the population of the small town of San Begonio. One day, local resident Adam comes to SBPL and asks for a copy of a recent article from the *San Begonio Times* about the town's early history, which Adam wants solely for his personal edification. Librarian makes one copy of the requested piece, writes "© 2008 San Begonio Times" at the top of the article, and gives it to Adam.

While Librarian is occupied with this project, Bob sneaks into SBPL and uses the library's photocopy machine to make a photocopy of the literary work *Novel*. The photocopy machine is situated under a sign that informs those using the machine that the making of a copy violates federal copyright law. Bob intends to scan *Novel* and put it online for the public to read free of charge.

Later that day, Archivist, an employee of the nearby La Garganta Public Library (LGPL), calls SBPL and asks Librarian if she could send a CD-ROM containing a rare and discontinued spoken-word version of *Dated Tome*, a difficult-to-find novel written by Lucy Jaylin, via inter-library loan. Archivist explains that SBPL's copy of the spoken-word version of *Dated Tome* has been stolen and SBPL needs to replace it so it can make the recording available to its borrowing public. Librarian burns a copy of SBPL's spoken-word recording of *Dated Tome* onto a CD-ROM, writes "Dated Tome, © Lucy Jaylin 2008" on the disc, and sends it to Archivist, along with SBPL's printed warning concerning copyright restrictions contained on its order form.

Which, if any, of these acts of reproduction will subject SBPL to infringement liability?

(A) Librarian's making a photocopy of the news article for Adam, and Bob's use of SBPL's photocopier to make an unauthorized copy of *Novel*.

(B) Bob's use of SBPL's photocopier to make an unauthorized copy of *Novel*, and Librarian's creation of a duplicate CD-ROM of *Dated Tome* for Archivist.

(C) Only Bob's use of SBPL's photocopier to make an unauthorized copy of *Novel*.

(D) None of these uses will expose SBPL to infringement liability.

134. Journalist, who is based in New York, pens an investigative essay that he markets to various news outlets. Finally, *Bi-Coastal Magazine* makes Journalist a publication offer of $10,000 in exchange for the exclusive right to publish the piece in its next issue. Journalist accepts. *Bi-Coastal Magazine* is a national publication that publishes separate East Coast and West Coast editions each month. Each of its two monthly editions contains 85 percent of the same material, including artwork and advertisements. Journalist's article appears in both editions. Journalist never specifically consented to this dual publication, and sues *Bi-Coastal Magazine* for reproducing the article in the West Coast edition without permission. Will Journalist prevail?

(A) Yes. Journalist will prevail because his agreement with *Bi-Coastal Magazine* included only the right to publish the article in one edition of the magazine.

(B) Yes. Journalist will prevail because *Bi-Coastal Magazine*'s use of his article in the West Coast edition amounts to an unauthorized public distribution of that work.

(C) No. Journalist will not prevail because *Bi-Coastal Magazine*'s use of the article in its West Coast edition falls within the federal privilege for publishers of collective works to republish individual contributions in different editions.

(D) No. Journalist will not prevail because by authorizing Bi-Coastal Magazine to use his article in one edition of its magazine, he also granted an implied license to Bi-Coastal Magazine to use the article in any other print medium.

135.   Consider question 134. Assume that *Bi-Coastal Magazine* licensed the content of its issues, including the article written by Journalist, to an online database. The online database allows users to search and retrieve articles that then appear in a text-only version, as opposed to being featured in the context of their original publication. How, if at all, would this affect Journalist's likelihood of success in a copyright infringement suit against *Bi-Coastal Magazine*?

136.   Composer writes a concerto for piano titled *Winter* that he performs and records on his own, and then sells the resulting sound recording in .mp3 form as a track titled *Composer Performs Winter*. Dilettante purchases an .mp3 copy *Composer Performs Winter*, and then, based only on hearing the track, performs and records the concerto herself. Without payment to or authorization from Composer, Dilettante then releases this latter sound recording under the title *Dilettante Performs Winter*. Composer sues Dilettante for copyright infringement. Will Composer succeed?

(A) Yes. Composer will succeed in showing that Dilettante infringed his copyright in both the *Winter* musical work and the *Composer Performs Winter* sound recording.

(B) Yes. Composer will succeed in showing that Dilettante infringed his copyright in the *Winter* musical work.

(C) No. Dilettante is free to make a new sound recording of the *Winter* musical work, so long as she does not duplicate the original; and she is free to reproduce the *Winter* musical work because it is subject to a compulsory mechanical license by statute.

(D) No. Dilettante must obtain a "master use" license to use the Composer Performs Winter sound recording, even if the musical work is subject to a compulsory mechanical license by statute.

137.   Consider question 136. Assume that instead of recording her own version of *Winter* without Composer's permission, Dilettante visited Attorney first and asked whether she needed to obtain Composer's permission in order to record *Dilettante Performs Winter*. Under these circumstances, what advice should Attorney give Dilettante?

138.   Composer composed musical work titled *Songbird*. She also performed and recorded it herself, resulting in a sound recording in which she owns the copyright. Her recording of *Songbird* has been available in .mp3 format only on Composer's personal website for a small fee. Techie runs indiecheap.com, a website where users can stream and download .mp3 versions of their favorite independent music tracks at a significant discount. Techie paid

to download a copy of *Songbird* from Composer's website. He then included it among the tracks that are available on indiecheap.com without Composer's permission.

Which of the following statements most accurately describes Techie's liability under the Copyright Act for his use of the *Songbird* musical work?

(A) Techie will be liable for copyright infringement under the Copyright Act only if he fails to obtain a mechanical license.

(B) Techie will be liable for copyright infringement under the Copyright Act only if he fails to obtain a public performance license.

(C) Techie will be liable for copyright infringement under the Copyright Act if he fails to obtain both a mechanical license and a public performance license.

(D) Techie will not be liable for copyright infringement under the Copyright Act because the recording of *Songbird* was not released in a physical copy; therefore, no license is necessary.

139. Which of the following statements most accurately describes Techie's liability under the Copyright Act for his use of the *Songbird* sound recording?

(A) Techie will be liable for copyright infringement under the Copyright Act, but not if he obtains a master use license.

(B) Techie will be liable for copyright infringement under the Copyright Act, but not if he obtains a public performance license.

(C) Techie will be liable for copyright infringement under the Copyright Act, but not if he obtains both a master use license and a public performance license.

(D) Techie will be liable for copyright infringement under the Copyright Act, but not if he obtains both a master use license and a license to digitally transmit the sound recording to the public.

140. Pal decides to make a mix CD to give to Friend as a gift. Pal does this by selecting several recordings of music that he has legally downloaded from the Internet to his home computer, which he then uses to burn the recordings onto a CD. How, if at all, does Pal's conduct violate the exclusive rights of the copyright owners in the musical works and sound recordings that comprise the tracks on the CD he burned for Friend?

(A) Pal's conduct violates the reproduction rights of the copyright owners of both the musical works and sound recordings.

(B) Pal's conduct violates the reproduction rights of the copyright in the musical works only.

(C) Pal's conduct violates the reproduction rights of the copyright in the sound recordings only.

(D) Pal's conduct does not violate the exclusive rights of any copyright owner.

141. Pomo is a contemporary "appropriation" artist whose work alters the creations of other artists in an effort to comment on those creations. Pomo acquires a print of *Idyll*, the latest work by Artist, who is a popular contemporary painter of oil landscapes. Pomo then composes an original paragraph decrying the mundane character of landscape painting, and writes the text all over his print of *Idyll*, which Pomo then displays in his art gallery for all to see, but not to purchase. When Artist learns about this, he becomes incensed and files a suit against Pomo for infringing his copyright in *Idyll*. Assuming that fair use is not an available defense, did Pomo's conduct violate any of Artist's exclusive rights in *Idyll*?

(A) Yes. Pomo's conduct violates Artist's exclusive right of public display.

(B) Yes. Pomo's conduct violates Artist's exclusive right of adaptation.

(C) No. Pomo's alteration of his copy of *Idyll* rather than the original means that none of Artist's exclusive rights are at issue.

(D) No. Pomo's conduct did not violate any of Artist's exclusive rights in *Idyll* because the work altered by Pomo was not offered for sale.

142. Consider question 141. Assume that, rather than composing an original text and altering *Idyll* using that text, Pomo had made a pleasing frame, placed his copy of *Idyll* in that frame, and then sold the framed copy of *Idyll* at an auction for a substantial sum. On these facts, would Pomo be subject to any copyright liability? No , not an adoption

143. Linguo is a language buff and avid reader. He buys a copy of Author's latest book, *Novel*, which is written in English. Linguo wants to impress his language-buff friends, and translates his copy of *Novel* into the Esperanto language. Linguo does this by photocopying his purchased copy of Novel on his employer's photocopier. He then makes notes on the photocopy, which he then uses to type up the Esperanto version of *Novel*. He then gives the translation to three of his close friends in order to show off his accomplishment. What exclusive rights in *Novel* did Linguo violate? Close friends

(A) Reproduction.

(B) Reproduction and public distribution.

(C) Reproduction and adaptation.

(D) Reproduction, adaptation, and public distribution.

144. Biglaw, LLC declines to promote Associate to partner, and Associate leaves the firm in anger. Associate surreptitiously steals several hundred copies of Biglaw's employee handbook with him on his last day of employment and stations himself outside the law firm's building, handing out copies of the handbook to strangers with a note attached to the front reading "Biglaw treats their employees like dirt—read all about it inside!" Biglaw discovers this,

and sues Associate for copyright infringement, alleging that Associate's conduct violated its exclusive right of public distribution. Is Biglaw's public distribution argument valid?

(A) Yes. Associate's making Biglaw's copies of the handbook available to the public without authorization violates Biglaw's public distribution right.

(B) Yes. As the owner of the copyright in its employee handbook, Biglaw has the right to control any dissemination of copies of the work.

(C) No. Associate's conduct is protected under the first sale doctrine.

(D) No. Associate cannot be held liable for violating Biglaw's right of public distribution in the handbook because he did not select a particular audience for his distribution, but rather made it generally available.

145.   Consider question 144. Assume that, instead of directly handing copies of the handbook to people, Associate made three copies of the handbook, gave each to close friends who specialized in employment law, and asked them to consider whether, in light of Biglaw's employment policies, it may create the basis for a wrongful termination lawsuit. On these facts, would Biglaw be able to successfully argue that Associate's conduct violated its exclusive right of public distribution in the employee handbook? No

146.   Consider question 144. Assume **for the purposes of this question only** that instead of giving copies of the employee handbook directly to people, Associate simply leaves copies all over the area near the law firm building, such as on park benches and at bus stops. Would these actions violate Biglaw's right of public distribution in the manual? Yes.

147.   Techie writes the original code for a computer program. Techie gives a copy of the program on a flash drive to his friend, Computo, saying, "I want you to have this program— I think you'll really like it!" Later, Techie is dismayed to learn that Computo was not impressed with the program, and that Computo gave the flash drive to the local public library in case any members of the public might have more interest in it. Techie sues Computo, arguing that Computo violated Techie's right of public distribution in the code of the computer program. Is Techie's argument correct?

(A) Yes. The first sale doctrine does not apply in this case because Techie did not sell the flash drive to Computo, but gave it to him as a gift.

(B) Yes. By facilitating the public library's distribution to the public of the flash drive containing Techie's protected code, Computo himself can be held liable for violating Techie's exclusive right of public distribution.

(C) No. Computo's conduct does not amount to public distribution of the source code that comprises the computer program.

(D) No. Computo's conduct amounts to public distribution of the source code that comprises the computer program, but it is permitted under the first sale doctrine.

148. Entrepreneur has an idea for a new business venture. He opens a business that purchases CD copies of all new major music releases and rents them to the public at a price much lower than it would cost to purchase the CD. This way, Entrepreneur theorizes, he can capture the market consisting of people who do not want to buy a CD outright, but still have enough interest in the music that they might pay a lower price to listen to it for a week or so. Entrepreneur's business presents no risk of music piracy. All of the rented CDs are heavily protected so that the tracks contained on them cannot be ripped. Soon, Entrepreneur finds himself sued by record companies who argue that his business violates their right of public distribution in the sound recordings embodied in the CDs that Entrepreneur rents. Will the record companies' argument succeed?

    (A) Yes. The first sale doctrine does not apply in this case because the Copyright Act was amended to exclude the rental of musical works embodied in phonorecords.

    (B) Yes. A purchaser of a CD cannot sell, lease, or give it to another person without running afoul of the copyright owner's exclusive right of public distribution.

    (C) No. The first sale doctrine immunizes Entrepreneur from liability because it entitles him to sell, lease, or give away the physical CDs in which he rightfully acquires ownership.

    (D) No. Because Entrepreneur has carefully crafted his business model to eliminate any risk of piracy, record companies cannot argue that they are harmed by his conduct.

149. Orchestra puts on a concert in New York City where it plays a piece of modern classical music. WCLX, an analog FM radio station, makes a simultaneous broadcast of the concert live. Fan, a big classical music aficionado in Hartford, Connecticut, tunes in to WCLX's broadcast of the concert and plays it on his home stereo system for an assembled group of 15 other music lovers. Which of these acts amounts to a "performance" within the meaning of the Copyright Act?

    (A) Orchestra's concert.

    (B) Orchestra's concert and WCLX's transmission of the concert.

    (C) WCLX's transmission of the concert and Fan's retransmission of the concert.

    (D) Orchestra's concert, WCLX's transmission of the concert, and Fan's retransmission of the concert.

150. Which of the following performances are "public" within the meaning of the Copyright Act?

I. An outdoor classical music concert at a municipal park;

II. A poetry reading at a café that is attended by 20 people;

III. A comedy routine at a private club that is by invitation only;

IV. A weekly presentation, which includes the performance of recorded music, by an employee of a private firm to a group of 15 fellow employees.

(A) I only

(B) I and II

(C) I, II, and III

(D) I, II, and IV

151. Hoteles Gigantes (HG) offers its numerous guests a distinctive in-room, on-demand movie service. Each HG location has an offsite server with hundreds of legally acquired digital versions of major motion pictures, including several for which Studio owns the copyrights. HG guests can use their in-room televisions to request any of these films, at which time the film is transmitted from the hotel's server to the guest's in-room television. Studio hears about HG's service and sues HG for copyright infringement, arguing that each transmission to a guest's room amounts to an unauthorized public performance of the copyrighted work. Will Studio prevail on this claim?

(A) Yes. Every time a user plays a digital version of a motion picture, it is a public performance of that work of authorship.

(B) Yes. HG's transmission of motion pictures from its central server to guest rooms amounts to an unauthorized public performance of those works of authorship.

(C) No. While HG's transmission of motion pictures from its central server to guest rooms amounts to an unauthorized performance of those works of authorship, it is not a public performance because the guest rooms are all private.

(D) No. Merely transmitting a work of authorship from one point to another does not amount to a performance of that work.

152. Consider question 151. Assume that, instead of offering an in-room on-demand movie service, HG offers its guests in-room Internet service at computer terminals located in each room. The Internet service is also routed through an off-site server to each HG site, so that whenever an HG guest requests a URL offering motion pictures on the guest's in-room computer, the HG server negotiates the request and passes it along to HG's Internet service provider, which sends the resulting information to the requesting guest's terminal. Assume that HG guests visit websites that show unauthorized versions of motion pictures. Could the studios that own the copyrights in those motion pictures successfully sue HG for publicly performing their works of authorship?

153. Restaurateur owns a restaurant that is 4,000 gross square feet in size. The restaurant has no stage or dance floor. Restaurateur has purchased a receiver, tuned it to a local FM radio station that broadcasts music, and attached the receiver to a sophisticated 10-speaker sound system installed by a sound engineering company at considerable expense. Restaurateur wants to take advantage of the Copyright Act's small business exception exempting certain commercial establishments from paying public performance fees for

musical works. Which of the following factors prevent Restaurateur from taking advantage of this section?

(A) The size of the restaurant is 4,000 gross square feet.

(B) The restaurant has an expensive, sophisticated sound system.

(C) The restaurant is a food service and not a drinking establishment.

(D) The restaurant is not a venue for live music.

154. The Children's Play Center is an advanced, music-focused preschool that features contemporary instrumental music as a background feature during breaks between learning sessions. The Center allows its students to choose which song they want to hear. The Center then plays the requested music for its students using a digital music player, a low power amplifier, two home-style speakers, and a library of .mp3 recordings of contemporary instrumental music. The Center has not asked for a license either from ASCAP or the owners of the copyrights in the works. Which of the following statements about these performances is accurate?

(A) They infringe the copyrights in the musical compositions, but only if the musical compositions had been distributed on phonorecords to members of the public for their private use.

(B) They infringe the copyrights in the musical compositions because the *Aiken* exception codified in section 110(5)(A) would not apply.

(C) They do not infringe the copyrights in the musical compositions because sound recordings do not have a public performance right.

(D) They do not infringe the copyrights in the musical compositions because the performances take place at the direction of the children.

155. Karma runs a store in the town of New Hayvensburg that sells tie-dyed prints and clothes made entirely from hemp. One day, officers of the New Hayvensburg Police Department (NHPD), acting on an anonymous tip, raid Karma's store looking for illegal drugs. The NHPD confiscates a substantial amount of material, including some of Karma's original pencil sketches of clothing designs, but ultimately finds nothing illegal. The NHPD delays in returning the confiscated items to Karma, and she ultimately files a series of legal actions against the NHPD based on its failure to return these items. Among these actions is a copyright infringement suit in which Karma argues that the NHPD's failure to return her pencil sketches amounts to a violation of her exclusive rights as the owner of the copyright on those protected works of authorship. Will Karma prevail on this copyright-based claim?

(A) Yes. The NHPD's failure to return the sketches violates Karma's exclusive right to control her work.

(B) Yes. The NHPD's failure to return the sketches violates Karma's exclusive rights to earn a profit from her copyrighted works by preventing her from selling them.

(C) No. The creator of an original pictorial or graphical work owns the copyright in the work of authorship contained in the work, but retains no rights in the physical object, so Karma has no right to have the drawings returned.

(D) No. Karma's ownership of the copyright in the drawings does not give rise to any copyright-based claim to have them returned.

156. Superfan is a schoolteacher and is also an enthusiast of Novelist's famed science fiction. Novelist releases a new literary work, *Ultraworld*, that Superfan is very excited about. She uses *Ultraworld* as a teaching tool for her sixth graders, reading them a chapter of the novel every day and engaging them in a discussion of how Novelist creates his distinctive tone and mood. Superfan also invites the 15 members of the local Novelist fan club to her home, where she regales them with a dramatic reading of her favorite passages from *Ultraworld*. One member of the fan club admires Superfan's readings and invites her to give a dramatic reading of *Ultraworld* at the open-mic night at the local coffeehouse. Superfan does a reading at the open-mic night, which is attended by a crowd of about 20 people, each of whom pay a fee of $5 to hear the various performers. Novelist hears about Superfan's conduct and sues her for violating Novelist's exclusive right of public performance of *Ultraworld*. Which of Superfan's readings violate Novelist's exclusive right of public performance in *Ultraworld*?

(A) Superfan's reading at the open-mic night only.

(B) Superfan's reading to the fan club and her reading at the open-mic night.

(C) Superfan's reading to her students and her reading at the open-mic night.

(D) Superfan's reading to her students, her reading to the fan club, and her reading at the open-mic night.

157. Musician performs and records an original version of *Delight*, a musical work that is in the public domain, which she then makes available on her website for download in .mp3 format for 99¢. Not wanting to pay anything for the recording, Pirate hacks into Musician's website, makes an unauthorized copy of the .mp3 file containing the recording of *Delight*, and places it onto his hard drive. Pirate then streams the recording of *Delight* over his own website so that any visitor can listen to (but not download) Musician's recording of *Delight* free of charge. Musician learns about Pirate's website and sues him for copyright infringement, arguing that Pirate has violated her exclusive rights to reproduce and publicly transmit a digital version of her sound recording. Will Musician's claim succeed?

(A) Yes. Both of Musician's bases for arguing that Pirate violated her exclusive rights are valid.

(B) Musician can successfully argue that Pirate violated her right of reproduction in her sound recording, but not her right of digital transmission.

(C) Musician can successfully argue that Pirate violated her right of digital transmission, but not her right of reproduction.

(D) No. Neither of Musician's bases for arguing that Pirate violated her exclusive rights is valid.

158. Consider question 157. Assume that instead of streaming Musician's *Delight* sound recording over his personal website, Pirate broadcast the sound recording over analog radio waves during his night shift at a local college radio station. In light of this variation, would Musician be able to successfully sue Pirate for violating her exclusive rights to reproduce and digitally transmit her sound recording?

159. The final installment in Novelist's popular graphic novel fantasy series, *Finality,* just came out, and Bookseller has stocked numerous copies of the volume. To encourage sales, he places a copy of *Finality* in his store window with the book open to a random page in order to show passersby a sample of the book's color illustrations and to give a brief taste of the plot. Bookseller also scans a copy of the same page he has shown to the public in his store window and puts it on his website to tempt readers to purchase copies of *Finality* through his online store. Novelist hears about Bookseller's conduct and sues him for copyright infringement on the theory that he has violated her exclusive right of public display in her graphic novel. Leaving the issue of fair use aside, will Novelist's claim succeed?

(A) No. There is no right of public display in literary works such as those embodied in Novelist's fantasy series.

(B) No. There is no violation of the right of public display unless the entire work of authorship, as opposed to just a small portion of that book, is displayed online.

(C) Yes. While both Bookseller's physical and online showing of parts of *Finality* amount to unauthorized public displays, the physical display is permissible while the online display is not.

(D) Yes. Both of Novelist's unauthorized displays of parts of Novelist's book amount to violations of her exclusive right of public display in the book.

160. BigMedia wants to enter the digital music business. It has various projects in the works. First, BigMedia plans to purchase a broadcast FM radio station and convert its operations from analog to digital form, while still serving the same geographical area. Second, Big-Media plans to set up a website called BigMedia.com, where 10 different digital radio stations will stream various genres of music online. Users will be able to go to the site and select which station's stream they want to tune in to, though BigMedia will choose which sound recordings it will stream. BigMusic's streaming music service is free, but it also plans to offer an on-demand music service on BigMusic.com called "BigMusic Plus" that will allow listeners, in exchange for a $10/month fee, to request particular sound recordings to

be played at any time. What kind of licenses does BigMedia need from the owners of the copyrights in the sound recordings it plans to transmit via these three means?

(A) None. There is no public performance right in sound recordings, so BigMedia needs no licenses from the owners of the copyrights in the sound recordings it plans to transmit.

(B) BigMedia needs no license to broadcast the sound recordings from its digital radio station or to stream the sound recordings from BigMedia.com, but it must negotiate a license with the owners of the sound recordings it plans to make available via its on-demand service.

(C) BigMedia needs a compulsory license to broadcast the sound recordings from its digital radio station and to stream the sound recordings from BigMedia.com, but must negotiate a license with the owners of the sound recordings it plans to make available via its on-demand service.

(D) BigMedia needs no license to broadcast the sound recordings from its digital radio station, needs a compulsory license to stream the sound recordings from BigMedia .com, and must negotiate a consensual license with the owners of the sound recordings it plans to make available via its on-demand service.

161. Writer pens a manuscript of a novel and then signs an agreement with Publisher. The agreement states that Publisher will publish the novel and pay a percentage of its revenues from the book sales to Writer, but that Writer retains the copyright in the work of authorship. After signing the agreement, Publisher decides that the book will sell more copies if it has the name of a more famous person attached to it, so the version of the book that is released wrongly lists Author, a well-known popular novelist, rather than Writer, on the front cover. Writer is incensed and sues Publisher for, among other things, copyright infringement. Will Writer succeed?

(A) Yes. Writer will succeed because Publisher created a derivative work by placing Author's name on the cover of Writer's book, thereby violating Writer's exclusive right of adaptation.

(B) Yes. Writer will succeed because Publisher failed to accurately attribute the book's origin to him, robbing Writer of his due recognition.

(C) No. Writer will fail because this is a moral-rights claim, and federal law does not recognize moral rights-based claims.

(D) No. Writer will fail because copyright law does not recognize a cause of action for copyright infringement based solely on failure to correctly attribute authorship.

162. Painter, a nationally renowned landscape artist, paints a picture of the Grand Canyon, which she then sells to Buyer. Buyer then delivers the painting to the local public art gallery in order to sell it. However, before he presents the painting to the gallery, Buyer puts

it in a frame that covers Painter's signature, and labels the work "Panorama of the Grand Canyon by Buyer." When the owner of the gallery asks if Buyer painted the picture himself, Buyer replies, "I sure did!" Painter then visits the gallery, tells the owner of the gallery that the work is actually hers, and the angry gallery owner demands that Buyer take back the painting. Buyer does so, and for a time hangs the painting in his living room. Eventually, though, Buyer feels so ashamed of his attempted subterfuge that he gives the painting back to Painter. When Painter takes it back, he notices that the work has faded because sunlight entered Buyer's living room through a skylight and the oil paints Painter used were particularly sensitive to degradation under those conditions.

Painter sues Buyer for violating his moral rights of attribution and integrity in the painting. Will he succeed?

(A) Yes. Painter will succeed on both claims.

(B) Painter will succeed on the right of attribution claim, but will fail on the right of integrity claim.

(C) Painter will succeed on the right of integrity claim, but will fail on the right of attribution claim.

(D) No. Painter will fail on both claims.

163. Consider question 162. Assume that instead of purchasing a painting of the Grand Canyon from Painter, Buyer acquired a photographic print of the Grand Canyon that was based on an original photo that Painters signed and intended to be shown in a gallery exhibition. Assume further that the photographic print Buyer acquired was one in a limited series of 250 photographic prints, all consecutively numbered and signed by Painter. If all other facts were the same, would Painter be able to successfully sue Buyer on a moral rights theory under VARA?

164. In 1992, Artist paints a canvas titled *DarkSyde* that depicts brutal police officers beating up innocent citizens. Artist sells the work to Collector, who loans it to the local museum of contemporary art. Artist dies in 2008. In his will, Artist states that he no longer agrees with the message conveyed in *DarkSyde* and wants the work destroyed as an expression of his repudiation of what the canvas depicted. The executor of Artist's estate files an action under VARA to have the painting returned to the estate's possession and destroyed as per its creator's wishes. Will Artist's executor's action succeed?

(A) Yes. To allow a picture to hang in a museum after an artist has repudiated it is considered a misrepresentation of the artist's views that violates the right of attribution.

(B) Yes. To allow a picture to hang in a museum after an artist has repudiated it is considered a mutilation of the artist's work that violates the right of integrity.

(C) No. Artist's VARA rights in *DarkSyde* expired upon his death in 2008.

(D) No. While Artist's VARA rights are still enforceable, a right to have the painting removed from existence is not among them.

165. Jam Records regularly sends its latest releases in CD form to local FM radio stations and DJs in order to encourage airplay. Jam includes a note on all such CDs indicating "This CD is licensed to its recipient for PROMOTIONAL USE ONLY. Jam Records retains the title to this CD, subject only to the limited-use license described herein."

Despite this limitation, Fly Guy, a local DJ, gave several promotional CDs to a local used record store in exchange for half the value of their eventual sales price. Jam Record sues him for violating their exclusive right of distribution. Who will win?

(A) Fly Guy, because the license term is unenforceable, and his conduct is permitted under the first sale doctrine.

(B) Fly Guy, because he has not actually distributed any of the CDs yet.

(C) Jam Records, because the first sale doctrine does not apply to online sales.

(D) Jam Records, because Fly Guy's conduct exceeds the terms of the license.

166. SoftCo sells the widely popular word processing program, PerfectWords. It makes this program available online for a one-time price of $250. Anyone who wants to use PerfectWords must both pay this fee and click "I accept" on a very long, web-based license agreement. The terms of the agreement stress that "users of PerfectWords are licensees, and are not owners of anything." They also state that users may not re-sell the program, and that users may not use PerfectWords outside the United States or Canada. Is this license agreement enforceable?

167. Artie is an Oakland-based painter who is famous for his iconic canvases depicting California's East Bay. In 2010, he sold a painting titled *Morning at Lake Chabot* to Gloria for $1,000. In 2011, Artie's fame increased significantly due to his work being featured in a high-profile art show. In 2016, Gloria publicly auctioned *Morning at Lake Chabot*, ultimately selling it to Nora for $1 million. Artie demanded that Gloria pay him a percentage of the profits from the 2016 sale, since the increase in value was due entirely to his own success.

Does Artie have a legal theory on which he can recover part of the proceeds from Gloria's sale of the painting to Nora?

(A) Yes. Artie can recover a percentage of the profits from the second sale under the Visual Artists Rights Act.

(B) Yes. Artie can recover a percentage of the profits from the second sale under the California Resale Royalties Act.

(C) No. Artie is limited to copyright infringement remedies against Nora, who engaged in an unauthorized distribution of his work.

(D) No. Artie cannot recover any of the proceeds from the second sale.

168.   Jack is a well-regarded artist who lives on the rural Oregon coast and constructs large artworks out of everyday cast-off items he finds. Recently, Jack bought a rickety old fishing dinghy for $100 and adorned it with all manner of outrageous decorations, including painting the vessel's newly given name, *The Invincible* on the side of the boat.

People came from all around the area to see *The Invincible*, which Jack sometimes motored around the marina to great fanfare. One wealthy art collector who admired Jack's work offered to buy *The Invincible* for $50,000, but as the collector and Jack were going back and forth about the terms of the purchase, a local prankster snuck onto the boat one night, tried to sail it out of the marina, and sank it.

Incensed, Jack sues the prankster on a variety of theories, including that by destroying Jack's artwork, the prankster violated Jack's rights under the federal Visual Artists Rights Act (VARA). Will Jack prevail on this claim?

(A)   Yes, because the prankster violated Jack's right of attribution in *The Invincible*.

(B)   Yes, because the prankster violated Jack's right of integrity in *The Invincible*.

(C)   No, because *The Invincible* is a form of "applied art" to which VARA does not apply.

(D)   No, because no court would hold that *The Invincible* is a "work of recognized stature."

169.   *Spartans Forever* is a recent hit movie about an underdog high school football team from a hardscrabble area that wins a state championship against long odds. The production company Fine Films owns the copyright in the film. The screenplay for *Spartans Forever* was loosely based on the true story of the St. Martin High School (SMHS) Spartans, a high school in a poor area that boasts a perennially successful football team. In the film *Spartans Forever*, the team rallies around the rousing slogan "St. Martin Spartans football forever!" Since the film's release and great popularity, the actual SMHS football team has been playing that iconic line from the film on the loudspeaker at football games to excite the crowd. In order to do this, SMHS personnel in the course of their employment for the school played a DVD copy of *Spartans Forever* and then used a digital audio recorder to make a digital sound recording of the line "St. Martins Spartans football forever!" The SMHS employees who work on audiovisual effects at the SMHS football stadium then play the audio recording over the loudspeaker at key points during Spartans football games. SMHS did not request permission from Fine Films to use the line from *Spartans Forever* at their football games.

Fine Films learns of SMHS's use of the line from *Spartans Forever*, and files a copyright infringement lawsuit against SMHS. Assuming the portion of the film used by SMHS was copyrightable, which, if any, of the following exclusive rights in *Spartans Forever* did SMHS violate?

I. Reproduction

II. Adaptation

III. Public display

IV. Public performance

(A) I and IV

(B) II, III, and IV

(C) I and IV

(D) II and IV

170. Bella is medical student studying in the United States. While visiting her family in Nigeria one recent summer, she notices that the medical textbooks assigned for her upcoming semester's courses are on sale in Nigeria for much less than the identical textbooks would cost in the United States. The publisher of those books manufactures some textbooks in Africa at a lower cost, then sells them in African markets, such as Nigeria, at a correspondingly lower price.

Bella decides to buy her own textbooks abroad, and also mentions this to several of her classmates, who express interest in the lower-cost textbooks, too. Bella buys 20 textbooks and ships them back to the United States, where she re-sells them to her classmates. She sells the books for a price higher than what she paid, but only to cover the cost of shipping.

One of Bella's other classmates, who purchased her textbooks in the United States at full price, considers this practice unfair, and reports Bella's resales to the publisher of the textbooks. The publisher sues Bella for violating their exclusive right of distribution.

Who will prevail, the publisher or Bella?

(A) The publisher, because the first sale doctrine applies only to copies lawfully acquired in the United States.

(B) The publisher, because Bella charged more for resale than she paid for the books abroad.

(C) Bella, because her conduct is permitted by the first sale doctrine.

(D) Bella, because she did not make a net profit on the resales.

171. AllGames is an Internet-based subscription service that allows its users to listen to live analog-radio sports broadcasts from 40 major media markets throughout the United States. AllGames does this by receiving those broadcasts via analog antenna in each of the cities it covers, and then converting the analog signals to digital, and finally retransmitting the digitized game broadcasts over the Internet to users. AllGames does not use a single antenna to receive broadcasts. Rather, it has stations with hundreds of antennae at each of the locations where it receives the analog signals. AllGames then retransmits to each user who requests a given broadcast the signals captured by one of the antennae. AllGames users

each receive separately captured and retransmitted broadcasts. That is, AllGames does not capture a single analog radio broadcast and retransmit it to all users requesting that broadcast.

AllGames does not pay the content owners of any of these broadcasts a fee for its use of their material. The owners of the copyrights in these broadcasts sue AllGames for infringement, arguing that AllGames' conduct amounts to an unauthorized public performance of their works. Assuming the broadcasts are validly copyrighted, who will prevail, the broadcasters or AllGames?

(A) The broadcasters, because AllGames' retransmission effects a public performance.

(B) The broadcasters, because AllGames intended to usurp their business model.

(C) AllGames, because courts should be careful not to let copyright law shut down the evolution of new technology.

(D) AllGames, because AllGames did not publicly perform the broadcasters' works.

Copyright Formalities

172.   Which of the following factors is most determinative of whether notice is a prerequisite for federal copyright protection in the United States?

(A)   The type of work of authorship.

(B)   The date the work was published.

(C)   The citizenship status of the author.

(D)   Whether the work is co-authored.

173.   Author wrote a novel, and recently assigned its registered copyright to Publisher A, who did not record the assignment with the Copyright Office. Three months later, Author assigned the copyright in the same novel to Publisher B, a good faith purchaser, for a large advance against royalties. Publisher B recorded the assignment immediately with the Copyright Office. While Publisher A continued to edit the manuscript of the novel in preparation for its release to bookstores, Publisher B printed and distributed the novel, which contained a copyright notice, to bookstores for sale to the public. Can Publisher A successfully sue Publisher B for copyright infringement?

(A)   Yes, because Publisher A was preparing the novel for publication.

(B)   Yes, because Publisher A was assigned the copyright first and thereafter Author had nothing left to assign.

(C)   No, because Publisher B's copyright interest in the novel is superior to Publisher A.

(D)   No, because Publisher B, not Publisher A, was the first to release the novel to the public with a copyright notice.

174.   In 1910, Designer's employer, the Anderson Print Shop, asked him to create a drawing of the building occupied by the print shop. This task was within the scope of Designer's employment. Designer worked for the company until he died in 1934. Gary Anderson, the owner of the Anderson Print Shop, kept the drawing in his personal safe. In 1954, Gary gave the original copy of the drawing, which did not contain a copyright notice, to his grandson. Gary died that same year. In 1960, Gary's grandson gave a copy of the drawing to each of his three fraternity brothers, with instructions to not copy the work. These copies did not contain a copyright notice. One of the fraternity brothers obtained proper authorization to publish the drawing in 2004 as part of a collection of turn-of-the-century

buildings. The collection contained a proper copyright notice. In what year was the drawing invested with federal copyright protection?

(A) 1910

(B) 1960

(C) 1978

(D) 2004

175. MelodyCo owns all the rights in the musical work *Executive Sweet*. In 1949, MelodyCo permitted a band to perform the musical work in a session closed to the public, but broadcast live over the radio. This performance created a demand for the work and, in 1950, MelodyCo created the first phonorecord of *Executive Sweet*, which it released to record stores for sale in a limited edition of 1,000 copies. In 1951, MelodyCo re-released the recording of *Executive Sweet*, this time on a larger scale, distributing tens of thousands of copies of the phonorecord to retail music establishments. Proper copyright notice accompanied each released phonorecord. By 1975, the entire inventory of *Executive Sweet* recordings had been sold by MelodyCo. When, if at all, was *Executive Sweet* generally published?

(A) 1949. The live performance of the musical work was sufficient to effect general publication.

(B) 1950. The limited-edition release effected general publication.

(C) 1951. The large-scale release effected general publication.

(D) Never. The Copyright Act deems all musical works distributed in phonorecords before January 1, 1978, not to have been published.

176. Consider question 175. Assume that all the acts described in that question took place in the 1990s, rather than in the 1940s and 1950s. In light of this change, at what stage, if at all, would publication have occurred?

177. In 1960, Writer penned an original manuscript for a novel titled *Clouded Sunset*, but told no one about it and placed the manuscript in his desk drawer. In 1961, Writer handed the manuscript over to Literary Agent, who sent a copy of the manuscript containing a proper copyright notice to each of five studio executives, seeking bids for motion picture rights to the novel. Literary Agent told each of the five executives, "You can have this copy to see if you want to bid on the novel, but keep it all very hush-hush." Shortly thereafter, the head of FilmCorp, one of the executives that reviewed the manuscript, called Literary Agent with a generous offer to buy the motion picture rights to the novel. Writer happily accepted.

In 1962, Robust Reader Publications published *Clouded Sunset* exclusively for the Bi-Monthly Book Club, which offered it for sale to its members. Following a year of production, FilmCorp released a motion picture in 1963 that featured the main character of

Clouded Sunset involved in a different story line. When, if at all, was the novel first generally published under the 1909 Copyright Act?

(A) 1960. The act of embodying the expression of a fictional idea in a tangible medium of expression effected general publication.

(B) 1961. The distribution of the manuscript to potential buyers effected general publication.

(C) 1962. The offering of copies of the novel exclusively to Bi-Monthly Book Club members effected general publication.

(D) 1963. The release of a motion picture resulting from the purchase of the motion picture rights to *Clouded Sunset* effected general publication.

178. In 1970, Zealot becomes convinced that he has found the one true path to enlightenment. That same year, he writes and self-publishes a pamphlet proclaiming this fact, and leaves 1,000 copies of the pamphlet at bus stops, libraries, and other public places throughout Zealot's local area. Soon thereafter, Zealot learns that he inadvertently failed to attach a copyright notice to 900 copies of the pamphlet. Zealot has never registered the copyright in the pamphlet's contents. Are the contents of the pamphlet forfeited to the public domain?

(A) Yes. By releasing physical copies of the pamphlet to the general public, the vast majority of which lacked notice, Zealot has forfeited the contents of the pamphlet to the public domain.

(B) Yes. Zealot's failure to register the copyright in his literary work prevented the curing of the omission of copyright notice.

(C) No. By including notice on even a single copy, Zealot preserved his copyright in the pamphlet's contents.

(D) No. Because Zealot's failure to include copyright notice was inadvertent, it cannot result in forfeiture of his copyright.

179. Consider question 178. Assume that instead of including notice on only 100 out of the 1,000 pamphlets, Zealot left notice off of only 10 of the 1,000 pamphlets. In light of this change, would the contents of Zealot's pamphlet still be forfeited to the public domain?

180. In 1982, Writer wrote a short story using her personal computer. In 1998, a thief stole her computer, discovered Writer's short story, and posted the file on the Internet, all without Writer's knowledge. Did this act amount to a publication of Writer's literary work?

(A) Yes, because it was a general release of a physical copy of the work.

(B) Yes, because the dissemination of a work on the Internet always constitutes a general publication.

(C) No, because posting material on the Internet does not count as publication since the 1976 Copyright Act did not explicitly contemplate it.

(D) No, because the dissemination of the short story was not with Writer's consent.

181. In 1980, Novelist released her self-published literary work, *American She*. Novelist failed to place copyright notice on any of the thousands of copies of her work sold to the public in California, though she did place copyright notice on the tens of thousands of copies sold outside California. Novelist registered the work in 1995. Which of the following statements most accurately describes the current status of Novelist's copyright in *American She*?

(A) *American She* is irrevocably part of the public domain.

(B) *American She* is in the public domain now, but Novelist can reclaim it if she takes steps sufficient to cure her original omission of copyright notice.

(C) The copyright in *American She* was restored to Novelist pursuant to section 104A of the 1976 Copyright Act on January 1, 1996.

(D) *American She* is protected by copyright and will remain so regardless of whether Novelist adds any copyright notice.

182. Consider question 181. Assume that all the facts remain the same, except that Novelist published *American She* in 1995 rather than 1980. How would this change in the facts affect the copyright status of the novel?

183. Under the 1976 Copyright Act, which of the following most accurately describes a copyright owner's obligations upon publication of a work of authorship?

(A) The copyright owner must register the work with the Copyright Office and deposit two copies of the work with the Library of Congress.

(B) The copyright owner must register the work with the Copyright Office.

(C) The copyright owner must deposit one copy of the work with the Library of Congress.

(D) The copyright owner is under no affirmative obligations pursuant to the 1976 Copyright Act.

184. Author writes a detailed outline of the plot for his next novel and unsuccessfully attempts to register the outline with the Copyright Office as a literary work. A few months later, Author discovers that Poseur has been claiming as his own a very similar plot outline. Author wants to sue Poseur for copyright infringement. Will Author be able to file his infringement suit?

(A) Yes. The act of registration is unrelated to Author's ability to file an infringement suit.

(B) Yes, but only if he notifies the Copyright Office of the lawsuit and provides it with a copy of the complaint.

(C) No. The Copyright Office's rejection of Author's application for registration means copyright has not vested in the work.

(D) No. Registration is a jurisdictional prerequisite for copyright enforcement, so Author's failure to attain registration means that he will not be able to file an infringement action in federal court.

185. Your client, Author, comes to you and says, "I've read a bit about copyright law, and it appears that I have a copyright without having to go through all the rigmarole of registration. I'm going to save myself the registration fee and a whole lot of hassle, and not register my latest novel." How should you advise Author? In particular, are there any specific advantages of copyright registration about which you should advise your client?

186. Owner sues Pirate for infringing the copyright in Owner's musical work. At trial, Owner places into evidence a copyright registration certificate, which she obtained two years after creation of the musical work in suit. What, if any, evidentiary advantage does Owner gain by doing this?

(A) The registration certificate is conclusive evidence of the copyright's validity.

(B) The registration certificate creates a rebuttable presumption of the copyright's validity.

(C) The registration certificate shifts the burden of proof to Pirate to show that he has not infringed Owner's copyright.

(D) The trial judge has the discretion to determine whether the registration certificate creates a rebuttable presumption of copyright validity.

187. Screenwriter spent several years polishing a screenplay, titled *Fast Track*, which she eventually licensed to De Marco Studios in 1961. This exclusive motion picture license encompassed the initial term of copyright protection, renewals, and all extensions. Pursuant to this license, De Marco Studios produced a motion picture, *Clashing Clouds*, which it released for exhibition in 1962. The motion picture included all of the copyrightable elements contained in *Fast Track* and was accompanied by a copyright notice that read: "© 1962, De Marco Studios." Screenwriter has never filed a document regarding her *Fast Track* screenplay with the Copyright Office. Screenwriter has never authorized any additional uses of *Fast Track*. De Marco Studios filed a timely and proper application for renewal of registration for the copyright in *Clashing Clouds* in 1989.

Recently, Cinemasters Publishing has published a compilation of highly regarded motion picture scripts from the 1960s, including *Fast Track*. Cinemasters Publishing has not obtained permission from Screenwriter to use *Fast Track*. Should Screenwriter decide to sue Cinemasters Publishing for copyright infringement, would her action be successful?

188. A prominent nature photographer takes a highly creative photograph of bison running in Yellowstone National Park using her own digital camera. She titles the resulting work

"Speeding Buffalo." She then includes "Speeding Buffalo" in the fall 2014 issue of "Scenes from the Wild." "Scenes from the Wild" is a serialized compilation of her best photography, with commentary and occasional other works she creates. The photographer publishes "Scenes from the Wild" herself and releases it exclusively to the publication's paid subscribers (in both hard-copy and digital format) four times yearly.

Prior to its release, the photographer then seeks to register the fall 2014 issue of "Scenes from the Wild" with the Copyright Office by completing and submitting registration Form SE. All the information she includes on her submitted Form SE regarding the authorship of "Speeding Buffalo" is accurate and more than sufficient to meet the minimum standards for copyrightability, and the photographer includes the requisite filing fee and deposit copy. Her submission of Form SE also includes a specific list of all the works of authorship in the issue that the photographer seeks to register, identified by title. This list includes all individual photographs that appear in the fall 2014 issue, including "Speeding Buffalo," as well as related textual commentary and several freehand sketches that photographer made of sunsets in New Mexico. The Copyright Office approves her registration application, and issues her a copyright registration certificate with the unique registration number SE-40-5006-12.

Soon after the certificate issues, the photographer learns that "Speeding Buffalo" appears as part of the home page of the popular, for-profit nature website, AmericaOutdoors.com. The website's management was aware that the copyright in "Speeding Buffalo" belonged to the photographer, but they did not seek her permission to use it. The photographer files a complaint for copyright infringement in the local federal district court. AmericaOutdoors.com moves to dismiss the complaint on the theory that the photographer's registration form is jurisdictionally insufficient.

Will AmericaOutdoors.com's motion to dismiss for lack of jurisdiction succeed?

(A) Yes. Form SE only applies to the selection, arrangement, and coordination of material in a serial work, not to the individual works—such as "Speeding Buffalo"—contained therein.

(B) Yes. In order to sue for an infringement of a work of authorship, that work must be registered using the appropriate form created by the Copyright Office, and the Copyright Office requires that photographs such as "Speeding Buffalo" be registered using Form VA.

(C) No. The form of registration is a mere technicality that can never have any effect on an owner's ability to sue for infringement.

(D) No. Photographer's detailed registration of all the works in the fall 2014 issue of "Scenes from the Wild" using Form SE is sufficient to enable her to sue for infringement of any of those works—including "Speeding Buffalo"—in federal court.

189. Assume **for the purposes of this question only** that when the photographer submitted her registration application for "Speeding Buffalo" to the Copyright Office, she did not include a list specifying the titles of the specific works for which she sought registration. Instead, the subject matter listed on the photographer's copyright registration application and the registration certificate issued by the Copyright Office identifies only "Scenes from the Wild fall 2014" as the registered subject matter. How would these changed facts affect the likelihood that AmericaOutdoors.com's motion to dismiss would succeed?

190. Esme wrote an essay online about her experiences as a young woman exploring Malaysia. The next year, Nemo Publishing released their annual "Best Travel Writing" anthology and included Esme's book. Nemo had, however, failed to secure permission from Esme to republish her essay, and Esme filed a complaint in federal district court against Nemo alleging copyright infringement and seeking actual damages as compensation. The parties filed cross-motions for summary judgment, and the judge denied Nemo's and granted Esme's, meaning that the only issue left to resolve was the amount of damages Nemo owed Esme for its infringement. At that point, Nemo offered a generous settlement to Esme, who accepted it.

As the court was preparing to review the settlement, though, Nemo's insurer filed a successful motion to intervene in the litigation, and then moved to dismiss the case for lack of subject matter jurisdiction. The insurer's motion argued exclusively that since the copyright in Esme's essay was not registered with the Copyright Office, the court lacked jurisdiction because of the statutory requirement that plaintiffs must register works prior to filing infringement suits.

Will the insurer prevail on its motion to dismiss Esme's infringement suit for lack of subject matter jurisdiction?

(A) Yes, because it waived the jurisdictional issue by failing to intervene and raise it during litigation.

(B) Yes, because registering a work of authorship is a prerequisite to a federal court exercising subject matter jurisdiction over a copyright infringement case.

(C) No, because registering a work of authorship is merely advisory, not mandatory, for plaintiffs in copyright infringement cases.

(D) No, because the copyright registration requirement does not bar courts from exercising subject matter jurisdiction over infringement cases.

191. In 1975, a famous novelist married her copyright lawyer. The novelist spent most of the next decade working on a manuscript she regarded as a masterpiece that will make millions. She wrote the draft of her manuscript longhand and kept it locked in a cabinet, never showing it to anyone. The manuscript did not contain a proper copyright notice.

In 1985, the marriage soured, and novelist demanded a divorce. In an act of revenge, the lawyer broke into the cabinet and took the novelist's manuscript. He then bought several hours' worth of airtime on a local radio station and read the manuscript during a live broadcast that was heard by tens of thousands of listeners. He then returned home and announced to the novelist that he had foiled her plans to make millions from her manuscript, because he had placed the work into the public domain by reading it on the radio when it was unprotected by a valid copyright notice.

Did the lawyer's actions place the manuscript in the public domain?

(A) Yes, because the lawyer published the manuscript without proper copyright notice.

(B) No, because the 1976 Copyright Act made notice irrelevant to copyright vesting and divesting.

(C) No, because this publication of the novel was not made with its author's consent.

(D) No, because mere performance of a work does not constitute a publication of it.

Duration, Renewal, and Termination of Transfers

192.   Architect created an original architectural drawing in 2001. Architect died in 2006. In her will, she left the copyright in the architectural drawing to the school from which she received her Bachelor of Architecture degree. Architect had no children. Architect's husband, Widower, has filed an action in United States District Court requesting that the court declare Widower the owner of the copyright in the architectural drawing. Will Widower be successful?

(A) No, because a state court must determine any legal issue regarding the interpretation of a bequest via will.

(B) No, because ownership of the copyright in the architectural drawing vested in Architect at the time the work was fixed in 2001.

(C) Yes, because Widower has priority of ownership as a statutory successor.

(D) Yes, because any bequest of a copyright via will must be made to a person, not an institution.

193.   A novel was both registered with the Copyright Office and published in 1922. The copyright in the novel was properly renewed. The author of the novel died in 1940. When did or will the copyright protection for the novel end?

(A) At the end of 2010.

(B) At the end of 2017.

(C) At the end of 1997.

(D) At the end of 1978.

194.   Poet wrote a poem in 1950. The poem was never published and its copyright was never registered. No renewal of copyright was ever filed with the Copyright Office. Poet died in 1970. The copyright in the poem did or will expire:

(A) At the end of 2047.

(B) At the end of 2002.

(C) At the end of 1978.

(D) At the end of 2040.

195.   Novelist published her novel with proper copyright notice in 1958, but never registered the copyright in the novel with the Copyright Office. Novelist died in 1984, survived only by her son. In her will, Novelist left the copyright in the novel, including the remainder of the initial term of copyright, as well as all renewals and extensions, to her neighbor. In 1986, the twenty-eighth year of the initial term of copyright, Novelist's son and neighbor each file a copyright renewal application with the Copyright Office. As of Novelist's death, who owns the copyright in the novel until it expires?

196.   A work was published with proper copyright notice in 1908 and properly renewed. The copyright in the work expired at the end of what year?

         (A)   1983

         (B)   1964

         (C)   2003

         (D)   1997

197.   Author wrote a novel in 1863. The manuscript was left in a desk drawer until Author's nephew discovered it in 1991. Author died in 1905. The novel was first published in 1994. Copyright protection for the novel:

         (A)   Never existed.

         (B)   Will expire at the end of 2047.

         (C)   Ended on January 1, 1978.

         (D)   Expired at the end of 2002.

198.   Composer composes a musical score in 1955 for a motion picture produced and released by Film Studio that same year. Composer created the score pursuant to a work made for hire agreement designating Film Studio as the author and owner of the work. Five years later, Film Studio assigned the copyright in the music score to Composer, who immediately assigned the copyright in the music score to Music Publisher. When the appropriate time arises, can Composer terminate the grant of rights to Music Publisher?

         (A)   Yes, because the agreement Composer seeks to terminate is not a work made for hire agreement.

         (B)   Yes, because Composer regained the status of author through the 1960 assignment from Film Studio.

         (C)   No, because grants of copyright in works made for hire are not eligible for termination.

         (D)   No, because only the first transfer of copyright after a work is created can be terminated.

199.   In 1905, Photographer took a photograph of a group of his fellow employees at a photography studio owned by Employer. The photograph was a work made for hire; Employer was the hiring party. Photographer died in 1934. The photograph was hung on the wall of Employer's private office until his death in 1954. The photograph was first published in 2004 as part of a collection of centuries-old photographs. At the end of what year did or will the photograph's copyright protection cease?

   (A) 1961   *1905 + 120*

   (B) 2004

   (C) 2025

   (D) 2099

200.   In 1980, Author and Collaborator write a screenplay together as joint authors. In 1985, Author and Collaborator both get into a car accident. Author dies immediately, while Collaborator lingers on for another five years, ultimately dying in 1990. Author and Collaborator have each left their estates, including all of their copyrights, to CharityCo, their favorite nonprofit organization. At the end of which year does the copyright in the screenplay expire?

   (A) 2050

   (B) 2055

   (C) 2060

   (D) It does not expire because its owner is now a corporation that lacks a natural life to create an expiration date.

201.   Author wrote a literary work in 1995. In 2000, Author finally published the work, albeit under the name "Pseudonym," which is also the name under which the work is registered with the Copyright Office. No one ever found out that Author actually wrote the work, and the secret died with Author in 2005. At the end of which year does the work's copyright expire?

   (A) 2065

   (B) 2075

   (C) 2095

   (D) 2115

202.   Consider question 201. Assume that in 2004, Author changed the name in which the work was registered from "Pseudonym" to his own, and then died the next year. Author's identity did not become widespread public knowledge until 2015, when a scholar researching Author's life discovers the revised copyright registration. In light of these revised facts, when would the work's copyright expire?

203.   Artist created a painting titled *Nocturne in Blue* on January 1, 1980, but kept the work in his private studio until May 1, 1985, when he included it in a public showing and registered it with the Copyright Office. Artist died on June 1, 1990, bequeathing all of his copyrights to his heirs. Fast forward to September 1, 2060, when Joe Future makes unauthorized reproductions of *Nocturne in Blue* and starts selling them to the public. The heirs of Artist's estate claim that Joe Future has infringed their copyright in the work. Assuming that United States copyright law regarding the length of copyright protection has not changed in the intervening years, will Artist's heirs prevail?

(A)   No, the work has been in the public domain since June 2, 2060.

(B)   No, the work has been in the public domain since 2055.

(C)   Yes, the unpublished work has perpetual copyright protection.

(D)   Yes, the work is protected through December 31, 2060.

204.   Writer composes a poem in 1930. He never shows it to anyone, instead keeping it in his desk drawer. Writer then dies in 1935. During, or at the end of, which year does the poem's federal copyright expire?

(A)   1958

(B)   1986

(C)   2002

(D)   2005

205.   Writer composes a play in 1910, but is not convinced of its quality, and puts it aside without ever showing it to anyone. It remains in his desk drawer through his death in 1920, and now exists only as a part of his personal effects. In 2005, one of Writer's heirs discovers the play and wonders whether it is still protected by copyright. As of that year, is it?

(A)   No, copyright in the play expired at the end of 1938.

(B)   No, copyright in the play expired at the end of 1990.

(C)   No, copyright in the play expired at the end of 2002.

(D)   Yes, the play is still protected by copyright as of 2005.

206.   Consider question 205. Assume instead that Writer's heir found his ancestor's play in 2000 and published it the next year. How, if at all, would this change the duration of copyright protection?

207.   Musician composes the musical work *Summer Rapture* in 1910 and registers the work the same year. He renews the copyright in 1938, then dies in 1950. During or at the end of what year does the copyright in *Summer Rapture* expire?

(A)   1966

 (B) 1985

 (C) 2002

 (D) 2020

208. Artist creates an original painting titled *House in the Woods* in 1960, and secures a valid federal copyright in the work that same year. Artist then dies intestate in 1985, survived only by his ex-wife, their son, and a single grandchild. In 1987, the twenty-eighth year of copyright protection, a dispute erupts as to which of Artist's heirs is entitled to renew the copyright in *House in the Woods* and possess the rights to its renewal term. Which of the following individuals will prevail?

 (A) Artist's son.

 (B) Artist's ex-wife.

 (C) The executor of Artist's estate.

 (D) Artist's grandson.

209. Consider question 208. Assume instead that Artist has an ex-wife, a widow, a son, a daughter, and two grandchildren. In light of this change, who owns the renewal rights to *House in the Woods*?

210. In 1955, BizCorp ordered one of its employees, Writer, to write a book chronicling the history of the company. BizCorp then assigned the rights in the literary work to Publisher, a natural person. Publisher died in 1970, leaving all of his estate to Heir. Assuming that the literary work was a work made for hire, who owns the rights in the renewal term?

 (A) BizCorp

 (B) Writer

 (C) Publisher

 (D) Heir

211. Consider question 210. Assume that the proprietor of·the copyright in the literary work at issue failed to renew the copyright in its twenty-eighth year of protection (1983). What are the implications of this failure?

212. Sculptor created a sculptural work in 1970, and obtained a valid federal copyright in the work that same year. In the twenty-eighth year of the work's copyright (1997), Sculptor did not file a renewal application with the Copyright Office. At the end of which year did or will the work enter the public domain?

 (A) 1998

 (B) 2026

 (C) 2045

(D) 2065

213.   Writer penned a screenplay in 1942, and registered it with the Copyright Office that same year. Writer subsequently fell on hard times and assigned to Shyster for $10,000 the remainder of the initial term, the renewal term, and the right of renewal in the copyright. Writer's downward spiral continued and ended with his death in 1958. During the twenty-eighth year of copyright in the screenplay (1970), a dispute arose between Shyster and Writer's statutory successor about which of them is the true owner of the copyright. Which of the following statements most accurately reflects the relative interests in the copyright as of that date?

(A) Writer's statutory successor owns the right of renewal; Shyster owns the initial term.

(B) Writer's statutory successor owns the right of renewal and the initial term; Shyster owns nothing.

(C) Writer's statutory successor owns the renewal term; Shyster owns the right of renewal and the initial term.

(D) Writer's statutory successor owns nothing; Shyster owns the right of renewal and the initial term.

214.   Consider question 213. Assume that Writer died in 1971 rather than 1958. How, if at all, would this change the analysis regarding ownership of the copyright?

215.   In 1966, Author published a novel titled *Empire* with valid copyright notice. The novel becomes a bestseller and, in 1970, De Marco Studios entered into a licensing agreement with Author. The agreement stated that, in exchange for a substantial fee, Author transferred to De Marco Studios the exclusive right to adapt *Empire* into a screenplay and to make a motion picture based on that screenplay. The studio released the resulting motion picture in 1973, and it became a critical and commercial success. In 1992, Author died without known heirs or a will. Then, in 1999, Daughter announced that she had just learned through a DNA test that she was Author's daughter, born out of wedlock. Daughter sued De Marco Studios for copyright infringement based on its continued exploitation of the film version of *Empire*. Will Daughter prevail on this argument?

(A) Yes. Author's death before the end of the initial term of protection means that his statutory successor acquired the copyright to *Empire*, which in turn means that Daughter controls the rights to *Empire*, including the exploitation of preexisting derivative works.

(B) Yes. Author's death before the end of the initial term of protection automatically terminated all licensing agreements he had with the makers of derivative works based on *Empire*, so that new licenses must be negotiated with his statutory successor.

(C) No. Author's death before the end of the initial term of protection gave his statutory successor control over preexisting derivative works only if the successor had affirmatively filed for renewal of the copyright in *Empire* during its twenty-eighth year of copyright protection.

    (D) No. Author's death before the end of the initial term of protection allows his statutory successor to exercise control only over future, not preexisting, derivative works based on *Empire*.

216.   Consider question 215. Assume that Daughter learned of her relationship to Author in 1996, and that she affirmatively filed for renewal of the copyright in *Empire* in the twenty-eighth year of protection (1997). How, if at all, would this change the analysis of her ability to force De Marco Studios to negotiate new licenses for its continued exploitation of preexisting derivative works based on *Empire*?

217.   Musician composed the musical work *Blue Betty* in 1980. In 1985, Musician granted to Production Company the exclusive right to use *Blue Betty* as theme music for the *Beautiful Betty* television series. In 1990, Musician died, leaving a widow and two sons. What is the earliest year in which the assignment can, if at all, be terminated?

    (A) 2015

    (B) 2020

    (C) 2041

    (D) It cannot be terminated because only a work's author may effect termination, and here the author is deceased.

218.   Consider question 217. In light of Musician's death, which of the following individuals can effect termination of the assignment to Studio?

    (A) Only Musician's widow can terminate the assignment.

    (B) Either Musician's widow acting alone or both of Musician's sons acting together can terminate the assignment.

    (C) Musician's widow acting together with one or both of Musician's sons can terminate the assignment.

    (D) Termination is not possible via any of these combinations.

219.   Consider question 217. Assume that Musician composed *Blue Betty* not in 1980, but in 1970, and that federal statutory copyright in the musical work vested that same year. How would this change effect the termination date of the grant?

220.   Author penned a novel titled *Molto Maria* in 1990. In 1995, Author died, and his copyright in *Molto Maria* was left to his sole heir, a son. On December 5, 2000, the son granted to a film producer an exclusive license to create a screenplay based on *Molto Maria*. When is the earliest date on which the son can terminate this license?

    (A) December 6, 2025.

    (B) December 6, 2030.

    (C) December 6, 2035.

(D) The license is not terminable.

221.   Consider question 220. Assume instead that Author's copyright in *Molto Maria* vested in 1960, that Author died in 1965, again leaving a son as his sole heir, and that the son executed an exclusive perpetual license to create a screenplay based on *Molto Maria* with Screenwriter on July 10, 1970. Assume further that Son exercised his right to renew the copyright in *Molto Maria* during its twenty-eighth year of copyright protection (1987). In light of these changes, what would be the earliest date on which the exclusive license could be terminated, if at all?

222.   Federal copyright in Poet's epic verse saga *Great Plains* vested in 1940. In 1950, Poet transferred all rights in the initial and renewal term, as well as the right of renewal, to Publisher. Publisher then commissioned, as a work made for hire, a prose version of *Great Plains* titled *Greater Plains*. Federal copyright in the derivative work *Greater Plains*, over which Publisher retains full ownership, vested in 1960. Publisher validly renewed the copyrights in both *Great Plains* and *Greater Plains* in the twenty-eighth year of their respective initial copyright terms. Poet died in 1990. Six years later his sole statutory successor, Heir, successfully terminated Poet's 1950 assignment of the copyright in *Great Plains* to Publisher. Heir seeks from Publisher all profits from any post-termination exploitation of *Greater Plains*. Will this argument succeed?

(A) Yes. The termination of the transfer in the underlying work, *Great Plains*, gives Heir full rights to any profits from the post-termination exploitation of derivative works, such as *Greater Plains*.

(B) Yes. The termination of the transfer in the underlying work, *Great Plains*, automatically causes copyright in any derivative works created pursuant to the 1950 agreement to revert to Heir.

(C) No. While termination of the transfer causes ownership of the copyright in the underlying work, *Great Plains*, to revert to Heir, this does not affect preexisting derivative works such as *Greater Plains*, which Publisher remains free to continue to exploit as it did pre-termination.

(D) No. Termination of transfer in underlying works like *Great Plains* does not prevent transferees from exploiting derivative works created pre-termination or creating new derivative works based on those pre-termination derivative works.

223.   Musician composed the musical work *Andalucia* in 1934 and the registered the work with the Copyright Office the same year. Five years later, Musician assigned all rights in the initial and renewal term of copyright to Publisher, which was also given a power of attorney to renew the copyright in *Andalucia* in Musician's name. Subsequently, Publisher licensed RecordCo, a recording company, to record *Andalucia* in 1940, which proved to be commercially successful. Publisher properly renewed the copyright in the musical work's twenty-eighth year of protection (1961). Musician died in 1970. In 1991, Musician's lone statutory successor, Heir, successfully terminated the transfer of *Andalucia* to Publisher.

After the termination, Heir assigned all right, title, and interest to the copyright in *Andalucia* to Music Town Publishing for a large advance against royalties. RecordCo has continued to sell its 1940 recording of *Andalucia*. Music Town Publishing now claims that it should receive the mechanical license fees generated by the post-termination sales of RecordCo's recording of *Andalucia*. Will Music Town Publishing prevail?

(A) Yes. Due to Heir's termination of the 1939 transfer to Publisher and post-termination assignment to Music Town Publishing, Music Town Publishing is entitled to all post-termination mechanical license fees generated by the exploitation of the copyright in the musical work *Andalucia*.

(B) No. Heir's termination of the 1939 transfer to Publisher and post-termination assignment to Music Town Publishing entitles Music Town Publishing to all mechanical license fees generated by any new use or new recording of the *Andalucia* musical work, but not recordings of the work exploited in the same manner that took place pre-termination.

(C) Yes. Heir's termination of the 1939 transfer to Publisher requires it to disgorge to Heir or his assigns all past and future mechanical license fees derived from the sales of recordings of *Andalucia*.

(D) No. Termination of the 1939 transfer to Publisher does not entitle Heir or his assigns to any of the mechanical license fees generated by any past or future exploitation of recordings of *Andalucia* permitted by Publisher, though it does entitle Heir or his assigns to license other record companies to use the work.

224. Composer created the musical work *Dancing Shoes*, in which federal copyright vested in 1933. Composer then assigned all rights in *Dancing Shoes* to MusicCo in 1935. In 1990, Composer sought to terminate the assignment of Dancing Shoes to MusicCo pursuant to section 304(c) of the Copyright Act. MusicCo claimed the attempted termination was invalid. To support this argument, it pointed to language in the 1935 assignment agreement stating that in addition to assigning the copyright in *Dancing Shoes*, Composer also assigned "any future rights of termination" to MusicCo as well. Because Composer no longer possesses any termination rights, MusicCo's lawyers reasoned, he cannot exercise them to terminate the assignment. Will this argument prevail?

(A) Yes. Termination rights, like all the statutory privileges granted to authors pursuant to the Copyright Act, can be freely sold, devised, or assigned.

(B) Yes. Termination rights can be alienated as long as the party alienating them is the original author.

(C) No. Termination rights can be assigned, but only to individuals, not to corporate entities.

(D) No. Termination rights are inalienable and cannot be assigned by contract.

225.   Consider question 224. In attempting to effect termination, Composer served on MusicCo a written, signed notification on July 31, 1986, stating, "I hereby give notice of my intent to terminate the 1935 transfer of all copyright interest in the musical work 'Dancing Shoes,' effective January 1, 1990." On January 2, 1990, Composer recorded the notice with the Copyright Office. Later in 1990, MusicCo argued that the termination was unenforceable because the notice was procedurally invalid. Will it prevail?

(A)   Yes. The notice was invalid because it was recorded after, not before, the effective date of the termination.

(B)   No. The intent of Composer to terminate the 1935 grant was sufficiently evidenced by the July 31, 1986 notice.

(C)   Yes. The notice was invalid because it was served too far in advance of the date of termination.

(D)   No. The notice was entirely valid.

226.   Consider question 224. If, for whatever reason, a court were to find that Composer's attempt to terminate the transfer of copyright in *Dancing Shoes* to MusicCo was invalid, would this mean that MusicCo would then be the owner of the copyright for the rest of its term?

227.   Screenwriter is a salaried employee of Wolf Entertainment, Inc. ("Wolf"), a film production studio. Screenwriter's primary work for Wolf is to develop original scripts at the studio management's direction, often in collaboration with co-authors. Wolf tells Screenwriter that her next project will be to develop an original screenplay in collaboration with Indy, a freelance screenwriter whose only compensation from Wolf will be a one-time, lump-sum payment of $25,000 upon completion of the script. Indy does not, however, sign any agreements with Wolf concerning her copyright ownership in the resulting screenplay.

Together, Screenwriter and Indy pen a screenplay titled *Alone*, about an explorer who is abandoned during an Antarctic expedition. Wolf reviews the screenplay upon its completion, and while they pay Indy her fee, they decide not to make a motion picture based on *Alone*. Deeply disappointed, Screenwriter and Indy agree to shop the screenplay to Zenith, a film production company that they believe may be interested in producing the script.

Zenith does indeed want to produce the film, and they offer to assign the copyright from Screenwriter and Indy for $50,000. The writers agree to the deal, but when Wolf hears about it, their lawyers tell Zenith that they have not validly acquired the rights to *Alone*, and that if Zenith produces a film based on the screenplay, Wolf will sue them for copyright infringement.

Should Zenith make a motion picture based on the *Alone* screenplay, will Wolf succeed in suing them for copyright infringement?

(A) Yes, because Wolf solely owns the copyright in *Alone* as a work made for hire that neither Screenwriter nor Indy had the right to assign.

(B) Yes, because Wolf owns a partial interest in the copyright in *Alone* that Screenwriter was not free to assign.

(C) No, because Wolf's decision not to produce *Alone* amounted to abandonment of any copyright interest in the screenplay it may otherwise have had.

(D) No, because Wolf's decision not to produce *Alone* allocated their ownership interest in the screenplay to Screenwriter, who was then free to assign it along with Indy.

228. Assume that *Alone* was completed in 2015. When does the copyright in the screenplay expire?

229. A songwriter pens a ballad in 1962 and publishes it with valid notice that same year. In 1970, he assigns the copyright in the ballad to his only child, a daughter, who then reassigns the copyright to a music publisher that same year. In 1979, the daughter executes an agreement with the music publisher clarifying that the 1970 agreement included transfer of the right to renew the copyright. The songwriter dies unmarried in 2005.

In 2016, the daughter files notice with the Copyright Office to terminate her 1970 transfer of the copyright in the ballad to the music publisher effective 2019. The music publisher files suit in federal district court seeking a declaration that the termination notice is invalid. Will the music publisher prevail?

(A) Yes, because window of time in which the daughter could terminate the 1970 assignment ended in 2010.

(B) Yes, because the 1979 agreement eliminated any termination rights the daughter would otherwise have had.

(C) No, because the 1979 agreement did not amount to a rescission and regrant of the 1975 assignment.

(D) No, because section 203 also entitles the daughter to terminate the 1979 agreement since it was executed after 1977.

230. Bo, a graphic artist, creates and publishes with valid notice in 1938 a comic book featuring the original superhero "Cat Man." That same year, Bo assigns the copyright in Cat Man to AB Comics for a mere $200. Cat Man becomes a huge success, earning AB Comics millions of dollars in licensing revenues alone. Bo dies in 1980 unmarried and with no children. In 1992, Bo's sister, Doris (who is also the executor and sole heir of Bo's estate), complains to AB Comics that they have done nothing for her or Bo despite making millions from the character Bo created.

In response to Doris' concerns, AB Comics offers her a deal. AB Comics promises to give Doris a "pension for life" of $25,000 per year in exchange for Doris' agreement to "fully settle all claims relating to any copyrights, trademarks, or other property right in any and all work created in whole or in part by Bo" and to "grant to AB Comics any such rights." Doris accepts the offer and she and AB Comics execute an agreement in 1992 memorializing their understanding and including this language.

In 2003, Doris files a notice with the U.S. Copyright Office indicating her intention to terminate, pursuant to section 304(d), Bo's 1938 transfer of the work to AB Comics. AB Comics responds that Doris lacks any enforceable termination rights under section 304. Who will prevail in this dispute?

(A) Doris, because as of 1992, executors and heirs had no termination rights to relinquish by contract.

(B) Doris, because the 1992 agreement does not clearly include language indicating her intent to revoke the 1938 transfer.

(C) AB Comics, because this is a valid renewal and regrant that eliminates the termination rights of any statutory successors under either section 203 or 304.

(D) AB Comics, because the 1998 revision of the Copyright Act did not retroactively extend to heirs and executors such as Doris.

231.   Musician wrote several famous hit songs, all during the 1950s. Musician transferred his copyrights in all of his musical works to Music Publisher, pursuant to an agreement whereby Music Publisher would exploit the copyrights and give Musician a substantial portion of the earned revenue. In 1975, Musician executed an agreement with his only child, a son, whereby his son agreed to relinquish "any and all rights, existing now or created in the future" with respect to Musician's musical works. Musician then established Foundation, a charitable organization devoted to helping the disabled, in 1980. In 1990, Musician died unmarried, survived by his son. Musician devised all his property, including the substantial revenue earned by his musical works, to Foundation, which since that time has used the money as its sole source of income to pursue its charitable aims.

In 2015, the son filed notice with the Copyright Office that he planned to terminate Musician's transfer of the copyrights in the musical works to Music Publisher. Foundation responded by filing suit in federal district court challenging the validity of the termination notices. The son responded by arguing that Foundation lacked standing to challenge the termination notices. Does Foundation have Article III standing to challenge the son's termination notices?

(A) Yes, because Foundation is a beneficial owner of the copyrights in Musician's musical works.

(B) Yes, because the termination of the transfers to Music Publisher lies within the Copyright Act's "zone of interests."

(C) No, because Foundation's injury is merely speculative since the terminations have not yet been effected.

(D) No, because the matter is not ripe for adjudication until the transfers have actually been terminated.

232. Van is a legendary graphic artist who participated in the creation of numerous iconic comic book characters during the mid-twentieth century. Van's most productive years were the early 1960s, when he worked closely with the staff of Spectacular Comics. During this time, Spectacular typically asked Van if he'd be interested in working on a given project, which they described in broad terms, expecting Van to fill in the details with his original style.

Van was at no time during this period a salaried employee of Spectacular. Rather, he worked from home using his own supplies and according to his own schedule, and was paid by Spectacular on a per-page basis for work that he submitted if it met with Spectacular's approval (which the vast majority of his work during this period did). Van also assigned to Spectacular any copyright interests in the works he created.

In 2015, Van's only statutory successor, a son, filed notice with the Copyright Office indicating his intention to terminate all of Van's assignments of the copyrights in his works to Spectacular. Spectacular responded by filing suit in federal district court seeking a declaratory judgment that the termination notices are invalid. Will they prevail?

(A) Yes, because any works Van created for Spectacular are works made for hire under the "instance and expense" test.

(B) Yes, because any works Van created for Spectacular are works made for hire as defined by the Copyright Act of 1976.

(C) No, because Van was the author of all the works he created for Spectacular under the "instance and expense" test.

(D) No, because Van was the author of all the works he created for Spectacular under the definition of "work made for hire" in the Copyright Act of 1976.

Infringement

233.   Studio has entered into an agreement with Distributor that grants Distributor an exclusive license to distribute DVD copies of a motion picture in the United States for five years. Five years have recently passed and the Distributor has continued to sell DVD copies of the motion picture in the United States without Studio's authorization. Can Studio successfully sue Distributor for copyright infringement?

(A)   No, because Studio no longer owns the distribution right to the motion picture.

(B)   No, because the termination right may be exercised by Studio only after 35 years from the date of the grant.

(C)   Yes, because copyright infringement is the only remedy available to Studio.

(D)   Yes, because Distributor has continued to distribute the motion picture after the license has terminated.

234.   Author pens a popular novel, then grants to Production Company an exclusive license to develop the novel into a screenplay for a flat fee. Later, Writer sells to Studio a screenplay that is based directly on Author's novel, which was created without permission. Who has standing to sue Writer for infringing the copyright in the novel?

(A)   Author alone.

(B)   Production Company alone.

(C)   Author and Production Company.

(D)   Neither Author nor Production Company.

235.   Consider question 234. Subsequent to granting the exclusive license to Production Company, Author has been approached by Book Publisher, which seeks an exclusive license to translate and publish the novel in Spanish. Does Author have the right to grant such a license to Book Publisher?

236.   Consider question 234. Assume that instead of assigning an exclusive license to Production Company to develop a screenplay based on his novel, Author assigned to Production Company a nonexclusive license to develop a screenplay based on his novel. In light of this variation, who would have standing to sue Writer?

237.   Composer created the musical work *Red Rhapsody* in 2000. Two years later, he assigned the copyright in the musical work in its entirety to Lyrical Publishing, a music publisher.

The agreement stated that in exchange for the assignment, Composer would receive 50 percent of the proceeds from any exploitation of the *Red Rhapsody* musical work. *Red Rhapsody* has not generated much revenue. Recently, it has come to the attention of Composer that a musical work written and recorded by Lil Flasher, *Blue Thug Lullaby*, includes melody and lyrics that are substantially similar to those in *Red Rhapsody*. When Composer brought his concerns to the attention of Lyrical Publishing, the company responded that it did not believe the two compositions were similar and that it would not file a copyright infringement action. Composer, noting that Lil Flasher recently signed a contract with a record company affiliated with Lyrical Publishing, has decided to bring a copyright infringement action against Lil Flasher and her music publishing company, Flasher Music. Will Composer be successful?

(A) No, because Lyrical Publishing has determined that the two music compositions were not substantially similar.

(B) No, because Composer has assigned the entirety of the copyright in *Red Rhapsody* to Lyrical Publishing and has no standing to bring a copyright infringement action.

(C) Yes, because Lyrical Publishing is merely administering Composer's music catalog and is not able to bring an action for copyright infringement.

(D) Yes, because Composer is a beneficial owner who has standing to sue Lil Flasher and Flasher Music for copyright infringement.

238. Big Biz is a rap artist whose recent single has enjoyed enormous popularity. Recently, Big Biz was sued in federal district court by his longtime collaborator, Penny Wise, who claims that she is entitled to a share of the royalties generated by the single. Wise claims that Biz assigned half the royalties in the musical work to her. Biz claims that the assignment agreement produced by Wise is invalid. Biz further argues that, even if the assignment agreement were valid, it cannot be construed to grant Wise more than 20 percent of the royalties generated by the single. Wise also argues in the alternative that she should receive half of the royalties generated by the single because she is a joint author of the musical work as defined by the Copyright Act. Biz has moved to have the case dismissed for lack of federal jurisdiction. How should the judge rule on Biz's motion?

(A) All of Wise's claims can be heard in federal court.

(B) A federal court can hear the claim based on a construction of the Copyright Act, but not the claims based on the validity of the assignment or the construction of the assignment.

(C) A federal court can hear the claim based on a construction of the Copyright Act and the claim based on the validity of the assignment, but not the claim based on the construction of the assignment.

(D) None of Wise's claims can be heard in federal court.

239.   Author has sued User for copyright infringement in federal district court. Author seeks both statutory damages from User and a permanent injunction ordering User to cease his allegedly infringing conduct. As the matter proceeds to trial, User moves to have the case heard by a jury rather than the judge. What will be the result of User's motion?

(A)   The judge will deny the motion and conduct a bench trial on both issues.

(B)   The judge will grant the motion for a jury trial as to statutory damages, but will rule on the issue of injunctive relief from the bench.

(C)   The judge will grant the motion for a jury trial as to injunctive relief, but will rule on the issue of statutory damages from the bench.

(D)   The judge will grant the motion and conduct a jury trial on both issues.

240.   DistroCo is a film distribution company, based in the United States, with both domestic and international operations. DistroCo's subsidiary, EuroDistro, has begun to distribute Studio's hit film on DVD to retail stores, though without obtaining permission from Studio to do so. EuroDistro obtained a copy of the film in France and manufactures its DVDs in Germany. EuroDistro's range of distribution extends only to Western Europe, and none of its conduct takes place in the United States. Studio sues DistroCo and EuroDistro in federal court for violating its exclusive right of public distribution. Will Studio prevail?

(A)   Yes. This is a clear violation of Studio's exclusive right of public distribution.

(B)   Yes. Although normally extraterritorial conduct is not actionable under United States copyright law, there is an exception where, as here, the conduct is that of a subsidiary whose parent is domestically based.

(C)   No. United States copyright law has no application to acts that take place entirely outside its borders.

(D)   No. EuroDistro's conduct does not amount to a "public distribution" within the meaning of the Copyright Act.

241.   Consider question 240. Assume that Studio discovers that DistroCo, acting out of its main office in New York, explicitly authorized EuroDistro to engage in the unlicensed reproduction and distribution of *Action Man* throughout Western Europe. How, if at all, does this affect Studio's ability to bring a copyright infringement suit, based on United States copyright law, against DistroCo in federal court?

242.   *Le Courant* is a French-language newspaper produced in Quebec City, Canada, and distributed almost exclusively within the Canadian province of Quebec. Yves Anglais, a freelance reporter, researched and wrote a devastating story about overfishing in the Great Lakes that was published in *Le Courant*. The next week, an English translation of the article appeared in the St. Louis *Post-Journal*, under the byline of *Post-Journal* reporter John Smith. Smith did not seek permission or a license from *Le Courant* or Anglais before

publishing the piece, instead assuming that no one would find out about his plagiarism, thereby allowing him to take credit for the story. Both *Le Courant* and Anglais, however, discovered Smith's conduct, and each filed suit against Smith in United States federal court. The district court judge joined the suits in order to address the related question whether *Le Courant* or Anglais owns the copyright in the original article. Which country's law applies to each of the critical issues in this case: ownership of the copyright and copyright infringement?

(A) Canadian copyright law governs the ownership issue; American copyright law governs the infringement issue.

(B) Canadian copyright law governs both the ownership and the infringement issue.

(C) American copyright law governs the ownership issue; Canadian copyright law governs the infringement issue.

(D) American copyright law governs both the ownership and the infringement issue.

243.   Hot Ten is a website that hosts photos of models in swimsuits. Hot Ten earns profits based on charging users a monthly fee to access its site. Payment of the fee provides users with access to view pictures only and does not extend to users the right to download or distribute Hot Ten's copyrighted photos. Hot Ten has discovered that one authorized user, Alex Brown, has been downloading Hot Ten's photos and storing them on his personal computer. Brown has not carefully read his user agreement with Hot Ten and knows nothing about copyright law, and believes in good faith that he is free to download the images to his own computer. Brown does not have any intention of distributing the photographs to the public. Hot Ten sues Brown, alleging that his unauthorized reproduction of its copyrighted photos amounts to infringement. Who will prevail?

(A) Brown. Personal use of copyrighted works is a full defense to infringement.

(B) Brown. Brown's intent not to distribute means that his downloading of the photos could cause Hot Ten no harm, therefore, his conduct does not amount to infringement.

(C) Hot Ten. While Brown's conduct would not normally amount to infringement, the fact that he violated the user agreement makes it a copyright issue.

(D) Hot Ten. Copyright infringement is a strict liability offense, so Brown's good faith is not a defense to what is otherwise a prima facie case of infringement.

244.   Consider question 243. Assume that in addition to suing user Alex Brown for copyright infringement, Hot Ten also sues NationOnLine (NOL), the Internet service provider that Alex uses to connect to the Internet. If all of Alex's allegedly infringing conduct related to his downloading Hot Ten's copyrighted photographs occurred while accessing the Internet over NOL, and if Alex's conduct amounts to infringement, would NOL also be liable to Hot Ten on a direct infringement theory?

245. Musician creates the melody and harmony for an original musical work. At Musician's request, Lyricist writes lyrics to accompany Musician's music. The resulting work is a musical composition for piano and vocalist titled *View From My Window*. Musician wastes no time in booking shows around the city where she performs both the musical and lyrical components of *View From My Window*, all without asking Lyricist's permission. When Lyricist confronts Musician about the issue, Musician tells him, "Too bad. It's my work too and I can do what I want with it. And the proceeds from the performances are all mine because I did the shows. If you want to make money performing our work, you're free to go out and do it." Incensed, Lyricist sues Musician. Will Lyricist prevail, and if so, on what theory or theories?

    (A) Lyricist can show that Musician violated his exclusive right of public performance.

    (B) Lyricist can show that Musician is obligated to give him half of the profits derived from the use of *View From My Window* in her public performances because of the common-law duties of co-owners.

    (C) Lyricist can show both that Musician violated his exclusive right of public performance, and also that Musician is obligated to give him half of the profits derived from the use of *View From My Window* in her public performances because of the common-law duties of co-owners.

    (D) Lyricist has no valid cause of action against Musician.

246. Author discovers that his novel has been infringed. The CEO of major movie studio G-M-G purchased one copy of Author's published novel, photocopied it several times, and distributed the copies to a team of five G-M-G-employed screenwriters, telling them to collaborate on a screenplay version of the literary work, all unbeknownst to Author. G-M-G has now produced a screenplay version of the novel, though it has yet to start production of the motion picture that will be based on it. Author files a copyright infringement suit against G-M-G's CEO, but not against G-M-G itself. Will he prevail?

    (A) Yes. CEO violated Author's right both to reproduce the novel, and to authorize adaptations of it.

    (B) Yes. Although CEO was entitled to make copies of Author's novel pursuant to the first sale doctrine, he violated Author's exclusive right to authorize adaptations of the literary work.

    (C) No. Where infringement by a corporation is at issue, only the corporate entity itself can be held liable, not any of the corporate officers who engage in the infringement.

    (D) No. Where infringement by multiple parties, such as, here, a corporation and one of its officers, is at issue, all parties must be joined or the suit lacks standing to proceed in federal court.

247. Author creates an original musical work in 1990, first publishing it that same year. He obtains registration for the work from the Copyright Office in 1993. In 1996, Author sues

User for sampling part of the work in User's sound recording. At the onset of litigation, Author produced his copyright registration certificate as evidence of his ownership of the work. Later, User moves for summary judgment, producing a valid agreement, dated 1995, transferring ownership of the musical work from Author to User. Author argues that his infringement suit should survive summary judgment on the strength of the registration certificate alone. Will he prevail?

(A) Yes. The presumption of valid ownership created by a copyright registration certificate can be overcome only at trial.

(B) Yes. Timely filing a registration certificate amounts to incontrovertible proof of copyright ownership.

(C) No. In order for a registration certificate to provide prima facie proof of validity, it must be filed within a year of first publication.

(D) No. Although a registration certificate filed within five years of first publication amounts to prima facie proof of copyright validity, this presumption may be overcome by the submission of evidence to the contrary.

248. Writer has filed an infringement suit against Pirate. Writer argues that Pirate's literary work *America* infringes Writer's literary work *USA*. Among the various arguments Pirate advances at trial to resist infringement liability is that Pirate had no access to *USA* prior to creating *America*. In opposition to this claim, Writer produces evidence indicating that Pirate had a reasonable opportunity to read *USA* prior to creating *America*, though Writer cannot show with certainty that Pirate actually did read *USA*. Who will prevail on the access issue?

(A) Pirate. In the absence of any evidence that Pirate actually read *USA* before creating *America*, an independent creation defense will succeed.

(B) Pirate. Writer bears a particularly high burden of proof on the access issue, which is clearly not met here.

(C) Writer. Writer need only produce evidence that Pirate had a reasonable opportunity to read *USA* before creating *America*, and he has met this burden.

(D) Writer. While Writer cannot successfully show access, this is irrelevant because access is a relatively minor consideration in copyright infringement suits.

249. Consider question VII-16. Assume instead that the only evidence of access that Writer produces is that when Writer first published *USA*, he sent a copy of the novel to Sid Bishop, a literary agent at Creative House Publishing, during the time Pirate worked part-time as a manuscript reviewer in Sid's department. Writer produces no direct evidence that Pirate actually saw or read *USA*. On these facts, could Writer successfully show that Pirate had a sufficient degree of access to *USA* to support a finding of infringement?

250. Consider question 248. Now, assume instead that the only evidence of access that Writer produces is that *USA* enjoyed commercial success, climbing into the top 10 of many nationally prominent bestseller lists and earning its author both literary and popular acclaim. Writer produces no direct evidence that Pirate actually saw or read *USA*. On these facts, and only these facts, could Writer successfully prove that Pirate had a sufficient degree of access to *USA* to support a finding of infringement?

251. Artist created an original painting titled *Man Overboard* that depicts a view of Niagara Falls. The background and major setting for the picture is the standard view of Niagara Falls that one sees when one stands on the main observation deck. However, Artist added to his picture a distinctive original element: a horrified-looking, black-haired man in a brown rowboat plunging to his demise, halfway down the waterfall. Artist has accused Painter of copying *Man Overboard*. Painter has created a painting, *The Fall*, which is also set in Niagara Falls from the perspective of the main observation deck. Painter's work also depicts a horrified-looking man in a rowboat plunging to his demise, halfway down the waterfall. Painter's work depicts the man identically, except that in Painter's work the man has brown (not black) hair, and is in a black (not brown) rowboat. Will Artist be able to successfully argue that Painter's *The Fall* is substantially similar to his *Man Overboard?*

    (A) Yes, because the setting Painter has chosen is identical to the one Artist has chosen.

    (B) Yes, because the falling man is an original element of Artist's work, and Painter's depiction of that element is substantially similar.

    (C) No, because the two works are not completely identical.

    (D) No, because the similarity of the two works consists largely of a public domain element.

252. Boney is an old-school skateboarder and filmmaker who created some of the original skateboarding movies back in the late 1970s. These films featured Boney and his cronies, nicknamed the "Boney Crew," performing advanced skateboard maneuvers on half-pipes. He later learned that some rogue skaters had gotten a hold of unauthorized copies of these movies, and had conducted a local screening of the old "Boney Crew" films for the general public without Boney's consent. Boney confronted Owner, the proprietor of the theater where the screening took place, about this event, and Owner replied, "Sure, I knew this was an illegal showing, and okay, I made a few bucks on it, but hey—I just rented the place to these guys and sold and collected some tickets. I didn't make the movie and I didn't own it, and I didn't even operate the projector, so I'm not on the hook. Go find the guys who rented the theater that night—if you can!"

    Assume that Boney owns a valid copyright in the "Boney Crew" motion pictures. Boney cannot find the person who showed the movie and wants to bring a copyright infringement lawsuit against Owner, the proprietor of the theater where the unauthorized screening took place. On what, if any, theory of secondary infringement is he likely to prevail against Owner?

(A) Owner is liable on both contributory and vicarious infringement theories.

(B) Owner is liable for contributory, but not vicarious, infringement.

(C) Owner is liable for vicarious, but not contributory, infringement.

(D) Owner is not liable on any secondary infringement theories.

253. Stealio Co. is a technology company that developed a hot new computer software application called VidCap. VidCap allows Internet users to easily select and download screenshot images from streaming videos. If a user is watching a streaming video on a site such as YouTube, and she has installed VidCap, she need only click on her computer screen as the desired image appears, and VidCap automatically downloads a high-quality JPEG image file to her computer's desktop. The primary use of VidCap is to create bootleg movie posters. Stealio promotes the VidCap application to users, running advertisements that state: "Why pay for pricey movie posters when you can create your own—for free— using VidCap?" G-M-G, a major motion picture studio, has filed a copyright infringement suit against Stealio. G-M-G argues that Stealio is liable on a theory of inducement. Will G-M-G prevail?

(A) Yes, because there is clear evidence that Stealio had knowledge of VidCap's infringing uses and that Stealio actively encouraged the application's infringing uses.

(B) No, because VidCap is capable of substantial noninfringing uses.

(C) Yes, because the Supreme Court's decision in *Metro-Goldwyn-Mayer Studios, Inc. v. Grokster* overruled its earlier decision in *Sony Corp. v. Universal City Studios, Inc.*

(D) No, because there is no evidence that Stealio profited financially from its creation of VidCap.

254. Matt is an experimental musician who specializes in electronic remixes of modern classical music. He contacted 10 of his favorite modern classical musicians and paid for nonexclusive licenses from each of them that gave Matt the right to use a 15-second sample of their most recent musical works. Matt then created a sound recording in which he compiled the music samples, calling the selection *Three-Bar Loop*. He did so by juxtaposing the 10 samples in different sequential orders in order to bring out new insights about the similarities and differences between the 10 works. Tiffany, a producer, heard *Three-Bar Loop* and wanted to include Matt's sound recording in a forthcoming album featuring recent examples of outstanding experimental music, but Matt refused outright. Tiffany then acquired assignments of all of the copyrights in the same 10 musical works that Matt included in *Three-Bar Loop*. She then included her recording of *Three-Bar Loop* on her album without Matt's permission. Matt sues Tiffany for infringement. Will he prevail?

(A) Yes. Matt's purchase of a nonexclusive license to use the samples gives him standing to sue for infringement of the works of authorship embodied in those samples.

(B) Yes. *Three-Bar Loop* is an original compilation based on the 10 licensed samples, and Tiffany's unauthorized use of that work violates Matt's copyright in the compilation.

(C) No. Because Matt's work is only a compilation of other authors' material, it does not possess any separate, copyrightable originality.

(D) No. Matt acquired only a limited use right to the samples that comprise *Three-Bar Loop*, which does not give him any rights in the underlying musical works from which those samples were taken.

255.   Consider question 254. Assume that instead of creating *Three-Bar Loop* by compiling copyrighted works of authorship, Matt used samples of classical music that belonged to the public domain and were wholly unprotected by copyright. Would this change the outcome of Matt's infringement suit against Tiffany for her unauthorized use of *Three-Bar Loop*?

256.   Studio owns the copyright in a motion picture. MovieCo releases a film that Studio believes infringes its copyright in Studio's motion picture. At trial, Studio and MovieCo jointly place only two facts in the record. A scientific survey of average people found that the survey participants regarded the two works as possessing largely the same aesthetic appeal; and that the same survey participants were each able to identify an average of five points of difference in the theme, plot, and mood of the two films. In terms of substantial similarity, which party has adduced more persuasive evidence to support a finding in its favor?

(A) MovieCo. Survey data is inadmissible to prove the presence of substantial similarity.

(B) MovieCo. Any points of difference between two films are enough to overcome a showing of substantial similarity.

(C) Studio. Because the two works possess the same essential aesthetic appeal, they are substantially similar.

(D) Studio. A copyright defendant must be able to show at least 10 points of salient difference between the two works in suit in order to overcome a finding of substantial similarity.

257.   Author penned a successful mystery novel in which he named the main female villain "Eva Destruction." Writer later wrote a romance novel, and named one of her characters "Eva Destruction." Writer's "Eva Destruction" character is otherwise entirely unlike Author's "Eva Destruction," and her romance novel bears no other similarities to Author's mystery novel. Author accosted Writer and said, "You're a thief! I know you took the name of your 'Eva Destruction' character directly from my book." Writer responded, "You're right, I did. Sue me." Author does. Will he prevail?

(A) Yes. Because Writer intentionally copied the name of Author's character, she is liable for copyright infringement.

(B) Yes. Because literary characters are copyrightable, their names are too.

(C)   No. This is at most a *de minimis* taking that does not rise to a level sufficient to trigger copyright infringement.

(D)   No. Literary characters are not copyrightable, so their names are not copyrightable either.

258.   Ray is a singer-songwriter, and the author and owner of both the musical work and the sound recording that comprise the minimalist vocal track *Only*. In 2014, two years after releasing the track to moderate critical and commercial success, Ray hears a track that is entirely identical to his. Titled *Number Three*, it is the work of Zao, a Buddhist monk in rural Laos who had no contact with western society until 2015, when he was discovered by explorers who recorded Zao's singing to bring it to a worldwide audience. All of Zao's vocal tracks on the CD were composed by Zao prior to his contact with the explorers. Incensed, Ray sues Zao for copyright infringement in United States federal court. Will Ray prevail?

(A)   Yes, because the author a work that possesses verbatim similarity to preexisting works is per se liable for infringement of the preexisting work.

(B)   Yes, because Zao's work will cut into the profitability and market share of Ray's work.

(C)   No, because any copying by Zao would have lacked conscious intent to infringe.

(D)   No, because Zao has independently created *Number Three* and thus has a complete defense to the claim that he infringed the copyright in *Only*.

259.   Consider question 258. Assume that Zao was not a monk in rural Laos cut off from western society, but an American who was part of mainstream society. In response to Ray's allegations of copyright infringement, Zao produces proof that despite the moderate popular success of Ray's *Only*, Zao had no conscious awareness of that work when he composed and recorded *Number Three*. Assuming that Zao's assertions are truthful, are they sufficient to escape copyright liability?   No

260.   Ben sells printing equipment to publishing companies such as book publishers, newspapers, and magazines. One day, Joe contacts Ben, seeking to purchase a large printing press. Ben recognizes Joe from a news item a year ago in which Joe was nabbed by federal authorities for printing unauthorized copies of novels, which he then sold cheaply to booksellers. Joe says to Ben, "I got out of that other infringement suit, and now I'm ready for another quick score. All I need is a printing press so I can—", at which point Ben interrupts and says, "What you plan to do with this printing press is your business; I don't want to know a thing about it." Joe buys the printing press, and several weeks later he runs into Ben and says, "Thanks for selling me that printing press, man—I'm making a killing selling bootleg copies of bestselling books!" Soon after, Joe is again caught using the press to make unauthorized copies of novels. This time, Ben is joined in the infringement suit against Joe on a theory of contributory infringement. Will Ben be held liable on a contributory infringement theory for the infringement of the copyrights in the novels?

(A) No. Ben's knowledge of the illegality of Joe's conduct arose only after Ben sold Joe the printing press that was used to engage in copyright infringement.

(B) No. Ben was conscious only of the fact that Joe was making copies of novels, not that this conduct was unlawful.

(C) Yes. Ben can be constructively charged with knowledge of the illegality of Joe's conduct.

(D) Yes. As long as the primary infringer was aware of the illegality of his conduct, that knowledge can be imputed to the secondary infringer.

261. Barry operates a website that provides visitors with information regarding other sites around the Internet where infringing digital music files can be downloaded for free. Barry's site has a disclaimer at the top that says, "Many of these sites are engaging in copyright infringement. Visit these sites at your own risk, and don't hold me responsible for your own actions!" Barry's site does not include links to the sites where the infringing music files are found. Rather, the site has descriptions that refer to each site with text that, when cut and pasted into a search engine, will return the site as the first result. Barry supports himself with the revenue he makes from selling advertising on his website. Can Barry be held liable on a contributory infringement theory?

(A) Yes, because Barry has a financial interest in directing visitors to infringing websites.

(B) Yes, because Barry's website materially contributes to copyright infringement with full knowledge of the illegality of the conduct.

(C) No, because Barry is not directly linking to the infringing websites, but merely providing information that allows users to locate them.

(D) No, because Barry notifies site visitors that the listed sites are infringing, and provides a full disclaimer of liability.

262. The Clean Channel Network is a radio network that has 50 independently owned affiliated AM radio stations throughout the United States. Each of these stations has agreed to Clean Channel's affiliate agreement pursuant to which the network agrees to provide programming in exchange for which the station agrees to broadcast the network's programming, give Clean Channel five minutes of advertising time each hour that Clean Channel can sell to national advertisers, and give Clean Channel approval rights to any other programming broadcast by the affiliate.

One of Clean Channel's affiliate radio stations, KXTM, is best known for its controversial local talk show host, Birch Barlow. Numerous listeners have complained to Clean Channel that they are offended by Barlow's show, but Clean Channel always responds by saying that local content is best determined by local affiliates. Barlow has introduced a new feature in which he reads entire chapters of books that express political views with which he disagrees, and then derides the opinions of the authors, none of whom have provided Barlow with permission to read from their works on air. Barlow's new feature has both increased listener share and advertising revenue associated with his show and has caused several of the authors to complain to Clean Channel about the unauthorized use of their literary works. Getting no response, the authors have sued both Barlow for direct infringement, and Clean Channel on a vicarious infringement theory. Assuming that Barlow is indeed directly liable for infringement, can Clean Channel also be held liable on a vicarious infringement theory?

(A) Yes. Clean Channel had knowledge of Barlow's infringing conduct, and provided him with the material means to engage in that infringement.

(B) Yes. Clean Channel both directly profited from Barlow's direct infringement and had the ability to control Barlow's public performance of the literary works.

(C) No. Clean Channel had no ability to control the conduct of its affiliate radio stations.

(D) No. Clean Channel may have profited from Barlow's performances, but only indirectly.

263.   James owns a vacant lot in Maine, though he lives in Oregon and has no family and friends anywhere in New England. James has owned the lot for years, refusing to develop or sell it, in the hope that someday the lot will increase in value and he can sell it for a profit. One day, James gets a call from Dan, who says, "Listen, if you want to make some cash on that old lot you've got, I'll pay you $1,000 to rent it for a month. I promise at the end of the time I'll be gone and the lot will be just as good as it was before. Just don't ask any questions, all right?" James replies, "Well, I've never done anything like this before, but sure—as long as you agree not to mess up the property, you've got a deal." A week later, James receives a check in the mail from Dan for $1,000, which he cashes, and then never thinks about it again. Six months later, James is joined in a copyright infringement suit against Dan. It turns out that throughout the month, during which James never set foot in Maine, Dan was using the lot to run an informal market where he sold bootleg copies of DVDs and CDs, all of which infringed their owners' copyrights. Assuming that Dan is liable on a direct infringement theory, will James be liable on a secondary infringement theory as well?

(A) Yes. James had constructive knowledge of Dan's infringing conduct, and provided him with the material means to engage in that infringement.

(B) Yes. James profited directly from Dan's infringing conduct, and had supervisory control over the infringing conduct as well.

(C) No. While James directly profited from Dan's infringement, he did not have control over or the ability to supervise Dan's infringing conduct on the lot.

(D) No. While James had supervisory control over Dan's infringing conduct, he did not profit directly from that infringement.

264.   Bill lost his job and was desperate to make ends meet. For a couple months, he made unauthorized copies of DVDs of recent blockbuster films, knowing full well that he was engaging in copyright infringement, and operated an illicit door-to-door business vending the bootleg DVDs for a fraction of what they sell for on the retail market. Unfortunately for Bill, one day he sold to an undercover FBI agent, who placed him under arrest for criminal copyright infringement. Over the course of his enterprise, Bill netted only $950 in sales. What criminal penalties might Bill face?

(A)   Bill will not be subject to criminal liability because his net sales did not exceed $1000.

(B)   Bill will not be subject to criminal liability because his conduct was not willful.

(C)   Bill may be subject to fines, but will not face imprisonment.

(D)   Bill may be subject to imprisonment and fines.

265.   Connex is a typical major provider of Internet access. Users pay Connex a monthly fee, and Connex provides those users with access to email and to the World Wide Web through its own network. For an added fee, Connex also allows users to store up to one terabyte of information on Connex's servers. Connex has adopted and publicized its policy of terminating any users who repeatedly use its service to engage in copyright infringement, and has an agent designated to receive and review takedown notices. Connex does not interfere with content owners' attempts to use standard technology protection measures.

Alice is a Connex user who frequently engages in illegal music filesharing, but has never been accused of copyright infringement. Alice transmits infringing music files back and forth to other users via email, all while using Connex as her Internet service provider. Also, pursuant to automated Connex procedures that apply to all its users, Alice's email transmissions, including attachments consisting of infringing music files, are typically archived on Connex's servers, sometimes for as many as five days. At no time do any of the owners of the material whose copyright Alice has infringed learn about or notify Connex of Alice's infringing conduct. Nor does any of Alice's conduct give rise to a reasonable suspicion that she is engaging in repeat infringement. Which, if any, of Alice's actions can render Connex liable for damages for copyright infringement on a secondary infringement theory?

(A)   Both Alice's email transmissions with infringing attachments and Connex's archiving of those emails subject Connex to liability on a secondary infringement theory.

(B)   Neither Alice's email transmissions with infringing attachments nor Connex's archiving of those emails subjects Connex to liability on a secondary infringement theory.

(C)   Alice's email transmissions with infringing attachments subject Connex to liability on a secondary infringement theory, but Connex's archiving of those emails does not.

(D) Connex's archiving of Alice's email communications with infringing attachments does not subject Connex to liability on a secondary infringement theory, but Alice's emails do.

266.   Consider question 265. Further assume that Alice has also paid for Connex's enhanced storage service, and takes advantage of it to store approximately 15 infringing music files on Connex's servers. Nothing about this storage reasonably gives rise to suspicion that Alice's conduct amounts to copyright infringement. Nor do any of the owners whose copyrights Alice infringes know of or notify Connex about her infringing conduct. In light of these facts, can Connex be held liable on a secondary infringement theory for Alice's storage of infringing files on its servers?

267.   Consider questions 265 and 266. Now assume that one of the copyright owners discovers Alice's infringing conduct, and sends a letter to Connex asking that it remove the infringing files from the Connex servers. The letter, composed by the copyright owner's attorney, specifically identifies Alice as the individual responsible for the infringement; provides Alice's full legal name, email address and phone number; identifies the infringed works and their particular location on Connex's servers; includes the signature of the owner's attorney as well as an attestation by the attorney, under penalty of perjury, that the information in the letter is accurate, and that she is legally authorized to act on the owner's behalf. Is this document sufficient to give rise to a duty on behalf of Connex to remove Alice's infringing files from its server?

(A) No. This notice is insufficient because it does not include a sworn attestation that Alice's use is unauthorized.

(B) No. This notice is insufficient because it does not include the owner's signature.

(C) No. This notice is insufficient because it does not include copyright registration certificates for all works that the owner seeks to have removed.

(D) Yes. This document meets all applicable statutory requirements and gives rise to a duty on behalf of Connex to remove Alice's infringing files from its server.

268.   Consider questions 265, 266, and 267. Now assume that Connex receives a takedown notice relating to Alice's storage of infringing material on its servers that is legally sufficient in all respects. Which, if any, of the following statements *incorrectly* describes Connex's obligations upon receipt of the takedown notice?

(A) Take reasonable steps to promptly notify the subscriber that it has removed or disabled access to the allegedly infringing material.

(B) Remove or disable access to the infringing material within a reasonable time.

(C) Cease to act as Alice's Internet service provider.

(D) Inform the copyright owner of Connex's receipt of a written communication from Alice contesting the denial of access.

269.   Cali is a singer and recording artist who reached her peak of fame during the 1960s and 1970s. She is best known for two tracks in particular, each of which is a soulful rendition of an ancient Celtic folk song: "Juniper" (recorded and released in 1969) and "Solitaire" (recorded and released in 1975). In 1980, Cali obtained a valid assignment of all rights and interest in the master versions of both sound recordings. Recently, Cali heard these two sound recordings played on the satellite radio station XM-100. XM-100, a typical subscription satellite radio station, schedules and broadcasts its own programming, and does not allow users to interactively choose what content it will broadcast. Cali, a lifetime Los Angeles resident, sued the radio station in the United States District Court for the Central District of California for performing her two sound recordings without obtaining her permission or paying her a royalty. Will Cali's lawsuit succeed?

(A) Cali's lawsuit will succeed, but only for the unauthorized performance of "Juniper."

(B) Cali's lawsuit will succeed, but only for the unauthorized performance of "Solitaire."

(C) Cali will probably succeed with respect to the unauthorized performances of both sound recordings.

(D) Cali will not succeed with respect to the unauthorized performance of either sound recording.

270.   Consider question 269. Now assume that, rather than playing the original master recordings of each of Cali's works, XM-100 played a digitally remastered version of the recordings. The sound engineer who created the remastered versions substantially improved the sound quality of Cali's analog master recordings and used a variety of mixing techniques to create an even more haunting affect to Cali's vocals. Under these facts, would Cali still be able to successfully argue that XM-100 violated her exclusive right of public performance in her recordings of "Juniper" and "Solitaire"?

271.   A famous actress performs a brief, three-minute cameo to a recent film in which she breaks into the board room of a major oil company during an executive meeting and delivers an impassioned speech about the risks of global warming. The actress did not sign an agreement with the film production studio that made the movie regarding assignment or ownership of copyright, though the studio received valid assignments from all other individuals—including the screenwriter—who worked on the film. The actress's only compensation for her contribution to the film was a one-time lump-sum payment of $30,000.

The actress's scene has gone viral, and unauthorized clips of it are now widely and freely available on Internet video portals. The actress implores the studio to either seek compensation for these unlicensed performances or take legal action to have them shut down. The studio, however, declines to take any action, since it believes the widespread availability of the scene on the Internet may help coalesce public opinion against global warming. The actress then identifies a man who has acquired a digital version of her scene, hosted it on his home computer, and is making it available on his personal website, all without permission or compensation. The actress sues him for violating her copyright in the scene. Will she prevail?

(A) Yes, because the man's unauthorized use violates her public performance rights in the scene.

(B) Yes, because she is a beneficial owner of the copyright in the film.

(C) No, because her performance within the film lacks the modicum of creativity required to meet copyright's originality threshold.

(D) No, because her performance within the film does not constitute a separately copyrightable work of authorship.

272. Joe writes a weekly humor column for his community newsletter, which appears in both print and online versions. One day he sees that a blogger named Kevin has reprinted the text of Joe's latest column on Kevin's blog verbatim and without permission. A local attorney approaches Joe and offers to take Joe's case on a contingency basis. Joe declines, saying that he does not want to be a party to any litigation. The attorney then offers to pay Joe to transfer to him for one year the exclusive right to sue for infringements of any of Joe's copyrights, for which the attorney will pay Joe $5,000 plus 25 percent of any net recoveries the attorney obtains from defendants during that time.

Joe agrees, and executes an agreement with the attorney reflecting these terms and formally defining the attorney as a "co-owner" of Joe's copyrights. The attorney then proceeds to sue Kevin for infringing the copyright in the column that Kevin reprinted on his blog. Kevin moves to dismiss the suit on the grounds that the attorney lacks standing to sue for infringement of Joe's copyright. Will Kevin prevail?

(A) Yes, because assignment of a bare right to sue for copyright infringement does not confer standing.

(B) Yes, because the right to sue for copyright infringement is non-transferable.

(C) No, because the agreement clearly designates the attorney as a "co-owner" of Joe's copyrights.

(D) No, because the agreement furthers the Copyright Act's policy of protecting owners' exclusive rights through infringement litigation.

273. Radio4U is a new technology that seeks to give users the ability to listen to terrestrial radio broadcasts from all over the United States via the Internet. Radio4U leases each of its users an individual remote antenna, which receives terrestrial radio broadcast signals, and then retransmits them to each individual user via the Internet. Radio4U users can listen to live radio broadcasts in real time, or record broadcasts to listen to them on demand or simply save them in an archive. Radio4U does not pay the broadcasters of the terrestrial radio signals for the right to retransmit their validly copyrighted content, and the owners of the

copyrights in the broadcast content sue Radio4U for infringement. Who will prevail, Radio4U or the owners?

(A) Radio4U, because their rebroadcasts are private, not public, performances, of the owners' copyrighted works of authorship.

(B) Radio4U, because their rebroadcasts are fair uses of the owners' copyrighted works of authorship.

(C) The owners, because Radio4U's rebroadcasts are unauthorized public performances of their copyrighted works of authorship.

(D) The owners, because Radio4U failed to pay the appropriate statutory license for rebroadcasting their copyrighted works of authorship.

274.   Star is a pop music artist who performs and produces all of her own work. Recently, she composed an original musical work titled "Elevate," which she then performed and engineered at her home recording studio. As part of "Elevate," she included a 1.5-second sample — i.e., a verbatim copy — of "Live," a copyright-protected track performed and owned by Arty, a famous hip-hop performer. "Elevate" becomes a hit, but when Arty hears the track, he threatens to sue Star for copyright infringement because she used a sample of "Live" without his permission.

Will Arty succeed in his copyright infringement lawsuit against Star?

Fair Use and Other Affirmative Defenses

275. Tanya owns the copyright in both the musical work and the sound recording that comprise the track *Fast Dog*. Don owns and operates a weblog on which he writes regular features about newly released music. Each of Don's weekly posts includes an unauthorized, 20-second audio stream of the new release he discusses. Recently, Don posted a review of Fast Dog, including an audio stream, without permission from Tanya. Tanya sues Don for copyright infringement, and Don counters by raising a fair use defense. Part of Don's argument is that his streaming of *Fast Dog* amounts to fair use because providing short streams on music review websites without licensing or compensation is customary practice in the music industry. Don further argues that courts should consider unauthorized uses that are also customary industry practices as more likely to be fair uses. May a court consider Don's argument about industry custom in its consideration of his fair use claim?

    (A) Yes. Customary use is one of the four statutory fair use factors that courts must consider.

    (B) Yes. Although customary use is not one of the four statutory fair use factors that courts must consider, the factors are not exclusive, so a court is permitted to take additional factors into account.

    (C) No. Customary use is not one of the four statutory fair use factors, so it may not enter into a court's analysis of the issue.

    (D) No. Fair use relates dominantly to the market effects the defendant's work has on the plaintiff's work, so the notion of custom cannot factor into a fair use analysis.

276. FreeBooks.com is a new web-based reading service. It is accessible only to subscribers who pay a membership fee. FreeBooks.com's paying members receive one new chapter of a book of their choice every month for a year, though the books can be read only in digital format. Accessing books through FreeBooks.com allows subscribers to read them for a fraction of the price they would pay for a hard copy of the same book in a traditional bookstore. All of the books FreeBooks.com makes available to readers are copyrighted, and at no time has FreeBooks.com licensed the use of any of these works. FreeBooks.com is sued for infringement by the owner of the copyright in a novel (*Grave Runner*) that it has made available on its site. The novel has, to date, been released only in physical, not digital form. FreeBooks.com responds by conceding the prima facie case for infringement and raising a fair use defense. Will this defense succeed?

(A) Yes. FreeBooks.com's use is transformative because it translates the physical novel into an online medium.

(B) Yes. FreeBooks.com's use would not harm any current or potential markets for sales of physical editions of the novel.

(C) No. FreeBooks.com's use does not transform the purpose of *Grave Runner*, and it would likely trade off with current or future markets for the novel.

(D) No. Courts have held that the fair use defense categorically does not apply to Internet uses of copyrighted works.

277.   John is a writer who loathes former President Bill Clinton. John composes a humorous, fictional work titled *The Trial of Slick Willie* in which he repeatedly mocks Clinton. John's literary work is an adaptation of the plot of *The Trial of Sick Billy*, a successful legal thriller published several years earlier. Betty, the author of *The Trial of Sick Billy*, is a fan of Bill Clinton and is upset by John's using her literary work to mock the former President, especially because John never asked her for permission to use that work. Betty contacts John and voices her distaste. John responds, "Don't take it personally, Betty. I'm not saying anything about you or your novel. I'm just using it to make fun of that jerk Clinton." Betty is not satisfied by this, and sues John for copyright infringement. John responds by raising a fair use defense. Assuming that a court agreed with John's descriptive assessment of his work, would John's fair use claim likely succeed?

(A) Yes. John's work is a parody, not a satire, and the Supreme Court has held that parodies are always fair uses.

(B) Yes. John's work is political commentary, and political commentary is always fair use.

(C) No. John's work is a satire, not a parody, and the Supreme Court has held that satire is never fair use.

(D) No. John's work is a satire, not a parody, and the Supreme Court has held that satire is less likely to merit a fair use defense.

278.   Consider question 277. Assume instead that when Betty contacted John, he told her, "I know why you're upset. It's not really that I made fun of Bill Clinton, but that I made fun of your dumb book. Well, that was my point—I think your book is awful and I wanted to show everyone just why." Assuming that a court agreed with John's descriptive assessment of his work, would he be likely to succeed on a fair use defense? *Yes, parody not, and fits*

279.   Which of the following statements most accurately describes the source of fair use law in the United States?

(A) The notion of fair use as a defense to copyright infringement was first articulated by Congress in the 1976 Copyright Act.

(B) Fair use is located explicitly in the United States Constitution and has also been passed as a federal statute.

(C) Fair use has long-standing common-law roots, but was first codified in statutory form in the 1976 Copyright Act.

(D) The fair use doctrine consists exclusively of judicial interpretations of explicit constitutional language.

280. *Eat at Joe's* is a very popular television situation comedy set at a greasy-spoon diner. In the seventh year of the show's run, two books are published about it. The first is *The Definitive Guide to "Eat at Joe's,"* which purports to be a complete compendium of all episodes of the show. The guide consists of plot summaries of each episode of Eat at Joe's from its seven-year run, all of which are factually detailed synopses of the episodes that also include several verbatim quotes from each episode that the author regards as especially funny or memorable.

The second publication is titled *Deconstructing "Eat at Joe's,"* and it consists of seven essays written by academic literary critics about *Eat at Joe's*. The essays each make different points about the social meaning of the show. Several of the essays include images or paragraph-long blocks of dialogue from *Eat at Joe's*, none of which were used with permission, in order to illustrate their points. The owner of the copyright in *Eat at Joe's* sues the publishers of each of the two books for copyright infringement. Each of the publishers responds by raising a fair use defense. With respect to whether the books' use of material from *Eat at Joe's* is transformative, how would a court likely rule?

(A) *The Definitive Guide to "Eat at Joe's"* is transformative, but *Deconstructing "Eat at Joe's"* is not.

(B) *Deconstructing "Eat at Joe's"* is transformative, but *The Definitive Guide to "Eat at Joe's"* is not.

(C) *Deconstructing "Eat at Joe's"* and *The Definitive Guide to "Eat at Joe's"* are both transformative.

(D) Neither *Deconstructing "Eat at Joe's"* nor *The Definitive Guide to "Eat at Joe's"* is transformative.

281. Kara is a commercial photographer who works in Africa, where she accompanies hunters on safaris and takes colorful pictures of the hunters with the game the hunters have killed. Jody is a visual artist and an environmentalist. She finds hunting odious and strongly dislikes that her fellow artist Kara capitalizes on the killing of wild animals to make a living. Jody lawfully acquires several prints of Kara's photographs, and makes paintings based on each of them. Jody's paintings depict exactly the same content as Kara's photographs—hunters and their recently killed prey—but in Jody's paintings she has given the hunters vicious expressions rather than smiles, and Jody has also written words like "murder" and "cruelty" in blood-red paint over each of the scenes. Kara is horrified when she learns about Jody's work, and she sues Jody for copyright infringement. Jody concedes that she created unauthorized adaptations of Kara's work, but argues that her infringement is defensible because it is a fair use. In considering Jody's fair use defense, how would a court rule on the issue of whether her adaptations are transformative of the originals?

(A) Jody's work is not transformative because she depicted exactly the same content in her paintings as Kara did in her photographs.

(B) Jody's work is transformative because she created paintings, while Kara created photographs.

(C) Jody's work is not transformative because she could have expressed her criticism of Kara's work via other means that did not entail unauthorized appropriation of Kara's work.

(D) Jody's work is transformative because it recasts Kara's work in a menacing rather than positive light, and does so in order to make a political point.

282.   SoundSearch.com is an online search engine that allows users to search for and locate sound files on the web. Users enter a search string in the form of text on SoundSearch.com's home page, and the site returns matches in the form of links. Clicking on one of these links then produces an automated, low-fidelity five-second version of the sound file. SoundSearch.com broadly combs the Internet for sound files to produce in response to user searches. It does not seek permission from the relevant copyright owners to use the sound files that embody their musical works or comprise part of their sound recordings. Several of those copyright owners now sue SoundSearch.com for its unauthorized copying and performance of these protected works of authorship. SoundSearch.com responds by conceding copying, but raising a fair use defense. Would a court considering this fair use defense regard SoundSearch.com's use as transformative?

(A) Yes. Any use of copyrighted material by a search engine amounts to fair use.

(B) Yes. By using only partial versions of the sound files, and by producing them for information and search, rather than entertainment, purposes, SoundSearch.com engaged in transformative use.

(C) No. Because SoundSearch.com did not offer any commentary on the sound files, their use cannot be transformative.

(D) No. Because SoundSearch.com did not alter the sounds in the five-second versions, their use cannot be transformative.

283.   The Sludge Retort is a libertarian website that aggregates news and information from around the web and provides acerbic commentary about it. Its founder, Cat Sludge, does not charge viewers a fee to access his site. He does sell ad space on the Sludge Retort, though the nominal revenues go almost entirely toward the costs of website maintenance. Rather, Cat's primary source of income is his day job as an information technology professional. Although the Sludge Retort typically posts only links to news items, some of Cat's editorials include large block quotes from other news outlets' articles, which Cat uses to frame his typically harsh commentary. Cat has never asked permission from any of these news outlets to link to or use block quotes from their articles. Several of the news outlets sue Cat for infringing the copyrights in their articles, and Cat responds by conceding unauthorized

copying, but raising a fair use defense. On the particular issue of whether Cat's unauthorized use of the selections from the news outlets' articles is commercial, how would a court be likely to rule?

(A) The use is commercial because Cat Sludge intends for it to increase his profit.

(B) The use is not commercial because Cat Sludge makes only a nominal amount on the Sludge Retort's advertising.

(C) The use is commercial because it helps enable the Sludge Retort to generate advertising revenue.

(D) The use is not commercial because users are not charged a fee for accessing the Sludge Retort.

284. Consider question 283. Assume **for the sake of this question only** that a court were to find that Cat Sludge's use was commercial. Would this finding have a dispositive effect on the outcome of the overall fair use analysis? No. You can go to the other factors as well

285. Janie is a nurse by day and an aspiring romance novelist by night. She has recently completed a manuscript of an original literary work entitled *Tempest at Sea*, which she hopes will be a great success. *Tempest at Sea* consists of a fictional story line, with fictional characters. It is, however, set in a realistic historical milieu, the New England whaling communities of the late nineteenth century, about which Janie has done much original historical research. Because she has never published a novel before, Janie arranges a meeting with her friend Alice, an established romance novelist, to ask about the ins and outs of the business. During their dinner, Janie gives Alice a copy of *Tempest at Sea*, saying, "I'd really appreciate your thoughts on this, but please don't show it to anyone else. You're the only person I've let see the manuscript." Alice reads and loves the manuscript, and a week or so later, without Janie's permission, Alice posts several paragraph-long excerpts from Janie's manuscript on her blog, praising them as "tantalizing bits from the work of America's next literary star." Janie is not pleased, despite Alice's praise, and sues Alice for copyright infringement. Alice concedes that posting the excerpts online amounted to unauthorized reproduction, but advances a fair use defense. When analyzing the second fair use factor, the nature of the protected work, the court is likely to find in favor of which party?

(A) Alice, because the historical character of Janie's work makes it factual, and because Janie published the manuscript by giving Alice a copy.

(B) Janie, because her manuscript is fictional, although she published it by releasing it to Alice.

(C) Janie, because her manuscript was unpublished and is fictional.

(D) Janie, because her manuscript was unpublished, although its historical character makes it factual.

286.   Consider question 285. Assume **for the purposes of this question only** that a court found that Janie's manuscript was unpublished. Would a court find this fact dispositive of Alice's fair use defense?

287.   Jayne Martel is a mystery writer with a large following. Her novels are distinctive in that they never reveal the mystery until the final page. Max is a huge Jayne Martel fan, and runs a website devoted to her work. Recently, Max has created a section of his website called "Solving the Puzzle," in which he publishes, without permission, the last page of each Jayne Martel novel, verbatim, for readers who can't wait to figure out the solution to the mystery. Jayne Martel discovers the website and sues Max for copyright infringement. Max counters with a fair use defense. In terms of the third factor, the amount and substantiality of the taking, in favor of which party would a court likely rule?

(A)   Max. His takings represented only a single page from each of Jayne Martel's books, and so represent only a small fraction of each literary work.

(B)   Jayne. Max's takings took the critical portion of each of her works, the ending, and are qualitatively, if not quantitatively, substantial.

(C)   Max. His takings were in good faith and would not undermine the market for Jayne Martel's novels.

(D)   Jayne. Max's takings were verbatim, so the amount they appropriated is irrelevant.

288.   Lloyd is a professor of film studies who specializes in horror movies. At an academic conference, Lloyd gives a lecture called "Text and Subtext in American Slasher Films." In his hour-long lecture, Lloyd plays three two-minute clips from his favorite horror movie, *Bloody Mary*, the running time of which is 90 minutes. During each of these clips, none of which were performed with permission, Lloyd continues to lecture as he illustrates in detail how each of the excerpts illustrates the three points that comprise the thesis of his academic paper. Shortly after the lecture, Gory Studios, the owner of the *Bloody Mary* audiovisual work, sues Lloyd for copyright infringement. Lloyd concedes that his conduct amounted to an unauthorized public performance of the audiovisual work, but counters with a fair use defense. In terms of the third element of a fair use defense, the amount and substantiality of the taking, in favor of which party would a court likely rule?

(A)   Gory Studios. By taking six minutes of a 90-minute film, Lloyd has appropriated the heart of Gory Studios' work.

(B)   Gory Studios. Taking more than five percent of an audiovisual work categorically results in the third fair use factor weighing against the defendant.

(C)   Lloyd. Because his taking was for the purpose of academic commentary, factor three weighs in his favor.

(D)   Lloyd. Because his taking took no more than was necessary to support his thesis, factor three weighs in his favor.

289.   Mark is a businessman specializing in emerging markets. He discovers a demand for independent films in China, and sets up businesses making unauthorized DVDs of independent films and selling them throughout China, without ever seeking the permission of the films' copyright owners. Mark makes the DVDs in and ships them from the United States. One of the movie studios complains to Mark about his practices, and Mark responds, "This is classic fair use. You don't have any distribution in Asian markets, and you haven't announced any plans to expand here. No harm, no foul." Assume that Mark's characterization of the studio's practices and plans is accurate. Would a court find Mark's argument convincing in terms of the fourth fair use factor, effect on current or future markets for or value of the owner's work?

   (A)   Yes. Because the studio is not currently exploiting the market that Mark has moved into, there is no harm to that market.

   (B)   Yes. Because the studio has no current plans to exploit the market that Mark has moved into, there is no harm to that market.

   (C)   No. Because Mark did not at least attempt to negotiate a license with the studio, the fourth factor necessarily weighs against him.

   (D)   No. Because the studio might reasonably choose to exploit Asian markets in the future, Mark's use harms its potential markets.

290.   Consider question 289. Assume **for the purposes of this question only** that a court found that the fourth factor of the fair use analysis weighed in favor of the film studio. Would this conclusion be dispositive of Mark's fair use defense? No. look at other factors

291.   *Ben* is a popular situation comedy on the television network CBA. Gina loves the show and invents a board game called *The Ben Game* that is structured around themes, characters, and facts about the show. The producers of *Ben* contact Gina and tell her that they love the game and want to use it as part of their marketing. For about a year, Gina sells CBA copies of *The Ben Game* at a deep discount. Then, without warning, CBA decides that it wants to produce its own version of a board game based on *Ben*, and seeks an injunction to stop Gina from producing *The Ben Game*. CBA argues that *The Ben Game* is an unauthorized derivative work, and thus amounts to infringement. Gina argues, among other things, that *The Ben Game* is defensible as a form of fair use. When analyzing the fourth factor of this fair use claim, which party is a court likely to favor?

   (A)   CBA, because fair use is not a valid defense when injunctive relief is at issue.

   (B)   CBA, because the market for *The Ben Game* is also a reasonably foreseeable potential future market for *Ben*.

   (C)   Gina, because at the time she first created *The Ben Game*, CBA had no pending plans to create a game based on *Ben*.

   (D)   Gina, because by allowing Gina to produce *The Ben Game* for a year without complaint, CBA implicitly conceded that the game did not harm its ability to exploit *Ben*.

292.   Consider question 291. Assume **for the purposes of this question only** that Gina adduces evidence that *The Ben Game* has increased the show's popularity, and, correlatively, its profitability, enough that any possible losses CBA suffered from the revenues it might have gained from a license were dwarfed by the revenue it gained by the game's existence. In other words, Gina can show that her unauthorized creation of *The Ben Game* helped rather than hurt the market for the show, on balance. Would this fact convince a court that the fourth factor of a fair use analysis should weigh in Gina's favor?

293.   Dolly Billionaire is a famous socialite who writes a mawkish self-help book titled *Yours for the Asking*. Wendy Wanamaker is a newspaper columnist who considers Dolly to be a loathsome dilettante and writes a book-length parody of Dolly's book titled *Mine for the Trashing*. Dolly is incensed and sues Wendy for copyright infringement, and Wendy responds by raising a fair use defense. In addressing the fourth fair use factor, Dolly argues that Wendy harmed a potential market by shortchanging Dolly's ability to license parodies and criticisms of her work. Will a court find this argument sufficient to conclude that the fourth fair use factor weighs in favor of Dolly?

(A)   Yes. Because the work at issue is one of nonfiction, the fourth factor must weigh in favor of Dolly.

(B)   No. There is no present or reasonably foreseeable market in parody or criticism, so Wendy's parody could not have supplanted any possible licensing deals for Dolly.

(C)   Yes. The fourth factor considers possible future markets as well as present ones, so the possibility that Wendy's parody may have supplanted these licensing deals means that the fourth factor weighs in favor of Dolly.

(D)   No. In the absence of evidence that Dolly was negotiating licensing deals, Dolly cannot plausibly argue that Wendy's parody supplanted a future market for derivative works.

294.   Jack loves the television program *Crime Dogs*, and he records every episode on his old-style VCR and keeps the videotapes in a locked cabinet. Jack never actually watches these taped programs, but just keeps them because he is an obsessive collector and is reassured by their mere presence. Jack's conduct clearly amounts to verbatim copying, but would it be defensible to charges of infringement via the fair use defense?

(A)   Yes. The Supreme Court held in *Sony Corporation of America v. Universal City Studios, Inc.* that videotaping television programs in order to create a library of tapes is fair use.

(B)   Yes. Because Jack's use is solely for personal purposes, it counts as a fair use.

(C)   No. The Supreme Court ruling in *Sony Corporation of America v. Universal City Studios, Inc.* concerning personal copying held only that videotaping television programs for purposes of time-shifting is a fair use.

(D) No. While the Supreme Court held in *Sony Corporation of America v. Universal City Studios, Inc.* that videotaping television programs is fair use, this holding was overruled by *Metro-Goldwyn-Mayer Studios Inc. v. Grokster, Ltd.*

295. Kendra is a biochemist who works for a major pharmaceutical company. During the course of her latest project, she has to make a presentation to a group of potential investors about the nature of the company's research. In preparing for this presentation, Kendra visits the company's library (which does not lend out physical copies of its holdings) and photocopies an article from a scientific journal. She then takes the article back to her office, where she uses the information contained in it to construct her presentation. Kendra's photocopying the article clearly amounts to verbatim copying, but is it likely defensible as fair use?

(A) Yes. Kendra's use is not transformative, but because it would have no effect on the copyright owner's market for exploiting their work, it is a fair use.

(B) Yes. Kendra's use was transformative and would have no negative effect on the copyright owner's market for exploiting its work, so it is a fair use.

(C) Yes. Kendra's use would have a negative effect on the copyright owner's market for exploiting its work, but because it is transformative, it is a fair use.

(D) No. This conduct is not transformative, and allowing the practice has a negative effect on the copyright owner's market for exploiting its work, so it is not a fair use.

296. Greco is a rock musician. In 2000, he composed and recorded the musical work *Only Me*. The track became a huge international success, and Greco, who retained ownership of both the musical work and sound recording that comprise the track, earned millions in royalties. "Strange Mel" Petrovic is a musician who is famous for his humorous send-ups of popular songs. In 2001, Strange Mel released the track *Golly Gee*, which parodied Greco's *Only Me*. That same year, Greco's agent told him about Strange Mel's unlicensed take-off of *Only Me*. Greco replied, "Whatever. I don't give a toss what that little twerp does." Greco never heard *Golly Gee*, and for years, he forgot about the issue. Strange Mel assumed that Greco had no objection to his parody, and relied on this assumption to create an expensive music video to promote *Golly Gee* in 2003. Then, in 2004, Greco happened to see the music video for *Golly Gee* and became incensed at what he thought was a disrespectful use of his works of authorship. Greco sued Strange Mel for copyright infringement in late 2008. Aside from fair use, what affirmative defenses might Strange Mel plausibly raise to Greco's lawsuit?

(A) Abandonment and statute of limitations.

(B) Abandonment and laches.

(C) Statute of limitations and laches.

(D) Abandonment, statute of limitations, and laches.

297. Chuck writes a poem and shows a copy of it to his friend Jeff, who is also a poet, to elicit Jeff's comments. Jeff thinks the poem is brilliant, but tells Chuck that it is awful because

he wants to claim credit for the poem himself. Jeff then registers the poem with the Copyright Office, listing himself as the work's author. Soon after, Mike releases an anthology of poetry that includes the poem, though he has not secured anyone's permission to do so. Jeff sues Mike for copyright infringement. Will Jeff prevail?

(A) Yes. Because he is the registered owner of the copyright in the poem, he has the right to sue for infringement, though Chuck may be able to join the action and recover any judgment.

(B) Yes. Because Chuck has failed to file a competing copyright registration, he has abandoned the copyright in the poem in favor of Jeff, making Jeff the valid owner.

(C) No. Only the original author of a copyrighted work of authorship is entitled to sue for infringement.

(D) No. Jeff's conduct amounts to fraud on the Copyright Office, and Mike can raise that point as a full defense to the infringement suit.

298. Seeking to broaden protection for the entertainment industry, California passes a law stating that its state laws will extend exclusive rights of reproduction, adaptation, public distribution, and public performance to creators of general ideas, in addition to the protection of the specific expression of those ideas already afforded by federal law. Would a court regard this California law as enforceable?

(A) No, a court would invalidate the California law because it is explicitly preempted by federal statute.

(B) No, a court would invalidate the California law because it creates a conflict whereby it is impossible to comply with state and federal law at the same time.

(C) Yes, states are permitted to provide authors with more, though not less, protection than prescribed by federal law, so the law is valid.

(D) Yes, a court would find the California law enforceable because Congress has decided it will not provide ideas with copyright protection.

299. In 1990, Harold Hermit, an artist specializing in depictions of architecture, created a detailed painting titled *Promises of Tomorrow*. The painting depicted a theme park in which each different section of the park was based on a different version of the future. Later that year, Hermit met with executives of Amusement Development, a large corporation involved in the building of amusement parks around the world. At that meeting, Hermit attempted to persuade Amusement Development to use his design for a new amusement park in the United States. Hermit provided the executives with a copy of *Promises of Tomorrow* as a prototype for such an amusement park. A few weeks later, Hermit was informed that the corporation was not interested in his design.

Shortly thereafter, Hermit moved to a small town in the remote, sparsely populated state of East Dakota. Hermit's wife became ill, and he spent most of his time caring for her. They both became isolated and disengaged from society. Hermit and his wife never left their town, had no children and did not own a television. Hermit was hospitalized for open-heart surgery throughout the fall of 2005. After his release from the hospital he remained a recluse, caring for his sick wife and tending to his own poor health.

In October 2005, Amusement Development opened a new theme park, "Futureland" in the state of South Virginia. Futureland, a park that specifically targets children as its patrons, is strikingly similar to the images contained in Hermit's *Promises of Tomorrow* painting. The opening of Futureland was accompanied by massive media attention and has been widely advertised since its opening.

Last month, Hermit filed suit in United States District Court against Amusement Development for infringing his copyright in *Promises of Tomorrow*. Hermit claims that he had not known of Futureland until he saw photos of it in a magazine article while visiting his local barbershop two months before filing suit. Amusement Development has moved for a dismissal of Hermit's lawsuit on the basis that the statute of limitations has run. Will Amusement Development's defense succeed?

300. Five years ago, Ripp-Off, Inc. manufactured and distributed 200,000 CDs featuring an unauthorized copy of a sound recording owned by MusicCo. Ripp-Off's unauthorized conduct earned a net profit of $1 million. MusicCo now has evidence that Ripp-Off is once again engaging in unauthorized copying of MusicCo's copyrighted sound recordings, manufacturing and distributing 35,000 phonorecords of the same compilation. This most recent infringement took place in the last year and earned a net profit of $175,000. All of the relevant copyrights owned by MusicCo were registered prior to Ripp-Off's initial infringements. MusicCo has filed a copyright infringement action against Ripp-Off and has successfully proven that Ripp-Off's conduct was willful. What is the likeliest measure of MusicCo's damages, assuming they want to seek the highest recovery possible?

(A) MusicCo will be awarded all of Ripp-Off's net profits: $1,175,000.

(B) MusicCo will be awarded all of Ripp-Off's net profits plus the maximum statutory damage amount: $1,325,000.

(C) MusicCo will be awarded the maximum statutory damage amount: $150,000.

(D) MusicCo will be awarded the net profits from Ripp-Off's most recent infringing activity: $175,000.

301. East Dakota is a state in the United States of America. Its state legislature has recently enacted legislation that creates a compulsory master use license for pre-1972 sound recordings transmitted by any website that transmits from a server located in the state of East Dakota. The legislation requires the website to pay 16¢ for each sound recording downloaded by users of the website to the owners of the master recordings. The legislation also mandates that pre-1972 sound recordings may be streamed by such websites without payment. Relying on this legislation, a website has been streaming pre-1972 sound recordings

without obtaining a license to do so. In addition, the website allows its users to download digital copies of pre-1972 sound recordings for 50¢. The website pays all necessary license fees to the owners of the musical compositions fixed in the recordings, as well as the state compulsory license fees for downloading digital copies of the pre-1972 sound recordings. A record company has brought a copyright infringement action against the website for its use of the record company's pre-1972 sound recordings, claiming that the East Dakota legislation is preempted by federal copyright law. Will the record company be successful with its preemption argument?

302.   *Welcoming the Sotos* was a popular television situation comedy from the 1970s that portrayed the daily life of a Latino family who moved into a wealthy, white neighborhood. *Welcoming the Sotos* was considered groundbreaking at the time, since it dealt with social issues such as race and class that had long been considered taboo. In the intervening four decades, however, much of the humor in *Welcoming the Sotos* would now be considered dated and even offensive. The show, considered a classic, continues to run in syndication (especially on cable comedy channels) and still generates significant royalties.

Recently, a playwright wrote and produced *The Sotos: Not Welcome*, a contemporary stage performance that uses the same basic elements of *Welcoming the Sotos*, such as settings and characters, but presents them in a darker, very serious light, emphasizing themes such as racial hostility and social class conflict. The playwright explained, "I want this work to unsettle viewers, and to spark serious conversation about the role of race in modern-day America. What better way to do that than by exposing the latent stereotypes at work in a purported 'classic' of American television?" At no time did the playwright seek or receive permission to use *Welcoming the Sotos*.

Megaverse, the production studio that owns the copyright to *Welcoming the Sotos*, sued the playwright for copyright infringement. The playwright counters by raising a fair use defense. Will she succeed?

(A) Yes, because *The Sotos: Not Welcome* is clearly a parody of *Welcoming the Sotos*.

(B) Yes, because *The Sotos: Not Welcome* transforms *Welcoming the Sotos* and operates in an entirely different market.

(C) No, because she could have addressed racism and other issues without making unauthorized use of *Welcoming the Sotos*.

(D) No, because plaintiffs who raise a fair use defense must show that they have sought and been denied permission to use the plaintiff's work.

303.   Consider Question 302. Assume **for the purposes of this question only** that *The Sotos: Not Welcome* becomes a national phenomenon and results in a change in popular opinion whereby *Welcoming the Sotos* becomes seen as an embarrassing relic of a racist past. Further assume that because of this backlash, television stations uniformly decide to stop

syndicating *Welcoming the Sotos*, and that sales of DVD copies of the show also plummet. In light of these facts, would the playwright's fair use argument come out differently? Yes... I

304. Ella Fox is a novelist famed for writing voluminous tomes depicting the tortured inner lives of average people in suburban America. One of her many voluminous books, written in 1970 and still validly copyrighted, contains the line "Men spend their whole lives trying to understand women, and all that proves is they don't understand themselves." A recent comedic film contains a scene in which one character taunts his hapless, recently divorced friend by saying, "You know what Ella Fox said, right? Men are always trying to understand women, and that just goes to show they don't understand themselves." Fox, upon learning of the unauthorized use of a quotation from her novel, sues the studio that produced the film for copyright infringement. The studio responds by conceding copying and substantial similarity and raising a fair use defense. Will their fair use defense succeed?

(A) Yes. The studio's unauthorized use is not a verbatim copy of the language in Fox's book, which makes it overwhelmingly likely that the court will find the use fair.

(B) Yes. The studio's unauthorized use transforms the meaning of the quote, represents only a tiny borrowing, and inflicts no meaningful economic harm on Fox.

(C) No. The studio's use was not transformative because it had the same artistic message as in Fox's novel, and cost Fox licensing revenue.

(D) No. The studio's use was *de minimis*, which by definition cannot be a fair use.

305. AllArt.com is a nonprofit website, produced by a consortium of universities and public-oriented arts foundations, that seeks to provide an online archive of all the great art in the history of the world. It aims to facilitate access to art in order both to enhance academic study of art and to bring great art works to less privileged audiences who would not otherwise have had the opportunity to see it. AllArt.com works primarily with museums, galleries, and private collectors to acquire digital scans of major works of art, which it then stores on its website in searchable form. AllArt.com does not, however, acquire permission from the copyright owners of any of the works. The many thousands of digital images stored on AllArt.com allow viewers to appreciate the art but do not enable full-scale reproductions of it that would be suitable for creating prints or decorations. Many of the museums and galleries who allow AllArt.com to create the digital versions have only limited licenses to display the reproduced works, and some of the copyright holders in those works sue AllArt.com for copyright infringement based on the unauthorized reproduction of their works on the website. AllArt.com responds by raising a fair use defense. Will such a defense be likely to succeed?

(A) Yes, because the galleries and museums have implicitly granted use licenses on behalf of the artists.

(B) No, because these are verbatim reproductions.

(C) Yes, because AllArt.com's use is transformative and inflicts no economic costs on copyright owners.

(D) No, because AllArt.com's use deprived the owners of licensing fees.

306.   Consider question 305. Assume **for the purposes of this question only** that as part of its fair use argument, AllArt.com argues that the court should tolerate its unauthorized use because doing so would advance the public interest by enhancing the academic study of art while also allowing access to art for underserved communities. Would a court consider this argument as part of the overall fair use calculus?

Remedies

307.   Publisher owns the copyright in a musical work. Pirate is a rogue online webcaster who streams music on his website without licenses or permission from the owners of those works. Publisher has issued numerous cease and desist letters to Pirate, but Pirate has ignored them all. Finally, Publisher sues Pirate in a United States District Court in New York, where Pirate is domiciled, for infringing its exclusive right to public performance. Soon after being served with Publisher's complaint for copyright infringement, Pirate goes bankrupt and ceases operations of his website. Publisher learns that Pirate has decided to cease his online operations and change the course of his life. Pirate joins a monastery in a remote area of Alaska for at least five years. Undaunted, Publisher presses its suit, seeking damages for Pirate's past infringements as well as an injunction in the event that Pirate ever decides to re-start his unlawful online operations. Will a court grant Publisher's request for an injunction?

(A)   Yes. Injunctions are appropriate to make sure that infringement will not recur, even if it has substantially ceased.

(B)   Yes. Injunctive relief follows automatically upon a showing of copyright infringement.

(C)   No. Because Pirate has ceased his unlawful operations and has given no indication that he will begin them again, a court will not enter an injunction.

(D)   No. A United States district court does not have national jurisdiction to enjoin a party that moves to another state.

308.   Consider question IX-1. Assume **for the purposes of this question only** that an injunction did issue, and Pirate argued that it was unconstitutional because it amounted to a prior restraint in violation of his free speech rights under the First Amendment of the U.S. Constitution. Would a court agree with Pirate's constitutional argument?

309.   Author is both the author and the copyright owner of the popular novel *Jezebel*. Author has recently discovered that Seller has produced thousands of unauthorized copies of *Jezebel* that Seller then sells online at cut-rate prices. Author sues Seller for copyright infringement, and in so doing immediately moves for a preliminary injunction. Author argues that because it has a nearly certain case against Seller for infringement, the injunction should issue as a matter of course. Seller does not contest the likelihood of Author's success on the merits, but argues that Author has failed to justify an injunction because Author did

not separately argue that the relevant balancing test warranted such relief. Would a court accept Seller's argument about irreparable harm?

(A) No. Because Author has a likelihood of succeeding on the merits of its copyright infringement case, it is entitled to an injunction as a matter of course.

(B) No. While preliminary injunctions are not issued as a matter of course in all cases, where, as here, the plaintiff's case is unusually strong, a court must grant such an injunction.

(C) Yes. Likelihood of success on the merits, without more, is insufficient to justify a preliminary injunction.

(D) Yes. Because Author's only injuries are financial, its harm is categorically not irreparable.

310. Consider question 309. Assume **for the purposes of this question only** that upon learning of Seller's infringement, Author waited six months to file suit, and that during those six months, Seller continued to sell unauthorized copies of *Jezebel*. Assuming **for the purposes of this question only** that the facts in question IX-3 would otherwise warrant a preliminary injunction, would a court still regard the harm inflicted on Author by Seller as irreparable if Author had waited this long to file suit?

311. Painter is a famed conceptual artist whose original canvases fetch millions in high-end art markets around the world. Mimic is a talented forger who produces nearly perfect knock-offs of famous paintings and sells them, with the buyers' full knowledge of their provenance, relatively cheaply. Painter learns that Mimic has painted a fake version of Painter's work, and sues Mimic for copyright infringement. Painter has a strong case against Mimic on the merits, but Mimic has both decent legal representation and a slim but not negligible chance of prevailing, based on one of several affirmative defenses to infringement. At the onset of litigation, Painter moves for a preliminary injunction, arguing, among other things, that he can show a reasonable likelihood of success on the merits. Is the trial court likely to find that Painter has met the likelihood of success element required for a preliminary injunction?

(A) Yes. All a movant need show on this element is a reasonable likelihood of success on the merits of their infringement claim, and Painter has done so.

(B) Yes. All a movant need show on this element is some plausible chance of success on the merits of its infringement claim, and Painter has done so.

(C) Yes. All a movant need show on this element is any conceivable chance of success on the merits of its infringement claim, and Painter has done so.

(D) No. Painter has failed to make a successful showing on this element of the test for a preliminary injunction because he has not shown a certainty of success on the merits of his claim.

312. Consider question 311. Assume **for the purposes of this question only** that a court were to find that Painter showed a reasonable probability of eventual success in his forthcoming litigation against Seller. If a court were to come to such a conclusion, what, if any, impact would it have on that court's analysis of the irreparable harm element of the preliminary injunction test?

313. Author pens a historical novel titled *Five Days in August*. A year later, Satirist writes an unauthorized parody of Author's novel called *Jive Ways in August*. Several weeks before it is due to be released, Satirist writes to Author to seek an approving quote about *Jive Ways in August* for the book's dust jacket. It turns out that Author did not know that Satirist was parodying *Five Days in August*, and Author is incensed by the unauthorized use. Author sues Satirist for copyright infringement, and immediately seeks preliminary injunctive relief in order to bar *Jive Ways in August* from ever being released to the public. In analyzing the public interest factor of the test for preliminary injunctive relief, in favor of which party would a court be likely to rule?

314. Al runs a bootleg DVD operation out of a warehouse where he uses a computer to download unauthorized digital copies of popular films from the Internet, and then creates hundreds of DVD copies of each film using a mass-producing device that he constructed. Al also keeps copies of his business records on the computer's hard drive, as well as hard-copy printouts of those files in a cabinet in the warehouse. Several of the studios that own the copyrights in the audiovisual works that Al is copying discover his activities and sue him for copyright infringement. At the outset of litigation, in addition to filing a motion seeking a preliminary injunction preventing Al from continuing his bootleg DVD business, the studios move for an ex parte order impounding the contents of Al's warehouse. Assuming that no showing has yet been made on the merits of the infringement suit, would a court be likely to order the requested impoundment?

(A) Yes. Pursuant to the Copyright Act, ex parte impoundment orders must issue upon a plaintiff's requesting them.

(B) Yes. Pursuant to rules issued by the United States Supreme Court, ex parte impoundment orders must issue upon a plaintiff's requesting them.

(C) No. Impoundment is not a remedy available to plaintiffs until a judgment of infringement has been entered.

(D) No. Impoundment lies in the discretion of the court, and courts tend not to order ex parte impoundment in light of reservations about the constitutional validity of such orders.

315. Consider question 314. Assume **for the purposes of this question only** that a court granted the studios' motion for impoundment. Which of the following materials in Al's warehouse could be validly included in the impoundment order?

(A) Al's bootleg DVDs.

(B) Al's computer and DVD-making device.

(C) The records contained in Al's file cabinet.

(D) All of the above.

316.   Composer is well known among Christians for his wholesome, religiously themed musical works. One of these works, in which Composer owns the copyright, is titled *Happy Springtime*. Recently, Composer learned that *Happy Springtime* was used ironically, and without authorization, as the background music in an adult film produced by Xplicit Entertainment. Composer is upset both that he lost the licensing fees that Xplicit should have paid him, and also that his work has been associated with material that is inconsistent with his religious beliefs. Indeed, since the release of Xplicit's adult film, many of Composer's fans have boycotted his records, and sales of copies of *Happy Springtime* have dropped precipitously. Composer sues Xplicit for copyright infringement, wins a default judgment, and seeks nonstatutory damages. Which answer best describes the appropriate measure of those damages?

(A) Composer is entitled to the profits that Xplicit earned through use of *Happy Springtime*.

(B) Composer is entitled to the profits that Xplicit earned through use of *Happy Springtime*, and to the lost revenues that Xplicit's unauthorized use caused by inflicting reputational harm.

(C) Composer is entitled to the lost revenues that Xplicit's unauthorized use caused by inflicting reputational harm.

(D) Composer is not entitled to nonstatutory damages.

317.   Consider question 316. Assume **for the purposes of this question only** that Composer discovers that Xplicit used *Happy Springtime* in its adult film knowing that the work was protected by copyright, and knowing that the composer and owner of the musical work was a devout Christian who would be particularly upset by the film's subject matter. Under these circumstances, if Composer requested punitive damages in his prayer for relief, would a court be likely to award them?

318.   Alice is a famed nature photographer. Betty is an aspiring nature writer. Betty recently self-published a very successful wildlife guide that featured her own writing as well as Alice's photographs, though Betty did not receive permission to use the latter. Alice sued Betty for copyright infringement and won a judgment in her favor. At trial, Alice sought nonstatutory damages, and produced evidence showing that Betty's gross revenues for her wildlife guide were $50,000, of which half were attributable to Alice's photographs. Betty responded by producing evidence that it cost her $10,000 in direct expenses to create the book. What is the most accurate measure of Alice's damages?

(A) $50,000

(B) $20,000

(C) $12,500

(D) $10,000

319. Consider question 318. Assume **for the purposes of this question only** that at trial, Alice adduced evidence of Betty's gross profits of $50,000, but that Betty did not produce evidence about the costs associated with producing the wildlife guide. Neither Alice nor Betty produced evidence about how much of Betty's gross profits were attributable to Betty's infringement. In light of this variation, what would the court order in nonstatutory damages?

(A) $50,000

(B) $25,000

(C) $20,000

(D) $0

320. Consider questions 318 and 319. Assume **for the purposes of this question only** that Alice adduces evidence that Betty used Alice's photographs despite being fully aware that they were validly copyrighted. In addition to the $10,000 in direct expenses, Betty produced evidence of $5,000 in overhead costs associated with the production of the wildlife guide. In light of this variation, would the measure of damages be any different?

321. Ed created a computer program called *Genius* and retains copyright ownership in both the object and source code that comprise the program. Ed sells *Genius* online, and as a condition of sale, requires sellers to enter into a contract stating that they will not copy Ed's program without his permission. Vic purchases a copy of *Genius* and proceeds to make hundreds of copies of it and sell them online at cut-rate prices. Ed sues Vic for copyright infringement and breach of contract, winning judgments in his favor on each claim. Based on undisputed evidence offered at trial, Ed seeks actual damages of $50,000 for lost profits related to the copyright infringement and $50,000 for lost profits related to the breach of contract. What amount of damages will a court award?

(A) $100,000

(B) $75,000

(C) $50,000

(D) $0

322. Hy completed his screenplay in January of last year. Hy's agent shopped the screenplay broadly around town in an effort to persuade a studio to acquire it for development. To assist with the publicity effort, Hy uploaded a .pdf copy of the screenplay to his personal website. In February of last year, Guy (a studio executive to whom Hy's agent pitched the screenplay) downloaded a copy of Hy's screenplay from the website, made several unauthorized copies of the script, and showed it to his colleagues, representing it as his own

work. Hy discovered Guy's subterfuge in March of last year, after which he immediately registered his work that same month and then sued Guy for infringing his exclusive right of reproduction. Hy seeks statutory rather than actual damages as a remedy. Will statutory damages be available to him?

(A) Yes. Registration is not a prerequisite for seeking statutory damages.

(B) Yes. By registering the screenplay within three months of its initial publication, Hy preserved the opportunity to seek statutory damages.

(C) No. Because he failed to register the screenplay before Guy infringed his copyright, Hy forfeited the opportunity to seek statutory damages.

(D) No. Hy cannot seek statutory damages because statutory damages are not available for unpublished works.

323. Consider question 322. Assuming **for the purposes of this question only** that Hy has registered in time to seek statutory damages, which of the following statements best describes Hy's options for seeking money damages?

(A) Hy can seek only statutory damages.

(B) Hy can seek both statutory and actual damages.

(C) Hy can seek either statutory or actual damages, but must elect one or the other when he files his initial complaint against Guy.

(D) Hy can seek either statutory or actual damages, but must elect one or the other prior to final judgment.

324. Zed is a composer and musician who owns the rights to several original zydeco musical compositions, including the undistributed musical work "King Cake." Yancey includes a version of Zed's "King Cake," without authorization and with full awareness that it was protected by copyright, on a CD compilation of zydeco music that he distributes widely for commercial sale. The CD sells hardly any copies, but Zed still sues Yancey for infringing his exclusive rights of reproduction and public distribution, and wins a judgment in his favor. Zed has properly elected to seek statutory damages, and following the judgment, moves that the court enter a damages award of $1.5 million dollars—$150,000 for each of the 10 copies of the zydeco CD Yancey sold. The judge orders Yancey to pay $150,000, and Zed appeals. Will he prevail?

(A) Yes. The judge's award failed to allocate damages for each of the 10 separate acts of infringement.

(B) No. The judge's award is within the appropriate range for the willful infringement that took place in this case.

(C) Yes. Statutory damages are capped at $30,000 per work infringed.

(D) No. Awards of statutory damages are subject to judicial discretion, so they cannot be upset on appeal.

325. Consider question 324. Assume **for the purposes of this question only** that when Yancey included Zed's "King Cake" on the compilation CD, Yancey was acting under the sincere, but mistaken, impression that Zed had executed a valid license permitting Yancey to include "King Cake" in the compilation. In light of this variation, what would be an appropriate measure of damages?

326. Wall of Reality is a television production company that has produced a dramatic miniseries focusing on the fictional lives of 12 different people involved in insurgent conflicts throughout the world. The miniseries consists of 12 episodes, each of which has been individually registered with the Copyright Office. Wall of Reality licensed the broadcast rights to the entire series to three independent television stations. Each license permitted the station to broadcast the entire series one time. All three stations, however, violated the license by re-broadcasting the series twice during the summer without permission. Wall of Reality has sued each of the stations for violating its exclusive right of public performance, and has sought statutory damages as a remedy. In calculating statutory damages, how many different acts of infringement are at issue?

(A) 1

(B) 3

(C) 12

(D) 36

327. Consider question IX-20. What is the maximum amount of statutory damages Wall of Reality could recover against the networks?

328. Tasty Cola, Inc., produces a popular carbonated soft drink. The company commissions as a work for hire an original intricate artistic design called the "Tasty Swoop" that it uses as the distinctive symbol associated with Tasty Cola. The company federally registered the "Tasty Swoop" as both a trademark and a copyrighted work of authorship. Mitch and Fred want to cash in on Tasty Cola's commercial success, and they seek to do so by purchasing a generic competitor soda that costs much less, repackaging it and selling it under the name "Tasty Cola." Mitch and Fred's repackaging extensively incorporates the Tasty Swoop, which they use, of course, without permission. Tasty Cola eventually discovers Mitch and Fred's subterfuge and sues them for both copyright and trademark infringement. Tasty Cola wins on both the copyright and trademark theories. Can a court order Mitch and Fred to pay damages on both theories?

(A) Yes. Because the interests protected by copyright and trademark are different, Tasty Cola can recover damages on each theory.

(B) Yes. Plaintiffs are entitled to recover damages on as many different theories as they can plausibly articulate.

(C) No. Because the interests protected by copyright and trademark are largely identical, Tasty Cola can recover damages on only one theory.

(D) No. Plaintiffs may recover on only one theory in intellectual property cases, though they are entitled to elect whichever theory of recovery will produce the highest award.

329.   Consider question 328. Assume **for the purposes of this question only** that Tasty Cola wins a $1 million judgment in statutory damages against Mitch and Fred for copyright infringement, and that shortly after the judgment is entered, but before any of the damages are recovered, Fred flees the country, leaving behind no assets and making him entirely judgment-proof. In light of this variation, what amount of damages can Tasty Cola recover from Mitch alone?

330.   Norm is suspected of running an online file-sharing operation in which he copies and distributes hundreds of copyrighted motion pictures without permission. De Marco Studios brings a civil copyright infringement action against Norm. The Department of Justice also brings a criminal copyright infringement action against Norm. The two cases are assigned to the same judge. At both trials, it becomes clear that the infringement allegations against Norm were based on a complete misunderstanding and that Norm is innocent of any wrongdoing. The court dismisses both the civil action filed by De Marco Productions and the criminal action filed by the Department of Justice. Following the dismissal, Norm moves to have the United States government reimburse him for the court fees and expert witness fees that he expended in defending the litigation. Will he succeed in recovering his costs of suit?

(A) Yes. Norm can recover his costs of suit, but that includes only court fees, not expert witness fees.

(B) Yes. Norm can recover the costs associated with the civil action, but not the costs associated with the criminal prosecution.

(C) No. Prevailing parties in copyright actions can typically recover costs of suit, but not against the United States government.

(D) No. Prevailing parties in copyright actions are entitled to expert witness fees, but not costs of suit.

331.   Jane finishes the novel *Norm's Diner* in January 2016, and the novel is published in physical copies only in March of that same year. In June 2016, rogue website InterPub.com starts offering for sale via its website digital versions of *Norm's Diner* at a much lower rate than the retail price of the hard-copy book. Jane becomes aware of InterPub.com's unauthorized use in July 2016 and files suit against the website for copyright infringement that same month. At the same time she files her complaint, Jane also registers *Norm's Diner* with the Copyright Office. Jane fails to win a preliminary injunction, and InterPub.com continues

to sell unauthorized copies of *Norm's Diner* over the Internet throughout the litigation. Ultimately, Jane prevails in her infringement suit against the website, and after judgment is entered in her favor, Jane seeks to recover attorney's fees from InterPub.com. Will she succeed?

(A) Yes, because many of InterPub's acts of infringement took place after *Norm's Diner* was registered.

(B) No, because *Norm's Diner* was not registered at the time of the initial infringement.

(C) Yes, because Jane registered *Norm's Diner* within three months of learning about Inter-Pub's infringement.

(D) No, unless Jane can show that InterPub's infringement was willful or malicious.

332. Jackson is an eminent historian. In 2005, he publishes a 700-page monograph titled *America in the Age of FDR*, in which he retains copyright ownership. Soon after, Henderson, another historian, publishes a negative review of Jackson's monograph in the scholarly journal *American Historical Review*. Henderson's five-page review contains five excerpts from Jackson's book, each about two sentences long, that Henderson included solely to support his criticisms of Jackson's book. Jackson is enraged at Henderson's negative view of his work and sues Henderson for copyright infringement.

In his complaint, Jackson alleges that by including the several sentences verbatim from Jackson's book in his review, Henderson violated Jackson's exclusive right of reproduction. Henderson moves for and wins summary judgment based on both a *de minimis* taking argument and, in the alternative, a fair use defense. In her ruling, the judge describes the outcome of the case as "an unambiguous one, both in terms of law and facts, in favor of the defendant." Following the entry of judgment in his favor, Henderson moves to have Jackson pay Henderson's attorney's fees. How will a court likely rule on this motion?

(A) Jackson will win. Because Jackson filed his lawsuit in good faith, he cannot be liable for Henderson's attorney's fees.

(B) Jackson will win. Because there was some chance, however remote, that Jackson might have prevailed, he cannot be liable for Henderson's attorney's fees.

(C) Henderson will win. Jackson's lawsuit was without sound factual or legal basis, Henderson's success was total, and an award of attorney's fees would help to discourage future baseless lawsuits.

(D) Henderson will win. Prevailing parties in copyright infringement lawsuits are entitled to attorney's fees as a matter of course.

333. Consider question 332. Assume **for the purposes of this question only** that Jackson were to prevail in his infringement suit against Henderson, and were to seek an award of

attorney's fees. Would Jackson's status as the plaintiff rather than the defendant affect the availability of an award of attorney's fees?

334.   Following entry of a successful copyright infringement judgment in their client's favor, the attorneys of Bram & Gower, LLC, filed a motion for an award of attorney's fees. Bram & Gower provided the court with documentation that showed that they expended 1,000 hours on the litigation, and that they normally bill $300 per hour, for a total requested fee award of $300,000. The court agreed that an award of attorney's fees was appropriate. However, after reviewing Bram & Gower's billing records, the court found 100 of the billed hours frivolous and excessive. The court thus entered an award of attorney's fees in favor of Bram & Gower's client, but only in the amount of $270,000. On appeal, is the court's order likely to stand?

(A)   Yes. A court is entitled to deviate from the fee request entered by the prevailing party where it finds that the hours or rates are unreasonable and/or excessive.

(B)   Yes. A court has absolute discretion to award whatever attorney's fees it deems appropriate, regardless of the parties' submissions.

(C)   No. Once a court finds that an award of attorney's fees is appropriate, it is required to enter the amount determined by applying the lodestar method (hours billed times hourly billing rate).

(D)   No. A court can reduce an attorney's fee award only upon motion from the non-prevailing party.

335.   West Company makes women's dresses based on original fabric designs in which it claims to own federal copyrights. All of West Company's five retail stores are located on the West Coast of the United States, and its sales are limited to that region. While displaying its new line of dresses at a fashion trade show in St. Louis, West Company discovered that East Company had infringed the fabric designs from West Company's new line. East Company, which also displayed its infringing fabric designs at the St. Louis trade show, limits its sales to retail stores on the East Coast of the United States. After the trade show, a rumor developed that West Company had stolen fabric designs from the East Company. As a result of this rumor, West Company lost sales in the amount of $25,000. West Company brought an action for copyright infringement against East Company. During trial, it was proven that East Company made a profit of $60,000 from its sales of dresses attributable to its use of the infringing fabric designs. To what amount of damages is West Company entitled?

(A) $25,000

(B) $35,000

(C) $60,000

(D) $85,000

336.   Consider question 335. Assume **for the purposes of this question only** that, in addition to the facts stated above, a consumer bought infringing dresses from East Company, for

which East Company made a profit of $20,000 attributable to its infringing activities. How would this additional fact change the amount of damages to which West Company is entitled?

337. Flower Publications, a major traditional print publisher, owns the copyright to the novel *Yesterday*, which it acquired by assignment in 2014 from the author of *Yesterday*. The assignment agreement included a clause in which the author represented that he had full ownership of the copyright and had not licensed any uses of it. In 2016, Flower learned that Gremlin Press, a small independent print publisher, was distributing for sale copies of *Yesterday*. Flower issued a cease-and-desist notice to Gremlin, and Gremlin insisted it had received permission to publish *Yesterday* from the work's author in 2013, the same year he finished writing the novel. Flower asked the author about this and he denied executing any such license in favor of Gremlin. Based on the author's assurances and the 2014 representation that he had not granted any such license, Flower rejected Gremlin's assertion as absurd and sued them for copyright infringement.

At summary judgment, Gremlin produced — to Flower's complete astonishment — a valid license from 2012 in which the author granted them the right to publish *Yesterday* in print form. The author later admitted to Flower that he had lied to them about not executing a license with Gremlin in 2012. Based on this evidence, the court entered summary judgment in favor of Gremlin. Gremlin then moved for the court to order Flower to pay its attorney's fees. The court denies Gremlin's motion, applying all of the factors outlined in *Fogerty v. Fantasy Records, Inc.* but stressing as paramount in its analysis the objective reasonableness of Flower's infringement suit. Gremlin appeals the denial of its motion. Will it succeed?

(A) Yes. The five *Fogerty* factors have to be granted equal weight.

(B) Yes. The district court erred because Flower's copyright infringement suit was both disingenuous and unreasonable.

(C) No. Objective reasonableness is a dispositive consideration within the *Fogerty* analysis.

(D) No. So long as a court considers all the *Fogerty* factors, it may place substantial weight on the objective reasonableness of the losing party's position.

338. Jones is an aspiring recording artist who has had some success in gaining attention to his music on social media, but has still not signed a deal with a recording company despite some initial interest from smaller labels. Nor does Jones currently seek to sell copies of his works. Dempsey is a fight promoter who hears Jones' track "Better" (which is not registered with the Copyright Office) and decides to include a substantial portion of it among the montage of music that Dempsey plays before fights to hype up the crowd. Dempsey plays a 30-second clip of "Better" as part of this "hype reel" at several major prize fights, all without permission from Jones. Jones discovers the unauthorized use, sues Dempsey for copyright infringement, and wins a judgment in his favor. In

subsequent proceedings about damages, Jones testifies that he thinks "Better" is a "sure platinum hit," and claims that he would have charged a licensing fee of $50,000 for each of Dempsey's uses. Jones also has an expert testify that fees for clips for "hype reels" in the prizefighting world range as high as $75,000 per clip. In response, Dempsey provides undisputed evidence that Jones has never licensed any uses of his music to any entity for any amount, and enters into the record the fact that Jones is not signed to any record label. Dempsey further testifies that if Jones had asked him for a license, Dempsey "would have moved on to use one of the other very good songs out there that emerging artists are happy to have me include in the hype reel for free — they just appreciate the free publicity." What is the appropriate measure of damages in this case?

(A) $250,000

(B) $75,000

(C) $50,000

(D) $0

339.   Repro is a company that makes high-quality art reproductions of works by contemporary artists. Since 2015, it has made reproductions of several works by the artist Hester. All of Hester's works are registered with the Copyright Office and include valid copyright notices. In 2016, Hester sues Repro for copyright infringement, alleging that it made all these reproductions without authorization. Hester joins in her infringement suit Wilma, Repro's Chief Executive Officer. Hester prevails on her substantive infringement claim, and the court enters judgment in her favor in the amount of $1.5 million in statutory damages against both Repro and Wilma. In subsequent proceedings, Repro informs the court that it has filed for bankruptcy and that it has debts far in excess of any assets. Hester seeks to recover the damages award from Wilma. Wilma counters by truthfully asserting that she had no knowledge of the unauthorized use because Repro's general counsel falsely represented to her that he had acquired a valid license from Hester. Which of the following statements most accurately represents Wilma's liability in light of these facts?

(A) Wilma will be fully liable for the $1.5 million damages award.

(B) Wilma will be liable for her half of the $1.5 million damages award.

(C) Wilma will be liable only for $200 in damages due to the innocent infringement defense.

(D) Wilma will not bear any financial liability.

340.   Gyasi is a comedian who is currently enjoying some early success in smaller comedy venues around Seattle. Matt is a blogger who reports on the Seattle entertainment scene. Matt acquires and streams on his blog, without permission, two videos that Gyasi made of himself performing different segments of his act. Gyasi, who owns and has registered the copyrights in both videos, sues Matt for copyright infringement. Gyasi prevails and seeks that the court award statutory damages of $3 million and attorney's fees of $100,000. Gyasi

provides affidavits and billing records from his attorneys substantiating the fee award he seeks. The court awards Gyasi statutory damages of $500, and attorney's fees of $50,000, reasoning that "while the plaintiff won a judgment on the merits, this case involved only two unauthorized performances of his videos, and cannot sustain a more substantial award." Gyasi appeals the award of statutory damages and attorney's fees, arguing that the court erred by awarding, in both cases, much lower amounts than those he had sought. Will Gyasi prevail?

(A) Gyasi will prevail on the statutory damages issue, but not on the attorney's fees issue.

(B) Gyasi will prevail on the attorney's fees issue, but not the statutory damages issue.

(C) Gyasi will prevail on neither issue.

(D) Gyasi will prevail on both issues.

341.   Consider question 340. Assume that Matt cross-appeals the court's final judgment on the theory that an award of attorney's fees that is substantially higher than the amount of statutory damages is per se error. Will he prevail?

Enhanced Protection for Digital Materials

342.   Which of the following statements most accurately and completely describes the Digital Millennium Copyright Act (DMCA)?

   (A)   The DMCA creates new exclusive rights that copyright owners have in their works of authorship.

   (B)   The DMCA creates a series of defenses that users can raise against infringement suits in online settings.

   (C)   The DMCA creates protections for copyright owners against circumvention of technical protection measures.

   (D)   The DMCA creates new rights that protect copyrights in online settings, and also limits the liability of certain digital service providers based on their users' infringing conduct.

343.   George owns and operates the website funfish.com, a compendium of information and resources for people who love keeping fish as pets, and that includes many of George's original essays about and photographs of exotic fish. George seeks to make funfish.com available only to paying members, so that web users can access the site only by entering a password. George charges members $10 per month for access to the site, and in exchange for the monthly fee, George gives each member the password that provides access for the current month.

   Jane is a computer programmer whose hobby is keeping fish as pets. She writes a software program that allows users to freely access funfish.com, bypassing George's attempts to password-protect the site. Jane uses the program to access funfish.com herself, and she has also emailed a copy of the program to her friend Harriet, so Harriet can access the site for free as well. Harriet has a lifetime membership to funfish.com, so she has not used the program to access the site. Harriet has, however, sent the program as an email attachment to 50 of her fish-loving friends, and tells each of them to send it along to anyone else who wants to access funfish.com without paying. Many of the recipients of Harriet's email use the program to do just that.

   George sues Jane and Harriet under the DMCA's anti-circumvention and anti-trafficking provisions. Will George succeed?

   (A)   Yes, Jane and Harriet are both liable under the DMCA.

   (B)   Yes, Jane is liable under the DMCA, but Harriet is not.

(C) Yes, Harriet is liable under the DMCA, but Jane is not.

(D) No, neither Jane nor Harriet is liable under the DMCA.

344. Consider question 343. Assume that when she hears of George's lawsuit, Jane says, "That's absurd, because the password-protection George used didn't provide any real protection at all. George used the most elementary password-protection system in existence to control access to funfish.com. A first-year computer science major could easily write a program to get around that thing." If Jane's observations about the rudimentary nature of George's password-protection efforts are correct, does that absolve her and Harriet of DMCA liability?

345. Greta is a well-known nature photographer who has recently started a website, Gretaspics.com, through which digital copies of her works can be purchased. The copies of Greta's photos are all encoded with a security device called Photo Security System (PSS), which assures that purchasers of digital copies of Greta's photos cannot make further copies or digitally manipulate them.

Warren is a fan of Greta's photos and also an amateur computer programmer. He was given a computer program called dePSS, which undoes the copy and use controls that PSS encodes into the digital copies of Greta's photos. Warren uses dePSS only to enable him to alter some of Greta's photos for use in a birthday card he makes for his wife. Separately, a hacker named Lloyd also obtains the dePSS program and makes the program available on his website, which makes available computer programs and information that Lloyd believes the programming community will find of interest. As a result, hundreds of users take advantage of dePSS to make unauthorized copies of Greta's photos. Greta learns of this, and files suit under section 1201 of the DMCA against Warren and Lloyd. Will she prevail?

(A) Yes, both Warren and Lloyd are liable under section 1201.

(B) Yes, but only Warren is liable under section 1201.

(C) Yes, but only Lloyd is liable under section 1201.

(D) No, neither Warren nor Lloyd is liable under section 1201.

346. Consider question 345. Assume that as part of his response to Greta's DMCA allegations, Lloyd argues that his inclusion of dePSS on his website constituted a fair use, and that this should shield him from liability. Assuming for purposes of this question that Lloyd's assertion that his use of the dePSS program would be considered fair use under the Copyright Act's statutory test, would this argument absolve him of any section 1201 liability for circumventing Greta's photo access controls using dePSS?

347. Vanna is an amateur computer programmer, and one of her favorite hobbies is writing software that seeks to circumvent the latest technology protection measures. Vanna

relishes these efforts because she strongly dislikes major corporations. One such technology protection measure is ContentKey, a digital lock developed by DynaCorp. ContentKey allows users to encrypt data on their laptops to prevent anyone else from accessing the contents of the hard drive. Vanna develops a program that circumvents DynaCorp's ContentKey by decrypting the encrypted material. Pleased with herself, Vanna posts an executable version of this program on her personal website under the title "Stick it to DynaCorp by Unlocking ContentKey." Although Vanna does not tell DynaCorp about this, DynaCorp discovers Vanna's site and brings a DMCA suit against Vanna. Who will prevail?

(A) Vanna, because her work was not for profit.

(B) Vanna, because encryption research is protected under the DMCA.

(C) DynaCorp, because there are no research safe harbors under the DMCA.

(D) DynaCorp, because Vanna's encryption research was not in good faith.

348.   Sculptor creates a bronze sculpture of a man's foot entitled *Step*, which Sculptor likes and keeps in his studio. Collector sees *Step* and asks if Sculptor will license Collector to show the sculpture in Collector's private gallery for three months. Sculptor agrees, and before handing *Step* over to Collector, affixes a label to the bottom of the statue that reads "Copyrighted material licensed to Collector for limited gallery showing only."

Collector places *Step* in his gallery, where he removes the label that Sculptor had applied, and promptly sells *Step* to a rich art aficionado for a large sum. Sculptor sues Collector under section 1202 of the DMCA. Will Sculptor prevail?

(A) Yes. By intentionally removing Sculptor's copyright management information from *Step*, Collector is liable under section 1202 of the DMCA.

(B) Yes. By violating the clear terms of the licensing agreement with Sculptor, Collector is liable under section 1202 of the DMCA.

(C) No. Section 1202 of the DMCA applies only to digital material.

(D) No. Collector is not liable under section 1202 of the DMCA because the information on the label did not identify Sculptor as the author of *Step*.

349.   Consider question 348. Assume **for the purposes of this question only** that when Collector receives "Step" from Sculptor, he cleans the sculpture, and in so doing, inadvertently causes the label with the licensing terms to fall off. Never aware of the label or its absence, Collector nevertheless sells "Step" to a rich art aficionado in violation of the licensing agreement with Sculptor, and Sculptor sues Collector under section 1202 of the DMCA. In light of this variation, will Sculptor prevail?

350.   Which of the following statements most accurately describes the penalties available to a court when a defendant is found to have violated sections 1201 and 1202 of the DMCA?

(A) Injunctive relief; actual or statutory damages; court costs; and attorney's fees.

(B) Injunctive relief; actual, statutory, or punitive damages; court costs; attorney's fees; criminal fines; and imprisonment.

(C) Injunctive relief; actual or statutory damages; court costs; attorney's fees; criminal fines; and imprisonment.

(D) Injunctive relief; actual or statutory damages; court costs; attorney's fees; and criminal fines.

351.   Steve and Olga are each found separately liable for several violations of section 1201 of the DMCA. A court initially concludes that both Steve's and Olga's civil liability amounts to $5,000. The court then learns that Olga violated these provisions without knowing she had done so, and with no reason to know she had committed the violation. The court also learns that Steve has violated section 1201 of the DMCA several other times in the past two years. How do these additional facts affect how the judge should impose damages on Steve and Olga?

(A) The judge must increase Steve's damages three times, and may lower Olga's by 50 percent.

(B) The judge may increase Steve's damages three times, and may lower Olga's by 50 percent.

(C) The judge must increase Steve's damages three times, and may lower Olga's by whatever amount he sees fit.

(D) The judge may increase Steve's damages three times, and may lower Olga's by whatever amount he sees fit.

352.   Christa is an eccentric filmmaker. She works for some time on a project for Vista Productions that she and she alone writes, directs, performs in, and edits. Then, a week before she is due to submit the final version of the film to Vista, she decides that it is a failure, and tells Vista that she will not submit it. The only copy of the film exists on Christa's computer's hard drive in an .mp4 file. Christa's refusal to show the film to Vista, or to the public generally, generates enormous curiosity. The film critic Eber Rogert hacks into Christa's computer, circumventing the technological protection of her content that she put in place, views the film, and considers it a triumph. Eber publishes an article about Christa's film, and includes three images directly taken from the .mp4 file to illustrate points made in his article. Christa is incensed and sues Eber for the unlawful circumvention of a technological measure under section 1201 of the DMCA. Eber counters with a fair use defense, arguing that the film images in his article were simply there in order to illustrate the points he made in his article. Will his defense succeed?

(A) No. Regardless of the validity of Eber's fair use argument, it is irrelevant here because fair use is not a defense to DMCA section 1201 liability.

(B) No. Fair use is categorically unavailable where it occurs in conjunction with wrong-ful behavior like computer hacking.

(C) Yes. Fair use is designed to assure broad access to material that authors would other-wise choose not to release publicly.

(D) Yes. Fair use gives critics a limitless right to access and use material regardless of autho-rial consent.

353. Kent, a long-time client, has called you. He is distressed about the fact that his daughter, Lexi, has "hacked" the eBooksOnline.com website from which she rents e-book titles to read on her e-book reader. Rented titles are placed in the memory of Lexi's e-book reader, but cannot be accessed after 30 days from the date of purchase. Apparently, Lexi has purchased a computer program, *Free Gutenberg*, that allows her to pay the rental fee for e-books, but upgrade the rented copy to a full-priced copy for free by circumventing the digital rights management installed in each e-book file. A full-priced copy of an e-book typically sells for three times the rental price. By manipulating the digital rights man-agement in the e-book file with the aid of *Free Gutenberg*, Lexi can access each "rented" e-book on her Digital Reader Book at any time. Kent wants to know whether his daughter has violated any laws.

354. Winsome Maxwell has recently created a website through which he makes rare and obscure films available to stream on a pay-per-view or subscription basis. Maxwell is scrupulous to assure that all of the copyrights in the films he features on his website have expired. Maxwell has also encrypted the films shown on his website to ensure that only those who pay can see them. One of the films available on the website is *The Dark Vegan*, an early science fiction film by the director Homer Chatsky. Winsome Maxwell recently purchased the only known analog copy of *The Dark Vegan* at a swap meet.

Qualitative Cinema, Inc. is a company specializing in the sale and distribution of high-quality DVDs of artistic films. Qualitative Cinema is currently seeking to release a DVD set of the films of Homer Chatsky. Qualitative Cinema has been unable, however, to find a copy of *The Dark Vegan*. Seeing that the film is streamed on Maxwell's website, Qualita-tive approached Maxwell and offered to pay him handsomely for one reproduction of his copy of *The Dark Vegan*. Maxwell refused to permit access to the motion picture or to license a copy of the film to Qualitative Cinema because Maxwell wanted to have sole pos-session of the only known analog copy of the film.

In response, the employees of Qualitative Cinema, acting within the scope of their employment, created a computer program that permitted the circumvention of Maxwell's encryption protection. The program gave Qualitative Cinema access to the films located on Maxwell's website without the payment of a fee and the ability to digitally reproduce those films. Employees of Qualitative Cinema were able to download a digital copy of *The Dark Vegan*, which was then included in the Chatsky DVD set that also contained six of Chatsky's films, a documentary about his life, and a film historian's analysis of Chatsky's film techniques. The DVD set was sold to the public. Maxwell has filed a lawsuit against Qualitative Cinema for the circumvention of his copyright protection system. Why will Maxwell's DMCA lawsuit fail?

(A) Qualitative Cinema had made a good faith effort to license the use of *The Dark Vegan* before it circumvented its encryption protection.

(B) Reasonable access must be provided to works that are in the public domain.

(C) The purpose of circumventing the encryption protection was to produce a creative work that provided a benefit to the public.

(D) The audiovisual works protected by the encryption are not protected by copyright.

355.   FotoLand is a photograph rights management company. FotoLand acquires the rights to photographs and then seeks to license them. A major part of FotoLand's business occurs via its website, FotoLand.com, which allows individuals to search FotoLand's catalog of photographs and purchase use licenses online. One of the works in the FotoLand catalog is an iconic photograph of former President Gerald Ford, which FotoLand licenses often and for a substantial fee. On FotoLand.com, the web page featuring the Ford photo lists "FotoLand" as both the author and the copyright owner of the photograph.

Ken, a then-famous photojournalist, took the Ford photo in 1975 and published it with proper copyright notice that same year. FotoLand is fully aware of these facts about the Ford photograph. He assigned "all right, title, and interest" in the work to FotoLand in 2000. Ken has since come to believe that FotoLand did not pay him enough for the 2000 copyright assignment. He now wants to sue FotoLand under section 1202(a) of the DMCA for misrepresenting the copyright management information related to the Ford photograph. Will his DMCA lawsuit succeed?

(A) Yes, because FotoLand has knowingly misrepresented both the copyright ownership and authorship information of the Ford photograph.

(B) Yes, because FotoLand has knowingly misrepresented the authorship information of the Ford photograph.

(C) No, because Ken's broad assignment of "all right, title and interest" would include his authorship of the work.

(D) No, because FotoLand did not misrepresent copyright management information with the intent to facilitate copyright infringement.

356.   Assume **for the purposes of this question only** that FotoLand did not take a valid assignment of copyright from Ken in 2000, but Ken still solely owns the work and that they are licensing it on their website without his permission. Assume further that FotoLand is fully aware that they do not hold a valid copyright in the Ford photograph. Ken would clearly have a cause of action against them on a copyright infringement theory under these circumstances, but would he also be able to state a claim under DMCA section 1202(a)?

357.   Jane is an amateur historian of the later Middle Ages and publishes a blog (using the popular web-based blog host Bloggy.com) on which she writes regular entries about the historical study of this period. She reads a recent article published in *Misericordia*, a scholarly journal devoted to medieval history, and finds the article to be inaccurate and misleading. Jane writes a scathing review of the article on her blog, and includes in her review several block quotes from the article that she thinks necessary to illustrate the author's many errors.

Flenderson, Inc. is the publisher of *Misericordia* and other academic journals. Per Flenderson's usual policy, the author of the *Misericordia* article that Jane eviscerated on her blog had assigned his copyright to Flenderson prior to publication. Flenderson issues a takedown notice to the registered DMCA agent of Bloggy.com asserting that the unauthorized use of substantial block quotes from the article violate Flenderson's copyright, and asking that Jane's blog post be taken down. Bloggy.com complies with Flenderson's request. Jane then sends a counter-notification to Bloggy.com indicating her belief that her use of the quotes was fair use and therefore not infringing. Bloggy.com notifies Flenderson of the counter-notification. If Flenderson fails to respond to the counter-notification, what do the DMCA's notice-and-takedown provisions require Bloggy.com to do with Jane's blog post?

(A)   Bloggy.com must keep the blog post offline until Jane submits a written request that the site re-post it.

(B)   Bloggy.com must keep the blog post offline until Jane files for a declaratory action in the local U.S. District Court to have the site re-post it.

(C)   Bloggy will be required to put Jane's blog post back online.

(D)   Bloggy.com will have the option to put Jane's blog post back online, but will not be required to do so.

358.   Assume **for the purposes of this question only** that Flenderson does file a copyright infringement suit against Jane, and that Jane both raises a fair use defense to Flenderson's copyright claim and files a counterclaim under the DMCA's provision imposing damages on copyright owners who "knowingly materially misrepresent" any information in takedown notices. 17 U.S.C. § 512(f). Assume further that the court enters summary judgment in Jane's favor on the copyright claim, holding that "this is a crystal clear case of fair use, an argument that Flenderson concedes it did not even consider before issuing its DMCA takedown notice." In light of the latter holding, will Jane succeed on her section 512(f) counterclaim against Flenderson?

359.   KommUnity.com is a social networking website used mostly by young people on which users create profiles that express their identity and provide ways to communicate with other users. KommUnity.com already boasts more than 500,000 users, and is growing more popular every day. The site allows users to post not only their own writing, but any kind of digital file they choose via uploading sound, image, or video files. Many of the files posted by KommUnity users include unauthorized copyrighted works of authorship; in fact, one

recent estimate suggested that 20 percent of all the files posted on KommUnity.com infringe a copyright.

TelCo, a production company that owns the copyrights in numerous films and television shows—many of which have been posted without its authorization on KommUnity.com—sues the site for infringing its copyrights in those works. KommUnity defends itself by arguing that it cannot be held liable because the safe harbor provisions of section 512 of the DMCA apply to it, and it was unaware of the particular infringing acts of which TelCo complains. TelCo concedes both that the safe harbor provisions of the DMCA apply to KommUnity, and that the site's operators were unaware of the specific infringing acts at issue. But TelCo also shows that KommUnity's directors were aware that their users were generally engaged in widespread infringement. TelCo argues that KommUnity's knowledge of this general practice of infringement disqualifies the site from taking advantage of the section 512 safe harbors. Will TelCo prevail on this argument?

(A) Yes, because the DMCA states that any service providers who are "generally aware" of infringement cannot take advantage of the safe harbor.

(B) Yes, because courts have held that general knowledge of infringing practices by users amounts to the kind of knowledge that disqualifies service providers from taking advantage of the DMCA safe harbor.

(C) No, because only actual knowledge of specific instances of infringing conduct disqualifies service providers from taking advantage of the DMCA's safe harbor provisions.

(D) No, because general knowledge of infringing practices by users does not suffice to meet the knowledge standard that disqualifies service providers from taking advantage of the DMCA's safe harbor provisions.

360. Consider question 359. Assume **for the purposes of this question only** that TelCo advances a different argument in an attempt to show that KommUnity had the kind of knowledge that disqualifies it from the DMCA safe harbors. TelCo argues that KommUnity was willfully blind to facts that would have made it aware of the widespread infringement on its site. In particular, TelCo shows that KommUnity considered but decided against implementing a highly effective system that would monitor users' accounts for copyright infringement. TelCo argues that KommUnity's failure to implement this monitoring scheme amounts to willful blindness sufficient to disqualify KommUnity from the DMCA safe harbor. Will KommUnity still be able to take advantage of the DMCA safe harbor despite TelCo's argument?

(A) Yes, because willful blindness can never comprise the kind of knowledge sufficient to disqualify a service provider from the DMCA safe harbor.

(B) Yes, because failure to monitor infringing conduct alone does not constitute willful blindness.

(C) No, because its failure to implement any kind of infringement monitoring system amounts to willful blindness.

(D) No, because its consideration of implementing an effective infringement monitoring system, and its eventual refusal to do so, amounts to willful blindness.

361. Consider questions 359 and 360. Assume **for the purposes of this question only** that TelCo argues also that KommUnity cannot take advantage of the DMCA because they receive a financial benefit directly attributable to their users' infringement and have the "right and ability to control" that activity. 17 U.S.C. § 512(c)(1)(B). In particular, TelCo argues that because KommUnity's terms of service allow them to "terminate users for any reason, including but not limited to illegal conduct such as . . . copyright infringement," they have both the right and ability to control users' unauthorized use of TelCo's copyrighted works of authorship. Assuming that KommUnity concedes that it derives a financial benefit from instances of unauthorized use of TelCo's copyrighted material, will KommUnity still be able to take advantage of the DMCA section 512 safe harbor despite TelCo's argument?

Practice Final Exam Multiple-Choice Questions

362. Bernard is a designer and tattoo artist. For years, he has been conceptualizing a graphic design in his imagination of a dragon eating a motorcycle. Bernard calls the design *Gorgon's Delight*. *Gorgon's Delight* is very clear and specific in Bernard's head but until this year he has never committed it to canvas or any other medium. Then, earlier this year, Bernard tattooed the design onto his friend Carlos' back. Bernard did not sketch *Gorgon's Delight* before tattooing Carlos, but worked entirely from memory and imagination. Carlos was very pleased with the way the tattoo came out, but unfortunately, just three minutes after Bernard completed the design, Carlos spontaneously combusted and turned into a pile of ash. Bernard was so traumatized by this freak tragedy that he has never tattooed or drawn *Gorgon's Delight* in any other context. Is *Gorgon's Delight* protected by federal copyright?

    (A) No, because it was never fixed in a tangible medium of expression.

    (B) No, because it was fixed in a tangible medium of expression for too brief a period of time.

    (C) Yes, because it was fixed in a tangible medium of expression.

    (D) No, because works of authorship fixed on human flesh are uncopyrightable as a matter of public policy.

363. Gene is an aspiring screenwriter who has been thinking about a new project. Gene pens a plot treatment that encapsulates this project, called *Seeing the Light*.

    > "'*Seeing the Light*' is about Melissa's journey to love. At the beginning, Melissa is dating Jack, a rich playboy who's lots of fun but doesn't treat Melissa well. Then one day, Melissa meets Alan, a shop worker who's poor and simple, but very sweet and kind to her. One day when Jack is being a drunk jerk, Melissa realizes Alan is the one for her. 'He may be poor but he has a heart of gold,' she says, 'and that's what really matters.' So Melissa dumps Jack and goes off with Alan. Alan and Melissa then get married, have lots of kids, and are happy as clams. The end!!!"

    Gene sends this plot treatment to Bill, a producer he met at a party. Bill reads the treatment, but tells Gene that there's no way any film company will be interested in producing *Seeing the Light*. Gene is so disappointed that he never develops the project further. But the next year Gene is shocked and angry when he learns that Bill wrote the screenplay for and produced a hit movie titled *The Last Runaway*. The main character in *The Last*

Runaway is a girl who runs away from home. But her parents are an unhappy couple. The father (who is named Jack) drinks a lot and is often abusive to the mother (who is named Melissa), and by the end of the movie Melissa gets sick of Jack's bad treatment and leaves him for another man.

Gene sues Bill in the U.S. District Court for the Southern District of New York, alleging that the "Jack" character in *The Last Runaway* infringed the copyright in the character of Jack in *Seeing the Light*. Who will prevail in the infringement suit, Gene or Bill?

(A)   Gene, because in the Second Circuit, literary characters enjoy distinctively broad copyright protection.

(B)   Gene, because the name "Jack" in combination with his other distinctive qualities created an original, and hence copyrightable, literary character.

(C)   Bill, because his use of the "Jack" character in *The Last Runaway*, which is a motion picture, could not infringe the "Jack" character in *Seeing the Light*, which is a literary work.

(D)   Bill, because the "Jack" character in *Seeing the Light* lacked sufficient originality to merit copyright protection.

364.   Cal, a self-employed computer programmer, composes and fixes in digital form the source code for *Iterate*, a computer program that will allow users to prioritize the tasks in their personal and professional lives. Cal does not publish in any analog form the source code for Iterate, though he does sell copies of the program's object code embedded in CD-ROMs for use on personal computers. Mal, a notorious hacker, buys a copy of *Iterate*, runs it on his computer, and then acquires the object code that has been compiled by his computer's operating system when executing *Iterate*. Mal studies this object code, eventually figures out how *Iterate* works, and then releases an equivalent of Cal's program, called *ReIterate*. *ReIterate* sells for much less than Iterate, and sales of *Iterate* plummet. Cal discovers what Mal has done, and sues him for infringing the copyrights Cal owns in *Iterate*. Assuming that Mal's conduct does not amount to fair use, who will prevail?

(A)   Cal will prevail because he copied without permission the *Iterate* object code, which is a protected literary work.

(B)   Cal will prevail because Mal violated an implied contract that he would use *Iterate* only in a personal, noncommercial manner.

(C)   Mal will prevail because Cal's copyright in *Iterate* extends only to the source code that Cal composed, not to the object code compiled by Mal's operating system.

(D)   Mal will prevail because it was Mal's computer that read the object code of *Iterate*, not Mal.

365.   Betty creates the lyrics and music that comprise an original musical composition for guitar and voice called *Summer Fugue*. Chris, a singer and guitarist, performs and makes a sound

recording of *Summer Fugue* in a home recording studio that he owns and operates entirely by himself. Chris' version of *Summer Fugue* hews very closely to Betty's original version, making no major changes in lyrics or arrangement. Chris distributes CDs containing his sound recording of *Summer Fugue* for self-promotion, and one of them becomes popular with the DJs at the local analog radio station KHIT, who play the track many times a day. Which statement best describes the obligations of the various parties under federal copyright law?

(A) Chris must pay a mechanical license fee to Betty for his reproduction of *Summer Fugue*, and KHIT must pay Chris royalties for their public performance of his sound recording of *Summer Fugue*.

(B) Chris must pay a mechanical license fee to Betty for his reproduction of *Summer Fugue*, and KHIT must pay Betty public performance royalties for its playing of Chris's sound recording of *Summer Fugue*.

(C) KHIT must pay Chris and Betty public performance royalties for its playing of Chris's sound recording of *Summer Fugue*.

(D) Chris must pay Betty a mechanical license fee for his reproduction of *Summer Fugue*, but KHIT need not pay public performance royalties to Chris or to Betty each time it plays Chris's sound recording of *Summer Fugue*.

366. MWB makes fine German cars. One day MWB tells its head designer to come up with a fanciful design for a futuristic car. The designer pens a sketch of a design for a hover-car called the "ZoomMeister," and the MWB management is so delighted that they arrange for very small, scale models of the ZoomMeister to be given to the company's top 20 employees as paperweights. The models do not work and do not represent serious or realistic aspirations for future cars, but are still very popular, simply because, in the words of one MWB manager, "They look so cool."

Then, when an executive from toy company FunCo is visiting a colleague at MWB, the executive notices one of the toy ZoomMeister models, commits its details to memory, and a year later FunCo releases an identical scale model of a hover-car it calls "Mr. Zoom." The executives at MWB are incensed and sue FunCo for copyright infringement. Will FunCo prevail?

(A) Yes, FunCo will prevail because the ZoomMeister is not a useful article, and thus not protected by federal copyright.

(B) Yes, FunCo will prevail because while the ZoomMeister is a useful article, its aesthetic features are not separable from its utilitarian ones, and it thus cannot be copyrighted.

(C) No, FunCo will not prevail because the ZoomMeister is not a useful article.

(D) No, FunCo will not prevail, because while the ZoomMeister is a useful article, its aesthetic features are separable from its utilitarian ones and may be copyrighted.

367.   Len pens the musical composition *Green Acres* in 1965; federal copyright in the work vested that same year. In 1967, Len's friend Janine performs and records a rendition of *Green Acres* with Len's permission in Janine's own home recording studio. Janine's rendition of *Green Acres* is released to the public on vinyl as a single that same year. As of 1980, who owns federal copyrights in the *Green Acres* musical work and sound recording?

   (A)   Len owns the federal copyright in the *Green Acres* musical work and sound recording.

   (B)   Len owns the federal copyright in the *Green Acres* musical work.

   (C)   Len owns the federal copyright in the *Green Acres* musical work, and Janine owns the federal copyright in the *Green Acres* sound recording.

   (D)   Len owns the federal copyright in the *Green Acres* musical work, and Len and Janine share the federal copyright in the *Green Acres* sound recording as joint authors.

368.   KaraokeCo releases a CD of music tracks for karaoke performers to sing along with. All the sound recordings on the CD are based on arrangements of popular musical works created by KaraokeCo employees, and were performed by session musicians who agreed to cede any rights in the resulting sound recordings to KaraokeCo. Each track of the CD also contains the lyrics of each musical work that could be read by those singing the tune. KaraokeCo did not ask any of the owners of the copyrights in the musical works for permission to make karaoke arrangements of their works.

   One day, a viral video circulates on YouTube of a man whose online moniker is Krooner Ken performing hilariously bad karaoke, using all of the tracks on KaraokeCo's CD. Ken then parlays his Internet stardom into lots of cash by selling DVDs of his awful singing, entitled *Krooner Ken Kills 'Em!* KaraokeCo wants a bite of Krooner Ken's DVD sale profits, and sues Ken for infringement, accurately pointing out that Ken did not get a license or permission to perform any of KaraokeCo's arrangements. Will KaraokeCo succeed in its infringement suit?

   (A)   Yes, because copyright is a strict liability offense, and Krooner Ken is liable regardless of whether his initial intent was to profit from his rendition of KaraokeCo's musical works.

   (B)   No, because Krooner Ken's renditions of KaraokeCo's arrangements were clearly fair use.

   (C)   No, because Krooner Ken's performances fell within section 115's "covering" privilege, which makes it unnecessary for recording artists and record companies to pay for creating renditions of musical works.

   (D)   No, because KaraokeCo had no copyright in the arrangements, since it unlawfully used the underlying musical works on which the karaoke arrangements were based.

369.   Lola loves Los Angeles, and especially its many restaurants. One day she decides to create a guide to her favorite L.A. eateries, called *The Lola Guide: Where to Eat in the City of Angels.*

Lola researches restaurants throughout Los Angeles County, chooses her favorites, writes distinctive descriptions of each venue, and lists them in her guide by alphabetical order. Which of the following statements most accurately describes the scope of Lola's copyright in *The Lola Guide*?

(A) Lola's guide has no copyright protection because it consists of uncopyrightable facts and research.

(B) The arrangement of information in Lola's guide, the selection of information in Lola's guide, and her original descriptions of restaurants are copyrighted.

(C) Both the arrangement of information in Lola's guide and her original descriptions of restaurants are copyrighted.

(D) Both the selection of information in Lola's guide and her original descriptions of restaurants are copyrighted.

370.   Melissa is an artist specializing in painting pictures of naturalistic scenes. She works part-time for the U.S. government, for whom she paints pictures of wild animals that adorn information centers in various national parks. The federal government gives her a monthly check from which it takes out taxes and health insurance costs, and provides her an office (stocked with supplies) where she can create the paintings the government requests. Melissa spends the rest of her work time in her home studio, painting pictures (with materials she supplies for herself) for private clients who request portraits of various nature scenes.

Because Melissa truly loves her work, she often paints portraits of nature in her free time, purely for her own enjoyment. During a recent weekend when Melissa had no obligations for the government or any private client, she created in her home studio a particularly compelling nature scene called *Against the Current*. This painting depicted salmon swimming upstream in Northern California's Klamath River, which she had recently observed while on vacation there.

Melissa's government boss, Albert, came over to Melissa's house one night to visit and was impressed by *Against the Current*. Albert said to Melissa, "Thanks for doing such great work for the feds." Melissa insisted that the copyright in the painting was hers, while Albert insisted that the copyright actually belonged to the United States. Who is right?

(A) Albert, because Melissa is an employee of the federal government.

(B) Melissa, because she is not an employee of any organization, but an independent contractor.

(C) Melissa, because she created *Against the Current* while acting outside the scope of her employment.

(D) Neither, because the U.S. government cannot own copyrights of works created by its employees.

371.   Hilda wrote the literary work *South Atlantic* in 1919, using ink pen and notebook paper. Two years later, in 1921, she published *South Atlantic* with proper copyright notice. Hilda validly renewed the copyright in the twenty-eighth year of its initial term. At the end of which year did the copyright in *South Atlantic* enter the public domain?

(A) 1975

(B) 1977

(C) 1994

(D) 1996

372.   Helen and Greg jointly author the musical composition *Prohibition Blues* in 1925. They never published the work, though they did register it with the Copyright Office as an unpublished work in 1928. In 1930, Helen died suddenly. The work was validly renewed in the twenty-eighth year of its initial term. Greg, in contrast to Helen, lived a long life, dying in 1970. At the end of which year did (or will) *Prohibition Blues* enter the public domain?

(A) 1984

(B) 2003

(C) 2023

(D) 2040

373.   In 1890, amateur artist Sam painted a self-portrait and hung it in the parlor of his private home, where it was seen only by small group of family and friends that came to Sam's home. Sam died in 1940, leaving his entire estate to his daughter, Juana. Juana placed the self-portrait in her attic for storage.

In 1990, Tracy approached Juana and informed her that many of Sam's other works have recently been discovered and made a splash in the art world. Juana told Tracy about the self-portrait, and Tracy bought the portrait and all copyrights in it from Juana for a handsome price. In 1992, Tracy unveiled Sam's self-portrait to the art world for the first time at a gallery opening in Manhattan to which all were invited, and that night more than 1,000 people viewed the portrait.

At the end of which year did (or will) the copyright in Sam's self-portrait enter the public domain?

(A) 1946

(B) 2002

(C) 2010

(D) 2047

374.   Sal is a struggling playwright who is currently developing a script titled *August Haze* while waiting tables to make a bare-bones living. One day, Sal strikes up a conversation with Ed,

a wealthy dilettante. Ed likes Sal's description of *August Haze*, and gives Sal $15,000 so Sal can quit his waiter job and focus exclusively on developing the script.

Sal accepts the offer, and makes enormous strides toward finishing *August Haze* in the next couple of months. During that time, Sal and Ed occasionally meet for coffee, and sometimes chat about the script. Ed constantly gives Sal writing suggestions, and though Sal usually ignores them, he does incorporate a few of Ed's proposed lines of dialogue verbatim. Ed eventually thinks of himself as Sal's collaborator, and Ed tells acquaintances that he's "co-writing a script with an up-and-coming playwright." Sal, by contrast, does not see Ed in this light, and tells friends that he "puts up with listening to this rich guy's lame ideas because he gives me money."

August Haze eventually makes a huge splash on Broadway, and Sal is surprised to find that Ed expects that he is entitled to half of the playwright's royalties, claiming that he is a joint author. Is Ed's claim to joint authorship of *August Haze* viable?

(A) No, because Sal did not consider Ed a joint author.

(B) Yes, because Ed's financial contributions were indispensable to Sal's completing *August Haze*.

(C) Yes, because Ed considered himself a joint author.

(D) Yes, because *August Haze* contained several lines of Ed's original, creative expression.

375. Which of the following circumstances gives rise to a jointly owned copyright?

I. A lyricist and a musician collaborate with each other to create a musical work.

II. The owner of the copyright in a lucrative literary work dies, leaving a will that devises all his property to his three children.

III. A woman who is married in a community property state solely creates a copyrighted work of authorship.

IV. Three friends create a partnership, and that partnership hires an employee to create a copyrighted work of authorship in the course of his employment.

(A) I only

(B) I and II

(C) I, II, and IV

(D) I, II, III, and IV

376. Kelly, a poet, composed a villanelle entitled *Good Friends* in 2007 using a word processor. Later that year, Kelly inscribed the text of *Good Friends* on parchment with ink, signed her name at the bottom of the parchment, framed it, and gave the framed copy of the villanelle to her friend Rosalind as a birthday present. When Kelly presented the gift to Rosalind, she said, "This poem is yours!"

In 2008, Kelly died, leaving a will devising all her worldly goods—including copyrights in all her poems—to James. In 2009, James published an anthology of Kelly's poetry that included *Good Friends*. Rosalind sues James for infringement of the copyright in *Good Friends*. Will she succeed?

(A) Yes. Kelly's signature on the parchment effected a transfer of the copyright in *Good Friends*, as well as transferring ownership of the object.

(B) Yes. Kelly's statement effects verbal transfer of the copyright in the poem.

(C) No. Kelly's gift of the framed copy of *Good Friends* gave Rosalind ownership of that physical copy of the poem, but did not effect transfer of the copyright in the poem.

(D) No. Kelly's devise to James voided the 2007 transfer of copyright in *Good Friends* to Rosalind, and vested ownership in James instead.

377. KLOQ is an analog radio station specializing in popular music. KLOQ broadcasts pursuant to a five-second delay, so that all of the content it broadcasts is saved digitally for five seconds, then immediately taped over. One day, the owner of one of the most popular musical works broadcast by KLOQ, *My Portrait*, sues the radio station for violating her exclusive rights of reproduction and public performance for the unlicensed broadcasts. The owner asserted that KLOQ's five-second tape-delay recordings amounted to unauthorized reproductions of her musical work. KLOQ had a valid license to publicly perform *My Portrait*, but the license did not extend to any other exclusive rights. Will the owner prevail on this argument?

(A) Yes. Copyright is a strict liability offense, so any unauthorized copying—however temporary—violates the owner's reproduction rights.

(B) No. KLOQ, as a transmitting organization entitled to transmit *My Portrait*, may make an ephemeral recording of the work.

(C) No. Courts have held that public performance licenses impliedly extend to reproduction by licensees as well.

(D) No. Because KLOQ did not copy the entirety of *My Portrait*, but rather only five-second snippets of it, they did not violate the owner's reproduction right.

378. Paramecium Records specializes in rare and specialized records, including obscure bootleg versions of live concerts. Paramecium does not create any bootlegs, but often buys bootlegs from sellers, and then re-sells them to the public. One day Paramecium receives a cease-and-desist letter from lawyers for the popular band Smack, demanding that Paramecium stop selling any more bootlegs of Smack's live musical performances. Paramecium has sold numerous Smack concert bootlegs in the past, and does not want to stop selling them. As a matter of federal law, does Paramecium's continued sale of Smack concert bootlegs expose them to liability?

(A) Yes, sale of the Smack bootlegs exposes Paramecium to both criminal and civil liability.

(B) No, because Paramecium's sale of the Smack bootlegs is excused from liability pursuant to the first sale doctrine.

(C) No, because concerts are not fixed, and thus cannot be the basis for federal copyright liability.

(D) No, because Paramecium did not engage in the initial copying of Smack's live performances, but only sold copies of the bootlegs.

379.   Grace is a well-known poet who is down on her luck, and she sells the copyrights in all of her poems to her brother, Deke, in exchange for a substantial amount of cash. Deke then grants a non-exclusive license to B.P. McGee, a publisher, to create an anthology of Grace's poems. B.P. McGee spends a few months culling out the weaker poems, decides to organize the selected works around a seasonal theme, and finally releases the anthology, called *Finding Grace*, which becomes a commercial success.

Several years later, B.P. McGee releases a second edition of *Finding Grace*, which includes the same poems, but adds a critical essay along with them and prints the new edition on higher-end paper stock. B.P. McGee did not negotiate a new license with Deke before releasing the second edition. As soon as the new edition comes out, Zed—a rogue publisher— makes thousands of unauthorized copies of it, and floods the market with lower-priced versions of the second edition of *Finding Grace*. Deke is outraged and sues both B.P. McGee and Zed for copyright infringement; B.P. McGee sues Zed as well. Against which, if any, of these parties, will Zed and B.P. McGee be liable?

(A)   Zed will be liable to both B.P. McGee and Deke, and B.P. McGee will be liable to Deke.

(B)   Zed will be liable to Deke.

(C)   Zed and B.P. McGee will both be liable to Deke.

(D)   Zed will be liable to both B.P. McGee and Deke.

380.   Ray is a budding media entrepreneur who wants to start a number of radio ventures. Ray seeks to own and operate an analog radio station, KRAY, which will also stream its content online over its website affiliate, www.kray.com. Ray also wants to branch out into two new digital radio services. The first is a satellite radio service, where he will offer digital streams of set playlists to subscribers via satellite. The second is an on-demand digital radio service, where he will offer listeners the opportunity to choose from a wide array of music titles, which will then be streamed instantly to them. Neither option will permit users to download any of the tracks. Ray comes to you and asks about his obligations to sound recording copyright owners for these four ventures. Which of the following answers most accurately describes his obligations under federal copyright law?

(A) Ray has no obligations to sound recording copyright owners for public performances of the works via his analog radio station, KRAY, but will have to negotiate a license with them for transmitting their works to the public via the other three means.

(B) Ray has no obligations to sound recording copyright owners for transmitting their works to the public via the analog or online versions of KRAY, but will have to pay them a compulsory license for transmitting their works to the public via the satellite radio and on-demand streaming services.

(C) Ray has no obligations to sound recording copyright owners for publicly performing their works via the analog version of KRAY, but will have to pay them a compulsory license for transmitting their works to the public via www.kray.com and via satellite radio, and will have to negotiate a license with them for transmitting their works to the public via the on-demand streaming service.

(D) Ray has no obligations to sound recording copyright owners for transmitting their works to the public via the analog or online versions of KRAY, but will have to pay them a negotiated license for transmitting their works to the public via the satellite radio and on-demand streaming services.

381. Bill takes an impromptu snapshot of Denise with his cellphone. He later prints out a copy of the photo and shows it to her. Denise hates the picture so much that she takes out a pen and scribbles all over it, ruining the copy. Bill is enraged, and claims that Denise has violated his moral rights by defacing the photograph. As a matter of law, does Bill have a claim under the Visual Artists Rights Act?

(A) Yes, because photographs are a protected work under VARA as long as the author does not print more than 200 copies.

(B) No, because this particular photograph is not a protected work under VARA.

(C) No, because VARA does not extend to authors a right of integrity.

(D) No, because Denise has an affirmative defense to violating VARA, because the photograph violated her right of publicity under state law.

382. In 1980, Iris composed an original pamphlet on her word processor about the health problems of eating fast food. In 1981, she printed the pamphlet in her home, made several hundred copies, and distributed them in person to passers-by outside Queen Burger, a local fast-food restaurant. The pamphlet identified Iris as its author, but did not contain a copyright notice. Recently, Queen Burger published a brochure called *Fighting the Lies*, in which it answers critics' objections to the health of its food. Included in the pamphlet is an exact reproduction of Iris' pamphlet. Iris sues Queen Burger for copyright infringement. Assuming Queen Burger's reproduction is not fair use, will Iris prevail?

(A) Yes, because federal copyright in her work vested upon fixation of her literary work in a tangible medium of expression in 1980.

(B) Yes, because federal copyright in her work vested when she distributed the pamphlet to the public in 1981.

(C) No, because while Iris' federal copyright vested when she first fixed the work in a tangible medium of expression in 1980, she ceded it to the public domain through failure to include proper notice, or cure that failure with a reasonable effort after the omission was discovered.

(D) No, because Iris' work was ceded irrevocably and immediately to the public domain in 1981, when it was published without proper copyright notice.

383. In 1950, Jean wrote a politically charged tract about the government, but kept the only copy in her desk and did not show it to anyone. In 1951, Jean posted a copy of the speech on the wall of the break room in her workplace, a small private company with about 20 employees. In 1952, Jean applied for and was permitted to read her speech during the "Citizen Editorial" segment of the local evening news broadcast. The speech became popular enough that in 1953, Jean created 100 copies of the speech using a makeshift printing press in her own home, handing them out only to close personal acquaintances who expressed an interest in her political beliefs and sought copies of the speech for their personal edification only. Finally, in 1954, Schriver & Co., a publisher, executed a contract with Jean to publish the speech in book form. Schriver & Co. released copies of the hardbound speech to bookstores for sale later that year. Proper copyright notice was affixed to all the aforementioned copies of the speech. Which of the foregoing acts amounted to publication under the then-applicable federal copyright law?

I. Posting the speech in the break room.

II. Reading the speech on the evening news.

III. Printing the speech and giving copies to interested acquaintances.

IV. Publishing the speech in book form.

(A) I and IV

(B) I, II, and IV

(C) I, III, and IV

(D) IV only

384. Logan writes a screenplay entitled *Max Furious*, and registers the work with the Copyright Office, listing himself as the copyright owner. Later, Logan assigns all rights in the Max Furious screenplay to Royal Studios, a film production company. Royal creates a motion picture largely based on Logan's screenplay, but never registers the copyright in the motion picture. A couple of years later, Royal learns that a bootlegger in Cleveland is making and

selling unauthorized DVDs of the *Max Furious* motion picture, selling them for cut-rate prices. Royal sues the bootlegger in the Northern District of Ohio for copyright infringement of the motion picture. The bootlegger moves to dismiss for lack of subject matter jurisdiction. Who will prevail?

(A) The bootlegger. Royal's failure to separately register the derivative work it created based on Logan's screenplay deprives the district court of jurisdiction.

(B) The bootlegger. Royal's failure to have Logan's initial copyright registration amended to reflect Royal as the new owner of the copyright in the original work deprives the court of jurisdiction.

(C) Royal Studios. Logan's registration of the original work gives the court jurisdiction of infringement suits concerning all derivative works.

(D) Royal Studios. The bootlegger's willful infringement waives the standard jurisdictional requirement of copyright registration.

385.   Initech is a Delaware corporation, incorporated in 1970, specializing in the creation of ergonomic computer keyboards. In 1980, one of its employees, Vince Virtual, acting within the scope of his employment, wrote a brochure called *The Ergonomic Advantage*, saving a copy of the brochure to a disk. Virtual died in 1990. In 1995, Initech released the brochure to the general public for the first time by uploading it onto its company website. In 2000, Initech becomes a casualty of the burst Internet bubble, goes out of business, and ceases to exist as a corporate entity. At the end of which year will *The Ergonomic Advantage* enter the public domain?

(A) 2060

(B) 2070

(C) 2090

(D) 2100

386.   Harriet is a screenwriter who wants to sell her script to a movie studio. She has a meeting with several executives at Acme Films, who consider her pitch and then decide to pass on the project. Harriet has no success selling her script at any other studio, and eventually decides to shelve it and work on other projects. A year later, Harriet is surprised to find that Zenith Pictures releases a movie that bears substantial similarity to her script. Although Harriet never had a meeting with Zenith, one of the executives in the room during her Acme meeting retired shortly after that meeting, but immediately after began working part-time as an independent consultant in the development division of Zenith Pictures. Harriet sues Zenith for infringement, and Zenith raises an independent creation defense, arguing that there is insufficient evidence that Zenith had access to Harriet's script. Which party will prevail on the access argument?

(A) Harriet, because access is presumed when two works are substantially similar.

(B) Harriet, because there is sufficient evidence here to infer that Zenith had access to her script.

(C) Harriet, because of the corporate receipt doctrine.

(D) Zenith, because a showing of copying must be based on direct, not circumstantial, evidence.

387. Ken is a botanist who writes a copyrighted 125-page treatise on ferns. A year later, Jamie, who is also a botanist, releases her own 150-page treatise on ferns. Jamie's treatise is distinct from Ken's except for page 86, where six paragraphs of text are identical to six original paragraphs that Ken wrote in his treatise. When Ken confronts Jamie about the uncanny similarity, Jamie is surprised, and responds that the taking must have been an unconscious product of her using Ken's treatise in researching her own. Assuming that Jamie's claim that she inadvertently incorporated the six paragraphs of Ken's work into her own treatise is truthful, does her conduct amount to infringement?

(A) No, because copying that is unconscious or inadvertent is not actionable.

(B) No, because Jamie's taking is *de minimis*.

(C) No, because Jamie's taking was small in relation to the overall size of Ken's treatise.

(D) Yes, Jamie infringed Ken's copyright.

388. New Biz is a profitable vendor that sells $5 music CDs at the First Waltz flea market. The flea market charges an entrance fee, a rental fee for vendor stalls, and sells food and beverages to shoppers. The New Biz CDs consist entirely of music that has been unlawfully downloaded. New Biz does not create these CDs, but accepts them from a distributor who sells the CDs to New Biz for $1 each. The distributor is able to make CDs so cheaply because he downloads .mp3 files from a foreign website that enables the unauthorized distribution of sound recordings, and then burns them onto blank CDs that he purchases in massive quantities. The owner of New Biz has said to the First Waltz management on several occasions, "You know how I get these songs I'm selling so cheap, right?" The First Waltz management consistently responds by saying, "I don't know, and I don't want to know, so keep your methods to yourself." First Waltz does not have any direct knowledge of the distributor's illegal activity, but it is aware that equivalent CDs created through legal means typically wholesale for at least $7. On what, if any, theory of secondary liability can First Waltz be held liable for the distributor's or New Biz's infringement?

(A) Contributory infringement and vicarious infringement.

(B) Contributory infringement, but not vicarious, infringement.

(C) Vicarious infringement, but not contributory, infringement.

(D) Neither contributory nor vicarious infringement.

389.   Tina is an amateur photographer. In her apartment hangs a framed copy of a photo she took of a particularly spectacular sunset. Tina's friend Quentin visits her, sees the photo, and tells Tina that he would like a copy of it. Tina declines, saying, "It may not be worth any money, but my pictures are mine and mine alone." Undeterred, Quentin sneaks into Tina's study, finds the .jpeg file containing the photograph on her computer, and downloads it to a portable hard drive. While Quentin originally intended to print a copy of the photograph to put in his private home, he eventually forgets all about the issue, and never even prints a copy of Tina's photograph. Does Quentin's conduct render him liable for criminal copyright infringement?

(A) Yes, because Quentin willfully copied Tina's photographic work.

(B) Yes, because Quentin acted in bad faith.

(C) No, because Quentin did not create the infringing copy for private financial gain, nor was the photograph worth more than $1,000.

(D) No, because Quentin never actually printed an infringing copy of the photograph.

390.   As a college student in 1978, Felice wrote a since-forgotten incendiary 30-page tract advocating the dissolution of all American government in favor of a completely unregulated market-based state. Now Felice serves as a moderate California state congresswoman. Edgar, a reporter for the San Francisco *Voice*, discovers Felice's old tract, and (without seeking permission) writes a five-page feature about it, using three separate quotes, ranging from 10–30 words, from the text to illustrate Felice's college-era beliefs. Edgar's boss at the *Voice* is so impressed with the piece that he gives Edgar a big raise. A few weeks after the article appears in the *Voice*, Felice sues Edgar for copyright infringement, and Edgar counters by raising the fair use defense. Does Edgar have a successful fair use defense to infringement liability?

(A) Yes. Edgar's article is news reporting, which is per se fair use.

(B) Yes. Edgar's article was a reportorial piece that did not harm Felice's economic interests (if any) in her tract, and Edgar's takings were not unreasonable in comparison to the initial work or his need to explain the character of the tract.

(C) No. Because Edgar received a raise after writing the article, it is commercial and thus not fair use.

(D) No. Because Edgar did not ask Felice for permission to use the tract, he is precluded from raising the fair use defense.

391.   Which of the following statements most accurately describes the fair use defense as embodied in 17 U.S.C. § 107?

(A) It is a codification of a constitutional right to which all users are entitled that outlines four nonexclusive factors that courts must consider.

(B) It is a codification of a constitutional right that outlines four exclusive factors that courts may consider.

(C) It is a codification of a common-law doctrine that outlines four nonexclusive factors that courts must consider.

(D) It is a codification of a common-law doctrine that outlines four exclusive factors that courts may consider.

392.   Dennis is a fundamentalist Christian, and rejects the biological idea of evolution completely. Genevieve is a schoolteacher who writes a biology text for sixth graders that assumes the veracity of evolution. Dennis is incensed by this, and posts the entirety of Genevieve's text on his personal website without her permission. Dennis urges visitors to his site to download the book rather than purchase it from Genevieve's publisher, and asks that users who do so give him voluntary donations. While several users do give him donations, most are outraged by Dennis' piracy, which creates a wave of positive publicity for Genevieve's book. As a result, in the following school year, thousands of teachers assign her text, increasing book orders and earning Genevieve substantial royalties. Soon after, Genevieve sues Dennis for infringement, and he counters by raising a fair use defense. Will Dennis prevail?

(A) Yes, because he transformed the text from an analog to digital medium by posting it online.

(B) Yes, because Dennis did not sell Genevieve's book, but sought only voluntary donations.

(C) Yes, because his unauthorized use of Genevieve's text helped her sell more books rather than harming the biology text's market share.

(D) No, because Dennis' use was essentially commercial, not meaningfully transformative, and aimed to undermine the market for Genevieve's book (even if it failed to do so).

393.   In 1978, Fran writes a screenplay called *One Man Down*. Fran gives a copy of the screenplay, with Fran's ownership of the copyright clearly indicated, to Zelda for comments, but never hears back from her. Then, in 1980, Lloyd, Fran's friend and an executive at D Films, calls Fran and tells her that Zelda has pitched *One Man Down*, claiming that the work is actually Zelda's. Moreover, Lloyd tells Fran, D Films loves the script and wants to produce it. Fran is angry, but never takes any action. By 1982, D Films assumes that Fran would have brought an infringement suit if she were so inclined, and begins production on *One Man Down*. D Films releases *One Man Down* in 1984, and it earns a healthy sum from box office proceeds and after-market sales over the next five years, after which D Films stops all exploitation of the motion picture. Fran keeps a close tab on all of these developments, but never gets around to retaining counsel to pursue infringement. Then, in 2005, Fran sues D Films for copyright infringement. Which affirmative defenses can D Films invoke to overcome Fran's infringement suit?

394.   Joe directs and produces an adult motion picture, *Bump in the Night*, and registers it with the Copyright Office as an audiovisual work. Joe does not disclose on the registration form

that the film includes explicit sex scenes. The motion picture is released on DVD, and is soon pirated and distributed without authorization and for free over various filesharing websites. Joe makes no effort to become aware of or stop this piracy until a year passes and he notices that the DVD sales of *Bump in the Night* have dropped to nearly zero. Joe then discovers the piracy and sues several of the parties who have created and distributed unauthorized copies of his motion picture. Shortly before Joe filed his copyright infringement action, a state court found *Bump in the Night* to be obscene. Will Joe succeed in his infringement suit against these parties, assuming that they are primarily liable for violations of Joe's exclusive rights in his audiovisual work?

(A) Yes. The infringers have no valid affirmative defenses to their conduct.

(B) No, because Joe's failure to disclose the adult content of his film constitutes a fraud on the Copyright Office.

(C) No, because Joe's film is obscene, and copyright is not available for such works.

(D) No, because Joe failed to carefully police infringements of his work for a year, he forfeited any right to bring suit against those infringements.

395. Helen recently painted a self-portrait, and then agreed to let the local Museum of Modern Art (MoMA) display it in its main hall for three weeks. Helen and MoMA agreed that she was granting only a license to permit the museum to display her self-portrait, and she has reserved all other exclusive rights in the work. Later, without Helen's permission, MoMA featured a digital copy of the self-portrait on its website, on a page entitled "New Work at the MoMA" that is designed to generate interest in the museum's collection. Helen sues MoMA in state court, claiming that MoMA's unauthorized reproduction and display of the portrait entitle her to recovery on three theories: right of publicity, conversion, and unfair competition. MoMA rejoins that federal copyright law preempts all of these causes of action. Which, if any, of Helen's causes of action actually are preempted?

(A) Right of publicity and conversion.

(B) Conversion and unfair competition.

(C) Conversion and right of publicity.

(D) Right of publicity, conversion, and unfair competition.

396. Hank engaged in early-stage discussions with Welter Publishing about an exclusive publication deal for Hank's novel, *Trains and Levees*. Early on in the negotiations, Welter grew so excited about the prospect of a deal that, without Hank's knowledge or approval, it printed 10,000 copies of Hank's novel to prepare for distribution and sale. The deal went bad, though, and Hank eventually took a better publication offer from Welter's competitor in publishing, Gladman Books. Gladman plans to release Hank's book in about a year. Welter is incensed, and tells Hank that it is going to sell the 10,000 copies of Hank's work

immediately. Hank then sues Welter for infringement in the U.S. District Court for the Northern District of Georgia, accurately stating that he never authorized Welter to make any of the copies of *Trains and Levees* that now sit in Welter's warehouse. Hank also moves for preliminary injunctive relief pending litigation. Will a court grant Hank's motion for a preliminary injunction?

(A) Yes, because Hank has shown all four elements necessary to warrant preliminary injunctive relief.

(B) Yes, because plaintiffs in infringement suits are presumptively entitled to preliminary relief, and Welter has not overcome this presumption.

(C) No, because the injury Hank would suffer in the absence of a preliminary injunction is solely financial, and therefore is not irreparable.

(D) No, because any injury Hank would suffer in the absence of a preliminary injunction would be offset by the injury that such an injunction would inflict on Welter.

397.   Madelyn is a folk musician who writes and performs her own musical compositions, and produces her own CDs as well, using her home recording studio. During 2009, Madelyn learns that her sales have declined precipitously and, after some investigating, she discovers that the cause for this is a digital locker website, owned and operated by the TekCo corporation, that allows users to download unauthorized copies of her sound recordings for free. Madelyn sues TekCo for copyright infringement, and wins a judgment in her favor. Madelyn submits evidence proving that her sales declined by $10,000 in 2009, and that this decline was attributable solely to sales that Madelyn would have made but for TekCo's infringement. Madelyn also submits evidence proving that in 2009, TekCo's gross profits were $1 million. TekCo then submits evidence proving that only $5,000 of its 2009 profits were attributable to its distribution of Madelyn's sound recordings, and that distributing those sound recordings required $1,000 in delivery costs. Assuming that Madelyn seeks actual damages from TekCo, what is the appropriate measure of those damages?

(A) $1 million

(B) $10,000

(C) $5,000

(D) $4,000

398.   Vic writes *Tales of Horror*, a book containing four separate stories about macabre themes. Vic registers *Tales of Horror* with the Copyright Office as a collective work, listing himself as the author of all four stories. Amy, Mike, and Jane are filmmakers who, without authorization, jointly write a screenplay based on Vic's *Tales of Horror*, and then co-produce and co-direct a motion picture based on that screenplay. Vic sues Amy, Mike, and Jane for copyright infringement, wins judgment in which the three defendants are named jointly

liable, and seeks statutory damages. The amount of statutory damages is set at $1,000 per infringement. What is the total amount of statutory damages for which Amy, Mike and Jane are jointly liable?

(A) $1,000

(B) $6,000

(C) $12,000

(D) $24,000

399.   Jane is a nature photographer living in Redwood Town. The Redwood Town Council contacts Jane and tells her they want to feature one of her photographs as the main image on the Redwood Town home page. In a brief, written agreement, Jane agrees to sell one copy of the photo to Redwood Town for $500, and to permit display of the photo on the Redwood Town home page. Jane retains copyright in the work. Pursuant to this agreement, Jane sends the Redwood Town Council a digital copy of her photograph as an email attachment. The photo that Jane sends has a digital watermark reading, "© Jane 2017." Jane receives payment from Redwood Town as per the agreement, but when she visits the town's site, Jane is surprised to find that the photo does not include the digital watermark. She contacts the Redwood Town Council about this issue, and it responds that it was free to remove the watermark, since it is the owner of the authorized copy. Jane sues Redwood Town under the DMCA. Will she prevail?

(A) No, because Redwood Town removed the watermark from a validly acquired copy of Jane's work for which it paid value.

(B) No, because Redwood Town is a state actor.

(C) No, because Redwood Town did not wrongfully identify itself, instead of Jane, as the author of the photograph.

(D) Yes. Redwood Town's unauthorized removal of Jane's copyright management information violates the DMCA.

400.   Youface is a popular social networking program created by software giant MacroHard. Because MacroHard wants Youface to create demand for its software, MacroHard limits the interactive elements of Youface by password, so that there is only one account per copy of the program. Moreover, MacroHard has engineered Youface so that the program cannot run on competing operating systems. Brad is a skilled hacker who dislikes MacroHard's market dominance. Brad develops two clever hacks. One allows him to access the interactive elements of Youface without getting a password, and the other allows the Youface software to run on his non-MacroHard operating system. Even though Brad develops these hacks only for his personal use, MacroHard somehow discovers them and brings suit against Brad under the DMCA for circumventing its copyright protection systems. On which, if any, theory of liability will MacroHard prevail?

(A) Brad's circumvention of MacroHard's use limitations.

(B) Brad's circumvention of MacroHard's access control measures.

(C) Brad's circumvention of MacroHard's use limitations and its access control measures.

(D) Brad has not engaged in any conduct actionable under the DMCA's provisions regulating circumvention of copyright protection systems.

An Inventor in Paradise

Harry Hopper wrote a fictional novel, titled *An Inventor in Paradise*, which was published with proper copyright notice in 1940, the same year it was registered with the United States Copyright Office. The novel depicted the fictional life of an inventor, Whitfield Diffie, who spent most of his life disassembling appliances and using them for experiments. After a tragic accident while playing poker, Diffie fell into a coma for several months. During his coma, Diffie's soul visited purgatory where the souls of the machines on which he had experimented had their revenge. When Diffie regained consciousness, he changed his ways and became a machine rights activist.

On September 2, 1942, Harry Hopper signed an exclusive motion picture license agreement with Left Coast Pictures to make a motion picture based on Hopper's novel. The agreement granted Left Coast Pictures the "exclusive right to make a motion picture based on *An Inventor in Paradise*, as well as remakes, sequels and prequels, in any medium now known or hereinafter devised." Left Coast Pictures was granted the exclusive license for the initial and renewal term of the copyright in *An Inventor in Paradise*. Left Coast Pictures was also given permission to "use the novel or any adaptation or version thereof for the purpose of advertising, publicizing or exploiting the motion picture." The agreement indicated that Harry Hopper, or his heirs and assigns, was to receive five percent of all gross revenues derived from the exploitation of the motion picture.

The motion picture, *Mr. Diffie's Soul*, was released in 1944 with proper copyright notice and was registered that year with the Copyright Office. The motion picture contained the characters and plot of *An Inventor in Paradise*. The copyright in the novel was properly renewed by Harry Hopper in the twenty-eighth year of its initial term of protection. The copyright in the motion picture was also properly renewed.

Harry Hopper died in 1985, leaving his daughter, Grace, as his only heir. On January 10, 1989, Grace Hopper sent a proper termination notice to Left Coast Pictures, notifying it that the September 2, 1942, agreement would be terminated as of January 5, 1999. Left Coast Pictures released *Mr. Diffie's Soul* on videocassette in 1990. Prior to the termination of the September 2, 1942, agreement, Left Coast Pictures had no Internet presence. On March 15, 1999, Left Coast Pictures released *Mr. Diffie's Soul* on DVD. The DVD version of *Mr. Diffie's Soul* resulted from a transfer of the entire original analog version of the motion picture into a digital version utilizing digital compression technology. No portion of the original motion picture was changed during the transfer process. No additional information or features were included in the *Mr. Diffie's Soul* DVD.

In July 1999, Left Coast Pictures premiered its website on the Internet. In addition to announcing its upcoming releases, Left Coast Pictures used its website to sell videocassette and DVD copies of its library of motion pictures. As a means of facilitating such sales, Left Coast Pictures created a web page containing a menu of the titles of its best-known motion pictures, including *Mr. Diffie's Soul*. By clicking on a title, visitors can access a single scene from that motion picture. At the end of the scene, the visitor sees a screen with the message: "If you liked this film, you would undoubtedly like one of the following films. Click on one of the titles listed below to order a copy." The visitor can then click on one of the suggested titles, including the motion picture that had been viewed in part. After the title is clicked, the visitor is given the opportunity to enter credit card and delivery information to purchase a videocassette or DVD copy of the selected motion picture.

The scene from *Mr. Diffie's Soul* that can be viewed by a visitor to Left Coast Pictures' website is the classic purgatory scene for which both the novel and motion picture are renowned. The motion picture's purgatory scene closely followed the written description of the scene found in the novel. Left Coast Pictures has continued to pay Grace Hopper five percent of the gross revenues derived from the sales of videocassette and DVD copies of *Mr. Diffie's Soul*.

Alan Cadabra created a musical composition, *Optical Rectosis*, that was used as the theme music for *Mr. Diffie's Soul*. *Optical Rectosis* was written in 1944 pursuant to a standard studio composer agreement that indicated *Optical Rectosis* would be created as a work made for hire. *Optical Rectosis* was not independently registered with the copyright office. The musical composition was listed as a work made for hire in the *Mr. Diffie's Soul* copyright registration.

Five years ago, Left Coast Pictures released *American Outback*, a motion picture that contained the musical composition *Piety and Iron*. The musical composition was created in 1995 by Winston James pursuant to a work made for hire agreement. The only use ever made of *Piety and Iron* was in the soundtrack of *American Outback*, which is now available on DVD. *Piety and Iron* was never released on a soundtrack album and has never been licensed to another party to record or distribute the musical composition.

Three of your clients have contacted you for advice.

1. Grace Hopper wants to bring a copyright infringement lawsuit against Left Coast Pictures. She believes Left Coast Pictures has no post-termination right to continue selling videocassette copies of *Mr. Diffie's Soul* without her consent. She also believes that Left Coast Pictures has no post-termination right to release *Mr. Diffie's Soul* on DVD, nor the post-termination right to use the three-minute film clip of the purgatory scene from her father's novel as a means of selling copies of *Mr. Diffie's Soul* or any other films. Since terminating the September 2, 1942, agreement, Grace Hopper has retained all of the rights to *An Inventor in Paradise*.

2. Alan Cadabra wants to terminate his 1944 agreement with Left Coast Pictures and obtain the rights to *Optical Rectosis*.

3. Bert Schreck, a record producer, wants to record a selection of musical compositions from various motion pictures and distribute the recordings on phonorecords. The original recordings of the musical compositions will not be used. He wants to include *Piety and Iron* in this compilation without negotiating directly with Left Coast Pictures.

Discuss and analyze the viability of your clients' requests. Do not address any possible fair use defenses or remedies.

Rick Rail

Rick Rail was the preeminent surfing music guitarist of the 1960s. Rail had several hits, including *Bail Before They Bite* ["*Bail*"], a musical composition he wrote in 1965 and immediately registered with the Copyright Office. He recorded the musical composition with his band, Rick Rail and the Bailettes, for Flusterated Records in 1966. The recording was distributed to retail stores throughout the country. Flusterated Records, which recorded all of Rail's recordings pursuant to a mechanical license from Rail, owns all rights in the *Bail* sound recording.

At the end of the 1960s, Rail left the music business and became a successful surfboard manufacturer. In 1975, Rail was approached by Anne Droid, a documentary film maker. Droid was interested in doing a documentary on the life of Rick Rail. Droid paid Rail $1,500 for the rights to use his life story, rights to use his musical compositions and his cooperation in the making of the documentary. The parties entered into a contract, which stated in relevant part:

> **6. Rick Rail hereby grants to Anne Droid a nonexclusive right to use any and all of his musical compositions in connection with a documentary. Anne Droid shall have the right to exhibit, distribute, exploit, market and perform said documentary perpetually throughout the world, including all renewals and extensions, by any means or methods now or hereafter known.**

* * * * *

> **9. Rick Rail reserves all rights and uses in and to said musical compositions, except those herein granted to Anne Droid.**

Before work on the documentary could begin but after he signed the agreement with Anne Droid, Rick Rail died in a freak surfing accident.

In 1990, Flusterated Records released a digital audio compact disc titled *Rick Rail's Greatest Hits*, which included *Bail*. To prepare this release, Flusterated Records made digital recordings of the original analog master recordings of Rick Rail and the Bailettes. The original analog master recordings had been recorded on ¼-inch reel-to-reel tapes which had been kept in a vault in Flusterated Records' headquarters. A computerized mastering machine, purchased by Flusterated Records from DigiCom, Inc., was used to convert the analog ¼-inch original master tapes into digital recordings. The mastering machine plays the analog tape on an analog tape deck, during which a computer program created by DigiCom samples the sounds on the analog tape at the rate of 44,100 times per second and records the digital information onto a ¾-inch digital tape. This process was conducted by Bobby Banger, a Flusterated Records employee acting within the scope of his employment, in Flusterated's recording studio.

Once the recording was completed, Banger "equalized" the digital recordings by listening to them while sitting at a sound board from which he could adjust the volume, tones and acoustics of the sounds captured on the digital tape. Banger raised the level of the bass guitar and reduced the level of the snare drum. No other adjustments were made to the digital recordings. Once the digital recordings had been equalized, the ¾-inch tape was sent to Flusterated Records' mastering plant, where the digital recordings were pressed into digital audio compact discs and distributed to retail stores.

Anne Droid now is the sole owner of Seedy Roms, a company that creates and markets multimedia CD-ROM computer programs for use in home computers. In 1993, the company released a CD-ROM program titled *Before California Fell Into the Ocean*. The program presents a history of California surfing music through the use of biographical textual material, photographs and sound recordings. One of the individuals featured in the CD-ROM program is Rick Rails. Anne Droid wrote the biographical material concerning Rails, obtaining the information from public domain sources. She paid a license fee for the use of 10 photographs taken of Rails in the 1960s. The section of the CD-ROM dealing with Rick Rails uses the digital recording of *Bail*. While using the CD-ROM, the computer user listens to the sound recording and has the option of reading Rail's biography, looking at the photographs of Rail in any order determined by the user, or reading the lyrics of the musical composition. In producing the CD-ROM program, Droid copied the digital recording of *Bail* from the 1990 *Rick Rail's Greatest Hits* compact disc, without obtaining permission. Droid, relying on her 1975 agreement with Rail, did not seek any additional permission to use the musical composition in the CD-ROM program.

When Rick Rail died in 1975, he had never married, had made no assignments of his copyrights and left no will. Unbeknownst to him, however, he had a daughter out of wedlock, Ambigua Peace, who was two years old at the time of his death. On her eighteenth birthday, Peace was informed that Rail was her birth father. At no time has Peace filed any document with the Copyright Office.

You have recently acquired Anne Droid as a client. She has received two cease-and-desist letters claiming federal copyright infringement. A letter from Flusterated Records threatens to sue for federal copyright infringement due to Droid's unauthorized use of the sound recording of *Bail*. Ambigua Peace has also sent a letter claiming that Droid's unauthorized use of the *Bail* musical composition is an infringement of Peace's copyright. Discuss the federal copyright issues raised by these letters.

Fiona Photog

Fiona Photog is a well-known photojournalist who has won numerous awards for her work. Fiona has authorized the appearance of her photographs in a variety of different publications over the course of her long career, but during the past five years, she has authorized the publication of her photographs only in the pages of the print news magazine *Tempo*.

Tempo, published by the media conglomerate PubliCo, regards itself as the premier news magazine in America. It has won acclaim for its unflinching, original coverage of major news events, and it always accompanies its articles with dramatic photographs, including, with some regularity, Fiona's. PubliCo has also refused to create an Internet presence, insisting that its high-quality content cannot be fully appreciated in an online medium.

One day, Fiona Photog visits the law office where you work to seek your advice with a complaint about PubliCo. She reports, "You remember those awful fires up in Blanco Valley last month? Well, I risked my life to be there, and I took a great pic of these cowboys saving some horses from a burning ranch. It was some of my best work yet. I titled the photograph 'Ranch Heroes.' As usual, *Tempo* loved my work and they ran 'Ranch Heroes' on a full page alongside an article they did about animal rescue during the Blanco Valley fires.

"I had no problem with that, as usual. PubliCo pays top dollar, and there's a lot of professional cachet in saying I'm a *Tempo* photographer. Plus, I like that they don't publish an online version of their magazine; that makes it harder for people to steal my work. But the agreement I sign every time I let them use one of my photos is very clear: they pay me a one-off fee for the picture, and I authorize them to use it in that issue of *Tempo*—and *only* in that issue.

"Then yesterday a friend texted me and said, 'I saw your picture of the horse-ranch evacuation on the Internet—great stuff!' So I follow the link he sent and it turns out that PubliCo started a website in order to seek Pulitzer Prizes. You know what the Pulitzer is, right? Well, I'll tell you anyway: it's the highest national honor in journalism. Winners of the award receive $10,000, a certificate, a medal, and an enormous amount of prestige. PubliCo's site is called 'The Best of PubliCo 2017,' and it has excerpts from all the stories in PubliCo magazines from the past year that they think deserve Pulitzer consideration. But they didn't just include the story part of the *Tempo* piece on the Blanco Valley fires; they also included my photograph.

"What's really annoying is that they bastardized my great photo in order to cram the article into an online format. The original version of 'Ranch Heroes' in *Tempo* was colorful and took up a whole page. But the one on the website was only a couple inches square, and in black-and-white too. They even cropped the top section off. That was the best part of the picture—it showed how the smoke from the fires made the horizon appear blurry and distorted."

"And you know, despite all that, I probably wouldn't even be here if the folks over at PubliCo weren't being such jerks about all this. I called them the other day to give them a piece of my mind, and they said I was overreacting. Then they made a bunch of lame excuses.

"First off, they said, 'Fiona, you know you're a *Tempo* photographer, so that means we can do whatever we want with your work.' But I don't know where they get that idea. Sometimes I call myself a '*Tempo* photographer,' but that's just to impress people or get media access when there's a tightly controlled scene. I do my own thing on my own schedule, not on *Tempo*'s or anyone's assignment. Sure, sometimes Tempo tips me off that an event is going down, and they've even given me a ride to event sites in their company helicopter. But whenever I cover an event, I choose whether I'm going to shop my photos to them — or anyone else if I feel like it. Plus, I work out of my own studio, not the *Tempo* offices, and all my equipment is my own. Well, most of it, anyway — actually, for the past three years, *Tempo* has given me a fancy new camera as an annual holiday gift, so about half of my cameras come from them, including the one I used to take 'Ranch Heroes,' now that I think about it.

"Then the PubliCo folks claimed that I gave them the go-ahead to use 'Ranch Heroes' on their website. What a crock! There was this one time two weeks ago at a party where one of their executives came up to me, reeking of booze, and mentioned something about doing a website only for Pulitzer publicity purposes. Then he said they thought the animal rescue article with my photo would be good on the site. I told this guy, 'Sure, whatever you say' — mainly to get him to go away. I didn't even remember the conversation until they brought it up the other day.

"But worst of all, they're telling me that *I* should be thanking *them* for putting 'Ranch Heroes' on the publicity site. I told them I don't think that dinky, shrunken version of my great photo is going to impress anyone. And just the other day, I got an angry call from the folks over at Eagle Prints, the company that I work with exclusively to create and sell limited-release prints of my best photographs. They'd seen 'Ranch Heroes' on PubliCo's website too, and they said that if I'm going to start publishing my work online where anyone can just download it, they'd have to reconsider their relationship with me.

"I'd love to sue these guys, but I don't want to go down that road unless I have a solid case. What do you think?"

Your task is to write a memo to your fellow law partners arguing for or against taking on Fiona's case. Your memo should address only the likelihood of Fiona Photog's success in a copyright infringement lawsuit against PubliCo. In answering this question, you should assume that PubliCo is the appropriate defendant and that "Ranch Heroes" is copyrightable subject matter. Limit your answer to theories of recovery based on the Copyright Act. DO NOT address moral rights theories based on the Visual Artists Rights Act.

The Gift

Sheila Barry, born in 1900, was a noted American writer. Her most famous work is a short story, *The Gift*, which Sheila wrote on paper using ink in 1927. As she did with all her writings, Sheila wrote a copyright notice — "© Sheila Barry 1927," in this instance — at the top of the manuscript's first page, but she never sought to register any copyrights in *The Gift* with the federal Copyright Office. Sheila created only the one single handwritten copy of *The Gift*, and she neither showed nor gave it to anyone.

For years, the only reason the public knew of the story's existence was that in 1928, Sheila read *The Gift* as part of a radio show broadcast by a local Los Angeles radio station. Only about 300 members of the radio station's general audience heard the broadcast, and because the broadcast was not recorded, only those 300 listeners ever heard Sheila's reading of *The Gift*. After the broadcast, Sheila put the copy of *The Gift* in her desk drawer, where it remained, unseen, until her death in 1930. Following Sheila's premature demise, the executors of her estate moved all of her personal papers into a private archive to which only the four members of Sheila's immediate family had access. During that time, the sole copy of *The Gift* never left the archive, and it was seen by only two of the four members of Sheila's immediate family, despite great public curiosity about the story.

Then, in 2000, Sheila's only living grandchild, Elise Barry, became the sole owner of Sheila's literary estate by devise. Elise's inheritance of the literary estate included sole ownership of any and all existing copyrights in Sheila's literary works, including any copyright that remained in *The Gift*.

That same year, Elise decided to commemorate the centennial of her grandmother's birth by reenacting the famous 1928 reading of *The Gift*. Reading from the same original copy of *The Gift* handwritten by Sheila, Elise created an .mp3 sound file of her reading the story, using her own personal computer. She then emailed a copy of that .mp3 sound file to her local paper, the San Sendero *Times*. Elise sent the email to info@sansenderotimes.com, which is the general-inquiry email address listed on the *Times* website. At the time she sent the email, the *Times* was a mid-size regional newspaper with a circulation of 300,000 readers and 500 editorial employees (these are employees responsible for creating content, such as editors, writers, and photographers). The email read:

I, Elise Barry, have read and recorded The Gift, *the famous story written by my grandmother, Sheila Barry, in 1927. This recording will be broadcast online on the same day and time as Sheila's birth in 1900, but a physical or digital copy of* The Gift *will not be made available. I want the San Sendero* Times *to be the first paper to report on this historic event, and to that end, I have attached an exclusive promotional copy of my reading* The Gift *in .mp3 format. You're free to listen, and even take a little quote here and there for the purpose of writing an article about my forthcoming Internet broadcast, but I hope you will not spread this copy outside the editorial staff of your paper. Part of* The Gift*'s magic is its mystery, and if that mystery were lost, it would be a devastating blow to me, my family, and the memory of my grandmother.*

The San Sendero *Times* indeed wrote a feature about Elise's forthcoming reading of *The Gift*, and included in that feature three quotes from *The Gift*, each less than a sentence long. The *Times* and its employees respected Elise's request that the .mp3 of *The Gift* not be given to anyone outside their editorial staff (though it circulated widely among the 500 editorial staff members). Then, as promised, Elise streamed the .mp3 of her reading of *The Gift* on the Internet exactly 100 years after the date and time that Sheila was born in 1900. Thanks to her publicity efforts, Elise's online broadcast of *The Gift* had an estimated audience of about 50,000 listeners. Elise encrypted the stream so that listeners could not record it. Nor did Elise make the .mp3 available to the public for sale or free download. As a result, no member of the public obtained even a single copy of the .mp3 containing Elise's reading at that time.

Later in 2000, Elise made five high-quality photocopies of the sole version of *The Gift* that Sheila had handwritten in 1927, and gave one to each of Sheila's five other living descendants at a family dinner. Quentin, one of the recipients, asked, "What are we supposed to do with these?" Elise replied, "Well, they're presents, Quentin, so you're free to do with them whatever you want. For example, you could put your copy on a mantelpiece, or read it to your children. I hoped they might be nice family heirlooms for each of us, especially considering that no one outside the family has ever laid eyes on Grandmother Sheila's handwriting."

Now, it is late 2017. Elise has just learned that copies of the .mp3 of *The Gift* that she recorded back in 2000 have been circulating all over the Internet. The party responsible for this is Joan Simon, a reporter for the San Sendero *Times*, who had worked on the article about *The Gift* back in 2000. Last year, Joan inadvertently forwarded the email containing the .mp3 file of Elise's reading of *The Gift* to her entire personal email contacts list, including friends, family, and even vague acquaintances. The .mp3 was soon after available for free download on websites around the world by the end of 2016.

Elise has also learned that Quentin, one of the few relatives to whom she gave one of the five copies of *The Gift*, executed in 2016 a lucrative agreement to publish *The Gift* in print form. After execution of the publishing agreement, Quentin himself typed the text of his copy of *The Gift* into his word processor, reducing the text of *The Gift* to a Microsoft Word file. Quentin then sent that file to his publisher. At no time did Quentin show his publisher or anyone else the original handwritten copy of *The Gift* from which he created the MS Word file. By March 2017, *The Gift* had been published pursuant to this agreement, and tens of thousands of print copies (featuring text in Times New Roman font) had already been sold.

Elise threatens to sue both Joan and Quentin for violating her exclusive rights of reproduction and public distribution in *The Gift*. Joan and Quentin both reply that they are entitled to distribute *The Gift* freely because the work has already fallen into the public domain. **Your task is to answer only a single question: Is *The Gift* in the public domain and, if so, when did it enter the public domain?** Your answer should thus be limited to issues relevant to the public domain status of *The Gift*; no credit will be given for discussing any extraneous issues.

The Dude Abides

Maude is a highly successful performance artist. In early 2015, she conceived of a new work that would, in her words, "Show how we're all slaves to media garbage. I want to make a video of me, just watching some awful schlock on TV, without food, water, or sleep, until I pass out—or die of disgust." Knowing nothing about how audiovisual technology actually works, Maude invited her friend Brandt (an expert videographer) to her studio apartment to record her performance. She had cleared out all the furniture and left only a hard wooden chair and a big tube television. Brandt asked where Maude wanted the digital video camera to be placed, and she responded, "I don't care. Just put it someplace where they can tell that I'm watching some awful junk on TV, and see how I'm reacting to it."

Brandt placed his camera at an angle behind the television, so that the video captured Maude sitting in the chair, the back of the television, and the audio (though not the video) from the television. Maude had selected the Treehorn Channel as the one she would watch during the performance art piece. The Treehorn Channel shows broadly appealing programming aimed at families and a somewhat politically conservative audience. Brandt asked Maude why she chose the Treehorn Channel, and she said, "I don't recall. All this stuff is so bad it doesn't even matter." Brandt turned on the camera and left, coming back to check on Maude every so often. A couple days after the recording started, he found Maude passed out in her chair with the Treehorn Channel still on.

After she came to, Maude told Brandt that she wanted the exhibition version of the video to feature only the time span between the moment when she started watching the Treehorn Channel and the moment when she passed out, 63 hours later. Brandt edited the video as Maude instructed, except that he added a time counter at the bottom of the screen so that viewers could discern exactly where Maude was at various moments in her TV-watching marathon. He then gave Maude a copy of the video recording in .mp4 format on a flash drive, and deleted all other copies made during the editing process. Maude properly registered the work with the Copyright Office, listing herself as the work's author, in November 2015. Maude then showed the resulting edited version of the original video recording under the title *TeaVee* at the local, public Sobchak County Museum of Art (SCMA) during December 2015. During this exhibition, *TeaVee* played on a constant loop in a theater at SCMA dedicated to art films. Patrons who paid the usual $2.50 general-admission charge to enter SCMA could freely wander into the theater that screened *TeaVee*, as well into any of SCMA's 12 other galleries. Shortly after the exhibition of *TeaVee* began, Treehorn Productions (the production company, known in the industry as "TP," owns all copyrights in all material shown on the Treehorn Channel), approached Maude and SCMA to ask for a licensing fee, since the audio portions of TP's programs were clearly audible throughout all 63 hours of *TeaVee*. Maude replied, "No dice. The stuff you make is garbage and I don't do business with hacks, as anyone who is familiar with my work would know." TP replied that its written policy was to seek only a $350 fee for "artistic, educational, or experimental" uses such as hers, but Maude refused, and TP's lawyers pressed the issue no further.

When the exhibition of *TeaVee* concluded at the end of December 2015, Maude took back her copy of *TeaVee* and put it in a closet. No other copies *TeaVee* (other than the one required by the Copyright Office for registration) existed, and the work was never shown to the public via any medium other than the exhibition at SCMA. Maude always said of all her work, "I don't want any copies of it out there circulating. I show you what I want, when I want, then it's over. If you miss it, too bad." In June 2016, though, Maude donated the contents of her closet to the local Goodwill Shop, inadvertently placing into their hands the flash drive with the sole existing copy of *TeaVee*, which they placed on sale with the rest of the closet's contents. A few months later, a Goodwill Shop customer bought the flash drive with the sole copy of *TeaVee* for $5. Realizing its contents, the shopper then sold the flash drive to the wealthy, privately owned Donny Kerabatsos Art Gallery (DKAG) for $15,000. In January 2017, DKAG began a widely publicized, for-profit exhibition of *TeaVee*. Because *TeaVee* was popular when it appeared at SCMA, and because Maude's work has never before been available after its first exhibition, demand for DKAG's showings of *TeaVee* was high, and by mid-2017, DKAG had made more than $1 million in admission fees.

Two parties objected to DKAG's showing of *TeaVee*. First, Jeff (Maude's self-appointed "biggest fan," who devotes all of his free time to studying her and her work) was deeply upset that DKAG would undermine Maude's desire not to have her work shown after its initial exhibition. Jeff notified Maude about this, and she responded (in a physical note written in purple lipstick), "Don't be fatuous, Jeffrey. First, I have oodles of money and don't need to squeeze any from the DKAG. Second, I honestly don't care that much. Third, it's beneath my dignity to litigate over art. But if you want to avenge my honor over this *TeaVee* fiasco, then I hereby entitle you—and you alone!—to do whatever you need to sue those nihilists for showing my art, whether by flogging them in court or just by punching one of those DKAG jerks in the nose. All love to you, Maudie." In October 2017, Jeff filed suit in the U.S. District Court for the District of Sobchak, alleging infringement of the copyright in *TeaVee*, and seeking only that the Court enjoin DKAG from any future public display of the audiovisual work.

Second, TP, despite its decision not to make an issue over the first exhibition of *TeaVee*, thought differently when it learned that DKAG had been making so much money for its more recent exhibition of the video. In November 2017, TP also filed suit in the U.S. District Court for the District of Sobchak, seeking both monetary and injunctive relief for DKAG's alleged violations of the copyrights in those of TP's audiovisual works that were featured in *TeaVee*.

Will Jeff and TP prevail in their respective copyright lawsuits against DKAG? Assume that all these events are governed by U.S. copyright law, and limit your answer to theories of recovery based on Title 17 of the U.S. Code.

Answers

Requirements for Copyright Protection

1.   **(A) is the correct answer.** The musical composition is not protected by a federal copyright because it lacks fixation. Federal copyright protection automatically attaches to a work once, and only if, it is "'fixed' in a tangible medium of expression . . . by or under the authority of the author. . . ." 17 U.S.C. § 101; *Community for Creative Non-Violence v. Reid*, 490 U.S. 730, 737 (1989). Since January 1, 1978, when the current federal copyright law came into effect, state law can protect only those original works of authorship that are *not* fixed in any tangible medium of expression. *See e.g.* Cal. Civ. Code § 980(a)(1).

The fact that Musician has sung the musical composition often and that a large number of her friends have heard this performance of the musical composition does not constitute fixation. A performance is not tangible. Not until Musician permits the composition to be placed in a tangible form will it be sufficiently fixed to meet the prerequisite for federal copyright protection. Until that time, the musical composition may only be protected by state common-law copyright.

(B) is incorrect because registration with the Copyright Office is not a prerequisite for federal copyright protection.

(C) and (D) are incorrect for the reasons given above.

2.   **(B) is the correct answer.** The musical composition is fixed in the tangible medium of the digital recording Musician has made. The digital recording is a phonorecord because it is an object containing sounds other than those accompanying an audiovisual work that can be perceived with the aid of a machine or device. *See* 17 U.S.C. § 101 (defining "phonorecord" to refer to fixations of sound recordings). The prerequisites of federal copyright have been met and federal copyright protection attaches immediately.

(A) is incorrect because the digital recording is not a copy for the reason explained above. If the musical composition had been fixed on a video recording depicting Musician as she performed the musical composition, the composition would have been fixed in a copy.

(C) is incorrect because, after 1977, copyright notice is no longer a prerequisite to the vesting of federal copyright. Prior to 1978, a work was invested with federal copyright protection when it was published with proper copyright notice, or when it was registered with the United States Copyright Office. Prior to publication, the work was protected by state common-law copyright. *See Goldstein v. California*, 412 U.S. 546, 562 (1973); *Capitol Records, Inc. v. Naxos of America, Inc.*, 372 F.3d 471, 477–78 (2d Cir. 2004).

(D) is incorrect because a work is sufficiently fixed if it can be "perceived, reproduced, or otherwise communicated, either directly or with the aid of a machine." 17 U.S.C. § 101. The human perceptibility doctrine enunciated in *White-Smith Music Pub. Co. v. Apollo Co.*, 209 U.S. 1 (1908), was thus overruled by statute and this will not prohibit copyright protection to a work fixed in a digital medium.

3.   **(C) is the correct answer.** At the moment the poem was fixed on the notebook page, it automatically received federal copyright protection. The destruction of the only copy of the poem creates problems in proving infringement or depositing a copy of the work with the Copyright Office, but these difficulties do not negate the federal copyright protection accorded the work from the date of its creation in a tangible form. *See Peter Pan Fabrics, Inc. v. Rosstex Fabrics, Inc.*, 733 F. Supp. 174, 177 (S.D.N.Y. 1990) (once work is fixed, its subsequent destruction does not vitiate its copyright).

(B) is incorrect for the reason just given.

(A) and (D) are incorrect because the aesthetic quality of a work has no bearing on its protection by copyright. *Bleistein v. Donaldson Lithographing Co.*, 188 U.S. 239, 250 (1903); *Campbell v. Acuff-Rose Music, Inc.*, 510 U.S. 569, 582–83 (1994).

4.   Songwriter's musical composition is likely unprotected under federal copyright law because the musical composition does not meet the fixation requirements of the Copyright Act. To be fixed, a work may be placed in a tangible medium by someone other than the author, but only with the author's authorization. Here, Songwriter did not give his authorization for Audience Member's recording of the musical composition, and federal copyright thus did not vest.

Regardless of the lack of fixation, however, Songwriter is protected by 17 U.S.C. § 1101. Section 1101 was enacted by Congress as part of the Uruguay Round Agreements Act that implemented the obligations of the United States under the Uruguay Round Agreement of GATT, the General Agreement on Tariffs and Trade. Section 1101 prohibits the unauthorized fixation of the sounds of a live musical performance, as well as its unauthorized reproduction, transmission, or distribution. This section protects the performance of a work that may not have been fixed within the definition of copyright law. It protects a live performance, rather than a work of authorship. And it provides this protection to a person, the performer, who may not be the author or copyright owner of the work being performed. *See Kiss Catalog v. Passport Int'l Prods.*, 405 F. Supp. 2d 1169 (C.D. Cal. 2005); *United States v. Martignon*, 492 F.3d 140 (2d Cir. 2007) (applying the federal anti-bootlegging statute and finding it validly enacted under commerce clause). The sale of unauthorized recordings of live performances may also be the subject of state criminal laws.

5.   **(D) is the correct answer.** The comedy routine is protected by California's state common-law copyright because it is original expression that has not been fixed. A comedy routine that is 10 minutes in length will undoubtedly include protectable expression. Cal. Civ. Code § 980(a)(1).

(A) and (B) are incorrect because the comedy routine cannot be protected by federal copyright law due to the lack of fixation.

(C) is incorrect because a performance is not protected by copyright; only the work being performed may be protected.

6.   **(A) is the correct answer.** Copyright acknowledges the possibility of independent creation, which is the notion that two authors could independently create the same work. *See Feist Publications, Inc. v. Rural Tel. Serv. Co., Inc.*, 499 U.S. 340, 345–46 (1991); *Grubb v. KMS Patriots, L.P.*, 88 F.3d 1, 3 (1st Cir. 1996); *Alfred Bell & Co. v. Catalda Fine Arts, Inc.*, 191 F.2d 99, 103 (2d Cir. 1951). "[I]f by some magic a man who had never known it were to compose anew Keats' 'Ode on a Grecian Urn,' he would be an 'author,' and, if he copyrighted it, others might not copy that poem, though they might of course copy Keats." *See also, e.g., Sheldon v. Metro-Goldwyn Pictures Corp.*, 81 F.2d 49, 54 (2d Cir. 1936); *Bryant v. Gordon*, 483 F. Supp. 2d 605, 616 (N.D. Ill. 2007) (independently produced photograph entitled to copyright protection despite its identical nature to prior work).

Of course, given the low probability that a later author actually could create the exact same work as that of an earlier author purely by coincidence, courts typically find strong similarities between two works highly probative of actual copying. *See Susan Wakeen Doll Co., Inc. v. Ashton-Drake Galleries*, 272 F.3d 441, 450 (7th Cir. 2001) ("The more a work is both like an already copyrighted work and . . . unlike anything that is in the public domain, the less likely it is to be an independent creation."); *Acuff-Rose Music, Inc. v. Josten's, Inc.*, 155 F.3d 140, 144 (2d Cir. 1998) (given the widespread usage of the phrase "You've got to stand for something," court held it exceedingly unlikely that composer had independently created the phrase).

Here, though, because the question stipulates that each of the novelists created fixed original expression, each owns a copyright in their separate work.

(B) is incorrect because copyright protection is based on the existence of fixed original expression, not on whether the work is new to the world, which is a patent law concept. *See Alfred Bell & Co. v. Catalda Fine Arts, Inc.*, 191 F.2d 99, 102 (2d Cir. 1951).

(C) is incorrect because copyright protection is vested due to the existence of fixed original expression, not on the date of publication, which could invest federal copyright protection in a work prior to 1978.

(D) is incorrect because copyright protection is vested due to the existence of fixed original expression, not on registration with the Copyright Office, which did vest federal copyright protection in a work prior to 1978.

7.   **(B) is the correct answer.** Copyright does not protect common geometric shapes. *See Bailie v. Fisher*, 258 F.2d 425 (D.C. Cir. 1958); *Atari Games Corp. v. Oman*, 888 F.2d 878 (D.C. Cir. 1989); 37 C.F.R. § 202.1 ("familiar symbols or designs" and "mere variations of typographical ornamentation, lettering or coloring" are not subject to copyright protection). Here, the work consists simply of a common shape with another common shape cut out of it.

This mere juxtaposition of two common shapes does not rise to the level of original copyrightable expression.

(A) is incorrect for the reason stated above, and because the square was cut out after the star was created, making the usefulness of the square separate from the overall shape of the star under the physical separability test. *See Mazer v. Stein*, 347 U.S. 201, 218 (1954).

(C) is incorrect for the reason stated above, and because the material used in creating a work may dictate the level of creativity of the work.

(D) is incorrect for the reason stated above.

8.   (C) is the correct answer. Videographer was not responsible for the situation she was filming, so she did not create any of the elements in front of the lens such as costuming, expression and lighting, which were the creative elements in a photograph recognized by the United States Supreme Court in *Burrow-Giles Lithographic Co. v. Sarony*, 111 U.S. 53 (1884). She had minimal control of the elements behind the lens such as aperture, selection of film medium, focus, audio and other automatic operations of the camera, which were the creative elements recognized in *Time, Inc. v. Bernard Geis Associates*, 293 F. Supp. 130 (S.D.N.Y. 1968). Videographer did select the cell phone and decided what to film and where to film it, as well as when to start and end the filming. However, a good argument could be made that these elements of originality are minimally creative in nature.

(A) is incorrect because no matter how artistically lacking a work may be, it is protectable by copyright. *See Bleistein v. Donaldson Lithographing Co.*, 188 U.S. 239, 250 (1903); *Campbell v. Acuff-Rose Music, Inc.*, 510 U.S. 569, 582–83 (1994).

(B) is incorrect because there is no required length for an audiovisual work to be protected by copyright, so long as there is more than one image and the images are related.

(D) is incorrect because making a copyrighted work available to the public does not dedicate the work to the public domain. Such an action by Videographer may be seen as an implied nonexclusive license to download the audiovisual work or possibly also to use it in other ways, but such action does not demonstrate an intent to abandon the copyright entirely in the audiovisual work. *See Micro Star v. Formgen, Inc.*, 154 F.3d 1107, 1114 (9th Cir. 1998).

9.   (D) is the correct answer. Copyright law does not preclude others from using the ideas revealed by the author's work. *See Nash v. CBS, Inc.*, 899 F.2d 1537, 1542 (7th Cir. 1990).

(A) is incorrect. Although it is true that "no plagiarist can excuse the wrong by showing how much of his work he did not pirate," *Sheldon v. Metro-Goldwyn Pictures Corp.*, 81 F.3d 49, 56 (2d Cir. 1936), this rule applies only to expression, not ideas.

(B) is incorrect because ideas are unprotected by copyright regardless of their novelty. The novelty of an idea may be relevant in some jurisdictions to the issue of whether the disclosure of the idea is deemed sufficient consideration for an implied-in-fact contract.

(C) is incorrect because a difference in medium, a questionable proposition in this case, is not a defense to copyright infringement. *See Walt Disney Prods. v. Filmation Assocs.*, 628 F. Supp. 871 (C.D. Cal. 1986) (copying of motion picture character onto storyboards constituted infringement).

10. No. Under the blank form doctrine resulting from the United States Supreme Court decision in *Baker v. Selden*, 101 U.S. 99, 107 (1879), forms that convey no information and serve only to provide blank space for recording information may not be protected by copyright. Therefore, the graph paper cannot be protected by copyright. *See Advanz Behavioral Mgmt. Resources, Inc. v. Miraflor*, 21 F. Supp. 2d 1179, 1189–91 (C.D. Cal. 1998). Further, as a cooperating part of a machine, the graph paper may not be protected by copyright. *See Brown Instrument Co. v. Warner*, 161 F.2d 910, 911 (D.C. Cir. 1947) (chart acting as a cooperating part of temperature monitoring machine held not copyrightable).

11. This scenario takes place prior to 1978. Therefore, the painting was initially protected by state common-law copyright at the time of its creation. By offering the painting for sale, Artist published the work, causing it to lose its common-law protection immediately. Federal copyright protection would have attached to the painting if Artist had written a copyright notice on the painting, front or back, that contained the term "copyright," Artist's name, and the year of publication. Another alternative would have been for Artist to apply to register the copyright in the painting with the Copyright Office. Such registration would have divested the common-law copyright in the work at the same time it invested the work with federal copyright protection. *See Goldstein v. California*, 412 U.S. 546, 562 (1973); *Capitol Records, Inc. v. Naxos of America, Inc.*, 372 F.3d 471, 477–78 (2d Cir. 2004); *Palmer v. DeWitt*, 47 N.Y. 532, 536–37 (1872).

12. **(D) is the correct answer.** The determination of whether the object in which a work is fixed is a copy or a phonorecord is dependent on what type of work is fixed. Phonorecords are material objects in which sounds, other than those accompanying an audiovisual work, are fixed and from which the sounds can be perceived, reproduced, or otherwise communicated, either directly or with the aid of a machine or device. 17 U.S.C. § 101; *see ABKCO Music, Inc. v. Stellar Records, Inc.*, 96 F.3d 60 (2d Cir. 1996) (karaoke CD-ROM on which sounds and visual representations of lyrics were fixed was a copy, not a phonorecord). Copies are material objects, other than phonorecords, in which a work is fixed and from which the work can be perceived, reproduced, or otherwise communicated, either directly or with the aid of a machine. 17 U.S.C. § 101; *see Midway Mfg. Co. v. Arctic Int'l, Inc.*, 547 F. Supp. 999 (N.D. Ill.), *aff'd*, 704 F.2d 1009 (7th Cir. 1982).

If the work is a sound recording, and it does not accompany an audiovisual work, it is fixed in a phonorecord. For example, a sound recording fixed in an audio CD is fixed in a phonorecord. If a sound recording has been fixed in a DVD as part of the soundtrack of a motion picture that is also fixed on that DVD, the sound recording is fixed in a copy. But if a sound recording alone is fixed on a DVD, then the sound recording is fixed in a phonorecord.

(A) and (B) are incorrect because it is not known what work is fixed.

(C) is incorrect because fixation offers only a binary choice. A work must be fixed in either a copy or a phonorecord.

13.   Sarah's detailed plans for the literary work seem to constitute sufficient original expression for federal copyright. The difficulty here is that Sarah did not fix her proposed literary work in a tangible medium of expression prior to her death. Although Fred has placed Sarah's expression into a tangible medium of expression, it was without Sarah's authorization. Therefore, Sarah's literary work is not fixed and is without federal copyright protection. 17 U.S.C. § 102(b). Sarah's mother would therefore not be able to pursue a copyright infringement suit against Fred for his writing and publication of the book.

However, Sarah's mother may be able to lay claim to Sarah's unfixed work to the extent that it is protected by state common-law copyright and can be devised by will. While federal copyright law does not protect unfixed works, state law may protect such works. *E.g.,* Cal. Civ. Code § 980(a)(1). *See also* Paul S. Bilker, *The Showdown Continues at the Circle C Ranch: Non-Preemption of State Copyright Protection for Unfixed Improvisational Works*, 18 Sw. U. L. Rev. 415, 436–39 (1989).

14.   **(C) is the correct answer.** Every image that can be seen on the plasma screen can be obtained from one of the computers used in the installation. The fact that the images are reproduced from different sources does not mean the individual images or the combination of images appearing on the screen are not fixed. *See Midway Mfg. Co. v. Arctic Int'l, Inc.,* 547 F. Supp. 999 (N.D. Ill.), *aff'd,* 704 F.2d 1009 (7th Cir. 1982) (audiovisual work component of video game properly fixed in several ROM chips).

(A) is incorrect because it is necessary only that the work be capable of being perceived or reproduced. There is no limitation on the number of sources needed to reproduce the work.

(B) is incorrect because the display of an audiovisual or pictorial work to the public does not cause the work to lose its copyright protection.

(D) is incorrect because the mere fact that a work is contained in a tangible medium of expression does not constitute fixation unless the author has placed them in the tangible medium herself, or has authorized that action.

15.   **(B) is the correct answer.** A live performance is fixed if it is recorded at the same time it is being transmitted. 17 U.S.C. § 101 (definition of "fixed"). *See National Football League v. McBee & Bruno's, Inc.,* 792 F.2d 726 (8th Cir. 1986) (live broadcast of football game was fixed because it was videotaped at the same time it was transmitted to viewers). Here, because Television Station did not simultaneously record its broadcast, it is unfixed and thus there was no federal copyright in it for Bar Owner to violate.

(A) is incorrect. It is very likely that the director's location of the cameras and the selection of which camera feed to include in the broadcast has sufficient originality for federal copyright protection. *See Los Angeles News Serv. v. Tullo*, 973 F.2d 791, 794 (9th Cir. 1992) (originality of videotape taken from a helicopter was found in "the choices of the heights and directions from which to tape"); *Baltimore Orioles, Inc. v. Major League Baseball Players Ass'n*, 805 F.2d 663 (7th Cir. 1986). However, regardless of the broadcast's originality, it will not be protected by federal copyright because it was not validly fixed.

(C) is incorrect because the location of the cameras and the selection of which camera feed to include in the broadcast provide sufficient originality for federal copyright protection, regardless of whether the broadcast contains statements of an announcer. Again, however, regardless of the broadcast's originality, it will not be protected by federal copyright because it was not validly fixed.

(D) is incorrect. Bar Owner will be liable for unauthorized reproduction if the broadcast is protected by federal copyright. The size of the bar is relevant to the question of whether a public performance license is required, see 17 U.S.C. § 110(5)(B), but has nothing to do with the primary infringement here.

16.   Probably. This situation initially concerns whether Professor's email messages are "sufficiently permanent or stable to permit [them] to be perceived, reproduced, or otherwise communicated for a period of more than transitory duration" to be within the section 101 definition of "fixed." There are at least four mediums in which Professor's email messages may have been fixed: the RAM (Random Access Memory) of Professor's computer; the RAM of Law Student's computer; the computer disk on which Law Student saved her questions and Professor's responses; and the printed copies sold by Law Student. Professor placed his messages in the first two of these mediums. Therefore, the first question is whether placing an email message in RAM is a sufficiently permanent embodiment of the Professor's messages.

The case law in this area indicates that capturing such messages in a computer's RAM satisfies the fixation requirement. These decisions have found that the booting up of a computer program into a computer's RAM creates a fixed copy of that program. The Copyright Act does not define what is meant by the phrase "for a period of more than transitory duration" used in the definition of fixation. These decisions also failed to provide a bright line rule, but found that information loaded into RAM may be contained in the RAM for extended periods of time. *See MAI Sys. Corp. v. Peak Computer, Inc.*, 991 F.2d 511 (9th Cir. 1993); *Ticketmaster v. RMG Technologies, Inc.*, 507 F. Supp. 2d 1096 (C.D. Cal. 2007) (RAM capture of website constitutes a copy of the website); *Advanced Computer Servs. of Mich. v. MAI Sys., Corp.*, 845 F. Supp. 356 (E.D. Va. 1994); Ira Brandriss, *Writing in Frost on a Window Pane: E-Mail and Chatting on Ram and Copyright Fixation*, 43 J. COPYRIGHT SOC'Y U.S.A. 237 (1996).

As for the third and fourth mediums in which the messages were embodied, Law Student's computer disk and the printed copies of the messages, Professor did not bring about the embodiment of his messages in those forms. Because someone else caused the embodiments other than the author and without his authorization, they did not result in fixation for copyright purposes. *See* 17 U.S.C. § 101 (defining "fixed" only to include fixations by or under the authority of the author).

17. **(A) is the correct answer.** The transposition of a musical composition from one key to another, where it is done with a formula with mathematical certainty, is accomplished with no variation or creativity. Under such circumstances there is insufficient originality for copyright protection. *See Jarvis v. A & M Records*, 827 F. Supp. 282, 291 (D.N.J. 1993) (easily arrived-at phrases and chord progressions are usually noncopyrightable).

(B) is incorrect because a change in the music of a musical composition may be sufficient for the creation of a derivative work, for example a new arrangement, even though no change has been made in the lyrics of the musical composition.

(C) is incorrect because even though the notes are different, they are in the same relationship to one another in the key of A as they were in the key of C. There is no creativity where the change in notes is done with mathematical certainty for the purpose of merely changing the key of the musical composition.

(D) is incorrect. Although the statement itself is true, it does not follow that every musical change made by a trained musician is necessarily sufficiently original to be protected by copyright. Mechanical transformations such as derivative works resulting from a simple molding process or obvious translations of a limited nature are not protected by copyright. *See Tempo Music, Inc. v. Famous Music Corp.*, 838 F. Supp. 162 (S.D.N.Y. 1994) (harmony that is a mechanical by-product of melody is not protected by copyright).

18. **(B) is the correct answer.** Verso will prevail not only because *Leaves of Autumn* is creative on its own terms, but also because that creativity originated with Verso. The originality requirement is satisfied if two tests are met: independent creation and a modicum of creativity. Proving that the work is the result of independent creation and, therefore, original, is required to meet the burden of proving copyright validity. *See Reader's Digest Ass'n v. Conservative Digest, Inc.*, 821 F.2d 800, 806 (D.C. Cir. 1987) ("Originality" means "only that the work owes its origin to the author—*i.e.*, that the work is independently created rather than copied from other works."). However, the concept of independent creation also recognizes the possibility that the defendant did not copy the plaintiff's work, but created the defendant's work independently. If that can be proven, the defendant will not be held liable for copyright infringement. *See Selle v. Gibb*, 741 F.2d 896 (7th Cir. 1984) (defendants' tape recording of the creative process by which defendants' musical work was composed constituted defense to infringement claim); *Murray Hill Publications, Inc. v. Twentieth Century Fox Film Corp.*, 361 F.3d 312, 326 (6th Cir. 2004) (elements of a defendant's work that were created prior to access to plaintiff's work found not to infringe); *Sturdza v. United Arab Emirates*, 281 F.3d 1287, 1297 (D.C. Cir. 2002) (elements present in submission by other architect before defendant had access to plaintiff's drawings excluded from liability).

(A) is incorrect. As indicated above, the plaintiff in every copyright infringement lawsuit must prove that the work at issue has a valid copyright. As part of that requirement, the plaintiff must prove that its work contains at least a modicum of creativity. However, evidence of creativity is insufficient to prove originality without additional evidence that the haiku was independently created by Verso.

(C) is incorrect. As indicated above, copyright law accepts the possibility that a person can create a work that is identical to a preexisting work without having copied that preexisting work. The fact that the second work is identical to the first does not preclude copyright protection for the second work. Verso's haiku is not denied copyright protection merely because it is identical to the previously created haiku.

(D) is incorrect. As a practical matter, proof that a defendant copied one source of a work, rather than another source, may be difficult to establish, though proof of access will likely decide that issue. In this case, the facts clearly indicate that Poetaster copied Verso's work. There are no facts that indicate Poetaster had access to, or even knew about, Quarto's *Rainbow Autumn* until after the copyright infringement suit was filed.

19. Ideas cannot be protected by copyright. *See* 17 U.S.C. § 102(b); *Baker v. Selden*, 101 U.S. 99 (1879); *Curtin v. Star Editorial Inc.*, 2 F. Supp. 2d 670, 674 (E.D. Pa. 1998) (plaintiff could not claim copyright protection for his "idea" to display photographs of Elvis Presley with celebrities); *Berkic v. Crichton*, 761 F.2d 1289, 1293 (9th Cir. 1985) (basic story ideas are not protectable by copyright, no matter how novel or distinctive). However, other legal theories are available to protect an idea itself or the use of an idea.

Trade secret law can protect an idea that has commercial value if reasonable steps have been taken to keep it secret. Under trade secret law, a formula, such as the formula for Coca-Cola®, may be protected. Some ideas, such as the title of a motion picture, novel or musical work, may be protected as a trademark.

Patent law may protect the application of an idea to an invention, if the invention meets the statutory requirements of utility, novelty and nonobviousness. The disclosure of ideas may be protected by contract, either express or implied by conduct. When a television writer pitches an idea for a television series to production company executive, an implied-in-fact contract may be created, for which the disclosure of the idea by the writer is deemed the writer's consideration for the contract and the executive's implied agreement to pay a reasonable fee for the use of the disclosed idea by the production company constitutes the consideration by the company.

20. **(A) is the correct answer.** In the majority of jurisdictions, an infringement of the adaptation right can occur only if the defendant has created a work that constitutes an unauthorized derivative work that contains sufficiently original new elements. The translation of a lengthy novel from French into English is a creative endeavor that is protected by copyright as a derivative work, separate from the copyright protecting the underlying French novel. The elements of creativity involved in the translation of the French novel into English by Publisher are not merely mechanical. Such a translation involves numerous choices of words to translate the novel, selecting proper grammar and phrasing, and rendering French slang terms and idioms into understandable English terms. Had the underlying French work been more limited, such as a list of 10 words needed to order in a restaurant, the

English word choices would be fewer. Such a mechanical translation would not be protected by copyright. *See Grove Press, Inc. v. Greenleaf Publishing Co.*, 247 F. Supp. 518 (E.D.N.Y. 1965).

(B) is incorrect. Although the statement in answer (B) is correct, it is not relevant to Translator's lawsuit. French Novelist retained the exclusive right of reproduction, and Publisher reached a settlement with him. Translator does not own the reproduction right in Novelist's work, nor has Translator created a derivative work that has its own reproduction right.

(C) is incorrect for reasons explained in the answer to the correct answer above.

(D) is incorrect. Translator owns the exclusive right to create an English translation of the French novel. This right is not dependent on whether Translator has yet to exercise that right.

21.　Yes. The interview tape is an object in which two copyrighted works are fixed: (1) the words spoken by Police Detective and Writer during the interview may be protected as a literary work; and (2) the recording of the sounds made during the interview may be protected as a sound recording. Writer no longer owns the copyright in the literary work fixed in the interview tape because she has assigned that copyright to Publisher. However, the assignment of print publishing rights to Publisher did not include any of the rights to the sound recording, which cannot be reproduced in print. Writer will have to prove that the sound recording at issue meets the originality requirement. The original elements of the sound recording are not the words uttered by Police Detective and Writer, they are the decisions made that allowed the sounds to be recorded in a particular way. These include the decisions as to what recorder to use, the type of recording tape, the positioning of the microphone, the determination of who and when to record, and the operation of the volume control. The creative decisions made by Writer during the sound recording of the interview with Police Detective are sufficiently original to merit copyright protection. Although the scope of protection afforded sound recordings under the 1976 Copyright Act are more limited than other categories of works, requiring proof of duplication and not mere substantial similarity, Audio Company has duplicated the Writer's sound recording verbatim. Writer has a successful cause of action against Audio Company.

22.　Because the analog sound recording was first fixed prior to 1972, it is not protected by federal copyright law, but may be protected under state common-law copyright or other state law theories, such as unfair competition. *See Capitol Records, Inc. v. Naxos of Am., Inc.*, 372 F.3d 471, 477 (2d Cir. 2004) (sound recordings fixed before February 15, 1972, are neither protected nor preempted by federal copyright law, until federal preemption occurs on February 15, 2067); *Daboub v. Gibbons*, 42 F.3d 285, 288 (5th Cir. 1995). The question is whether Record Company could successfully sue Website for *federal* copyright infringement. To do so, Record Company would have to prove that it owns a federal copyright in the digital version of the *Megaron* sound recording—that is, the digital reissue of the original analog recording. The digital reissue has clearly been fixed in a tangible medium by Record Company.

However, Record Company can successfully sue for federal copyright infringement of its recent digital reissue only if it is sufficiently original. If the creation of the digital reissue had simply been a conversion process utilizing the computerized mastering machine without creative human intervention, the digital reissue would lack sufficient originality for copyright protection. If such were the case, the digital recording would be no more original than the duplication of the 1965 analog recording onto an analog cassette tape. It is also clear that if Record Company's employee had digitally "remastered" the original analog recording by changing the volume, tone and acoustics of each of the instruments on each of the recording tracks, the resulting digital recording would be sufficiently creative for copyright protection.

In most jurisdictions, Record Company will have to prove that the digital reissue of the *Megaron* sound recording constitutes more than a mere trivial variation of the 1965 analog sound recording. In this case, the employee engaged in more than a mere mechanical transfer of the analog recording to the digital recording. He listened to the recording and made a creative decision to only change the levels of the bass guitar and snare drum. Record Company will argue that such a change is sufficiently creative and that the employee's decision not to change the sound of the other instruments also constituted creative input. Pirate.com will argue that such decisions are less than minimal and lack sufficient creativity, resulting in a digitized sound recording that is almost identical to the original analog sound recording of *Megaron*. Pirate.com will also question the policy of extending copyright protection to unprotected subject matter through digitization. Website has clearly reproduced the digital reissue without authorization and would be found liable for federal copyright infringement if a court finds the digital reissue protected as a derivative work.

23. **(B) is the correct answer.** Titles of books are not protected by copyright, because they are not sufficiently original for copyright protection or are deemed to constitute mere ideas. Although a well-known book title may be protected as a trademark, it cannot be protected by copyright. *See, e.g., Shaw v. Lindheim*, 919 F.2d 1353, 1362 (9th Cir. 1990) (title of "The Equalizer" television series not protected by copyright); *Trenton v. Infinity Broadcasting Corp.*, 865 F. Supp. 1416, 1426 (C.D. Cal. 1994) (title of "Loveline" radio program not protected by copyright); *Morgan Creek Prods Inc. v. Capital Cities/ABC Inc.*, 22 U.S.P.Q.2d 1881, 1883 (C.D. Cal. 1991) (title of film "Young Guns" cannot be protected by copyright); *Perma Greetings, Inc. v. Russ Berrie & Co., Inc.*, 598 F. Supp. 445, 448 (E.D. Mo. 1984) ("Clichéd language, phrases and expressions conveying an idea that is typically expressed in a limited number of stereotypic fashions, are not subject to copyright protection."). *But see Universal City Studios, Inc. v. Kamar Industries, Inc.*, 217 U.S.P.Q. 1162, 1166 (S.D. Tex. 1982) ("I Love You, E.T." and "E.T. Phone Home" protected by copyright).

(A) is incorrect. Composer's concern was for the similarity in the titles, not the contents of the works.

(C) is incorrect. The identical nature of the titles is not relevant for the reasons stated above.

(D) is incorrect. The fact that the title was first used in connection with the book has no bearing on a possible copyright infringement action for the reasons stated above.

24.   **(A) is the correct answer.** Individual recipes comprising lists of required ingredients and directions for combining them to achieve final products, without expressive elaboration, constitute a "procedure" and are not entitled to copyright protection. 17 U.S.C. § 102(b). There can be a monopoly neither in the ideas for producing foodstuffs nor in the method of preparing and combining the necessary ingredients. *See Publications Int'l, Ltd. v. Meredith Corp.*, 88 F.3d 473, 480–81 (7th Cir. 1996).

(B) is incorrect. The useful article exception to copyright protection only applies to pictorial, graphic or sculptural works, not literary works. In addition, something that merely conveys information is not deemed a useful article. *See* 17 U.S.C. § 101 (defining "useful article"); *Pivot Point Int'l, Inc. v. Charlene Prods., Inc.*, 372 F.3d 913, 919 (7th Cir. 2004).

(C) is incorrect. Copyright infringement is not based on a comparison of final products, but on the similarity of protected expression. Beet dishes are not copyrightable subject matter.

(D) is incorrect. Although the recipes may be substantially similar, they are not protected by copyright for the reasons stated above.

25.   Depending on the jurisdiction in which the case is brought, the Owner of *Space Station* may be successful for part of its claim of infringement. Owner will argue that *Space Station* is protected by copyright as an audiovisual work. As such, the sequence of images on the screen is protected. The number and sequence of the game elements presented in the video game, regardless of the exact image used, are protected expression, not merely ideas. The possible variety of game elements in such a game are unlimited, therefore, the merger doctrine would not apply. However, even if the merger doctrine were found to be applicable, the majority rule grants copyright protection to one of a limited number of expressions against the type of identical copying engaged in by Manufacturer. And recent authority has suggested that courts may find substantial similarity plausible where, as here, a second video game takes the basic scheme of a preexisting video game — even a relatively simple one — and copies it verbatim save for graphics, icons, and avatars. *See Spry Fox LLC v. LOLapps, Inc.*, 2012 WL 5290158 (W.D. Wash. Sept. 18, 2012) (denying motion to dismiss copyright infringement action against defendant who copied essential scheme of casual video game while changing its graphical context and avatars).

Irrespective of infringement of the audiovisual elements of Space Station, the majority rule, stated in *Herbert Rosenthal Jewelry Corp. v. Kalpakian*, 446 F.2d 738, 742 (9th Cir. 1971) (jeweled bee deemed limited expression, but deserving limited copyright protection), would also protect the expression of the *Space Station* game rules, which are almost identical to the rules stated in *Hangar*.

Manufacturer will argue that games cannot be protected by copyright, because only images and other independently protected expression associated with the game are protectable. Therefore, the number and sequence of the game elements presented in the video game are integral to the game itself and constitute an unprotected system or process under section 102(b) of the Copyright Act. It is especially true in this case where the images on the screen are so completely different. In addition, the number and sequence of game elements available for use in such a video game are limited. Therefore, under the minority view of *Morrissey v. Procter & Gamble Co.*, 379 F.2d 675 (1st Cir. 1967) (copyright will not protect any of the limited number of expressions), they merge with the idea of obstacles presented on a video game screen and remain unprotected by copyright. And courts have recently stressed that copying just a few basic elements of a game does not amount to copyright infringement. *See DaVinci Editrice S.R.L. v. ZiKo Games, LLC*, 183 F. Supp. 3d 820 (S.D. Tex. 2016) (concluding that defendant's video game did not infringe plaintiff's video game even though it had several similar features, such as set of abilities and number of life points).

The same is true for the simple game rules that appear on the screen in *Space Station*. As a general principle, the rules by which games are played are not copyrightable, though their expression may be. Particularly here, where the game rules are so basic, the merger doctrine may limit or bar copyright protection. Even if the game rules are deemed to be expression, the limited number of forms of expressing the rules causes the expression to be merged with the idea of the rules themselves. This is true under the minority view that would deny all copyright protection. It is also true under the majority view that would grant copyright protection only against verbatim or near-verbatim copying. As can be seen from a comparison of the two statements of game rules, the rules for *Hangar* are not identical, nor nearly identical, to the rules for *Space Station*.

26. **(D) is the correct answer.** Where the subject matter of the copyright is a depiction of an object that appears in nature, the scope of copyright protection is limited. To prove copyright infringement, the owner of the copyright must prove that the defendant's work is a verbatim or near-verbatim copy of the plaintiff's work. In this case, Hunter is only able to show that Competitor's decoys are substantially similar. *See Streeter v. Rolfe*, 491 F. Supp. 416 (W.D. La. 1980); *Satava v. Lowry*, 323 F.3d 805, 812–13 (9th Cir. 2003) (realistic depictions of live animals were "first expressed by nature, are the common heritage of humankind, and no artist may use copyright law to prevent others from depicting them"); *Franklin Mint Corp. v. National Wildlife Art Exchange, Inc.*, 575 F.2d 62 (3d Cir. 1978) (paintings of cardinals). *But see Mattel, Inc. v. Goldberger Doll Mfg. Co.*, 365 F.3d 133, 135–36 (2d Cir. 2004) ("There are innumerable ways of making upturned noses, bow lips, and widely spaced eyes [for dolls]."); *Hamil Am., Inc. v. GFI*, 193 F.3d 92, 100–01 (2d Cir. 1999) (where the plaintiff's work is a stylized floral pattern, mere substantial similarity need be shown).

(A) is incorrect. It is true that sculptural works are copyrightable subject matter, but the protection is limited because the accurate depiction of a turkey limits the possible number of means of expression.

(B) is incorrect. Substantial similarity is the traditional infringement test used in connection with the reproduction right. However, the more demanding test of verbatim or near-verbatim copying is employed where natural objects are the subject of the reproduction.

(C) is incorrect. The statement is true, but Hunter is not complaining of Competitor copying a natural turkey. Hunter is claiming that Competitor has copied Hunter's decoy, which is protected by copyright.

27.   **(A) is correct.** Copyright law does not preclude others from using the ideas revealed by the author's work. *See Nash v. CBS, Inc.*, 899 F.2d 1537, 1542 (7th Cir. 1990). And even if Studio borrowed its basic premise from Novelist's work, those ideas operate at too high a level of generality to support an infringement cause of action. At most, *The Collapsible Tower* and *All Fall Down* share only the general notion of a building being built out of material that collapses, creating disaster. This is not particularized enough expression to be copyrightable.

        (B) is incorrect. So long as the resulting use is substantially similar to the copyrightable elements in the plaintiff's work, the medium used by the defendant is not a bar to liability. In addition, defendant Studio in this case did not reproduce any of the protectable elements contained in plaintiff's novel.

        (C) is incorrect. As indicated above, ideas can freely be taken from a work that has been disclosed to the public.

        (D) is incorrect. Although it is presumed that Studio had access to the novel, it was free to use any of the ideas contained in the novel.

28.   **(B) is the correct answer.** When a person uses a work protected by copyright in a manner commensurate with the manner the copyright owner intended the work to be used, an implied license will be recognized as a complete defense to a claim of copyright infringement. In this case, the intended purpose for a collection of legal forms is to provide templates to assist in the drafting of legal agreements, including the reproduction of the language published in the collection. If a person were to reproduce the entire collection of forms published as the *Entertainment Law Form Book* and market them under a different title, such use would constitute infringement because it was not the intent of the copyright owner to permit the copying of the forms *en masse*.

        (A) is incorrect. Although there was no express authorization by Publisher to allow Young Attorney to make reproductions of the copyright mortgage agreement, the publication of the agreement in a form book intended to be used by attorneys when drafting agreements for clients constituted an implied license to reproduce the agreement for that purpose.

        (C) is incorrect. The use doctrine is not limited to copies of works owned by the person making the use of the protected work. Form books are intended to be used by practicing attorneys in this manner, whether they are owned by the attorney or are made available by libraries.

        (D) is incorrect. A contract is protectable as a literary work. The practice of transactional law often requires attorneys to customize or make changes to preexisting contracts obtained from various sources. Under such circumstances, an attorney would be unable to claim ownership of the copyright in the underlying contract. However, there is nothing stated in the facts that places the originality of the contract at issue.

29.   **(C) is the correct answer.** The doctrine of copyright estoppel is an exception to the general rule that fictional elements in a work are protectable under copyright law. Once a

plaintiff's work has been held out to the public as factual, the copyright owner cannot then claim that the work is, in actuality, fiction and thus entitled to copyright protection. *See Houts v. Universal City Studios, Inc.*, 603 F. Supp. 26, 28 (C.D. Cal. 1984).

(A) is incorrect. This statement of law is correct, but the material at issue is not factual. It is the fictional product of Author's creativity.

(B) is incorrect. This statement of law is correct as a general rule, but the copyright estoppel exception is applicable in this case.

(D) is incorrect. No matter how important stated facts are to a work, they will not be protected by copyright. The same holds true for fictional elements, presented as fact, which are therefore treated as though they were actual facts.

30.   **(D) is the correct answer.** An individual line of dialogue from a motion picture is not protected by copyright. It does not contain sufficient originality and in some cases is merely an idea. *See Murray Hill Publications, Inc. v. ABC Communications, Inc.*, 264 F.3d 622, 633 (6th Cir. 2001).

(A) is incorrect. This is an incorrect statement of law. Motion pictures are audiovisual works that do enjoy a public performance right. In addition, the downloading of a recording of the dialogue is a reproduction.

(B) is incorrect. As indicated above, a single line of dialogue is not protected by copyright. The fact that the line of dialogue is the most memorable of the motion picture may make it protectable under trademark law, but not copyright law.

(C) is incorrect. A line of dialogue is not protected by copyright. In addition, the copying of a single line of dialogue would be considered to be a *de minimis* taking that is not actionable as an infringement. *See Ringgold v. Black Entertainment Television*, 126 F.3d 70, 76 (2d Cir. 1997) (where "the allegedly infringing work makes such a quantitatively insubstantial use of the copyrighted work as to fall below the threshold required for actionable copying, it makes more sense to reject the claim on that basis and find no infringement . . . .").

31.   It is unlikely that Uncle Unique will have any legal remedy and certainly no copyright infringement claim. First, he has no copyright interest in the photograph that formed the basis for the Uncle Natural character. The subject of a photograph is not a copyrightable element and is not the author of the work, unless it has been created as a work made for hire, which is not the case here. *See Masterson Marketing, Inc. v. KSL Recreation Corp.*, 495 F. Supp. 2d 1044, 1048 (S.D. Cal. 2007) ("[A] photograph does not and cannot create a copyright in the underlying subject matter. The subject matter is factual material, available for use by all photographers."); *Natkin v. Winfrey*, 111 F. Supp. 2d 1003, 1008–10 (N.D. Ill. 2000) (photographs of Oprah Winfrey); *Gentieu v. John Muller & Co.*, 712 F. Supp. 740, 742 (W.D. Mo. 1989) (photographs of babies).

Secondly, Uncle Unique has no copyright in his personal appearance. Copyright does not protect human beings. *See Downing v. Abercrombie & Fitch*, 265 F.3d 994, 1003–04 (9th Cir.

2001); *Brown v. Ames*, 201 F.3d 654, 658 (5th Cir. 2000). Lastly, Uncle Unique has not presented himself as a fictional character and has not used his distinctive appearance as a fictional character. He has created a persona, not a copyrightable character. *See Columbia Broad. Sys., Inc. v. DeCosta*, 377 F.2d 315 (1st Cir. 1967).

32.   **(C) is the correct answer.** The elements that appear in both motion pictures are elements that are necessary for a work dealing with the genre of vampire stories. As such, they constitute *scènes à faire* that are not protected by copyright and may be copied without permission.

(A) is incorrect. The elements at issue are sufficiently detailed to constitute expression. However, these elements are necessary for a motion picture dealing with the genre of vampire stories. As such, they constitute *scènes à faire* and are not protectable. The difference between the unprotectability of ideas and the unprotectability of elements that constitute *scènes à faire* is that ideas are never protectable. The elements at issue in this case would have been protectable had they been used for the first time in a story about vampires. Given, however, that genre of vampire stories has existed for at least 150 years, these elements have no copyright protection and are treated similarly to ideas. *See Twentieth Century-Fox v. MCA*, 6 Media L. Rep. 2016 (C.D. Cal. 1980).

(B) is incorrect. The similarity of the elements at issue is not relevant because the elements constitute *scènes à faire* and are not protected by copyright.

(D) is incorrect. Priority of use is generally not relevant in a copyright infringement action and is completely irrelevant where the material at issue is not protected by copyright.

33.   To be protected by copyright, the drawings must constitute fixed original expression. The paper on which the drawings are fixed constitutes a tangible medium. They are not copied from another source, so the independent creation requirement is met. As for the required minimum level of creativity, the fact that purchasers pay $15,000 per drawing is a strong indication, though not conclusive proof, of sufficient creativity. The variety of the created designs and images constitutes more than a mere idea and would be viewed as creative enough to meet the low bar for originality sufficient to merit copyrightability. *Feist Publications v. Rural Tel. Serv. Co.*, 499 U.S. 340, 345 (1991) ("the requisite level of creativity is extremely low; even a slight amount will suffice").

The main issue under these facts, however, is the question of authorship. To be protected by copyright, a human must have created the work. *Urantia Foundation v. Maaherra*, 114 F.3d 955, 958 (9th Cir. 1997) (to be protected by copyright a work must be the product of some element of human creativity); *Naruto et al. v. Slater et al.*, no. 15-CV-04324 (N.D. Cal. January 28, 2016) (photograph taken by a monkey not copyrightable). Programmer would argue that the computer program she wrote for Picabrandt made the creation of every drawing possible and that the protocols she included in the computer program affected the content of each of the drawings. In addition, the drawings could not exist without the ink and paper loaded into Picabrandt. According to Programmer, these contributions constituted sufficient human creativity to make these drawings protected by copyright.

A contrary argument could be raised that the provision of ink and paper are merely supplying the tools needed for the work to be created, but in no way could be viewed as providing creativity. *Cf. Naruto, supra* (merely supplying camera and other photography equipment to monkey insufficient to create authorship claim on behalf of individual who supplied those materials). An art supply store does not have authorship status merely because it sells paints and brushes to an artist. The computer program addresses what cannot be drawn, such as a third eye. It is questionable whether such negative instruction can be the basis for a claim of human creativity. A purchaser who asks a painter to make a landscape without buildings would not be considered an author of the pictorial work.

34.   **(D) is the correct answer.** Network's claim of copyright protection of the colorized version of *Style Over Substance* is limited to the original new elements that make it a protected derivative work. The portions of the black and white version of the motion picture that entered the public domain remain in the public domain.

(A) is incorrect. Because the original black and white version of *Style Over Substance* is in the public domain, anyone may use it, including all broadcast and cable channels and stations. While it is true that the colorized version of *Style Over Substance* contains all of the elements of the original motion picture, Network can only preclude others from using the new elements created by the colorization. Network's claim of copyright protection is limited to those new elements. Anyone who has a copy of the black and white version of the motion picture remains free to transmit it without authorization from Network.

(B) is incorrect. Although Network does have a copyright in the colorized version of *Style Over Substance* as a derivative work, only the original elements added to the underlying work—the color added to the original images—are owned by Network, which is insufficient to preclude the use of the underlying work.

(C) is incorrect. The black and white version of the motion picture is in the public domain, but that does not preclude the protection of the original new elements created by Network. Any reproduction or transmission to the public of the colorized version of *Style Over Substance* requires Network's permission.

35.   **(B) is the correct answer.** Elements or sequences of events that necessarily result from a chosen concept do not enjoy copyright protection. The setting of a dinosaur zoo or adventure park, with electrified fences, automated tours, dinosaur nurseries, uniformed workers, and placing dinosaurs on a prehistoric island far from the mainland "are classic *scènes à faire* that flow from the uncopyrightable concept of a dinosaur zoo." *Williams v. Crichton*, 84 F.3d 581, 589 (2d Cir. 1996).

(A) is incorrect. Although the elements are very similar, they are not protected by copyright because they constitute *scènes à faire* for the reasons stated above.

(C) is incorrect. As indicated above, the elements are not protected by copyright.

(D) is incorrect. Although the fact that two works are intended for different audiences may have relevance to a jury in determining whether there is substantial similarity between two works, this is not the case where the elements in question are nearly identical. More important is the question whether the elements at issue are protected by copyright. In this case, they are not, because the elements necessarily flow from the novel's high concept of a dinosaur zoo and, therefore, are deemed unprotected *scènes à faire*.

36.   **(B) is the correct answer.** While copyright law does require some "spark of creativity" in order to meet the originality requirement for copyrightability, this has traditionally been held a very low standard that is easy to meet. *See Feist Publications v. Rural Tel. Serv. Co.*, 499 U.S. 340, 345 (1991) ("the requisite level of creativity is extremely low; even a slight amount will suffice"). The B-Loko warning label is not highly creative, but does seem to possess enough distinctive phrasing in terms of its grammatical structure and word choice that it meets this low bar — but only just.

In a case involving very similar warning labels on energy shots, one federal district court so held, stating that, "Because the medical caution statements appearing on the energy shots have appreciable differences, and stylistic flourishes may be inserted in the statement, the medical caution label has the minimum level of originality necessary to warrant copyright protection as a matter of law." *Innovation Ventures LLC v. N2G Distributing, Inc.*, 635 F. Supp. 2d 632, 640 (E.D. Mich. 2008).

(A) is incorrect because copyright is a strict liability tort that does not require any showing of intent. Nor is B-Krazy's similar name relevant to the copyright infringement analysis; that would raise at most a trademark issue.

(C) is incorrect because copyright originality is a low, not a high, standard. *See Feist*, 499 U.S. at 345.

(D) is incorrect because the warning does not lack *any* creativity or originality; it possesses a very small quantum of both that is evident in its word choice and grammatical usage.

37.   Beth does not have a cause of action for federal copyright infringement. While BCS used without permission her idea for a reality TV show about overly competitive cat owners, ideas are not protected by federal copyright law. 17 U.S.C. § 102. Federal courts have held that even in cases where a television studio uses an idea from a pitch meeting without authorization, that does not amount to copyright infringement. *See Montz v. Pilgrim Films & Television, Inc.*, 649 F.3d 975, 979 (9th Cir. 2011) (en banc) (holding, in case brought by writer against studio who used his idea from a pitch meeting without authorization to develop a TV series, that "[s]ince an idea cannot be copyrighted, a concept for a film or television show cannot be protected by a copyright").

California state law, on the other hand, may provide an avenue for Beth to sue BCS Studios. Under that state's law, writers who disclose script ideas to production studios may have an implied contract that they will be compensated if the idea is used. *See Desny v. Wilder*, 46 Cal.2d 715 (1956). Such claims are not preempted by federal copyright law. *See Grosso v. Miramax Film Corp.*, 383 F.3d 965 (9th Cir. 2004); *Montz*, 649 F.3d at 977 ("We again hold that copyright law does not preempt a contract claim where plaintiff alleges a bilateral expectation that he would be compensated for use of the idea[.]"). Assuming, then, that Beth can show there was an implied mutual understanding with BCS Studios that she would be paid if they used her idea, then she could seek relief against the studio on this California state law theory.

38.   (C) is the correct answer. The studio copied the physical "facts" reflected in the photograph — the fact that Jones was standing on a particular street corner in a particular place surrounded by people who looked a particular way. The studio did not copy the tourist's photograph verbatim, and the re-creation was very similar to but still clearly distinguishable from the tourist's photograph. The tourist could argue that the framing, timing, and other elements of her photograph amounted to copyrightable expression, but this is unlikely for a pair of reasons. First, this was not a carefully posed and crafted photograph such as the kind that has often been held copyrightable, *e.g., Burrow-Giles Litho. Co. v. Sarony*, 111 U.S. 53, 60–61 (1884), but just a "quick, informal" cell phone picture. Second, the fact that Jones was even in the photograph was an "accident," and not the result of any conscious intention by the tourist in taking the photograph.

Courts have recently held on facts much more favorable to plaintiffs that re-creations of factual news photographs do not infringe any copyright that may subsist in the photograph. *See Harney v. Sony Pictures TV, Inc.*, 704 F.3d 173, 184 (1st Cir. 2013) (rejecting a plaintiff photographer's copyright claim because the plaintiff's "creation consists primarily of subject matter — 'facts' — that he had no role in creating"); *cf. Satava v. Lowry*, 323 F.3d 805, 812–13 (9th Cir. 2003) (realistic depictions of live animals were "first expressed by nature, are the common heritage of humankind, and no artist may use copyright law to prevent others from depicting them").

(A) is incorrect because while photographs have long been considered copyrightable subject matter, *see Sarony*, 111 U.S. at 60–61, that does not mean that *all* photographs — or all of any particular kind of work — are copyrightable.

(B) is incorrect because a defendant's intent to infringe is not relevant to the legal question whether infringement actually happened. Copyright infringement does not include an intent element. In fact, courts have repeatedly found infringement even where defendants unconsciously infringed the plaintiff's work. *See Three Boys Music Corp. v. Bolton*, 212 F.3d 477 (9th Cir. 2000); *Bright Tunes Music Corp. v. Harrisongs Music, Ltd.*, 420 F. Supp. 177 (S.D.N.Y. 1976), *aff'd sub nom. ABKCO Music, Inc. v. Harrisongs Music, Ltd.*, 722 F.2d 988 (2d Cir. 1983).

(D) is incorrect because verbatim copying is not the only conceivable kind of copying that may result in copyright infringement. As Learned Hand famously put it, copyright "cannot be limited literally to the text, lest a plagiarist would escape by immaterial variation." *See Nichols v. Universal Pictures Corp.*, 45 F.2d 119, 121 (2d Cir. 1930).

39.   (A) is the correct answer. Blooey's face makeup design was clearly creative and original to him, hence its description as "outrageous and distinctive." It was also fixed in a tangible

medium of expression. The human face is certainly tangible. And while his makeup was eventually removed, fixation does not require that the work persist forever. On the contrary, while ephemeral fixations may not be protected, *see Cartoon Network v. CSC Holdings, Inc.*, 536 F.3d 121 (2d Cir. 2008) (holding that data that persists in digital medium for no longer than 1.2 seconds fails the duration element of the fixation requirement), the standard for the sufficiency of a fixation is that it persist for long enough to be perceived. Midway. Blooey's makeup easily meets this standard, since it typically is fixed for at least an hour and then ceases to exist only when Blooey takes it off. By the same token, a poet who writes a poem on paper, then decides an hour later that the poem is terrible and throws the paper into the fire has created a fixed work of authorship even though the original fixation itself has ceased to exist.

(B) is incorrect because there are no court cases explicitly holding that makeup designs, on clowns or otherwise, are valid fixations solely by virtue of their being applied to the human body. While the best reading of the Copyright Act is that they are, this is an interpretation of the statutory text, not an extrapolation from case law.

(C) is incorrect because, for reasons explained above, Blooey's work was fixed in a tangible medium of expression.

(D) is incorrect because Blooey's makeup likely does fall into one of the categories of works of authorship listed in the Copyright Act. It is a pictorial or graphical work, *see* 17 U.S.C. § 102(a)(5). And even if this were not the case, the categories of works of authorship listed in the Copyright Act are inclusive, not exclusive. *See id.* § 102(a) ("Works of authorship include the following categories[.]").

Copyrightable Subject Matter

40.   **(D) is the correct answer.** The expression of factual information is protected by copyright. Factual works, however, are more susceptible to a claim of fair use than are works of fiction. Furthermore, there may be more limitations on the protection given to the organization and structure of a nonfiction literary work.

(A) is incorrect. Although facts are not protected by copyright, the original expression of facts is protected. For example, the Encyclopedia Britannica is protected by copyright because its entries contain original expression as well as factual information.

(B) is incorrect. The short history would not be deemed a derivative work of the newspaper articles because only unprotected facts were taken from the articles, therefore, the short history cannot be said to constitute a derivative work as it did not substantially copy protectable expression from the prior work.

(C) is incorrect. The nonprotection of facts and the protection of the expression of facts by copyright have remained constant before, during and after 1978.

41.   **(D) is the correct answer.** The sound contained in the DVD accompanies a series of related images. As such, the work fixed in the DVD is an audiovisual work, not a sound recording.

(A) is incorrect. As explained in the answer above, the DVD contains an audiovisual work, not sound recordings.

(B) is incorrect. The statement of the law is correct, but not relevant to Record Company's incorrect claim that the filmed performance constituted a sound recording.

(C) is incorrect. If the DVD did contain sound recordings owned by Record Company, the absence of any contractual relationship between Club Owner and Record Company would prohibit Club Owner from distributing the copyright protected sound recordings without the permission of Record Company. However, the DVD contained only six musical works and an audiovisual work, not sound recordings.

42.   Federal copyright protection for sound recordings is more limited than that accorded other categories of copyrightable subject matter, including musical works. There is no federal copyright protection for United States sound recordings that were first fixed prior to February 15, 1972. It should be noted that a pre-1972 sound recording created by a foreign author may be protected under section 104A. The reproduction right of section 106(1) offers protection only against duplication of the sound recording, although a musical composition is generally protected against substantial similarity. This means that simulation of

a work may constitute infringement, but not if the protected work is a sound recording. For a violation of the adaptation right, section 106(2), the unauthorized derivative work must contain a portion of the plaintiff's actual sound recording, not an imitation. The public distribution right of sound recordings is not limited by the first sale doctrine of section 109 in the case of rental, lease or lending of sound recordings, except for nonprofit libraries and educational institutions, whereas musical works not fixed in sound recordings may be rented, leased or lent. Sound recordings enjoy no public performance right under section 106(4) or public display right under section 106(5), though musical works have the protection of both the public performance and public display rights. Sound recordings are the only works protected by section 106(6), the digital transmission right.

43.   **(C) is the correct answer.** Letters may not be regarded as literature in a colloquial sense, but this is irrelevant to the question whether they are considered works of authorship for the purpose of copyright analysis. Courts have consistently held that letters are copyrightable so long as they contain sufficient original expression. *See, e.g., Salinger v. Random House, Inc.,* 811 F.2d 90, 94–95 (2d Cir. 1987) (author of the letter owns the copyright in its contents). So Publisher's unauthorized publication of Author's copyrighted material amounts to infringement.

(A) is incorrect because expository materials certainly do count as "literary works" within the meaning of the Copyright Act. The term "literary works" is not given a narrow or colloquial construction to refer only to works of literature. Rather, courts construe it broadly to refer to any work that is composed in words or numbers. *See* 17 U.S.C. § 101 ("Literary works") ("'Literary works' are works, other than audiovisual works, expressed in words, numbers, or other verbal or numerical symbols or indicia.").

(B) is incorrect because Author explicitly asked Publisher not to publish the existing manuscript or new ending until after she had the opportunity for revision. There is no way this language could be construed as implied or explicit permission to publish the copyrighted material contained in the letter.

(D) is incorrect for much the same reasons given for answer (A). Remember, a work need not amount to "literature" to count as a literary work or a work of authorship within the meaning of the Copyright Act.

44.   Although, as the answer to II-4 makes clear, Author owns the copyrighted material contained in the letter (the work of authorship), this does not mean that Author also owns the physical object in which that material is fixed (the copy). Thus, the letter, which Author gave to Publisher, is owned by Publisher; but the copyrighted material contained in that letter is owned by Author. Publisher is thus under no obligation to return the letter to Author. *See Salinger v. Random House, Inc.,* 811 F.2d 90, 94–95 (2d Cir. 1987) (author of the letter owns the copyright in its contents, while the recipient of the letter retains ownership of the physical document).

45.   **(D) is the correct answer.** Agent did not copy the particular expression contained in Author's email, only the general plot outlines that Author had suggested. However, that

plot outline was expressed at such a high level of generality that it did not amount to copyrightable subject matter. *See Shipman v. RKO Pictures*, 100 F.2d 533, 538 (2d Cir. 1938) (bare plots are not protected by copyright). The ideas suggested are familiar themes from world literature dating at least to Shakespeare's *Romeo and Juliet*: young, star-crossed lovers whose desire for each other is thwarted by venal family ambitions. Such *scènes à faire* (stock events and characters) are not copyrightable. *See Nelson v. Grisham*, 942 F. Supp. 649, 653 (D.D.C. 1996), *aff'd*, 132 F.3d 1481 (D.C. Cir. 1997).

(A) is incorrect because it misstates the facts of the question. Agent did not copy the particular expression contained in the email. Rather, Agent merely relied on the general ideas contained in the email when creating her own subsequent work.

(B) is incorrect because copyright law does not protect a work simply because it is created from the "sweat of the brow." This theory was rejected by the Supreme Court in *Feist Publications, Inc. v. Rural Telephone Service Company, Inc.*, 499 U.S. 340, 359 (1991).

(C) is incorrect because although verbatim copying is evidence of infringement, it is not required to show infringement. The traditional test of the infringement of the reproduction right is whether the defendant's work is substantially similar, not verbatim.

46.   **(C) is the correct answer.** All of the expression contained in the material taken by Employee amounts to copyrightable subject matter. The brochure, video, and memorandum all contain at least a modicum of creative expression, and are fixed in tangible media of expression. While these materials may not be typical subjects of copyright, the fact that they were produced in a business context does not deprive them of protection. *See, e.g., Khandji v. Keystone Resorts Mgmt., Inc.*, 140 F.R.D. 697 (D. Colo. 1992) (settlement brochure is copyrightable); *Rexnord, Inc. v. Modern Handling Sys., Inc.*, 379 F. Supp. 1190 (D. Del. 1974) (manufacturer's catalogue is copyrightable).

(A), (B), and (D) are incorrect because they state that some of the material at issue is not copyrightable.

47.   **(D) is the correct answer.** Student took only generally available facts, such as names, addresses, and phone numbers, from the University's directory. Facts are not copyrightable. *See Harper & Row Publishers, Inc. v. Nation Enters.*, 471 U.S. 539, 556 (1985) ("No author may copyright . . . the facts he narrates."). While the University may have had a claim if Student had copied any original selection or arrangement of these facts, that was not the case here, because Student used only the facts in the University's directory and infused them with his own selection and arrangement.

(A) is incorrect because while Student copied certain elements of the directory verbatim, those elements were uncopyrightable facts, not protectable expression.

(B) is incorrect because the University's copyright in the directory is actually very thin. *See Kregos v. Associated Press*, 937 F.2d 700 (2d Cir. 1991). It extends no farther than the selection and arrangement of facts, and certainly does not include "the idea of all student directories for their employees."

(C) is incorrect because some elements of directories, such as their selection and arrangement of facts, are copyrightable. 17 U.S.C. § 103(a) (compilations are copyrightable); *see, e.g., Feist Publications, Inc. v. Rural Tel. Serv. Co., Inc.*, 499 U.S. 340, 357 (1991).

48.   Student would likely prevail in his copyright infringement suit against Compatriot. This would be a case involving wholesale, verbatim copying of a compilation of data. While the facts in Student's compilation are not copyrightable, any originality reflected in Student's selection or arrangement of those facts likely would be. Here, it appears that Student made an effort to select names from the database according to his own subjective evaluation of which University students are most popular. This evinces originality in his selection and thus would likely be copyrightable. *See, e.g., Eckes v. Card Prices Update*, 736 F.2d 859 (2d Cir. 1984) (choosing 5,000 premium cards out of a universe of 18,000 baseball cards constituted sufficient "selection" for copyright protection). By contrast, Student's arrangement of those facts is merely in alphabetical order, and this natural and predictable ordering does not merit copyright protection. Still, because Compatriot copied Student's directory without permission, and because the directory's selection of facts reflects a minimally sufficient quantum of creativity, Compatriot's copying likely amounts to infringement.

49.   **(A) is the correct answer.** While courts generally do not consider conversations to be copyrightable, they have, by contrast, held that prepared speeches are copyrightable literary works. *See, e.g., Jackson v. MPI Home Video*, 694 F. Supp. 483, 490 (N.D. Ill. 1988) (Jesse Jackson's speech at the 1988 Democratic Party Convention found protectable as a literary work). Because Professor's speech was composed in written form beforehand, and because his delivery followed the written text precisely, it is a copyrightable work, and Student's unauthorized reproduction and display of it would amount to infringement.

(B) is incorrect because no court has ever held that memorization amounts to fixation in a tangible medium of expression.

(C) is incorrect because lectures based on a written text are treated differently than extemporaneous spoken word performances, which typically are not protected by federal copyright because they are not fixed in a tangible medium of expression.

(D) is incorrect because courts do not treat prepared lectures as a form of extemporaneous conversation, since the former are written down in a tangible medium while the latter is not. Independently, some courts have implied that conversation may be copyrightable under certain circumstances, so the broad statement "conversation . . . is never copyrightable" inaccurately states the law. *See Estate of Hemingway v. Random House, Inc.*, 23 N.Y.2d 341, 244 N.E.2d 250 (1969); *Falwell v. Penthouse Int'l, Ltd.*, 521 F. Supp. 1204 (W.D. Va. 1981).

50.   Student's unauthorized reproduction of Professor's casual cocktail party banter would be very unlikely to incur copyright liability. Courts generally have a narrow view regarding the copyright protection of conversations. *See Falwell v. Penthouse International, Ltd.*, 521 F. Supp. 1204, 1207–08 (W.D. Va. 1981). In *Estate of Hemingway v. Random House, Inc.*, 23 N.Y.2d 341, 244 N.E.2d 250 (1969), the New York Court of Appeals held that conversation was

presumed to be unprotected by copyright. The court noted that this presumption could be rebutted under the following conditions: First, the speaker must indicate that she intended to mark off the utterance from the ordinary stream of speech. Second, the speaker must indicate that she meant to adopt the utterance as a unique statement. Third, the speaker must indicate that she wished to exercise the control over the statement's publication. *Estate of Hemingway*, 23 N.Y.2d at 349, 244 N.E.2d at 256. There is nothing in the fact pattern that suggests Professor meets any of these conditions, let alone all three of them.

51.   **(D) is the correct answer.** Neither Amateur nor Nemesis copied copyrightable subject matter. Where Archaeologist's dig took place and what was discovered are scientific and historical facts, which are not copyrightable, so there is no infringement claim against Amateur's reporting these facts on his website. *See Rosemont Enters., Inc. v. Random House, Inc.*, 366 F.2d 303 (2d Cir. 1966). Similarly, the interpretation of those historical and scientific facts is also not copyrightable, *Hoehling v. Universal City Studios, Inc.*, 618 F.2d 972 (2d Cir. 1980), so the element of Nemesis' article that recounts Archaeologist's interpretation of his discoveries also does not amount to an infringement. Had Nemesis copied the particular words Archaeologist used when articulating his new theory, that would likely amount to infringement, but the facts specify that Nemesis did not do this, but instead expressed Archaeologist's theory entirely in his own words.

(A), (B), and (C) are incorrect because they wrongly assume that Nemesis, Amateur, or both, took copyrighted material.

52.   **(B) is the correct answer.** Courts have consistently held that characters are copyrightable as long as they are represented with sufficient distinctness, and are not represented in a generic or commonplace manner. *See Nichols v. Universal Pictures Corp.*, 45 F.2d 119, 121 (2d Cir. 1930) ("[T]he less developed the characters the less they can be copyrighted, that is the penalty an author must bear for marking them too indistinctly."). Characters depicted graphically (i.e., visually rather than in literature) are particularly likely to merit copyright protection. *See Walt Disney Prods. v. Air Pirates*, 581 F.2d 751 (9th Cir. 1978). Here, the SuperCop character has a clearly recognizable image that has been appropriated without permission, so Cartoonist's infringement suit against Publisher will likely prevail.

(A) is incorrect because it describes the scope of Cartoonist's rights in SuperCop too broadly. Cartoonist enjoys statutorily enumerated exclusive rights in the character, but does not have a broad right to control every subsequent graphic depiction of a heroic policeman.

(C) is incorrect because placing a copyrighted literary character in a different context does not obviate a plaintiff's claim for infringement. The copyright in the character persists as long as the character is reproduced without permission, regardless of the context in which it is featured. *See Walt Disney Prods. v. Air Pirates*, 581 F.2d 751 (9th Cir. 1978); *Walt Disney Prods. v. Filmation Assocs.*, 628 F. Supp. 871 (C.D. Cal. 1986).

(D) is incorrect because courts have consistently held that graphical characters are copyrightable. *See Metro-Goldwyn-Mayer v. Am. Honda Motor*, 900 F. Supp. 1287 (C.D. Cal. 1995).

53.   Cartoonist will likely fail in his infringement suit against Republisher. While there are some similarities between the two series, they all operate on the level of general, stock qualities or ideas, rather than distinct features that may be copyrighted. *See Nichols v. Universal Pictures Corp.*, 45 F.2d 119, 121 (2d Cir. 1930) ("[T]he less developed the characters the less they can be copyrighted, that is the penalty an author must bear for marking them too indistinctly."). Indeed, the notion of the bumbling cop has a long pedigree (e.g., the *Police Academy* series of films and Chief Wiggum from *The Simpsons*), and cannot be said to be original to Cartoonist's work. It is not relevant that Republisher may have been inspired to create PooperCop in part by the SuperCop series. As long as Republisher has not taken any copyrightable expression from the SuperCop series, Cartoonist has no infringement claim.

54.   **(B) is the correct answer.** All circuits, except the Ninth Circuit, have clearly held that literary characters depicted in novels are copyrightable as long as they are sufficiently distinctive. That is, they must be sufficiently fleshed out with recognizable physical traits, backstory, or personality traits in order to be copyrightable. *Filmvideo Releasing Corp. v. Hastings*, 509 F. Supp. 60 (S.D.N.Y. 1981), *aff'd*, 668 F.2d 91 (2d Cir. 1981); *Silverman v. CBS, Inc.*, 870 F.2d 40, 50 (2d Cir. 1989). Here, the Judy McGee character is clearly distinctive in terms of her appearance and behavior, so she is copyrightable, and Studio's use of the character without seeking a license from Author amounts to infringement.

(A) **is incorrect** because literary characters are not always copyrightable. Rather, they must be sufficiently well developed to be distinctive and recognizable in order to merit copyright protection. *See Nichols v. Universal Pictures Corp.*, 45 F.2d 119, 121 (2d Cir. 1930).

(C) **is incorrect** because it refers to the minority view, the Ninth Circuit test for protectability of literary characters. This test sets a higher bar. It looks to whether the character at issue represents the actual story being told or is merely a plot device used to move the story along. Only if the character is sufficiently central to the narrative does it merit protection under this test. *See Warner Bros. Pictures, Inc. v. Columbia Broad. Sys., Inc.*, 216 F.2d 945, 950 (9th Cir. 1954) (literary character Sam Spade held not protected by copyright); *Rice v. Fox Broad. Co.*, 330 F.3d 1170, 1176 (9th Cir. 2003) ("Mystery Magician" held to be merely a chess piece in the game of telling the story of how magic tricks are performed). Some courts in the Ninth Circuit have, however, moved away from exclusively applying the "Sam Spade" test. *See Shaw v. Lindheim*, 908 F.2d 531 (9th Cir. 1990); *Metro-Goldwyn-Mayer, Inc. v. American Honda Motor Co., Inc.*, 900 F. Supp. 1287 (C.D. Cal. 1995).

(D) **is incorrect** because literary characters are copyrightable if they meet the standards described in the discussion of answer (B) above.

55.   **(A) is the correct answer.** Copyright protection is extended to a component part of a character that significantly aids in identifying the character. *See, e.g., New Line Cinema Corp. v. Eastern Unlimited, Inc.*, 17 U.S.P.Q.2d 1631, 1633 (E.D.N.Y. 1989) (glove with razor fingers significantly aided in identifying Freddy Krueger character). Because Judy McGee is distinctively recognized by the oversized, pink-handled magnifying glass that she uses in all the novels, that magnifying glass is protected as part of the copyright in the character.

(B) is incorrect because it overstates the scope of the law. Copyright in literary characters extends to distinctive, identifying features of those characters, but does not extend to everything that could possibly be associated with them.

(C) is incorrect. Although it is true that claiming copyright in the idea of using a magnifying glass would be untenable, that is not what Author claims here. Rather, she claims copyright protection only for a particular, very distinctive magnifying glass, and only because it is uniquely associated with a character she has created.

(D) is incorrect. Although the statement is correct as a general matter, a useful article can be used to flesh out a character, e.g. Indiana Jones' bullwhip and fedora hat. The useful article can be protected as part of the copyright in the character if it significantly aids in identifying the character.

56. Ninth Circuit law creates a higher bar for the protectability of literary characters. That circuit looks to whether the character at issue represents the actual story being told or is merely a plot device used to move the story along. Only if the character is sufficiently central to the narrative does it merit protection under this test. *Warner Bros. Pictures, Inc. v. Columbia Broad. Sys., Inc.*, 216 F.2d 945, 950 (9th Cir. 1954). Under this test, a court would look to see whether the story in Author's novels was primarily the character Judy McGee herself, or whether Judy was merely a "chess piece" used to advance the plot along. If the former, a court would conclude that the character were copyrightable. If the latter, a court would conclude that the character were not copyrightable. *See Metro-Goldwyn-Mayer, Inc. v. American Honda Motor Co., Inc.*, 900 F. Supp. 1287, 1296 (C.D. Cal. 1995) (James Bond character protected under the "story being told" test because "audiences do not watch Tarzan, Superman, Sherlock Holmes, or James Bond for the story, they watch these films to see their heroes at work. A James Bond film without James Bond is not a James Bond film."). Courts within the Ninth Circuit have applied both the story being told and fleshing out tests. *See, e.g., Metro-Goldwyn-Mayer v. American Honda Motor*, 900 F. Supp. 1287, 1296 (C.D. Cal. 1995). The Ninth Circuit itself has indicated an acceptance of the majority rule of literary character protection. *See Shaw v. Lindheim*, 908 F.2d 531 (9th Cir. 1990).

57. **(C) is the correct answer.** Characters, including graphic characters, fall into the public domain as soon as any work in which they are depicted falls into the public domain. A character will enter the public domain when the work in which the character was initially sufficiently delineated enters the public domain. *See Klinger v. Conan Doyle Estate, Ltd.*, 755 F.3d 496 (7th Cir. 2014) (holding that Sherlock Holmes character is in the public domain because initial versions of the character are in the public domain); *Silverman v. CBS, Inc.*, 870 F.2d 40, 50 (2d Cir. 1989). Mikey the Mouse thus became public domain material when the first *Mice-a-Roni* comic became part of the public domain. Mikey the Mouse is no longer protected, so Publisher is free to use it without a license. That other elements of the series, such as new stories, characters, images and dialogue, remain protected by copyright does not matter.

(A) is incorrect. It gets the law exactly backwards: if any one literary work in which a character is sufficiently well delineated becomes part of the public domain, then the character becomes part of the public domain as well. It does not matter if there are other works depicting the public domain character that contain other copyrighted material.

(B) is incorrect because it misstates the law. The period of protection for characters depicted in any works of authorship is no longer than it is for those works of authorship.

(D) is incorrect. The reason that Mikey the Mouse is not protected is that Animator failed to preserve his copyright in the character, not because a court would look askance at his failure to follow those formalities on some equitable theory. Publisher will not have to rely on an affirmative defense, such as laches, when the subject matter at issue, the character of Mikey the Mouse, is no longer protected by copyright.

58.   **(B) is the correct answer.** The source code that comprises computer programs is copyrightable, *Apple Computer, Inc. v. Franklin Computer Corp.*, 714 F.2d 1240, 1248–49 (3d Cir. 1983), but the functionality of computer programs is not, because it amounts to an unprotectable idea. *See Computer Assocs. Int'l, Inc. v. Altai, Inc.*, 982 F.2d 693 (2d Cir. 1992). Programmer can successfully sue Pirate for infringing the source code, which Pirate copied verbatim, but the idea of a program that catalogs bird sightings operates at too high a level of generality to be protectable. The cataloging function may be protectable by patent law, if it is sufficiently novel, nonobvious and useful, but not by copyright law.

(A), (C), and (D) are incorrect because they falsely assume either that source code is not protectable or that ideas are.

59.   **(A) is the correct answer.** The structure of computer chips enjoys *sui generis* protection by the Semiconductor Chip Protection Act of 1984, 17 U.S.C. §§ 901–14. The duration of such protection is 10 years, 17 U.S.C. § 904, therefore the federal protection of the chip will expire in 2000, because Techie created his chip in 1990. The structure of the computer chip is protected separately from the computer program embodied in the chip. The computer program is protected for the duration of works protected by copyright.

(B) is incorrect because it incorrectly assumes the protection offered by the Semiconductor Chip Protection Act of 1984 lasts 20 years, which is the period of protection for patents.

(C) is incorrect because it incorrectly assumes the protection offered by the Semiconductor Chip Protection Act of 1984 lasts for the life of the author plus 70 years, which is the period of protection for copyrights.

(D) is incorrect because computer chips are protectable under federal law for the reasons discussed in explaining answer (A).

60.   **(C) is the correct answer.** The 1976 Copyright Act provides for the unauthorized copying of a computer program by the owner of the computer program when it is an essential step in the utilization of the program in conjunction with the computer or when the copy is used for archival purposes. 17 U.S.C. § 117. *See Allen-Myland, Inc. v. Int'l Business Machines Corp.*, 746 F. Supp. 520, 536 (E.D. Pa. 1990).

(A) is incorrect because, although object code is a copyrightable literary work, this answer fails to take into account the section 117 exception.

(B) is incorrect because object code is copyrightable. *See Apple Computer, Inc. v. Franklin Computer Corp.*, 714 F.2d 1240, 1248–49 (3d Cir. 1983) (computer programs are copyrightable subject matter regardless of whether they are expressed in human-readable source code or machine-readable object code); *Apple Computer, Inc. v. Formula Int'l, Inc.*, 725 F.2d 521, 523 (9th Cir. 1984).

(D) is incorrect because User's intent is irrelevant; copyright infringement is a strict liability tort.

61. **(D) is the correct answer.** The owner of a computer program is permitted to make an adaptation of the computer program, without authorization from the copyright owner, as an essential step in the utilization of the computer program. 17 U.S.C. § 117; *see Aymes v. Bonelli*, 47 F.3d 23, 26–27 (2d Cir. 1995) (adaptation permitted where the changes were necessary to keep program current and to maintain its viability with an upgraded computer system).

(A) is incorrect. While User's alteration of the source code that comprises *DethKlok 2000* does create an unauthorized derivative work, this particular conduct falls within a narrow statutory exemption from liability.

(B) is incorrect. Even if User made a copy of the *DethKlok 2000* source code in revising it, that reproduction would also fall within the section 117 statutory exemption.

(C) is incorrect. User's ownership of an authorized copy of *DethKlok 2000* does not obviate the adaptation right enjoyed by the owner of the copyright in the source code that comprises the program. It merely permits a limited exception to the copyright owner's adaptation right.

62. **(D) is the correct answer.** Though some typefaces may have sufficient originality to be copyrightable, Congress, as a matter of public policy, has determined that the design of typefaces will not be protected by copyright, though they may be protected by the law of unfair competition. *See Monotype Corp. PLC v. Int'l Typeface Corp.*, 43 F.3d 443 (9th Cir. 1994); *Eltra Corp. v. Ringer*, 579 F.2d 294 (4th Cir. 1978).

(A) and (B) are incorrect; whether pictorial, graphical, or literary works, fonts are not protectable by federal copyright.

(C) is incorrect. Fonts could certainly possess the requisite degree of originality to merit copyright protection. Although the letters of the alphabet themselves are in the public domain, they could be depicted with enough creative expression that the result easily crosses the low bar of originality.

63. **(B) is the correct answer.** Though the Copyright Act does not define "musical works," *see* 17 U.S.C. § 102(a)(2), courts have construed this term to include the harmony, melody, and accompanying words that comprise a musical composition. *See Mills Music, Inc.*

v. Arizona, 187 U.S.P.Q. 22 (D. Ariz. 1975), *aff'd per curiam*, 591 F.2d 1278 (9th Cir. 1979). By contrast, the recording of a performance of a musical work constitutes a fixation of sounds in a phonorecord, which is a sound recording. *See* 17 U.S.C. § 101 (definition of "sound recordings"). Thus, Polly Math owns a copyright in both elements of the musical work, melody and lyrics, which together comprise *Only Me*, while her recorded performance of *Only Me* constitutes a sound recording in which she owns a separate copyright.

(A) is incorrect because it fails to recognize that Polly Math also owns the copyright in the sound recording of *Only Me*.

(C) is incorrect because it wrongly states that Polly Math owns the copyright in the melody of *Only Me* as a sound recording, not a musical work.

(D) is incorrect because it wrongly states that Polly Math owns the copyright in the recorded performance of *Only Me* as a musical work. Further, the recording of a performance of *Only Me* would constitute a sound recording, not a musical work. The performance of a work is not copyrightable subject matter. The work being performed and the recording of that performance are copyrightable subject matter.

64.　**(A) is the correct answer.** Choreographic works are copyrightable. 17 U.S.C. § 102(a)(4). Although Dancer's performance of her choreographic works was spontaneous and unplanned, even spontaneous choreographic works can be fixed in a tangible medium of expression if they are recorded by the author or under her authority. *See Martha Graham School and Dance Foundation, Inc. v. Martha Graham Center of Contemporary Dance, Inc.*, 380 F.3d 624, 632 (2d Cir. 2004). Dancer's choreographic works that were performed in Carnegie Hall were recorded with her authorization. As a result, they were sufficiently fixed to meet the requirement for federal copyright protection.

(B) is incorrect for two reasons. First, unless the audiovisual work contained in the original DVD was a work made for hire, Dancer does not own the copyright in the audiovisual work. And second, the copyright in the audiovisual work contained in the original DVD cannot prevent the creation of an independent recording of the same performance. There is no indication that the second unauthorized DVD contained any of the creative elements that made the first audiovisual work protected by copyright.

(C) is incorrect because Dancer's performance was fixed in a tangible medium of expression: the authorized recording that served as the basis for the first DVD. If Dancer had not authorized any of the recordings of her Carnegie Hall performance, federal copyright law would not have protected her choreographic works, and she would have to rely on state common-law copyright.

(D) is incorrect because choreographic works are clearly copyrightable, as noted in the explanation to answer (A) above, whether they communicate a story or not. Under the 1909 Act, a choreographic work could only be protected as a dramatic work, and only if it communicated a story. Under the 1976 Act, there is no such limitation.

65. **(B) is the correct answer.** Photog has an enforceable copyright in his original photograph. However, the infringement claim applies to the photograph only; Photog does not have any copyright interest in the shirt, which is an uncopyrightable useful object. *See Poe v. Missing Persons*, 745 F.2d 1238 (9th Cir. 1984) (clothing not protectable by copyright). But Knockoff's reproduction of the image on a shirt, as opposed to selling copies of it as a photograph, does not negate Photog's argument that his exclusive right of reproduction was infringed. Although courts consider clothing an uncopyrightable useful object, aesthetic features of utilitarian objects that are physically or conceptually separable from the objects on which they appear, such as, here, the kitten photograph on the shirts, are considered copyrightable. *See Mazer v. Stein*, 347 U.S. 201 (1954); *Esquire, Inc. v. Ringer*, 591 F.2d 796, 804 (D.C. Cir. 1978).

    (A) is incorrect because Photog's copyright is limited to his original photograph and does not extend to the utilitarian object on which it is depicted.

    (C) is incorrect. Although clothing is indeed not copyrightable, where, as here, a separate image or design is depicted on clothing, that image is copyrightable.

    (D) is incorrect because the copyrightable status of protectable images that have been appended to utilitarian objects is preserved by the separability doctrine.

66. **(C) is the correct answer.** Video game screen displays are registrable as an audiovisual work. *Atari Games Corp. v. Oman*, 979 F.2d 242 (D.C. Cir. 1992). This illustrates that the term "audiovisual work" does not encompass only motion pictures or television programs, and is construed broadly by courts to allow copyright protection for new forms of technology. *See Midway Manufacturing Co. v. Arctic International, Inc.*, 704 F.2d 1009, 1011 (7th Cir. 1982) (term "audiovisual work" should be broadly construed "to refer to any set of images displayed as some kind of unit"). The sounds associated with *A-Maze-ment* are also subsumed by the copyright in the audiovisual work. 17 U.S.C. § 101 (defining "audiovisual work" to encompass "accompanying sounds, if any").

    (A) and (B) are incorrect because they misstate the work of authorship at issue.

    (D) is incorrect because courts consistently have held that computer screens, including video game screen displays, are copyrightable. The elements appearing on the screen have been created and fixed by the author, even though each individual player may manipulate the elements differently. Although the musical work may be separately protected and registered, a sound recording created for an audiovisual work is deemed part of that audiovisual work, not a separate sound recording.

67. **(C) is the correct answer.** The Copyright Act's definition of "sound recording" does not include the sounds accompanying a motion picture or other audiovisual work. A motion picture's music soundtrack is protected under the motion picture copyright. 17 U.S.C. § 101; *Maljack Productions, Inc. v. Goodtimes Home Video Corp.*, 81 F.3d 881, 888 (9th Cir. 1996).

    (A) and (B) are incorrect because they falsely presume that music soundtracks accompanying motion pictures must be separately registered.

(D) is incorrect because the Copyright Act's registration provisions apply equally to all works of authorship.

68.   (C) is the correct answer. Pianoman's unauthorized recording and public distribution of his performance of the concerto infringes the copyright in the musical work that comprises the concerto. However, Pianoman did not infringe the copyright in the *Musician's Concerto Live* sound recording. The imitation or simulation of the sounds captured in the sound recording is permitted, so long as an actual duplication of the sound recording itself is not made. 17 U.S.C. § 114(d); *Bridgeport Music, Inc. v. Dimension Films*, 410 F.3d 792, 800 (6th Cir. 2005).

(A), (B), and (D) are incorrect because they state either that Pianoman infringed the sound recording or that he did not infringe the musical work.

69.   (A) is the correct answer. Donny Dank owns the federal copyright in the musical work, but Big Waves has no federal copyright ownership interest in the recording of that work. Federal copyright law does not protect sound recordings fixed prior to February 15, 1972. Because the sound recording that resulted from Big Waves' studio performance of *Sir Surfs-a-Lot* took place in 1969, that sound recording is unprotected by federal copyright law. Pre-1972 sound recordings may, however, be protected by state common-law copyright, property, unfair competition, or criminal law. *Capitol Records, Inc. v. Naxos of America, Inc.*, 372 F.3d 471, 477–78 (2d Cir. 2004).

(B), (C), and (D) are incorrect because they wrongly state that it is possible to have a federal copyright in a sound recording prior to February 15, 1972.

70.   (A) is the correct answer. Prior to 1990, architectural structures generally were not copyrightable because they were deemed useful articles, though the blueprints on which they were based were copyrightable as pictorial works. *Robert R. Jones Associates, Inc. v. Nino Homes*, 858 F.2d 274, 278 (6th Cir. 1988). The Architectural Works Protection Act of 1990 created the new subject matter category of "architectural works," 17 U.S.C. § 102(a)(8), and copyright law now protects buildings as part of that category of work of authorship. Protection is extended to individual original design elements and to the overall form of the building, as well as the arrangement and composition of spaces, protected elements, and unpredictable elements in the design. 17 U.S.C. § 101. *See Shine v. Childs*, 382 F. Supp. 2d 602, 609 (S.D.N.Y. 2005). In addition to being protected as architectural works, architectural plans, drawings, and models continue to be protectable as pictorial, graphic, or sculptural works under section 102(a)(5). *See Hunt v. Pasternack*, 192 F.3d 877, 880 (9th Cir. 1999). Thus (A) correctly identifies that the blueprints are protectable as both pictorial and architectural works, and that the external design of the house as well as the interior staircase are protectable as an architectural work.

(B), (C), and (D) are incorrect because they fail to correctly identify the kinds of works of authorship at issue as explained in the discussion of answer (A) above.

71.   (C) is the correct answer. A work prepared by an officer or employee of the United States government as part of that person's official duties cannot be protected by

copyright. 17 U.S.C. § 105. *See Matthew Bender & Co., Inc. v. West Publishing Co.*, 158 F.3d 674, 679 (2d Cir. 1998). However, the section 105 prohibition does not affect the copyrightability of works created by employees of state governments. Rather, for copyright purposes, state and local government entities are treated the same as non-governmental entities. *See, e.g., McKenna v. Lee*, 318 F. Supp. 2d 296, 301 (E.D.N.C. 2002) (State of North Carolina owned copyright in "First in Flight" license tag design), *aff'd*, 53 Fed. App'x 268 (4th Cir. 2002). In this case, the painting prepared by Fed in his official capacity as a federal employee would not be copyrightable, but the poem prepared by Statie in his official capacity as a state employee would be.

(A), (C), and (D) are incorrect because they falsely state either that Fed's painting was protectable or that Statie's poem was not.

72.   **(A) is the correct answer.** Publisher has violated Novelist's exclusive rights by copying and publicly distributing an unauthorized derivative work based on Publisher's original copyrighted work of authorship. Although Critic created the derivative work, it was unauthorized, therefore no copyright interest in the work arose. The new elements of a derivative work that has been based on a copyrighted underlying work, without authorization, will be denied copyright protection. *See* 17 U.S.C. § 103(a); *Watkins v. Chesapeake Custom Homes, L.L.C.*, 330 F. Supp. 2d 563, 572 (D. Md. 2004) (a derivative copyright that is based on a copyrighted work requires the authorization of the copyright owner in order to be "lawful" and thus valid).

(B), (C), and (D) are incorrect because they wrongly state either that Novelist will not prevail or that Critic will.

73.   **(B) is the correct answer.** Fan has clearly infringed the *PoundSigne* creator's copyright in the Le Mec character. Distinctive characters, especially graphic characters such as Le Mec, are copyrightable. *Walt Disney Productions v. Air Pirates*, 581 F.2d 751 (9th Cir. 1978). Publisher has created an authorized derivative work based on the original *PoundSigne* comics, but its copyright in this work extends only to the original contributions it made. The copyright in a derivative work extends only to the original new elements added by the author of the derivative work. 17 U.S.C. §§ 101, 103; *G. Ricordi & Co. v. Paramount Pictures, Inc.*, 189 F.2d 469 (2d Cir. 1951). Because the only original contribution added by Publisher was the new English text of the comics, Publisher has no copyright interest in the graphic character of Le Mec itself. Thus, *PoundSigne's* creator has a valid infringement suit against Fan, but Publisher does not, because Fan infringed the character copyright in Le Mec, not the translation created by Publisher.

(A), (C), and (D) are incorrect because they wrongly state either that Publisher will prevail or that PoundSigne's creator will not.

74.   **(C) is the correct answer.** If a freelance artist allows his copyrighted work of authorship to be used in a collective work, the section 201(c) privilege requires the collective work owner to get a new license if it seeks to release the collective work in a manner that is outside its original context. *See New York Times Co., Inc. v. Tasini*, 533 U.S. 483,

499–500 (2001) (inclusion of articles written by freelance authors for newspapers and magazines in electronic data bases and CD-ROM programs held not to be revisions of the collective works permitted by section 201(c)). However, where the original work is subsequently used in a revision of the collective work, or a later collective work in the same series, the section 201(c) privilege applies and collective work owners are free to engage in such reproduction and distribution without seeking an additional license from the owner of the work of authorship. *Greenberg v. Nat'l Geographic Soc'y*, 533 F.3d 1244, 1249 (11th Cir. 2008) (digital version of collective work constitutes a privileged revision if each page of the collective work appears as it did in the print version). In this case, because Photog's lion photograph was presented in the DVD in exactly the same context it was presented in the original print version of the magazine, the section 201(c) privilege applies and permits *Adventure* to release the DVD without seeking permission.

(A) **is incorrect** because it fails to reflect that this use would not be covered by the section 201(c) privilege.

(B) **is incorrect** because the Copyright Act imposes no such requirement.

(D) **is incorrect** because licenses to use works of authorship in one manner or medium do not imply licenses to use those same works in a different manner or medium. On the contrary, licenses to use a work for a particular purpose or in a particular context suggest that the licensor did not grant a right to use the work for any other purpose or in any other context.

75.   **The correct answer is (B).** The transmission of a musical composition that is audible to a computer user is deemed a performance. When the transmission is audible to a number of computer users, it constitutes a public performance pursuant to the transmit clause of the definition of public performance in section 101.

(A) **is incorrect.** Although the computer file containing the musical composition is divided into packets, transmitted through telephone lines, cables and routers, and reassembled at the user's computer, this change in the computer file does not constitute a change in the musical composition that has resulted in the creation of any new elements. Therefore, a derivative work has not been created.

(C) **is incorrect.** The musical composition has not appeared on the screen of the user's computer, so no display has been made of the musical composition. If the music and lyrics of the musical composition appeared on the computer screen, that would constitute a public display.

(D) **is incorrect.** The digital transmission right of section 106(6) only applies to sound recordings, not musical compositions.

76.   **The correct answer is (D).** Section 106(6) creates a digital transmission right that applies only to sound recordings. Here a sound recording has been transmitted, in digital form, to the public.

(A) is incorrect. Although the computer file containing the sound recording is divided into packets, transmitted through telephone lines, cables, and routers, and reassembled at the user's computer, this change in the computer file does not constitute a change in the sound recording that has resulted in the creation of any new elements. Therefore, a derivative work has not been created.

(B) is incorrect. Although the transmission of a work over the Internet is generally deemed to be a public performance under section 106(4), sound recordings do not have public performance rights.

(C) is incorrect. The act of streaming does not create a display. In addition, sound recordings do not have public display rights.

77. **(C) is the correct answer.** While The Curve clearly had aesthetic appeal, its particular shape was also dictated by functional considerations. As the PI advertisement stated, changing the design even a little bit would alter the quality of the smoking experience delivered by The Curve. In a very similar case, the Ninth Circuit recently held that a hookah water pipe was not subject to copyright protection because while it had a pleasing aesthetic, its design was not separable from its utility because if the shape of the water pipe changed, the pipe would work differently. *Inhale, Inc. v. Starbuzz Tobacco, Inc.*, 739 F.3d 446 (9th Cir. 2014); *see also Bonazoli v. R.S.V.P. Int'l, Inc.*, 353 F. Supp. 2d 218, 225 (D.R.I. 2005) (heart and arrow shaped measuring spoons not protected by copyright because "[e]verything about their size and shape is designed to measure material accurately and to scoop effectively").

By contrast, if the designer of The Curve had added the S-shaped stem to the pipe solely due to aesthetic considerations, it would be copyrightable. *See Brandir Int'l, Inc. v. Cascade Pacific Lumber Co.*, 834 F.2d 1142 (2d Cir. 1987) (conceptual separability exists "where the design elements can be identified as reflecting the designer's artistic judgment exercised independently of functional influences"); *Pivot Point Int'l, Inc. v. Charlene Prods., Inc.*, 372 F.3d 913, 931 (7th Cir. 2004) (conceptual separability exists where the design elements can be identified as reflecting the independent, artistic judgment of the designer, exercised independently of functional influences).

(A) and (D) are incorrect because they misstate the correct legal standard. No conceptual separability doctrine states that the presence of aesthetic appeal alone gives rise to a valid copyright. Nor does any doctrine state that the presence of utilitarian function alone negates copyright. Rather, the doctrines seek to determine what elements of works that possess both aesthetic and functional features are copyrightable. *See Pivot Point Int'l, Inc. v. Charlene Products, Inc.*, 372 F.3d 913, 921–29 (7th Cir. 2004) (discussing the problem of conceptual similarity as the challenge of determining copyrightability in objects that possess both aesthetic and functional elements).

(B) is incorrect because a valid registration certificate only creates a presumption of a copyright's validity. That presumption can be overcome by a showing that a work is not copyrightable. *E.g., Aalmuhammed v. Lee*, 202 F.3d 1227, 1236 (9th Cir. 1999) (validity of film consultant's certificate of registration containing claim that he was co-creator, co-writer, and co-director of *Malcolm X* rebutted on summary judgment); *Fonar Corp. v. Domenick*, 105 F.3d 99, 104 (2d Cir. 1997) (evidence that work is copied from work in the public domain or is non-copyrightable may be sufficient to rebut presumption of validity).

78.   **(C) is the correct answer.** The point of RG's "master down, 3 up" model was solely to distribute living space in a particular way, namely separating out parents from children. This is a purely functional aspiration, and indicates that the relevant features of RG's model are utilitarian, not aesthetic. They thus lack the requisite creativity to merit copyright protection. *See Medallion Homes Gulf Coast, Inc. v. Tivoli Homes of Sarasota, Inc.*, 656 Fed. App'x 450, 454 (11th Cir. 2016) (holding that a home design with "four-three split plans, that is, four-bedroom, three-bathroom plans with a master bedroom on one end and three other rooms at the other end" represented only a functional way to distribute space, not an instance of aesthetic expression meriting copyright protection).

(A) is incorrect because Alvernaz' intentions with respect to RG are not relevant to copyright infringement, which is a strict-liability tort.

(B) is incorrect because, as RG itself explained, the main inspiration of the "master down, 3 up" design is functional, not aesthetic. Also, the design is a simple idea composed of simple, preexisting elements (master bedrooms and regular bedrooms in a two-story house), and such generic floor plans do not merit copyright protection as architectural works. *See Home Design Servs. v. Turner Heritage Homes, Inc.*, 825 F.3d 1314, 1326–27 (11th Cir. 2016); *see also* 17 U.S.C. § 101 (defining "architectural work" to exclude "individual standard features").

(D) is incorrect because building a structure based on protected architectural plans without the permission of the owner of those plans amounts to infringement. *Cf. Shine v. Childs*, 382 F. Supp. 2d 602 (S.D.N.Y. 2005) (holding that an architectural model infringed copyright in an architectural work embodied only in a model). In this case, though, this issue is moot because the features Alvernaz copied were not protected by copyright because they were functional.

79.   **(D) is the correct answer.** The en banc Ninth Circuit recently considered whether actors own a separate copyright in their performances in a very similar case regarding the controversial film, "The Innocence of Muslims." The court resoundingly rejected this argument, holding that actors do not own a separate copyright in their performances. *Garcia v. Google, Inc.*, 786 F.3d 733, 740–41 (9th Cir. 2015) (en banc). The court explained that not everything will qualify as a distinct work of authorship, and stressed the list of works of authorship in the Copyright Act as an exclusive enumeration of types of works that could merit copyright protection. *Id.* at 742. The court also emphasized the practical problems that would arise if all works of authorship could be subdivided infinitely into smaller units of creativity. Instead, it held that any creative expression by performers in films was subsumed by the copyright in the audiovisual work itself.

In light of *Garcia v. Google*, Extra would be out of luck. His acting performance, however effective, did not give rise to a separate copyright. Instead, it was subsumed by Producer's ownership of the copyright in the film itself.

(A) is incorrect because Producer did not need to seek a waiver of Extra's copyright interest in his performance copyright. There is no such performance copyright.

(B) is incorrect because regardless of the creativity inherent in Extra's performance, performers have no separate copyright in their performances.

(C) is incorrect because no courts have so held. Nor would they need to, since there is no separate copyright interest in actors' performances.

80.   **(B) is the correct answer.** Non-human objects can be subject to a character copyright when they meet the same standards that apply to all character copyrights. That is, they must have physical and conceptual qualities that are sufficiently delineated to be recognizable in repeated situations, and must not be a stock character. *DC Comics v. Towle*, 802 F.3d 1012, 1021–22 (9th Cir. 2015). Lightning clearly meets these standards, since it has numerous distinctive and recognizable features that distinguish it from a standard pogo stick — like a face, a catchphrase, and a particular design. BizMo's unauthorized copying of Lightning's essential features thus infringes Producer's copyright in that character.

(A) is incorrect because it is not clear whether Lightning is copyrightable as a sculptural work, since it has both functional and aesthetic features. In any event, the issue is moot since Producer advanced the argument that BizMo's use violates its graphical character copyright in Lightning, not any sculptural copyright it might have.

(C) is incorrect because this proposition was specifically rejected in *Towle*, 802 F.3d at 1021–22.

(D) is incorrect because character copyrights are not subject only to verbatim copying. Such a rule would be impossible to enforce since characters invariably shift and change over time; there is frequently not one single version of a literary or graphic character. *See Toho Co. Ltd. v. William Morrow & Co., Inc.*, 33 F. Supp. 2d 1206, 1215–16 (C.D. Cal. 1998) (although Godzilla shifted from evil to good over time, there remains an underlying set of attributes that remain in very film); *Metro-Goldwyn-Mayer v. Am. Honda Motor*, 900 F. Supp. 1287, 1296–97 (C.D. Cal. 1995) (James Bond graphic character consisted of identifiable set of traits developed over course of 16 films).

81.   Probably not. Betty did not make a verbatim copy of Boomer's video, so Boomer has to argue that she copied some other protected feature of "The Boom Method." The exercises themselves can clearly not qualify for copyright protection. They are standard movements that are not original to Boomer. Nor is "Get Pumped!" substantially similar to "The Boom Method" on a total concept and feel theory; if anything, it is dramatically different in its setting, style, and overall mood. Betty's video seeks to distract the viewers with energetic music and varied backgrounds, while Boomer's video focuses solely on the workout itself.

The best claim Boomer has to copyrightable subject matter in "The Boom Method" is that the sequence of exercises he used in his video is a copyrightable compilation. Boomer could, for example, argue that these movements, in their particular sequence, amount to a copyrightable compilation that might be termed a choreographic work.

While plausible, this argument would likely also fail. The order of operations for the exercises chosen by Boomer does not necessarily exhibit creativity. On the contrary, Boomer portrays his video as a spare, no-frills way to work out that is designed only to increase muscle mass. The sequence of exercises thus does not exhibit the kind of expressive creativity that characterizes dance choreography, but is largely functional. On similar facts, a federal appeals court recently held that a series of yoga poses does not amount to copyrightable subject matter because it lacks the kind of creative originality that is characteristic of choreographic works. *Bikram's Yoga Coll. of India, L.P. v. Evolution Yoga, LLC*, 803 F.3d 1032, 1035–27 (9th Cir. 2015). The same result would very likely obtain here.

82.   **(C) is the correct answer.** While landscape design, including the creation of topiary sculptures such as Jane's, is highly creative, courts have held that because plants are constantly changing, artistic expression that uses plants or flowers as its medium is not sufficiently fixed for the purpose of copyright. As the Seventh Circuit recently explained, "A garden's constituent elements are alive and inherently changeable, not fixed." *Kelley v. Chicago Park Dist.*, 635 F.3d 290 (7th Cir. 2011).

(A) is incorrect because the "Larry the Lion" topiaries are not fixed in a tangible medium, as explained above.

(B) is incorrect because a work must separately meet each of the copyright prerequisites of originality and fixation. They do not operate in a sliding scale where an excess of one can make up for the lack of another.

(D) is incorrect because Jane's "Larry the Lion" does not merely depict wildlife verbatim. Her topiaries are "whimsical," and Larry in particular features a "toothy grin," each of which evidences that Jane added substantial creative originality beyond the mere image of a lion.

Ownership of Copyright

83.   **(C) is the correct answer.** The computer program is subject to the 1976 Act presumption that the copyright in any work created by an independent contractor, such as Programmer in this case, is owned by the independent contractor. This presumption can be rebutted only if the parties have signed a written work made for hire agreement and the work to be created is included in one of the nine categories of works listed in section 101's definition of work made for hire. See 17 U.S.C. § 101 (defining "work made for hire"). A computer program is not listed among those nine categories.

    (A) is incorrect. Under the 1909 Act, any work created at the instance and expense of another would be considered a work made for hire and the hiring party would be considered the author of the work and its initial copyright owner. The computer program in this case was created "recently," thus not under the 1909 Act. Even under the 1976 Act, Programmer is not an employee, therefore, Florist would not be deemed the author due to his status an employer. Programmer is an independent contractor who is presumed to be the copyright owner for the reason stated above.

    (B) is incorrect. Even if the parties had signed a written work made for hire agreement, a computer program is not included in the nine categories of works that can be deemed a work made for hire when created by an independent contractor.

    (D) is incorrect for the reasons stated above.

84.   **(C) is the correct answer.** While Frontera is the rightful owner of the books themselves, those are only copies—i.e., the objects in which the work of authorship, Author's novel, is fixed. See 17 U.S.C. § 101 (defining "copies" as "the material objects, other than phonorecords, in which a work is fixed by any method now known or later developed, and from which the work can be perceived, reproduced, or otherwise communicated, either directly or with the aid of a machine or device."). By contrast, the literary work of authorship that is the subject of copyright remains Author's intellectual property, regardless of who owns the physical copies in which that work is fixed. 17 U.S.C. § 202 ("Ownership of a copyright, or of any of the exclusive rights under a copyright, is distinct from ownership of any material object in which the work is embodied."). *See Salinger v. Random House, Inc.*, 811 F.2d 90 (2d Cir. 1987) (explaining that the author owns the copyright in the content of a letter as a literary work, the recipient of the letter owns the paper on which the literary work is written, and the transfer of ownership of one does not transfer the ownership of the other). Therefore, the only party who can sue for copyright infringement is the owner

of the copyright, Author. Frontera Bookstore may, of course, be able to sue Envy for replevin to recover the actual books, or for damages to compensate Frontera Bookstore for its loss, but not for copyright infringement.

(A), (B), and (D) are incorrect because they wrongly state either that Author will not prevail in an action for copyright infringement or that Frontera will.

85. **(D) is the correct answer.** By virtue of the fact that Painter made the work himself, he is its creator. However, he may not be its author under the Copyright Act if the painting was a work made for hire. 27 U.S.C. § 201(b) ("In the case of a work made for hire, the employer or other person for whom the work was prepared is considered the author for purposes of this title[.]"). In that circumstance, the party that hired Painter to create the painting would be the author, not Painter. Finally, Painter may not be the owner of the work. Merely because he created the work does not mean that he retained an ownership interest in its copyright. For example, he could have assigned its copyright to another person.

(A), (B), and (C) are incorrect because they falsely state that Painter is either the author or the owner of the work.

86. Sculptor is the creator of the work because he is the one who conceived and executed it. Left Coast Studios is the author of the work, because the sculpture was a work made for hire. The work is deemed a work made for hire because it was created by an employee acting within the scope of his employment. The Copyright Act defines the hiring party as the "author" of any work made for hire. 17 U.S.C. § 201(b). Finally, Museum is the owner of the physical sculpture itself because it purchased the object, but not the work of authorship embodied in that object. Museum thus would not be able to exploit the sculpture through photographs or replicas without Left Coast's permission. The ownership of the object is separate from the ownership of the copyright in the sculptural work. 17 U.S.C. § 202. Left Coast Studios remains the owner of the copyright in the sculptural work after the Museum's purchase.

87. **(B) is the correct answer.** First, it is important to note that this fact pattern takes place in 1950. It is thus governed by the law regarding work made for hire under the 1909 Copyright Act, not the work made for hire provisions of the 1976 Copyright Act. Authorship is determined at the time of its creation. Works created before January 1, 1978, are subject to the 1909 Copyright Act, and those created on or after January 1, 1978, are subject to the 1976 Copyright Act. *See Roth v. Pritikin*, 710 F.2d 934, 938–39 (2d Cir. 1983) (work made for hire rules of the 1976 Copyright Act are applied prospectively, not retroactively).

Under the 1909 Copyright Act, the party at whose "instance and expense" a work was created was presumed to be its legal "author" for copyright purposes because it was a work made for hire. *Martha Graham Sch. & Dance Found., Inc. v. Martha Graham Center of Contemporary Dance, Inc.*, 380 F.3d 624, 634–35 (2d Cir. 2004). That Fritzlinger directed Poet to create the poem means that it was created at Fritzlinger's "instance." *See Siegel v. National Periodical Publications, Inc.*, 508 F.2d 909, 914 (2d Cir. 1974). The fact that Fritzlinger paid Poet to write the poem means it was created at Fritzlinger's "expense." *See Playboy Enters.,*

Inc. v. Dumas, 53 F.3d 549, 555 (2d Cir. 1995). Under the 1909 Act "instance and expense" test, then, Fritzlinger is the poem's author.

(A) and (D) are incorrect because a creator's status as an independent contractor is not relevant to the 1909 Act work made for hire standard. That standard made no distinction between an employer and an independent contractor by the "instance and expense" test.

(C) is incorrect because, under the 1909 Act, the amount of creative control exercised over the project was not as important as who initiated the work and who paid for its creation.

88. The work for hire status and authorship of the poem is the same, regardless of Poet's status as an independent contractor or Fritzlinger's employee. Under the 1909 Act, the standard for whether a work was a work made for hire was whether it was made at the "instance and expense" of the hiring party, and this was true regardless of whether the creator was an employee or an independent contractor. *See Murray v. Gelderman*, 566 F.2d 1307 (5th Cir. 1978); *Easter Seal Society for Crippled Children & Adults of La., Inc. v. Playboy Enters.*, 815 F.2d 324, 325–27 (5th Cir. 1987).

89. **(A) is the correct answer.** For a work created by an employee to be deemed a work made for hire, it must be created by the employee while she was acting within the scope of her employment. 17 U.S.C. §§ 101, 201(b). While Worker would be considered an employee of Manufacturer during her vacation, her work was clearly outside the scope of her employment. It was not performed at her employer's direction, had nothing to do with her job description or the subject matter of her employment and was created away from her employer's place of business. The mere fact that the creator of a work happens to be an employee does not allow the employer to claim authorship of every work created by the employee. "[N]o one sells or mortgages all the products of his brain to his employer by the mere fact of employment." *Public Affairs Assocs. v. Rickover*, 177 F. Supp. 601, 604–05 (D.D.C. 1959), *rev'd on other grounds*, 284 F.2d 262 (1960), *vacated for insufficient record*, 369 U.S. 111 (1962), *on remand*, 268 F. Supp. 444 (D.D.C. 1967).

(B) is incorrect because Worker would not be considered an independent contractor because the novel was not created at the instance and expense of the hiring party.

(C) is incorrect because it is overly broad. A work made for hire created by an employee must be made not just by the employee, but by the employee while acting within the scope of her employment.

(D) is incorrect because it misstates the law. There is no such presumption about the ownership of works made for hire.

90. **(C) is the correct answer.** Polly clearly worked as an independent contractor: she used her own materials, acted with little or no influence from Big Press, created the work at her home, and was paid in a manner inconsistent with employee status. In the absence of an agreement, this would mean the English translation is not a work made for hire, and Polly would be its author. However, the agreement signed by both Polly and Big Press indicates that Big Press is to be considered the author of the translation. Although the phrase "work

made for hire" was apparently not contained in the agreement, such language is not required if the agreement reflects the parties' intent that the work to be created is to be a work made for hire. *See Armento v. Laser Image, Inc.*, 950 F. Supp. 719, 731 (W.D.N.C. 1996) (copyright statute does not demand that specific words "work made for hire" appear in the writing). In this case, the agreement did not state that Big Press is to be the "copyright owner," which would be consistent with an assignment of the copyright. Rather, the agreement stated that Big Press is to be the "author of the work," language with significance only to the issue of whether the work is to be a work made for hire. Therefore, the writing requirement has been met. Also because this work, a translation, is one of the nine categories of works for which such agreements are enforceable, the statutory category requirement has also been met. Therefore, the presumption that Polly, as an independent contractor, was the author of the English translation was overcome by the signed work made for hire agreement and the fact that the work fell within the statutory work made for hire categories. This makes the hiring party, Big Press, the author of the English translation. *See* 17 U.S.C. § 101 (defining "work made for hire"); *Quintanilla v. Texas Television Inc.*, 139 F.3d 494, 497 (5th Cir. 1998).

(A) is incorrect because the 1976 Copyright Act specifically provides for certain written agreements that determine authorship status in situations where the work is to be created by an independent contractor. An agreement to create a translation is such an agreement.

(B) is incorrect because Polly's creation of the translation alone does not determine the answer to the question. The 1976 Copyright Act's work made for hire provisions mean that the creator of a work is not always its author. *See* 17 U.S.C. § 201(b); *Lulirama Ltd, Inc. v. Axcess Broadcast Servs., Inc.*, 128 F.3d 872 (5th Cir. 1997).

(D) is incorrect because Polly was clearly an independent contractor, not an employee acting within the scope of her employment.

91.   **(B) is the correct answer.** Works created by an officer of a corporation in the course and scope of her employment are considered works made for hire. *See Lulirama Ltd, Inc. v. Axcess Broad. Servs., Inc.*, 128 F.3d 872, 875 n.1 (5th Cir. 1997). The fact that Lucy made the memo at home rather than at the office is irrelevant, since she was acting on a direct order from the DynaCorp board of directors when drafting the memo. Works created by employees at their homes, on their own time, are usually found to be works made for hire when the employee is a supervisor and the work is related to the supervisor's employment duties. *See Miller v. CP Chemicals, Inc.*, 808 F. Supp. 1238 (D.S.C. 1992) (computer program created by employee at home, on the employee's own computer, on the employee's own time and without extra pay, was deemed within the scope of employment).

(A) is incorrect because it is overly broad. DynaCorp is not the owner of *anything* that Lucy writes while she is employed, but only those copyrightable works of authorship that she creates in the course and scope of her employment. For example, if Lucy wrote a love poem for her husband during the period of her employment, it would not be a work made for hire because it would be unrelated to her job.

(C) is incorrect because CEOs are salaried employees, not independent contractors.

(D) is incorrect because memoranda, while not "literature" in a colloquial sense, are still potential subjects of copyright protection if they meet the low bar of originality. *See Salinger v. Random House, Inc.*, 811 F.2d 90 (2d Cir. 1987) (letters); *Grundberg v. Upjohn Co.*, 137 F.R.D. 372, 19 U.S.P.Q.2d 1590 (D. Utah 1991) (litigation documents); *City Consumer Services, Inc. v. Horne*, 100 F.R.D. 740 (D. Utah 1983) (business records). Here the memo was long and detailed, and therefore would certainly have met the originality requirement.

92.   ConsultCo will prevail. ConsultCo is clearly an independent contractor because it was hired on a one-time basis, paid in a single lump sum, and was asked to do an independent report rather than one whose content was directed or determined by DynaCorp. *See Community for Creative Non-Violence v. Reid*, 490 U.S. 730, 751–52 (1989) (listing factors relevant to determination of independent contractor status). In the absence of a work made for hire agreement, ConsultCo is the author and copyright owner of the report and can do with it what it wants.

93.   (A) is the correct answer. Under the 1976 Act, in the absence of a signed work made for hire agreement, determining whether a work is made for hire depends on the creator's status as an employee. In order to determine that status, courts look to a multifactor test drawn from the law of agency. *See Community for Creative Non-Violence v. Reid*, 490 U.S. 730, 751–52 (1989). Here, because most of the factors (Fuchsia using her own design, GiantCo relinquishing creative control, a lump sum payment, no ongoing relationship) weigh in the direction of Fuchsia's not being an employee. Only one factor (Fuchsia using GiantCo's materials) weighs in the direction of Fuchsia's being an employee, it is clear that Fuchsia is not an employee and that she is thus the author of the mural. Because the mural was created at the instance and expense of GiantCo, Fuchsia is an independent contractor who is deemed the author of the mural because there was no work made for hire agreement.

(B) is incorrect because no single factor is dispositive in this analysis; rather, it is a context-sensitive, multifactor test.

(C) is incorrect because the test does not require that all factors weigh in the same direction in order to determine whether a given creator is an independent contractor or an employee.

(D) is incorrect because it is not necessary to know about the provision of health benefits in order to determine whether Fuchsia is an employee or independent contractor. The *CCNV* analysis does not make any one factor dispositive.

94.   (C) is the correct answer. There are two ways a work can be regarded as a joint work under the Copyright Act. One way is for the work to be the product of a simultaneous collaboration, as was the case with *Spring*, where Writer and Author actively worked with one another as they wrote the piece. Another means by which a work can be regarded as a joint work, though, is for two creators to contribute to the work with the intent that it be merged with

the contribution of other authors as "inseparable, e.g. as in a novel or painting, or interdependent, e.g. as in words and music of a musical composition, parts of a unitary whole." 17 U.S.C. § 101 (definition of "joint work"). This is the means by which Writer and Musician created the final version of *Autumn*. Although there was no active collaboration, i.e., meetings or mutual revisions, during the process of creating *Autumn*, the authors' mutual expectation that their work be merged into a unified whole makes it a joint work as well. In both cases, the material contributed by each of the putative joint authors was fixed and original, and therefore copyrightable.

(A), (B), and (D) are incorrect because they assume either that *Spring* or *Autumn* is not a joint work.

95. **(D) is the correct answer.** W.C. and E.C. each contributed to a collaborative work with the intent that it would be merged into a single, unified whole. In addition, each contributed copyrightable material to the project. This is enough to make it a joint work; it is not necessary that the authors know one another's identities. *Systems XIX, Inc. v. Parker*, 30 F. Supp. 2d 1225, 1229 (N.D. Cal. 1998) (as long as intent to create a joint work is present, the authors of that work need not know one another's identities).

(A) and (B) are incorrect because it is irrelevant to a work's status as a joint work that a particular contributor began or completed the project.

(C) is incorrect because in the absence of a written work made for hire agreement, assignment, or exclusive license agreement securing the rights in the work, Producer owns nothing. Copyright vests initially in a work's creator, not in a work's producer, regardless of who is the "creative force" behind the project.

96. **(B) is the correct answer.** Joint authorship requires that all joint authors mutually recognize one another's status as joint authors at the time of the collaboration. *Childress v. Taylor*, 945 F.2d 500 (2d Cir. 1991). Here, neither Haul nor Screenwriter considered Haul a co-author at the time of the collaboration. This is clear because Haul was paid up front in a single lump sum, rather than evincing any expectation of compensation resulting from the sale of the screenplay. Screenwriter offered to credit Haul only as a "consultant," not an equal co-author, a designation that Haul happily approved. Further, Haul described himself as merely "chip[ping] in" to the project. It is clear that neither party intended a full co-authorial relationship. Similar consultant work on motion pictures has been held by courts not to constitute joint authorship on the part of the consultant. *See Aalmuhammed v. Lee*, 202 F.3d 1227, 1233 (9th Cir. 1999).

(A) is incorrect because it falsely assumes that there must be a written agreement in order for a work to be jointly authored. The Copyright Act contains no such requirement.

(C) is incorrect because contributing substantially to a creative work is only one of the requirements for a determination of joint authorship and does not necessarily make one a joint author. The courts also look to the intent of the collaborators at the time of the collaboration as to the joint authorship status for all putative co-authors.

(D) is incorrect because, although both Screenwriter and Haul intended their contributions to be merged into inseparable parts of a unitary whole, they did not share an intent to make Haul a joint author.

97.   On these facts, Haul has a much stronger claim to joint authorship. Whether collaborators are joint authors is determined primarily by the parties' intent to contribute to a joint work and their actual contribution to the work. The rules regarding joint authorship that were codified by the 1976 Copyright Act required that joint authors must intend, at the time of the creation of the component materials, to create a joint work. Each author must intend her contribution to constitute a part of a total work to which another will make or has made a contribution. *See Weissmann v. Freeman*, 868 F.2d 1313 (2d Cir. 1989); *Systems XIX, Inc. v. Parker*, 30 F. Supp. 2d 1225, 1229 (N.D. Cal. 1998). In addition, each putative joint author was required to contribute material that was more than *de minimis*. *See M.G.B. Homes, Inc. v. Ameron Homes, Inc.*, 903 F.2d 1486, 1493 (11th Cir. 1990).

A majority of courts have since adopted more stringent requirements. The putative joint authors must mutually intend that each be a co-author at the time the work was created. *See Childress v. Taylor*, 945 F.2d 500 (2d Cir. 1991); *Thomson v. Larson*, 147 F.3d 195, 201–02 (2d Cir. 1998). In addition, the contribution of each joint author must be copyrightable. *See Erickson v. Trinity Theatre, Inc.*, 13 F.3d 1061 (7th Cir. 1994) (actors participating in improvisational scenes did not provide independently copyrightable expression and were held not to be joint authors); *S.O.S., Inc. v. Payday, Inc.*, 886 F.2d 1081, 1087 (9th Cir. 1989); *Natkin v. Winfrey*, 111 F. Supp. 2d 1003, 1008–10 (N.D. Ill. 2000) (producer of television show did not provide copyrightable subject matter to photographs of the television set or individuals).

Factors to determine co-authorship status are "the contributor's decision-making authority over what changes are made and what is included in a work, the way in which the parties bill or credit themselves with regard to the work, any written agreements with third parties, and any other additional evidence." *BTE v. Bonnecaze*, 43 F. Supp. 2d 619, 624–25 (E.D. La. 1999). Because Haul had complete control over the very substantial revisions he made, and because Screenwriter implicitly approved Haul's referring to himself as a co-author on the front page of the script, Haul can make a much stronger case for co-authorship on these revised facts.

98.   **(D) is the correct answer**. The putative joint authors must intend, at the time of the creation of each of their component materials, to create a joint work. Moreover, the putative joint authors must mutually intend that each be a co-author at the time the work was created. *See Childress v. Taylor*, 945 F.2d 500 (2d Cir. 1991). Author never had any intent that Advisor would be a co-author, therefore, no joint authorship relationship ever arose.

(A) is incorrect because the relative importance of a creative contribution to the completion of a work of authorship, without more, does not create a joint authorship relationship.

(B) is incorrect because one party's unilateral subjective belief that he was a co-author is insufficient to create a joint authorship relationship. Rather, both parties must mutually intend that they are co-authors in order for such a relationship to arise.

(C) is incorrect because the relative significance of various contributors' contributions to a work of authorship is not dispositive of joint authorship status.

99.   (B) is the correct answer. The presence of a consensual, enforceable written agreement defining the contributors to a work of authorship as joint authors is, in the absence of any evidence to the contrary, determinative of their status as joint authors. *Cf. Childress v. Taylor*, 945 F.2d 500 (2d Cir. 1991) (listing written agreement between collaborators as factor in analysis for whether joint authorship relationship exists). As joint authors, the parties own the copyright in the work as tenants in common, and each has an equal, undivided share of the whole, unless expressly reapportioned in a written agreement signed by all the joint copyright owners. 17 U.S.C. § 201(a); *Glovaroma, Inc. v. Maljack Productions, Inc.*, 71 F. Supp. 2d 846, 853 (N.D. Ill. 1999); *Papa's-June Music, Inc. v. McLean*, 921 F. Supp. 1154, 1158 (S.D.N.Y. 1996) (writing requirement of section 204 applicable to transfers between joint authors).

(A) is incorrect. Although it is presumed that all joint authors will share profits in equal amounts, judges will recognize any reapportionment authorized by the joint authors made in a signed written agreement. *See Papa's-June Music, Inc. v. McLean*, 921 F. Supp. 1154, 1158 (S.D.N.Y. 1996) (writing requirement of § 204 applicable to transfers between joint authors).

(C) is incorrect. The amount of each author's contribution is not dispositive of joint authorship status, at least in light of an agreement clearly identifying the contributors as joint authors. In addition, once a person is acknowledged as a joint author, she is presumed to share equally in all profits derived from the use or licensing of the jointly owned work, unless the joint authors decide otherwise in a signed written agreement.

(D) is incorrect. As explained above, the relative substantiality of each co-author's contribution is not a factor in how profits from the work are allocated. They are presumptively split equally among all co-authors, as tenants in common, absent an agreement to the contrary.

100.   He is not. Each co-author need not contribute equal amounts of authorship, however, the contribution of each must be more than *de minimis*, and in the majority of jurisdictions must be copyrightable. Here, Neighbor's contribution would certainly not be copyrightable. Even in the minority of jurisdictions, where the contribution need not be copyrightable but must be more than *de minimis*, Neighbor's contribution would not cross the *de minimis* threshold because it is such a minor addition to the musical composition. Even in *Gaiman v. McFarlane*, 360 F.3d 644, 658–59 (7th Cir. 2004), in which joint author status for the contribution of ideas for a comic book character was permitted, the ideas established the basis for the character and deemed to be more than *de minimis*.

101. **(D) is the correct answer.** Artistic collaboration, i.e., joint authorship, is not the only means by which co-ownership of a work may arise. Rather, creation of a joint work is only one method of creating co-ownership of the copyright in a work. The assignment of less than the entire interest in copyright, or the transfer of the copyright to a partnership, also creates co-ownership of the copyright in a work. *See Oddo v. Ries*, 743 F.2d 630, 632 (9th Cir. 1984). Additional methods include willing the copyright to more than one person, or through state community property laws. *See In re Marriage of Worth*, 195 Cal. App. 3d 768, 241 Cal. Rptr. 135 (1987) (non-authoring spouse is joint owner of copyright in any work created by authoring spouse during the marriage). Thus, Author's transfer of part ownership to Wife, or his creation of a partnership with Wife with the copyright as an asset, are both valid means of creating co-ownership status.

    (A) and (B) are incorrect because they are not the only means by which valid co-ownership may arise.

    (C) is incorrect because merely attributing abstract support to another person does not make her a joint author and the introductory note is not a sufficient transfer of copyright ownership.

102. **(B) is the correct answer.** As joint authors of the musical work, Biggie and Smalls are tenants in common, which means that they each share equally in the ownership of the copyright in the work. *Glovaroma, Inc. v. Maljack Productions, Inc.*, 71 F. Supp. 2d 846, 853 (N.D. Ill. 1999); *Denker v. Twentieth Century-Fox Film Corp.*, 223 N.Y.S.2d 193, 195 (1961). However, because Smalls performed and recorded the track on his own, he owns the copyright in the sound recording outright. This does not mean that sales of the sound recording would not redound to Biggie's benefit as well. As a co-owner of the underlying musical work, Biggie would share in the mechanical license fees for the use of the musical work, but would have no claim to the profits generated by the sale of the sound recording.

    (A) is incorrect because it wrongly states that Biggie and Smalls co-own the copyright in the sound recording.

    (C) is incorrect because it wrongly states that Biggie alone owns the musical work.

    (D) is incorrect because it does not distinguish between the two works at issue, the musical work and the sound recording, the copyrights in which are owned by different individuals as indicated above.

103. **(A) is the correct answer.** Unless there is an agreement to the contrary, each co-owner has the independent right to use the work or to grant a nonexclusive license to non-owners to use the work. *See Oddo v. Ries*, 743 F.2d 630, 633 (9th Cir. 1984); *Cassidy v. Lourim*, 311 F. Supp. 2d 456, 459 (D. Md. 2004) (each band member who collaborated on album could license and promote the album). Thus, Guitarist was free to nonexclusively license Pianist to record and distribute her new arrangement of *Fighty Aphrodite*.

    However, Guitarist must share the profits generated by the license with the other members of the Midnights. A joint owner must abide by the rule of mutual accountability.

A joint owner is under a duty to account to other joint owners of the work for their proportional share of profits realized from the use or licensing of the work. The right of accounting may be enforced only against the joint owner-licensor, not against the licensee. *Oddo v. Ries*, 743 F.2d 630, 633 (9th Cir. 1984) (duty to account is derived from general principles of law governing the rights of co-owners).

(A) is incorrect because it incorrectly states that co-owners do not owe one another a duty of accounting.

(C) and (D) are incorrect because they wrongly state that a single owner cannot grant a nonexclusive license.

104.   If the license Guitarist granted to Pianist was exclusive rather than nonexclusive, Guitarist's unilateral grant would make the license unenforceable. An assignment of copyright or an exclusive license may be effected only by a grant in which all of the co-owners join. *See Glovaroma, Inc. v. Maljack Prods., Inc.*, 71 F. Supp. 2d 846, 853 (N.D. Ill. 1999); *Denker v. Twentieth Century-Fox Film Corp.*, 223 N.Y.S.2d 193, 195 (1961). Thus, a single joint owner, such as Guitarist in this case, may not unilaterally grant an exclusive license. A court would regard the grant as invalid and thus unenforceable.

105.   **(B) is the correct answer.** An agreement entered into by all of the co-owners cannot be rescinded by fewer than all of the co-owners. *Denker v. Twentieth Century-Fox Film Corp.*, 223 N.Y.S.2d 193, 195 (1961). Thus, here, because both co-authors agreed to exclusively license Singer to publicly perform and record *Temptations*, that license cannot be rescinded without their mutual consent. Composer's refusal to assent in the rescission means that the license remains valid.

(A) is incorrect because it is an overly broad statement of the law. Exclusive licenses to exploit copyrighted works of authorship, like any other licenses, may be rescinded, so long as applicable legal requirements are met.

(C) is incorrect because it wrongly states that a single co-owner's desire to rescind is sufficient to effect rescission of an exclusive license, when in fact all co-owners must agree to its rescission.

(D) is incorrect because one co-owner's desire to rescind a license is not sufficient evidence to support an inference that all co-owners want to rescind the license. Indeed, here, Lyricist wanted to rescind, but Composer strongly disagreed.

106.   **(D) is the correct answer.** When a musical composition has been licensed by its copyright owner for a recording, and the distribution of the recording on phonorecords or digital phonorecord delivery to the public for its private use, section 115 of the Copyright Act permits a new recording and distribution of the musical composition without the permission of the owner of the copyright in the musical composition. In exchange for this compulsory mechanical license, the statutory rate set by the Copyright Office must be paid for each unit that is distributed. *See Leadsinger, Inc. v. BMG Music Publishing*, 512 F.3d 522 (9th Cir. 2008). Singer's licensed digital downloads of her recording constituted digital

phonorecord deliveries of the musical composition that changed the status of *Temptations* to a distributed musical composition, making section 115's compulsory mechanical license available to Record Company. Of course, Record Company must actually take advantage of these provisions in order to avoid liability, which it has not done yet.

(A) is incorrect. It is true that the reproductions of the *Temptations* musical composition were unauthorized, but they did not constitute copyright infringement because they were permitted under section 115 of the Copyright Act.

(B) is incorrect because Record Company did not rely on Singer's agreement because it could be licensed under section 115 of the Copyright Act.

(C) is incorrect because section 115 of the Copyright Act does not simply obviate liability for unauthorized reproductions of musical works. Rather, it permits reproduction and distribution of phonorecords containing musical works when certain conditions, such as appropriate filings with the Copyright Office and payment of the compulsory license fee, have been met.

107. The first issue is whether Studio and Clark have infringed any of Michael's copyrights. The only work in which Michael has a copyright ownership is the novel. Michael did not supply any of the new elements that made up the screenplay or the two revisions to the screenplay, which are all derivative works. The Studio owns the copyright in the screenplay as a result of Clark's assignment of all right, title, and interest in the screenplay. Studio also owns the copyrights in the two revisions because Clark rendered those services as Studio's employee, making the revisions works made for hire and Studio the author and copyright owner of the revisions.

As for the claim that Studio has infringed the copyright in the novel, of which Michael, as joint author, owns 50 percent, Clark assigned his copyright interest in the novel to Studio. As a result, the Studio stepped into the shoes of Clark and has all of the rights in the novel that were previously possessed by Clark. As a co-owner of the copyright in the novel, Studio cannot be sued for copyright infringement for any use it makes of the novel. One joint owner cannot be liable for copyright infringement to another joint owner of the work. *Richmond v. Weiner*, 353 F.2d 41 (9th Cir. 1965); *Donna v. Dodd, Mead & Co., Inc.*, 374 F. Supp. 429 (S.D.N.Y. 1974). *See Gaiman v. McFarlane*, 360 F.3d 644, 652 (7th Cir. 2004). Therefore, Michael's copyright infringement claims will not be successful.

Michael will likely have limited success with his accounting claims. For such claims, Michael must identify the profits in which he believes he is entitled to share. A joint owner must abide by the rule of mutual accountability. A joint owner is under a duty to account to other joint owners of the work for a proportional share of profits realized from the use or licensing of the work. The right of accounting may be enforced only as against the joint owner-licensor, not against the licensee. *See Davis v. Blige*, 505 F.3d 90, 100 (2d Cir. 2007) (licensee need not pay any royalties or other consideration to co-owners not parties to license agreement); *Oddo v. Ries*, 743 F.2d 630, 633 (9th Cir. 1984) (duty to account is derived from general principles of law governing the rights of co-owners).

Michael's first claim will likely be for a share of the money received by Clark from Studio. Clark had received $100,000 for his copyright interest in the novel. Michael has no right to share in this payment because it did not flow from the use or licensing of the novel. One co-owner of a copyright is permitted to transfer her share of that copyright to a third party without the permission of the other co-owners and with no obligation to share the proceeds of that transfer. *See Glovaroma, Inc. v. Maljack Prods., Inc.*, 71 F. Supp. 2d 846, 853 (N.D. Ill. 1999); *Maurel v. Smith*, 271 F. 211, 214 (2d Cir. 1921).

The same is true for the $50,000 Clark received for revising the script. This payment was for the personal services rendered by Clark as an employee. Michael has no interest in the new material prepared by Clark as part of that employment.

The use of the novel in the screenplay and the motion picture, however, does require the application of the rule of mutual accountability. If Michael had a co-ownership interest in the copyright of the screenplay, then he would have a valid claim for $125,000 (50 percent of the $250,000 sale price of the screenplay) from Clark. However, because Michael only has a copyright interest in the novel, not the screenplay, his accounting claim is relevant only to the portion of the sale price attributable to the elements in the novel that appeared in the original script.

Similarly, Studio must account to Michael for 50 percent of the profits from the motion picture that are attributable to the use of the novel. Michael is not entitled to half of the $10 million profit made by the motion picture. The elements of the novel that were included in the motion picture are one of the numerous components that went into the creation of a commercially successful motion picture, including the performances of the actors, the skill of the director, the production values and the marketing campaign. The difficulty with such an apportionment is a major reason why motion picture studios will rarely, if ever, enter into unilateral agreements with a co-owner of a screenplay or its underlying work. Although copyright law may permit such agreements, business realities counsel against it.

108.   **(D) is the correct answer.** Under the 1976 Copyright Act, a copyright is fully divisible. A copyright is now viewed as a bundle of exclusive rights. Any of the section 106 exclusive rights that make up a copyright, and any subdivision of them, can be transferred and owned separately, whether or not the transfer is limited in time, media or geographic area. 17 U.S.C. § 201(d); *see, e.g., Gamma Audio & Video, Inc. v. Ean-Chea*, 11 F.3d 1106 (1st Cir. 1993). Thus, the various limitations placed by Studio on Distributor's exploitation of *Tiger Woman* are all valid and enforceable.

(A), (B), and (C) are incorrect because they wrongly state that certain kinds of limitations on copyright licensing terms are invalid. While there is some debate that certain licensing terms, such as those included in shrink-wrap and click-wrap licenses that restrict fair use or first sale privileges may be invalid, the limitations at issue in the Studio-Distributor license are undeniably valid.

109.   **(B) is the correct answer.** Any transfer of statutory copyright ownership other than by operation of law, such as by assignment or exclusive license, must be in writing and signed

by the owner of the rights conveyed or her authorized agent. 17 U.S.C. § 204; *Glovaroma, Inc. v. Maljack Prods., Inc.*, 71 F. Supp. 2d 846, 853 (N.D. Ill. 1999); *Billy-Bob Teeth, Inc. v. Novelty, Inc.*, 329 F.3d 586, 592 (7th Cir. 2003). Thus the oral transfer of rights in the novel from Writer to Speculator was never enforceable. Therefore, Writer can continue to act as the owner of the copyright, though Speculator can recover his $500 on a contract theory.

(A) is incorrect because it wrongly states that creators who transfer their copyrights retain licensing rights; unless there is some agreement specifying an express reservation of such rights, no such reservation takes place on these facts.

(C) is incorrect because the transfer in this case was invalid and never effectively shifted rights in the novel from Writer to Speculator.

(D) is incorrect because there is no evidence here to suggest bad faith, and that issue is not dispositive anyway.

110.   This would not change the outcome, because the law requires that a transfer of statutory copyright ownership must be in writing and signed by the owner of the rights conveyed or her authorized agent. 17 U.S.C. § 204. Here, while there is a written agreement memorializing the transfer, and while it is signed, it is still unenforceable because it is signed by the transferee, Speculator, and not by the owner of the copyright, Writer. If Writer had signed the agreement, the transfer would have been enforceable, though the use of the term "transfer" in the agreement is ambiguous. The term "transfer" could mean an assignment or an exclusive license. In either case, the rights conveyed would likely be sufficient to meet the needs of Speculator, though the scope of his rights could be questioned.

111.   **(B) is the correct answer.** The Copyright Act does not dictate specific language or form needed to satisfy the writing requirement of section 204. Rather, the writing need only demonstrate the owner's intent to transfer the copyright. *See Radio Television Espanola S.A. v. New World Entertainment, Ltd.*, 183 F.3d 922, 927 (9th Cir. 1999) ("No magic words must be included in a document to satisfy § 204(a)."); *Effects Assocs., Inc. v. Cohen*, 908 F.2d 555, 557 (9th Cir. 1990) ("It doesn't have to be the Magna Carta; a one-line pro forma statement will do."); *Natkin v. Winfrey*, 111 F. Supp. 2d 1003, 1011 (N.D. Ill. 2000) (written invoice with "buy out" notation may be sufficient writing for exclusive license). *But see Playboy Enters., Inc. v. Dumas*, 53 F.3d 549, 564 (2d Cir. 1995) (writing that did not expressly mention copyright failed to meet requirements of section 204(a)); *Saxon v. Blann*, 968 F.2d 676, 680 (8th Cir. 1992) ("[T]he conveyance of 'ownership rights' to a book will not convey the copyright of the book. To transfer ownership of a copyright, the parties must state in writing that they intend to transfer a copyright.").

In light of this, it is clear that the check in this case suffices as the kind of "written memorandum" of transfer required by section 204(a). It is in writing, clearly indicates what is being transferred, specifies the amount of consideration, and is signed by the owner of the rights. Any ambiguity as to whether Artist's endorsement on the back of the check counts as a valid endorsement of the terms of the transfer is eliminated by Artist's inclusion of her initials next to the written memorandum on the front of the check.

(A) is incorrect because it incorrectly states that the reason the written memorandum is valid and enforceable is that it was signed by the transferee, Publisher. In fact, the criterion for validity is that the written memorandum be signed by the transferor copyright owner, in this case, Artist.

(C) is incorrect because a minimal degree of formality is not required to satisfy the "written memorandum" requirement of section 204(a). Courts have consistently held that as long as the memorandum clearly memorializes the transfer and is signed by the owner, it is enforceable. *See Effects Assocs., Inc. v. Cohen*, 908 F.2d 555, 557 (9th Cir. 1990).

(D) is incorrect because section 204(a) does not require that the transferor copyright owner write the memorandum, but only that the copyright owner signs it.

112.   (A) is the correct answer. First, these events took place prior to the effective date of the 1976 Act, so the copyright in Screenwriter's script is governed by the 1909 Act. Prior to 1978, the transfer of such copyrights could be oral or inferred from conduct. *See Magnuson v. Video Yesteryear*, 85 F.3d 1424, 1428–29 (9th Cir. 1996); *Houghton Mifflin Co. v. Stackpole Sons*, 104 F.2d 306 (2d Cir. 1939) (mere delivery of manuscript by Adolf Hitler to publisher was sufficient to show transfer of the copyright in the manuscript). In this case, both the oral agreement between Executive and Screenwriter, as well as the course of conduct between the two, amply evidence their mutual understanding that a complete transfer of rights in the script should take place. Because the work of authorship at issue was both unpublished and unregistered, and because the situation occurred prior to 1978, this is sufficient to effectuate a complete transfer of copyright in the script.

(B) is incorrect because it misstates the rule under the 1909 Copyright Act. For any work that was invested with federal copyright under the 1909 Act, any transfer of copyright in the work was required to be in writing. In this case, the script was not invested with federal copyright protection, so the statutory writing requirement was not applicable. The script was protected by state common-law copyright that permitted oral transfers of copyright.

(C) is incorrect because it wrongly assumes that prior to 1978, agreements to transfer ownership of common-law copyrights had to be signed by transferor copyright owners.

(D) is incorrect because the term "copyright" need not be mentioned where the conduct of the parties so clearly implies the transfer of copyright. *See Urantia Found. v. Maaherra*, 114 F.3d 955 (9th Cir. 1997) (delivery of printing plates implied transfer of copyright in literary work).

113.   (C) is the correct answer. Once the copyright owner has granted an assignment of a copyright or an exclusive right, the copyright or the exclusive right belongs to the assignee, not the assignor. *See Walker v. University Books, Inc.*, 602 F.2d 859, 862 (9th Cir. 1979). An assignee therefore has the right to transfer its rights to a third party without the consent of the assignor. *See Gardner v. Nike, Inc.*, 279 F.3d 774, 780 (9th Cir. 2002). In light of this, ShoeCo is free to assign the copyright, validly transferred from Designer, to whatever third

party it chooses. Designer's distaste for BigCorp is immaterial in light of Designer's complete cession of his rights.

(A) is incorrect because it wrongly states that a complete assignment of copyright does not include the right to subsequently assign the copyright to third parties.

(B) is incorrect because assignees retain no such right of first refusal unless specifically provided for in the assignment agreement.

(D) is incorrect because nothing suggests that the assignment from ShoeCo to BigCorp was invalid. Even if it were invalid, this would not mean that Designer would prevail, because he would still have validly assigned away his rights to ShoeCo and would have no standing to contest their subsequent disposition by ShoeCo.

114.   The case would come out differently if Designer had granted an exclusive license to ShoeCo rather than assigning the copyright. An exclusive license does not permit the licensee to sub-license the copyright without the consent of the original licensor. This is a key difference between an assignment and an exclusive license under the 1976 Copyright Act. *See Gardner v. Nike, Inc.*, 279 F.3d 774, 780 (9th Cir. 2002). Thus if Designer had granted ShoeCo an exclusive license to use the copyrighted logo with no sub-licensing provision, ShoeCo's attempt to sub-license rights in the logo to BigCorp would be invalid because ShoeCo lacked the consent of the original licensor, Designer.

115.   **(B) is the correct answer.** When created by an independent contract, a work made for hire is a work that is created pursuant to a written work made for hire agreement, not a work that has already been created. *See* 17 U.S.C. § 201(b) (work made for hire is deemed authored by "the employer or other person for whom the work was prepared"). In such cases, the copyright in the created work would be obtained through an assignment or exclusive license. *Cf. Teevee Toons, Inc. v. MP3.com, Inc.*, 134 F. Supp. 2d 546, 549 (S.D.N.Y. 2001). Further, there was no written agreement signed by both parties in this case. As a result, the musical composition could not be deemed a work made for hire.

(A) is incorrect because the agreement entered into by the parties was never reduced to a signed writing.

(C) is incorrect because mere payment does not make a work a work made for hire. Payment may also be made for an assignment or license of copyright. Here the statutory requirements for a work made for hire were not met. In addition, the statement that Musician was paid to create the musical composition is false; he was paid to deliver musical compositions, not to compose original ones.

(D) is incorrect because the focus of the work made for hire statutory categories is the type of work created pursuant to the work made for hire agreement. Here, Musician created the musical composition before AdAgency requested the compositions. Moreover, this answer is wrong because if the musical composition had been created pursuant to AdAgency's request, that request would have been for use in a television commercial, an audiovisual work that is one of the statutory categories.

116.   **(C) is the correct answer.** Although the parties intended that the copyright in the musical composition be assigned to AdAgency, the attempted assignment was ineffective because it failed to meet the Copyright Act's writing requirement. 17 U.S.C. § 204(a). No exclusive license exists for the same reason. However, the writing requirement does not apply to nonexclusive licenses. A nonexclusive license can be oral, or implied from conduct. *See John G. Danielson, Inc. v. Winchester-Conant Properties, Inc.,* 322 F.3d 26, 40 (1st Cir. 2003) (nonexclusive license may be implied from conduct that indicates owner's intent to allow a licensee to use the work); *Nelson-Salabes, Inc. v. Morningside Development, LLC,* 284 F.3d 505, 514 (4th Cir. 2002). Factors indicating the presence of a nonexclusive license include: the putative licensee asking the creator to provide the work; the creator delivering the work to the putative licensee; and the creator intending that the putative licensee use and/or distribute the work. *See Effects Assocs., Inc. v. Cohen,* 908 F.2d 555, 558–59 (9th Cir. 1990).

In this case, AdAgency requested that Musician provide the musical composition, along with 11 other compositions, which Musician delivered. It was intended by the parties that the musical composition would be used in the television commercial for AdAgency's storage company client. By entering into an intended, albeit invalid, assignment of all rights to the musical composition, the parties demonstrated their intent to give AdAgency the ability to use the composition in as many commercials as it wanted on behalf of any number of clients. Therefore, the scope of the implied nonexclusive license that was created by the conduct of the parties included the use in a radio commercial for a bank as well as a television commercial for a storage company.

(A) is incorrect. The absence of a written memorandum memorializing an assignment of the copyright in the musical composition means that the attempted assignment was invalid. 17 U.S.C. § 204(a).

(B) is incorrect. As stated above, although the agreement between Musician and AdAgency did constitute an assignment or exclusive license, the conduct of the parties created an implied nonexclusive license that gave AdAgency the lawful right to use the musical composition in both commercials.

(D) is incorrect. Although AdAgency's request to Musician was for a musical composition to be used in a television commercial for a storage company, the request envisioned the possibility of AdAgency selecting all 12 compositions, not all of which would be used in the storage company commercial. Therefore, it was foreseeable that the delivered musical compositions would be used for more than one commercial and for more than one AdAgency client. Furthermore, the handshake agreement establishes the intent of the parties that AdAgency would own some interest in the copyright in the musical composition, thereby giving AdAgency the ability to use the composition in as many commercials as it wanted on behalf of any number of clients. The fact that the Copyright Act does not permit the transfer of copyright under these circumstances does not change the intent of the parties, which shapes the scope of the implied nonexclusive license that was created by their conduct.

117.   **(D) is the correct answer.** In the case of conflicting transfers, the first good faith recorded transfer of a registered copyright is given priority unless an earlier transfer is recorded within one month after the earlier transfer's execution in the United States, or two months after its execution outside the United States. 17 U.S.C. § 205(d). Thus, while Collector recorded her transfer agreement and Publisher did not, Collector's knowledge of a prior transfer of the copyright in the poem means that she is not a good faith transferee, and the recordation cannot give her superior rights to Publisher.

(A) is incorrect because recordation is not a precondition to validity of transfers of copyright ownership. Rather, it is a permissive, though advisable, means of memorializing transfers.

(B) is incorrect because the first party to record a transfer does not have rights superior to all other purported transferees. Here, for example, Collector's status as a bad faith transferee means that recordation cannot give her rights that are superior to Publisher.

(C) is incorrect because earlier transfers do not necessarily create rights superior to subsequent transfers.

118.   **(B) is the correct answer.** In the absence of evidence of the specific intent of the parties, a court will attempt to identify any indicia of a mutual general intent to include rights to uses in new technological formats. These indicia may be discerned from the language of the license, the surrounding circumstances, and trade usage. *Rey v. Lafferty*, 990 F.2d 1379 (1st Cir. 1993). Here, because the contractual clause is narrowly limited to "printed form," and because digital media did not exist at the time the agreement was executed, a court would almost certainly construe this agreement not to include the right to publish *Holidaze* in digital media. This interpretation of the agreement is strongly bolstered by the presence of the reservation of rights clause.

(A) is incorrect because it overstates the scope of the law. There are circumstances under which a licensing agreement executed in the context of analog media will be construed to grant rights to use the work at issue in the context of digital media as well. This is particularly true where the granting clause uses particularly broad language, such as a new technology clause. *See, e.g., Rooney v. Columbia Pictures Indus., Inc.*, 538 F. Supp. 211 (S.D.N.Y. 1982), *aff'd*, 714 F.2d 117 (2d Cir. 1982) (license to exhibit films "by any present or future methods or means"); *Platinum Record Co. v. Lucasfilm, Ltd.*, 566 F. Supp. 226, 227 (D.N.J. 1983) (synchronization license to perform a musical composition "perpetually throughout the world by any means or methods now or hereafter known").

(C) is incorrect because it is by no means always true that an agreement to publish a work in analog format implies a license to publish the same work in digital format. *See, e.g., Tele-Pac, Inc. v. Grainger*, 570 N.Y.S.2d 521, *appeal dismissed*, 580 N.Y.S.2d 201, 588 N.E.2d 99 (1991) (broadcast rights do not encompass videocassette film rights).

(D) is incorrect because a failure to explicitly exclude a reference to digital media does not imply an intent to include new media. This would be a particularly perverse approach where, as here, digital media did not exist at the time of the agreement's execution.

119.   **(C) is the correct answer.** The date of creation of *Sunrise Over Shatto* is important to this analysis as it determines the rules to be applied to the issue of copyright ownership. The 1970 date indicates that the law to be applied is that of the 1909 Act and the corresponding common-law rules regarding the status of copyright authorship and ownership. *Sunrise Over Shatto* was not created at the instance and expense of Collector, therefore the painting was not a work for hire. Avant created *Sunrise Over Shatto* for himself, though he likely created it for subsequent sale. This means that Avant was the creator and author of the work. Collector's subsequent purchase of *Sunrise Over Shatto* gave her the ownership of the canvas containing the copyrighted image, but not the ownership of the copyright. *See* 17 U.S.C. § 202 (ownership of copyright is distinct from the ownership of the material object in which the copyrighted work is embodied). Avant retained the ownership of the copyright in the painting.

Note that this answer would be somewhat more complicated in one jurisdiction — New York — that developed a presumption prior to the 1976 Act's passage that sales of works of art such as paintings or sculptures implied the transfer of reproduction rights as well. *See Pushman v. New York Graphic Soc'y, Inc.*, 39 N.E.2d 249 (1942).

(A) is incorrect. For the reasons stated above, Collector purchased the painting, not the copyright in the painting.

(B) is incorrect. For the reasons stated above, the painting was not a work for hire, therefore, Collector could not be deemed its author. In addition, Collector purchased the painting, not the copyright in the painting.

(D) is incorrect. *Sunrise Over Shatto* was painted by Avant, who is the creator of the work, not Collector.

120.   **(B) is the correct answer.** The date of creation of *Sunrise Over Palms* is important to this analysis as it determines the rules to be applied to the issue of copyright ownership. The 1970 date indicates that the law to be applied is that of the 1909 Act and the corresponding common-law rules regarding the status of copyright authorship and ownership. *Sunrise Over Palms* was a commissioned work created at the instance and expense of Collector, therefore the painting was a work made for hire. This means that the hiring party, Collector, is deemed the author of the work and the initial copyright owner of the work. *See Martha Graham School & Dance Found., Inc. v. Martha Graham Ctr. of Contemporary Dance, Inc.*, 380 F.3d 624, 634–35 (2d Cir. 2004) ("[W]ith respect to works for hire, the employer is legally regarded as the 'author,' as distinguished from the creator of the work.").

(A) is incorrect. Because *Sunrise Over Palms* is a work for hire, the hiring party, Collector, is deemed the author of the work.

(C) is incorrect. Because *Sunrise Over Palms* is a work for hire, the hiring party, Collector, is deemed the author of the work and the initial copyright owner of the work.

(D) is incorrect. *Sunrise Over Palms* was painted by Avant, who is the creator of the work, not Collector.

121.   **(C) is the correct answer.** The date of creation of *Moonlight Over the Bay* is important to this analysis as it determines the rules to be applied to the issue of copyright ownership. The recent date indicates that the law to be applied is that of the 1976 Copyright Act regarding the status of copyright authorship and ownership. Avant Jr. was not an employee of Collector, therefore, *Moonlight Over the Bay* was not a work made for hire created by an employee within the scope of his employment. Avant Jr. created *Moonlight Over the Bay* for himself, though he likely created it for subsequent sale. This means that Avant was the creator and author of the work. Collector's subsequent purchase of *Moonlight Over the Bay* gave her the ownership of the canvas containing the copyrighted image, not the ownership of the copyright. *See* 17 U.S.C. § 202 (ownership of copyright is distinct from the ownership of the material object in which the copyrighted work is embodied). Avant Jr. retained the ownership of the copyright in the painting.

The *Pushman* doctrine, which somewhat complicated the answer to III-37, *see Pushman v. New York Graphic Soc'y, Inc.*, 39 N.E.2d 249 (1942), has no relevance here. The 1976 Act was intended to create complete separation between copies and works of authorship, and therefore explicitly abrogated any doctrines to the contrary. And even before the passage of the 1976 Act, the *Pushman* doctrine had been overturned by statutes in New York and California. *See* N.Y. Gen. Bus. Law §§ 223–224; Cal. Civ. Code § 982(c).

(A) is incorrect. For the reasons stated above, Collector purchased the painting, not the copyright in the painting.

(B) is incorrect. For the reasons stated above, the painting was not a work made for hire, therefore, Collector could not be deemed its author. In addition, Collector purchased the painting, not the copyright in the painting.

(D) is incorrect. Avant, who painted *Moonlight Over the Bay*, is the creator of the work, not Collector.

122.   **(C) is the correct answer.** The date of creation of *Sunset Boulevard* is important to this analysis because it determines the rules to be applied to the issue of copyright ownership. The recent date indicates that the law to be applied is that of the 1976 Copyright Act rules regarding the status of copyright authorship and ownership. Avant, Jr. was not an employee of Collector, therefore, *Sunset Boulevard* was not a work made for hire created by an employee within the scope of his employment. However, *Sunset Boulevard* is a commissioned work created at the instance and expense of Collector, therefore, the Avant, Jr. was acting as an independent contractor when he created the painting. Unlike the law under the 1909 Copyright Act, where a commissioned work was presumed to be a work made for hire, under the 1976 Copyright Act, a commissioned work created by an independent contractor is presumed not to be a work made for hire. The independent contractor is presumed to be the author and initial owner of the copyright in the work created. This presumption can be overcome only if there is a work made for hire agreement signed by both the creator and the hiring party, and the work to be created falls within one of the nine statutory work made for hire categories set forth in the definition of work made for hire in section 101 of

the 1976 Copyright Act. Here there was no writing and the painting does not fall within one of the statutory categories. Therefore, *Sunset Boulevard* is not a work made for hire. Avant, Jr. is deemed the author and copyright owner of the painting.

(A) is incorrect. For the reasons stated above, Collector purchased only the physical painting itself, not copyright in the painting.

(B) is incorrect. For the reasons stated above, the painting was not a work made for hire; therefore, Collector could not be deemed its author.

(D) is incorrect. Avant, who painted *Sunset Boulevard,* is the creator of the work, not Collector.

123.   **(C) is the correct answer.** Vanessa and Angie created *Dirt Wars* as a jointly made work, as evidenced by their mutual intention to combine their original creative efforts into an inseparable and interdependent whole. *See* 17 U.S.C. § 101 (defining "joint work"); *id.* § 201(a) ("The authors of a joint work are co-owners of the copyright in the work."); *Childress v. Taylor*, 945 F.2d 500 (2d Cir. 1991) (elaborating Copyright Act standards for joint authorship). Angie, however, was an employee acting in the scope of her employment with GreatGames, so her joint ownership interest in the work vests with her employer. *See* 17 U.S.C. § 201(b) ("In the case of a work made for hire, the employer or other person for whom the work was prepared is considered the author for purposes of this title, and, unless the parties have expressly agreed otherwise in a written instrument signed by them, owns all of the rights comprised in the copyright."). Joint authors are tenants in common of the work of authorship they create, and are thereby entitled to equal shares of the profits produced by the work, regardless of the relative percentages of their respective contributions. 17 U.S.C. § 201(a); *Glovaroma, Inc. v. Maljack Productions, Inc.*, 71 F. Supp. 2d 846, 853 (N.D. Ill. 1999). So the two co-authors of *Dirt Wars*, Vanessa and GreatGames, would each be entitled to half of the $10 million profits it earned, even though Vanessa wrote most of the code.

(A) is incorrect because co-owners own equal interests in a copyright regardless of the relative percentage of their contribution. *Janky v. Lake County Convention & Visitors Bureau,* 576 F.3d 356 (7th Cir. 2009) (finding a songwriter who contributed only 10 percent to a musical composition to be a fully equal co-author).

(B) is incorrect because, as explained above, GreatGames, not Angie, co-owns the copyright in *Dirt Wars* with Vanessa, because Angie wrote her portion of the code while working as an employee in the scope of her employment.

(D) is incorrect because Vanessa is an independent contractor, not an employee of Great-Games. Nor is there an agreement between Vanessa and GreatGames indicating that *Dirt Wars* is a work made for hire (and if there were one, it would not likely be valid because it is not one of the kinds of works that parties can render a work made for hire by contract). So Vanessa retains a separate joint ownership interest in *Dirt Wars* that is independent of GreatGames' interest. *See* 17 U.S.C. § 101 (defining "work made for hire").

124. **(B) is the correct answer.** Vanessa was an original co-author of "Dirt Wars," and authorship is a fact about works of authorship that does not change and cannot be assigned. Ownership, however, is assignable, and by this agreement Vanessa transferred her copyright interest in the game to its other co-owner, GreatGames. As a result, she remains the co-author of "Dirt Wars," but GreatGames now owns all of the copyright in the game.

   (A) is incorrect because the question clearly states that Vanessa assigned all, not part, of her copyright in *Dirt Wars* to GreatGames.

   (C) is incorrect both because by virtue of the transfer, Vanessa is no longer a co-owner of *Dirt Wars* because she transferred away her entire copyright, and also because authorship is not transferable, so Vanessa will always be a co-author of the work.

   (D) is incorrect because, as explained above, authorship is not transferable, so GreatGames must remain a joint author of the work along with Vanessa.

125. These facts would make it a closer issue, but would still likely not change Vanessa's status as a co-owner of *Dirt Wars*. As the author of 75 percent of the game's source code, Vanessa is the dominant author, and this consideration alone strongly weighs in favor of categorizing her as an author of the game regardless of factors courts often entertain to resolve co-authorship status. *See Thomson v. Larson*, 147 F.3d 195 (2d Cir. 1998).

   Moreover, the fact that Vanessa was not explicitly billed as a co-creator of the game is not fatal to her claim of co-authorship. Courts have held a work to be jointly authored even where one co-author failed to credit the other, so long as significant enough evidence points in the direction of co-authorship. *See, e.g., Huurman v. Foster*, 2010 WL 2545865 (S.D.N.Y. 2010) (finding joint authorship in the absence of equal billing where numerous other factors established joint authorship). Here, Vanessa's authorship of the majority of the source code, her ongoing collaboration with Angie on an equal basis, and her shared decisionmaking control over the content of the game all point strongly enough to her status as a co-author that any evidence to the contrary from GreatGames' failure to give her due credit will be unlikely to undermine that claim.

   Finally, the fact that the founder and CEO of GreatGames was unaware of Vanessa's contribution also does not cancel out her claim to co-authorship. Many (though not all) courts have held that co-authorship requires both parties to believe the other to be a co-author. *E.g., Childress v. Taylor*, 945 F.2d 500, 507–08 (2d Cir. 1991) (requiring that parties mutually regard each other as co-authors for joint authorship to arise); *but see CSC Pub., Inc. v. Vibra Screw, Inc.*, 2003 WL 21180419, *2 (D. Minn. May 9, 2003) (defining joint authorship to require only that multiple people make independently copyrightable contributions that they intend to merge into inseparable or interdependent parts of a unitary whole). One could thus argue that since GreatGames is Vanessa's purported co-author, the company's total ignorance of Vanessa's contributions necessarily undermines her co-authorship claim. However, subjective beliefs about co-authorships are questions that must be proved by "objective manifestations of a shared intent to be co-authors." *Aalmuhammed v. Lee*, 202 F.3d 1227, 1234–35 (9th Cir. 2000). In light of this evidentiary standard, the substantial number of ways that Vanessa can actually prove she was a co-author mean that Jane's lack of knowledge about these facts will not eliminate her status as a co-author. Moreover, this is an unusual case where GreatGames is a co-author of the work only by virtue of the work made for hire doctrine; the actual creative contributions on their behalf were made by Angie, who was well aware of the substantiality of Vanessa's role in creating *Dirt Wars*. On an agency theory, this knowledge can likely be imputed to GreatGames as Angie's principal.

126.   **(B) is the correct answer.** Ed and Sesilia's co-ownership in the screenplay copyright arose by operation of federal law. Ed and Sesilia are thus co-owners of the copyright as tenants in common, and they are equally entitled to any profits produced by the copyright—including the $1 million fee Tantamount paid for the option to produce the screenplay.

The Copyright Act does not, however, provide a freestanding federal cause of action that would allow co-owners such as Ed to recover their fair share of profits earned by the work when the other co-owner has failed to pay them. For that, co-owners must turn to state law. Courts have held that state-law actions for accounting are the appropriate vehicle for co-owners seeking to recover profits from works of authorship wrongly withheld by other co-owners.

(A) is incorrect because there is no federal cause of action entitling co-owners such as Ed to recover funds wrongly withheld by other co-owners. For such relief, co-owners must turn to state law, as explained above.

(C) is incorrect because as co-owners, both Ed and Sesilia are free to use the work however they want, subject to the duty to account to each other for half of any profits generated by the work. Since Sesilia, as a co-owner, has a right to use the work however she wants, she would not need—and Ed could not grant—a license to use the screenplay. Owners of a work may grant a license (implied or otherwise) only to non-owners; they may not be granted between owners. *See Bubble Pony, Inc. v. Facepunch Studios, Ltd.*, 2017 WL 1379326, *2 (D. Minn. Apr. 4, 2017) ("[P]ermission to use a work is inherent to joint authorship.").

(D) is incorrect because, at most, Ed expressed words of discouragement with the project. Mere words are not enough to effect abandonment of a copyright.

127.   **(D) is the correct answer.** Co-owners of copyrighted works of authorship are free to use them however they choose, without permission from other co-owners, subject only to a duty to account to other co-owners for any profits earned by those uses. Co-owners are also free to grant non-exclusive licenses without the permission of other co-owners. *See Oddo v. Ries*, 743 F.2d 630, 633 (9th Cir. 1984); *Cassidy v. Lourim*, 311 F. Supp. 2d 456, 459 (D. Md. 2004). So here, Sesilia was free to transfer a non-exclusive option right to Tantamount unilaterally, regardless of Ed's objections.

(A) is incorrect because only a single co-owner's permission is required to effect a valid transfer of an interest in a co-owned copyrighted work of authorship.

(B) is incorrect because Ed's grant or withdrawal of permission to Tantamount to use the screenplay is irrelevant, since the studio has a valid grant of authority from the screenplay's other co-owner, Sesilia.

(C) is incorrect because Sesilia did not need Ed's permission to use the screenplay in any respect, either to show the screenplay to Tantamount or to sign a nonexclusive option deal with them.

Protection of Exclusive Rights

128. **(A) is the correct answer.** The exclusive right of reproduction is defined as the right to produce a material object in which the work is duplicated, transcribed or simulated in a fixed form. It is irrelevant whether the duplication is of only a portion of the protected work or that the reproduction is never released to the public. In either case, the right of reproduction is violated if a substantial amount of the plaintiff's work has been taken. *See, e.g., Walt Disney Prods. v. Filmation Assocs.*, 628 F. Supp. 871 (C.D. Cal. 1986) (copying of Disney animation as part of an intermediate step in Filmation's development of a motion picture was held to constitute an infringement).

In this case, Animator's mere act of reproducing some elements of the animation cels he created for Studio violates its exclusive right of reproduction, regardless of the fact that Animator never publicly released the short film or that he reproduced only segments of the background images from Studio's original cels.

(B) is incorrect because the right of public display is not at issue here. Animator never displayed his short film to the public.

(C) is incorrect because it is not a prerequisite for copyright protection that the images Animator created for Studio appeared in the animated feature film on which he was working at that time. As long as the images were fixed in a tangible medium of expression, they merited copyright protection.

(D) is incorrect because the right of reproduction applies to all protected elements of a work. It is not a defense that only subsets of the original work were copied.

129. **(C) is the correct answer.** Copying of a computer program into the RAM of a computer constitutes an infringing reproduction. *See MAI Sys. Corp. v. Peak Computer, Inc.*, 991 F.2d 511 (9th Cir. 1993); *Advanced Computer Servs. of Mich. v. MAI Sys. Corp.*, 845 F. Supp. 356 (E.D. Va. 1994). Here, by effecting the creation of a copy of the Bonestorm object code in the RAM of his computer, Bo violated SoftCo's reproduction right in that object code.

(A) is incorrect because courts have consistently rejected arguments that RAM copies of object code are too evanescent to count as copyrightable fixations, as illustrated by the cases cited above.

(B) is incorrect because while the Digital Millennium Copyright Act held that unauthorized RAM copies of object code made for the purpose of repair or maintenance do not violate the reproduction right, 17 U.S.C. § 117(c), Bo's use was not for one of these purposes, and thus does not fall within the DMCA safe harbor provision. The DMCA abrogated the application of the *MAI* cases to computer repair, but the legal principle established in those cases remains in force.

(D) is incorrect because in order to violate SoftCo's adaptation right, Bo would have to make a derivative work based on the object code, but Bo made an exact copy of the object code.

130.   Under these facts, Bo would not be liable for copyright infringement. While courts initially held that any RAM copies of a computer program's object code infringed the reproduction right, *MAI Sys. Corp. v. Peak Computer, Inc.*, 991 F.2d 511 (9th Cir. 1993), this holding was abrogated by the Digital Millennium Copyright Act. The DMCA held that RAM copies of computer programs' source code made for the purposes of repair or maintenance are not infringing. 17 U.S.C. § 117(c). Here, because Bo made the copy of the Bonestorm object code solely to diagnose and repair a problem with his personal computer, the reproduction of that object code would fall within the DMCA safe harbor and thus would not infringe SoftCo's reproduction right in the object code.

131.   **(C) is the correct answer.** The ability to use a work, generally a musical composition or sound recording, in the soundtrack of an audiovisual work, in synchronization with the images in the audiovisual work, has been deemed part of the reproduction right. *See Agee v. Paramount Comm'ns, Inc.*, 59 F.3d 317 (2d Cir. 1995); *Angel Music, Inc. v. ABC Sports, Inc.*, 631 F. Supp. 429, 433 n.4 (S.D.N.Y. 1986). In practice, when a musical composition is synchronized in an audiovisual work, a "synch" license is required. A "master use" license is necessary when a sound recording is synchronized in an audiovisual work.

(A), (B), and (D) are incorrect because they incorrectly state the exclusive right that is at issue prior to the exhibition of the motion picture. The distribution of copies of the motion picture containing the musical composition and sound recording to theater owners would be considered a public distribution. The performance of the musical composition in theaters would be considered a public performance. Sound recordings have no analog public performance rights. *See* 17 U.S.C. § 114.

132.   **(B) is the correct answer.** Although Band's live performance was unfixed and thus not copyrightable, Congress has amended federal law to prevent the unauthorized fixation of musical performances. One who fixes the sounds or images of a live musical performance, without the consent of the performer, is subject to the same remedies as a copyright infringer. 17 U.S.C. § 1101. Groupie's unauthorized recording of Band's performance runs afoul of the federal anti-bootlegging statute and would incur liability for this reason.

(A) is incorrect because the sounds that comprise Band's live performance are unfixed, and thus cannot merit federal copyright protection. The musical composition that was performed was in the public domain, with no copyright protection, and thus cannot be infringed.

(C) is incorrect because while Band's live performance is not copyrightable and the musical works performed were in the public domain, Groupie's recording of the performance can incur liability due to federal anti-bootlegging provisions that operate separately from standard copyright analysis.

(D) is incorrect because liability on an anti-bootlegging theory does not require that the copy was sold or distributed.

133.   **(D) is the correct answer.** None of these acts will expose SBPL to copyright liability. Libraries and archives are specially privileged to make reproductions under certain circumstances. *See generally* 17 U.S.C. § 108. Public libraries may make copies of protected works for patrons so long as the copy is not made for commercial advantage and the copy clearly indicates that the work is protected by copyright. *Id.* § 108(a). Thus Librarian's making of the single copy of the news article for Adam's personal use does not amount to infringement. A library or archive will also not be held liable for any copyright infringement resulting from the unsupervised use of reproducing equipment located on its premises, provided that such equipment displays a notice that the making of a copy may be subject to copyright law. *Id.* § 108(f). Thus Bob's surreptitiously using SBPL's photocopier to make an unauthorized reproduction of *Novel* does not expose SBPL to infringement liability, though it will almost certainly expose Bob to infringement liability. Finally, libraries may make unauthorized reproductions of copyrighted works for other libraries or archives so long as (1) the copy will become the property of the requesting institution; (2) the library making the copy has no reason to think that it will be used for other than archival and/or borrowing purposes; (3) it has been determined that a copy or phonorecord of the copyrighted work cannot be obtained at a fair price; and (4) the library displays prominently on its order form a warning concerning copyright restrictions. Because Librarian's copy for Archivist meets all four of these criteria, it also does not expose SBPL to copyright liability. *Id.* § 108(d).

    (A), (B), and (C) are incorrect because they wrongly state that any of the acts described in the question IV-6 will expose SBPL to copyright infringement liability.

134.   **(C) is the correct answer.** The owner of the copyright in a collective work has the right to reproduce and publicly distribute an individual contribution as part of that particular collective work, and has a statutory privilege to reproduce and distribute the individual contribution in any revision of that collective work and any later collective work in the same series. 17 U.S.C. § 201(c). Because *Bi-Coastal Magazine* published Journalist's article in its West Coast edition in substantially the same form as it appeared in the East Coast edition of the magazine, its use falls within the privilege, and Journalist's copyright infringement suit must fail.

    (A) is incorrect because it does not take into account the section 201(c) privilege that is available to Bi-Coastal Magazine.

    (B) is incorrect because the section 201(c) privilege permits the public distribution of an individual contribution in another edition of the collective work.

    (D) is incorrect because the privilege provided by section 201(c) is a limited privilege and does not create a license to use the individual contribution in all print mediums.

135.   Under these facts, Journalist would likely succeed in a copyright infringement suit against *Bi-Coastal Magazine*. The collective work revision privilege, 17 U.S.C. § 201(c), applies only to the reproduction and public distribution of works in their original context, while works that are denuded of that context do not fall within the privilege. *See New York Times Co. v. Tasini*, 533 U.S. 483, 496–97 (2001) (use of individual newspaper articles in electronic database, retrievable separately from newspaper, deemed not to constitute a revision under section 201(c)). Here, because the online database presents users with articles separated from their original context, divorced from accompanying articles, photographs and advertisements, the unauthorized use of Journalist's article would not fall within the privilege, and a copyright infringement suit by Journalist against Magazine would likely succeed. *See Faulkner v. Nat'l Geographic Enters. Inc.*, 409 F.3d 26, 38 (2d Cir. 2005) (searchable electronic replica of magazines held to be a permissible revision where new elements did not substantially alter the original context of the magazines).

136.   **(B) is the correct answer.** Dilettante is free to make a new sound recording of the *Winter* musical work so long as she does not duplicate the original sound recording *Composer Performs Winter*. However, Dilettante's unauthorized and uncompensated reproduction of the *Winter* musical work infringes Composer's copyright in the musical work. Dilettante did not need to acquire Composer's permission to reproduce the *Winter* musical work so long as he paid the statutory compulsory mechanical license. 17 U.S.C. § 115. However, Dilettante's failure to do this means that her reproduction and public distribution of the musical work amounts to infringement.

(A) **is incorrect** because it wrongly states that Dilettante's conduct violates Composer's copyrights in the sound recording and the musical work, when in fact it only violates Composer's *Winter* musical work copyright.

(C) **is incorrect** because the fact that the *Winter* musical work is subject to a compulsory mechanical license by statute does not mean that Dilettante is simply entitled to reproduce Composer's musical work without compensation. It merely means that Dilettante need not seek Composer's permission to reproduce the musical work so long as she pays the statutorily fixed licensing fee.

(D) **is incorrect** because a "master use" license is only necessary when a sound recording is duplicated in whole or in part. Here, Dilettante did not duplicate *Composer Performs Winter*.

137.   Attorney should advise Dilettante that she needs a license to record and distribute the *Winter* musical work. One option is to negotiate a consensual license with Composer. A second option is also available. Because Composer has recorded and distributed the *Winter* musical work to the general public, on phonorecords made for private use, Dilettante also has the option of using the compulsory license instead. Should he choose that route, Dilettante need not obtain Composer's permission to use the work. However, Attorney should emphasize that this is only true if Dilettante remits to Composer the statutory compulsory mechanical licensing fee for Dilettante's use of the *Winter* musical work and follows the other procedures outlined in section 115.

The Copyright Act provides that a non-dramatic musical composition that has been reproduced and distributed with the authorization of the copyright owner thereafter may be reproduced and distributed without the consent of the copyright owner pursuant to a compulsory mechanical license. 17 U.S.C. § 115. Under this compulsory license, the composition can be recorded, manufactured in phonorecords, and sold to the public for its private use, as long as the statutory royalty of 9.1¢ per unit is paid to the copyright owner. Stylistic changes to the composition are permitted, as long as the composition is not perverted or distorted, and the fundamental character of the work is not changed. *See ABKCO Music, Inc. v. Stellar Records, Inc.*, 96 F.3d 60 (2d Cir. 1996) (karaoke CD-ROM did not fall within section 115's compulsory mechanical license); *Rodgers & Hammerstein Organization v. UMG Recordings Inc.*, 60 U.S.P.Q.2d 1354, 1360 (S.D.N.Y. 2001) (compulsory mechanical license does not permit reproduction onto servers or streaming of composition over the Internet).

138.   **(C) is the correct answer.** Techie clearly owes a mechanical license fee to Composer for the reproduction and distribution of Composer's copyrighted musical work via an electronic phonorecord, known as a digital phonorecord delivery. 17 U.S.C. § 115. Such licenses may be consensual or may be obtained as a compulsory mechanical license under section 115. Until 1995, there was ambiguity as to whether the digital delivery of music, e.g., via .mp3 files, would trigger the compulsory mechanical license provisions of section 115. However, in that year, Congress settled the question when it passed the Digital Performance Right in Sound Recordings Act of 1995, which expanded the compulsory mechanical license to include "digital phonorecord delivery." Currently, the statutory fee set for digital phonorecord delivery is the same as the statutory fee set for sale and distribution of traditional physical phonorecords. 17 U.S.C. § 115(c)(3)(A).

In addition, the streaming of the *Songbird* musical work on Techie's website constitutes a public performance that must be separately licensed to avoid a copyright infringement claim. The section 115 compulsory license applies only to the reproduction and distribution of musical works in phonorecords, not to the public performance of musical works.

(A) is incorrect because it does not recognize the need to obtain a public performance license.

(B) is incorrect because it does not recognize the need to obtain a mechanical license.

(D) is incorrect because, as explained above, a mechanical license is required for a digital download and the streaming of the musical work constitutes a public performance, whether or not the musical work at issue has been released in a physical copy.

139.   **(D) is the correct answer.** Reproducing a sound recording and making it available as a digital download requires the authorization of Composer, the owner of the copyright in the sound recording. *See* 17 U.S.C. § 106(1). This authorization generally takes the form of a master use license, pursuant to which the licensee is given the right to make phonorecords of the sound recording. In addition, Techie is streaming the sound recording of *Songbird*. This constitutes a digital transmission of the sound recording to the general public, an exclusive right owned by Composer. *See* 17 U.S.C. § 106(6). To avoid a claim of copyright infringement regarding the sound recording of *Songbird*, Techie must obtain

either a statutory license pursuant to section 114 of the Copyright Act, or obtain a consensual license from Composer.

(A) is incorrect because it overlooks the digital transmission right of the sound recording of *Songbird*.

(B) is incorrect on two grounds. First, a master use license is necessary to offer downloads of the sound recording of *Songbird*. Second, sound recordings have no public performance rights under section 106(4).

(C) is incorrect because sound recordings have no public performance rights under section 106(4) and it does not address the need for a digital transmission license to stream the sound recording.

140. **(A) is the correct answer.** This conduct violates the reproduction rights of the copyright owners of all the musical works and sound recordings included on the CD Pal created for Friend. Pal might argue that his conduct falls within the home taping provisions of the Audio Home Recording Act ("AHRA"). *See* 17 U.S.C. § 1008. But this argument would fail because the reproduction of the copyrighted material onto the CD was done with a computer, which does not constitute a "digital audio recording device" under the AHRA. *See Recording Indus. Ass'n of Am. v. Diamond Multimedia Sys., Inc.*, 180 F.3d 1072, 1078 (9th Cir. 1999) (computers do not constitute "digital audio recording devices" under AHRA); *A&M Records, Inc. v. Napster, Inc.*, 239 F.3d 1004, 1024–25 (9th Cir. 2001) (AHRA immunity for noncommercial taping held inapplicable to .mp3 music file sharing program that does not involve a digital audio recording device).

(B) is incorrect because it does not address Pal's reproduction of the sound recordings.

(C) is incorrect because it does not address Pal's reproduction of the musical works.

(D) is incorrect. The Audio Home Recording Act of 1992 permits unauthorized audio recording for noncommercial use, 17 U.S.C. § 1008, but only when the recording is done with a digital audio recording device. Computers are not deemed digital audio recording devices, so Pal's use of his computer makes section 1008 inapplicable, even though his use was clearly noncommercial because the CD was merely an interpersonal gift.

141. **(B) is the correct answer.** The copyright owner has the exclusive right to prepare a derivative work that recasts, transforms or adapts the underlying original work of authorship. 17 U.S.C. § 106(2); *see, e.g., Grove Press, Inc. v. Greenleaf Publishing Co.*, 247 F. Supp. 518 (E.D.N.Y. 1965). By modifying Artist's painting through the addition of substantial original creative material, Pomo violated Artist's exclusive adaptation right. *See Peker v. Masters Collection*, 96 F. Supp. 2d 216 (E.D.N.Y. 2000) (painting over a poster of an oil painting deemed an infringement).

(A) is incorrect because the public display right is not at issue here due to the statutory exception that permits owners of lawfully made copies of copyrighted works of authorship to display them publicly without the owner's consent. *See* 17 U.S.C. § 109(c).

(C) is incorrect because it is immaterial whether Pomo altered the original version or a copy of Artist's work because the alteration was of the copyrighted image. In either case, there would be substantial recasting of the work of authorship sufficient to violate the adaptation right.

(D) is incorrect because copyright infringement does not depend on whether a work is offered for sale.

142. Most courts would hold that Pomo would not be subject to liability because his frame mildly resituated the work without adding anything original to it. A majority of jurisdictions require that the defendant must have created a work with sufficient originality to be deemed a derivative work to violate the adaptation right. *See Lee v. A.R.T. Co.*, 125 F.3d 580 (7th Cir. 1997); *C.M. Paula Co. v. Logan*, 355 F. Supp. 189 (N.D. Tex. 1973) (placing the work in a new context must be sufficiently original to be protectable as a derivative work for such action to be found an infringement of the adaptation right).

Some courts, however, would hold that even a slight recasting of a work, without the addition of any original material, would amount to infringement of the adaptation right. The Ninth Circuit, for example, has held that placing a work in a new context in which the work is "recast, transformed or adapted" is sufficient to infringe the adaptation right without a showing that the change contained sufficient originality. *See Mirage Editions, Inc. v. Albuquerque A.R.T. Co.*, 856 F.2d 1341 (9th Cir. 1988) (removing prints from a book, pasting them onto a tile, and framing the print constitutes an infringement). In such a jurisdiction, Pomo's conduct may be held to infringe Artist's work.

143. **(C) is the correct answer.** Linguo clearly violated the reproduction right in *Novel* by photocopying it without permission. *See* 17 U.S.C. § 106(1). Linguo also violated the adaptation right by creating an unauthorized translation of *Novel*. 17 U.S.C. § 106(2). *See, e.g., Grove Press, Inc. v. Greenleaf Publ'g Co.*, 247 F. Supp. 518 (E.D.N.Y. 1965).

(A) is incorrect because it fails to state that Linguo's conduct violated the adaptation right.

(B) and (D) are incorrect because they falsely state that Linguo's conduct violated the public distribution right in *Novel*. What Linguo did was likely not a public distribution because it was not public, but was distributed only to a small circle of known friends. *See Bagdadi v. Nazar*, 84 F.3d 1194, 1198–99 (9th Cir. 1996) (public distribution requires distribution of copies to the public, or the offering to distribute copies to a group of persons for purposes of further distribution, public performance, or public display).

144. **(A) is the correct answer.** Although the Copyright Act provides no definition of "distribution," the statutory provision creating the exclusive right of public distribution refers to an owner's right to "distribute copies . . . of the copyrighted work to the public by sale or other transfer of ownership, or by rental, lease, or lending." 17 U.S.C. § 106(3).

Here, Associate's conduct clearly amounts to public distribution because he disseminated numerous copies of Biglaw's employee handbook to the public, which amounted to an unauthorized "transfer of ownership." One might counter that because Associate purloined the copies, he could not effect valid transfers of their ownership (since he did not own them himself). Even so, a copyright owner's rights include not only the rights "to do" the acts enumerated in section 106, but also "to authorize" those acts, so that by purporting to authorize transfers of ownership in copies of Biglaw's work, Associate would have violated their exclusive right of public distribution on this theory as well.

(B) is incorrect because it contains an incorrect statement of law. Pursuant to the first sale doctrine, a copyright owner has only an exclusive right to make the initial transfer of copies of their work, without any right to the further distribution of that copy.

(C) is incorrect because Associate was not the owner of the copies he distributed. Therefore, he cannot take advantage of the first sale doctrine. 17 U.S.C. § 109(a).

(D) is incorrect because an infringer need not know the particular members of the public to whom an unauthorized dissemination is made in order to violate the public distribution right; a general dissemination is sufficient.

145.   Probably not. The answer remains unclear, however, because Biglaw's success depends on the meaning of "public" in connection with the exclusive right of public distribution. The term "public" is not defined in the Copyright Act. Its meaning, however, can be determined by looking at two analogous terms: "To perform or display a work 'publicly'" and "publication."

The phrase "[t]o perform or display a work 'publicly'" is used in connection with the public performance (section 106(4)), public display (section 106(5)), and public digital audio transmission (section 106(6)) exclusive rights. In those situations, the exclusive right is violated if the performance or display occurs in a place open to the public, or at any place "where a substantial number of persons outside of a normal circle of a family and its social acquaintances is gathered." 17 U.S.C. § 101. To the extent that the latter part of this definition governs the term "public" in "public distribution," it would exclude any distribution to members of one's family or social acquaintances. Under this view, the distribution of copies of the employee handbook to close friends would not constitute a distribution to the public. *See Bagdadi v. Nazar*, 84 F.3d 1194, 1198–99 (9th Cir. 1996).

Another defined term that may be relevant is "publication." Under the common law, a publication occurs when a possessory interest in tangible copies of the work is made available to the general public with the consent of the copyright owner. *See Shoptalk, Ltd. v. Concorde-New Horizons Corp.*, 168 F.3d 586, 590 (2d Cir. 1999); *Burke v. Nat'l Broad. Co.*, 598 F.2d 688, 691 (1st Cir. 1979). The definition of "publication" in section 101 of the Copyright Act expands the common-law definition to include "offering to distribute copies or phonorecords to a group of persons for purposes of further distribution, public performance, or public display." Under this view, the distribution of the three copies of the employee handbook to close friends would not have made the tangible copies available to the general public. This is particularly true where the copies are to be used for a specific purpose, to establish the viability of a proposed lawsuit. While it is true that under this definition a publication may be found where only one copy reaches a member of the general public, *see Ford Motor Co. v. Summit Motor Prods., Inc.*, 930 F.2d 277, 299 (3d Cir. 1991), a distribution to three close friends likely would not be deemed a distribution to members of the general public.

146. Probably not. On these facts, we know only that copies of the handbook were made available to the public, not that any members of the public actually acquired them. Most courts have held that merely making a copy available to the public, without more, does not amount to public distribution. *National Car Rental Sys., Inc. v. Computer Assocs. Int'l, Inc.*, 991 F.2d 426, 430–31 (8th Cir. 1993). *Capitol Records, Inc. v. Thomas*, 579 F. Supp. 2d 1210, 1225 (D. Minn 2008) (concluding that the plain language of the Copyright Act precludes the "making available" interpretation).

Some courts have held that merely making a work available to the public amounts to a public distribution, as where a library places a work in its catalog for users to freely access. *E.g.*, *Hotaling v. Church of Jesus Christ of Latter-Day Saints*, 118 F.3d 199 (4th Cir. 1997) (listing work in library's catalog system, adding it to library's collection, and making it available to the public constituted "distribution" of the work). This holding represents the minority of opinion, though, and has been specifically considered and rejected by subsequent courts as inconsistent with the plain language of the Copyright Act. *Capitol Records*, 579 F. Supp. 2d at 1217 ("Congress explains the manners in which distribution can be effected: sale, transfer of ownership, rental, lease, or lending. The provision does not state that an offer to do any of these acts constitutes distribution. Nor does § 106(3) provide that making a work available for any of these activities constitutes distribution.").

147. **(D) is the correct answer.** Computo's conduct clearly amounts to public distribution because he facilitated the public library's dissemination of Techie's protected computer code to the public. However, pursuant to the "first sale doctrine," the copyright owner's distribution right ceases with respect to a particular authorized copy once the copyright owner has parted with ownership of that particular copy. 17 U.S.C. §§ 109(a), 109(b) (emphasizing that first sale doctrine applies to computer programs, except when they are made available for rental, lease, or lending); *cf. also Mirage Editions, Inc. v. Albuquerque A.R.T. Co.*, 856 F.2d 1341 (9th Cir. 1988) (sale of initial copy exhausts owner's public distribution right). Therefore, any owner of a lawfully made copy of a work may sell or transfer the possession of that copy. Here, Techie parted with the CD-ROM on which his program was embodied when he gave it to Computo. This means that Computo was free to sell or transfer the flash drive, so long as it did not constitute disposing of the copy by rental, lease, or lending for commercial advantage. As a result, Computo's gift to the library is not actionable.

(A) is incorrect because the first sale doctrine applies to any circumstance under which an owner of the physical instantiation of a copyrighted work of authorship gives it to another. By giving the flash drive to Computo, Techie parted ownership with it, triggering the application of the first sale doctrine.

(B) is incorrect because it fails to note that while Computo's conduct may in itself amount to a violation of Techie's public distribution right, that conduct is immunized from liability pursuant to the first sale doctrine.

(C) is incorrect because Computo's conduct clearly amounts to a public distribution of the computer program for the reasons explained above.

148.   **(A) is the correct answer.** While the first sale doctrine generally allows purchasers of the physical objects in which copyrighted works of authorship are embodied to sell, rent, or give away those objects, the first sale doctrine no longer applies to the rental, lease, or lending of a sound recording of a musical composition embodied in a phonorecord. 17 U.S.C. § 109(b)(1)(A); *see A & M Records, Inc. v. A.L.W., Ltd.*, 855 F.2d 368, 370 n.6 (7th Cir. 1988) (buy-back program pursuant to which customers purchased a record for $2, plus a $5 deposit, which was returned at the customer's choice within a specified time limit, held to constitute a disguised rental). Because Entrepreneur's enterprise falls squarely within this exception to the first sale doctrine, the doctrine does not apply and the record companies have a valid cause of action against Entrepreneur for violating their exclusive right of public distribution in the sound recordings embodied in the CDs.

(B) is incorrect because the first sale doctrine does allow purchasers of music CDs to sell or give them away without running afoul of the copyright owner's exclusive right of public distribution. In addition, nonprofit libraries and educational institutions may also rent, lease, or lend sound recordings. 17 U.S.C. § 109(b)(1)(A).

(C) is incorrect because it wrongly states that the first sale doctrine immunizes Entrepreneur's conduct of renting sound recordings. It does not, for the reasons explained above.

(D) is incorrect because Entrepreneur's attempts to insulate the record companies from piracy are unrelated to the question of whether he has infringed any exclusive rights in the copyrighted works of authorship.

149.   **(D) is the correct answer.** To "perform" a work within the meaning of the Copyright Act means to recite, render, play, dance or act it. 17 U.S.C. § 101 (defining "perform"). This means that Orchestra's presentation of the modern classical music piece is a "performance" within the meaning of the Copyright Act. However, a transmission and even a "secondary transmission" (the simultaneous retransmission of a primary transmission), is a performance. *See Sailor Music v. Gap Stores, Inc.*, 668 F.2d 84 (2d Cir. 1981); *Broadcast Music, Inc. v. Claire's Boutiques, Inc.*, 949 F.2d 1482 (7th Cir. 1991). This means that Radio Station's primary transmission of the concert and Fan's retransmission of that broadcast in Hartford both amount to "performances" as well.

(A) is incorrect because it does not include Radio Station's primary transmission and Fan's secondary transmission.

(B) is incorrect because it does not include Fan's secondary transmission.

(C) is incorrect because it does not include Orchestra's concert.

150.   **(C) is the correct answer.** A performance is "public" if it occurs at a place open to the public or at any place where a substantial number of persons outside of a normal circle of a family and its social acquaintances is gathered. *Sailor Music v. Gap Stores, Inc.*, 668 F.2d 84 (7th Cir. 1981). Under this standard, the outdoor concert clearly counts as a public performance. The poetry reading, while a less clear case, also counts as a public performance because it takes place at a public venue. The performance would be deemed to be public even if no one attended the reading because the focus is on the public nature of the venue. *See* 17 U.S.C. § 101 (defining "To perform or display a work 'publicly'") ("place open to the public"); *Video Views, Inc. v. Studio 21, Ltd.*, 925 F.2d 1010, 1020 (7th Cir. 1991) ("proper inquiry is directed to the nature of the place . . . and whether it is a place where the public is openly invited."). The comedy routine is a harder call still because a private club seems hard to define as public. Yet performances at "semi-public" places such as clubs, lodges and schools are now found to be public performances. *See Bourne Co. v. Hunter Country Club, Inc.*, 990 F.2d 934 (7th Cir. 1993). The presentation is thus the only one of these performances that is not public, because the legislative history of the Copyright Act indicates that routine meetings of businesses and governmental personnel do not represent a gathering of a "substantial number of persons." *See* H.R. Rep. No. 94-1476, 94th Cong., 2d Sess. 64 (1976).

   (A), (B), and (D) are incorrect for the reasons explained above.

151.   **(B) is the correct answer.** Pursuant to the transmit clause in the Copyright Act's definition of "to perform . . . a work publicly," a performance is "public" if it is transmitted to a place specified by the "public place" clause, or to a place or separate places where the public is capable of receiving the transmission at the same time or at different times. 17 U.S.C. § 101. The transmit clause applies only when images or sounds are transmitted from one place to another place, but this is the case here because HG's transmission begins at its central server and terminates in numerous individual guest rooms. *See Columbia Pictures Indus., Inc. v. Aveco, Inc.*, 800 F.2d 59 (3d Cir. 1986) (holding that site-to-site transmissions are public performances within the meaning of the Copyright Act).

   (A) is incorrect because the Copyright Act does not define every performance of a motion picture as a public performance. For example, many times motion pictures are performed in private homes and are not deemed to be "public" performances. *See Columbia Pictures Indus., Inc. v. Redd Horne Inc.*, 749 F.2d 154, 157 (3d Cir. 1984).

   (C) is incorrect because courts have held that electronically transmitting a motion picture from a central device to individual hotel rooms constitutes a public performance. *See On Command Video Corp. v. Columbia Pictures Indus.*, 777 F. Supp. 787, 789–90 (N.D. Cal. 1991).

   (D) is incorrect because the transmit clause explicitly states that the transmission of a work of authorship from one site to certain types of other sites is a public performance of that work.

152.   No. As we saw in question IV-24, the transmit clause in the Copyright Act's definition of "to perform . . . a work publicly" states that a performance is "public" if it is transmitted to

a place specified by the public place clause, or to a place or separate places where the public is capable of receiving the transmission at the same time or at different times. 17 U.S.C. § 101 (defining "to perform . . . a work 'publicly'"). On these facts, HG is merely providing a conduit to the Internet. *See* 17 U.S.C. § 512(a). None of the copyrighted material at issue resides on HG's server. Any website that offered the streaming of copyrighted motion pictures without a public performance license would be liable for copyright infringement. *See Playboy Enters., Inc. v. Frena*, 839 F. Supp. 1552 (M.D. Fla. 1993) (transmission of an image from a computer bulletin board, an on-line service or the Internet constitutes a public performance). But HG, which did not copy, select, or request the delivery of the motion pictures would not suffer liability for the unauthorized public performance of the motion pictures. *See Perfect 10, Inc. v. Amazon.com, Inc.*, 487 F.3d 701, 715–19 (9th Cir. 2007).

153.   **(A) is the correct answer.** The Copyright Act exempts only commercial establishments of fewer than 3,750 gross square feet from the requirement to license public performances of musical works. Larger establishments can still take advantage of this exemption if they a total of not more than six loudspeakers, with no more than four loudspeakers located in any one room or adjoining outdoor space. But since her establishment is 4,000 gross square feet and uses 10 speakers, Restaurateur has to either stop using the receiver or obtain public performance licenses from ASCAP and BMI, and perhaps SESAC.

(B) is incorrect. The sophistication of an establishment's sound system and the cost of its installation are not factors under section 110(5)(B). They are factors for the *Aiken* exception of section 110(5)(A) that offers an exemption to the public performance right where the reception of television and radio broadcasts is by way of home-style receivers that may be seen or heard by the public, so long as no direct charge is made. *Twentieth Century Music Corp v. Aiken*, 422 U.S. 151 (1975).

Many of the cases involving the *Aiken* exemption limit its application to establishments with four or fewer speakers.

(C) is incorrect because section 110(5)(B) distinguishes between non-food service or drinking establishments and food service or drinking establishments, regarding requirements for an exception from the public performance right. The section does not distinguish between food service and drinking establishments.

(D) is incorrect because section 110(5)(B) does not apply to the performance of live music. The fact that the restaurant does not provide live music makes it more, not less, likely to qualify for an exception to the public performance right.

154.   **(B) is the correct answer.** The *Aiken* exception applies only to retransmissions of television and radio broadcasts. It does not apply to live performances. Playing music fixed in a digital file via an amplifier and speakers is a live performance. Therefore, section 110(5)(A) does not apply to these facts.

(A) is incorrect. Every musical composition protected by copyright enjoys the exclusive right of public performance, regardless of whether it has been distributed to the public.

Whether a musical composition has been distributed on phonorecords is relevant to whether the compulsory mechanical license provisions of section 115 apply, but not to whether the limitations on the public performance right provided by section 110 apply.

(C) is incorrect. The fact that sound recordings do not have a public performance right has no impact on the public performance right enjoyed by musical compositions.

(D) is incorrect. Even though the children select the musical compositions they want to hear, it is still the employees of the Children's Play Center who actually cause the performance of the musical composition. As a result, the employees' conduct directly infringes the copyrights in the musical compositions.

155.   (D) is the correct answer. The NHPD's failure to return Karma's drawings, however wrongful, does not violate her copyright-based exclusive rights in those works. Copyright law does not provide the copyright owner with a right of access to her work. *See Shell v. City of Radford*, 351 F. Supp. 2d 510, 511 (W.D. Va. 2005) (Copyright Act did not provide photographer with means to force police department to return photographs). Karma may, of course, have other, non-copyright-based causes of action against the NHPD, such as the tort of conversion.

(A) is incorrect because the Copyright Act does not give owners a broad right of control over their work, but only the six enumerated exclusive rights over those works set forth in section 106.

(B) is incorrect because the Copyright Act does not give owners an exclusive right to profit from their works.

(C) is incorrect because the creator of a work may well have some rights in the physical embodiment of that work, as Karma does on these facts. It is not the case, as this answer falsely states, that the creator never has an interest in the physical instantiation of the work.

156.   (A) is the correct answer. Even if one assumes that Superfan's reading to her students and to the fan club are public performances within the meaning of the Copyright Act, they are each subject to statutory exemptions from copyright infringement liability. Specifically, face-to-face classroom teaching activities, such as Superfan's using *Ultraworld* to educate her sixth graders, are exempt from copyright infringement liability even if they do amount to public performances. 17 U.S.C. § 110(1). Certain nonprofit performances, such as Superfan's reading to her small group of fellow fans for no profit, enjoy a similar exemption. 17 U.S.C. § 110(4). However, Superfan's reading at the open-mic night clearly violates Novelist's public performance right in the novel because it is an unauthorized reading of sections of *Ultraworld* for a paying audience of the general public, and is not subject to a section 110 exemption. It is thus the only of Superfan's three readings of *Ultraworld* that may infringe Novelist's copyright in the work.

(B), (C), and (D) are incorrect because they falsely assume either that Superfan's reading to her students or the fan club (or both) are actionable.

157.   **(A) is the correct answer.** Pirate has clearly violated Musician's right of reproduction in the *Delight* sound recording by copying the .mp3 file containing the Sound Recording from her website to his hard drive without authorization. And while there is no analog public performance right in sound recordings, 17 U.S.C. § 114(a), sound recordings are provided with a digital transmission right, *id.* § 106(6). Because Pirate's unauthorized transmission of the *Delight* sound recording took place over a digital medium, that transmission did violate her section 106(6) digital transmission right, and Pirate can be held liable for infringement on that theory as well.

        (B), (C), and (D) are incorrect because they wrongly state that there is no violation of either the reproduction or the digital transmission right.

158.   Under these facts, Musician would still be able to successfully argue that Pirate violated her exclusive right of reproduction in the *Delight* sound recording, for the straightforward reasons explained in the answer to question IV-30. However, Musician would not be able to sue Pirate for infringement on the theory that Pirate violated her digital transmission right in the *Delight* sound recording, because there is no general right of public performance in sound recordings. 17 U.S.C. § 114(a). *See Agee v. Paramount Commc'ns, Inc.*, 59 F.3d 317, 320 (2d Cir. 1995). The narrow digital transmission right for sound recordings, 17 U.S.C. § 106(6), does not apply here because the broadcast took place over an analog medium.

159.   **(C) is the correct answer.** The exclusive right to publicly display a work extends to literary works; musical works; dramatic and choreographic works; and pictorial, graphic, or sculptural works, including the individual images of a motion picture or other audiovisual work. 17 U.S.C. § 106(5). Bookseller's unauthorized display of the physical copy of *Finality* clearly constitutes a public display. The online display does as well. Courts have held that placing the digitized version of a work on a website to which the public has access via the Internet constitutes a public display of the work. *See Playboy Enters., Inc. v. Webbworld, Inc.*, 991 F. Supp. 543, 552–53 (N.D. Tex. 1997). However, there would be no liability in this case for the physical display because Bookseller, as the owner of the displayed lawful copy of *Finality*, is entitled to display that copy publicly. 17 U.S.C. § 109(c) (lawful owners of copies of works of authorship are entitled to display such copies publicly).

        This limitation does not apply to the online display, however. The Copyright Act permits the owner of a lawfully made copy of the work to display that copy by projection as well as by means of the physical copy itself, but copy owners may display no more than one image at a time, and only to viewers present at the place where the physical copy is located. 17 U.S.C. § 109(c). This exception does not apply to Bookseller's unauthorized online display for two reasons. First, to be placed on Bookseller's website, the page of *Finality* had to be scanned. Bookseller's scanning created an unauthorized copy, making the copy that was actually displayed on the website one that was not "lawfully made," therefore placing it outside the scope of the section 109(c) exception. In addition, material that is displayed on the Internet does not fall within the exception because viewers are not present at the place where the copy is located (i.e., the server used to operate the website). *See Bryant v. Gordon*, 483 F. Supp. 2d 605, 613 (N.D. Ill. 2007) (section 109(c) does not entitle the owner of a copy to publicly display images from that copy on the Internet); *Ringgold v. Black Entertainment Television, Inc.*, 126 F.3d 70 (2d Cir. 1997) (unauthorized use of copyrighted pictorial work on set of cable show transmitted to public did not fall within section 109(c) exception).

(A) is incorrect because there is a public display right in literary works. 17 U.S.C. § 106(5).

(B) is incorrect because the Copyright Act does not require that an entire work be displayed in order to violate the exclusive right to public display.

(D) is incorrect because the physical display of *Finality* is not actionable pursuant to section 109(c), as explained above.

160.   **(D) is the correct answer.** The Digital Performance Right in Sound Recordings Act of 1995 provides protected sound recordings with a digital transmission right that gives the copyright owner of a sound recording the exclusive right to perform the copyrighted work publicly by means of a digital audio transmission. This right applies only to sound recordings that are transmitted digitally to the public. This right operates differently with respect to different forms of digital transmission. Some digital transmissions of sound recordings have been exempted, such as radio broadcasts within the service area of the radio station's FCC license. 17 U.S.C. § 114(d)(1). *See Bonneville Int'l Corp. v. Peters*, 347 F.3d 485, 495 (3d Cir. 2003) (media exemption has been limited to the geographic area set forth in the broadcaster's FCC license and does not exempt broadcast signals transmitted over the Internet). Thus, BigMedia needs no license from the owners of the copyright in sound recordings to transmit their works over the radio station that BigMedia plans to purchase and convert to digital form.

Public performances of sound recordings by a noninteractive digital transmission may qualify for a compulsory license (sometimes referred to as a "statutory license"). 17 U.S.C. § 114(d)(2). To qualify for this license the transmission must meet several conditions, including a limitation on the number of recordings from a single album or artist transmitted during a specified period and a prohibition of advance announcements of playlists. If the numerous requirements for the compulsory license are not met, a negotiated consensual license from the owner of the copyright in the sound recording must be obtained. Thus, BigMedia needs to pay either the compulsory license fee, or obtain a consensual license from sound recording owners in order to stream the sound recordings over BigMedia.com.

Finally, streaming sound recordings by an interactive digital transmission requires a negotiated consensual license from the owner of the copyright in the sound recording. Thus, BigMedia will need to negotiate licenses with sound recording owners for any works it wants to make available via its on-demand "BigMedia Plus" service.

(A) is incorrect because, although the traditional public performance right set forth in section 106(4) does not apply to sound recordings, the digital transmission right set forth in section 106(6) does apply to BigMedia's planned use of sound recordings.

(B) and (C) are incorrect because they wrongly characterize BigMedia's licensing obligations as explained above.

161.   **(D) is the correct answer.** Writer's objection in this case is that Publisher violated his right of attribution, but this is not a basis for copyright infringement under federal copyright law. As a general rule, United States copyright law does not recognize a right of attribution. *See Graham v. James*, 144 F.3d 229, 236 (2d Cir. 1998) (author who sells or licenses her work does not have an inherent right to be credited as its author). Although section 106A does provide for a right of attribution, it only applies to works of visual art, not literary works. Writer may have other causes of action against Publisher, such as common-law fraud, breach of contract, or false advertising, but copyright infringement is not among them.

(A) is incorrect because merely changing the name of the author does not create a derivative work, and therefore does not violate the adaptation right.

(B) is incorrect because a violation of the right of attribution is not a basis for a copyright infringement claim, for the reasons explained above.

(C) is incorrect because it misstates the scope of the law. Federal law does recognize some moral rights, including an attribution right, through the Visual Artists Rights Act (VARA), codified in section 106A of the Copyright Act.

162.   **(B) is the correct answer.** Moral rights have been specifically accorded only to a limited category of "works of visual art" pursuant to the Visual Artists Rights Act of 1990 ("VARA"), but Painter's painting is clearly among them. 17 U.S.C. §§ 106A (limiting scope of federal moral rights protection to "works of visual art"), 101 (defining "work of visual art"). An author of a qualifying work has the right to claim authorship in her work, to prevent the use of her name as the author of any work she did not create, and to prevent the use of her name as the author of a work she did originally create, but that has been mutilated. 17 U.S.C. § 106A(a)(1)–(2); *see Berrios Nogueras v. Home Depot*, 330 F. Supp. 2d 48, 50 (D.P.R. 2004). Thus, Painter can successfully sue Buyer for his attempt to pass himself off as the author of the painting.

An author also has the right to prevent the intentional distortion, mutilation, or other modification of her work that would be prejudicial to her honor or reputation. 17 U.S.C. § 106A(a)(3)(A). However, modification of a work of visual art that is a result of conservation or the public presentation of the work, including lighting and placement, is not actionable unless the modification is caused by gross negligence. 17 U.S.C. § 106A(c)(2). Here, the reason that the painting degraded was due both to the inherent fragility of the paint used and to non-negligent environmental factors, so Painter cannot successfully sue Buyer for violating Painter's right of integrity in the painting.

(A), (C), and (D) are incorrect because they incorrectly state either that Painter cannot successfully sue Buyer on a right of attribution theory, or that Painter can successfully sue Buyer on a right of integrity theory.

163.   On these facts, Painter would have no moral rights cause of action under VARA. The Visual Artists Rights Act applies only to certain qualifying works. Although photographs may be protected by VARA as works of visual art, VARA applies only to photographs where the initial rendering of a still photographic image was produced for exhibition purposes only and signed by the author. Any copy in a limited edition of 200 copies or fewer is also protected if the copies are signed and consecutively numbered by the author. Here, the photograph taken by Painter meets all of these standards except one: the limited series numbered 250 rather than 200. As a result, the prints at issue here do not qualify for protection under VARA, therefore, Painter cannot successfully sue Buyer for a violation of section 106A.

164.   **(C) is the correct answer.** For works of visual art created on or after June 1, 1991, the duration of rights under section 106A is life of the author. 17 U.S.C. § 106A(d)(1). Artist's VARA rights died with him and can no longer be enforced.

        (A) and (B) are incorrect because no courts have interpreted the rights of attribution or integrity to include a right of removal.

        (D) is incorrect because it wrongly states that Artist's rights under VARA remain enforceable. It is worth noting, however, that the second half of the statement is correct: VARA does not confer on artists a right to remove their work from circulation should they decide they no longer agree with it. This is in contrast to most continental European moral rights regimes, where artists do have a right of removal.

165.   **(A) is the correct answer.** Fly Guy's attempted resale of the promotional CDs from Jam Records does represent an unauthorized distribution. While no sale has taken place, Fly Guy's giving the CDs to the used record store may represent the kind of "transfer of ownership" or "lending" that still amounts to a distribution. 17 U.S.C. § 106(3). Alternatively, the fact that Fly Guy authorized the used record store to sell the CDs amounts to distribution as well. *See* 17 U.S.C. § 106 (copyright owners have "the exclusive rights to do *and to authorize*" the six enumerated rights) (emphasis added).

        The first sale doctrine, however, permits owners of copies and phonorecords—such as CDs—from liability for reselling them. 17 U.S.C. § 109(a) ("Notwithstanding the provisions of section 106(3), the owner of a particular copy or phonorecord lawfully made under this title . . . is entitled, without the authority of the copyright owner, to sell or otherwise dispose of the possession of that copy or phonorecord.").

        Jam Records will argue that they did not transfer ownership of the promotional CDs, but rather retained ownership of them and granted only a limited use license to recipients such as Fly Guy's. But this argument will fail because courts have held such license terms written on CDs to be unenforceable. Particularly where, as here, the parties did not mutually agree on the terms, courts have been unwilling to create a licensing agreement in what looks much more like a garden-variety transfer of ownership. *See UMG Recordings, Inc. v. Augusto*, 628 F.3d 1175 (9th Cir. 2011) (declining to enforce license terms written onto promotional CDs).

(B) is incorrect because Fly Guy's has both effected a kind of transfer of ownership, and has authorized the sale of the CDs. As explained above, each of these actions amounts to an unauthorized distribution.

(C) is incorrect because the Copyright Act's statutory first sale doctrine nowhere limits its effect to analog sales.

(D) is incorrect because, as explained above, the license is unenforceable.

166.   Yes, SoftCo's license is probably enforceable. In *Vernor v. Autodesk, Inc.*, 621 F.3d 1102 (9th Cir. 2010), the Ninth Circuit upheld the validity of an agreement defining a software user as a licensee where three conditions were met: (1) the agreement specified that the user was granted only a license; (2) the agreement placed significant restrictions on the user's ability to transfer the program; and (3) the agreement placed other significant use restrictions on the user.

Here, SoftCo's license quite clearly meets all three of these criteria. It unambiguously states that it grants the user only a license. It also restricts resale of the program, and further limits use to a particular geographic area. These conditions satisfy each of the *Vernor* factors, thereby rendering the license enforceable under that standard. Not all circuits have embraced the *Vernor* approach, though, so this outcome may not obtain outside the Ninth Circuit. Some courts have favored a broader approach that looks more generally to the "economic realities" of the situation, and in particular whether the transaction has more of the traditional indicia of a sale rather than a license. *See, e.g., Krause v. Titleserv, Inc.*, 402 F.3d 119, 124 (2d Cir. 2005) ("absence of formal title may be outweighed by evidence that the possessor of the copy enjoys sufficiently broad rights over it to be sensibly considered its owner").

167.   **(D) is the correct answer.** Federal law allows purchasers of copies of works of authorship to resell them without restriction pursuant to the first sale doctrine. 17 U.S.C. § 109(a). Some states have passed laws allowing visual artists a percentage royalty of each subsequent sale of their paintings. The California Resale Royalty Act (CRRA), for example, allows artists to collect five percent of the sales price of any resale of "fine art" in excess of $1,000, so long as the artist lives in California or the sale takes place in California. Cal. Civ. Code §§ 986(a), 986(b)(2), 986(c)(2).

While the CRRA does seem to give Artie an option for recovering some of the value of the second sale of his painting, this option was foreclosed by recent federal cases holding that the Copyright Act preempted the CRRA because the latter conflicted with the former's first sale doctrine. *Estate of Graham v. Sotheby's, Inc.*, 178 F. Supp. 3d 974, 988 ("Because the CRRA disrupts Congress's efforts to balance the interests of copyright holders and downstream consumers, it must be preempted.").

(A) is incorrect because VARA guarantees creators of fine art some attribution and integrity rights, but does not promise them any resale royalties.

(B) is incorrect because the CRRA has been invalidated due to its preemption by the Copyright Act.

(C) is incorrect because Nora's unauthorized distribution is immunized from liability under the first sale doctrine. 17 U.S.C. § 109(a).

168. **(C) is the correct answer.** VARA applies only to "works of visual art." 17 U.S.C. § 106A(a). The Copyright Act excludes "applied art" from its definition of "works of visual art." *Id.* § 101(A)(i) (listing exclusions from definition of "works of visual art"). Although the Copyright Act does not also define "applied art," courts have held that "applied art" means "two- and three-dimensional ornamentation or decoration that is affixed to otherwise utilitarian objects." *Carter v. Helmsley-Spear*, 71 F.3d 77, 84–85 (2d Cir. 1995); *see also Pollara v. Seymour*, 344 F.3d 265, 269 (2d Cir. 2003) ("VARA may protect a sculpture that looks like a piece of furniture, but it does not protect a piece of utilitarian furniture, whether or not it could arguably be called a sculpture.").

Here, the work in question was a boat that was heavily decorated and, though rickety, still capable of sailing. This falls squarely within the Second Circuit's definition of "applied art"—an everyday useful object that has been decorated but still retains its utility. Along these lines, the Ninth Circuit recently held that an elaborately decorated but still functional bus was "applied art" and therefore not within the scope of VARA. *Cheffins v. Stewart*, 825 F.3d 588, 594 (9th Cir. 2016) ("We therefore hold that an object constitutes a piece of 'applied art'—as opposed to a 'work of visual art'—where the object initially served a utilitarian function and the object continues to serve such a function after the first artist made embellishments or alterations to it."). *The Invincible* was a functional boat with lots of decorations. It was thus "applied art" within the meaning of the Copyright Act, and therefore not a "work of visual art" subject to VARA.

(A) and (B) are incorrect because they assume VARA applies to *The Invincible*, when for reasons explained above, it doesn't. That said, if VARA did apply, the prankster's conduct would violate only Jack's right of integrity, not his right of attribution. The integrity right protects against such acts as "distortion," "mutilation," and "destruction" of a work of visual art. 17 U.S.C. § 106A(a)(3). Sinking a decorated boat certainly falls into one or all of these categories. By contrast, the attribution right allows creators to "claim authorship" of works of visual art, *id.* § 106A(a), an issue that is not raised by the prankster's sinking *The Invincible*.

(D) is incorrect because VARA does not apply for a different reason. And there are numerous reasons that a court would regard *The Invincible* as a "work of recognized stature." 17 U.S.C. § 106A(a)(3)(B). Jack is a "well-regarded" artist; people came from all around to see *The Invincible*; and a major collector was willing to pay $50,000 for the work before it was destroyed.

169. **(C) is the correct answer.** SMHS violated Fine Films' exclusive right of reproduction in *Spartans Forever* by making an unauthorized, verbatim copy of the audio portion of part of the film. That SMHS made only an audio recording does not change the analysis. Unauthorized reproduction of any part of a work of authorship that is separately copyrightable infringes the owner's copyright in the work.

SMHS's use also infringed Fine Films' exclusive right of public performance in their film by playing the .mp3 of the famous line at Spartans football games. This is clearly a performance because "[t]o "perform" a work means to recite, render, play, dance, or act it, either directly or by means of any device or process or, in the case of a motion picture or other audiovisual work, to show its images in any sequence or to make the sounds accompanying it audible." 17 U.S.C. § 101 (defining "perform"). By playing an audio portion of *Spartans Forever*, SMHS made a portion of the sounds accompanying the film audible.

SMHS's use did not violate Fine Films' adaptation right. The audio recording was a verbatim copy of part of the film, and in no way constituted a derivative work. 17 U.S.C. § 106(2) (defining the adaptation right as the right to "prepare derivative works"). It did not involve the kinds of "modifications" amounting to a separate "work of authorship" that is required to create a derivative work. *Id.* § 101 (defining "derivative work"); *The Bridgeman Art Library, Ltd. v. Corel Corp.*, 25 F. Supp. 2d 421, 426–27 (S.D.N.Y. 1998).

Nor did SMHS's use violate Fine Films' adaptation right. "To 'display' a work means to show a copy of it, either directly or by means of a film, slide, television image, or any other device or process or, in the case of a motion picture or other audiovisual work, to show individual images nonsequentially." 17 U.S.C. § 101. Here, SMHS only performed audio from *Spartans Forever*. The school did not show a copy of the film itself, or show images from the film.

(A), (B), and (D) are incorrect because they misstate the exclusive rights SMHS violated.

170.   **(C) is the correct answer.** This is in one sense a classic example of a resale privileged by the first-sale doctrine, which allows owners of copies to resell them regardless of the copyright owner's exclusive right of distribution. 17 U.S.C. § 109(a). While the Copyright Act bars unauthorized importation of copies into the United States. 17 U.S.C. § 602(a)(1) ("Importation into the United States, without the authority of the owner of the copyright under this title, of copies or phonorecords of a work that have been acquired outside the United States is an infringement of the exclusive right to distribute copies or phonorecords under section 106[.]"), the Supreme Court has held that the first sale doctrine permits unauthorized importation of lawfully acquired copies, *see Quality King Distributors, Inc. v. L'anza Research Int'l, Inc.*, 523 U.S. 135 (1998). And though *Quality King* held only that the first-sale doctrine permitted reimportation into the United States of copies that had been made domestically, the Supreme Court later expanded this interpretation to hold that the first-sale doctrine also permitted the importation of lawfully acquired copies that had been made overseas. *Kirtsaeng v. John Wiley & Sons, Inc.*, 568 U.S. 519 (2013).

(A) is incorrect because the Supreme Court rejected this "geographic interpretation" of the first-sale doctrine in *Kirtsaeng*.

(B) and (D) are incorrect because whether the owner of the copy profited from their resale of it is not relevant to the application of the first-sale doctrine.

171.   **(A) is the correct answer.** The Copyright Act is clear that the transmission and retransmission of copyrighted works, including radio broadcasts, amounts to a performance if it is "to the public." 17 U.S.C. § 101 (defining "perform publicly"). AllGames would argue that its transmissions, though, are not "to the public" because they are each separately captured and then directed at a particular user, not generally retransmitted to all users at once. *See Cartoon Network, LP v. CSC Holdings, Inc.*, 536 F.3d 121 (2d Cir. 2008). The Supreme Court, however, has rejected this argument in the context of technology very similar to that used by AllGames. It held that the use of technological innovations to meet the *Cablevision* standard did not obscure the fact that such systems bear an "overwhelming likeness to cable companies," and that they thus "perform . . . works 'publicly.'" *American Broad. Cos. v. Aereo, Inc.*, 573 U.S. __, 134 S. Ct. 2498 (2014).

(B) is incorrect because copyright infringement is a strict liability tort, so that the intentions of infringers — good, bad, or otherwise — are irrelevant.

(C) is incorrect because the *Aereo* majority acknowledged the concern that copyright law should sustain, not retard, the development of new technology, but concluded that its holding did not impede this aim. 134 S. Ct. at 2510 ("We agree that Congress, while intending the Transmit Clause to apply broadly to cable companies and their equivalents, did not intend to discourage or to control the emergence or use of different kinds of technologies. But we do not believe that our limited holding today will have that effect.").

The *Aereo* dissent, however, based its disagreement with the Court largely on the basis that judges should take particular care not to interfere with as-yet poorly understood new technologies. *Id.* at 2518 (Scalia, J., dissenting) ("We are in no position to judge the validity of those self-interested claims or to foresee the path of future technological development. Hence, the proper course is not to bend and twist the Act's terms in an effort to produce a just outcome, but to apply the law as it stands and leave to Congress the task of deciding whether the Copyright Act needs an upgrade.").

(D) is incorrect because the prevailing rule articulated by the *Aereo* Court is that systems like AllGames do affect public performances.

Copyright Formalities

172.   **(B) is the correct answer.** The date of publication plays a central role in determining whether there is a need for a copyright notice. Different rules apply depending on whether the work was published under the 1909 Act (from 1909 through 1977), during the decennial period (from January 1, 1978, to February 28, 1989), or on or after March 1, 1989.

(A), (C), and (D) are incorrect because the factors they identify are unrelated to the need for notice.

173.   **(C) is the correct answer.** In the case of conflicting transfers of copyright ownership, the first good faith recorded transfer of a registered copyright will be given priority. 17 U.S.C. § 205(d). The Copyright Act gives priority to the transfer of copyright executed first if that transfer is recorded prior to the recordation of any conflicting transfer, or if the recordation is made within one month after its execution in the United States or within two months after its execution outside the United States, even if another transfer has been recorded during that time. *Id.* Outside of that one-to-two month grace period, a later transfer prevails if it is recorded first, taken in good faith and without notice of the earlier transfer. *Id.*

(A) is incorrect for the reason stated above. It is not relevant that Publisher A had acted on its contractual rights. When there is a recordation of assignment of a copyright, section 205(d) of the Copyright Act resolves the conflict in favor of the earlier-recorded transfer.

(B) is incorrect for the reason stated above. The Copyright Act does not favor the first party to take assignment, but the first to record the assignment or other transfer of copyright.

(D) is incorrect for the reason stated above. Publication with proper copyright notice no longer vests federal copyright in a work, as it did prior to 1978.

174.   **(C) is the correct answer.** Under the 1909 Copyright Act, the unpublished drawing was protected by state common-law copyright until it was either published, registered with the Copyright Office, or had its state protection preempted by federal copyright law. The 1960 distribution of the drawing constituted a limited publication that did not require a copyright notice, and thus did not divest the work of its state common-law protection. *See Academy of Motion Picture Arts & Sciences v. Creative House Promotions, Inc.*, 944 F.2d 1446 (9th Cir. 1991) (holding that limited publication did not divest common-law copyright). Because the drawing was a fixed work, federal copyright law preempted its common-law protection on January 1, 1978, when the 1976 Copyright Act took effect.

(A) is incorrect. In 1910, federal copyright in a work vested either when it was published with proper copyright notice or registered with the Copyright Office. The creation of a work did not vest the work with federal copyright protection. State common-law copyright protected the work at the time of its creation.

(B) is incorrect. The distribution of the work to three individuals as a gift with limitations placed on its further distribution was not a publication to the general public. It was a distribution to a limited number of individuals for a specific purpose. As such, it was a limited publication that permitted state common-law protection of the drawing to continue. *See Academy of Motion Picture Arts and Sciences*, 944 F.2d at 1451–52 ("Oscar" statuette underwent only limited publication and thus did not fall into the public domain); *White v. Kimmell*, 193 F.2d 744, 746–47 (9th Cir. 1952). Furthermore, the copies distributed did not contain a copyright notice. Therefore, even if the distribution constituted a publication, the absence of a copyright notice would have foreclosed the vesting of federal protection while, at the same time, divesting the work of its common-law protection. *See Letter Edged in Black Press, Inc. v. Public Bldg. Comm'n of Chicago*, 320 F. Supp. 1303 (N.D. Ill. 1970); *J.A. Richards, Inc. v. New York Post, Inc.*, 23 F. Supp. 619 (S.D.N.Y. 1938).

(D) is incorrect. By the time the work was published with proper copyright notice, it had been vested with federal copyright on January 1, 1978, as a fixed original work. *See* 17 U.S.C. § 303(a); *Martha Graham School & Dance Found., Inc. v. Martha Graham Center of Contemporary Dance, Inc.*, 380 F.3d 624, 632–33 (2d Cir. 2004).

175.   **(D) is the correct answer.** The Ninth and Second Circuits split on the question whether the distribution to the public of phonorecords containing a musical composition is a general publication that requires the use of a proper copyright notice to protect the copyright in the musical composition. *Compare La Cienega Music Co. v. ZZ Top*, 53 F.3d 950 (9th Cir. 1995) (distribution effects general publication) *with Rosette v. Rainbo Record Mfg. Corp.*, 354 F. Supp. 1183 (S.D.N.Y. 1973), *aff'd per curiam*, 546 F.2d 461 (2d Cir. 1976) (distribution does not effect general publication because phonorecord held not to be a copy of musical composition). Congress responded to this disagreement by amending the Copyright Act to state that any distribution of a phonorecord before January 1, 1978, did not constitute a publication of a musical composition embodied within it. 17 U.S.C. § 303(b). Subsequent courts also held that section 303(b) has retroactive effect. *ABKCO Music, Inc. v. LaVere*, 217 F.3d 684 (9th Cir. 2000).

(A) is incorrect. Under the 1909 Act, a performance did not constitute a publication. *See Estate of Martin Luther King, Jr., Inc. v. CBS, Inc.*, 194 F.3d 1211, 1215–16 (2d Cir. 1999).

(B) and (C) are incorrect because, under section 303(b) of the 1976 Copyright Act, the release of a phonorecord containing a musical work prior to January 1, 1978, does not constitute a publication of the musical work embodied in it.

176.   Under this analysis, publication would have occurred with the limited-edition release of *Executive Sweet*. Under the 1976 Copyright Act, a general publication occurs when copies or phonorecords are distributed "for purposes of further distribution, public performance,

or public display." 17 U.S.C. § 101 (defining "publication"); *Shoptalk, Ltd. v. Concorde-New Horizons Corp.*, 168 F.3d 586, 590 (2d Cir. 1999) (holding that a general publication occurred when a possessory interest in tangible copies of the work is made available to the general public with the consent of the copyright owner). Thus, the post-1977 release of 1,000 phonorecords of *Executive Sweet* would amount to a general publication of the musical works fixed in the phonorecords, even though the same acts would not have effected general publication prior to 1978.

177.   **(B) is the correct answer.** You may have overlooked this answer believing that the distribution of a work in 1961 to merely five individuals for the purpose of deciding whether to bid on a novel's motion picture rights constituted a limited publication and not a general publication. If the manuscript of the novel had not contained a copyright notice, a limited publication that saved the novel's copyright from divestment would likely be found. Here, however, the issue is whether there was sufficient publication, with proper copyright notice, to vest the work with federal copyright protection. The answer is likely to be "yes," due to the case law under the 1909 Act that it takes "more" publication to destroy a common-law copyright, thereby divesting the work of copyright protection, than it takes to vest a work with federal statutory copyright, assuming a proper copyright notice is present. *See Dolman v. Agee*, 157 F.3d 708, 713–714 (9th Cir. 1998) ("[I]t takes 'more' publication to destroy a common-law copyright than to perfect a statutory copyright."); *American Visuals Corp. v. Holland*, 239 F.2d 740, 744 (2d Cir. 1956) ("The doctrine of limited publication . . . has generally been invoked by courts to protect the common law remedy where the statutory remedy is unavailable."). In light of this principle, the relatively small distribution of *Clouded Sunset* would likely have sufficed to vest federal copyright in the novel, even though the same act would not have been likely to divest it of any copyright protection had it lacked proper copyright notice.

   (A) is incorrect because this answer states the requirement for federal copyright protection under the 1976 Copyright Act, which does not apply to these pre-1978 facts. Under the 1909 Copyright Act, merely embodying a creative work in a tangible medium of expression was insufficient to effect publication.

   (C) is incorrect. The distribution of copies of the novel to book club members in 1962 certainly would constitute a general publication, but a court would likely view the 1961 distribution of the manuscript of the novel to potential buyers as a sufficient publication to vest the novel with federal copyright protection.

   (D) is incorrect because the release of the film effected a general publication of the motion picture and, under the majority view, all of the copyrightable elements contained in it. This act would not have effected publication of the entire work *Clouded Sunset*, though, because only a single copyrightable element from the novel (its main character) was published with the release of the motion picture.

178.   **(A) is the correct answer.** The 1909 Act required that a proper copyright notice be placed on all copies of any work that underwent a general publication. Failure to meet the notice

requirement led to harsh results. General publication of a work without proper copyright notice immediately and irreversibly divested the work of copyright protection, placing it into the public domain. *See Letter Edged in Black Press, Inc. v. Public Bldg. Comm'n of Chicago*, 320 F. Supp. 1303 (N.D. Ill. 1970); *J.A. Richards, Inc. v. New York Post, Inc.*, 23 F. Supp. 619 (S.D.N.Y. 1938). Here, there is clearly a general publication because Zealot released physical copies of his work broadly and not for any narrow purpose. *See Shoptalk, Ltd. v. Concorde-New Horizons Corp.*, 168 F.3d 586, 590 (2d Cir. 1999); *Burke v. National Broad. Co.*, 598 F.2d 688, 691 (1st Cir. 1979). Thus Zealot's failure to include notice on the vast majority of his pamphlets forfeits his copyright in those pamphlets to the public domain.

(B) is incorrect because there was no curing provision under the 1909 Copyright Act.

(C) is incorrect because under the 1909 Act, notice must be included on all, or nearly all, copies of a work in order to preserve an author's copyright.

(D) is incorrect because failure to include proper notice effects forfeiture regardless of the copyright owner's intent. Inadvertent failure to provide notice was actually a very common way to forfeit copyright. *See Sanga Music, Inc. v. EMI Blackwood Music, Inc.*, 55 F.3d 756, 759–61 (2d Cir. 1995); *Twin Books Corp. v. Walt Disney Co.*, 83 F.3d 1162, 1165–66 (9th Cir. 1996).

179.   On these facts, the contents of Zealot's pamphlet likely would not be forfeited to the public domain. Though the notice requirement of the 1909 Act was strict, it was excused where the notice was omitted from no more than a relatively small number of copies. Here, because the notice was left off 10 copies, constituting only 1% of the pamphlets, it would be unlikely that this small omission would result in the total forfeiture of Zealot's copyright.

180.   **(D) is the correct answer.** Under the 1976 Copyright Act, a general publication is the "distribution of copies or phonorecords of a work to the public by sale or other transfer of ownership, or by rental, lease, or lending." 17 U.S.C. § 101 (definition of "publication"). However, the dissemination must be with the consent of the copyright owner. *See John G. Danielson, Inc. v. Winchester-Conant Properties, Inc.*, 322 F.3d 26, 38 (1st Cir. 2003). Here, because the dissemination of Writer's work was without her consent, that act does not amount to publication of the short story.

(A) is incorrect because a general release of a copy of a work of authorship is not always a publication, including where, as here, that release was without the owner's consent.

(B) is incorrect because the work was placed on the Internet without Writer's consent.

(C) is incorrect because courts interpret the 1976 Copyright Act flexibly to adapt to new technologies, and the fact that the Internet did not exist when that legislation was passed does not mean that publication was limited to existing media.

181.   **(A) is the correct answer.** During the decennial period, which lasted from the effective date of the 1976 Copyright Act (January 1, 1978) to the effective date of the Berne Convention Implementation Act (March 1, 1989), failure to include proper copyright notice

on validly published copies caused those works to fall into the public domain. 17 U.S.C. § 401(a). However, the omission of copyright notice could be cured under certain circumstances, saving the work from the public domain. 17 U.S.C. § 405; *see Hasbro Bradley, Inc. v. Sparkle Toys, Inc.*, 780 F.2d 189 (2d Cir. 1985). Where notice of copyright was omitted from a large number of copies, that omission could be cured if an author registered her work with the Copyright Office within five years of publication, and made a reasonable effort within a reasonable period to attach copyright notice to all domestically distributed copies from which it was missing. 17 U.S.C. § 405(a)(2). Here, Novelist published *American She* in 1980 and did not register it within five years. Therefore, the curing provision of section 405(a)(2) is not available to Novelist.

(B) is incorrect because, as explained above, Novelist cannot take advantage of the cure provisions due to her failure to register the work within five years of first publication.

(C) is incorrect because Novelist is a United States author, therefore the restoration provisions of section 104A do not apply to her.

(D) is incorrect because *American She* is in the public domain, not protected by copyright.

182.   The answer is different in this case because the decennial period ended on February 28, 1989. The failure to include copyright notice on any work published after that date does not cause the work to fall into the public domain. *Martha Graham School & Dance Found., Inc. v. Martha Graham Center of Contemporary Dance, Inc.*, 380 F.3d 624, 633 n.14 (2d Cir. 2004). It is strongly advised, however, for copyright owners to use copyright notice, in part because copyright notice precludes a defendant from mitigating damages pursuant to an innocent infringement defense. 17 U.S.C. §§ 401(d), 402(d).

183.   **(C) is the correct answer.** The Copyright Act has a mandatory deposit provision that requires the copyright owner to deposit one copy of a published work with the Library of Congress. 17 U.S.C. § 407.

        (A), (B), and (D) are incorrect because they fail to accurately describe the obligations of copyright owners under the 1976 Copyright Act. Registration and deposit are not, however, required to acquire a federal copyright in a work. *See Raquel v. Education Mgmt. Corp.*, 196 F.3d 171, 176 (3d Cir. 1999). Such protection automatically exists at the time of fixation. *See Kodadek v. MTV Networks, Inc.*, 152 F.3d 1209, 1211 (9th Cir. 1998).

184.   **(B) is the correct answer.** Although it is true that registration is a jurisdictional prerequisite for filing a copyright infringement suit, this refers to attempted registration, not actual registration. An unsuccessful applicant is entitled to file an action for copyright infringement so long as the Copyright Office is notified of the lawsuit and provided with a copy of the complaint. 17 U.S.C. § 411(a); *see Iconbazaar, L.L.C. v. America Online, Inc.*, 308 F. Supp. 2d 630, 632 n.2 (M.D. N.C. 2004). The Copyright Office has the statutory authority to join in such a lawsuit for the purpose of contesting registrability of the work for which registration was denied. *See Norris Industries, Inc. v. Int'l Tel. & Tel. Corp.*, 696 F.2d 918, 920 (11th Cir. 1983).

(A) **is incorrect.** Registration, at least attempted registration, is a prerequisite for filing a copyright infringement suit.

(C) **is incorrect** because copyright vests upon fixation in a tangible medium of expression, not upon registration with the Copyright Office.

(D) **is incorrect** because it fails to take into account the possibility that a failed applicant can file suit in federal court pursuant to section 411.

185.   You should advise Author to register the copyright for several reasons. First, registration or, at least, attempted registration, is a prerequisite to filing a suit for copyright infringement. So if Author ever wants or needs to protect his copyright via lawsuit, he will need to file for registration. 17 U.S.C. § 411; *see Xoom, Inc. v. Imageline, Inc.*, 323 F.3d 279, 283 (4th Cir. 2003). Second, registration prior to the infringement of a work or within three months from a work's initial publication is a prerequisite for seeking statutory damages and attorneys' fees. 17 U.S.C. § 412; *see Bouchat v. Baltimore Ravens Football Club, Inc.*, 346 F.3d 514, 517 n.2 (4th Cir. 2003). Statutory damages not only may be higher than actual damages in a particular case, but seeking statutory damages also carries with it the advantage of not having to prove the specific amount of actual damages, which can be very time-consuming and expensive. Third, timely registrants enjoy the evidentiary advantage of several presumptions: the validity of the copyright itself; the validity of all facts stated in the certificate of registration; and that the registrant is the copyright owner. 17 U.S.C. § 410(c); *Evans & Assocs. Inc. v. Continental Homes, Inc.*, 785 F.2d 897, 903 (11th Cir. 1986). *See Boisson v. Banian, Ltd.*, 273 F.3d 262, 268 (2d Cir. 2001) (registration certificates established statutory presumption that works are original); *Smith v. Jackson*, 84 F.3d 1213, 1219 (9th Cir. 1996).

186.   (B) **is the correct answer.** This certificate constitutes prima facie evidence of the validity of the copyright and of the facts stated in the certificate, so long as registration was obtained before or within five years after the first publication of the work. 17 U.S.C. § 410(c); *see Evans & Assocs. Inc. v. Continental Homes, Inc.*, 785 F.2d 897, 903 (11th Cir. 1986); *Boisson v. Banian, Ltd.*, 273 F.3d 262, 268 (2d Cir. 2001) (registration certificates established statutory presumption that works are original). The presumptive validity of the certificate of registration may be rebutted and defeated. *See, e.g., Aalmuhammed v. Lee*, 202 F.3d 1227, 1236 (9th Cir. 1999) (validity of film consultant's certificate of registration containing claim that he was co-creator, co-writer and co-director of *Malcolm X* rebutted on summary judgment).

(A) **is incorrect** because while the registration certificate is presumptive evidence of the copyright's validity, the presumption of validity raised by a registration certificate may be overcome by a sufficient contrary showing. *E.g., Fonar Corp. v. Domenick*, 105 F.3d 99, 104 (2d Cir. 1997) (evidence that work is copied from work in the public domain or is non-copyrightable may be sufficient to rebut presumption of validity).

(C) **is incorrect** because the certificate does not shift all burdens of proof onto the defendant, but only creates a presumption of validity. The plaintiff retains the burden of proving the defendant infringed the plaintiff's copyright.

(D) is incorrect because the trial judge has such discretion only when the registration is made five years after the initial publication of the work.

187.   These facts raise the issue of whether the distribution of a motion picture constitutes a publication of its underlying screenplay. Although the issue remained unresolved for some time, the majority of courts analyzing this issue have reached a consensus. Most courts have found that any copyrightable elements that are contained in a motion picture are published when the motion picture is released. The result of this determination is that any elements of a screenplay that are contained in a motion picture that is published with a proper copyright notice prior to 1978 vested those screenplay elements with federal statutory protection that is separate from the copyright in the motion picture itself. Elements of the screenplay that were not included in the motion picture, and were not independently published, remained protected by common-law copyright until January 1, 1978, when they received federal copyright protection. *See Shoptalk, Ltd. v. Concorde-New Horizons Corp.*, 168 F.3d 586, 591–92 (2d Cir. 1999); *Batjac Prods. Inc. v. GoodTimes Home Video Corp.*, 160 F.3d 1223, 1233–35 (9th Cir. 1998); *Classic Film Museum, Inc. v. Warner Bros., Inc.*, 597 F.2d 13, 14–15 (1st Cir. 1979).

Under this approach and the facts stated above, all of the elements of the *Fast Track* screenplay were included in the *Clashing Clouds* motion picture, which was distributed with a proper copyright notice, vesting the entire screenplay with federal statutory copyright protection upon the film's release in 1962. This provided the screenplay with an initial 28-year federal copyright term. However, Screenwriter's expectancy interest in the screenplay's renewal term of copyright did not materialize because Screenwriter did not affirmatively renew the copyright in *Fast Track*. The renewal of the *Clashing Clouds* copyright applied only to the motion picture, not the underlying screenplay. Moreover, the 1992 Automatic Renewal Amendment to the 1976 Copyright Act was not in effect at the time the initial term of copyright in *Fast Track* was in its twenty-eighth year. As a result, the copyright in *Fast Track* entered the public domain on December 31, 1989.

In *Richlin v. Metro-Goldwyn-Mayer Pictures, Inc.*, 531 F.3d 962 (9th Cir. 2008), the Ninth Circuit took the position that the inclusion of elements of an underlying work in a published motion picture did not secure a federal statutory copyright for the underlying work as an independent work. *Id.* at 975–77. Under this view, the underlying work could be invested with federal copyright protection only if it was separately registered or published as an independent work.

The facts at issue state that Screenwriter has never authorized a use of the *Fast Track* screenplay other than in connection with *Clashing Clouds*. Under the Ninth Circuit view as expressed in *Richlin*, this means that *Fast Track* remained protected by state common-law copyright and was not invested with federal copyright protection until January 1, 1978, when that common-law protection was preempted by federal law. That federal protection will end 70 years after Screenwriter's death. Therefore, Screenwriter continues to have a copyright in *Fast Track* and its unauthorized use by Cinemasters Publishing would constitute an actionable infringement.

188.   **(D) is the correct answer.** The Copyright Office created Form SE specifically for authors of serial publications, like the photographer, to apply for copyright of the works contained therein. Nor does it undermine photographer's ability to bring an infringement suit in which she listed many different works in a single application. On the contrary, the Copyright Office has made it clear that it actually it prefers that multimedia works that are created by a single author and released in a single unit of publication—such as, here, the fall 2014 issue of *Scenes from the Wild*—be registered in a single certificate. This furthers both authors' and the Copyright Offices' interests in streamlining the registration process. 37 C.F.R. §202.3(b)(4)(i) (expressing a preference that works released as part of a single "unit of publication, and in which the copyright claimant is the same" be registered on a single certificate).

         (A) is incorrect because it simply misstates the character of Form SE. The Copyright Office has spoken unambiguously to this issue and has stated that "[t]he claimant registering a serial may claim copyright not only in the collective-work authorship for which the claimant is responsible, but also in any independently authored contributions" for which the claimant owns the copyright. "Copyright Registration for Single Serial Issues," U.S. Copyright Office Circular No. 62.

         (B) is incorrect because it is similarly foreclosed by the language quoted in the discussion of incorrect answer A. The Copyright Office specifically intended Form SE to cover both the copyright in the selection, coordination, and arrangement of material in a collective work, but also to the individual contributions in that work where the claimant also owns the copyright in those works. Requiring the photographer to register "Speeding Buffalo" using Form VA separately would undermine this policy and contradict the Copyright Office's own clear interpretation of its regulations.

         (C) is incorrect because it suggests that the Copyright Office's registration categories are *never* relevant. The Copyright Act does state that "[t]he administrative classification of works has no significance with respect to the subject matter of copyright or the exclusive rights provided by this title." 17 U.S.C. §408(c)(1). But this means only that the Copyright Office's administrative classifications are not relevant to the copyrightability of the work as defined by the Copyright Act. This clause does not necessarily mean that those administrative categories cannot negatively affect registration.

         Indeed, some courts have held that mistakes in registration filings can undermine an owner's ability to sue for infringement of the work they sought to register. In *Valley Entertainment, Inc. v. Friesen*, 691 F. Supp. 2d 821 (N.D. Ill. 2010), the plaintiff accused the defendant of infringing its copyrighted musical works. The defendant pointed out that the plaintiff's works were registered using Form PA (for works related to the performing arts, including musical compositions), not Form SR (for sound recordings). The court dismissed the plaintiff's complaint, because the defendant copied only the plaintiff's sound recording and did not copy from any sheet music.

189.   On these facts, the photographer will have a harder time successfully arguing that her registration is jurisdictionally sufficient. One concern is that neither the registration

application or the certificate list "Speeding Buffalo" as a protected work. Standing alone, this is probably not fatal to the photographer's ability to sue for infringement of that work. Indeed, the Copyright Act does state that a valid registration certificate "shall include . . . the title of the work." 17 U.S.C. § 409(6). And several district courts have held that plaintiffs whose works are not identified by title in their copyright registration certificate lack jurisdiction to sue for infringement of those works. *E.g., Muench Photography, Inc. v. Houghton Mifflin Harcourt Publ'g Co.*, 712 F. Supp. 2d 84, 94 (S.D.N.Y. 2010); *Alaska Stock, LLC v. Houghton Mifflin Harcourt Publ'g Co.*, 2010 WL 3785720, at *4 (D. Alaska Sept. 21, 2010).

On the other hand, the only court of appeals to consider this issue has held that compilation registrations suffice to authorize suits even if they do not specifically identify underlying works by title. *See Metro. Reg'l Info. Sys., Inc. v. Am. Home Realty Network, Inc.*, 722 F.3d 591, 598–600 (4th Cir. 2013). And several district courts have concurred with this conclusion. *E.g., Panoramic Stock Images, Ltd. v. McGraw-Hill Cos., Inc.*, 961 F. Supp. 2d 918, 926–27 (N.D. Ill. Aug. 9, 2013); *Masterfile Corp. v. Gale*, 2011 WL 4702862, at *2 (D. Utah Oct. 4, 2011). Moreover, the United States in amicus curiae briefs has taken this position on behalf of the Copyright Office. *See* Br. for the United States of America as Amicus Curiae in Support of Reversal, *Alaska Stock, LLC, v. Houghton Mifflin Harcourt Publ'g Co.*, Appeal No. 10-36010 (9th Cir. 2010).

So while there is still a split of opinion on the issue, the emerging weight of authority currently — but narrowly — favors the view that a registration certificate need not identify a work within a compilation by title in order to allow a claim for infringement of that work to proceed. If this position prevailed, the photographer would be able to proceed with her claim.

190.   **(D) is the correct answer.** The Copyright Act states that "no action for infringement of the copyright in any work shall be instituted until registration of the copyright claim has been made in accordance with this title." 17 U.S.C. § 411(a). The Supreme Court has held, though, that this requirement is not an absolute jurisdictional bar, but rather a mere "claim-processing rule," and that copyright registration is thus not a prerequisite for subject-matter jurisdiction. *Reed-Elsevier, Inc. v. Muchnick*, 559 U.S. 154, 163–66 (2010) ("Section 411(a) thus imposes a type of precondition to suit that supports nonjurisdictional treatment under our precedents."). Here, then, the court did not lack subject-matter jurisdiction to adjudicate Esme's copyright infringement lawsuit even though her essay was unregistered, and in turn the insurer's argument that her lawsuit was a sure loser would fail.

(A) is incorrect because subject-matter jurisdiction cannot be waived. *E.g., La Resolana Architects, PA v. Clay Realtors Angel Fire*, 416 F.3d 1195, 1198 (10th Cir. 2005) (holding, in the course of a copyright infringement matter, that "it is axiomatic that subject matter jurisdiction, which gives courts the power to adjudicate cases, cannot be waived").

(B) is incorrect because this is the very proposition the Court rejected in *Reed-Elsevier*.

(C) **is incorrect** because the Court stopped well short of describing the copyright registration requirement as merely "advisory." On the contrary, they left open the possibility that the requirement was a mandatory precondition to a lawsuit that courts should enforce sua sponte, even though the nature of this requirement was not jurisdictional. *Id.* at 170–71.

191. (D) **is the correct answer.** The lawyer publicly performed the literary work by reading it aloud over the radio. This performance, though, does not amount to publication of a work. *See Estate of Martin Luther King, Jr., Inc. v. CBS, Inc.*, 194 F.3d 1211, 1215–16 (2d Cir. 1999); *American Vitagraph, Inc. v. Levy*, 659 F.2d 1023, 1027 (9th Cir. 1981); *Burke v. National Broad. Co.*, 598 F.2d 688 (1st Cir. 1979). So while valid publication of the manuscript without proper notice would have divested its federal copyright, since this all took place during the decennial period, no such divestiture took place because the lawyer's actions did not amount to publication.

(A) **is incorrect** because, as explained above, the lawyer merely performed the novelist's literary work, and performance does not effect publication.

(B) **is incorrect** because the 1976 Act did not make notice irrelevant to copyright divesting (though it did make it irrelevant to copyright vesting). Until the effective date of the Berne Convention Implementation Act (March 1, 1989), publication of a work without proper copyright notice caused the work to enter the public domain, subject to cure provisions.

(C) **is incorrect** because it assumes that the lawyer's actions published the manuscript, which they did not. That said, it is true that valid publication requires an author's consent. *See John G. Danielson, Inc. v. Winchester-Conant Properties, Inc.*, 322 F.3d 26, 38 (1st Cir. 2003).

Duration, Renewal, and Termination of Transfers

192.   **(B) is the correct answer.** Because the work was created after 1977, its copyright was vested in the author at the time of creation. Once ownership of a copyright has vested, the owner of the copyright is free to devise the copyright via will to any person or institution the copyright owner desires.

(A) is incorrect. Although state law determines probate matters, a federal court has jurisdiction to hear cases that require the court to interpret the Copyright Act. *See Bell v. Combined Registry Co.*, 397 F. Supp. 1241, 1246 (N.D. Ill. 1975) (federal courts have exclusive jurisdiction to determine questions of title to a copyright, even when the issue arises out of a bequest in a will).

(C) is incorrect because the statutory successor provisions of the Copyright Act pertain to ownership of renewal terms of copyright in works created before 1978 that had not yet vested or the ownership of termination rights after the death of the author. Neither of these issues arises from this fact pattern.

(D) is incorrect for reasons stated earlier.

193.   **(C) is the correct answer.** The work received an initial term of copyright protection of 28 years. Upon renewal, the work received an additional 28 years of protection. On January 1, 1978, that renewal term was extended by 19 years. Because the copyright in the novel was no longer in effect as of October 27, 1998, the 20-year extension offered by the Copyright Term Extension Act of 1998 did not apply to the copyright in the novel. And while we do not know the precise date in 1922 when the copyright vested, the copyright will expire at the end of 1997 (not exactly 75 years after its date of vesting) due to the Copyright Act's provision that "[a]ll terms of copyright provided by sections 302 through 304 run to the end of the calendar year in which they would otherwise expire." 17 U.S.C. § 305.

(A) is incorrect because the duration of the copyright in the novel was not based on the life of the author, but on the rules of bifurcated copyright term duration that applied to works invested with federal copyright protection prior to January 1, 1978.

(B) is incorrect because the 20-year extension created by the Copyright Term Extension Act of 1998 did not apply to the copyright in the novel because it was not protected by federal copyright as of October 27, 1997.

(D) is incorrect because the copyright in the novel was in its renewal term on January 1, 1978. As a result, the renewal term was automatically extended 19 years.

194.   **(D) is the correct answer.** Because the work was protected by state common-law copyright as of January 1, 1978, the appropriate durational rule for the copyright in the poem is life of the author plus 70 years. 17 U.S.C. § 303(a). Poet died in 1970. Seventy years after that date is 2040. All terms of copyright extend until the end of the year in which they otherwise would have expired. 17 U.S.C. § 305. The second statutory minimum provided by the Copyright Act that provides for protection at least through 2047 does not apply because the poem was not published between January 1, 1978, and December 31, 2002. 17 U.S.C. § 303(a).

(A) is incorrect for the reason stated above.

(B) is incorrect because the proper durational analysis stated earlier provided protection for a longer period of time than the first statutory minimum protection, to the end of 2002, offered to all works that had been protected by state common-law copyright on January 1, 1978.

(C) is incorrect because works that had been protected by state common-law copyright on January 1, 1978, did not enter the public domain immediately once the 1976 Copyright Act took effect. Rather, such works were granted the more favorable of the applicable 1976 Act term or a statutory alternative minimum. 17 U.S.C. § 303(a).

195.   Upon publication with proper copyright notice, the novel was invested with statutory copyright protection. Novelist owned the initial term of the copyright. The remaining two years of the initial term of copyright protection (1984–1986) are owned by Neighbor, to whom Novelist devised her vested copyright interest via will. Novelist's intent also to give Neighbor the renewal term of copyright protection is not relevant under federal copyright law because Novelist did not own the renewal term of copyright at the time of his own death. The Copyright Act, not state law, determines the ownership of renewal copyright terms. Where the author dies before the final year of the initial term of the copyright, the Copyright Act sets the priority of statutory succession in such cases as surviving spouse and children, then to the surviving spouse if there are no children, then to the children if there is no surviving spouse, then to the executor of the will to disperse the property pursuant to the will if there is no surviving spouse or children, then to the next of kin if there is no will. 17 U.S.C. § 304(a). Here there is no surviving spouse, but there is a surviving son who has the right to renew the copyright, which he did. The son owns the renewal term of copyright until the end of 2053 (28-year initial term, 28-year renewal term, 19-year extension, and an additional 20 years provided by the Copyright Term Extension Act of 1998).

196.   **(A) is the correct answer.** The work was given an initial copyright term of 28 years. Upon renewal, the owner of the copyright received an additional 28 years of protection. The copyright would have expired at the end of the fifty-sixth year of protection (1964), but for the interim renewal term extension that, in effect, applied the 19-year extension of the renewal term to any work whose renewal term ended between 1962 and 1977. After the

19-year extension was applied to the renewal term, the work was protected by copyright through 1983.

(B) is incorrect because the work fell with the interim renewal term extension as explained above.

(C) is incorrect because the 20-year extension provided by the Copyright Term Extension Act of 1998 did not apply to this work, which entered the public domain before October 27, 1998.

(D) is incorrect because the interim renewal term extension brought this work into the 1976 Copyright Act, but applied the 19-year renewal extension from 1964, not 1978.

197.   **(B) is the correct answer.** Because the novel had been neither published with proper notice nor registered with the Copyright Office as of January 1, 1978, the applicable durational rule is either life of the author plus 70 years or the minimum protections provided by the Copyright Act. 17 U.S.C. § 303(a). Here, the durational rule would result in novel's copyright protection ending at the end of 1975 (death of author in 1905 plus 70 years). As a result, the minimum protection available to all works in this category ensures the copyright protection for this work until December 31, 2002. Because the novel was published between January 1, 1978, and December 31, 2002, the second statutory minimum of duration through December 31, 2047, applies here. 17 U.S.C. § 303(a).

(A) is incorrect because state common law protected the novel until January 1, 1978, because it had not been published or registered prior to that date.

(C) is incorrect because although state common-law copyright for the novel ended on January 1, 1978, the Copyright Act vested the work with federal copyright on that date.

(D) is incorrect because the second statutory minimum applies here for the reasons explained above.

198.   **(C) is the correct answer.** Because this is a grant that was executed prior to January 1, 1978, termination is available only under section 304(c) of the Copyright Act. Pursuant to section 304(c), the grant of a copyright in a work made for hire is not subject to termination.

(A) is incorrect because the exemption from termination of grants of copyright in works made for hire applies to any grant of a copyright in a work made for hire. It is not limited to any particular kind of agreement. Here, because the work was one made for hire, any transfers of that work—including Composer's assignment of the work to Music Publisher—are exempt from the Copyright Act's termination provisions. 17 U.S.C. § 304(c).

(B) is incorrect because the status of authorship of a work is determined at the time of the creation of the work and cannot be subsequently altered.

(D) is incorrect because the right to terminate applies to any eligible grant of copyright and is not limited to the initial grant, nor is the right limited to transfers of copyright. Grants of nonexclusive licenses may also be terminated.

199.   **(C) is the correct answer.** The duration of copyright for a work created as a work made for hire that had been created prior to 1978, but had not been published or registered prior to 1978, is 120 years from the date of creation, or 95 years from the date of first publication, whichever computed date is earlier. In this case, the earlier of these two dates is 2025 (120 years from creation in 1905), rather than 2099 (95 years from the first publication in 2004). Neither of the minimum terms that apply to common-law copyrighted works invested with federal copyright as of January 1, 1978, is relevant here because the photograph was not published by the end of 2002. *See* 17 U.S.C. § 303(a) (guaranteeing such works a term lasting through December 31, 2047, if the work was published before January 1, 2003).

(A) is incorrect because the applicable rule of duration is not the standard 1909 Act full term of 56 years from the date of creation. Federal copyright did not vest in the photograph until January 1, 1978. It had been protected by state common-law copyright until that date.

(B) is incorrect because the photograph was created as a work made for hire. Therefore, Employer was the author and initial owner of the copyright in the photograph, not Photographer, who was the creator of the photograph, but not its author. As a result, the appropriate 1976 Act rule of duration is the rule applicable to works made for hire, not life of the author plus 70 years. 17 U.S.C. § 303(a).

(D) is incorrect because the date of 2099, computed by adding 95 years to the date of first publication, is later than the date of 2025, which is computed by adding 120 years to the date of creation.

200.   **(C) is the correct answer.** The term of protection for the screenplay is 70 years after the death of the author. 17 U.S.C. § 302(a). In the case of joint works, the term is measured from the date of the last surviving author. 17 U.S.C. § 302(b). Because Collaborator lived longer than Author, the term is measured from the end of her life: 70 years after 1990, or through the year 2060.

(A) is incorrect. The term of copyright protection is not measured from the date of creation, but from the date of the author's death, or the last author's death in the case of joint works.

(B) is incorrect. The term of copyright protection in the case of joint authors is measured from the death of the last surviving co-author, not the first one to decease.

(D) is incorrect. The author's life determines the length of the copyright, regardless of who, or what, subsequently owns that copyright.

201.   **(C) is the correct answer.** For pseudonymous works, the term of copyright protection is 95 years after the work's first publication or 120 years after its creation, whichever computed date is earlier. 17 U.S.C. § 302(c). Here, 95 years from publication would be 2095 (2000 + 95), while 120 years after creation would be 2115 (1995 + 120). Because the earlier of the two computed dates is 2095, the copyright will expire at the end of that year.

(A) **is incorrect**. There is no reason to think the operative term would be the date of creation plus 70 years.

(B) **is incorrect**. Although normally the term of copyright is life of the author plus 70 years, in the case of pseudonymous works, this term is not applicable.

(D) **is incorrect** for the reasons explained above.

202. By changing the name on the copyright registration from a pseudonym to his own name, Author has converted the term to the standard life plus 70 term. The Copyright Act states that such changes in registration, if made before the otherwise applicable term expires, change the term from that which governs pseudonymous works to that which governs standard works written by a known author. 17 U.S.C. § 302(c). This means that in light of the revised facts, the work's copyright will expire 70 years from Author's death, in 2075.

203. (D) **is the correct answer.** The term of copyright runs to the end of the calendar year in which it would otherwise expire. 17 U.S.C. § 305. This means that the life plus 70 years term that *Nocturne in Blue* enjoys does not expire on the 70-year anniversary of Artist's death, but extends to the end of that calendar year. Thus the work was still protected when Joe Public tried to make use of it, and the heirs can bring a viable copyright infringement suit against him.

(A) **is incorrect** for the reasons set forth above.

(B) **is incorrect** because it falsely presumes that the term of protection is dated from registration. It is in fact dated from the author's death.

(C) **is incorrect** because only common-law copyright had perpetual protection. However, common-law copyright is not available to a work fixed after January 1, 1978.

204. (D) **is the correct answer.** The unpublished and unregistered poem was initially protected by state common-law copyright. Works protected by common-law copyright when the 1976 Copyright Act took effect on January 1, 1978, lost their perpetual common-law protection and received the same duration of federal protection as those works created on or after January 1, 1978. These works were also provided certain statutory minimum protections not applicable under these facts. 17 U.S.C. § 303; *Martha Graham School & Dance Found., Inc. v. Martha Graham Ctr. of Contemporary Dance, Inc.*, 380 F.3d 624, 632–33 (2d Cir. 2004). The term is life of the author plus 70 years, so the term of protection for this work, whose author died in 1935, continues through 2005. Neither of the minimum terms that apply to common-law copyrighted works invested with federal copyright as of January 1, 1978, are relevant here. *See* 17 U.S.C. § 303(a) (guaranteeing such works a term lasting at least through December 31, 2002, or through December 31, 2047, if—as was not the case here—the work was published before December 31, 2002).

(A) **is incorrect** because it assumes that the federal term of protection under the 1909 Act applies to the poem. It does not because this poem was not published or registered, and was thus protected by common-law copyright.

(B) **is incorrect** for the reasons explained above.

(C) **is incorrect** because the automatic statutory minimum copyright term lasting through December 31, 2002, applies only to works that were due to expire before on or before that date, when converted to the life-based term of the 1976 Copyright Act. 17 U.S.C. § 303(a). Works whose copyrights would last beyond that date under the 1976 Act enjoy that longer term of protection instead.

205.   (C) **is the correct answer.** Because Writer never registered the work nor published his work with valid copyright notice, it never took on the federal term of protection available under the 1909 Act, but was instead protected by state common-law copyright. Works protected by state common-law copyright when the 1976 Copyright Act took effect on January 1, 1978, have now lost their perpetual common-law protection and receive the same duration of protection as those works created on or after January 1, 1978. *See Martha Graham School & Dance Found., Inc. v. Martha Graham Ctr. of Contemporary Dance, Inc.*, 380 F.3d 624, 632–33 (2d Cir. 2004). In no case, however, did the protection of any of these works expire prior to December 31, 2002. 17 U.S.C. § 303(a). Because the life-plus-70 term would result in the copyright in Writer's play ending in 1990, the work instead is protected through 2002. In any event, though, this means that by the time Writer's heir discovered the play, its protection had expired.

(A), (B), and (D) **are incorrect** for the reasons explained above.

206.   Writer's heir's publishing the play in 2001 changes the duration of protection. The copyright in the play will now expire at the end of 2047. Works protected by state common-law copyright as of the effective date of the 1976 Copyright Act were converted to a federal copyright by that Act, and given a term of copyright protection lasting either for the applicable 1976 Act term, or through December 31, 2002, whichever computed length of protection is greater. However, where the previously unpublished and unregistered work is published between January 1, 1978, and December 31, 2002, the minimum term of copyright protection is extended through December 31, 2047. 17 U.S.C. § 303(a). The publication of the play by Writer's heirs in 2001 meets this latter criterion and, by doing so, extends the play's protection until the end of 2047.

207.   (B) **is the correct answer.** Any renewal terms of federal copyright protection that would have expired between September 19, 1962, and December 31, 1977, were automatically continued through December 31, 1977, and brought into the new Act. Congress periodically passed these interim extensions of copyright protection in anticipation of the "new" Copyright Act that was expected to extend the renewal term. As of January 1, 1978, these works, which were previously protected by the 1909 Copyright Act, obtained the protection of the 1976 Act. Specific duration rules are then applied that provide copyright protection for 75 years from the date federal protection initially vested, unless the renewal occurred after 1950, in which case copyright protection is provided for 95 years from the date federal protection initially vested, due to the 20-year increase provided by the Copyright Term Extension Act of 1998 to any copyright in existence in 1998. 17 U.S.C. § 304. Thus,

Summer Rapture enjoys a term of 75 years after its initial vesting in 1910, so that its copyright will expire at the end of 1985. *See* 17 U.S.C. § 305 (year-end expiration of copyright terms).

(A) is incorrect because it fails to account for the fact that the renewal term was extended for copyrights due to expire between 1962 and 1977.

(C) is incorrect for the reasons explained above. As a registered work, *Summer Rapture* was invested with a federal statutory copyright, not common-law copyright. Therefore, the statutory minimum protections do not apply here.

(D) is incorrect because it wrongly assumes that a life-based term applies to the work at issue.

208. **(A) is the correct answer.** If an author of a 1909 Act work died during the work's first copyright term and prior to renewal, the author's statutory successors succeeded to the second term if the work's copyright was validly renewed. Valid statutory successors were the author's surviving spouse and any children. If no such persons existed at the time of the author's death, then the author's executor was deemed the statutory successor. If the author left no will, then the statutory successor was deemed the author's remaining next of kin under state law. 17 U.S.C. § 304(a)(1)(C); *Music Sales Corp. v. Morris*, 73 F. Supp. 2d 364, 373 (S.D.N.Y. 1999). In light of this statutory scheme, only Artist's son would prevail. Artist's ex-wife does not have a place in this scheme because she is not a widow. Artist's grandchild is not a valid statutory successor in the Copyright Act's succession scheme.

(B), (C), and (D) are incorrect because they identify individuals other than the ones identified in the statutory scheme. (C), in particular, makes no sense, because Artist died intestate, so there was no will in which to name an executor. In terms of (D), while Artist's grandson may be a valid statutory successor under state law, any hypothetical interest the grandson may have had was superseded by the statutory scheme, which vests all ownership in the renewal term in an author's children and surviving spouses.

209. In terms of the right to apply for a renewal with the Copyright Office, the Artist's widow, his son, or his daughter may do so. Any one of these individuals may apply for the renewal. That renewal application will be deemed to include all of the statutory owners of the renewal term of copyright. In terms of who owns what share of the renewal term, as statutory successors, the surviving spouse holds a 50 percent share in the renewal copyright and the surviving children hold equal divided shares in the remaining 50 percent. *See Broadcast Music, Inc. v. Roger Miller Music, Inc.*, 396 F.3d 762, 782 (6th Cir. 2005). In this case, Artist's widow owns a 50 percent interest in the renewal term, and his son and daughter each own equal shares of the other half-interest in the renewal term, 25 percent each.

210. **(D) is the correct answer.** In the case of a work made for hire, the proprietor of the copyright (i.e., the employer or its assignee) in the original term is entitled to the renewal term. 17 U.S.C. § 304(a)(1)(B). *See Estate of Hogarth v. Edgar Rice Burroughs, Inc.*, 342 F.3d 149,

157 (2d Cir. 2003). Heir is the proprietor of the rights in this literary work, because he acquired them by devise after a valid transfer from BizCorp to Publisher.

(A) is incorrect. BizCorp is no longer the proprietor, having assigned away the rights in the literary work.

(B) is incorrect. This was a work made for hire, and Writer thus had no interest in the copyright.

(C) is incorrect. Publisher's demise and subsequent devise to Heir means that Publisher is no longer the proprietor of rights in the work.

211.   For works in the first term of copyright protection as of the effective date of the 1976 Act, and whose twenty-eighth year of protection occurred prior to 1992, failure to affirmatively renew the copyright resulted in the work entering the public domain. *See Martha Graham School & Dance Found., Inc. v. Martha Graham Ctr. of Contemporary Dance, Inc.*, 380 F.3d 624, 633 (2d Cir. 2004). The public may freely use a work that has entered the public domain. *See Frederick Warne & Co., Inc. v. Book Sales Inc.*, 481 F. Supp. 1191, 1197 (S.D.N.Y. 1979). Thus, the proprietor's failure to renew the copyright term in 1983 placed the literary work in the public domain and resulted in the work's being available for anyone to use.

212.   (D) is the correct answer. In 1992, the Copyright Act was amended to make renewal automatic. This automatic renewal applies to any work that was initially invested with federal protection from 1964 through 1977. *Martha Graham School & Dance Found., Inc. v. Martha Graham Ctr. of Contemporary Dance, Inc.*, 380 F.3d 624, 633 & n.15 (2d Cir. 2004); *Dimensional Music Publishing v. Kersey*, 435 F. Supp. 2d 452, 458 (E.D. Pa. 2006). Sculptor's failure to affirmatively renew the copyright may have had other negative implications, but it did not result in the work entering the public domain at the end of the initial term of copyright protection. The copyright is thus protected for the full 95-year term established by the 1976 Copyright Act and its amendments (i.e., a 28-year initial term, 28-year renewal term, 19-year renewal term extension, and an additional 20 years for works protected by copyright in 1998). 17 U.S.C. § 304(a).

(A) is incorrect because it assumes that the work will fall into the public domain unless a renewal application is filed. The 1992 Copyright Renewal Act amended the 1976 Copyright Act so that works in their first term as of the effective date of the former statute automatically enjoy a second term.

(B) is incorrect because it assumes that the 1909 Copyright Act's 56-year term (28-year initial term and 28-year renewal term) still prevails.

(C) is incorrect because it assumes that the original 75-year term for preexisting works established in the 1976 Copyright Act (28-year initial term, 28-year renewal term and 19-year renewal term extension) still applies. This ignores the term's 20-year extension in 1998 that was established by the Copyright Term Extension Act of 1998.

213.   (A) is the correct answer. In the event of the death of the author prior to the renewal of the copyright, the ownership of the renewal term of copyright is determined by the

statutory successors provision of the Copyright Act, not the testamentary intent or the contractual obligations of the author. *See Miller Music Corp. v. Charles N. Daniels, Inc.*, 362 U.S. 373, 375 (1960); *Broadcast Music, Inc. v. Roger Miller Music, Inc.*, 396 F.3d 762, 774 (6th Cir. 2005) ("A renewal copyright will automatically vest as of the last day of the original copyright in any person entitled to the renewal copyright even absent an affirmative act by any such person."). Thus, Writer's assignment of the initial term to Shyster is enforceable because Writer had a vested interest in the initial term of copyright at the time he contracted with Shyster. However, the assignment of the right of renewal and the renewal term itself is not enforceable because it has been obviated by Writer's death before the vesting of his interest in the renewal term.

(B) and (D) are incorrect because, for the reasons explained above, neither Writer nor Shyster own anything.

(C) is incorrect because, on the above facts, no one yet owns the renewal term. At the time of these events (i.e., prior to the 1992 Copyright Renewal Act), it was a mere expectancy interest that would vest only upon valid renewal. Writer's statutory successor thus does not yet own the renewal term because it has not yet vested in anyone.

214.   Under these facts, if a renewal application was filed by Writer or on his behalf, Shyster would own the right of renewal, the renewal term, and the initial term, while Writer's statutory successors would own nothing. The author may, during the first term of copyright, assign her expectancy interest in the renewal rights to a third party by contract. If, as here, the author survives until the renewal copyright vests, the assignment to the third party is binding. *Music Sales Corp. v. Morris*, 73 F. Supp. 2d 364, 371 (S.D.N.Y. 1999); *see also Fisher Music Co. v. W. Witmark & Sons*, 318 U.S. 643, 658–59 (1943). But if Writer, or Shyster on his behalf, failed to affirmatively renew the copyright in the screenplay, it would enter the public domain at the end of the initial term of copyright protection.

215.   **(C) is the correct answer.** The Supreme Court held in *Stewart v. Abend*, 495 U.S. 207 (1990), that the creator of a derivative work could not continue to utilize the derivative work after the copyright in the underlying work was renewed by a statutory successor, unless it was licensed by that statutory successor. Congress, however, modified *Abend* in 1992 when it required that a statutory successor must affirmatively renew the copyright in the twenty-eighth year of the copyright term in order to take full advantage of the *Abend* decision. 17 U.S.C. § 304(a)(4)(A). So here, Daughter's failure to file for renewal means that she cannot require De Marco Studios to negotiate a new license to exploit the preexisting derivative works based on Author's novel. De Marco Studio may continue to exploit its derivative work (i.e., the film based on *Empire*) created during the initial term of copyright, but it is precluded from making any new uses of them.

(A) is incorrect because it is overly broad. Author's statutory successor could gain the ability to control preexisting derivative works only if she had affirmatively filed for renewal in the twenty-eighth year of the initial term.

(B) is incorrect because an author's death in the initial term of protection does not automatically terminate licenses, though it may affect those agreements.

(D) is incorrect because, although Daughter cannot take full advantage of *Abend*, she has control over any new uses of preexisting derivative works, as well as the creation of all future derivative works.

216.   In light of these facts, Daughter could require De Marco Studios to negotiate new licenses for its continued exploitation of preexisting derivative works based on *Empire*. The Supreme Court held in *Stewart v. Abend*, 495 U.S. 207 (1990), that the creator of a derivative work could not continue to utilize its derivative work after the copyright in the underlying work was renewed by a statutory successor, unless it was licensed by that statutory successor. As of 1992, statutory successors must file for renewal in the twenty-eighth year of the copyright term in order to take advantage of the *Abend* decision. 17 U.S.C. § 304(a)(4)(A). But here, Daughter has fulfilled this latter condition, so she can take advantage of the *Abend* decision and require De Marco Studios to enter into new license agreements if it wants to continue exploiting the film version of *Empire*. As a result, even if De Marco Studios had released the motion picture on DVD and permitted its broadcast on television during the initial term of copyright protection of the *Empire* novel, this continued exploitation would constitute copyright infringement without a license from Daughter.

217.   **(B) is the correct answer.** The author or the author's statutory successor is permitted to terminate the grant of rights beginning 35 years after the date of the initial grant. The grant may be terminated any time during the five-year period beginning at the end of the 35 years from the day of execution of the grant. 17 U.S.C. § 203(a)(3). Here, the assignment took place in 1985, so the termination period begins 35 years later, in 2020.

(**A) is incorrect** because the termination window for grants entered into after 1977 begins 35 years from the date of the grant, not 35 years from the date of the creation of the work.

(**C) is incorrect** because, for grants entered into after 1977, the termination window does not begin 56 years from the date the work was vested with federal copyright protection. For such works, the termination window begins 35 years after the date of the executed grant.

(**D) is incorrect** because in the event of an author's death, termination can be effected by his statutory successors. This answer highlights a common source of confusion with section 203 terminations: only grants by authors may be terminated under section 203, but either an author or her statutory successors can terminate them.

218.   **(C) is the correct answer.** Where the author is dead, her termination interest is owned and may be exercised by the widow, widower, children, grandchildren, executor, administrator, personal representative or trustee as set forth in 17 U.S.C. § 203(a)(2). The termination interest may be exercised only with the support of a majority of the termination interest shares. 17 U.S.C. § 203(a)(1). Where the surviving spouse and children own the termination right, a 50 percent share of the termination interest vests in the surviving

spouse and the surviving children divide the remaining 50 percent in equal divided shares. *See Broadcast Music, Inc. v. Roger Miller Music, Inc.*, 396 F.3d 762, 771 (6th Cir. 2005).

Here, Musician's widow owns 50 percent of the termination right, and his sons each own 25 percent. In order to exceed the 50 percent minimum required to effect termination, the widow can exercise the termination right only if she has the support of at least one of the sons. *See, e.g., Penguin Group (USA) Inc. v. Steinbeck*, 537 F.3d 193, 202–03 (2d Cir. 2008).

(A) and (B) are incorrect because Musician's widow acting alone amounts to only 50 percent of the termination interest, which is insufficient because it is not a majority interest. Musician's sons acting alone similarly fail to constitute a majority because together they reach, but do not exceed, 50 percent of the termination interest.

(D) is incorrect because termination is clearly possible via the combination described above.

219.   It would not affect the termination date at all. For purposes of section 203, only the date of execution of the conveyance, not the date on which the original copyright vested, has significance. *See Broadcast Music, Inc. v. Roger Miller Music, Inc.*, 396 F.3d 762, 772 (6th Cir. 2005). Thus, while the revised facts would mean that the work would be governed differently in terms of its length of protection, this distinction is irrelevant to the date on which termination could begin, which continues to be in the year 2020.

220.   **(D) is the correct answer.** For grants made after January 1, 1978, transfers made by authors can be terminated beginning 35 years after the date of the transfer. However, grants conveyed by statutory successors cannot be terminated. 17 U.S.C. § 203(a). *See Broadcast Music, Inc. v. Roger Miller Music, Inc.*, 396 F.3d 762, 771 n.9 (6th Cir. 2005). Because the exclusive license to base a screenplay in *Molto Maria* was executed not by Author himself, but by his statutory successor, it cannot be terminated.

(A), (B), and (C) are incorrect because they assume the grant by the son can be terminated, when for the reasons explained above, it cannot.

221.   Unlike the facts in question VI-29, section 304(c), not section 203, governs this termination scenario. This is because the grant was executed prior to 1978. Unlike section 203 terminations, section 304 terminations do apply to grants made by statutory successors. 17 U.S.C. § 304(c). Thus, pursuant to the terms of section 304(c), the termination window begins 56 years after the copyright's original vesting. And under the 1976 Copyright Act, the term of copyright runs to the end of the calendar year in which it would otherwise expire, 17 U.S.C. § 305, the earliest date of termination would be the first day of the 57th year of copyright protection. So because the copyright in *Molto Maria* in the revised scenario vested in 1960, the earliest possible termination date would be January 1, 2017.

222.   **(C) is the correct answer.** "A derivative work prepared under authority of the grant before its termination may continue to be utilized under the terms of the grant after its termination." 17 U.S.C. § 304(c)(6)(A). Because Publisher created the derivative work *Greater Plains* before the termination of the transfer of the copyright in the underlying work *Great Plains*, Publisher remains entitled to exploit the latter in the same manner. Publisher is

precluded from making any new uses of the existing derivative works and from creating and exploiting any new derivative works without permission from Heir.

(A) and (B) are incorrect because they misstate the law. Terminating a transfer neither entitles the terminating party to all profits derived from the derivative work nor transfers ownership of that work to the terminating party.

(D) is incorrect because the derivative works privilege "does not extend to the preparation after the termination of other derivative works based upon the copyrighted work covered by the terminated grant." 17 U.S.C. § 304(c)(6)(A). If Publisher wants to create new derivative works based on *Great Plains*, it must obtain the right to do so from Heir.

223.   **(B) is the correct answer.** A music publisher may continue to receive its share of royalties derived from the sale of pre-termination licensed recordings of a musical composition after the termination of the grant to the music publisher of the copyright in the musical composition. 17 U.S.C. § 304(c)(6)(A); *Mills Music, Inc. v. Snyder*, 469 U.S. 153 (1985). Therefore, Publisher may continue to collect mechanical royalties from the post-termination sales of any recordings of *Andalucia* that were made pre-termination.

(A) is incorrect because the Supreme Court held just the opposite in *Mills Music*. The Court determined that when a music publisher facilitates the creation of a derivative work by permitting the use of a musical composition, the music publisher is allowed to take advantage of the Copyright Act's continuing use exception for derivative works. 17 U.S.C. § 304(c)(6)(A).

(C) is incorrect both because it is inconsistent with *Mills Music* and because transferees never have to disgorge past profits earned from works for which transfers have been terminated.

(D) is incorrect because termination of the 1939 transfer does entitle Heir or his assigns to profit from new uses of the 1940 *Andalucia* recording by RecordCo or any new post-termination recording.

224.   **(D) is the correct answer.** The Copyright Act unambiguously states that termination of copyright assignments may be effected notwithstanding any agreement to the contrary. 17 U.S.C. § 304(c)(5). As such, an agreement not to terminate is invalid. *See Stewart v. Abend*, 495 U.S. 207, 230 (1990) ("The 1976 Copyright Act provides . . . an inalienable termination right"); *Music Sales Corp. v. Morris*, 73 F. Supp. 2d 364, 372 (S.D.N.Y. 1999) ("[A]ny contract provision that purports to assign [the termination] right is void."). Thus, the provision of the 1935 assignment in which Composer is purported to have alienated his termination rights to MusicCo is invalid and MusicCo cannot rely on it to oppose Composer's termination of the 1935 assignment of the copyright in *Dancing Shoes*.

(A) is incorrect because it is directly contrary to the plain language of the Copyright Act, which makes terminations of transfers inalienable.

(B) is incorrect because the termination right is never alienable, regardless of the transferring party.

(C) is incorrect because termination cannot be assigned to any party, individual or corporate.

225.   (A) is the correct answer. The termination notice must be recorded in the United States Copyright Office prior to the date of termination. 37 C.F.R. § 201.10. Because this notice was served after the date of termination, it is not valid.

(B) is incorrect because it is not merely the intent to terminate that must be communicated to the grantee. The party attempting to terminate must meet the requirements set forth in the regulations of the Copyright Office.

(C) is incorrect because a termination notice must be issued at least two, but not more than 10 years, prior to the effective date of the termination. 37 C.F.R. § 201.10. The notice sent by Composer fell within the required time span.

(D) is incorrect because the notice was invalid for the reasons explained above.

226.   Not necessarily. Typically, an unlimited grant of rights that is not terminated will continue in effect for the duration of the term of copyright. 17 U.S.C. § 304(c)(6)(F). In this case, however, Composer would have sufficient time to give another termination notice to MusicCo within the five-year termination window that began on January 1, 1990. Composer would have until December 30, 1992, to give a termination notice that is two years in advance of the termination date, the minimum period of notice required for termination. In addition, in the case of pre-1978 assignments such as this one, there is an additional opportunity to terminate the final 20 years of the copyright's 95-year term even if the owner of the termination right does not take advantage of the initial opportunity to terminate the transfer. In 1998, Congress created a second termination opportunity for some pre-1978 grants that had not been terminated after the fifty-sixth year of copyright protection, but now benefit from a 20-year extension of the renewal term. 17 U.S.C. § 304(d). *See Music Sales Corp. v. Morris*, 73 F. Supp. 2d 364, 372, 380 (S.D.N.Y. 1999). Under this provision, Composer could also effect termination of the final 20 years of the copyright in *Dancing Shoes* for a five-year period beginning on January 1, 2009.

227.   (B) is the correct answer. *Alone* is a jointly made work, *see* 17 U.S.C. § 101 (defining "joint work"), which means that the copyright in the screenplay is jointly owned by its co-authors as tenants in common. *Id.* § 201(a); *Thomson v. Larson*, 147 F.3d 195 (2d Cir. 1998). Part of that interest belongs to Wolf, because *Alone* was created by Wolf's employee, Screenwriter, in the scope of her employment. *See* 17 U.S.C. § 101 (defining "work made for hire"). The other part belongs to Indy, since she was an independent contractor. *See Community for Creative Non-Violence v. Reid*, 490 U.S. 730 (1990) (holding that works produced by independent contractors are not works made for hire, and therefore are owned by their creators, not the entity that commissioned them). And while Indy consented to Zenith's assignment of the copyright, that alone is insufficient because the consent of all joint owners is required to effect a valid copyright assignment. *See Glovaroma, Inc. v. Maljack Productions, Inc.*, 71 F. Supp. 2d 846, 853 (N.D. Ill. 1999); *Denker v. Twentieth Century-Fox Film Corp.*, 223 N.Y.S.2d 193, 195 (1961).

(A) is incorrect because Wolf did not solely own the copyright in *Alone*, but owned only a part interest as a tenant in common.

(C) is incorrect because Wolf's decision not to make a derivative work based on the screenplay does not amount to abandonment. If anything, just the opposite is true. By exercising selectivity about whether *Alone* would be made into a motion picture, and then threatening Zenith with infringement litigation, Wolf indicated its intent to maintain active ownership and management of the work. This is the opposite of abandonment.

(D) is incorrect because nothing about a decision not to make a derivative work based on the screenplay reallocates ownership. Moreover, there is no written transfer of ownership, which the Copyright Act would require for any transfer of Wolf's rights in *Alone* to Screenwriter. 17 U.S.C. § 204(a).

228.   This is a hard question. The copyright term in jointly authored works that vest after 1977 lasts for 70 years after the death of the last living co-author. 17 U.S.C. § 302(b) ("In the case of a joint work prepared by two or more authors who did not work for hire, the copyright endures for a term consisting of the life of the last surviving author and 70 years after such last surviving author's death.").

In this case, though, *Alone* was jointly authored by an individual (Indy) as well as a corporate entity (Wolf), the latter by operation of the work made for hire doctrine. Here, the language of § 302(b)—"such last surviving author's death"—does not seem to track onto corporations, which are not natural persons.

While there is no case law directly addressing this issue, one plausible answer is simply to use the applicable copyright term for each author, and then apply the later expiration date. The duration of copyright for a work made for hire is the earlier of 100 years after the date of creation or 75 years after the date of publication. So if Wolf's copyright term were used, that would mean that *Alone* would enter the public domain at the end of 2115, unless it were published in or before 2049, in which case it would expire earlier. If Screenwriter's copyright term were used, *Alone* would enter the public domain at the end of the seventieth year following Screenwriter's death, whenever that may be.

Since much of the relevant information is not yet available, it is not possible to say with certainty when *Alone* will enter the public domain. And while the Copyright Act does not explicitly address the problem of works jointly authored by natural and artificial persons, it would likely follow the approach implied for most joint works and simply use the longer of the two joint authors' terms.

229.   (C) is the correct answer. The daughter is seeking to effect termination of transfer under section 304(c), which applies to transfers executed prior to 1978, such as the 1970 assignment. She is the only statutorily entitled individual with the right to terminate transfers of the ballad's copyright, since the work's author died unmarried and she is his only daughter. An argument that the 1979 agreement eliminated her transfer rights would fail because that agreement did not rescind the 1970 agreement but only clarified it. *See*

Classic Media, Inc. v. Mewborn, 532 F.3d 978, 989 (9th Cir. 2008) (agreement that did not rescind but only highlighted meaning of preexisting transfer did not rescind that transfer); *Brumley v. Albert Brumley & Sons, Inc.*, 822 F.3d 926 (6th Cir. 2016). As a result, the 1970 agreement remained the operative assignment of copyright in the ballad, and the daughter's timely filing of notice to terminate that transfer would survive the music publisher's objections.

(A) is incorrect because under section 304(c), the five-year window of time to terminate transfers opens 56 years after the copyright's vesting. In this case, since the copyright vested in 1962, the termination window would open in 2018. (A) appears to wrongly assume that the five-year termination window opened in 2005, 35 years after the transfer—which is the timing relevant to section 203 terminations, not section 304 terminations.

(B) is incorrect because the 1979 agreement did not rescind the earlier transfer and regrant it to the music publisher. When a pre-1978 assignment is rescinded and re-granted in this manner during or after 1978 by a statutory heir, that has the effect of obviating the heir's termination rights because the operative agreement is subject to section 203's termination provisions (since it was executed during or after 1978), while transfers by statutory heirs are not subject to section 203 terminations (only transfers by authors may be terminated under section 203). *See Penguin Group (USA) Inc. v. Steinbeck*, 537 F.3d 193, 202–04 (2d Cir. 2008); *Milne ex rel. Coyne v. Stephen Slesinger, Inc.*, 430 F.3d 1036, 1043–45 (9th Cir. 2005). But where, as here, an agreement merely clarifies a point from a preexisting agreement, it does not count as the kind of rescission and re-grant that can undo an heir's termination rights. *See Classic Media, Inc. v. Mewborn*, 532 F.3d 978, 989 (9th Cir. 2008).

(D) is incorrect for at least two reasons. First, any termination rights that would apply to the 1979 agreement would arise under section 203, and would be unrelated to attempts to terminate the 1970 assignment under section 304. And second, the daughter could not terminate the 1979 agreement even if it were a transfer of copyright because she is a statutory heir, and only transfers by authors may be terminated under section 203.

230.   **(C) is the correct answer.** The 1992 agreement amounted to a rescission and re-grant that effectively eliminated Doris' 304(d) termination rights by revoking any pre-1978 transfers of the copyright in Cat Man. *See Penguin Group (USA) Inc. v. Steinbeck*, 537 F.3d 193, 202–04 (2d Cir. 2008); *Milne ex rel. Coyne v. Stephen Slesinger, Inc.*, 430 F.3d 1036, 1043–45 (9th Cir. 2005). While the 1992 agreement does not explicitly use the term "revoke" or "rescind" with respect to the 1938 transfer, courts have held that this kind of formulaic language is not required to effect a valid rescission and re-grant. *See D.C. Comics v. Pacific Pictures Corp.*, 545 Fed. Appx. 678, 680–81 (9th Cir. Nov. 21, 2013) (holding that a similarly worded agreement effected revocation of an earlier transfer and that courts do not require "magic . . . words" but instead look to the parties' intent when construing such agreements). Courts have also held that a party need not have effective termination rights at the time of a rescission and re-grant. *D.C. Comics v. Pacific Pictures Corp.*, 2012 WL 4936588 at *11– 12 (C.D. Cal. Oct. 17, 2012); *but see D.C. Comics*, 545 Fed. Appx. at 682–83 (Thomas, J.,

dissenting) (arguing that parties without statutory termination rights cannot make binding agreements with respect to those rights).

(A) is incorrect because courts have held that parties can prospectively bind themselves with respect to termination rights that have not yet been created by statute. *E.g., D.C. Comics v. Pacific Pictures Corp.*, 2012 WL 4936588 at *11–12 (C.D. Cal. Oct. 17, 2012).

(B) is incorrect because the language of an agreement need not resolve this point, so long as there is evidence of the parties' intent to rescind and re-grant an earlier transfer.

(D) is incorrect because the 1998 revision did extend termination rights to heirs and executors such as Doris.

231.   **(B) is the correct answer.** The question is whether the issue raised by the Foundation lies within the "zone of interests" of the Copyright Act's termination provisions, i.e., "injuries *to precisely the sorts of . . . interests the Act protects.*" *Ray Charles Found. v. Robinson*, 795 F.3d 1109, 1123 (9th Cir. 2013). While these provisions were designed primarily for the benefit of statutory heirs, such as Musician's son, the statute's zone of interests also encompasses the interests of parties, such as Foundation, who rely on royalties that may be eliminated by terminations of transfer. As a federal appeals court put it when resolving a case on virtually identical facts, "the Foundation alleges injury to its interest in continuing to receive the royalty stream generated by [Musician's] works, which is . . . the one Congress contemplated, regulated, and protected in enacting the termination provisions." *Id.*

(A) is incorrect because the beneficial ownership gives rise to standing only in copyright infringement cases, not cases involving the validity of copyright termination notices. 17 U.S.C. § 501(b) ("The legal or beneficial owner of an exclusive right under a copyright is entitled . . . to institute an action for any infringement of that particular right committed while he or she is the owner of it.").

(C) is incorrect because the termination notices threaten Foundation with a very real injury-in-fact: the potential loss of all its operating revenue. *Id.* at 1118–19.

(D) is incorrect because there are no more facts a court would need to adjudicate the validity of the termination notices. *Id.* at 1116–17.

232.   **(A) is the correct answer.** Van contributed to Spectacular comics in the early 1960s, so the relevant test for whether a work is one made for hire is the "instance and expense" test that prevailed during the Copyright Act of 1909 regime. *See Estate of Burne Hogarth v. Edgar Rice Burroughs, Inc.*, 342 F.3d 149, 156–63 (2d Cir. 2003). "Instance" refers to who initiated the creation of a work. *Marvel Characters, Inc. v. Kirby*, 726 F.3d 119, 139 (2d. Cir. 2013) ("'Instance' refers to the extent to which the hiring party provided the impetus for, participated in, or had the power to supervise the creation of the work."). Here, Spectacular suggested that Van work on given projects, so the works he created were clearly at Spectacular's instance. "Expense" refers to both who paid for the material necessary to create the work as well as the distribution of financial risk between the commissioning party and the creator. *Id.* at 139–40. In this case, while Van used his own supplies, he bore

little risk that Spectacular would not buy his work, because Spectacular asked Van to contribute to their projects, and because they almost always accepted and paid for the work he created. Spectacular bore relatively more financial risk than Van, because if a given comic failed, they would lose money but Van would already have been paid. *See id.* at 140–43 (holding, on virtually identical facts, that the contributions of famed graphic artist Jack Kirby to Marvel Comics titles were works made for hire under the instance and expense test).

(B), (C), and (D) are incorrect for the reasons explained above.

Infringement

233. **(D) is correct.** By continuing to distribute the motion picture on DVD after the expiration of the license, Distributor is doing so without the consent of the copyright owner. This constitutes infringement of the public distribution right owned by Studio. *See Jarvis v. K2 Inc.*, 486 F.3d 526, 530 (9th Cir. 2007) (use of photographer's images after expiration of contractual usage term constituted infringement); *Powell v. Green Hill Publishers, Inc.*, 719 F. Supp. 743 (N.D. Ill. 1989) (continued publication of book following termination of license found to be copyright infringement).

    (A) is incorrect because ownership of the distribution right to the motion picture reverted to Studio at the end of the five-year agreement, pursuant to the agreement.

    (B) is incorrect because a contractual termination provision of an agreement that is of shorter duration than the statutory termination provided by the Copyright Act is enforceable and makes statutory termination inapplicable. *See Walthal v. Rusk*, 172 F.3d 481, 485 (7th Cir. 1999).

    (C) is incorrect because copyright infringement is not the only remedy available to Studio. On these facts the Distributor could be sued for breach of contract. *See Effects Associates, Inc. v. Cohen*, 817 F.2d 72, 73 (9th Cir. 1987) ("plaintiff is master of his claim and in some cases will have the choice of framing his action either as one for infringement or for breach of contract").

234. **(B) is the correct answer.** A copyright owner has the right to sue any unauthorized user for infringement, but only of exclusive rights that they possess. 17 U.S.C. § 501(a) ("Anyone who violates any of the exclusive rights of the copyright owner . . . is an infringer of the copyright"). An owner of an exclusive right obtained via an exclusive license thus has standing to sue for infringement of that right, though the assignor/author does not. 17 U.S.C. § 501(b). *See Gamma Audio & Video, Inc. v. Ean-Chea*, 11 F.3d 1106 (1st Cir. 1993). Thus, only Production Company, as the exclusive licensee, would have standing to sue Writer for infringement.

    (A), (B), and (D) are incorrect for the reasons explained above.

235. Author does have the right to grant the license Book Publisher seeks. An exclusive right, such as the adaptation right, can be divided into different types of derivative works as well as different types of media. Any of the section 106 exclusive rights that make up a copyright and any subdivision of them can be transferred and owned separately, whether or

not the transfer is limited in time, media, or geographic area. 17 U.S.C. § 201(d); *see Gamma Audio & Video, Inc. v. Ean-Chea*, 11 F.3d 1106 (1st Cir. 1993).

In this case, Author has relinquished the right to authorize the creation of a screenplay based on the novel, but has retained the right to other types of derivative works based on the novel, such as the Spanish translation right for use in a published novel.

236.   In light of these changed facts, only Author would have standing to sue Whanna Bee. Although an owner of the copyright, or subsequent assignee, or an exclusive licensee of an exclusive right, has standing to sue for copyright infringement of that right, a nonexclusive licensee does not have standing to sue. 17 U.S.C. § 501(b). *See Gamma Audio & Video, Inc. v. Ean-Chea*, 11 F.3d 1106 (1st Cir. 1993). As the copyright's owner, Author would have standing to sue, but as the nonexclusive licensee, Production Company would not.

237.   **(D) is the correct answer.** Composer can sue Lil Flasher and Flasher Music for copyright infringement, because although Composer is no longer a legal owner of the copyright in *Red Rhapsody*, he is a beneficial owner of that copyright. A beneficial owner is one who, like Composer, has relinquished legal ownership in exchange for an economic interest in the exploitation of the copyright. *See Cortner v. Israel*, 732 F.2d 267 (2d Cir. 1984). And a beneficial owner of an exclusive right under a copyright is entitled to sue for infringement. 17 U.S.C. § 501(b).

(A) is incorrect because the views of private parties regarding the similarity between two works do not determine the outcome of a copyright infringement action. The finder of fact will make that determination as part of the litigation. Further, Lyrical Publishing may be protecting its affiliated record company by using the lack of similarity as an excuse not to file an infringement action.

(B) is incorrect because it does not take into account Composer's status as a beneficial owner.

(C) is incorrect. Composer assigned all of his copyright interest in *Red Rhapsody* to Lyrical Publishing, making the music publisher the legal owner of the copyright in the musical work, not merely its administrator.

238.   **(A) is the correct answer.** Federal district courts have exclusive original jurisdiction over actions that arise under the Copyright Act. 28 U.S.C. § 1338(a). An action "arises under" the Copyright Act if the complaint is for a remedy expressly granted by the Act, the claim requires a construction of the Act, or a distinctive policy of the Act requires that federal principles control the disposition of the claim. *T.B. Harms Co. v. Eliscu*, 339 F.2d 823, 828 (2d Cir. 1964). Here, Wise's claim that she is a joint author clearly belongs before a federal court because it requires a construction of the Copyright Act.

It is true that state law governs both construction of the assignment of royalty interests, *see Yount v. Acuff Rose-Opryland*, 103 F.3d 830, 835 (9th Cir. 1996), and the validity of ownership transfers themselves, *see Eliscu*, 339 F.2d at 827. However, federal courts have the authority to hear state as well as federal causes of action pursuant to their supplemental jurisdictional authority. 28 U.S.C. § 1367. The test for whether supplemental jurisdiction is appropriate is whether the state and federal claims arise out of the same case or controversy. 28 U.S.C. § 1367(a). Here, it is clear that they do. Both claims concern Wise's entitlements to the royalties generated by *In tha Biz*. Additionally, the state and federal claims each require interpretation of the same instrument. For these reasons, adjudication in state and federal courts would be inefficient, and an exercise of supplemental jurisdiction by the federal court is appropriate.

(B) and (C) are incorrect because they wrongly assume that supplemental jurisdiction in this matter is not appropriate, and that the matter would be better adjudicated separately by state and federal courts.

(D) is incorrect because the construction of the Copyright Act is clearly a matter a federal court is jurisdictionally competent to hear.

239.   **(D) is the correct answer.** Although a party has no right to a jury trial when the relief sought is solely equitable (i.e., when only an injunction is being sought), when the relief sought is both equitable and legal (i.e., when both an injunction and money damages are being sought), the Constitution requires that the entire matter be tried by a jury if either party so requests. U.S. CONST. Amend. XII. There had been some question as to whether statutory damages are deemed a legal or equitable remedy, because the statute creating the right to statutory damages does not define them as either. *See* 17 U.S.C. § 504(c). However, the Supreme Court considered this issue and held unequivocally that "if a party so demands, a jury must determine the actual amount of statutory damages under section 504(c) in order to preserve the substance of the common-law right of trial by jury." *Feltner v. Columbia Pictures Television, Inc.*, 523 U.S. 340, 355 (1988).

         (A), (B), and (C) are incorrect for the reasons explained above.

240.   **(C) is the correct answer.** United States copyright law has no application to infringements that occur wholly outside the United States. *Subafilms, Ltd. v. MGM-Pathe Communications Co.*, 24 F.3d 1088 (9th Cir. 1994); *Armstrong v. Virgin Records, Inc.*, 91 F. Supp. 2d 628, 634 (S.D.N.Y. 2000). Because DistroCo's conduct was entirely extraterritorial, it is not actionable in federal court.

         (A) is incorrect because, while the conduct alleged would normally amount to a clear violation of the right of public distribution, that does not resolve this question because of the extraterritoriality issue.

         (B) is incorrect because there is no such exception for international subsidiaries with domestic parents.

         (D) is incorrect because EuroDistro's conduct clearly amounts to a "public distribution" within the meaning of the Copyright Act. Here, the infringing act of unauthorized distribution occurs entirely outside the United States, where the Copyright Act does not apply.

241.   Studio still cannot sue DistroCo in United States federal court for violations of United States copyright law, even though it authorized its subsidiary, EuroDistro, to engage in unlicensed

distribution of the film. Because the conduct alleged is not actionable under the Copyright Act due to its extraterritoriality, there can be no liability for authorizing that conduct. *See* 17 U.S.C. § 106. Thus, the mere authorization of extraterritorial acts of infringement does not state a claim under the Copyright Act. *Subafilms, Ltd. v. MGM-Pathe Communications Co.*, 24 F.3d 1088, 1090–95 (9th Cir. 1994).

242.   **(A) is the correct answer.** Ownership of copyright issues is determined by the law of the country with the most significant relationship to the work and the parties. *See Itar-Tass Russian News Agency v. Russian Kurier, Inc.*, 153 F.3d 82, 90 (2d Cir. 1998) (Russian law deemed appropriate source of law to determine issues of ownership of rights in works created by Russian nationals and first published in Russia). Whether the copyright in a work has been infringed is determined by the law of the place, the situs, where the alleged violation occurred. *See id.* at 91.

Here, the country with the most significant relationship to the work and the parties is clearly Canada. The original article was published in a Canadian newspaper, and its author was Canadian as well. Thus, Canadian law must determine the ownership issue. However, the alleged violation of the work took place in the United States when Smith published an unauthorized translation of Anglais' article. As a result, United States law governs the infringement issue.

(B), (C), and (D) are incorrect for the reasons explained above.

243.   **(D) is the correct answer.** Copyright infringement is a strict liability tort. A defendant need not have intended the infringement in order to be held liable. *See Shapiro, Bernstein & Co. v. H.L. Green Co.*, 316 F.2d 304, 308 (2d Cir. 1963). Brown's lack of awareness that his conduct amounted to infringement does not provide a defense to that infringement.

(A) is incorrect. Personal use of copyrighted works may be permitted under some circumstances, but is certainly not always a full defense to infringement.

(B) is incorrect. Copyright infringement is a strict liability offense, as explained above, so Brown's innocent state of mind cannot negate his liability. Here, the actionable conduct lies in violating Hot Ten's exclusive right of reproduction, whether or not a commercial use is subsequently made of the works.

(C) is incorrect. The user agreement may create a contract cause of action, but it does not create an infringement cause of action.

244.   No. Direct copyright infringement requires volitional conduct that directly results in the violation of an exclusive right. *See Cartoon Network LP, LLP v. CSC Holdings, Inc.*, 536 F.3d 121, 131–33 (2d Cir. 2008) (volitional conduct of cable customer who makes copy of protected material on cable operator's digital video recorder system that reproduces the material on central hard drives housed and maintained by cable operator at a remote location, results in no direct infringement by cable operator). Courts have held that Internet service providers are not liable for direct infringement of copyrighted works posted on the Internet, so long as they did not take any affirmative action that directly resulted in copying.

See Costar Group, Inc. v. Loopnet, Inc., 373 F.3d 544, 549–52 (4th Cir. 2004) (Copyright Act requires conduct by a person who causes an infringement); *Religious Technology Center v. Netcom On-Line Communication Services, Inc.*, 907 F. Supp. 1361, 1368 (N.D. Cal. 1995); *Hendrickson v. Amazon.com, Inc.*, 298 F. Supp. 2d 914, 915 (C.D. Cal. 2003) (online retailer that facilitated sale of infringing motion picture by independent third-party seller held not to be a direct infringer); *see also Bernstein v. J.C. Penney*, 50 U.S.P.Q.2d 1063 (C.D. Cal. 1998) (website owner not liable for linking to a second website that in turn linked to an infringing third website). *But cf. Kelly v. Arriba Soft Corp.*, 280 F.3d 934, 947 (9th Cir. 2002) (owner of Internet visual search engine acted as more than a passive conduit of images by trolling the web, finding the images, and having its program inline link and frame those images within its own website).

245. **(B) is the correct answer.** A co-owner of a copyright cannot be liable to another co-owner for infringement of the copyright. *Oddo v. Ries*, 743 F.2d 630, 632–33 (9th Cir. 1984). However, while this means that Lyricist would not be able to sue Musician on a copyright theory, under the rule of mutual accountability of joint copyright owners, Lyricist would still be able to sue Musician on a state property-law theory because co-owners of property are obligated to share the profits generated by that property with the other joint owners. *See Harrington v. Mure*, 186 F. Supp. 655, 657–58 (S.D.N.Y.1960) (superseded by the 1976 Copyright Act on other grounds). This would not entitle Lyricist to all of the proceeds from Musician's shows. Rather, the rule of mutual accountability requires Musician to account to Lyricist for any profits he earns from the use of the copyright. *See Shapiro, Bernstein & Co. v. Jerry Vogel Music Co.*, 221 F.2d 569, *modified*, 223 F.2d 252 (2d Cir. 1955). Lyricist has a right to share in the proceeds attributable to the public performance of the musical work, but not in the proceeds attributable to Musician's personal services, such as the performance of additional musical works not owned by Lyricist. As a practical matter, this would require the determination of a reasonable public performance license for the proportion of Musician's shows featuring *View From My Window*, of which Lyricist would receive half.

(A) is incorrect because as a joint owner of *The View From My Window*, Musician is entitled to publicly perform it without running afoul of Lyricist's exclusive rights. Musician and Lyricist, as joint owners, each have ownership of the entirety of the copyright, including all of the exclusive rights protected by the copyright.

(C) is incorrect because Musician has not violated any of Lyricist's exclusive rights.

(D) is incorrect because Lyricist does have a valid cause of action against Musician based on a state-law theory of mutual accountability.

246. **(A) is the correct answer.** CEO is individually liable to Author for violations of both the right of reproduction (as a direct infringer because he made unauthorized photocopies of the novel embodying the literary work) and the right of adaptation (as a contributory infringer because he authorized adaptations of the literary work without permission and facilitated that adaptation), *see* 17 U.S.C. § 106 (granting copyright owners the right "to do or to authorize" each of the six enumerated exclusive rights).

(B) is incorrect. The first sale doctrine does not apply here, because it entitles users only to further distribute the original authorized copy of the work they purchased, not to make unauthorized reproductions of that work. 17 U.S.C. § 109(a).

(C) is incorrect because a corporate officer who personally participates in infringing activity may be personally liable for the infringement. *See Southern Bell Tel. & Tel. v. Associated Tel. Directory Publishers*, 756 F.2d 801, 811 (11th Cir. 1985); *Columbia Pictures Indus., Inc. v. Redd Horne, Inc.*, 749 F.2d 154, 160 (3d Cir. 1984) ("An officer or director of a corporation who knowingly participates in the infringement can be held personally liable, jointly and severally, with the corporate defendant.").

(D) is incorrect because a copyright owner is free to choose which infringer to sue and is not required to sue all infringers. *Bassett v. Mashantucket Pequot Tribe*, 204 F.3d 343, 360 (2d Cir. 2000).

247.   **(D) is the correct answer.** Production of a copyright registration certificate is prima facie proof of the ownership of a valid copyright if the owner of the copyright filed the registration before or within five years of the date of first publication. 17 U.S.C. § 410(c); *Evans and Assocs. Inc. v. Continental Homes, Inc.*, 785 F.2d 897, 903 (11th Cir. 1986). However, the presumptive validity of the certificate of registration may be rebutted and defeated. *See Aalmuhammed v. Lee*, 202 F.3d 1227, 1236 (9th Cir. 1999) (validity of film consultant's certificate of registration containing claim that he was co-creator, co-writer and co-director of *Malcolm X* rebutted on summary judgment); *Glovaroma, Inc. v. Maljack Productions, Inc.*, 71 F. Supp. 2d 846, 854 (N.D. Ill. 1999). Here, the submission of a valid agreement assigning copyright ownership of the work in suit from Author to User clearly suffices to overcome that presumption.

(A) is incorrect because proof of valid ownership need not be produced or contested only at trial.

(B) is incorrect because timely registration gives rise only to a presumption of validity, and is not incontrovertible proof of validity.

(C) is incorrect because a registration certificate need only be filed within five years of publication in order to amount to prima facie proof of validity.

248.   **(C) is the correct answer.** Access can be proven by evidence that the defendant had actually read or heard plaintiff's work, or had a reasonable opportunity to view or hear the plaintiff's work. *See Peel & Co. v. The Rug Market*, 238 F.3d 391, 394 (5th Cir. 2001) (requiring only a "reasonable opportunity to view the copyright work" as sufficient to show access to the plaintiff's work).

(A) is incorrect because it is not necessary to show actual access, only a reasonable opportunity for access.

(B) is incorrect because the standard of proof regarding access is not "particularly high." Rather, courts require merely a reasonable opportunity for the defendant to view or hear the plaintiff's work. *See Jason v. Fonda*, 698 F.2d 966 (9th Cir. 1983) (finding access based on the "bare possibility" that the producers and broadcasters of the motion picture had access to the author's book was insufficient to prove access).

(D) is incorrect because access is invariably an important consideration in copyright infringement suits regarding unauthorized reproduction; in fact, it can be the most important consideration.

249. Although access considerations are always fact-specific, there is a good chance that a court would regard these facts as establishing a sufficient degree of access to support a finding of infringement. The reasonable opportunity for defendant to view or hear the plaintiff's work may be established by showing a particular chain of events by which the alleged infringer might have gained access through an intermediary. *See Swirsky v. Carey*, 376 F.3d 841, 844 n.3 (9th Cir. 2004) (fact that a number of individuals involved in the recording of plaintiff's musical work also were involved in recording of defendant's work found sufficient to prove access); *Bouchat v. Baltimore Ravens, Inc.*, 241 F.3d 350 (4th Cir. 2001); *Towler v. Sayles*, 76 F.3d 579, 583 (4th Cir. 1996) (court may infer that alleged infringer had a reasonable possibility of access if the author sent the copyrighted work to a third party intermediary who has a close relationship with the infringer, such as one who supervises or works in the same department as the infringer or who contributes creative ideas to the infringer); *Moore v. Columbia Pictures Indus., Inc.*, 972 F.2d 939, 942 (8th Cir. 1992); *Gaste v. Kaiserman*, 863 F.2d 1061, 1067 (2d Cir. 1988). *But see Shaw v. Lindheim*, 809 F. Supp. 1393 (C.D. Cal. 1992) (relationship between two "co-creators" of allegedly infringing television series held insufficient to prove access); *Weygand v. CBS, Inc.*, Copyright L. Rep. (CCH) ¶ 27,660 (C.D. Cal. 1997) (access by producer not imputed to co-producer).

The fact that Pirate was only a part-time employee in Sid's department at Creative House Publishing lessens the probability that Pirate had a reasonable opportunity to read *USA*. An investigation as to whether *USA* was reviewed at Creative House Publishing, and by whom, would be very important in making a determination of access. For example, if Sid Bishop testifies that he assigned the review of *USA* to a reviewer other than Pirate, and that reviewer testifies that no one else in the department had possession of *USA* or its review, access would be difficult for Writer to prove.

250. Yes. Access may be presumed where the plaintiff's work has been widely distributed to the public. *Bright Tunes Music Corp. v. Harrisongs Music, Ltd.*, 420 F. Supp. 177 (S.D.N.Y. 1976), *aff'd sub nom. ABKCO Music, Inc. v. Harrisongs Music, Ltd.*, 722 F.2d 988 (2d Cir. 1983). *But see Three Boys Music Corp. v. Bolton*, 212 F.3d 477 (9th Cir. 2000) (limited record sales and regionally sporadic radio and television broadcasts sufficient evidence for jury to find access where defendant admitted to closely following band's career). The fact that *USA* had sold enough copies to appear on several bestseller lists increases the likelihood that Pirate read *USA* to create a rebuttable presumption that Pirate had a reasonable opportunity to do so.

251. **(B) is the correct answer.** In a copyright infringement action, the court must distill the material in the plaintiff's work that is not protected by copyright, such as ideas, facts, *scènes à faire*, or elements dictated by efficiency or non-original material, from the material in

plaintiff's work that is protected by copyright. This latter material constitutes the only elements for which plaintiff may press her claim. *See Incredible Technologies, Inc. v. Virtual Technologies, Inc.*, 400 F.3d 1007, 1011 (7th Cir. 2005) ("copyright laws preclude appropriation of only those elements of the work that are protected by the copyright"); *Kohus v. Mariol*, 328 F.3d 848, 855 (6th Cir. 2003) (court is required to identify which aspects of the artist's work, if any, are protectable by copyright); *Fisher-Price, Inc. v. Well-Made Toy Mfg. Corp.*, 25 F.3d 119, 123 (2d Cir. 1994); *Landsberg v. Scrabble Crossword Game Players, Inc.*, 736 F.2d 485, 489 (9th Cir. 1984); *Jarvis v. A & M Records*, 827 F. Supp. 282, 291 (D.N.J. 1993) (because it is not unlawful to copy noncopyrightable portions of a plaintiff's work, noncopyrightable elements must be factored out in an inquiry into infringement).

Here, the setting, Niagara Falls, is clearly a public domain element and cannot be considered in a substantial similarity analysis. However, the distinctive image of the man in a rowboat, which is substantially similar because it is depicted with only trivial differences in Painter's version, is an original and protectable element, and Painter's appropriation of that significant original element of Artist's work renders the two substantially similar.

(A) is incorrect because Painter is entitled to choose a setting that is in the public domain, even if Artist has already done so.

(C) is incorrect because verbatim similarity is not a requirement in this type of copyright infringement action. Here, Artist can prevail even if he proves only substantial similarity.

(D) is incorrect because the mere presence of a public domain element alone does not preclude a finding of substantial similarity between plaintiff's protected elements and the defendant's work.

252.   **(A) is the correct answer.** Contributory infringement can be imposed when a party has knowledge of the infringing activity of another and induces, causes or materially contributes to that infringing conduct. *Gershwin Publishing Corp. v. Columbia Artists Management, Inc.*, 443 F.2d 1159 (1971). Owner meets both elements of contributory infringement. He had knowledge that the performance of the motion pictures constituted an infringement, and materially contributed to the infringement by providing the physical means for it to take place.

Vicarious liability can be imposed when a party has the right and ability to supervise the infringing activity and also has a direct financial interest in such activities. *Shapiro, Bernstein & Co., Inc. v. H.L. Green Co., Inc.*, 316 F.2d 304 (2d Cir. 1963). Owner also meets both elements of vicarious infringement. He profited financially from the showing of the motion pictures, while, as the proprietor of the theater, he also exercised control over the performance of the motion pictures because he had the right to permit or prohibit showings.

(B), (C), and (D) are incorrect for the reasons explained above.

253.   **(A) is the correct answer.** Stealio clearly meets the standard for secondary liability under the theory of inducement as articulated in *Grokster*. *See Metro-Goldwyn-Mayer Studios Inc. v. Grokster, Ltd.*, 545 U.S. 913, 940–41 (2005). Stealio was clearly aware of the illegality

that its application, VidCap, enabled. It also actively encouraged the infringing uses as illustrated by its posters, which exhorted users to make bootleg posters using the Vidcap application

(B) is incorrect because the Supreme Court in *Grokster* rejected the argument that it is a full defense to secondary liability for copyright infringement via inducement merely to show that a device is capable of substantial noninfringing uses.

(C) is incorrect because the Supreme Court in *Grokster* did not overrule its earlier decision in *Sony*. It merely held that the manufacturer of a device that is capable of substantial noninfringing uses may still be held liable on a secondary infringement theory where there is evidence that the manufacturer knew about and induced the direct infringer to engage in the substantial infringing uses to which its device was put.

(D) is incorrect because a showing of financial gain is not required by the inducement theory of secondary liability.

254. **(B) is the correct answer.** There is original expression in the selection and arrangement of the 10 samples that Matt used to comprise *Three-Bar Loop*. Tiffany's unauthorized use of *Three-Bar Loop* infringes those protected elements of Matt's work. The fact that Tiffany acquired the copyrights in the works of authorship that Matt used in creating *Three-Bar Loop* does not entitle her to use, without permission, a legally created compilation based on those works.

(A) is incorrect because purchasing a nonexclusive license to use a protected work of authorship does not confer an ownership interest in that copyrighted work or standing to sue for infringement of that work.

(C) is incorrect because Matt's selection and arrangement of the samples constitutes sufficient originality for independent copyright protection, even though he did not create the underlying works of authorship himself.

(D) is incorrect because, while it is true that Matt acquired only a limited use right in the samples, his creation of an original compilation gave rise to copyright in the compilation that exists independently of the copyrights in the underlying works.

255. No. A sufficiently original compilation of unprotectable elements may be protected by copyright. *See Metcalf v. Bochco*, 294 F.3d 1069, 1074 (9th Cir. 2002) ("The particular sequence in which an author strings a significant number of unprotectable elements can itself be a protectable element. Each note in a scale, for example, is not protectable, but a pattern of notes in a tune may earn copyright protection."); *Three Boys Music Corp. v. Bolton*, 212 F.3d 477, 485 (9th Cir. 2000) (unique compilation of unprotectable musical elements held to be protected). A compilation such as Matt's that is comprised of unprotected elements is thus still protectable in its entirety. *See Yurman Design, Inc. v. Golden Treasure Imports*, 275 F. Supp. 2d 506, 517 (S.D.N.Y. 2003).

256. **(C) is the correct answer.** There is substantial similarity between the defendant's infringing work and the plaintiff's protected work where "the ordinary observer, unless he set

out to detect the disparities, would be disposed to overlook them, and regard their aesthetic appeal as the same." *Peter Pan Fabrics, Inc. v. Martin Weiner Corp.*, 274 F.2d 487, 489 (2d Cir. 1960). *See Atari, Inc. v. North American Philips Consumer Elecs. Corp.*, 672 F.2d 607, 614 (7th Cir. 1982) (holding that the relevant test is "whether the accused work is so similar to the plaintiff's work that an ordinary reasonable person would conclude that the defendant unlawfully appropriated the plaintiff's protectable expression by taking material of substance and value"). Here, it is an undisputed fact that both works possess the same aesthetic appeal. That is enough to support a finding of substantial similarity.

(A) is incorrect because survey evidence is not categorically prohibited as evidence in copyright infringement trials.

(B) and (D) are incorrect because the focus of an infringement inquiry is on the similarities between the plaintiff's and defendant's works, and cannot be overcome simply by enumerating differences between the two. *See Sheldon v. Metro-Goldwyn Pictures Corp.*, 81 F.2d 49, 56 (2d Cir. 1936) ("[N]o plagiarist can excuse the wrong by showing how much of his work he did not pirate.").

257.   **(C) is the correct answer.** The names of characters are generally not protected by copyright. *See* 37 C.F.R. § 202.1(a) (identifying names as a subject matter that are typically not copyrightable). And even if what Writer copied were protected by copyright, not every instance of copying constitutes actionable infringement. The copying must be substantial and material, either quantitatively or qualitatively, to constitute an infringement. *See Arnstein v. Porter*, 154 F.2d 464, 468–69 (2d Cir. 1946); *Newton v. Diamond*, 388 F.3d 1189, 1195 (9th Cir. 2004) ("Substantiality is measured by considering the qualitative and quantitative significance of the copied portion in relation to the plaintiff's work as a whole."). Here, the taking of a two-word name consisting of only 14 letters clearly falls below the *de minimis* threshold. Therefore, Writer's taking, however intentional, is not actionable on a copyright infringement theory.

(A) is incorrect because copyright infringement does not depend on whether the alleged infringer intentionally copied the plaintiff's work. Thus, even where the fact of copying is conceded, the copying must be substantial to be actionable. *See Newton v. Diamond*, 388 F.3d 1189, 1193 (9th Cir. 2004).

(B) is incorrect because, although literary characters are copyrightable where sufficiently detailed and distinctive, *Nichols v. Universal Pictures Corp.*, 45 F.2d 119 (2d Cir. 1930), this does not mean that every feature or trait associated with those characters is separately copyrightable. Here, Writer copied only a single feature associated with Author's "Eva Destruction" character. This does not amount to actionable appropriation, even if "Eva Destruction" is sufficiently fleshed out to merit copyright protection.

(D) is incorrect because literary characters are copyrightable, at least where they are sufficiently fleshed out.

258.   **(D) is the correct answer.** Independent creation is a complete defense to copyright infringement. Even if two works are entirely identical, if the second author did not copy the first

author's work, but created it by mere coincidence, that lacks the element of copying that is requisite to copyright infringement. "[I]f by some magic a man who had never known it were to compose anew Keats' Ode on a Grecian Urn, he would be an 'author,' and, if he copyrighted it, others might not copy that poem, though they might of course copy Keats'." *Sheldon v. Metro-Goldwyn Pictures Corp.*, 81 F.2d 49, 54 (2d Cir. 1936). Here, there is no way that Zao could have copied Ray's work, even though the two are identical, because Zao had no contact whatsoever with Western society, including Ray's track *Only*, at the time he created and subsequently recorded *Number Three*.

(A) is incorrect because independent creation is a complete defense to a claim of copyright infringement even where the defendant's work possesses verbatim similarity to the plaintiff's work.

(B) is incorrect because copyright infringement is not determined by market share or financial impact, but by proof of access and substantial similarity.

(C) is incorrect because intent to infringe is not an element of copyright infringement.

259. No. That Zao was not conscious of Ray's work at the time he composed *Number Three* does not preclude the possibility that Zao may have subconsciously copied Ray's work. Copyright infringement is a strict liability tort, thus, the fact that a person has subconsciously copied a work protected by copyright does not preclude a finding of liability. *See Three Boys Music Corp. v. Bolton*, 212 F.3d 477 (9th Cir. 2000); *Bright Tunes Music Corp. v. Harrisongs Music, Ltd.*, 420 F. Supp. 177 (S.D.N.Y. 1976), *aff'd sub nom. ABKCO Music, Inc. v. Harrisongs Music, Ltd.*, 722 F.2d 988 (2d Cir. 1983); *Sheldon v. Metro-Goldwyn Pictures Corp.*, 81 F.2d 49, 54 (2d Cir. 1936); *Fred Fisher, Inc. v. Dillingham*, 298 F. 145, 147–48 (S.D.N.Y. 1924). Ray will still be required to prove that Zao had a reasonable opportunity to see or hear *Only*. The fact that Ray's recording of *Only* had only moderate success may not be sufficient, by itself, to prove access by Zao. *See Repp v. Webber*, 132 F.3d 882 (2d Cir. 1997).

260. (C) is the correct answer. The knowledge requirement may be met with proof of constructive knowledge. *See UMG Recordings, Inc. v. Sinnott*, 300 F. Supp. 2d 993, 999 (E.D. Cal. 2004). Here, the facts clearly indicate that Ben was aware of Joe's previous use of printing presses to engage in copyright infringement, which, along with Joe's reference to a "another quick score," clearly suggests that Joe is going to use the printing press to infringe again. Additionally, Ben's telling Joe that Ben did not want to hear about Joe's purposes further suggests that he was constructively aware of the illegality of Joe's purposes. Willful blindness to the infringing actions of the direct infringer may be construed as evidence of actual knowledge. *See UMG Recordings, Inc. v. Sinnott*, 300 F. Supp. 2d 993, 1000 (E.D. Cal. 2004) (not reading cease and desist letter deemed evidence of knowledge).

(A) is incorrect. Although it is true that Ben must have been aware of the illegality of Joe's conduct prior to the infringing conduct, *see UMG Recordings*, 300 F. Supp. 2d at 998, Ben did have such knowledge, for the reasons explained above.

(B) is incorrect because Ben clearly knew of the illegality of Joe's conduct in light of Joe's previous infringement, Joe's statement regarding a "quick score" and Ben's statement that he did not want to know any of the details of Joe's planned project.

(D) is incorrect because knowledge of illegality cannot be imputed from primary to secondary infringers.

261.   **(B) is the correct answer.** Directing users to sites where infringing content may be found, with full knowledge of the illegality of the conduct, is sufficient to show secondary infringement. *Intellectual Reserve, Inc. v. Utah Lighthouse Ministry, Inc.*, 75 F. Supp. 2d 1290, 1294 (D. Utah 1999) (proprietor of website that listed website addresses where infringed work could be found and who posted emails to third parties suggesting they log onto the infringing website was deemed a sufficient contribution for a finding of contributory infringement).

(A) is incorrect because financial profit from direct infringement is not an element of contributory infringement; it is an element of vicarious infringement.

(C) is incorrect because Barry has provided clear directions to the infringing websites even in the absence of actual links.

(D) is incorrect because Barry cannot absolve himself of liability on a secondary liability theory simply by disclaiming it.

262.   **(B) is the correct answer.** Clean Channel directly profited from Barlow's conduct because its affiliate, KXTM, gained listener shares and advertising revenue due to Barlow's inflammatory feature. *Cf., e.g., Famous Music Corp. v. Bay State Harness Racing and Breeding Ass'n*, 554 F.2d 1213 (1st Cir. 1977) (racetrack owner found to financially benefit from unlicensed music performed by contractor between races); *Polygram Int'l Publishing v. Nevada/TIG, Inc.*, 855 F. Supp. 1314, 1333 (D. Mass. 1994) (trade show organizer found to have direct financial interest in infringing activity of exhibitors by attracting attention to infringer's booth). Clean Channel also had the ability to control Barlow's conduct because it had contractual approval rights over the content of KXTM's local programming. *See Hard Rock Café Licensing Corp. v. Concession Servs., Inc.*, 955 F.2d 1143, 1150 (7th Cir. 1992); *Jobete Music Co., Inc. v. Johnson Communications, Inc.*, 285 F. Supp. 2d 1077, 1083–84 (S.D. Ohio 2003).

(A) is incorrect because it lists the elements of contributory, not vicarious, liability.

(C) is incorrect because Clean Channel clearly possessed a significant degree of control over the conduct of their affiliates due to Clean Channel's contractual approval rights.

(D) is incorrect because Clean Channel profited directly, not indirectly, from Barlow's performances. As the KXTM affiliate of Clean Channel gained market share and ratings due to Barlow's increasing popularity, Clean Channel's advertising time became more profitable.

263.   **(C) is the correct answer.** James clearly profited from Dan's infringement, because he earned a rental fee for letting Dan sell infringing CDs and DVDs on the vacant lot in Maine. James

did not, however, have supervisory control over Dan's conduct on the lot. James lived in another state, had no knowledge of Dan's infringing activities, nor any reason to know about them, had never supervised activity on the lot in any way, and did not place conditions on or create rules governing Dan's conduct on the lot. *Compare, e.g., Fonovisa, Inc. v. Cherry Auction, Inc.*, 76 F.3d 259 (9th Cir. 1996) (operator of swap meet that had the right to terminate vendors who rented space, promoted the swap meet and controlled customer access, was held to have sufficient ability to control the activities of the vendors who were selling counterfeit sound recordings at the swap meet); *Metro-Goldwyn-Mayer Studios v. Grokster*, 380 F.3d 1154, 1160 (9th Cir. 2004), *rev'd on other grounds*, 545 U.S. 913 (2005) (ability to exclude individual participants, a practice of policing aisles, ability to block individual users directly at the point of log-in or ability to delete individual filenames from one's own computer is the sort of monitoring and supervisory relationship that supports a finding of vicarious liability); *UMG Recordings, Inc. v. Sinnott*, 300 F. Supp. 2d 993, 1001 (E.D. Cal. 2004) (rules of flea market owner prohibiting vendors from selling certain classes of goods constituted right and ability to supervise and control the vendors selling infringing recordings); *Polygram Int'l Publishing v. Nevada/TIG, Inc.*, 855 F. Supp. 1314 (D. Mass. 1994) (trade show organizer found to have the ability to supervise the infringing activity of exhibitors).

(A) is incorrect because it states the elements of contributory, not vicarious, infringement.

(B) and (D) are incorrect for the reasons explained above.

264.   **(D) is the correct answer.** Criminal liability may attach where a person "infringes a copyright willfully and for purposes of commercial advantage or private financial gain . . . or by the reproduction or distribution . . . of 1 or more copies or phonorecords of 1 or more copyrighted works, which have a total retail value of more than $1,000. . . ." 17 U.S.C. § 506(a)(1)–(2). In addition, Bill's conduct was willful because he was well aware that he was infringing multiple copyrights. And Bill was clearly engaging in these sales for "private financial gain," since he was selling bootleg DVDs because he faced financial distress. This alone suffices for criminal copyright infringement liability to attach. In addition, however, while Bill's infringing acts did not total more than $1,000 in sales, he was selling them for well below their retail value, so the actual retail value of the copies he sold was likely more than $1,000. Bill's unlawful conduct thus subjects him to the full range of penalties available under the Copyright Act's criminal provisions. Penalties for criminal copyright infringement, which may be deemed a felony, include up to six years in prison and heavy monetary fines. *See* 18 U.S.C. § 2319.

(A), (B), and (C) are incorrect for the reasons explained above.

265.   **(B) is the correct answer.** ISPs can take advantage of the statutory immunity for secondary liability based on their users' conduct if they adopt, reasonably implement, and inform subscribers of a policy that provides for termination of repeat infringers, and do not interfere with content owners' standard technology protection measures. 17 U.S.C. § 512(i). When an ISP meets these qualifications, as Connex has done here, it cannot be held liable

for monetary relief if it is acting as a mere conduit for infringing communications. 17 U.S.C. § 512(a). *See In re Charter Comm., Inc. Subpoena Enforcement Matter*, 393 F.3d 771, 775 (8th Cir. 2005). This is even true where, as here, the ISP also automatically stores those communications for a brief period of time due to technical processes. *See, e.g., Ellison v. Robertson*, 357 F.3d 1072, 1081 (9th Cir. 2004) (AOL found to have functioned as a conduit service provider even though it stored Usenet messages for 14 days).

(A), (C), and (D) are incorrect for the reasons explained above.

266.   Probably not. Connex has met several of the elements that immunize ISPs from liability for the infringing conduct of their users. Connex has implemented a notice-and-takedown regime; it has neither actual nor constructive knowledge of Alice's infringing conduct; and it has not received a takedown notice from any of the owners whose copyrights Alice has infringed. In order, however, to avoid secondary liability for users' storage of infringing material, an Internet service provider must also show that it has not received a financial benefit directly attributable to the infringing activity where the service provider has the right and ability to control such activity. 17 U.S.C. § 512(c)(1)(B).

Connex clearly received a financial benefit from Alice's conduct, since she paid them to store the infringing material, but it is less clear whether merely allowing users to store files amounts to the "right and ability to control [infringing] activity." Current authority suggests that the ability of a service provider to remove or block access to materials posted on its website or stored in its system does not mean that the service provider has the right and ability to control the infringing activity. *See Hendrickson v. eBay Inc.*, 165 F. Supp. 2d 1082, 1093 (C.D. Cal. 2001) (infringing activity of the sale and distribution of pirated copies of motion picture by sellers via auction website are consummated offline and are not controlled by service provider); *Costar Group Inc. v. Loopnet, Inc.*, 164 F. Supp. 2d 688, 704 (D. Md. 2001), *aff'd*, 373 F.3d 544 (4th Cir. 2004). In light of these cases, a court would likely hold that Connex did not have the "right and ability to control [Alice's infringing] activity." In that case, the safe harbor would apply, immunizing Connex from liability on a secondary infringement theory.

267.   **(A) is the correct answer.** Although this notice meets nearly all the requirements imposed by statute, *see* 17 U.S.C. § 512(c)(3)(A), it is incomplete because it does not include an attestation that the owner believes Alice's conduct to be unauthorized, *see* 17 U.S.C. § 512(c)(3)(A)(v). A notice that fails to substantially comply with any of these requirements is insufficient to give rise to a duty on behalf of the ISP to remove the allegedly infringing material. 17 U.S.C. § 512(c)(3)(B). *See Hendrickson v. eBay Inc.*, 165 F. Supp. 2d 1082, 1089–90 (C.D. Cal. 2001) (failure to include statement that use of the materials is not authorized renders notification of claimed infringement deficient). Thus, in light of this omission, Connex would have no obligation to remove Alice's infringing material from its servers.

(B) and (C) are incorrect because neither identify statutory requirements applicable to notice and takedown letters.

(D) is incorrect for the reasons explained above.

268.   **(C) is the correct answer.** Although Connex has met the safe harbor provisions of the DMCA, such as the requirements that Connex adopt, reasonably implement, and inform subscribers of a policy that provides for termination of repeat infringers, *see* 17 U.S.C. § 512(i)(1)(A); *Ellison v. Robertson*, 357 F.3d 1072, 1080 (9th Cir. 2004), Connex is not under an obligation to terminate its services to Alice after a single claim of copyright infringement, which has already taken place here.

        (A), (B) and (D) are incorrect because they describe only some of Connex's obligations that arise upon receipt of the takedown notice. Where a valid takedown notice is issued to an ISP, the ISP must remove the identified material and notify the user that it has done so. Upon receipt of a counter notification, the ISP must promptly provide the copyright owner with a copy of the counter notification and inform the copyright owner that the ISP will replace the removed material or cease disabling access to it in 10 business days. 17 U.S.C. § 512(g).

269.   **(C) is the correct answer.** XM-100's performance of "Solitaire" without compensating Cali clearly violates the station's obligation to pay a compulsory statutory license to the owners of the copyrights in the sound recordings it performs. 17 U.S.C. § 114(d)(2) ("The performance of a sound recording publicly by means of a subscription digital audio transmission . . . that is made by a preexisting satellite digital audio radio service shall be subject to statutory licensing.").

        XM-100's unauthorized performance of "Juniper" may not violate Cali's federal copyright in the sound recording, since there are no such rights. Federal copyrights in sound recordings apply only to recordings created on or after February 15, 1972, *see* Sound Recording Act of 1971, Pub. L. No. 92-140, 85 Stat. 391, and "Juniper" was made in 1969. The unauthorized performance may, however, violate Cali's state common-law rights in the "Juniper" recording. California law extends common-law copyright protection to sound recordings made before February 15, 1972. Cal. Civ. Code § 980(a)(2). And several courts, including in the Central District of California, have recently held that unauthorized public performances by satellite radio stations of pre-1972 sound recordings infringe the state common-law copyrights in those works. *E.g., Flo & Eddie Inc. v. Sirius XM Radio Inc.*, 2014 WL 4725382 (C.D. Cal. Sept. 22, 2014).

        If this case had been decided under New York law, however, the result would have been different. The Second Circuit, applying that state's law, found that common-law copyrights did not include public performance rights. *See Flo & Eddie, Inc. v. Sirius XM Radio, Inc.*, 849 F.3d 14, 16 (2d Cir. 2017) ("[W]e certified this question to the New York Court of Appeals. The Court of Appeals accepted certification, and on December 20, 2016, responded that New York common law does not recognize a right of public performance for creators of pre-1972 sound recordings.") (citations omitted).

        (A), (B), and (D) are incorrect for the reasons explained above.

270.   This is a harder question. XM-100 has a good argument that by remastering the works, the version that they publicly performed is simply not Cali's work anymore, and therefore

does not violate her copyrights in the master recordings. Sound recording copyrights are distinctive in that the copyright inheres in the fixed sounds themselves. See 17 U.S.C. § 101 (defining "sound recording" as "works that result from the fixation of a series of musical, spoken, or other sounds"). So unlike with musical works, imitations of a sound recording that seem substantially similar are not infringing. *Cf.* 17 U.S.C. § 114(b) (limiting copyright ownership in sound recording to the particular sounds fixed in a given medium of expression). And especially where, as here, a remastering changes a sound recording substantially, the inclusion of additional original material may convince a court that XM-100 publicly performed a different work than the masters Cali owned, thus undermining her infringement claim. *Cf. ABS Entertainment v. CBS Corp.*, 2016 WL 4259846, (C.D. Cal. May 30, 2016) (entering summary judgment in favor of entity that performed remastered versions of plaintiff's pre-1972 sound recordings because remastered versions did not comprise the same work of authorship the plaintiff owned).

Even if Cali were to lose on this argument, though, she may have a claim that the sound engineer who remastered the recordings without her permission infringed her copyrights in them by creating an unauthorized derivative work. *See* 17 U.S.C. § 114(b) ("The exclusive right of the owner of copyright in a sound recording under clause (2) of section 106 is limited to the right to prepare a derivative work in which the actual sounds fixed in the sound recording are rearranged, remixed, or otherwise altered in sequence or quality.").

271.   **(D) is the correct answer.** An acting performance, such as the actress's cameo here, is not a "work of authorship" within the meaning of the Copyright Act. 17 U.S.C. § 102(a) ("Copyright protection subsists . . . in original works of authorship fixed in any tangible medium of expression."). "[M]otion picture or other audiovisual work" is a category of work of authorship, but this work consists of the screenplay and the group of "related images" that derive from it, 17 U.S.C. § 101 (defining "audiovisual work" as "consisting of a series of related images which, when shown in succession, impart an impression of motion, together with accompanying sounds, if any"), not the individual performances of the actors, *see Garcia v. Google, Inc.*, 786 F.3d 733, 740–43 (9th Cir. 2015) (explaining that an acting performance is not a "work of authorship" in any sense of the term). The en banc Ninth Circuit recently held on very similar facts that as a matter of both copyright law and sound policy, acting performances did not constitute separately copyrightable works of authorship owned by actors. *Id.* at 742 (warning that a holding otherwise would generate a "legal morass" and would make "Swiss cheese of copyrights" by vesting ownership rights in countless contributors to highly collaborative works like motion pictures).

(A) is incorrect because, for the reasons explained above, the actress has no public performance rights in the scene since she lacks any valid copyright interest.

(B) is incorrect because the actress is not a beneficial owner of the film's copyright. Beneficial owners have some direct interest in exploitation of the film, such as a right to a royalty stream. *See Cortner v. Israel*, 732 F.2d 267, 270–71 (2d Cir. 1984). The actress has no such legal interest in profiting directly from the exploitation of the film.

(C) **is incorrect** because the actress's performance appears to be highly creative. The reason it is not copyrightable is because acting performances do not comprise works of authorship within the meaning of the Copyright Act, not because it lacks creativity.

272.   (A) **is the correct answer.** It is not possible for anyone to sue for infringement of a copyright; the Copyright Act limits the right to sue for infringement to actual and beneficial owners. 17 U.S.C. § 501(a). Entities that have sought to acquire no more than a right to sue on behalf of an owner's copyright without acquiring a meaningful ownership interest in the copyright itself have been consistently found to lack standing. *Righthaven LLC v. Hoehn*, 716 F.3d 1166, 1169–72 (9th Cir. 2013) (holding that an agreement that does not assign substantive section 106 rights cannot confer standing on the assignee); *Righthaven LLC v. Wolf*, 813 F. Supp. 2d 1265, 1272 (D. Colo. 2011) (finding that assignee who was assigned only a bare right to sue "lack[ed] standing to institute an action for copyright infringement").

Here, Joe's assignment to the attorney conferred no substantive ownership rights such as reproduction, adaptation, or performance. The agreement did formally designate the attorney as a "co-owner" of the copyright, but courts have seen through formalistic language and rejected such attempts to create ownership status in the absence of actual exclusive rights. *E.g., Hoehn*, 716 F.3d at 1169 ("When determining whether a contract has transferred exclusive rights, we look not just at the labels parties use but also at the substance and effect of the contract.").

(B) **is incorrect** because the right to sue for infringement is entirely transferable. It transfers along with the transfer of any valid assignment or exclusive right. The reason the attorney lacks standing is not that the right to sue for infringement cannot be transferred, it is that the right to sue cannot be transferred separately from substantive ownership rights.

(C) **is incorrect** because merely referring to an assignee as a co-owner of a copyright does not make the assignee a co-owner. As the Ninth Circuit colorfully put it in a similar case, "Abraham Lincoln told a story about a lawyer who tried to establish that a calf had five legs by calling its tail a leg. But the calf had only four legs, Lincoln observed, because calling a tail a leg does not make it so. Before us is a case about a lawyer who tried to establish that a company owned a copyright by drafting a contract calling the company the copyright owner, even though the company lacked the rights associated with copyright ownership. Heeding Lincoln's wisdom, and the requirements of the Copyright Act, we conclude that merely calling someone a copyright owner does not make it so." *Hoehn*, 716 F.3d at 1167–68.

(D) **is incorrect** because whether or not the agreement furthered the policies of the Copyright Act, it failed to confer ownership (and therefore standing) as a matter of law.

273.   (C) **is the correct answer.** It is beyond dispute that Radio4U's unauthorized retransmission of the owners' copyrighted broadcasts amounts to a "performance" of those broadcasts. *See* 17 U.S.C. § 101 (defining the exclusive right to "perform" as including "to transmit or otherwise communicate a performance or display of the work to . . . the public, by means

of any device or process"). The harder question is whether this is a "public" performance. Radio4U will argue that the performance is not public because they merely receive terrestrial radio broadcasts that they receive through standard means, see 17 U.S.C. § 110(5) (excepting "mere reception of broadcasts in a public place" from infringement liability), and then transmit those broadcasts to subscribers through individually dedicated antennae. I.e., Radio4U will argue that they do not make a public performance as a cable television station does, by retransmitting content to all users at the same time, but that they make many different private performances, by retransmitting content to each user individually.

There is some support for this in the Copyright Act's definition of "perform . . . a work 'publicly,'" which specifies that it means "to transmit or otherwise communicate a performance . . . of the work . . . to the public, by means of any device or process, whether the members of the public capable of receiving the performance or display receive it in the same place or in separate places and at the same time or at different times." 17 U.S.C. § 101 (defining "perform . . . a work 'publicly'"). This definition could be read to exclude individualized retransmissions such as the one Radio4U engages in, which are not made "to the public" but instead to specific subscribers.

The Supreme Court, though, rejected this view in *American Broadcasting Cos. v. Aereo, Inc.*, 134 S. Ct. 2498 (2014), which evaluated a service nearly identical to Radio4U except that it rebroadcast analog television transmissions rather than radio transmissions. The Court held that rebroadcasting in this manner is effectively the same as cable television, which has long been considered a public performance. *Id.* at 2505–06 (discussing intention of 1976 Act revisions to clarify that cable retransmissions were public performances). The Court further held that the technical distinction between making one broadcast to a group of subscribers versus many separate broadcasts to individual subscribers was a formalistic, technical distinction that should not have any legal weight. *Id.* at 2508–10. In light of *Aereo*, then, the service provided by Radio4U would amount to an unauthorized public performance that would infringe the exclusive rights of the owners of the copyrights in those broadcasts.

(A) is incorrect because, as explained above, the Supreme Court considered this issue and held that multiple individual retransmissions to subscribers are public, not private, performances.

(B) is incorrect because Radio4U does not transform the broadcasts it retransmits in any way; it engages in retransmission wholly for commercial purposes; and harms the market for providers of content via paid means (e.g., satellite radio). This is clearly not a fair use in light of the relevant factors. *See* 17 U.S.C. § 107. *Sony Corp. of America v. Universal City Studios, Inc.*, 464 U.S. 417 (1984), is not to the contrary because Radio4U allows users to archive radio broadcasts, a form of use that the Court held to be unfair in that case. *But cf. Aereo, Inc.*, 134 S. Ct. at 2517–18 (Scalia, J., dissenting) (drawing parallels between Aereo's service and the VCR, and cautioning against rendering novel technology illegal at an early stage before it is fully understood).

(D) is incorrect because there are no provisions for compulsory licenses relating to radio retransmissions, though there are such provisions relating to cable television retransmissions. *See* 17 U.S.C. § 111.

274. It depends on what law applies. Star has used Arty's copyrighted sound recording without permission, violating his exclusive rights to reproduction and possibly to adaptation (though not public performance, since sound recordings do not come with public performance rights, *see* 17 U.S.C. § 114(d)). Some circuit courts have held that any sampling without a license is copyright infringement, regardless of the sample's length, emphasizing that sampling is verbatim copying. *See, e.g., Bridgeport Music, Inc. v. Dimension Films*, 410 F.3d 792 (6th Cir. 2005) ("Get a license or do not sample.").

More recently, though, other courts have taken a different approach to this issue, holding that very brief samples may represent *de minimis* copying, and therefore that their unauthorized use does not amount to copyright infringement. *See, e.g., VMG v. Ciccone*, 839 F.3d 168 (2d Cir. 2016) (holding that an 0.23-second sample of horns from an earlier song amounted to *de minimis* use that did not infringe the owner's copyright). *VMG* may be distinguishable from *Bridgeport*, though, because the sample in *VMG* was slightly modified, while the sample in *Bridgeport* was not. On this theory, one could conclude that the sample in *VMG* did not amount to verbatim copying.

Fair Use and Other Affirmative Defenses

275.   **(B) is the correct answer.** The four statutory fair use factors are not exhaustive. The statute states that a court "must consider" those four factors, but does not state that the court must consider *only* those factors. 17 U.S.C. § 107. Indeed, some courts have considered custom in analyzing fair use issues. *Cf., e.g., Harper & Row Publishers, Inc. v. Nation Enters.*, 471 U.S. 539, 550 (1985) (observing that the fair use doctrine was originally "predicated on the author's implied consent to 'reasonable and customary use'").

(**A**) **is incorrect** because customary use is not one of the four statutory fair use factors that courts must consider.

(**C**) **is incorrect** because the four fair use factors are not exclusive, as explained above.

(**D**) **is incorrect** because fair use does not relate exclusively to economic considerations. While the Supreme Court stated in *Sony Corp. of America* v. *Universal City Studios, Inc.*, that "every commercial use of copyrighted material is presumptively . . . unfair," 464 U.S. 417, 451 (1984), the Court later held that this approach to fair use was erroneous. *See Campbell v. Acuff-Rose Music, Inc.*, 510 U.S. 569, 577 (1994) ("The task is not to be simplified with bright-line rules, for the statute, like the doctrine it recognizes, calls for case-by-case analysis.").

276.   **(C) is the correct answer.** The purpose and character of FreeBooks.com's unauthorized use of the literary works is not sufficiently transformative because it merely transforms the medium in which those works are expressed. *See, e.g., Castle Rock Entertainment, Inc. v. Carol Publishing Group, Inc.*, 150 F.3d 132, 142–43 (2d Cir. 1998) (holding that translating content from a television show into a quiz book is not sufficiently transformative). The use is further unlikely to be fair because FreeBooks.com would likely harm present markets for sales of the owners' literary works, and would harm future markets for potential digital sales of the work, such as e-books. *See* 17 U.S.C. § 107(4) (requiring consideration of "the effect of the use upon the potential market for or value of the copyrighted work").

(**A**) **is incorrect** because transformation from one medium to another, without more, does not make a use transformative. *See A & M Records, Inc. v. Napster, Inc.*, 239 F.3d 1004, 1015 (9th Cir. 2001) (downloading MP3 files does not transform the copyrighted work); *Infinity Broad. Corp. v. Kirkwood*, 150 F.3d 104, 108 n.2 (2d Cir. 1998) (retransmitting radio transmissions over telephone lines deemed not transformative); *UMG Recordings, Inc. v. MP3.com, Inc.*, 92 F. Supp. 2d 349, 351 (S.D.N.Y. 2000) (defendant's claim that its service provided "space shifting" of sound recordings was deemed to merely be a repackaging of the recordings to facilitate their transmission through another medium that was not transformative); *Video Pipeline, Inc. v. Buena Vista Home Entertainment, Inc.*, 342 F.3d 191, 199 (3d Cir. 2003) (defendant's database of unauthorized film clips held not to improve access to authorized material on the Internet). *But see Kelly v. Arriba Soft Corp.*, 280 F.3d 934, 941 (9th Cir. 2002) (use of digital thumbnail images of photographs found to be transformative in that it was intended to facilitate searching images on the Internet); *Bill Graham Archives v. Dorling Kindersley Ltd.*, 448 F.3d 605, 611 (2d Cir. 2006) (featuring reduced-size concert posters for use on a historical timeline in biographical book on the Grateful Dead was transformative because it was a historical not advertorial use).

(B) is incorrect because placing literary works online at a discount is likely to undercut both traditional markets for physical versions of those same works and present or future markets for digital versions of the works.

(D) is incorrect because courts have never held that the fair use defense does not apply in online contexts. *See, e.g., Kelly v. Arriba Soft Corp.*, 280 F.3d 934, 941 (9th Cir. 2002) (applying the fair use defense to permit the unauthorized use of plaintiff's image as a thumbnail image in an Internet visual search engine).

277. **(D) is the correct answer.** In *Campbell v. Acuff-Rose*, 510 U.S. 569 (1994), the Supreme Court held that the distinction between parody and satire has special significance in the fair use context. The Court viewed parody as unauthorized use that targets the plaintiff's work, at least in part, as the object of the critique. *See, e.g., Leibovitz v. Paramount Pictures Corp.*, 137 F.3d 109 (2d Cir. 1998) (teaser ad for motion picture deemed a fair use because it targeted photograph of nude pregnant Demi Moore as an object of parody).

By contrast, the *Campbell* Court viewed satire as a more generalized social commentary that uses the plaintiff's work merely as a vehicle for social criticism without commenting on the copyrighted work through which the criticism is expressed. Although a work of satire could possibly make a successful claim of fair use, it is not deemed deserving of the special consideration given to parody. *See MCA, Inc. v. Wilson*, 677 F.2d 180 (2d Cir. 1981); *Dr. Seuss Enters., L.P. v. Penguin Books USA, Inc.*, 109 F.3d 1394 (9th Cir. 1997) (defendant's work, which mimicked Dr. Seuss' style, did not target it for comment or criticism, and therefore did not constitute a fair use); *Columbia Pictures Indus., Inc. v. Miramax Films Corp.*, 11 F. Supp. 2d 1179, 1188 (C.D. Cal. 1998) ("Miramax has merely used [Columbia's poster] as a vehicle to poke fun at another target — corporate America. It has not used its advertising to comment on or criticize the copyrighted work.").

Here, John's work is clearly satire, not parody, because he explains to Betty that he was not seeking to comment on her novel, but only to use it as a vehicle for criticizing Bill Clinton. As such, John's work is less likely to be considered a fair use.

(A) is incorrect because John's work is a satire, not a parody, for reasons explained above.

(B) is incorrect because political commentary is not categorically immune from copyright infringement via the fair use defense. While "purposes such as criticism, comment, [and] news reporting" are listed as examples of fair use, 17 U.S.C. § 107, these categories are merely illustrative and do not represent a bright-line approach to fair use that obviates the need to apply the categories. *Campbell v. Acuff-Rose Music, Inc.*, 510 U.S. 569, 577 (1994) (warning that the preamble provides "only general guidance about the sorts of copying that courts and Congress most commonly had found to be fair uses").

(C) **is incorrect** because the Supreme Court did not hold in *Campbell* that satires are categorically not fair uses, merely that satires are less likely to be fair uses. 510 U.S. at 580 n.14 ("looser forms of parody may be found to be fair use, *as may satire*") (emphasis added).

278.   Yes. If John's work poked fun at Betty's novel as well as at Bill Clinton, then it would be a parody under the definition of parody articulated in *Campbell v. Acuff-Rose Music, Inc.* 510 U.S. 569, 579 (1994) (defining parody as an unauthorized use that comments critically on the plaintiff's work). Although parody is not categorically considered a form of fair use, courts have historically favored parodic uses as fair ones. *See id.*; *see also, e.g., Mattel Inc. v. Walking Mountain Prods.*, 353 F.3d 792, 802 (9th Cir. 2003) (holding defendant photographer's depicting Barbie as being harmed by kitchen appliances or in sexually suggestive contexts to be fair use because defendant was commenting on Barbie's influence on gender roles and the position of women in society).

279.   (C) **is the correct answer.** Although fair use was first codified in the Copyright Act of 1976, 17 U.S.C. § 107, it has long common-law roots prior to the passage of that statute. *See, e.g., Folsom v. Marsh*, 9 F. Cas. 342 (1841).

(A) **is incorrect** because the common-law history of fair use pre-dates the passage of the Copyright Act of 1976.

(B) **is incorrect** because the Constitution's Intellectual Property Clause, U.S. Const. art. I, sec. 8, cl. 8, does not explicitly mention fair use and courts have never interpreted the clause to require the fair use defense. *See Universal City Studios, Inc. v. Corley*, 273 F.3d 429, 458 (2d Cir. 2001) (fair use is not a constitutional requirement).

(D) **is incorrect** because fair use is modernly a matter of judicial interpretation of *statutory* language. As explained above, it does not have an explicit constitutional source.

280.   (B) **is the correct answer.** Courts have held that merely recasting the facts that comprise a television show without adding any original content or commentary is not transformative. *See Castle Rock Entertainment, Inc. v. Carol Publishing Group, Inc.*, 150 F.3d 132, 143 (2d Cir. 1998) (book containing trivia questions about *Seinfeld* television series had "little, if any, transformative purpose"); *cf. Ty, Inc. v. Publications Int'l, Ltd.*, 292 F.3d 512, 517–18 (7th Cir. 2002) (holding that a guide to Beanie Babies featuring nothing more than pictures of all the stuffed animals in the series was not a fair use); *Infinity Broad. Corp. v. Kirkwood*, 150 F.3d 104, 108 n.2 (2d Cir. 1998) (retransmitting radio transmissions over telephone lines deemed not transformative). *The Definitive Guide to "Eat at Joe's"* thus would not be considered transformative.

By contrast, academic commentary about a television show would be much more likely to be considered transformative because it takes the material presented in the television show and recasts it in the context of original expression. The unauthorized takings of text and images would thus be viewed as a paradigmatic fair use in order to support the associated academic commentary; indeed "commentary" is one of the illustrative categories of fair use listed in the preamble to the statutory fair use factors. 17 U.S.C. § 107; *see Ty, Inc.*, 292 F.3d at 522 (holding that a different guide to Beanie Babies that included original commentary, such as estimated value of each stuffed animal, was fair use). Thus a court would be very likely to regard *Deconstructing "Eat at Joe's"* as transformative.

(A), (C), and (D) are incorrect for the reasons explained above.

281.   **(D) is the correct answer.** Although courts have expressed some ambivalence about whether artists who appropriated and recast others' work had transformed it, *see Rogers v. Koons*, 960 F.2d 301, 310 (2d Cir. 1992), more recent decisions suggest that "appropriation art" is transformative, at least where it clearly expresses a different message than the original, *see Blanch v. Koons*, 467 F.3d 244, (2d Cir. 2006) (finding defendant's appropriation of fashion photographs into large canvas painting to be transformative because it had an "entirely different purpose and meaning" than the original). Here, Jody recasts Kara's work entirely by seeking to make a strongly negative political point about it; these two factors suggest that a court would regard Jody's work as transformative.

(A) is incorrect because one artist's appropriating another's content does not categorically preclude a fair use defense. In addition, the content of Jody's paintings is not "exactly the same" as the content of Kara's photographs.

(B) is incorrect because recasting work in a different medium, without more, is not transformative. *See A & M Records, Inc. v. Napster, Inc.*, 239 F.3d 1004, 1015 (9th Cir. 2001) (downloading MP3 files does not transform the copyrighted work); *Infinity Broad. Corp. v. Kirkwood*, 150 F.3d 104, 108 n.2 (2d Cir. 1998) (retransmitting radio transmissions over telephone lines deemed not transformative).

(C) is incorrect because a defendant is not required to show that the use was necessary in order for it to be transformative.

282.   **(B) is the correct answer.** SoundSearch.com's use is transformative in two ways. First, it has transformed the sound files from full-length versions into brief, low fidelity five-second versions. Second, and related, it has presented those versions for the purpose of information rather than entertainment, transforming the manner in which the Internet can be used. Although a mere change in format is not transformative, courts have held, in the context of search engines, that where unauthorized takings possess these two features, the use is transformative. *Kelly v. Arriba Soft Corp.*, 280 F.3d 934, 941 (9th Cir. 2002) (use of plaintiff's image as a thumbnail image in an Internet visual search engine held to be a fair use because the thumbnails were much smaller, lower-resolution images that served an entirely different function, improving access to information on the Internet, than the plaintiff's original image); *see also Author's Guild v. Google, Inc.*, 804 F.3d 202 (2d Cir. 2015)

(holding that making unauthorized digital reproductions of literary works for the purpose of research and information, rather than entertainment, constituted a fair use).

(A) is incorrect because courts have never held that any use of copyrighted works of authorship by a search engine is categorically a fair use.

(C) is incorrect because it is possible (though not likely) that a use can be transformative without the addition of critical commentary.

(D) is incorrect because a use need not alter the content of the copyrighted work of authorship in order to be transformative. For example, in many instances of fair use, the defendant has only added material. *See, e.g., Mattel, Inc. v. Walking Mountain Prods.*, 353 F.3d 792, 800–03 (9th Cir. 2003) (placing Barbie dolls in unusual contexts held to constitute a fair use). Even so, SoundSearch.com does alter the sound files by automatically cutting each of them down to a five-second version.

283.   **(C) is the correct answer.** The operation of a web site that produces income has been found to be a commercial use even where it does not charge an access fee. The fact that the web site operator seeks to attract a sufficiently large subscription base to charge advertising fees and otherwise generate revenue has been found to make its purpose commercial. *See UMG Recordings, Inc. v. MP3.com, Inc.*, 92 F. Supp. 2d 349, 351 (S.D.N.Y. 2000). That Cat Sludge could have charged a licensing fee but chose not to in order to attract more users, further weighs in favor of a conclusion that this is a commercial use. *See A & M Records, Inc. v. Napster, Inc.*, 239 F.3d 1004, 1015 (9th Cir. 2001).

(A) is incorrect because the actual revenue generated by the Sludge Retort, not Cat's intent to profit, is determinative of the commercial character of his use.

(B) is incorrect because the amount of Cat's net profit is not determinative of the commercial character of his use, and in any event the Sludge Retort clearly generated significant revenue.

(D) is incorrect because sites that do not charge a fee, but earn profits in other ways, have been found to engage in commercial use, as explained above.

284.   No. Although the United States Supreme Court stated in *Sony Corp. of America v. Universal City Studios, Inc.*, 464 U.S. 417, 451 (1984), that "every commercial use of copyrighted material is presumptively an unfair exploitation of the monopoly privilege that belongs to the owner of the copyright," the Court subsequently retreated from this strongly stated position. The mere fact that a use is commercial does not bar a finding of fair use. *Campbell v. Acuff-Rose Music, Inc.*, 510 U.S. 569, 583–84 (1994) (holding that the only "presumption" of market harm supported by *Sony* would apply in a case involving mere duplication for commercial purposes). The mere fact that an unauthorized user is a commercial enterprise does not preclude the possibility of that user's stating a successful fair use defense. *See Kelly v. Arriba Soft Corp.*, 280 F.3d 934, 940 (9th Cir. 2002); *Warner Bros., Inc. v. Am. Broad. Cos., Inc.*, 523 F. Supp. 611 (S.D.N.Y. 1981), *aff'd*, 654 F.2d 204 (2d Cir. 1981).

285.   **(C) is the correct answer.** The second fair use factor weighs against a finding of fair use where a work is close to the "core" of copyright protection. This means that the scope of the fair use defense tends to be greater when the plaintiff's work constitutes an informational type of work, as opposed to a more creative product. *Marcus v. Rowley*, 695 F.2d 1171 (9th Cir. 1983); *see Stewart v. Abend*, 495 U.S. 207, 237–38 (1990) ("[F]air use is more likely to be found in factual works than in fictional works"). Also pursuant to the second section 107 factor, unauthorized uses of published works are more likely to qualify as fair uses because the first appearance of the author's expression has already occurred. *See Kelly v. Arriba Soft Corp.*, 280 F.3d 934, 943 (9th Cir. 2002).

Here, both of these aspects of the second factor of the fair use analysis weigh in favor of Janie. Although her work has a historical setting, it is still predominantly a work of fiction, which lies very close to the core of copyright. *See Harper & Row Publishers, Inc. v. Nation Enters.*, 471 U.S. 539, 563 (1985) ("The law generally recognizes a greater need to disseminate factual works than works of fiction or fantasy"). And while Janie gave her manuscript to Alice, this single act of explicitly limited sharing is insufficient to undermine the work's status as unpublished. *See Academy of Motion Picture Arts & Sciences v. Creative House Promotions, Inc.*, 944 F.2d 1446, 1451–52 (9th Cir. 1991) (holding that a limited publication occurs when tangible copies of the work are distributed to a limited class of persons and for a limited purpose).

(A), (B), and (D) are incorrect for the reasons explained above.

286.   No. At common law, fair use was not recognized as a defense to the unauthorized copying of an author's unpublished works. *Harper & Row Publishers, Inc. v. Nation Enters.*, 471 U.S. 539, 550–55 (1985). Some courts held that this rule survived the codification of fair use, but Congress disagreed. To clarify that an unauthorized use may be fair even though the plaintiff's work is unpublished, Congress amended the Copyright Act to add: "The fact that a work is unpublished shall not itself bar a finding of fair use if such finding is made upon consideration of all the above factors." 17 U.S.C. § 107; *see Sundeman v. The Seajay Society, Inc.*, 142 F.3d 194, 204–05 (4th Cir. 1998) (concluding that unauthorized use of an unpublished work was a fair use). Thus whether Janie's work is published would not be dispositive of the fair use issue overall, though a finding that it is unpublished would still weigh against fair use under the second factor, *see Kelly v. Arriba Soft Corp.*, 280 F.3d 934, 943 (9th Cir. 2002).

287.   **(B) is the correct answer.** The third fair use factor focuses on the amount and substantiality of the defendant's taking of the plaintiff's work. This factor requires an analysis of both the quantity and quality of the alleged infringement. *Marcus v. Rowley*, 695 F.2d 1171 (9th Cir. 1983); *Salinger v. Random House, Inc.*, 818 F.2d 252 (2d Cir. 1987). Use of the "heart" of the plaintiff's work reduces the likelihood that a fair use will be found. *See Harper & Row Publishers, Inc. v. Nation Enters.*, 471 U.S. 539, 565–66 (1985) (discussion of Nixon pardon was "heart" of Gerald Ford's memoir); *Elvis Presley Enterprises, Inc. v. Passport Video*, 349 F.3d 622, 630 (9th Cir. 2003) (using key portions of Elvis Presley's classic television appearances extracted the most valuable part of plaintiff's copyrighted television

shows); *Los Angeles News Serv. v. Reuters Television Int'l, Ltd.*, 149 F.3d 987, 994 (9th Cir. 1998).

Max's taking one page from each of Jayne Martel's novels may not be quantitatively large, but it is qualitatively significant because it appropriates the most salient part of each work, the mystery's end. Courts have suggested that giving away the ending of any literary work amounts to appropriation of the "heart" of that work. *Cf. Video Pipeline, Inc. v. Buena Vista Home Entertainment, Inc.*, 342 F.3d 191, 201 (3d Cir. 2003) (defendant's unauthorized two minute clips taken only from first half of plaintiff's films and did not "give away" ending of films, thereby used "to whet customer's appetite, not to sate it," held not designed to reveal the heart of the films).

(A) is incorrect because even quantitatively small takings can be qualitatively significant, as this one clearly was.

(C) is incorrect because good faith and market effect are not relevant to factor three of the fair use analysis, which focuses exclusively on the amount and substantiality of the taking.

(D) is incorrect because the fact that a taking is verbatim is relevant to, but not dispositive of, its status under a factor three analysis. Max would most likely not be liable if he had made a verbatim reproduction of a single sentence.

288. (D) is the correct answer. When analyzing factor three of the fair use defense, courts are sympathetic to takings that appropriate no more than necessary of the plaintiff's work. *See Bill Graham Archives v. Dorling Kindersley Ltd.*, 448 F.3d 605, 611 (2d Cir. 2006) (reducing size of posters for use on a timeline in biographical book on the Grateful Dead permitted readers to recognize historical significance of posters, but inadequate to offer more than a glimpse of their expressive value); *Kelly v. Arriba Soft Corp.*, 280 F.3d 934, 943 (9th Cir. 2002) (use of thumbnail image of plaintiff's photographs deemed a fair use because it was necessary to copy plaintiff's entire image to allow users of visual search engine to recognize the image). Also, courts may permit a defendant to take a greater amount of the copyrighted work where there is a special need for accuracy in reporting or other factual uses. *See Meeropol v. Nizer*, 560 F.2d 1061, 1071 (2d Cir. 1977).

Here, Lloyd appropriated only the three scenes from *Bloody Mary* necessary to support his academic thesis, as illustrated by the modest lengths of the clips and the fact that he continued to lecture through each of them rather than simply sitting back and observing while they were playing. In light of these facts, a court would be likely to conclude that factor three militates in favor of Lloyd.

(A) is incorrect because the quantity of taking is not relevant to the qualitative question whether the heart of the defendant's work has been appropriated.

(B) is incorrect because there are no absolute rules as to how much of a copyrighted work may be copied and still be considered a fair use. *See, e.g., Sony Corp. of America v. Universal City Studios, Inc.*, 464 U.S. 417, 449–50 (1984) (fact that entire work is reproduced by defendant does not have its ordinary effect of militating against a finding of fair use when the viewer has been invited to witness the work in its entirety free of charge); *Higgins v. Detroit Educ. Television Found.*, 4 F. Supp. 2d 701, 707 (E.D. Mich. 1998) (use of 35 seconds of musical composition, without lyrics, as background music in an educational television program held to be a fair use).

(C) is incorrect because the purpose of Lloyd's use is not relevant to the amount and substantiality of his taking.

289.   **(D) is the correct answer.** Although the studio is not exploiting Asian markets currently, and has not announced any plans to do so, this does not mean it may not exploit those markets in the future. The fourth factor does not require that a plaintiff show a negative effect from the unauthorized use on markets that it currently exploits or even that the plaintiff has current plans to exploit a market in the future. The factor also encompasses negative effects on markets that may reasonably or likely be developed. 17 U.S.C. § 107(4) (referring to "the effect of the use upon the *potential market* for or value of the copyrighted work") (emphasis added); *American Geophysical Union v. Texaco, Inc.*, 60 F.3d 913, 921 (2d Cir. 1995) ("[A]n impact on potential licensing revenues for traditional, reasonable, or likely to be developed markets should be legally cognizable when evaluating a secondary use's 'effect upon the potential market for or value of the copyrighted work.'"). Because film companies are increasingly exploiting Asian markets, it is entirely reasonable that this studio would eventually do so. The fourth factor would thus weigh in favor of the studio, and against Mark.

(A) and (B) are incorrect because the fourth factor does not only require current exploitation or current plans to exploit a potential market, but also includes markets that are reasonably likely to be developed.

(C) is incorrect because whether or not a defendant has attempted to negotiate a license is not conclusive with respect to the fourth factor of a fair use analysis.

290.   No. Earlier decisions suggested that the fourth factor was particularly important, though none went so far as to state that it was dispositive of fair use analysis altogether. *See Harper & Row, Publishers, Inc. v. Nation Enters.*, 471 U.S. 539, 566 (1985) (calling the fourth factor "undoubtedly the single most important element of fair use"). Subsequent decisions have pulled back from the position that the fourth factor should be disproportionately important in a fair use analysis. *See Campbell v. Acuff-Rose Music, Inc.*, 510 U.S. 569, 590 n.21 (1994) ("Market harm is a matter of degree, and the importance of this factor will vary, not only with the amount of harm, but also with the relative strength of the showing on the other factors."). Thus, if the fourth factor were to weigh against Mark, that would tend to indicate that the use was not fair, but would not be determinative of the fair use defense on its own.

291.   **(B) is the correct answer.** Regardless of whether CBA originally expressed approval of or indifference to Gina's unauthorized creation of *The Ben Game*, it is entitled to raise an infringement claim at any time because copyright is a strict liability tort. In terms of the

Strict liability

fourth factor of a fair use analysis, Gina's unauthorized creation of the board game may not interfere with the primary market for *Ben*, such as syndicated broadcasting, but it does undermine the creation of secondary markets that CBA might have exploited through licensing. *Campbell v. Acuff-Rose Music, Inc.*, 510 U.S. 569, 590 (1994) ("The licensing of derivatives is an important economic incentive to the creation of originals.").

(A) is incorrect because the availability of the fair use defense does not depend on the kind of relief sought.

(C) is incorrect because an owner need not have current plans to exploit a market in order to prevail on the fourth factor.

(D) is incorrect because an owner's initial acquiescence in an unauthorized use does not preclude that owner from making a successful claim on factor four of a fair use analysis at a later time. *See, e.g., Castle Rock Entertainment v. Carol Publishing Group, Inc.*, 150 F.3d 132, 145 (2d Cir. 1998); *Warner Bros. Entertainment Inc. v. RDR Books*, 575 F. Supp. 2d 513 (S.D.N.Y. 2008).

292. Probably, though not certainly, not. Most courts have held that the fact that the defendant's use may have a positive impact on copyright holder's market does not exonerate that use. *See Ringgold v. Black Entertainment Television*, 126 F.3d 70, 81 n.16 (2d Cir. 1997) (even if use in television program increased poster sales, plaintiff retained right to licensing fee); *UMG Recordings, Inc. v. MP3.com, Inc.*, 92 F. Supp. 2d 349, 352 (S.D.N.Y. 2000) ("Any allegedly positive impact of defendant's activities on plaintiffs' prior market in no way frees defendant to usurp a further market that directly derives from reproduction of the plaintiffs' copyrighted works."); *Los Angeles Times v. Free Republic*, 2000 U.S. Dist. LEXIS 5669, at * 73 (C.D. Cal. March 31, 2000) ("Courts have routinely rejected the argument that a use is fair because it increases demand for the plaintiff's copyrighted work.").

However, recently some courts have begun to take more seriously the argument that the unauthorized but financially beneficial uses of a copyrighted work may help a defendant's fair use case. The Ninth Circuit has suggested, though by no means clearly held, that it is relevant in the context of the fourth factor to consider whether the purportedly fair use would increase demand for the owner's work. *See Kelly v. Arriba Soft Corp.*, 280 F.3d 934, 944 (9th Cir. 2002) (concluding that unauthorized use was fair in part because inclusion of thumbnail images of plaintiff's photographs in visual search engine would guide users to plaintiff's website rather than away from it); *Brownmark Films LLC v. Comedy Partners*, 682 F.3d 687, 693 (7th Cir. 2012) (observing that defendant's parody did not harm the market for plaintiff's work, and that if anything, "[i]t seems to this court that the parody's likely effect, ironically, would only increase ad revenue" associated with plaintiff's work); *Hofheinz v. AMC Prods., Inc.*, (E.D.N.Y. 2000) ("[defendant's use] may increase market demand for plaintiff's copyrighted works and make more people aware of the influence that [plaintiff] had in developing the 'B' movie genre").

293. **(B) is the correct answer.** Although in theory, any possible use might be licensed, plaintiffs can only make arguments that a defendant's use creates market harm within the

You weren't going to license people to make fun of you.

Trans > licensing market

meaning of the fourth fair use factor where the market is actual or reasonably likely to develop. Parody and criticism comprise a special case where courts have consistently held that licensing markets are neither present nor reasonably likely to develop. *See Campbell v. Acuff-Rose Music, Inc.*, 510 U.S. 569, 592 (1994); *Mattel Inc. v. Walking Mountain Prods.*, 353 F.3d 792, 805 (9th Cir. 2003) (not likely that Mattel would license an artist to create a work that is critical of Barbie); *Sundeman v. The Seajay Society, Inc.*, 142 F.3d 194, 207 (4th Cir. 1998). Thus, Dolly's argument that Wendy's parody infringed on her market to license parodies of her work will fail. Relatedly, courts have held that there are no markets in transformative users. I.e., if an unauthorized use is transformative, the plaintiff cannot advance an argument that the fourth factor favors them because the defendant deprived them of a licensing fee. *See, e.g., Bill Graham Archives, Inc. v. Dorling Kindersley Ltd.*, 448 F.3d 605, 614 (2d Cir. 2006) (rejecting a claim that an owner lost license fees under fair use's factor-four analysis because the use at issue was transformative).

(A) is incorrect because whether a work is fiction or nonfiction relates to the second fair use factor, nature of the plaintiff's work, and not to the fourth factor, market effects. And in any event, the non-fiction status of a work means that fair use would be more likely for the defendant, not the plaintiff. *See Kelly v. Arriba Soft Corp.*, 280 F.3d 934, 943 (9th Cir. 2002).

(C) is incorrect because courts have consistently held that no such licensing markets exist or are reasonably likely to emerge.

(D) is incorrect because a plaintiff need not produce evidence of pending negotiations to prove that a licensing market is reasonably likely to emerge.

294.   **(C) is the correct answer.** Although the Supreme Court held in *Sony* that manufacturers of video recording devices were not liable for infringement on a secondary liability theory, this did not mean that the underlying act, unauthorized videotaping, did not constitute primary infringement. The *Sony* Court held that while "time-shifting" (recording television programs for the purpose of watching them at a more convenient time) was fair use, it did not address whether the practice of recording television programs for the purpose of keeping a permanent videotape library of them constituted a fair use. *See Sony Corp. of America v. Universal City Studios, Inc.*, 464 U.S. 417, 423 n.3 (1984). Jack's conduct clearly falls into the category of library building because he records *Crime Dogs* solely for the purpose of keeping a permanent videotape library of the show. Therefore, his conduct does not fall within the holding of *Sony*.

(A) is incorrect because it misstates the Court's holding in *Sony*.

(B) is incorrect because courts have not conclusively held that a use is fair simply because it is made solely for personal purposes. *E.g., A&M Records, Inc. v. Napster, Inc.*, 239 F.3d 1004, 1017 (9th Cir. 2001) (rejecting a fair use defense even though all the unauthorized uses facilitated by the defendant's service were personal).

(D) is incorrect because it misstates the relationship between *Sony* and *Grokster*. Not only did *Grokster* not explicitly overrule *Sony*, it did not address the question whether copying works for the purpose of creating a personal archive amounts to fair use.

295.   **(D) is the correct answer.** Kendra's photocopying was minimally transformative because it represents a bare change in medium at best (she converted the physical version of a literary work to loose-leaf). Moreover, courts have held that the existence of the Copyright Clearance Center suggests that there is a present, plausible licensing market for individual photocopies. In a case very similar to this one, the Second Circuit held that photocopying a journal article by an industrial scientist was not a fair use. *See American Geophysical Union v. Texaco, Inc.*, 60 F.3d 913, 918 (2d Cir. 1994); *see also Cambridge Univ. Press v. Patton*, 769 F.3d 1232, 1284 (11th Cir. 2014) (reversing and remanding district court's holding that unauthorized copying of academic books by university professors for student coursepacks was fair use).

   (A), (B), and (C) are incorrect for the reasons explained above.

296.   **(C) is the correct answer.** There is a three-year statute of limitations for copyright infringement actions. 17 U.S.C. §507(b). Because Greco was well aware of Strange Mel's unauthorized use in 2001, but waited a total of seven years to bring an infringement suit, Strange Mel would be able to argue that he was liable only for infringements that took place within the three years prior to Greco's filing suit. This may rule out infringement liability for acts of copying *Only Me* made by Strange Mel when creating *Golly Gee*, though Strange Mel would still be liable for any public distribution of unauthorized copies, such as copy sales, that took place between late 2005 and late 2008.

   The equitable defense of laches may apply in the copyright setting when there has been a sufficient passage of time between the plaintiff's knowledge of the injury and the date of bringing suit, as well as the presence of prejudice to the defendant. *See Broadcast Music, Inc. v. Roger Miller Music, Inc.*, 396 F.3d 762, 783 (6th Cir. 2005) (laches is an affirmative defense for claims asserted under the Copyright Act). Strange Mel can raise a plausible laches defense because Greco waited seven years to bring an infringement suit, *cf. Trust Company Bank v. Putnam Publishing Group, Inc.*, 5 U.S.P.Q.2d 1874 (C.D. Cal. 1988) (19-month delay in bringing action against alleged infringing novel was deemed sufficient to constitute laches), and because Strange Mel relied to his detriment on Greco's delay in bringing a lawsuit by investing time and money in the music video, *see id.* (subsequent to plaintiff's knowledge of the infringing nature of the novel, defendants acquired the softcover rights to the novel and expended substantial sums promoting and publishing the novel). Strange Mel's likely success on the laches defense would not, however, obviate Greco's ability to recover for infringements that took place within the three-year statute of limitations period. *See Petrella v. Metro-Goldwyn-Mayer, Inc.*, 134 S. Ct. 1962, 1967 (U.S. 2014) ("Laches, we hold, cannot be invoked to preclude adjudication of a claim for damages brought within the three-year window.").

   Abandonment of copyright may also be a valid affirmative defense to copyright infringement, but can be raised only if there is an intent by the copyright proprietor to surrender the rights in her work. *Dam Things From Denmark v. Russ Berrie & Co., Inc.*, 290 F.3d 548, 560 (3d Cir. 2002) ("[T]here must be either an act, or a failure to act, from which we can readily infer an intent to abandon the right"). The mere failure to pursue third-party infringers is not an indication of abandonment. *See Capitol Records, Inc. v. Naxos of Am., Inc.*, 372 F.3d 471, 484 (2d Cir. 2004). Here, Greco's general indication of contemptuous indifference toward "Strange Mel" and *Golly Gee* does not come close to the level of indicating a general relinquishment of all rights in the musical work and sound recording that comprise *Only Me*. "Strange Mel" could thus not raise an abandonment defense.

(A), (B), and (D) are incorrect because they inaccurately state the affirmative defenses available to "Strange Mel."

297.   **(D) is the correct answer.** A plaintiff's knowing failure to advise the Copyright Office of material facts is grounds for holding the registration invalid and incapable of supporting an infringement action. *See Masquerade Novelty, Inc. v. Unique Indus., Inc.*, 912 F.2d 663, 667 (3d Cir. 1990). Here, Jeff made an intentional misstatement on his registration by claiming that he, not Chuck, is the author of the poem. This is also clearly a material misrepresentation because it caused registration to issue in his name rather than the name of the true author. In light of these facts, Mike has a valid affirmative defense of fraud on the Copyright Office.

(A) is incorrect because Jeff's status as the registered owner of the copyright in the poem does not give rise to standing since it is fraudulent.

(B) is incorrect because non-registration does not constitute abandonment.

(C) is incorrect because any valid owner of a copyright can sue for infringement, and the owner may well not be the author.

298.   **(A) is the correct answer.** The Copyright Act explicitly preempts state laws where the subject matter of the law comes within the subject matter of copyright as defined by sections 102 and 103 of the 1976 Copyright Act, and the right asserted under the state law is the equivalent to a right protected by federal copyright law. 17 U.S.C. § 301; *see Mayer v. Josiah Wedgwood & Sons, Ltd.*, 601 F. Supp. 1523 (S.D.N.Y. 1985); *Facenda v. N.F.L. Films, Inc.*, 542 F.3d 1007, 1027–28 (3d Cir. 2008) (person's voice is outside the subject matter of copyright); *Valente-Kritzer Video v. Pinckney*, 881 F.2d 772 (9th Cir. 1989) (state fraud claim requirement of misrepresentation constituted an extra element).

Ideas have been held to come within the subject matter of copyright as defined by the Copyright Act. 17 U.S.C. § 102(b); *see Katz, Dochtermann & Epstein, Inc. v. Home Box Office*, 1999 Copy. L. Dec. (CCH) ¶ 27,907 (S.D.N.Y. 1999) (holding that the uncopyrightable idea that underlies copyrightable expression falls within "subject matter of copyright" for preemption purposes). In addition, the rights provided by the California statute—reproduction, adaptation, public distribution and public performance—are among the same rights protected by the Copyright Act. *See* 17 U.S.C. § 106; *Daboub v. Gibbons*, 42 F.3d 285, 288, 289–90 (5th Cir. 1995). Therefore, a California state law that seeks to protect general ideas as an exclusive right incident to authorship would be deemed preempted and unenforceable.

(B) is incorrect. It is true that where state and federal law conflict, federal law prevails pursuant to the U.S. Constitution's Supremacy Clause. U.S. Const. art. IV, cl. 2. *See*

Goldstein v. California, 412 U.S. 546 (1973) (state penal law protection of pre-1972 sound recordings did not conflict with federal copyright law). However, in this case, one could comply with both laws at the same time even though they are otherwise in tension.

(C) is incorrect because states are not generally permitted to provide more copyright protection to authors, especially where, as here, that protection conflicts with both the text and policy of federal law.

(D) is incorrect because the California law is unenforceable for the reasons explained above.

299.   This is a difficult question for which there are at least two plausible answers. The Copyright Act provides a three-year statute of limitations for civil actions, though the statute of limitations begins to run only when the plaintiff's claim accrues. 17 U.S.C. § 507(b) ("No civil action shall be maintained under the provisions of this title unless it is commenced within three years after the claim accrued."). Amusement Development will argue that Hermit's claim actually accrued when it created Futureland's plans and blueprints, which Hermit claims were based on *Promises of Tomorrow*. Amusement Development will argue that failing that, Hermit's claim would have accrued at the latest upon the opening of Futureland. Because both of these events occurred more than three years prior to Hermit filing his lawsuit, and assuming there are no subsequent acts of infringement alleged, Amusement Development will claim that the District Court has no subject matter jurisdiction to hear the case. *See Broadcast Music, Inc. v. Roger Miller Music, Inc.*, 396 F.3d 762, 783 (6th Cir. 2005) (statute of limitations is an affirmative defense for claims asserted under the Copyright Act).

The vast majority of courts, however, apply the discovery rule in copyright infringement actions, under which a claim accrues only when a plaintiff knows or has sufficient reason to know of the conduct on which the claim is grounded. *See Warren Freedenfeld Assocs., Inc. v. McTigue, D.V.M.*, 531 F.3d 38, 44 (1st Cir. 2008); *see also Bridgeport Music, Inc. v. Diamond Time, Ltd.*, 371 F.3d 883, 889 (6th Cir. 2004). Under this rule, a claim accrues only when a reasonably prudent plaintiff would have discovered, or acquired an awareness of, the putative infringement. *See Stone v. Williams*, 970 F.3d 1043, 1048 (2d Cir. 1992). The reasonable person standard incorporates a duty of due diligence, under which plaintiffs can be charged with inquiry notice sufficient to start the limitations clock once they possess information fairly suggesting some reason to investigate whether they may have suffered an injury at the hands of a putative infringer. *Warren Freedenfeld Assocs., Inc. v. McTigue, D.V.M.*, 531 F.3d 38, 44–45 (1st Cir. 2008) ("Typically, inquiry notice must be triggered by some event or series of events that comes to the attention of the aggrieved party.").

Pursuant to the discovery rule, Hermit will argue that he has been preoccupied with his and his wife's health issues and that, because of his remote residence, his removal from media coverage and his reclusive nature, the statute of limitations should be tolled until he discovered the photographs of Futureland shortly before filing suit. The opening of Futureland took place when Hermit was undergoing open-heart surgery, at a time when he was clearly focused on staying alive. In addition, Hermit will note that the absence of children in his life made it unlikely that he would pay any attention to an amusement park directed at children.

Amusement Development will counter that a reasonably prudent person would have become aware of the massive publicity surrounding Futureland, as well as the pervasive advertising campaign that has continued since its opening. Even though Hermit did not have a television, he apparently had access to print media over the years when visiting his barber. As a result, the corporation will argue that the three-year statute of limitations should not be tolled and the lawsuit should be dismissed.

300.   **(D) is the correct answer.** Recovery in copyright infringement suits is allowed only for those acts occurring within three years of the filing of the lawsuit, and is disallowed for earlier infringing acts. 17 U.S.C. § 507(b); *see Roley v. New World Pictures, Ltd.*, 19 F.3d 479 (9th Cir. 1994); *Stone v. Williams*, 970 F.2d 1043 (2d Cir. 1992); *Hoste v. Radio Corp. of America*, 654 F.2d 11 (6th Cir. 1981). MusicCo can thus not recover any damages for Ripp-Off's initial infringing conduct, which took place five years ago.

Moreover, while Ripp-Off made thousands of copies of MusicCo's sound recording, they are limited to one count of statutory damages, since only one work was at issue. 17 U.S.C. § 504(c)(1) ("[T]he copyright owner may elect . . . to recover . . . an award of statutory damages for all infringements involved in the action, *with respect to any one work*[.]") (emphasis added). Thus even though maximum statutory damages are available to MusicCo, since they timely registered their work and since Ripp-Off's conduct was willful, they can recover at most $150,000 in statutory damages. MusicCo would be better off recovering the actual damages inflicted on them by Ripp-Off's infringement in the past three years is greater: $175,000.

(A) is incorrect because MusicCo could not obtain Ripp-Off's net profits from its infringing acts of five years ago.

(B) is incorrect because MusicCo cannot recover Ripp-Off's net profits from its infringing acts of five years ago. In addition, MusicCo cannot receive both statutory and non-statutory damages for the same infringement.

(C) is incorrect because MusicCo would elect to receive the larger amount of $175,000 in non-statutory damages.

301.   It is clear that the record company has no basis for bringing a federal copyright infringement lawsuit because pre-1972 sound recordings have no federal copyright protection. *See* 17 U.S.C. § 301(c) ("[N]o sound recording fixed before February 15, 1972, shall be subject to copyright under this title."). That means that the only recourse for the record company is to bring an action under East Dakota state law. States offer various protections for pre-1972 sound recordings, including common-law copyright, unfair competition, and criminal laws against piracy and bootlegging. In the absence of any legislation to the contrary, it is plausible that the record company would have a viable

claim against the website for the infringement of the common-law copyright in the sound recordings. *See, e.g., Capitol Records, Inc. v. Naxos of America, Inc.*, 372 F.3d 471, 477–78 (2d Cir. 2004).

The possibility of such an action for common-law copyright infringement, though, has been explicitly precluded by the East Dakota legislation. If the record company can, however, prove that federal copyright law preempts the recent legislation, then it may be able to proceed with a common-law copyright theory under East Dakota state law. Such a preemption argument would invalidate the recent legislation, leaving the record company free to proceed on its common-law copyright theory. *See Goldstein v. California*, 412 U.S. 546 (1973) (holding, in the absence of any state statutory law to the contrary, that federal copyright law does not preempt common-law copyright claims).

The record company may seem to have a viable claim of preemption under section 301(a). Such a claim would require it to argue that pre-1972 sound recordings may not be protected by federal copyright, but are still within the subject matter of copyright, and that the downloading or streaming involve the exclusive rights of reproduction, public performance, and public transmission of sound recordings. But such a claim is prohibited by section 301(c) of the Copyright Act, which states that federal copyright law cannot preempt any state laws regarding pre-1972 sound recordings. *See* 17 U.S.C. § 301(c) ("With respect to sound recordings fixed before February 15, 1972, any rights or remedies under the common law or statutes of any State shall not be annulled or limited by this title until February 15, 2067."). This means that the record company must live with the East Dakota law that provides for a compulsory master license for pre-1972 sound recording downloads and the free streaming of such recordings.

302.   **(B) is the correct answer.** Fair use requires consideration of a number of factors, principally including the purpose and character of the unauthorized use and the effect of the use of the market for or value of the plaintiff's work. 17 U.S.C. § 107. *The Sotos: Not Welcome* substantially transforms *Welcoming the Sotos* by recasting a light-fare television situation comedy into a serious social commentary about racism. *See Campbell v. Acuff Rose Music, Inc.*, 510 U.S. 569, 581–82 (1994) (holding that recasting a light pop song about romance into a ribald rap number about urban gender relations amounted to transformative use); *Adjmi v. DLT Entertainment, Ltd.*, 97 F. Supp. 3d 512, 529–32 (holding that an unauthorized stage adaptation of 1970s comedy *Three's Company* that raised serious social issues about homophobia was a transformative fair use).

The Sotos: Not Welcome is also very unlikely to be a market substitute for *Welcoming the Sotos* because it operates in a different market (stage as opposed to television), has different creative aims (serious commentary rather than light comedy), and appeals to a different audience (people interested in difficult social issues rather than consumers of mainstream entertainment). *See Adjmi*, 97 F. Supp. 3d at 534–35 (holding that a "hard-edged" stage adaptation of a mainstream television situation comedy inflicted no economic harm on the latter because it was aimed at an entirely different audience).

(A) **is incorrect** because it wrongly assumes that parody is synonymous with fair use. This is a common misreading of *Campbell*. That case held merely that parodies are more likely than satires to be fair uses, not that a finding of parody ended the fair use inquiry. Indeed, *Campbell* echoed the Supreme Court's earlier rejection of "rigid, bright-line approach[es] to fair use." 510 U.S. at 584 (citing *Sony Corp. of Am. v. Universal City Studios, Inc.*, 464 U.S. 417, 449 n.31 (1984). The Copyright Act clearly requires judges to apply all four fair use factors, and even courts that find an unauthorized use to be parodic regularly apply all the factors to determine the validity of the asserted fair use defense. So while *The Sotos: Not Welcome* is clearly a parody of *Welcoming the Sotos*, that issue alone does not determine the outcome of playwright's fair use defense.

(C) **is incorrect** because while playwright may have addressed these themes in other ways, that is not a relevant consideration for the fair use defense. If the four statutory factors favor the defendant, they have a full defense to infringement regardless of whether they could have expressed their ideas in a different way. And in any event, *The Sotos: Not Welcome* is clearly a parody of *Welcoming the Sotos*, which means that the playwright could not have expressed her ideas as well without referencing the television show, since part of her message was to critique that show.

(D) **is incorrect** because there is no procedural requirement that defendants must seek and be denied a license prior to raising a fair use defense.

303.   Probably not. These facts likely do create a closer case on fair use because they indicate that playwright's unauthorized use did inflict significant harm to the value of Megaverse's work. But the Supreme Court has stressed that not all economic costs inflicted by an unauthorized use cause the fourth fair use factor to favor the plaintiff. "[W]hen a lethal parody, like a scathing theater review, kills demand for the original, it does not produce a harm cognizable under the Copyright Act. Because parody may quite legitimately aim at garroting the original, destroying it commercially as well as artistically, the role of the courts is to distinguish between [b]iting criticism [that merely] suppresses demand [and] copyright infringement[, which] usurps it." *Campbell*, at 591–92 (citations and internal quotation marks omitted).

So while *The Sotos: Not Welcome* undoubtedly inflicts economic harm on Megaverse's work in this revised factual scenario, it does so not because it is a direct market substitute (which would harm the case for fair use) but because it is the kind of "lethal parody" that may harm demand in a way that does not help the plaintiffs' factor-four argument.

304.   **(B) is the correct answer.** Factor one favors fair use because the studio used the quote for comedic purposes while Fox's novels were serious. Factor three favors fair use because the taking consisted of one sentence from a "voluminous" novel. And factor four favors fair use because the line of dialogue in the film was so brief that it would have had at most a marginal effect on the film's economic success, and thus would have fetched only a very small license fee. *See Faulkner Literary Rights, LLC v. Sony Pictures Classics, Inc.*, 953 F. Supp. 2d 701 (N.D. Miss. 2013) (holding that film's use of one sentence of dialogue from William Faulkner's "Requiem for a Nun" was a fair use for similar reasons).

(A) is incorrect because nonliteral similarity is not a factor that makes an unauthorized use "overwhelmingly likely" to be fair use. While the degree of similarity could possibly affect the first factor analysis, *see* 17 U.S.C. § 107(1) (requiring courts to consider, inter alia, the "purpose and character of the use"), it would not be a dispositive consideration and in any event that issue is foreclosed here since the studio conceded both copying and substantial similarity.

(C) is incorrect because on very similar facts, a federal court recently held that use of an attributed quotation from a famous novel in a film is transformative to the extent that different artistic context changes the purpose and character of the sentence. *Faulkner Literary Rights*, 953 F. Supp. 2d at 708. Moreover, the minuscule and transformative nature of the use militates against a finding that the use robbed Fox of any meaningful licensing revenue. *Id.* at 710–11.

(D) is incorrect because the studio's use was not necessarily *de minimis*. The sentence from Fox's work, while brief, clearly contains originality in phrasing and expression and thus likely exceeds the *de minimis* threshold because it could be recognized as part of her work even out of context. *See Newton v. Diamond*, 388 F.3d 1189, 1193 (9th Cir. 2003) ("[A] use is *de minimis* only if the average audience would not recognize the infringement."). Regardless, numerous courts have found an unauthorized use to be both *de minimis* and fair use. *See, e.g., Compaq Computer Corp. v. Ergonome Inc.*, 387 F.3d 403, 406 (5th Cir. 2004) (affirming jury verdict rendered based on *de minimis* and fair use grounds).

305.   **(C) is the correct answer.** While this is a close question, recent precedent suggests the answer is yes. AllArt.com's use is transformative in that it does not seek to reproduce the art for aesthetic experience, but rather to create an archive to advance the study and appreciation of art. While the reproductions show the entire works, this is necessary to advance the aims for which AllArt.com exists. And there is little or no economic harm to the copyright owners, since the digital versions on AllArt.com cannot be used to make the kinds of full-scale reproductions that would supplant the market for licensed reproductions. If anything, the site might boost sales of art reproductions by stimulating interest in artists' works. Courts have recently held that unauthorized uses in other contexts (i.e., the unlicensed reproduction of literary works to create archives for public access) to be fair uses. *See Author's Guild v. Google, Inc.*, 804 F.3d 202 (2d Cir. 2015).

These facts may present a somewhat harder case than *Author's Guild*, though, because in that case viewers could not access the entire text of books freely online, while AllArt.com is making full artworks available to viewers. Still, though, because merely viewing a digital version of a painting or sculpture on the Internet cannot deliver the same experience as seeing the work in person, the likelihood that a court would find this unauthorized use substitutive remains small, and the factors would still likely favor fair use overall.

(A) is incorrect because the galleries and museums possess copies of the works pursuant to narrow use licenses regarding the right to display the works; this does not allow them to sublicense the owners' rights to reproduce the works in digital form. In any event, an implied license argument is not a fair use argument.

(B) is incorrect because courts have frequently held that unauthorized uses that entail verbatim reproductions are fair uses. *See, e.g., Seltzer v. Green Day, Inc.*, 725 1170 (9th Cir. 2013) (holding that a band's unlicensed display of an artist's work as part of the stage backdrop during a concert was fair use).

(D) is incorrect because it is not clear that AllArt.com, a nonprofit website, would have been able to pay licensing fees to many thousands of copyright holders. Moreover, whereas here an unauthorized use is transformative, courts are loath to hold that the owner would have been entitled to a licensing fee in the first instance. *See Bill Graham Archives, Inc. v. Dorling Kindersley Ltd.*, 448 F.3d 605, 614 (2d Cir. 2006) (rejecting a claim that an owner lost license fees under fair use's factor-four analysis because the use at issue was transformative).

306. Possibly, but not necessarily. Courts are certainly free to consider any relevant issues raised by the parties in the context of fair use, because the statutory factors are inclusive, not exclusive. And at least one court has considered the public value of an unauthorized use in upholding a fair use defense. *See Author's Guild, Inc. v. Google, Inc.*, 954 F. Supp. 2d 282, 293–95 (S.D.N.Y. 2013) (noting that the Google Books project "provides significant public benefits" in ruling that the unlicensed copying in that case was fair use). That said, a court is certainly not required to consider the public interest in fair use cases, since it is not a statutorily enumerated factor. Whether the court would credit AllArt.com's public interest argument in this case thus remains a possibility but not a certainty.

Remedies

307.   **(C) is the correct answer.** Injunctive relief is a traditional remedy for copyright infringement. *See, e.g., Cable/Home Comm. Corp. v. Network Productions, Inc.*, 902 F.2d 829, 849 (11th Cir. 1990); *United Feature Syndicate, Inc. v. Sunrise Mold Co., Inc.*, 569 F. Supp. 1475 (S.D. Fla. 1983). However, a court may not issue an injunction where a defendant has ceased its infringing actions and shows no inclination to infringe in the future. *See Harrison Music Corp. v. Tesfaye*, 293 F. Supp. 2d 80, 83 (D.D.C. 2003). Here, the request for injunctive relief is no longer appropriate because Pirate has ceased his infringing conduct and radically changed the course of his life so that there is no reasonable expectation that the infringement will recur.

(A) is incorrect for the reasons explained above.

(B) is incorrect because injunctive relief does not follow automatically on a showing of copyright infringement, but rather only where the plaintiff convinces a court that it is appropriate under the circumstances. The elements a court will analyze when determining whether to grant an injunction include: (1) whether the plaintiff would suffer irreparable harm if a preliminary injunction does not issue; (2) whether the plaintiff can show a likelihood of success on the merits; (3) balancing competing claims of injury to the parties; and (4) consideration of the public interest. *See Warren Pub., Inc. v. Microdos Data Corp.*, 115 F.3d 1509, 1516 (11th Cir. 1997); *see also Salinger v. Colting*, 607 F.3d 68, 79 (2d Cir. 2010) (preliminary injunction does not issue automatically upon showing of infringement).

(D) is incorrect because the federal courts have jurisdiction to enjoin the actions of parties regardless of their geographic location, at least within the territorial limits of the United States.

308.   No. Traditionally, courts have consistently held that injunctions against future copyright infringement do not violate the First Amendment. *See Elvis Presley Enters., Inc. v. Passport Video*, 349 F.3d 622, 626 (9th Cir. 2003) ("[I]f the use of the alleged infringer is not fair use, there are no First Amendment prohibitions against granting a preliminary injunction."); *Intellectual Reserve, Inc. v. Utah Lighthouse Ministry, Inc.*, 75 F. Supp. 2d 1290, 1295 (D. Utah 1999).

More recently, some courts have voiced concerns that the blunt force of the traditional rule may diminish free speech. One court has gone so far as to vacate, on First Amendment grounds, a preliminary injunction against purportedly infringing conduct. *See Suntrust Bank v. Houghton Mifflin Co.*, 252 F.3d 1165, 1166 (11th Cir. 2001) (holding that a preliminary injunction enjoining the publication of *The Wind Done Gone*, a parody of *Gone With the Wind*, amounted to an unlawful prior restraint in violation of the First Amendment). *Suntrust* is likely distinguishable from the facts in questions IX-1 and IX-2, though, because the purportedly fair use in that case—a parody of the novel *Gone With the Wind*—was highly expressive, while merely performing another author's work without authorization, the activity engaged in by Pirate, is not.

309.   **(C) is the correct answer.** While courts used to grant preliminary injunctive relief in copyright cases based solely on a showing of likely success on the merits, more recent authorities have abandoned this approach. "The court must not adopt a 'categorical' or 'general' rule or presume that the plaintiff will suffer irreparable harm (unless such a departure from the long tradition of equity practice was intended by Congress). Instead, the court must actually consider the injury the plaintiff will suffer if he or she loses on the preliminary injunction but ultimately prevails on the merits, paying particular attention to whether the remedies available at law, such as monetary damages, are inadequate to compensate for that injury." *Salinger v. Colting*, 607 F.3d 68, 79–80 (2d Cir. 2010) (quoting *eBay v. MercExchange, Inc.*, 547 U.S. 388, 391–94 (2005)).

(A) **is incorrect** because this is the position rejected by federal courts in *Colting* and numerous other cases. *E.g., Flexible Lifeline Sys. v. Precision Lift*, 654 F.3d 989 (9th Cir. 2011).

(B) **is incorrect** because no cases create an exception for particularly strong merits cases.

(D) **is incorrect** because the availability of money damages alone does not rebut the presumption of irreparable harm. *Cadence Design Systems, Inc. v. Avanti! Corp.*, 125 F.3d 824, 827 (9th Cir. 1997). A handful of courts have disagreed, *see, e.g., Belushi v. Woodward*, 598 F. Supp. 36, 37 (D.D.C. 1984) ("If a legal remedy will adequately compensate for any infringement, then injury, if any, is not irreparable."), but they represent a vanishingly small minority of opinion.

310.   Possibly, but not necessarily. Undue delay in seeking a preliminary injunction may rebut the presumption of irreparable harm. *See Richard Feiner & Co. v. Turner Ent. Co.*, 98 F.3d 33, 34 (2d Cir. 1996); *Metro-Media Broad. Corp. v. MGM/UA Entertainment Co.*, 611 F. Supp. 415, 427 (C.D. Cal. 1985) (four-month delay in seeking injunctive relief supported denial of plaintiff's motion for preliminary injunction).

These authorities represent rough rules of thumb rather than bright-line rules, though. So here, if Author could advance some convincing explanation that justified his waiting six months to request the injunction after learning of the infringement to file suit, a court might still find that the harm was irreparable. But absent some such saving explanation, an otherwise unjustified six-month delay in filing suit may well cause a court to conclude that the harm inflicted by Seller on Author was not irreparable.

311.   **(A) is the correct answer.** In order to obtain a preliminary injunction the movant must show a reasonable probability of eventual success in the litigation. *See Value Group, Inc. v.*

Mendham Lake Estates, L.P., 800 F. Supp. 1228, 1232 (D.N.J. 1992). Painter has done this, so he should prevail on this element of the test for a preliminary injunction.

(B) and (C) are incorrect because they describe this element of the test for a preliminary injunction too loosely.

(D) is incorrect because it describes this element of the test for a preliminary injunction too broadly.

312.   Such a conclusion would not be dispositive with respect to the outcome of the preliminary injunction motion. While courts used to presume irreparable harm when plaintiffs showed a likelihood of success on the merits of copyright infringement suits, recent cases have reversed this approach. *See Salinger v. Colting*, 607 F.3d 68, 79–80 (2d Cir. 2010); *Flexible Lifeline Sys. v. Precision Lift*, 654 F.3d 989 (9th Cir. 2011).

313.   This is a hard question. On one hand, Author can invoke the public interest by arguing that the public generally has a strong interest in seeing that copyright laws are enforced and that infringement is limited. Courts have often expressed solicitude for this position, stressing that mere infringement cannot advance the public interest. *See, e.g., Intellectual Reserve, Inc. v. Utah Lighthouse Ministry, Inc.*, 75 F. Supp. 2d 1290, 1295 (D. Utah 1999); *Value Group, Inc. v. Mendham Lake Estates, L.P.*, 800 F. Supp. 1228, 1234 (D.N.J. 1992) ("The public has no interest in permitting one company to copy another company's work.").

On the other hand, Satirist can argue that there is a strong public interest favoring the publication of books and novels, especially those that express novel or controversial opinions. *Trust Company Bank v. Putnam Publishing Group, Inc.*, 5 U.S.P.Q.2d 1874 (C.D. Cal. 1988); *Belushi v. Woodward*, 598 F. Supp. 36, 37–38 (D.D.C. 1984) (promotion of free expression and robust debate is a competing public interest to the public interest that favors maintaining the integrity of copyright laws). In particular, where the work at issue is not a verbatim copy, but possesses substantial original material, courts recently have been inclined to find that preliminary relief is not in the public interest. *See, e.g., Suntrust Bank v. Houghton Mifflin Co.*, 252 F.3d 1165, 1166 (11th Cir. 2001).

314.   **(D) is the correct answer.** Although the Copyright Act clearly places impoundment within the discretion of courts, 17 U.S.C. § 503(a) ("the court *may* order impounding") (emphasis added), courts have been unwilling to issue ex parte impoundment orders due to concerns that such orders may unduly burden property rights without due process. *See Paramount Pictures Corp. v. Doe*, 821 F. Supp. 82, 87 (E.D.N.Y. 1993) ("[A] literal reading of the rules [regarding *ex parte* seizures] would result in procedures of dubious constitutional validity in light of Supreme Court decisions handed down since the time of the rules' adoption."). In light of this, a court would likely not order the studios' requested impoundment.

(A) is incorrect because the plain language of the Copyright Act clearly makes impoundment discretionary, not mandatory.

(B) **is incorrect** because, while the Rules of Practice in Copyright Cases promulgated under the 1909 Act appeared to make impoundment mandatory upon a plaintiff's motion, those rules have since been abrogated by the Supreme Court and are no longer in force. *See AdobeSystems, Inc. v. South Sun Prods., Inc.,* 187 F.R.D. 636, 640 (S.D. Cal. 1999).

(C) **is incorrect** because the Copyright Act makes impoundment available "at any time while an [infringement] action . . . is pending." 17 U.S.C. § 503.

315.   (D) **is the correct answer.** The Copyright Act enables impoundment of infringing "copies or phonorecords," such as Al's infringing DVDs, 17 U.S.C. 503(a)(1)(A); "articles by means of which such copies . . . may be reproduced," *id.* § 503(a)(1)(B), such as Al's computer and DVD-making device; and "records documenting the manufacture, sale, or receipt of things involved in any such violation," *id.* § 503(a)(1)(C), such as the records contained in Al's file cabinet.

(A), (B), and (C) **are incorrect** because they fail to account for all the materials a court may impound in a copyright infringement matter, for the reasons explained above.

316.   (B) **is the correct answer.** A plaintiff in a copyright infringement action is entitled to recover actual damages suffered as a result of the infringement as well as any of the defendant's profits that are attributable to the infringement. *See Frank Music Corp. v. Metro-Goldwyn-Mayer, Inc.,* 772 F.2d 505 (9th Cir. 1985). Thus, here, Composer would be entitled to any profits that Xplicit generated attributable to its use of *Happy Springtime*, as well as any revenue composer lost due to the boycott of that work.

(A) **is incorrect** because it does not take Composer's actual damages into account.

(C) **is incorrect** because it does not take Xplicit's profits into account.

(D) **is incorrect** because any plaintiff who proves infringement is entitled to nonstatutory damages, including actual damages and defendant's profits, if proven.

317.   No. The overwhelming majority of courts have held that punitive damages are not available in federal copyright infringement actions. *Oboler v. Goldin,* 714 F.2d 211 (2d Cir. 1983). *See also Budget Cinema, Inc. v. Watertower Associates,* 81 F.3d 729, 733 (7th Cir. 1996); *Viacom Int'l, Inc. v. YouTube, Inc.,* 540 F. Supp. 2d 461, 464 (S.D.N.Y. 2008); *Calio v. Sofa Express, Inc.,* 368 F. Supp. 2d 1290, 1291 (M.D. Fla. 2005). The lone exception is *TVT Records v. Island Def Jam Music Group,* 262 F. Supp. 2d 185, 186 (S.D.N.Y. 2003), which has been described as a "rogue decision" that runs counter to the overwhelming majority of contrary cases.

318.   (B) **is the correct answer.** The appropriate measure of damages is Betty's net profits (gross profits minus costs, or $50,000–$10,000=$40,000), though only to the extent that they are attributable to her infringement of Alice's work. 17 U.S.C. § 504(b) ("The copyright owner is entitled to recover the actual damages suffered by him or her as a result of the infringement, and any profits of the infringer *that are attributable to the infringement* and are not taken into account in computing the actual damages.") (emphasis added). Because half of the profits for Betty's wildlife guide were attributable to her unauthorized use of

Alice's work, half of those profits, $20,000, are the best measure of Alice's nonstatutory damages. *See id.* ("In establishing the infringer's profits, the copyright owner is required to present proof only of the infringer's gross revenue, and the infringer is required to prove his or her deductible expenses and the elements of profit attributable to factors other than the copyrighted work.").

(A), (C), and (D) are incorrect because they give the wrong measure of actual damages, for the reasons explained above.

319. **(D) is the correct answer.** Alice is required to prove not only the gross revenues resulting from the sales of Betty's wildlife guide, but also the gross revenues that are attributable to defendant's infringing activities. 17 U.S.C. § 504(b). *See Bouchat v. Baltimore Ravens Football Club, Inc.*, 346 F.3d 514, 524–26 (4th Cir. 2003) (plaintiff unable to recover any damages for infringing use of his logo design by professional football team because sales of tickets, sponsorships, broadcast rights, trading cards, video games and merchandise in the absence of proof that these profits were responsive to his logo design); *John G. Danielson, Inc. v. Winchester-Conant Properties, Inc.*, 322 F.3d 26, 47 (1st Cir. 2003).

Betty's failure to show how much she expended in making her wildlife guide means that she forfeits the opportunity to do so, *see Russell v. Price*, 612 F.2d 1123, 1130–01 (9th Cir. 1979) (holding that the gross revenue figure proven by the plaintiff stands as the profit factor if the defendant fails to prove deductible expenses), but Alice's failure to provide evidence that any of the gross revenues earned by the sale of the wildlife guide were due to her photographs precludes any award of nonstatutory damages.

(A), (B), and (C) are incorrect because they misstate the appropriate amount of actual damages.

320. This is a difficult question, the answer to which would depend on the jurisdiction in which the case was filed. On this variation of the question, Betty would be a willful infringer because she used Alice's photographs knowing of their protected status, and still made no effort to secure a license. Some circuits do not allow willful infringers to deduct overhead from their costs. *See Saxon v. Blann*, 968 F.2d 676, 681 (8th Cir. 1992) (willful infringers cannot deduct overhead); *Frank Music Corp. v. Metro-Goldwyn-Mayer, Inc.*, 772 F.2d 505 (9th Cir. 1985) (disallowing deduction of overhead expenses). Other circuits, however, do allow willful infringers to deduct expenses in this calculation. *See, e.g., Hamil Am., Inc. v. GFI*, 193 F.3d 92, 106–07 (2d Cir. 1999) (overhead expenses may be deducted, though subject to heightened scrutiny of proof of sufficient nexus and allocation formula).

Whether Betty's status as a willful infringer would affect the damages calculation thus varies circuit-by-circuit. The Second Circuit would allow her to reduce the gross profits by the amount of her overhead, resulting in a relatively lower award; while the Eighth and Ninth Circuits would not permit this, resulting in a relatively higher award.

321. **(C) is the correct answer.** Multiple recoveries are permitted for the violation of two distinct rights resulting from the same conduct, but only to the extent that two different types

of harm have been suffered. *See Nintendo v. Dragon Pacific Int'l*, 40 F.3d 1007 (9th Cir. 1994) (recovery for statutory damages under Copyright Act and additional award for trebled profits under Lanham Act permitted because the interests protected by copyright law are separate from the interests protected by trademark law); *Sparaco v. Lawler, Matusky, Skelly Engineers LLP*, 313 F. Supp. 2d 247, 250–51 (S.D.N.Y. 2004). By contrast, multiple damages are not permitted where the harm suffered as a result of each legal wrong is identical. *See Bowers v. Baystate Techs, Inc.*, 320 F.3d 1317, 1328 (Fed Cir. 2003) (no double recovery where breach of contract damages arose from same copying and lost sales that formed the basis for copyright damages); *Computer Associates Int'l v. Altai, Inc.*, 982 F.2d 693, 720 (2d Cir. 1992) (double recovery not permitted where damages for copyright infringement and trade secret misappropriation are coextensive).

Here, the injury that Ed claims to have suffered as a result of Vic's conduct, lost profits, is the same, even though there are two theories of legal wrongs: breach of contract and copyright infringement, that could frame this injury. As a result, Ed can only recover the actual damages he suffered—$50,000.

(A), (B), and (D) are incorrect for the reasons explained above.

322.   **(B) is the correct answer.** Typically, registration with the Copyright Office at the time of the infringement is a condition precedent to obtaining statutory damages. 17 U.S.C. § 412; *see Bouchat v. Baltimore Ravens Football Club, Inc.*, 346 F.3d 514, 517 n.2 (4th Cir. 2003). Registration within three months after the first publication of the work will satisfy the registration requirement even though the infringement commenced after the first publication, but before the registration. 17 U.S.C. § 412(2). So because Hy registered within three months of first publication, he can still seek statutory damages against Guy.

(A) is incorrect because registration certainly is a prerequisite for seeking statutory damages.

(C) is incorrect because the general rule that registration must precede infringement does not apply where, as here, registration is made within three months of publication.

(D) is incorrect because it is possible to obtain statutory damages for published as well as unpublished works. In addition, the script was published when Hy placed it on his personal website prior to Guy's infringement.

323.   **(D) is the correct answer.** Plaintiffs in copyright infringement suits may always seek money damages. If, as is the case here, the plaintiff is entitled to statutory damages, it is the plaintiff's election to receive either statutory or actual damages, not both. 17 U.S.C. § 504(c)(1); *see Hamil Am., Inc. v. GFI*, 193 F.3d 92, 103 (2d Cir. 1999); *Jordan v. Time, Inc.*, 111 F.3d 102 (11th Cir. 1997). This election can be made any time before final judgment, and so certainly does not need to be made in the initial complaint. 17 U.S.C. § 504(c)(1); *see Feltner v. Columbia Pictures Television, Inc.*, 523 U.S. 340, 347 n.5 (1998) ("election may occur even after a jury has returned a verdict on liability and an award of actual damages");

Business Trends Analysts v. Freedonia Group, Inc., 887 F.2d 399, 403–04 (2d Cir. 1989) (election may be made at any time before final judgment).

(A), (B), and (C) are incorrect for the reasons explained above.

324. **(B) is the correct answer.** Yancey's infringement was willful because he engaged in the conduct with actual knowledge that he was infringing a copyright. *See Peer Int'l Corp. v. Pausa Records, Inc.*, 909 F.2d 1332, 1335 n.3 (9th Cir. 1990) (infringement is "willful" if the actions of the defendant were taken "with knowledge that the defendant's conduct constitutes copyright infringement"). Courts have discretion to increase the statutory damages to $150,000 in the case of willful infringement. 17 U.S.C. § 504(c)(2). However, Zed is only entitled to one count of statutory damages because only one of his works was infringed; multiple acts of infringement of the same work by the same defendant do not merit multiple damage awards. *See Venegas-Hernandez v. Sonolux Records*, 370 F.3d 183, 194 (1st Cir. 2004); *Walt Disney Co. v. Powell*, 897 F.2d 565, 569 (D.C. Cir. 1990).

(A) is incorrect because statutory damages are calculated with respect to different works infringed, not by enumerating different acts of infringement with respect to the same work.

(C) is incorrect because a court may order willful infringement statutory damages of up to $150,000 per work infringed.

(D) is incorrect because even matters that lie within judicial discretion may be overturned on appeal where they constitute clear error or abuse of discretion.

325. The precise amount of damages is not certain because it lies within the judge's discretion, but the ultimate award will certainly be lower than in question IX-18. Yancey's conduct in this instance amounts to innocent infringement, where the defendant "was not aware and had no reason to believe that [its] acts constituted an infringement of copyright." 17 U.S.C. § 504(c)(2); *Los Angeles News Serv. v. Reuters Television Int'l, Ltd.*, 149 F.3d 987, 995 (9th Cir. 1998). The court has the discretion to reduce the minimum statutory damages award to $200 per work in the case of innocent infringement. 17 U.S.C. § 504(c)(2); *see Jobete Music Co., Inc. v. Johnson Comms., Inc.*, 285 F. Supp. 2d 1077, 1084 (S.D. Ohio 2003), but even if it chose not to do this, an award at the lower end of the statutory damage range ($750–$30,000) would be appropriate.

326. **(D) is the correct answer.** Statutory damages are calculated according to the number of works infringed, not the number of individual acts that infringed those works. *See Walt Disney Co. v. Powell*, 897 F.2d 565, 569 (D.C. Cir. 1990). Each episode of a television series is a separate work for purposes of statutory damages, particularly if each episode can stand on its own by telling an individual story and is separately registered. *See Columbia Pictures Television v. Krypton Broadcasting of Birmingham, Inc.*, 106 F.3d 284, 295 (9th Cir. 1997), *rev'd and remanded on other grounds*, 523 U.S. 340 (1998); *MCA Television Ltd. v. Feltner*, 89 F.3d 766 (11th Cir. 1996). Each separately liable infringer involved in the suit acts as a multiplier. *See Columbia Pictures Television v. Krypton Broadcasting, Inc.*, 106 F.3d 284, 294 (9th Cir. 1997) (each television station broadcasting unlicensed television program

held to be separate defendants for purposes of statutory damages), *rev'd and remanded on other grounds*, 523 U.S. 340 (1998).

In light of all this, there are three separate actors (each of the television stations) who have committed 12 separate acts of infringement (broadcasting each of the 12 episodes of the series), which means there are a total of 36 acts of infringement. The fact that the stations each re-broadcast the miniseries twice is irrelevant to this calculus. The relevant metric for determining statutory damages is works infringed, not individual acts of infringement.

(A), (B), and (C) are incorrect for the reasons explained above.

327.   Statutory damages in this case could possibly be as high as $5.4 million. The standard range for statutory damages is from $750 to $30,000 per work infringed, per infringing defendant. 17 U.S.C. § 504(c)(1). Here, however, the television stations broadcast the miniseries during the summer, knowing full well that their actions constituted infringement of Wall of Reality's copyrights. This likely makes their conduct willful infringement. *See Peer Int'l Corp. v. Pausa Records, Inc.*, 909 F.2d 1332, 1335 n.3 (9th Cir. 1990) (infringement is "willful" if the actions of the defendant were taken "with knowledge that the defendant's conduct constitutes copyright infringement"). In light of that, a judge could award damages as high as $5.4 million ($150,000 times 36 acts of infringement).

328.   **(A) is the correct answer.** Plaintiffs are entitled to multiple recoveries for the same conduct where that conduct inflicts different harms. Here, Mitch and Fred inflicted two separate kinds of harm on Tasty Cola. They violated Tasty Cola's exclusive rights to reproduce and to publicly display the Tasty Swoop, and they also diminished the consumer goodwill associated with the Tasty Cola brand. This is not considered a double recovery because the interests protected by the copyright law are separate from the interests protected by trademark law. *See Nintendo v. Dragon Pacific Int'l*, 40 F.3d 1007 (9th Cir. 1994) (permitting recovery on both copyright and trademark theories for the same conduct).

(B) is incorrect because plaintiffs are not entitled to recovery on any number of theories, but only theories that articulate different kinds of harm.

(C) is incorrect because the interests protected by copyright and trademark are quite different, for the reasons explained above.

(D) is incorrect because plaintiffs are not limited to only one theory of recovery in intellectual property cases.

329. $1 million. All defendants who engage in the same act of copyright infringement are jointly and severally liable for plaintiff's statutory damages. *See Fitzgerald Publ'g Co., Inc. v. Baylor Publ'g Co., Inc.*, 807 F.2d 1110, 1116 (2d Cir. 1986). Therefore, even though Fred is judgment-proof, Tasty Cola can still seek the full amount of the recovery from Mitch alone.

330.   **(C) is the correct answer.** The court has the discretion to allow the recovery of full costs by or against any party other than the United States or its officers. 17 U.S.C. § 505.

(A) is incorrect because, in this case, Norm cannot recover the costs of suit. However, expert witness fees are typically recoverable. Recoverable expenses include court fees, printing, photocopying, expert fees, interpreter costs, long-distance telephone calls, and parking. *See Invessys, Inc. v. McGraw-Hill Cos., Ltd*, 369 F.3d 16, 22 (1st Cir. 2004); *Brewer-Giorgio v. Bergman*, 985 F. Supp. 1478, 1485 (N.D. Ga. 1997).

(B) is incorrect because Norm cannot recover any of the fees associated with the suit from the U.S. government. He may, however, be able to recover costs and fees from De Marco Studios.

(D) is incorrect because prevailing parties in infringement actions are entitled to both expert witness fees and costs. 17 U.S.C. § 505.

331. (B) is the correct answer. Registration with the Copyright Office at the time of the commencement of infringement is a condition precedent to obtaining attorney's fees. 17 U.S.C. § 412. *See M.G.B. Homes, Inc. v. Ameron Homes, Inc.*, 903 F.2d 1486, 1493 (11th Cir. 1990). Moreover, infringement is commenced as of the first act of infringement, even though a series of separate infringements of the work by the defendant may later take place. *See Mason v. Montgomery Data, Inc.*, 967 F.2d 135, 143 (5th Cir. 1992). Therefore, because *Norm's Diner* was not registered at the time of the initial infringement, Jane forfeited the opportunity to recover attorney's fees.

(A) is incorrect because even though some acts of infringement took place after registration, the relevant measuring point is the *initial* infringement, and this took place prior to registration.

(C) is incorrect because registration within three months of the initial infringement does not necessarily enable recovery of attorney's fees. However, registration within three months after the first publication of the work will satisfy the registration requirement even though the infringement commenced after the first publication, but before the registration. 17 U.S.C. § 412(2).

(D) is incorrect because willful or malicious infringement is not a prerequisite for recovery of attorney's fees.

332. (C) is the correct answer. The court in its discretion may award reasonable attorney's fees to the prevailing party. 17 U.S.C. § 505; *Harrison Music Corp. v. Tesfaye*, 293 F. Supp. 2d 80, 84 (D.D.C. 2003). When determining whether to grant attorney's fees, courts in the Ninth Circuit consider five "*Fogerty* factors." *See Fogerty v. Fantasy Inc.*, 510 U.S. 517 (1994) (enumerating these factors); *Jackson v. Axton*, 25 F.3d 884, 890 (9th Cir. 1994) (applying these factors). These factors include the degree of success obtained; frivolousness; motivation; objective reasonableness; and considerations of deterrence and compensation. A court's consideration of attorney's fees is not limited to the five factors. *Smith v. Jackson*, 84 F.3d 1213, 1221 (9th Cir. 1996).

Here, four of the factors strongly weigh in favor of granting attorney's fees to Henderson. Jackson's suit was largely frivolous and lacked legal foundation, as the court explained when issuing its judgment. Henderson's success was complete because the award of summary judgment in his favor was not equivocal. Deterrence considerations weigh in favor of awarding attorney's fees to Henderson as well, because it will send a message to plaintiffs in Jackson's situation that they should not confuse copyright infringement with negative criticism.

(A) is incorrect because while motivation is one of the *Fogerty* factors, an innocent state of mind does not categorically preclude an award of attorney's fees.

(B) is incorrect because merely showing that there is a nonzero chance of prevailing in an infringement suit does not preclude a finding of attorney's fees.

(D) is incorrect because in the Ninth Circuit, prevailing parties in copyright infringement suits are not entitled to attorney's fees as a matter of course. By contrast, courts in some other circuits have held that an award of attorney's fees in copyright cases is the rule, rather than the exception, and should be awarded routinely. *See, e.g., Eagle Servs. Corp. v. H2O Indus. Servs., Inc.*, 532 F.3d 620, 625 (7th Cir. 2008) (defendants in copyright infringement cases have a very strong presumptive entitlement to an award of attorney's fees); *Compaq Computer Corp. v. Ergonome Inc.*, 387 F.3d 403, 411 (5th Cir. 2004) (affirming award of $2.7 million against corporation and one of its principals).

333.   No. The Supreme Court has rejected any dual standard that treats prevailing plaintiffs differently than prevailing defendants under § 505. *See Fogerty v. Fantasy, Inc.*, 510 U.S. 517 (1994). Courts thus cannot treat prevailing defendants categorically differently than they treat prevailing plaintiffs when considering a fee award.

334.   **(A) is the correct answer.** Courts have wide discretion to award attorney's fees, 17 U.S.C. § 505, but the award must be reasonable, *see Moorish Vanguard Concert v. Brown*, 498 F. Supp. 830 (E.D. Pa. 1980). The "reasonable" fees are based on a lodestar figure represented by the reasonable hourly rate multiplied by the hours expended in the litigation, but the court retains discretion to adjust this figure. *See Crescent Publ'g Group, Inc. v. Playboy Enters., Inc.*, 246 F.3d 142, 150 (2d Cir. 2001).

When considering adjustment of the lodestar figure, excessive, redundant, or unnecessary hours should be excluded. *See Harrison Music Corp. v. Tesfaye*, 293 F. Supp. 2d 80, 85 (D.D.C. 2003) (number of requested attorney hours deemed excessive for straightforward case where plaintiffs admitted liability); *Queenie, Ltd. v. Nygard Int'l*, 204 F. Supp. 2d 601, 609 (S.D.N.Y. 2002) (court found it unreasonable to shift more than 50 percent of pre-trial attorney's fees to plaintiff in light of straightforward factual issues and absence of novel legal issues or case dispositive motions).

Here, the court was acting well within its discretion to reduce the fee amounts submitted by Bram & Gower, particularly because the hours the firm submitted were viewed as excessive.

(B) is incorrect because a court's discretion to award fees is not absolute, but is constrained by reasonableness.

(C) is incorrect because a court should use the lodestar amount as a starting point when considering a fee award, but is not absolutely constrained by that amount.

(D) is incorrect because a court is free to exercise its discretion to reduce fee awards regardless of whether a motion has been filed by the non-prevailing party.

335.   **(D) is the correct answer.** A prevailing plaintiff is entitled to recover its actual damages and the profits attributable to the infringement. *See* 17 U.S.C. § 501(b). Therefore, West Company is entitled to its actual damages of $25,000, which are not speculative because it has sold to this retailer for a long time. West Company is also entitled to the $60,000 in profits of East Company attributable to its infringing activity. Because the two companies market their goods to different retailers, the defendant's sales are not to be taken into account when establishing plaintiff's actual damages. West Company is entitled to $85,000, the sum of the $25,000 in actual damages and the $60,000 in profits.

(A) is incorrect because it does not include the profits of the defendant attributable to its infringement.

(B) is incorrect because the lost sales of West Company and the profits from sales made by East Company are not the same sales made to the same retailer.

(C) is incorrect because it does not include the lost sales suffered by West Company.

336.   West Company remains entitled to its actual damages, which consist of its lost profits of $25,000, and to the $60,000 in profits attributable to the infringing activities of East Company. These profits were derived from the sale of dresses on the East Coast and have no effect on the actual damages of West Company. As for the $20,000 profit from East Company's sale to the consumer, that profit was derived from the same sale that West Company had lost. Therefore, East Company's profit from that sale cannot be taken into account. To do so would count the profit from the consumer sale twice. Such double-counting is not permitted. As a result, the amount of damages to which West Company is entitled remains $85,000, even in light of this new fact.

337.   **(D) is the correct answer.** The Supreme Court recently held in *Kirtsaeng v. John Wiley & Sons, Inc.*, No. 15-375 (U.S. June 16, 2016) that federal courts are permitted to place "substantial weight" on the objective reasonableness factor within the *Fogerty* analysis, so long as "all other relevant factors" are taken into account. This is clearly a case where a losing party made an objectively reasonable argument. Flower had no idea that the author had executed a preexisting license to publish with Gremlin, but had been lied to by the author, who wrongfully lied about the existence of the earlier license. In light of this, it was entirely reasonable for Flower to sue Gremlin for infringement, since they had no reason to believe that Gremlin's publication of *Yesterday* was authorized. In light of this, the objective reasonableness factor within the *Fogerty* analysis clearly favors denial of Gremlin's motion for attorney's fees. And in light of *Kirtsaeng*, the district court did not err by placing substantial weight on this factor, and thus did not commit reversible error.

(A) **is incorrect** because in crafting the *Fogerty* factors, the Court held just the opposite, stressing that they are "nonexclusive" factors that "may be used to guide courts' discretion" in deciding whether to award attorney's fees, "so long as such factors are faithful to the purposes of the Copyright Act and are applied to prevailing plaintiffs and defendants in an evenhanded manner." *Fogerty v. Fantasy Records, Inc.*, 510 U.S. 517, 534 n.19 (1994).

(B) **is incorrect** because Flower's infringement suit was clearly reasonable and in good faith, for the reasons explained above.

(C) **is incorrect** because the *Kirtsaeng* court held that there are no dispositive factors within the *Fogerty* analysis, but rather all are "relevant factors" courts must consider.

338.   (D) **is the correct answer.** Prevailing plaintiffs seeking actual damages in copyright infringement cases must prove that they have suffered economic harm as a result of the infringement. This could take the form of lost sales, which are not relevant here since Jones is not currently seeking to sell copies of his works. This could also take the form of lost licensing fees, but this requires the plaintiff to prove via objective evidence that the plaintiff would have been able to charge such a fee. *On Davis v. The Gap, Inc.*, 246 F.3d 152, 166 (2d Cir. 2001) ("In order to make out his claim that he suffered actual damage because of the infringer's failure to pay the fee, the owner must show that the thing taken had a fair market value.").

Here, Jones cannot prove via objective evidence that Dempsey's unauthorized uses cost him a licensing fee. Jones' own assertions that "Better" was a major hit and that he would have charged a high fee amount only to his own subjective assertions rather than objective evidence. Jones' expert's testimony only shows that some works fetch high licensing fees for "hype reel" uses; this does not mean that Jones' work would have fetched such a fee. Moreover, Dempsey's uncontested evidence that Jones' tracks have no current market value, and that Dempsey would have declined to use them had Jones sought a fee both prove that Jones did not actually lose any money. Because he has suffered no economic harm, then, Jones cannot recover any actual damages.

(A), (B), and (C) **are incorrect** for the reasons explained above.

339.   (A) **is the correct answer.** Copyright defendants are jointly and severally liable if they are held liable for the same act of infringement, *Fitzgerald Publ'g Co., Inc. v. Baylor Publ'g Co., Inc.*, 807 F.2d 1110, 1116 (2d Cir. 1986), so Hester is entitled to recover any and all of the judgment from either Wilma or Repro. And regardless of the veracity of Wilma's claims that she was unaware of the infringement, as CEO of Repro, she is constructively on notice of their misconduct. Corporate officers may be held liable for infringement by their companies regardless of their actual knowledge. "[T]he right and ability to supervise coalesce with an obvious and direct financial interest in the exploitation of copyrighted materials — even in the absence of actual knowledge that the copyright monopoly is being impaired — the purposes of copyright law may be best effectuated by the imposition of liability upon the beneficiary of that exploitation." *Shapiro, Bernstein & Co. v. H. L. Green Co.*, 316 F.2d

304, 307 (2d Cir. 1963); *see also Star Pacific Corp. v. Star Atlantic Corp.*, 574 Fed. App'x 225 (3d Cir. 2014) (holding corporate officer liable for infringement by corporation regardless of his subjective knowledge of infringing conduct).

(B) is incorrect because it appears to assume that Hester's statutory damages are to be equally apportioned between Wilma and Repro, when in fact they are jointly and severally liable.

(C) is incorrect because Wilma's position as CEO of Repro makes her constructively knowledgeable of the corporation's infringement, as explained above. Moreover, the innocent infringer defense is unavailable in cases where the copyright owner has included valid copyright notices on her work. 17 U.S.C. § 401(b)(3).

(D) is incorrect because, for the reasons given above, Wilma will bear substantial liability.

340. **(C) is the correct answer.** "The court has wide discretion in determining the amount of statutory damages to be awarded, constrained only by the specified maxima and minima." 17 U.S.C. § 504(c)(1) (permitting awards of statutory damages, per act of infringement, in "a sum of not less than $750 or more than $30,000 as the court considers just"); *Peer Int'l Corp. v. Pausa Records, Inc.*, 909 F.2d 1332, 1336 (9th Cir. 1990). Courts also have broad discretion in fashioning attorney's fee awards. 17 U.S.C. § 505; *Harrison Music Corp. v. Tesfaye*, 293 F. Supp. 2d 80, 84 (D.D.C. 2003). This discretion enables courts to award lower amounts of statutory damages and attorney's fees than prevailing plaintiffs may seek, so long as they give some indication for why they are exercising their discretion to do so.

Here, the court reasonably pointed out that because the infringement was relatively minor, an award in the seven figures seemed excessive, so it accordingly reduced the statutory damages and attorney's fees to more plausibly reflect the economic scale of the case. Such a decision clearly lies within the court's statutorily granted discretion. *See, e.g., Teller v. Dogge*, 2014 WL 4929413, *4, *7 (Sept. 30, 2014) (reducing award of statutory damages from $150,000 sought by prevailing plaintiff to $30,000, and reducing award of attorney's fees from $989,568.60 sought by prevailing plaintiff to $500,000).

(A), (B), and (D) are incorrect for reasons explained above.

341. No. Courts have wide discretion, per statute, to determine both statutory damages and attorney's fees. 17 U.S.C. §§ 504(c)(1), 505. The Copyright Act specifies no required ratio between damages and attorney's fees. Courts have routinely demonstrated no compunction about awarding attorney's fees that far exceed statutory or actual damages in a case. *See, e.g., Princeton Univ. Press v. Michigan Doc. Servs., Inc.*, 869 F. Supp. 521, 523–24 (E.D. Mich. 1994) (awarding plaintiff $326,318.52 in attorney's fees and costs on a statutory damages award of $30,000); *Branch v. Ogilvy & Mather, Inc.*, 772 F. Supp. 1359 (S.D.N.Y. 1991) (awarding plaintiff $116,700 in attorney's fees on a damages award of $10,001); *Landsberg v. Scrabble Crossword Game Players, Inc.*, 212 U.S.P.Q. 159 (C.D. Cal. 1980) (awarding plaintiff $233,026.27 in attorney's fees on lost profits award of $87,086.47);

Teller v. Dogge, 2014 WL 4929413, *4, *7 (Sept. 30, 2014) (awarding plaintiffs $500,000 in attorney's fees on statutory damages award of $30,000). As one court has noted, "[a]lthough the statutory damages awarded are significantly less than the attorney fees sought, the court notes the success achieved is more than the financial gain and that the recovery of fees is necessary to protect copyright law and to encourage the litigation of meritorious infringement claims." *Princeton Univ. Press*, 869 F. Supp. at 523–24.

Enhanced Protection for Digital Materials

342.   **(D) is the correct answer** because it correctly describes in general terms both the copyright-protective and liability-limiting aspects of the DMCA.

   (A) is incorrect because the DMCA did not create any new exclusive rights of copyright owners. It created, inter alia, "paracopyright" provisions that protect but do not expand copyright owners' exclusive rights in their works.

   (B) is incorrect because it describes only the liability-limiting provisions of the DMCA, *see generally* 17 U.S.C. § 512, without acknowledging its anti-circumvention, anti-trafficking, and copyright management information provisions, *see generally* 17 U.S.C. §§ 1201–03.

   (C) is incorrect because it describes only the anti-circumvention, anti-trafficking, and copyright management information provisions of the DMCA, *see generally* 17 U.S.C. §§ 1201–03, without acknowledging its liability-limiting provisions, *see generally* 17 U.S.C. § 512.

343.   **(A) is the correct answer.** section 1201 of the DMCA prohibits the act of circumvention of a technological measure, such as scrambling, encryption or password protection, put in place by a copyright owner to effectively control access to a copyrighted work, without the authority of the copyright owner. 17 U.S.C. § 1201(a)(1); *see Chamberlain Group, Inc. v. Sky-link Technologies, Inc.*, 381 F.3d 1178, 1203 (Fed. Cir. 2004). Thus Jane would be liable to the extent that she used the program to circumvent the access-control measures (i.e., the password protections) that George put in place.

   This section of the DMCA also prohibits the manufacture and distribution of products and services used to defeat a technological measure that effectively controls access to a work protected by copyright. 17 U.S.C. § 1201(a)(2); *see Universal City Studios, Inc. v. Corley*, 273 F.3d 429 (2d Cir. 2001) (posting of decryption software on website and linking to other sites posting decryption software is actionable). Thus, although Harriet herself did not use the program to circumvent the access-control measures protecting funfish.com, she can be held liable for distributing the program to others and enabling them to do so. Jane would also be found liable for her creation and distribution of the software program.

   (B), (C), and (D) are incorrect because they wrongly state the parties who can be held liable under DMCA section 1201.

344.   No. It is true that section 1201 of the DMCA applies only to technology protection measures that "effectively control access" to digital material, *see* 17 U.S.C. § 1201(a), and some

defendants have argued that if an access-control device is weak or facile, it does not "effectively" control access to the protected digital material. *See, e.g., RealNetworks, Inc. v. Streambox, Inc.*, 2000 U.S. Dist. LEXIS 1889 (W.D. Wash. 2000). Courts have rejected this argument, however, and in so doing have developed a broad definition of what it means to "effectively control access" to digital material. A technological measure effectively controls access to a work if the measure, in the ordinary course of its operation, requires the application of information, or a process or a treatment, with the authority of the copyright owner, to gain access to the work. *Id.* § 1201(a)(3)(B); *see 321 Studios v. Metro Goldwyn Mayer Studios, Inc.*, 307 F. Supp. 2d 1085, 1094 (N.D. Cal. 2004).

In light of this broad definition, a court would regard it as immaterial that programmers would regard George's access control efforts as technically poor. The password-protection would ordinarily have required entry of information provided by George in order to permit access, and this is all courts require in order to find that a technology protection measure "effectively" controls access to the underlying material.

345.   **(C) is the correct answer.** Section 1201 of the DMCA prohibits the manufacture and distribution of products and services used to defeat technological measures that impose limitations on the use of a copyrighted work. 17 U.S.C. § 1201(b); *see 321 Studios v. Metro Goldwyn Mayer Studios, Inc.*, 307 F. Supp. 2d 1085, 1094 (N.D. Cal. 2004) (DVD content encryption is a copy control system to which section 1201(b)(1) applies); *United States v. Elcom Ltd.*, 203 F. Supp. 2d 1111, 1120 (N.D. Cal. 2002) (developer and marketer of software program that allowed users to remove use restrictions on ebook files, thereby making the e-book file copyable, printable and easily distributed electronically without the permission of the copyright owner, violated section 1201(b)).

Congress did not, however, ban the act of circumventing use restrictions, only the trafficking in and marketing of devices used to circumvent use restrictions. *See United States v. Elcom Ltd.*, 203 F. Supp. 2d 1111, 1120–21 (N.D. Cal. 2002) ("circumventing use restrictions is not unlawful").

Warren cannot be held liable because the law does not create liability for the use of the device. By contrast, Lloyd can be held liable for his conduct, because even though he did not create or use dePSS, he did make it available to others, which amounts to the kind of trafficking rendered unlawful by section 1201 of the DMCA.

(A), (B), and (D) are incorrect because they wrongly state the parties who can be held liable under section 1201 of the DMCA.

346.   No. It is not a defense to a violation of the anti-trafficking provisions of section 1201(b) that the defendant used the copyrighted material legally. *See 321 Studios v. Metro Goldwyn Mayer Studios, Inc.*, 307 F. Supp. 2d 1085, 1097–98 (N.D. Cal. 2004). And while the statutory text does state that remedies, limitations, or defenses to copyright infringement, including fair use, are not to be affected by the DMCA, 17 U.S.C. § 1201(c)(1), this means merely that Lloyd would still have a fair use defense were Greta also to seek liability on a

copyright infringement theory of liability. It does not absolve Lloyd for any DMCA theories of liability.

347.   **(D) is the correct answer.** Section 1201 of the DMCA permits the circumvention of a technological measure in furtherance of good faith encryption research. *See* 17 U.S.C. § 1201(g). Here, Vanna's work was clearly in bad faith because she decrypted ContentKey not in a sincere attempt to discover security flaws in DynaCorp's software, but rather to inflict harm on DynaCorp, one of many corporations she dislikes. Moreover, Vanna took no steps to notify DynaCorp about the results of her research, *see Universal City Studios, Inc. v. Reimerdes*, 111 F. Supp. 2d 294, 321 (S.D.N.Y. 2000), *aff'd sub nom. Universal City Studios, Inc. v. Corley*, 273 F.3d 429 (2d Cir. 2001) (Internet posting of software used to decrypt DVD encryption technology deemed evidence of absence of good faith encryption research), and did not disseminate it in a manner likely to result in advancing the state of encryption research generally (i.e., in a research journal or a credible website as opposed to her personal website).

(A) **is incorrect** because encryption research can be in good faith regardless of whether it is undertaken for profit.

(B) **is incorrect** because, while section 1201 of the DMCA protects encryption research, it does so only for good-faith encryption research, and Vanna's work does not fall into that category for the reasons explained above.

(C) **is incorrect** because there are various research safe harbors under section 1201 of the DMCA, including but not limited to the encryption one discussed above.

348.   **(A) is the correct answer.** Section 1202 of the DMCA prohibits the provision or distribution of false copyright management information ("CMI"), 17 U.S.C. § 1202(a), and the removal or alteration of CMI, *id.* § 1202(b). "Copyright Management Information" includes information that identifies a copyrighted work, its author, its copyright owner, its creator, as well as terms and conditions for use of the work. *Id.* § 1202(c).

Here, the notice that Sculptor placed on *Step* is clearly CMI because it identifies that the work is copyrighted as well as the terms and conditions for the use of the work, and Collector has violated section 1202 of the DMCA by removing the label.

(B) **is incorrect** because violating the licensing agreement may give rise to a cause of action on a breach of contract or copyright infringement theory, but does not implicate section 1202 of the DMCA.

(C) **is incorrect** because nothing in section 1202 of the DMCA indicates that they are limited to digital material only.

(D) **is incorrect** because CMI need not identify the author, but can include information about the author of the work, the owner of the work, the creator of the work, or terms and conditions of its use. *Id.* CMI need only list one of these features, not all of them.

349.   Section 1202 of the DMCA requires that in order to be actionable, any removal or alteration of CMI must be intentional. 17 U.S.C. § 1202. Because Collector's eradication of the label in this question was a mere inadvertent by-product of cleaning the statue, Sculptor cannot recover against Collector on a DMCA section 1202 theory. This does not mean that Sculptor is entirely out of luck, of course. Collector's conduct was still wrongful because it violated the terms of the license, and so Sculptor may have a valid breach of contract cause of action, as well as a copyright infringement claim for the unauthorized public distribution of "Step."

350.   **(C) is the correct answer.** Courts have broad discretion to impose a variety of penalties when a defendant is found to have violated sections 1201 or 1202 of the DMCA. These include injunctive relief, 17 U.S.C. § 1203(b); actual or statutory damages, *id.* § 1203(c); court costs and attorney's fees, *id.* § 1203(b); and criminal fines and imprisonment, *id.* § 1204(a).

   (A) is incorrect because it fails to include any of the criminal penalties available for violations of sections 1201 and 1202.

   (B) is incorrect because it includes punitive damages, which are not available for violations of sections 1201 and 1202.

   (D) is incorrect because it does not include imprisonment, which is available for violations of sections 1201 and 1202.

351.   **(D) is the correct answer.** In cases of repeated violations of sections 1201 or 1202 of the DMCA, courts have the discretion, but are not required, to increase the damages award up to three times. 17 U.S.C. § 1203(c)(3). In cases of innocent violations of those sections, courts may, but are not required to, reduce or remit the total award of damages. *Id.* § 1203(c)(5).

   (A), (B), and (C) are incorrect for the reasons explained above.

352.   **(A) is the correct answer.** Fair use is a defense to copyright infringement, 17 U.S.C. § 107, but not DMCA liability. Here, Christa's claim against Eber is based only on the DMCA, alleging that Eber's accessing her film constitutes an unlawful circumvention of a technological measure put in place by a copyright owner to effectively control access to a copyrighted work. Eber's invocation of fair use is thus irrelevant. *See Universal City Studios, Inc. v. Corley*, 273 F.3d 429, 459 (2d Cir. 2001) (rejecting applicability of fair use defense to DMCA actions).

   (B) is incorrect because while bad-faith behavior like hacking might make a court less disposed to find that a use is fair, it does not categorically preclude a finding of fair use.

   (C) is incorrect because fair use is actually less available where authors have not yet published their works of authorship. *See* 17 U.S.C. § 107(3); *Harper & Row, Publishers, Inc. v. Nation Enterprises*, 471 U.S. 539, 554 (1985) ("The unpublished nature of a work is a key, though not necessarily determinative, factor tending to negate a defense of fair use.").

(D) is incorrect because courts have never held that fair use gives users an unlimited right of access, for the reasons explained above.

353.   Your client can rest easy tonight. Lexi has not violated any copyrights because she has not made any unauthorized copies or displays of the e-books. In terms of possible DMCA liability, the only plausibly relevant provisions are the anti-circumvention provisions. *See generally* 17 U.S.C. § 1201–03. Lexi, however, has not manufactured or distributed the *Free Gutenberg* program, nor has she used the program to gain access to e-book files, because she has paid the rental fee for each. Therefore, Lexi has not violated 17 U.S.C. § 1201(a). Lexi has, though, used the *Free Gutenberg* program to manipulate the use limitations set in place by the technological measures installed by eBooksOnline.com. But still, because Lexi has not manufactured or distributed the *Free Gutenberg* program, she has not violated 17 U.S.C. § 1201(b). Lexi's use of the *Free Gutenberg* program to gain greater use of a file to which she already has access is not unlawful.

354.   **(D) is the correct answer.** Circumvention of a technological measure that effectively controls access to a work is prohibited only when that work is protected by copyright. 17 U.S.C. § 1201(a). All of the works that are protected by Maxwell's encryption are no longer protected by copyright. Therefore, the anti-circumvention protections of section 1201 do not apply.

    (A) is incorrect because making a good faith effort to license a work does not absolve a defendant of DMCA liability.

    (B) is incorrect because the owner of a copy of a work has the right not to grant access to that work, even if the work has entered the public domain.

    (C) is incorrect because, unless it is expressly permitted by the exceptions listed in section 1201, the mere fact that the unauthorized use of an accessed work benefits the public does not excuse the circumvention of a technological measure that made that access possible.

355.   **(D) is the correct answer.** FotoLand has represented that it, not Ken, is the author of the photo, which is clearly false. The author of a work is the person or entity in whom the copyright initially vests. 17 U.S.C. § 201(a) ("Copyright in a work protected under this title vests initially in the author or authors of the work."). And FotoLand made this false representation knowingly because it knew that Ken originally took the Ford photograph. But section 1202(a) requires that a misrepresentation of copyright management information be not only knowing (which this one is, since FotoLand is fully aware that Ken, not it, was the author of the Ford photograph), but also done "with the intent to induce, enable, facilitate, or conceal infringement." 17 U.S.C. § 1202(a). Here, FotoLand was not engaging in any copyright infringement because they were selling valid licenses of a photograph to which they owned a valid copyright. So their misrepresentation of the authorship of the Ford photograph does not violate the DMCA's provisions against the falsification of copyright management information.

(A) is incorrect because FotoLand has not misrepresented the copyright ownership information of the Ford photo. Ken validly assigned "all right, title and interest" in the work to FotoLand in 2000, thus making FotoLand the copyright owner.

(B) is incorrect because while FotoLand did knowingly misrepresent the authorship of the Ford photograph, they did not do so "with the intent to induce, enable, facilitate, or conceal infringement," which is a required element of this cause of action. 17 U.S.C. § 1202(a).

(C) is incorrect because authorship is not assignable. The author of a work is the person or entity in whom the copyright initially vests. 17 U.S.C. § 201(a) ("Copyright in a work protected under this title vests initially in the author or authors of the work."). Authorship is thus a fact about a work that is fixed at the moment the work vests, and cannot be transferred by contract or changed by any means.

356.   Possibly. On these facts, Ken can again easily show two of the three elements of a DMCA section 1202(a) cause of action. As explained in XI-14, *supra*, FotoLand clearly misrepresented the authorship of the work by stating that it, not Ken, was the author of the Ford photograph. In addition, if FotoLand had not taken a valid assignment of the work, its assertion that it was the copyright owner of the photograph would amount to an additional basis for showing a violation of section 1202(a). 17 U.S.C. § 1202(c)(3) ("The name of, and other identifying information about, the copyright owner of the work, including the information set forth in a notice of copyright."). Moreover, FotoLand is entirely aware both that they did not take the Ford photograph (and hence that they are not its author) and that they did not validly acquire a copyright in the photograph (and hence that they are not its owner). These facts mean that FotoLand clearly misrepresented the work's copyright management information, and that they did so knowingly.

It is a harder question, though, whether FotoLand knowingly misrepresented these facts about the work "with the intent to induce, enable, facilitate, or conceal infringement," which is required to state a cause of action for falsification of copyright management information. That FotoLand represented itself as the author and owner of the work is some evidence that they were seeking to conceal its actual authorship and ownership to avoid any inquiries about the validity of their offer to license it. But without more than just the misrepresentation, Ken may not have enough evidence to meet the intent element of section 1202(a).

357.   (C) is the correct answer. After a user files a counter-notification stating her good-faith belief that the material was wrongly taken down, the service provider must notify the copyright owner of the counter-notification. The service provider must then place the material back online within 10 days of its receipt of the counter-notification unless the owner gives the service provider notice within that time frame that it has filed a complaint for copyright infringement. 17 U.S.C. § 512(g)(2) (requiring service providers to give notice to owners upon receipt of counter-notification that they "*will replace* the removed material or cease disabling access to it in 10 business days") (emphasis added).

(A), (B), and (D) are incorrect because they misstate the requirements of the DMCA, as explained above.

358.   Yes. The DMCA requires that copyright owners have "a good faith belief that use of the material in the manner complained of is not authorized by the copyright owner, its agent, or the law." 17 U.S.C. § (c)(3)(A)(v). Courts have held that this language requires owners to consider the possibility that an unauthorized use may be fair use before issuing a DMCA takedown notice. *Lenz v. Universal Music Corp.*, 801 F.3d 1126, 1138 (9th Cir. 2015) ("Copyright holders cannot shirk their duty to consider—in good faith and prior to sending a takedown notification—whether allegedly infringing material constitutes fair use, a use which the DMCA plainly contemplates as authorized by the law."). Flenderson's failure to even consider fair use before issuing the takedown notice clearly runs afoul of their obligations under the DMCA to consider this issue in good faith.

359.   **(D) is the correct answer.** Knowledge of infringing conduct by users can indeed disqualify a service provider from taking advantage of the DMCA safe harbor, but the statute requires either actual knowledge of specific acts of infringement or awareness "of facts or circumstances from which infringing activity is apparent." 17 U.S.C. § 512(c)(1)(A)(ii). The former is clearly not present here because KommUnity was not aware of specific acts of infringement, but only a general practice of unauthorized use by its users. TelCo may argue that KommUnity's awareness of this general practice amounts to the latter, which has become known as "red flag" knowledge. Yet courts have repeatedly rejected this argument, holding that red flag knowledge requires awareness of "facts or circumstances" related to specific acts of infringement, not just general consciousness of infringing activity. *See Viacom Int'l, Inc. v. YouTube, Inc.*, 676 F.3d 19, 32 (2d Cir. 2012) (holding that only "actual knowledge or awareness of facts or circumstances that indicate *specific and identifiable instances of infringement* will disqualify a service provider from the safe harbor") (emphasis added); *accord UMG Recordings, Inc. v. Shelter Capital Partners LLC*, 667 F.3d 1022, 1037 (9th Cir. 2011).

(A) is incorrect because that language appears nowhere in the DMCA.

(B) is incorrect because courts have held just the opposite: that general knowledge of infringing activity by users does *not* meet the knowledge standard sufficient to disqualify a service provider from taking advantage of the DMCA safe harbors. *See, e.g., Viacom Int'l*, 676 F.3d at 32.

(C) is incorrect because either actual or red flag knowledge of infringing conduct would disqualify a service provider from taking advantage of the DMCA safe harbors. *See* 17 U.S.C. § 512(c)(1)(A)(i)–(ii).

360.   **(B) is the correct answer.** The DMCA clearly indicates that it does not oblige service providers to actively monitor infringement by users in order to take advantage of the safe harbor. 17 U.S.C. § 512(m) ("Nothing in this section shall be construed to condition the applicability of [the safe harbor] on . . . a service provider monitoring its service or affirmatively seeking facts indicating infringing activity."); *see Viacom Int'l v. YouTube, Inc.*,

676 F.3d 19, 35 (2d Cir. 2012) ("Section 512(m) is explicit: DMCA safe harbor protection cannot be conditioned on affirmative monitoring by a service provider."). And while litigants have raised the argument that failure to implement basic safeguards against copyright infringement by users can amount to willful blindness sufficient to give service providers knowledge of infringing activity, courts have consistently rejected this claim as inconsistent with section 512(m). *See id.* at 35 ("[W]illful blindness cannot be defined as an affirmative duty to monitor.").

(A) is incorrect because courts have stressed that willful blindness may constitute a form of knowledge sufficient to remove the safe harbor protection of the DMCA. *See UMG Recordings, Inc. v. Shelter Capital Partners, LLC*, 718 F.3d 1006, 1023 (9th Cir. 2013) ("Of course, a service provider cannot willfully bury its head in the sand to avoid obtaining such specific knowledge."). Courts have held that the common-law theory of willful blindness is limited but not entirely abrogated by DMCA section 512(m), so that parties may invoke willful blindness but not in ways that undermine the statutory provision against monitoring obligations. *Viacom Int'l v. YouTube, Inc.*, 676 F.3d 19, 35 (2d Cir. 2012) ("Because the statute does not 'speak[ ] directly' to the willful blindness doctrine, § 512(m) limits — but does not abrogate — the doctrine. Accordingly, we hold that the willful blindness doctrine may be applied, in appropriate circumstances, to demonstrate knowledge or awareness of specific instances of infringement under the DMCA.").

(C) and (D) are incorrect because they misstate the legal principle discussed above that a service provider's failure to monitor copyright infringement by its users, standing alone, cannot suffice to show knowledge sufficient to disqualify service providers from taking advantage of the DMCA safe harbor.

361.   Yes, because these facts still do not show that KommUnity had the "right and ability to control" specific instances of infringement as required by the statute. As with the actual and red flag knowledge provisions of the DMCA, the "'right and ability to control' under § 512(c) requires control over specific infringing activity the provider knows about. A service provider's general right and ability to remove materials from its services is, alone, insufficient." *UMG Recordings, Inc. v. Shelter Capital Partners LLC*, 667 F.3d 1022, 1043 (9th Cir. 2011); *see also UMG Recordings, Inc. v. Shelter Capital Partners LLC*, 718 F.3d 1006, 1027–28 (9th Cir. 2013). Here, the mere fact that KommUnity had the ability to cut off users' access for violating the terms of use — which is true of nearly all social media websites — does not suffice to meet this standard, since KommUnity did not have knowledge of the specific instances of infringing activity of which TelCo complained.

Practice Final Exam Answers

Multiple-Choice Answers

362.   (C) is the correct answer. *Gorgon's Delight* is a pictorial work that was fixed in a tangible medium of expression: the skin on Carlos' back. That this "copy" is unusual does not mean that it is not a copy. Copies are "material objects, other than phonorecords, in which a work is fixed and from which the work can be perceived, reproduced, or otherwise communicated, either directly or with the aid of a machine." 17 U.S.C. § 101. Carlos' back meets all of these criteria.

The fixation requirement demands only that the work persist in the medium for more than a transitory duration, and most tattoos last for the duration of their recipient's life. Hence the adage: "Love lasts forever, but a tattoo lasts six months longer." In this case, of course, that did not happen; rather, Carlos (and his body) ceased to exist shortly after the fixation of *Gorgon's Delight*. That this particular medium of expression happened to disintegrate quickly, though, does not mean that at the time of fixation it was not tangible. A poem written in ink on paper is clearly sufficiently fixed in order for copyright to vest, even if its author burns the paper seconds after completing the poem. *See Peter Pan Fabrics, Inc. v. Rosstex Fabrics, Inc.*, 733 F. Supp. 174, 177 (S.D.N.Y. 1990) ("Once a work is fixed, its subsequent destruction does not vitiate its copyright.").

(A) is incorrect because *Gorgon's Delight* was fixed, and in a tangible medium of expression: Carlos' back.

(B) is incorrect because the length of fixation in a tangible medium of expression is not relevant to whether the initial fixation was in a tangible medium of expression.

(D) is incorrect because courts have not held that tattoos are objectionable as a matter of public policy. Some commentators have suggested this public policy objection, but courts have rejected such points as "silly," and the consensus of scholarship on this issue embraces the conclusion that tattoos fixed on human skin are validly copyrighted. *See* Aaron Perzanowski, *Tattoos & IP Norms*, 98 Minn. L. Rev. 511, 527–30 (2012) (reviewing authorities on this point and dismissing objections to fixation of tattoos).

363.   (D) is the correct answer. Gene's plot treatment is likely an uncopyrightable *scène à faire*, because it is nothing more than a collection of familiar plot clichés. *See, e.g., Nelson v. Grisham*, 942 F. Supp. 649, 653 (D.D.C. 1996) (holding that the author's use of media, politicians, jail house personnel, and frenzied last-minute appeals in novel *The Chamber*, "are all stock events and scenes that are expected in any book about the representation of a death row inmate"). In addition, the Jack character in *Seeing the Light* is insufficiently developed in the

plot treatment to merit copyright protection. The drunk, abusive husband is a stock character that appears in numerous literary works (consider *A Streetcar Named Desire*, for just one example), and Gene has done nothing to make Jack more than just a stereotype. That the characters share the same name is some evidence that Bill may have been affected by Gene's plot treatment in writing *The Last Runaway*, but this is irrelevant because Gene's character did not possess enough originality to merit copyright protection. *See Nichols v. Universal Pictures Corp.*, 45 F.2d 119 (2d Cir. 1930) (characters must be "sufficiently fleshed out" to merit copyright protection).

(A) is incorrect. While the rule governing the copyrightability of literary characters in the Second Circuit—and indeed, the majority of federal circuits—is broader than the minority rule (which may require that, in order to gain copyright protection, literary characters constitute the story being told rather than a mere plot device, *see Rice v. Fox Broadcasting Co.*, 330 F.3d 1170, 1176 (9th Cir. 2003) ("Mystery Magician" held to be merely a chessman in the game of telling the story of how tricks are performed)), the prevailing test for copyrightability of literary characters is not nearly broad enough to encompass the Jack character in *Seeing the Light*.

(B) is incorrect because Jack is not nearly original enough to merit copyright protection, even when all of the character's features are taken into account. That Bill used the name "Jack" in his screenplay does not change matters. Names are typically not copyrightable. U.S. Copyright Office Circular No. 34 (Nov. 2009) ("Copyright law does not protect names[.]").

(C) is incorrect because the unauthorized use of a copyrighted work of authorship in any tangible medium of expression amounts to infringement, regardless of the medium in which the author fixed the initial work.

364.   **(A) is the correct answer.** Mal copied Cal's object code for *Iterate* without permission. The literal elements of computer operating programs and application programs—such as object code—are copyrightable subject matter, protectable as literary works. *Apple Computer, Inc. v. Formula Int'l, Inc.*, 725 F.2d 521, 523 (9th Cir. 1984) (object code held to be copyrightable). Mal's unauthorized copying thus amounts to infringement.

(B) is incorrect, because Cal's argument is a breach of contract claim, and (regardless of its validity), it cannot give rise to a copyright infringement cause of action.

(C) is incorrect because both object and source code amount to copyrightable literary works. *Apple Computer, Inc. v. Franklin Computer Corp.*, 714 F.2d 1240, 1248–49 (3d Cir. 1983) (computer programs are copyrightable subject matter regardless of whether they are expressed in human-readable source code or machine-readable object code).

(D) is incorrect because Mal reproduced Cal's computer code and sold it as *ReIterate*.

365.   **(B) is the correct answer.** Chris can reproduce and distribute Betty's musical work if he is licensed to do so. Chris must either obtain a consensual mechanical license from Betty, or

he can reproduce and distribute *Summer Fugue* without her permission so long as he pays her the applicable mechanical license fee and complies with the other formalities required by the Copyright Act. 17 U.S.C. § 115 (creating limitation on exclusive rights of owners of musical works whereby via compulsory license the composition can be recorded, manufactured in phonorecords and sold to the public for its private use, as long as the statutory royalty per unit is paid to the copyright owner). KHIT must also pay royalties to Betty for publicly performing her musical work, though it need not pay royalties to Chris for publicly performing his sound recording. Sound recording owners do not have a right of public performance via analog media. *See* 17 U.S.C. § 106(4) (excluding sound recordings from public performance right); *but cf. id.* § 106(6) (creating digital public performance right for sound recording owners).

(A), (C), and (D) are incorrect because they inaccurately describe the owners' rights and users' obligations described above.

366.   **(C) is the correct answer.** The "ZoomMeister" model is not a useful article, but an aesthetic object. *See* 17 U.S.C. § 101 (definition of "useful article"); *Pivot Point Int'l, Inc. v. Charlene Products, Inc.*, 372 F.3d 913, 919 (7th Cir. 2004) ("A work that merely portrays a useful article or conveys information is not deemed a useful article and may be protected by copyright."). It was not built as a serious design prototype, but simply as a fanciful aspiration for what an imaginary futuristic vehicle might look like. Nor does the model have any utilitarian functions (except as a mere paperweight), and it is clear that it is valued primarily for its aesthetic, not utilitarian functions (hence the executives' saying that the models "[l]ook so cool"). In light of this, the model is simply an aesthetic object, similar to a sculpture or painting, and falls well within the ambit of copyright protection. This means that FunCo's unauthorized reproduction of the model is actionable, and MWB can bring a successful infringement suit.

(A) is incorrect because it gets the law exactly backward. It is where objects are *not* useful articles that they are clearly protected by copyright law.

(B) and (D) are incorrect because a separability analysis is unnecessary where an object is not a useful article.

367.   **(B) is the correct answer.** Assuming that Len has not transferred ownership in the musical work *Green Acres*, he still owns the copyright in it as of 1980, because the work will still be in the initial 28-year term of protection. Janine, by contrast, is out of luck. Her rendition of *Green Acres* did not vest any federal copyright in the sound recording. Sound recordings fixed prior to February 15, 1972, are not protected by federal copyright law. Such works may be protected, if at all, by state common-law copyright, property, unfair competition, or criminal law. *See Capitol Records, Inc. v. Naxos of America, Inc.*, 372 F.3d 471, 477–78 (2d Cir. 2004).

(A), (C), and (D) are incorrect because they inaccurately describe the rights of the respective federal ownership interests at issue.

368.   **(D) is the correct answer.** A derivative work that has been based, without authorization, upon an underlying work that is protected by copyright, may be denied copyright protection. *See* 17 U.S.C. § 103(a); *Pickett v. Prince*, 207 F.3d 402, 406 (7th Cir. 2000) (creator of an unauthorized guitar shaped like a copyrighted symbol has no claim to copyright); *Watkins v. Chesapeake Custom Homes, L.L.C.*, 330 F. Supp. 2d 563, 572 (D. Md. 2004) (a derivative copyright that is based on a copyrighted work requires the authorization of the copyright owner in order to be "lawful" and thus valid). Because KaraokeCo did not acquire the permission of the musical work owners before it made its karaoke arrangements of those works, KaraokeCo forfeits any copyright protection in its works, and does not have any rights to enforce against Krooner Ken, though the owners of the musical works may well be able to sue Ken for infringement.

(A) is incorrect, because while copyright infringement is a strict liability offense, KaraokeCo has no enforceable copyrights since it used the initial musical works unlawfully.

(B) is incorrect, because Krooner Ken need not invoke the fair use privilege in light of KaraokeCo's having no enforceable copyrights in its arrangements. That said, Krooner Ken's obvious profit motivation in releasing his DVD and the existence of licensing procedures would cast doubt on any fair use claims.

(C) is incorrect because the section 115 covering privilege does not apply where, as here, the lyrics are separately provided, making the CD a copy, rather than a phonorecord, that falls outside the ambit of section 115. *See ABKCO Music, Inc. v. Stellar Records, Inc.*, 96 F.3d 60 (2d Cir. 1996) (karaoke CD-ROM did not fall within section 115's compulsory mechanical license). Moreover, section 115 does not give users carte blanche to reproduce and distribute musical works without limit. Rather, it allows them to do so only where they remit a mechanical license to the musical work owners, which KaraokeCo did not do here.

369.   **(D) is the correct answer.** Lola's personal, descriptive reviews of restaurants are fixed literary works that easily exceed the constitutional minimum for originality. Moreover, her selection of particular restaurants is separately copyrightable as a compilation because it evinces originality insofar as Lola personally chose restaurants to feature (and not feature) in her guide. 17 U.S.C. § 103; *Feist Publications, Inc. v. Rural Telephone Service Company, Inc.*, 499 U.S. 340, 357 (1991) (copyright in factual compilations is limited to selection or arrangement of material).

(A) is incorrect because while facts and research are not copyrightable on their own, *Hoehling v. Universal City Studios, Inc.*, 618 F.2d 972 (2d Cir. 1980) (historical facts are not copyrightable), compilations of facts can be copyrightable to the extent that the author contributes original expression about, or selection or arrangement of, those facts, *Feist Publications, Inc. v. Rural Tel. Serv. Co., Inc.*, 499 U.S. 340, 357 (1991), as Lola did here.

(B) and (C) are incorrect because the arrangement of the information in Lola's guide did not evince sufficient originality to be copyrightable. Lola merely placed the reviews in alphabetical order, which is a commonplace organizational scheme that does not reflect any original input. *Feist Publications, Inc. v. Rural Telephone Service Company, Inc.*, 499 U.S.

340, 357 (1991) (organizing a compilation alphabetically does not reflect any original input by the author).

370. **(C) is the correct answer.** Regardless of Melissa's status relative to the U.S. Government (i.e., whether she is an employee or independent contractor), *Against the Current* cannot be a work made for hire because it was created outside the scope of her employment. 17 U.S.C. § 101 ("A 'work made for hire' is . . . a work prepared by an employee within the scope of his or her employment.").

Factors used in determining the scope of employment include whether the creation of the work is within the employee's job description; whether the work is of a type traditionally created by a person in the employee's position; whether it was created during official hours; on the employer's premises; using the employer's equipment; with the aid of the employer's support personnel; or using information available to the employee as part of the employee's employment; and whether the work was related to the employer's projects. *See Scherr v. Universal Match Corp.*, 417 F.2d 497, 500–01 (2d Cir. 1969); *Shaul v. Cherry Valley-Springfield Central School Dist.*, 363 F.3d 177, 186 (2d Cir. 2004) (educational materials produced in furtherance of employment duties of teacher deemed work made for hire). Here, Melissa created *Against the Current* during her free time, in her own studio, using her own art supplies. In light of all this, the painting was not within the scope of her part-time employment for the U.S. government, and the author of the copyright is Melissa.

(A) is incorrect because while Melissa may be an employee of the federal government, she was not acting in the scope of her employment when she created *Against the Current*, so that the painting cannot be a work made for hire.

(B) is incorrect because Melissa is, at least to some extent, an employee of the federal government, though this does not dispose of the work made for hire status of *Against the Current*, for reasons explained above.

(D) is incorrect because, while works of the U.S. Government are not subject to copyright protection, *see* 17 U.S.C. § 105, works created for the U.S. Government by independent contractors, *United States v. Washington Mint, LLC*, 115 F. Supp. 2d 1089 (D. Minn. 2000) (design of Sacajawea coin created by independent contractor authored by the independent contractor, not U.S. Government) or by U.S. Government employees outside the scope of their employment, *see* 17 U.S.C. § 101 ("A 'work of the United States Government' is a work prepared by an officer or employee of the United States Government as part of that person's official duties."), can be copyrighted.

371. **(D) is the correct answer.** The copyright in *South Atlantic* vested in 1921, upon publication with proper copyright notice, and its renewal in the twenty-eighth year of its initial term initially entitled the copyright owner to 56 years of copyright protection, which would have meant that the work entered the public domain in 1977. However, the Interim Copyright Term Renewal Act specified that renewal terms of federal copyright protection that would have expired between September 19, 1962, and December 31, 1977, were automatically continued through December 31, 1977, and brought into the 1976 Act. Congress

periodically passed these interim extensions of copyright protection in anticipation of the "new" Copyright Act extending the renewal terms still further. As of January 1, 1978, these works, which were previously protected by the 1909 Copyright Act, obtained the protection of the 1976 Act. Specific duration rules are then applied which provide copyright protection for 75 years from the date federal protection initially vested, unless the renewal occurred after 1950, in which case copyright protection is provided for 95 years from the date federal protection initially vested. 17 U.S.C. § 304. Thus, the total coverage for *South Atlantic* is 75 years from its date of vesting, so that it would have entered the public domain at the end of 1996.

(A) is incorrect because it wrongly assumes a vesting date of 1919, when *South Atlantic* was fixed in a tangible medium of expression. Under the 1909 Act, copyright did not vest until publication with proper notice or, in the case of unpublished works, registration with the Copyright Office.

(B) is incorrect because it fails to take into account the term extensions effected by the Interim Copyright Term Renewal Act, as explained above.

(C) is incorrect because while it does take into account the term extensions effected by the Interim Copyright Term Renewal Act, it wrongly assumes a vesting date of 1919, rather than the actual vesting date of 1921.

372.   **(C) is the correct answer.** Federal copyright vested in *Prohibition Blues* in 1928, when the authors registered the unpublished work with the Copyright Office. The renewal term of the copyright was due to expire in 1984, but was extended by the 1976 Act and 1998 Copyright Term Renewal Act, so that the total copyright term for *Prohibition Blues* will be 95 years, set to expire at the end of 2023.

(A) is incorrect because it fails to take into account the two extensions of the renewal term effected by the 1976 Act and 1998 Copyright Term Extension Act.

(B) is incorrect because it fails to take into account the 20-year extension to the renewal term effected by the 1998 Copyright Term Extension Act.

(D) is incorrect because it wrongly assumes that a life-based 1976 Act copyright term applies, measuring 70 years from the death of the latest surviving joint author. Because this copyright vested prior to the effective date of the 1976 Act, this is not the case.

373.   **(C) is the correct answer.** Because Sam's self-portrait was unpublished, it was initially unprotected by federal copyright, but was protected by perpetual state common-law copyright. Works such as the self-portrait were protected by state common-law copyright when the 1976 Copyright Act took effect on January 1, 1978. At that time they lost their perpetual common-law protection and received the same duration of protection as those works created on or after January 1, 1978. *See Martha Graham School & Dance Found., Inc. v. Martha Graham Center of Contemporary Dance, Inc.*, 380 F.3d 624, 632–33 (2d Cir. 2004). In no case, however, did the protection of these works expire prior to December 31,

2002. If the work was published between January 1, 1978, and December 31, 2002, copyright protection will not expire before December 31, 2047. 17 U.S.C. § 303(a).

On January 1, 1978, the copyright term of Sam's self-portrait was converted into a term of the author's life plus 70 years, or 2010. The display of the self-portrait at the gallery by Tracy did not constitute a publication, because it was not a public offering to sell or otherwise transfer ownership of the canvas, 17 U.S.C. § 101 ("Publication is the distribution of copies or phonorecords of a work to the public by sale or other transfer of ownership, or by rental, lease, or lending."). Therefore, the second statutory minimum period of protection does not apply.

(A) is incorrect because it assumes that a standard 1909 Act bifurcated term applies to the self-portrait. It does not, because federal copyright never vested in the work.

(B) is incorrect because the first statutory minimum period of protection for unpublished works converted to federal copyright by the 1976 Act does not apply where, as here, the standard 1976 Act term would be longer.

(D) is incorrect because Tracy's display of the self-portrait in 1992 did not extend the copyright term through 2047, as explained above.

374.   (A) is the correct answer. In order for a work to be a joint work, the authors must intend, at the time of the creation of the component materials, to create a joint work. Each author must intend her contribution to constitute a part of a total work to which another will make or has made a contribution. As long as this intent is present, the authors need not even know one another. *Edward B. Marks Music Corp. v. Jerry Vogel Music Co.*, 140 F.2d 266 (2d Cir. 1944). *See Weissmann v. Freeman*, 868 F.2d 1313 (2d Cir. 1989); *Systems XIX, Inc. v. Parker*, 30 F. Supp. 2d 1225, 1229 (N.D. Cal. 1998). Here, Sal did not intend to create a joint work with Ed; indeed, Sal did not even consider Ed to be a meaningful contributor to the work. Because there was no mutual intent to create a joint work, Ed's claim to joint authorship must fail.

(B) is incorrect because mere financial contributions do not suffice to make the contributor a joint author. Rather, the contribution of each joint author must be copyrightable material. *E.g., Natkin v. Winfrey*, 111 F. Supp. 2d 1003, 1008–10 (N.D. Ill. 2000) (producer of television show did not provide copyrightable subject matter to photographs of the television set or individuals).

(C) is incorrect because Ed's self-perception as a joint author is insufficient, on its own, to give rise to joint authorship status. Courts require that both authors think of themselves as joint authors. *Childress v. Taylor*, 945 F.2d 500 (2d Cir. 1991) (stressing the centrality of mutual intent to create a joint work).

(D) is incorrect because the jointly authored status of a work turns on the intent of the respective authors, not on the amount or substantiality of the relative contributions. Even a significant contribution to the work by the alleged co-author does not automatically suffice to confer co-authorship status on that contributor. *See Aalmuhammed v. Lee*, 202 F.3d 1227, 1233 (9th Cir. 1999). Even if the dialogue contributed by Ed were copyrightable, this would not suffice to make Ed a co-author.

375.   **(D) is the correct answer.** These are all valid ways of creating joint ownership in a work of authorship. Note that the question dealt with joint ownership, not joint authorship. Creation of a jointly authored work is the most familiar way to give rise to joint ownership, but it is only one way of doing so. Other methods include transferring or willing the copyright to more than one person, or through state community property laws. *See In re Marriage of Worth*, 195 Cal. App. 3d 768, 241 Cal. Rptr. 135 (1987) (non-authoring spouse is joint owner of copyright in any work created by authoring spouse during the marriage). *But cf. Rodrigue v. Rodrigue*, 218 F.3d 432 (5th Cir. 2000) (under state community property laws, the authoring spouse retains copyright ownership and management, while nonauthoring spouse retains right to enjoy one-half interest in the economic benefits of the copyrighted works). When the copyright is owned by a partnership, each partner is a co-owner of the copyright. *See Oddo v. Ries*, 743 F.2d 630, 632 (9th Cir. 1984).

(A), (B), and (C) are incorrect because they do not take into account all the ways that a joint ownership can be created.

376.   **(C) is the correct answer.** While Kelly clearly transferred to Rosalind ownership over the copy of *Good Friends* that she gave to her as a present, this gift did not effect transfer of the copyright in the poem. Therefore, the poem was part of Kelly's estate when she died and became James' by devise. Any transfer of statutory copyright ownership (assignment or exclusive license), other than by operation of law, must be in writing and signed by the owner of the rights conveyed or her authorized agent. 17 U.S.C. § 204.

(A) is incorrect. While the copy of the poem Kelly gave Rosalind was signed, the signature did not attest to a statement of copyright ownership transfer, but was only a way of authenticating the work, much like an artist may sign a portrait.

(B) is incorrect. Transfers of copyright ownership must be written and signed; verbal transfers are insufficient. *Effects Assocs., Inc. v. Cohen*, 908 F.2d 555 (9th Cir. 1990) (producer's argument that moviemakers do lunch, not contracts, was insufficient to make an oral agreement an exclusive license); *Weinstein Co. v. Smokewood Entertainment Group LLC*, 664 F. Supp. 2d 332, 339 (S.D.N.Y. 2009). Moreover, Kelly's statement to Rosalind does not clearly seek to transfer ownership over the poem's copyright, and may more sensibly be thought to refer to Rosalind being the owner of that *copy* of *Good Friends*.

(D) is incorrect because there was no 2007 transfer of the copyright in *Good Friends*. Had there been such a transfer, though, the devise would not have extinguished it.

377.   **(B) is the correct answer.** A transmitting organization that has the right to transmit any work may make an "ephemeral recording," a single copy of a particular program that must be subsequently destroyed if not preserved for archival purposes. 17 U.S.C. § 112; *Agee v. Paramount Communications, Inc.*, 59 F.3d 317 (2d Cir. 1995).

(A) **is incorrect** because while copyright infringement is indeed a strict liability offense, this does not take into account the limitations on owners' rights imposed by section 112.

(C) **is incorrect** because no courts have so held; public performance licenses are construed to extend only to public performance rights.

(D) **is incorrect** because copying a part of any protected work amounts to a violation of the reproduction right, as long as the copying is more than *de minimis*. *See Walt Disney Productions v. Filmation Assocs.*, 628 F. Supp. 871 (C.D. Cal. 1986).

378.   (A) **is the correct answer.** One who distributes or offers to distribute copies or phonorecords containing the sounds or images of a live musical performance, made without the consent of the performer, is subject to the same remedies as an infringer of copyright. 17 U.S.C. § 1101. By distributing copies of the unauthorized Smack bootlegs, then, Paramecium becomes liable under these provisions of federal law, even though its conduct does not violate any copyrights. Criminal liability exists for such conduct pursuant to 18 U.S.C. § 2319A.

    (B) **is incorrect.** The first sale defense applies only to copyright infringement, which is not the basis for Paramecium's federal liability.

    (C) **is incorrect**, because while lack of fixation makes the concerts unavailable as a basis for liability on a copyright infringement theory, this does not obviate the possibility that Paramecium could be liable under the federal anti-bootlegging provisions. In addition, many concerts are fixed by the band and are sold at the end of the concert or subsequently streamed on a band's website.

    (D) **is incorrect**, because selling is a form of distribution, and distribution of unauthorized bootlegs is a basis for liability under the federal anti-bootlegging provisions.

379.   (D) **is the correct answer.** Zed is clearly liable to Deke because he reproduced copies of many of the poems to which Deke owned the copyright without authorization. Zed is also liable to B.P. McGee, because he copied the original selection and arrangement of poems that the publisher added to *Finding Grace* when McGee created the collective work. B.P. McGee is not, however, liable to Deke, because the owner of copyright in a collective work has the right to distribute to the public individual contributions as part of that particular collective work, any revision of that collective work, and any later collective work in the same series. 17 U.S.C. § 201(c). This privilege entitled B.P. McGee to create the second edition of *Finding Grace* without fear of an infringement suit from Deke.

    (A), (B), and (C) **are incorrect** because they misstate the correct liability of the respective parties, as explained above.

380.   (C) **is the correct answer.** Sound recording owners do not have a right of public performance via analog means, such as radio stations, so Ray will not have to pay any royalties for publicly performing sound recordings via KRAY. Under the Digital Performance Right in Sound Recordings Act of 1995, copyright owners of sound recordings have a limited

exclusive right to transmit their works to the public by means of digital audio transmissions. 17 U.S.C. § 106(6). Transmissions of sound recordings to the public by a noninteractive digital transmission may qualify for a "statutory license" (compulsory license). 17 U.S.C. § 114(d)(2). Courts have held that Internet transmissions fall into this category, even when originated by a local radio station exempted from section 106(6). *Bonneville Int'l Corp. v. Peters*, 347 F.3d 485, 495 (3d Cir. 2003). Ray will thus have to pay sound recording copyright owners a compulsory license for publicly performing their works via www.kray.com and via the satellite radio service. Finally, transmissions of sound recordings to the public by an interactive digital transmission require a negotiated license from the owner of the copyright in the sound recording, so Ray will have to negotiate with sound recording copyright owners in order to transmit their works to the public via the on-demand streaming service.

(A), **(B)**, **and (D)** **are incorrect** because they misstate Ray's obligations to sound recording copyright owners as described above.

381.   **(B) is the correct answer.** Only certain still photographs are protected by VARA, depending on their intended use. *See Pollara v. Seymour*, 344 F.3d 265, 269–70 (2d Cir. 2003) ("Congress explicitly limited VARA's protection to works 'intended for exhibition only,' as opposed to works intended for use in a publication or the photographer's photo album."). Photographs are protected only where the initial rendering of a still photographic image that was produced for exhibition purposes only and signed by the author. Any copy in a limited edition of 200 copies or fewer is also protected if the copies are signed and consecutively numbered by the author. 17 U.S.C. § 101 (defining the kind of "work of visual art" that is protected by VARA). Bill's casual cellphone picture of Denise clearly does not qualify, because it was not meant for exhibition and was not signed.

(A) is incorrect because the photograph was not produced for exhibition purposes. In addition, the protection of a "limited edition" applies only where there is a series of photographs that number 200 or fewer, and they are signed and numbered by the author. 17 U.S.C. § 101.

(C) is incorrect because VARA does vest a right of integrity in authors of works of visual art. An author has the right to prevent the intentional distortion, mutilation, or other modification of her work that would be prejudicial to her honor or reputation. 17 U.S.C. § 106A(a)(3)(A); *see Berrios Nogueras v. Home Depot*, 330 F. Supp. 2d 48, 50 (D. Puerto Rico 2004).

(D) is incorrect because there is no such affirmative defense.

382.   **(C) is the correct answer.** During the decennial period (1/1/1978–2/28/1989), federal copyright vested in original works fixed in tangible mediums of expression, but could be forfeited to the public domain through general publication without inclusion of proper copyright notice, though owners had an opportunity to cure the lack of notice by registering the work before or within five years of publication without notice and making a reasonable effort to add notice to all copies publicly distributed in the United States after the

omission has been discovered. 17 U.S.C. §§ 401(a), 405(a)(2). Here, Iris' copyright vested upon fixation in a tangible medium of expression in 1980, but was ceded to the public domain for failure of notice, and a corresponding failure to cure that notice, by the time Queen Burger published its brochure in 1986.

(A) is incorrect because it fails to take into account the copyright notice requirement that prevailed during the decennial period.

(B) is incorrect because Iris' publication of the work without proper copyright notice divested (not vested) federal copyright in the work.

(D) is incorrect because, unlike the situation under the 1909 Act, Iris' omission of copyright notice from a published work in 1981 was curable, not irrevocable.

383. **(D) is the correct answer.** A general publication occurred when a possessory interest in tangible copies of the work was made available to the general public with the consent of the copyright owner. *See Shoptalk, Ltd. v. Concorde-New Horizons Corp.*, 168 F.3d 586, 590 (2d Cir. 1999). Posting the work in her break room did not effect publication because it constituted a mere display and did not make tangible copies of the speech available to her co-workers. Moreover, that group of co-workers constituted a limited group of 20 people, not the general public. Reading the speech during a broadcast did not effect publication because it did not cause copies of the work to be available to the public. A performance does not constitute a publication. *See Estate of Martin Luther King, Jr., Inc. v. CBS, Inc.*, 194 F.3d 1211, 1215–16 (2d Cir. 1999). Jean's distribution of individual copies did not effect a general publication, because the distribution was carefully limited to personal acquaintances, rather than to the public at large and for a limited purpose, thus constituting a limited publication. *See White v. Kimmell*, 193 F.2d 744, 746–47 (9th Cir. 1952). Schriver & Co.'s offering the book to the public for sale did constitute a general publication, though, because it met all the applicable criteria for publication that prevailed under the 1909 Act.

(A), (B), and (C) are incorrect for the reasons explained above.

384. **(A) is the correct answer.** Registration is a prerequisite to the filing of a copyright infringement action. 17 U.S.C. § 411. Most courts require that a copyright owner formally register a derivative work with the Copyright Office as a prerequisite to filing a suit for infringement of that derivative work. *See, e.g., Murray Hill Publications, Inc. v. ABC Communications, Inc.*, 264 F.3d 622, 630–32 (6th Cir. 2001); *Creations Unlimited, Inc. v. McCain*, 112 F.3d 814, 816 (5th Cir. 1997).

(B) is incorrect because amending the registration for the screenplay would not have enabled the court to exercise jurisdiction over the motion picture.

(C) is incorrect because registration of an individual work does not give courts jurisdiction over derivative works without a separate registration of the latter.

(D) is incorrect because federal subject-matter jurisdiction cannot be waived.

385.   **(C) is the correct answer.** This is a work made for hire because its creator was Vince Virtual, an Initech employee acting within the scope of his employment. 17 U.S.C. § 101 (defining "work made for hire"). The term of copyright protection for such works is 95 years after the work's first publication or 120 years after its creation, whichever is earlier. 17 U.S.C. § 302(c). The work was created in 1980, but generally published in 1995. The brochure will enter the public domain in the earlier of (1980 + 120) or (1995 + 95), which is 2090.

    (A), (B), and (D) are incorrect because they specify the wrong date upon which the work will enter the public domain.

386.   **(B) is the correct answer.** Access can be proven by evidence that the defendant had actually read or heard plaintiff's work, or had a reasonable opportunity to view or hear the plaintiff's work. *See Peel & Co. v. The Rug Market*, 238 F.3d 391, 394 (5th Cir. 2001) (requiring only a "reasonable opportunity to view the copyright work" to enable an inference of access). Here, the Acme employee who became a consultant at Zenith shortly after leaving Acme had heard about Harriet's script in detail during the pitch meeting. This is sufficient evidence to enable an inference of access, since that employee easily could have discussed the script with Zenith.

    (A) is incorrect because substantial similarity does not suffice to enable an inference of access. Such a rule would fail to take account of the possibility that two works are similar because of independent creation.

    (C) is incorrect because the corporate receipt doctrine applies only to employees, *Moore v. Columbia Pictures Indus., Inc.*, 972 F.2d 939, 942–43 (8th Cir. 1992), while the source of access at Zenith was an independent consultant. A reasonable possibility of access can be established where a supervisory employee or an employee within the work unit from which the corporate defendant's work was developed had the opportunity to view or hear the plaintiff's work.

    (D) is incorrect because copying is typically proven by circumstantial evidence, because direct evidence of copying is characteristically difficult to find. *Swirsky v. Carey*, 376 F.3d 841, 844 (9th Cir. 2004) ("element of copying is rarely the subject of direct evidence").

387.   **(D) is the correct answer.** That Jamie's copying was inadvertent or unconscious does not amount to a defense to infringement. *See Three Boys Music Corp. v. Bolton*, 212 F.3d 477 (9th Cir. 2000) (holding that subconscious copying amounts to infringement). Nor is Jamie's taking *de minimis*. A taking is *de minimis* if it is so meager and fragmentary that the average audience would not recognize the misappropriation. *Fisher v. Dees*, 794 F.2d 432, 435 n.2 (9th Cir. 1986). Here, by contrast, Jamie took six full paragraphs of original expression from Ken's treatise. It also diminishes Jamie's *de minimis* argument that Ken immediately recognized the taking. *See Jobete Music Co., Inc. v. Johnson Communications, Inc.*, 285 F. Supp. 2d 1077, 1088–89 (S.D. Ohio 2003) (*de minimis* defense not available where anyone familiar with the musical work would recognize it instantly). Finally, it is not relevant that the portion of Ken's treatise that Jamie took was small in relation to the whole. The focus is on the similarities between the plaintiff's and defendant's works.

Sheldon v. Metro-Goldwyn Pictures Corp., 81 F.2d 49, 56 (2d Cir. 1936) ("[N]o plagiarist can excuse the wrong by showing how much of his work he did not pirate."). Because she does not have a defense, Jamie's unauthorized taking of Ken's protected literary work amounts to infringement.

(A), (B), and (C) are incorrect for the reasons explained above.

388.   **(A) is the correct answer.** Vicarious liability can be imposed when a party has the right and ability to supervise the infringing activity and also has a direct financial interest in such activities. *Shapiro, Bernstein & Co., Inc. v. H.L. Green Co., Inc.*, 316 F.2d 304 (2d Cir. 1963). Here, First Waltz clearly has vicariously infringed because it has the right and ability to stop New Biz from selling the infringing CDs at the flea market. In addition, First Waltz has a financial interest in those sales because it profits from the entrance fees of those who purchase the CDs, from the rental fee paid by New Biz and its sales of food and beverages at the flea market. *See Metro-Goldwyn-Mayer Studios Inc. v. Grokster, Ltd.*, 125 S. Ct. 2764, 2776 (2005) ("One . . . infringes vicariously by profiting from direct infringement while declining to exercise a right to stop or limit it"). Contributory infringement can be imposed when a party has knowledge of the infringing activity of another and induces, causes or materially contributes to that infringing conduct. *Gershwin Publishing Corp. v. Columbia Artists Management, Inc.*, 443 F.2d 1159 (1971).

Here, First Waltz has also contributorily infringed. While First Waltz did not have actual knowledge of the distributor's illegal activity, it had constructive knowledge because the wholesale prices of the CDs were suspiciously low, and because First Waltz engaged in willful ignorance by preventing New Biz from discussing his illegal acquisition of the sound recordings. Willful blindness to the infringing actions of the direct infringer may constitute actual knowledge. *See UMG Recordings, Inc. v. Sinnott*, 300 F. Supp. 2d 993, 999–1000 (E.D. Cal. 2004). First Waltz contributed to the infringing activity by providing a site for the sale of the infringing CDs.

(B), (C), and (D) are incorrect for the reasons explained above.

389.   **(C) is the correct answer.** Criminal liability may attach either where a person "infringes a copyright willfully and for purposes of commercial advantage or private financial gain," or "by the reproduction or distribution . . . of 1 or more copies or phonorecords of 1 or more copyrighted works, which have a total retail value of more than $1,000. . . ." 17 U.S.C. § 506(a). Here, while Quentin's infringement was willful, it was not done for the purpose of commercial advantage or private financial gain. Nor was Tina's photograph worth more than $1,000; rather, as Tina conceded, it was not worth anything financially.

(A) is incorrect because willful infringement alone is not a sufficient basis for criminal copyright infringement.

(B) is incorrect because bad faith is not the statutory standard for criminal copyright infringement.

(D) **is incorrect** because Quentin infringed Tina's copyright in the picture as soon as he made an unauthorized digital copy of it; whether he actually printed the photograph is not relevant to whether he can be held criminally liable.

390.　(B) **is the correct answer.** Edgar's use clearly meets the four fair use factors codified by Congress in the 1976 Act. 17 U.S.C. § 107. His use is transformative because it recasts a political tract in the context of an expository article. The tract written by Felice is not creative. The amount of the tract Edgar took is reasonable in relation to the purpose and scale of his article. Finally, there does not seem to be any market for the tract, so his use of unauthorized quotations cannot damage any economic interests Felice may have in it.

(A) **is incorrect** because while reporting is one of the examples of fair uses featured in the preamble to section 107, no court has held that these categories are entitled to a per se fair use defense. The preamble provides "only general guidance about the sorts of copying that courts and Congress most commonly had found to be fair uses." *Campbell v. Acuff-Rose Music, Inc.*, 510 U.S. 569, 577 (1994).

(C) **is incorrect** because Edgar's receiving a financial award for his article does not make that article wholly commercial. The mere fact that the use takes place in the context of a nominally commercial enterprise will not preclude the applicability of the fair use defense. *See Kelly v. Arriba Soft Corp.*, 280 F.3d 934, 940 (9th Cir. 2002).

(D) **is incorrect** because seeking permission before use is not a prerequisite to claiming the fair use defense. *See, e.g., Campbell v. Acuff-Rose Music, Inc.*, 510 U.S. 569 (1994).

391.　(C) **is the correct answer.** The fair use defense has long common-law roots, *see, e.g., Folsom v. Marsh*, 9 F. Cas. 342 (1841), and was finally codified in the 1976 Act at 17 U.S.C. § 107. The Copyright Act requires judges to consider all four enumerated factors when evaluating a fair use defense, but the factors are nonexclusive. *See id.* ("In determining whether the use made of a work in any particular case is a fair use the factors to be considered *shall include* . . . .") (emphasis added). In other words, judges must consider at least all four listed factors, but can include other factors in their analysis (though they rarely do so).

(A) **and** (B) **are incorrect** because courts have never held that fair use is a constitutional right. *See Universal City Studios, Inc. v. Corley*, 273 F.3d 429, 458 (2d Cir. 2001).

(D) **is incorrect** because courts *must* (not may) consider all four fair use factors when evaluating such a defense, for the reasons explained above.

392.　(D) **is the correct answer.** Dennis' use was essentially commercial, even if he did not formally sell the book, because he sought to have users give him money in exchange for downloading the text from his website. Nor was Dennis' use meaningfully transformative, because it was a mere change in medium, rather than a change in purpose or content. A mere change of format has been held not to be transformative. *See A & M Records, Inc. v. Napster, Inc.*, 239 F.3d 1004, 1015 (9th Cir. 2001) (downloading .mp3 files does not transform the copyrighted work); *Infinity Broadcast Corp. v. Kirkwood*, 150 F.3d 104, 108 n.2 (2d Cir. 1998) (retransmitting radio transmissions over telephone lines deemed not transformative). Finally, it is not a defense that Dennis' use ultimately increased demand for Genevieve's work. The fact that the defendant's use may have a positive impact on the copyright holder's market does not exonerate that use. *See Ringgold v. Black Entertainment Television*, 126 F.3d 70, 81 n.16 (2d Cir. 1997) (even if use in television program increased poster sales, plaintiff retained right to licensing fee).

(A), (B), and (C) are incorrect for the reasons explained above.

393.　There is a three-year statute of limitations for copyright infringement actions. 17 U.S.C. § 507(b). The limitations period had more than lapsed by the time Fran brought her infringement suit in 2005, with all arguably infringing acts taking place decades before. As a result, Fran will not be able to bring an infringement action until D Films once again exploits the *One Man Down* motion picture.

The equitable defense of laches applies when there has been a sufficient passage of time between the plaintiff's knowledge of the injury and the date of bringing suit, and the presence of prejudice to the defendant. *Kling v. Hallmark Cards*, 225 F.3d 1030, 1036–37 (9th Cir. 2000). The Supreme Court recently held, though, that the common-law laches defense is not available to copyright defendants in claims for damages, *Petrella v. Metro-Goldwyn-Mayer, Inc.*, 134 S. Ct. 1962 (2014), so while this defense would not do much for Fran given the lapse in the statute of limitations, it would also not bar her from bringing an infringement suit for any future infringing conduct that would not be statutorily time-barred.

Abandonment of copyright occurs only if there is intent by the copyright proprietor to surrender the rights in her work. *Dam Things from Denmark v. Russ Berrie & Co., Inc.*, 290 F.3d 548, 560 (3d Cir. 2002) ("there must be either an act, or a failure to act, from which we can readily infer an intent to abandon the right"). Here, there is no overt act on Fran's part evidencing abandonment. D Films may argue that Fran abandoned her copyright when she gave a copy of the script to Zelda, but this argument will certainly fail. Fran gave Zelda the copy for comments only, and that copy had a clear indication of Fran's reservation of copyright ownership in the underlying literary work.

394.　**(A) is the correct answer.** None of these purported affirmative defenses are availing. First, obscenity is not a defense to copyright infringement. The general rule is that copyright protection is to be accorded a work that has met the statutory prerequisites, even if it is obscene. *See Mitchell Brothers Film Group v. Cinema Adult Theater*, 604 F.2d 852 (5th Cir. 1979). Second, fraud on the Copyright Office arises only where a plaintiff knowingly fails to advise the Copyright Office of material facts related to the copyrightability of the work. *See Masquerade Novelty, Inc. v. Unique Industries, Inc.*, 912 F.2d 663, 667 (3d Cir. 1990). In light of the fact that the work's obscenity did not compromise its copyrightability, Joe had no obligation to disclose it, and his failure to do so cannot be construed as fraudulent. Finally, Joe's failure to police his work does not, without more, deprive him of the ability to bring suit for infringement. The failure to pursue third-party infringers is not a defense to copyright infringement. *See Capitol Records, Inc. v. Naxos of America, Inc.*, 372 F.3d 471, 484 (2d Cir. 2004).

(B), (C), and (D) are incorrect for the reasons explained above.

395.   **(B) is the correct answer.** Most courts have found that the Copyright Act preempts state law claims of conversion. *See, e.g., United States ex rel. Berge v. Board of Trustees of Univ. of Alabama*, 104 F.3d 1453 (4th Cir. 1997). Courts also regard unfair competition claims based on the unauthorized reproduction of the plaintiff's copyrightable work as preempted. *See, e.g., Kodadek v. MTV Networks, Inc.*, 152 F.3d 1209, 1212–13 (9th Cir. 1998). By contrast, an action for the violation of the right of publicity is generally deemed not to be preempted. *See Facenda v. N.F.L. Films, Inc.*, 542 F.3d 1007, 1026–28 (3d Cir. 2008) (right of publicity statute's requirement of proof of commercial value provides an additional element beyond what copyright infringement claim requires); *Waits v. Frito-Lay, Inc.*, 978 F.2d 1093 (9th Cir. 1992) (tort of appropriation of voice is not preempted); *Landham v. Lewis Galoob Toys, Inc.*, 227 F.3d 619, 623 (6th Cir. 2000) (actor's right of publicity suit against toy manufacturer for marketing an action figure based on actor's screen persona was held to evoke the actor's personal identity, an inchoate idea not amenable to copyright protection).

(A), (C), and (D) are incorrect for the reasons explained above.

396.   **(A) is the correct answer.** When considering a motion for a preliminary injunction in a copyright infringement case, most courts—including those in the Eleventh Circuit—traditionally analyze four elements. Those elements are the movant's likelihood of success on the merits, the irreparable harm that the movant would suffer in the absence of an injunction, balancing of these harms to the movant against the harm that the injunction would inflict on the nonmoving party, and public policy. *See Warren Pub., Inc. v. Microdos Data Corp.*, 115 F.3d 1509, 1516 (11th Cir. 1997).

Here, all four elements weigh in favor of entering preliminary injunctive relief in favor of Hank. Hank has an extremely high likelihood of success on the merits because Welter unambiguously violated Hank's exclusive rights in *Trains and Levees* by making thousands of unauthorized copies of the literary work. Second, the injury is irreparable because Hank has shown that the actions of Welter Publishing caused Hank to lose control over his work, the time and manner in which it is to be presented to the public, as well as the effectiveness of Gladman's marketing campaign. Third, the balance of harms weighs in Hank's favor because an injunction would only delay Welter's releasing *Trains and Levees*, while the release of the book before its authorized publication date with Gladman would cost Hank much more in terms of lost revenue and decreased publicity. Fourth, courts typically find that it is in the public's interest to protect the copyright laws and the interests of copyright holders. *See, e.g., Intellectual Reserve, Inc. v. Utah Lighthouse Ministry, Inc.*, 75 F. Supp. 2d 1290, 1295 (D. Utah 1999).

(B) is incorrect because there is no presumptive right to a preliminary injunction. On the contrary, Hank, as the nonmoving party, bears the burden of proof on this issue (though he has carried that burden, as explained above). The Supreme Court's decision in *eBay,*

Inc. v. MercExchange, L.L.C., 547 U.S. 388, 391 (2006), which disallowed a presumption of irreparable harm on a showing of likelihood of success on the merits, has been applied to copyright infringement actions. *See Metro-Goldwyn-Mayer Studios, Inc. v. Grokster, Ltd.*, 518 F. Supp. 2d 1197, 1211 (C.D. Cal. 2007) (plaintiff seeking injunctive relief in copyright infringement action has the burden of proving the four traditional factors).

(C) **is incorrect** because loss of control of a copyrighted work and its release to the public likely constitutes an irreparable harm.

(D) **is incorrect** because an injunction would only delay Welter's publishing *Trains and Levees*, while the release of the book before its authorized publication date with Gladman would cost Hank much more in terms of lost revenue and decreased publicity.

397.   **(B)** **is the correct answer.** A prevailing plaintiff in a copyright infringement action is entitled to recover actual damages suffered as a result of the infringement and any of the defendant's profits that are attributable to the infringement. *See Frank Music Corp. v. Metro-Goldwyn-Mayer, Inc.*, 772 F.2d 505 (9th Cir. 1985). Where, however, giving a prevailing plaintiff both actual damages *and* infringer's profits would amount to double-counting, the prevailing plaintiff is entitled only to the greater of the two figures. *See Abeshouse v. Ultragraphics, Inc.*, 754 F.2d 467 (2d Cir. 1985) (improper double-counting arises "when an infringing seller has to disgorge profits on sales that a copyright holder might have made and for which he may therefore claim damages in the form of lost profits").

Here, Madelyn's actual damages attributable to TekCo's infringement are $10,000. TekCo's profits attributable to that infringement are $4,000 ($5,000 in gross profit less $1,000 in manufacturing expenses). Here, though, Madelyn's actual damages *are* TekCo's profits, and giving Madelyn both would amount to double-counting. She is thus entitled to the greater of the two figures, or $10,000.

(A), (C), and (D) **are incorrect** because they state the wrong amount of damages.

398.   **(A)** **is the correct answer.** Statutory damages are to be calculated according to the number of works infringed, not the number of infringements. *See Venegas-Hernandez v. Sonolux Records*, 370 F.3d 183, 194 (1st Cir. 2004); *Walt Disney Co. v. Powell*, 897 F.2d 565, 569 (D.C. Cir. 1990). So here, the existence of two separate infringing works (screenplay and motion picture) does not increase statutory damages. Moreover, while multiple defendants may multiply statutory damages where they act separately, *Columbia Pictures Television v. Krypton Broadcasting, Inc.*, 106 F.3d 284, 294 (9th Cir. 1997), joint acts of infringement do not multiply statutory damages, so the presence of three individuals who contributed to the infringements (Amy, Mike, and Jane) also does not increase statutory damages. Finally, all the parts of a compilation or derivative work constitute one work for purposes of statutory damage calculations. 17 U.S.C. §504(c)(1); *see UMG Recordings, Inc. v. MP3.Com, Inc.*, 109 F. Supp. 2d 223 (S.D.N.Y. 2000) (statutory damages computed on the basis of number of audio CDs, not individual recordings). So here, the existence of separate short stories within Vic's book (a collective work) does not multiply the statutory damages.

Ultimately, we have multiple infringements by joint infringers of a single work. This amounts to a single infringement as defined by the Copyright Act, so the total amount of statutory damages is (only) $1,000.

(B), (C), and (D) are incorrect for the reasons explained above.

399. **(D) is the correct answer.** The DMCA prohibits the providing or distribution of false copyright management information, 17 U.S.C. § 1202(a), and the removal or alteration of CMI, *id.* § 1202(b). Copyright management information includes information that identifies a copyrighted work, its author, its copyright owner, its creator, as well as terms and conditions for use of the work, *id.* § 1202(c). Because this definition clearly includes Jane's digital watermark, and because Redwood Town removed the watermark without permission, its conduct is liable under the DMCA.

(A) is incorrect because there is no exemption under the DMCA for owners of copies.

(B) is incorrect because there is no exemption under the DMCA for state actors, though there is one for "lawfully authorized investigative, protective, information security, or intelligence activity of federal, state or local law enforcement or intelligence agencies." 17 U.S.C. § 1202(d).

(C) is incorrect because, while the imposition of misleading copyright management information is actionable, it is not the only cause of action created by the DMCA. Removal or alteration of CMI is also actionable on its own. 17 U.S.C. § 1202(b).

400. **(B) is the correct answer.** The DMCA prohibits the act of circumvention of a technological measure, such as scrambling or encryption, put in place by a copyright owner to effectively control access to a copyrighted work, without the authority of the copyright owner. 17 U.S.C. § 1201(a)(1). Brad will be liable on that basis, because he circumvented the password-protection that MacroHard used to restrict access to YouFace.

The DMCA also prohibits the manufacture and distribution of products and services used to defeat technological measures that impose limitations on the use of a copyrighted work. 17 U.S.C. § 1201(b). Brad did not violate this provision. Brad did create a hack that allowed YouFace to operate on a non-MacroHard operating system, but this provision of the DMCA only regulates *trafficking* in such circumventions of use limitations, not the use or creation of such measures. Brad is thus only liable for circumventing MacroHard's access control measures, not its use-limitation measures.

(A), (C), and (D) are incorrect for the reasons explained above.

Practice Final Exam: Essay Answers

Answer to: An Inventor in Paradise

I have been asked to advise three of my clients concerning issues with Left Coast Pictures:

Grace Hopper

If Ms. Hopper is to bring a copyright infringement action against Left Coast Pictures, she must prove that her father's novel, *An Inventor in Paradise*, continues to be protected by copyright, that she is the current owner of that copyright and that Left Coast Pictures has infringed one or more of her exclusive rights set forth in section 106 of the Copyright Act.

The novel was invested with federal copyright protection in 1940 when it was published with a proper copyright notice, as well as registered with the copyright office. The facts indicate that the work was renewed by the author in 1968. On January 1, 1978, the renewal term of the novel's copyright was extended by 19 years to 2015. The renewal term was further extended in 1998 by 20 years pursuant to the Sonny Bono Copyright Term Extension Act. As a result, the novel will enter the public domain in the United States at the end of 2035.

Harry Hopper died in 1985, without a surviving spouse. As his only child, Grace Hopper is his statutory successor for purposes of exercising the termination right for the copyright in the novel. The author had granted an exclusive motion picture license, for both the initial and renewal terms of the copyright in the novel, to Left Coast Pictures on September 2, 1942. Because the grant was executed prior to 1978, section 304(c) of the Copyright Act dictates the termination right that Grace is entitled to exercise. Under section 304(c), the five-year termination window began in 1996 and extended through 2001. Grace selected a termination date within that window, January 5, 1999, and sent a proper termination notice on January 10, 1989, which was more than the required two years' notice prior to termination and less than the 10-year maximum period of notice allowed. Therefore, Grace's termination of the September 2, 1942, agreement was valid. Grace now owns the exclusive right to make and exploit a motion picture based on the novel.

Pursuant to the continued use of a derivative work provision of section 304(c), Left Coast Pictures is permitted to continue to exploit its derivative motion picture, *Mr. Diffie's Soul*, in the same manner that it had before Grace Hopper's termination on January 5, 1999. Left Coast is not permitted to create a sequel, prequel or remake of *Mr. Diffie's Soul* post-termination, nor can the studio make any other new uses of its existing motion picture. *See Fred Ahlert Music Corp. v. Warner/Chappell Music, Inc.*, 155 F.3d 17 (2d Cir. 1998).

Grace Hopper has raised concerns about three post-termination uses of *Mr. Diffie's Soul*: the selling of the motion picture on videocassette copies; the release of *Mr. Diffie's Soul* on DVD; and the use of a three-minute film clip of the purgatory scene from *Mr. Diffie's Soul* on Left Coast's website.

Sale of videocassette copies of the film

Grace Hopper will have a difficult time with this argument. *Mr. Diffie's Soul* was created pre-termination pursuant to a grant to Left Coast Pictures from the author of the underlying work, Harry Hopper, which included the renewal term of the novel. The motion picture constitutes a derivative that was released on videocassette prior to Grace Hopper's termination. Pursuant to the derivative work exclusion of section 304(c), Left Coast may continue to release the motion picture on videocassette, thereby helping to ensure that Left Coast recoups its investment in the film. Left Coast is obligated to continue to pay Grace Hopper the royalty that was paid prior to her termination. *See Mills Music, Inc. v. Snyder*, 469 U.S. 153 (1985).

DVD release

The release of *Mr. Diffie's Soul* on DVD is a somewhat closer issue than the continued sales of the motion picture on videocassettes. To stop the DVD release of *Mr. Diffie's Soul*, Grace Hopper must prove that the DVD release constitutes a new use of her father's novel. The facts surrounding the release indicate that the analog motion picture has been digitized, without changing the substance of the motion picture, and is being released with no additional information or features. This allows Left Coast to argue that its DVD release does not contain any new elements, is not a new derivative work and does not constitute a new use. In addition, changes in media, particularly mechanical translations into digital media, are generally viewed as lacking the originality necessary to create a new work. As such Left Coast would be permitted to release the DVD of the motion picture post-termination. To bolster its argument, Left Coast will point to the cases where new performances of pre-termination works have been found not to constitute new uses. *See Woods v. Bourne Co.*, 60 F.3d 978 (2d Cir. 1995).

Grace Hopper will want to investigate the DVD and its packaging to determine whether they contain a copyright notice with the current date by which Left Coast is claiming a derivative work copyright in the DVD version of the motion picture. If such a new copyright notice is used, Left Coast will be hard pressed to deny that the DVD release constitutes a new use. However, even if the DVD release does not contain a new copyright notice, Grace Hopper will argue that for purposes of section 304(c), there is a difference between adding new elements to a post-termination version of the motion picture and making a new use of the motion picture. New types of exploitation of a work, post-termination, should be deemed new uses, regardless of whether the new uses are found to be new derivative works, because such new exploitations provide new sources of revenue that the termination provisions of the Copyright Act are meant to ensure are given to the author of the author's statutory successors. *See Broadcast Music, Inc. v. Roger Miller Music, Inc.*, 396 F.3d 762 (6th Cir. 2005). Grace will point to the cases where the use of a musical composition in a motion picture or soundtrack CD created post-termination have been found to be new uses. *See, e.g., Fred Ahlert Music Corp. v. Warner/Chappell*

Music, Inc., 155 F.3d 17 (2d Cir. 1998). The release of *Mr. Diffie's Soul* on DVD likely constitutes a new use and an infringement of the copyright in the novel.

The fact that the 1942 agreement between Harry Hopper and Left Coast Pictures contained a new technology clause merely granted Left Coast the right to use the novel in new media while the grant was still in effect. That right ceased to exist once the grant was terminated by Grace Hopper. Therefore, the existence of the new technology clause does not provide Left Coast with an argument that the DVD release is not a new use.

Use of clip on website

Many of the same arguments raised in connection with the DVD release would also apply to the use of the novel on the website. It is clear from the facts that the portion of the motion picture included on the website constitutes a use of the novel as well. In addition to the fact that this constitutes a new method of exploitation, post-termination, which is likely to be deemed a new use, only a portion of the novel is being used. Apparently this is the first time the novel has been used in a clip. This fact adds to Grace Hopper's argument that the website use constitutes a new use.

Left Coast Pictures may argue that its agreement with Harry Hopper gave it the right to use any version of the novel "for the purpose of advertising, publicizing or exploiting the motion picture." It is unclear whether that right survives post-termination. Grace Hopper argues that her termination has ended the existence of the 1942 agreement and that any right of Left Coast to continue to use its derivative motion picture is derived from the termination provisions of the Copyright Act, which do not permit any new uses of the derivative motion picture post-termination. Left Coast can argue that its right to advertise its motion picture through use of the novel should survive termination. It makes little sense to have the continuing right to sell its motion picture in videocassettes if it is not permitted to advertise the motion picture, which contains elements of the novel.

Grace Hopper may answer that, while it makes sense for the owner of a derivative work to be able to advertise its exploitation post-termination, that right should be limited only to pre-termination uses, not new uses such as the website. In addition, Left Coast's website does not use the classic purgatory scene from *Mr. Diffie's Soul* to sell only videocassette copies of the motion picture, but DVD copies also, as well as other motion pictures in Left Coast's film library that are also offered for sale on the website and are linked to the viewing of the purgatory scene. The use of the clip from *Mr. Diffie's Soul* on the website constitutes a new use and an infringement of the copyright in the novel.

Alan Cadabra

Mr. Cadabra has no right to terminate his 1944 composer agreement with Left Coast Pictures. The work created pursuant to that agreement, the musical work titled *Optical Rectosis*, was a work made for hire. It was created prior to 1978 at the instance and expense of Left Coast Pictures. *See Martha Graham School and Dance Foundation, Inc. v. Martha Graham Center of Contemporary Dance, Inc.*, 380 F.3d 624 (2d Cir. 2004). In addition, the composer agreement expressly stated that *Optical*

Rectosis would be created as a work made for hire. Grants involving works made for hire are not subject to statutory termination. *Marvel Characters, Inc. v. Simon*, 310 F.3d 280 (2d Cir. 2002).

Bert Schreck

The musical work *Piety and Iron* is still protected by copyright. Therefore, the only way Mr. Schreck could record and distribute the musical work without negotiating directly with its copyright owner, Left Coast Pictures, would be to take advantage of the compulsory mechanical license provided by section 115 of the Copyright Act. Section 115 permits the recording and distribution via phonorecord or digital phonorecord delivery to the public for its private use, without the permission of the copyright owner, of any nondramatic musical work that had previously been recorded and distributed via phonorecord or digital phonorecord delivery to the public for its private use. In return, the party taking advantage of the compulsory mechanical license is required to pay a license fee at the current statutory fee set by the Copyright Office. Although Mr. Schreck's planned recording and distribution would meet the requirements of section 115, that section is not applicable to the musical work *Piety and Iron*. The musical work has only been distributed to the public as part of the *American Outback* motion picture, which has been released on copies, not phonorecords. Nondramatic musical works that have only been released on copies do not fall within the ambit of section 115. Therefore, no compulsory mechanical license is available to Mr. Schreck. *See Leadsinger, Inc. v. BMG Music Publishing*, 512 F.3d 522 (9th Cir. 2008).

Answer to: Rick Rail

Flusterated Records v. Anne Droid

Flusterated Records owns two versions of the sound recording of *Bail Before They Bite*: the 1966 analog recording and the 1990 digital release. The 1966 analog recording by Rick Rail and the Bailettes was made at the instance and expense of Flusterated Records prior to 1978, therefore, it is deemed a work for hire. However, the recording was initially fixed prior to February 15, 1972. Therefore, it was not protected by federal copyright, which attaches only to sound recordings first fixed on or after that date. *Capitol Records, Inc. v. Naxos of America, Inc.*, 372 F.3d 471 (2d Cir. 2004). The call of the question asks for a discussion of federal copyright issues only. As a result, any state common-law copyright protection for the 1966 analog recording is not relevant to this exam.

The federal copyright infringement claim raised by Flusterated Records must be based on the 1990 digital recording. The digital recording was first fixed after February 15, 1972, but it must contain sufficient originality to meet the statutory requirements for federal copyright protection. To prove originality, Flusterated Records must prove that the digital recording contains elements that were independently created by Flusterated Records and that the elements were sufficiently creative to be deserving of copyright protection. The vast majority of the elements contained in the 1990 digital recording were copied from the 1966 analog recording of *Bail*. Flusterated Records will have to prove that it added or changed elements to the analog recording and that those additional elements are sufficiently original to protect the 1990 digital recording as a derivative work. *See Maljack Productions, Inc. v. UAV Corp.*, 964 F. Supp. 1416 (C.D. Cal. 1997), *aff'd*, 160 F.3d 1223 (9th Cir. 1998).

There is no evidence that Flusterated Records has obtained a copyright registration for the 1990 digital recording, therefore, if Flusterated Records wanted to sue Anne Droid for copyright infringement, it would have to apply for a registration. Flusterated Records would have to show that its digital reissue of *Bail Before They Bite* was fixed in a tangible medium of expression that is sufficiently permanent to permit it to be reproduced for a period of more than transitory duration. The reproduction of the sounds from the sound recording in a digital computer file is sufficiently fixed to meet the statutory fixation requirement because the sound can be replayed each time the file is accessed. *See Midway Manufacturing Co. v. Arctic International, Inc.*, 547 F. Supp. 999 (N.D. Ill.), *aff'd*, 704 F.2d 1009 (7th Cir. 1982).

Flusterated Records will claim that its employee, Bobby Banger, did not merely make a mechanical recording of the 1966 analog *Bail* recording, but made several creative decisions to augment the digital recording that resulted from the transfer of the analog sounds via the DigiCom computer program. These decisions involved whether the volume, tones and acoustics of the sounds contained in the digital recording should be adjusted. In addition to these decisions, Banger actually made adjustments at the sound board by raising the level of the bass guitar and lowering the level of the snare drum. These decisions and actual adjustments resulted in variations between the sounds of the 1966 analog recording and the 1990 digital recording. Flusterated Records must prove that these variations were more than merely trivial variations to protect the digital recording as a derivative work. *See Alfred Bell & Co. v. Catalda Fine Arts, Inc.*, 191 F.2d 99, 102–03 (2d Cir. 1951). These variations were deemed necessary by a music professional and were variations that can be heard throughout the 1990 digital recording. As such they are not merely trivial. All that is required is proof of a modicum of creativity and this was clearly evidenced by the changes that resulted from Banger's actions.

Anne Droid will counter that Flusterated Records is attempting to protect a pre-1972 sound recording with federal copyright protection by merely copying the sound recording in a new digital medium, thereby ensuring copyright protection of the recording to the end of 2085. Courts have found that the act of merely mechanically reproducing a work in another medium is insufficiently creative to meet the statutory originality requirement. *See Entertainment Research Group, Inc. v. Genesis Creative Group, Inc.*, 122 F.3d 1211 (9th Cir. 1997). Although Droid would likely concede that an analog sound recording that is fully digitally remastered is worthy of federal copyright protection as a derivative work, the bare tweaking of the volume of a bass guitar and a snare drum is merely a trivial variation that does not meet the level of creativity required by the originality requirement.

If the digital recording satisfied the statutory requirements for copyright protection, Flusterated Records will be the author and initial copyright owner of the derivative work. The facts indicate that Bobby Banger was an employee acting within the scope of his employment when he created the digital sound recording. Therefore, the sound recording constituted a work made for hire. *See Community for Creative Non-Violence v. Reid*, 490 U.S. 730 (1989). Flusterated Records would likely be able to prove that Droid has infringed its copyright in the digital sound recording when she reproduced and publicly distributed the digital sound recording in her CD-ROM program *Before California Fell Into the Ocean*.

Ambigua Peace v. Anne Droid

To succeed in her threatened copyright infringement action against Anne Droid, Ambigua Peace will have to prove that she owns a valid copyright in the musical composition *Bail Before They Bite* and that Droid has infringed one or more of the exclusive rights of section 106 protected by that copyright.

The copyright validity of the *Bail* musical work is really not at issue. The work was first invested with federal copyright protection in 1965 at the time of its registration with the Copyright Office. This gave the work 28 years of initial copyright protection. The first issue is whether the copyright in the composition was renewed. The facts state that Peace never filed a document with the Copyright Office, which means that she never filed an application to renew the copyright. However, because the twenty-eighth year of the initial term was 1993, such an affirmative act of renewal was no longer required. The automatic renewal amendment to the Copyright Act went into effect in 1992. Under this amendment, affirmative renewal of the copyright in the twenty-eighth year by the owner of the renewal right is no longer required. Whoever owns the renewal right at the end of the twenty-eighth year is automatically vested with the renewal copyright. In this case, Rick Rail died in 1975, before he was able to renew the copyright. He had never married, therefore there is no spouse who would be recognized as a valid statutory successor to the renewal right. The next statutory successor category is children. Ambigua Peace is the only child of Rick Rail. Under the 1976 Copyright Act, children born out of wedlock are included in the statutory successor category of children. Therefore, she was automatically vested with the renewal term at the end of 1993. This renewal term is for a period of 67 years: the 28-year traditional term of the renewal copyright, the 19-year extension to the renewal term that was added by the 1976 Copyright Act and the additional 20 years added by the Sonny Bono Copyright Term Extension Act to any work still protected in 1998, which includes the *Bail* musical work.

The facts of this case present a problem similar to that in *Stewart v. Abend*, 495 U.S. 207 (1990). In that case, the United States Supreme Court held that when the author of an underlying work had licensed its use as the basis for a derivative work for both the initial and renewal terms of the copyright in the underlying work and the author died before renewing the copyright, the statutory successor who owns the renewal copyright is not in privity of contract with the creator of the derivative work and is not bound by the earlier license. In this case, the author, Rick Rail, had entered into a license agreement in 1975 with Anne Droid to use the *Bail* musical work during the initial and renewal terms and any extensions. At the time he entered into the license, however, Rick Rail owned only an expectancy interest in the renewal term for the *Bail* musical work. His expectancy interest was not realized because Rail died before he was able to renew the copyright, thus it never vested in him. As stated earlier, the renewal term did vest in Ambigua Peace. Because she was not a party to the 1975 license, Peace owns the renewal term without any obligations under the agreement. Under the *Abend* case, this ownership would have given Peace the right to sue Droid for copyright infringement, because Peace is not bound by the 1975 license agreement. However, the 1992 automatic renewal amendment to the Copyright Act modified the application of the *Abend* decision. Pursuant to that amendment, a statutory successor can take advantage of the *Abend* decision only if the statutory successor affirmatively filed a renewal application with the Copyright Office in the twenty-eighth year of copyright protection. For those statutory successors who did not affirmatively renew the copyright in the twenty-eighth year, but own the renewal copyright because of automatic renewal, the creator of a derivative work, created pursuant to a grant that included the renewal term, is permitted to continue using the derivative work during the renewal term, under the provisions of the original grant.

In this case, Peace cannot take advantage of the *Abend* decision because she did not affirmatively renew the copyright in *Bail* in its twenty-eighth year. That means that Anne Droid has the statutory right to use the *Bail* musical composition in her CD-ROM program if the 1975 license gives her that right.

Whether the CD-ROM program meets the requirement of "in connection with a documentary"

Droid argues that the 1975 grant gives her a nonexclusive right to use the *Bail* musical composition "in connection with a documentary" and that her CD-ROM program, *Before California Fell Into the Ocean*, is a documentary because it presents a history of California surfing music. It utilizes biographical material, photographs and music to inform viewers and listeners of that history. The 1975 license used the term "documentary" in its general sense and did not use it as a defined term, the use of which would have been capitalized. Therefore, her use falls within the parameters of the 1975 license.

Peace responds that the intent of the parties to the 1975 license was to permit the use of *Bail* in a documentary on the life of Rick Rail, not a general work on California surfing music. This intent is evidenced by the fact that Rick Rail also permitted the use of his life story and agreed to cooperate in the making of the motion picture. If a court finds that the term "documentary" in the license is not ambiguous, it is likely that the court will interpret the license to permit the use of the *Bail* composition in any documentary created by Droid. This would allow Droid to continue to exploit the *Before California Fell Into the Ocean* derivative work.

New technology issue

Ambigua Peace will likely argue that the 1975 license does not extend to the use of the *Bail* composition in a CD-ROM, because the parties did not know of that technology at the time they entered into the license. Droid will successfully argue, however, that the 1975 license contained the language "by any means or methods now or hereafter known," which is a new technology clause that permits the use of the *Bail* composition in connection with technology that was not known at the time. A court will be faced with the issue of whether the reservation of rights clause (paragraph 9), by which Rail reserved all rights and uses to *Bail* "except those herein granted to Anne Droid," would be sufficient to counter the new technology clause. Because the use of the composition in unknown technology was granted to Droid in paragraph 6, it is likely that a court would find that the new technology clause would control, though that is not certain.

Application of the compulsory mechanical license of section 115

If the 1975 license were found to be inapplicable to Droid's CD-ROM program, the compulsory mechanical license provision of section 115 of the Copyright Act would not be available to her. First, she is using the *Bail* musical work in an audiovisual work that is distributed in a copy. Section 115 only applies to musical works that are distributed in phonorecords. *See ABKCO Music, Inc. v. Stellar Records, Inc.*, 96 F.3d 60, 65 (2d Cir. 1996). Second, even if she were distributing the *Bail* composition in a phonorecord, she is distributing it in connection with a preexisting sound recording. Section 115 will not permit a compulsory mechanical license for such a use unless a license to use the preexisting sound recording has been obtained. In this case Droid has not obtained a license to the sound recording from Flusterated Records.

Answer to: Fiona Photog

Fiona Photog (FP) is the creator of "Ranch Heroes," a copyrighted work of authorship that falls into the category of pictorial, graphical, or sculptural work. Her claim is that PubliCo's (PC) use of "Ranch Heroes" on its Pulitzer website without FP's explicit authorization amounts to a violation of her exclusive rights as the owner of the copyright in the photograph. If FP's claim is accurate, PC's actions would violate her exclusive rights of reproduction, public display and, possibly, adaptation. The reproduction right is at issue because this is a near-verbatim copy of the original "Ranch Heroes." By placing a version of "Ranch Heroes" on its website, PC has displayed the work to the public. It is a harder question whether the adaptation right is at issue because there may not be enough originality in the online version of "Ranch Heroes" to make that version a derivative work. *See L. Batlin & Son, Inc. v. Snyder*, 536 F.2d 486 (2d Cir. 1976).

Because PC used FP's work without her permission, violating at least two of her exclusive rights, it seems that FP would have a strong case for copyright infringement against PC. But PC can advance three arguments to resist FP's allegations of infringement.

PC may own the "Ranch Heroes" copyright because the photograph was a work made for hire

Although FP is clearly the creator of "Ranch Heroes," that does not mean she is necessarily the author or the owner of the copyright in that work. If "Ranch Heroes" is a work made for hire, then the Copyright Act defines the hiring party, not the creator, as the author. 17 U.S.C. § 201(b). So if "Ranch Heroes" is a work made for hire, that means that PC (not FP) is the author, and also copyright owner (in the absence of a transfer), and FP cannot object to its use without her consent.

A work made for hire is one prepared by an employee in the scope of her employment. 17 U.S.C. § 101. Here, if FP is not an employee, but rather an independent contractor, then "Ranch Heroes" cannot be a work made for hire unless both FP and PC signed a work made for hire agreement and "Ranch Heroes" falls within one of the nine statutory work made for hire categories. The fact that FP has not signed a work made for hire agreement precludes "Ranch Heroes" from being deemed a work made for hire if FP is found to be an independent contractor.

Numerous factors suggest that FP is an independent contractor rather than an employee. FP works out of her own studio as an independent contractor would, not the *Tempo* offices as an employee would. FP also covers events on her own schedule and at her own instance as an independent contractor would, rather than taking assignments from *Tempo* as an employee would. Finally, FP's financial relationship with *Tempo* is not an employee-like regular paycheck arrangement, but a series of one-off, individually negotiated contracts.

PC can point to several factors that may suggest instead that FP is its employee. FP consistently refers to herself as a "*Tempo* photographer," which suggests identification with a particular publication rather than freelance status. FP's equipment comes to a large extent from *Tempo* as well—the camera she used to take Ranch Heroes was a holiday gift from *Tempo*—and this could be taken to indicate that *Tempo* supplies FP with equipment as it would any other employee. Moreover, the fact that *Tempo* regularly gives FP a gift during the holidays suggests the presence of an ongoing relationship with her. Finally, *Tempo* sometimes gives Fiona tips about events and even a ride to sites in their company helicopter, which is the kind of service that employers typically provide to employees.

Examined more closely, though, none of these factual assertions resisting independent contractor status bear scrutiny. FP referred to herself as a "*Tempo* photographer" not because it reflected her actual status, but just to gain professional cachet or to get access to tightly controlled news areas. And even if FP uses the cameras she got from *Tempo*, they are still hers (given as gifts), so she is not using *Tempo* equipment when she takes pictures with them. Nor does the fact of gift-giving necessarily mean that FP is a PC employee; the cameras likely reflect PC's appreciation of her good work and represent an incentive to keep up an otherwise informal relationship. Finally, the occasional tip or ride does not mean that FP is in PC's employ, but merely that PC has provided some degree of assistance that is overwhelmed by the independence FP maintains in all other respects. Nor is it unusual for any hiring party to provide assistance to an independent contractor; a freelance writer may receive copyediting help from a publication, but that does not automatically convert her status into an employee.

So, although there is no dispositive factor on this issue—for example, we do not know whether PubliCo takes taxes out of the checks they issue to FP—these facts strongly indicate that FP is an independent contractor for two reasons. First, the factors suggesting her independent contractor status—payment arrangements and professional relationship—are core matters that go to the heart of the work relationship between FP and *Tempo*, while the ones that militate in the other direction—a holiday gift or ride to an event site here or there—are far more marginal in their significance. Also, the factors arguably militating in favor of employee status are far weaker when examined closely because they are all subject to explanations that render them less probative of employee status. In light of all this, "Ranch Heroes" is very likely not a work made for hire, so FP, not PC, would be its author and owner.

PC's use of "Ranch Heroes" may not be improper to the extent that FP authorized it

Even though FP, not PC, is likely the author and owner of "Ranch Heroes," PC's use of the photograph on its website will not amount to infringement if it can mount an argument that FP permitted that use. There are two possible arguments that FP permitted this use.

PC's use of "Ranch Heroes" may fall within the scope of the original license pursuant to the section 201(c) collective work privilege

FP's license clearly allowed PC to use "Ranch Heroes" only in that single edition of *Tempo*. The Copyright Act, however, permits owners of collective works to reproduce and distribute validly acquired works of authorship in future editions and revisions of the original collective work in which the licensed work of authorship was used. 17 U.S.C. § 201(c). *Tempo* is clearly a collective work because, like a newspaper, it consists of a variety of different separately copyrighted works of authorship such as FP's "Ranch Heroes." *E.g., New York Times Co., Inc. v. Tasini*, 533 U.S. 483 (2001).

The difficult question, though, is whether PC's Pulitzer website counts as the kind of revision or new edition that falls within the section 201(c) privilege. FP will argue that the website is not a new revision or edition because it is a different medium. This argument will fail, however, because the Supreme Court held that mere reissuance in the context of a digital medium from an analog one does not automatically preclude application of the section 201(c) privilege. *See New York Times Co., Inc. v. Tasini*, 533 U.S. 483 (2001).

FP will also argue that the use of "Ranch Heroes" on the website is not within the section 201(c) privilege because the website takes the picture out of its original context. This argument has a stronger legal foundation because the Supreme Court has held that the standard for whether a new use falls within the section 201(c) privilege is whether it is presented in its original context. Here, "Ranch Heroes" is presented outside its original context for two reasons. First, the website does not merely post full-text versions of *Tempo* articles online, but only excerpts and does not include the Blanco Valley fire article in the context of the other articles in that issue of *Tempo. C.F. Greenberg v. Nat'l Geographic Society*, 533 F.3d 1244 (11th Cir. 2008). Second, "Ranch Heroes" itself is not presented in its original version, but is rather shrunken, cropped, and in black-and-white (as opposed to color). In light of all this, PC's argument that its website is a revision or new edition that falls within the section 201(c) privilege, and thus moots the need to ask FP for permission for the new use, would very likely fail.

FP granted PC a non-exclusive license to use "Ranch Heroes" on the Pulitzer website

In light of the above, there is no argument that FP's original license allowing PC to use "Ranch Heroes" in *Tempo* extends to PC's use on the Pulitzer website. There may, however, be an argument that FP subsequently licensed PC to do so.

PC will argue that FP granted a license to use "Ranch Heroes" on its website when she was approached by a PC executive at a party who mentioned the Pulitzer website and FP responded, "Sure, whatever you say."

An argument that this exchange amounts to a transfer (i.e., assignment or exclusive license) by FP to PC will certainly fail, because transfers of copyrights must be written. 17 U.S.C. § 204(a). However, nonexclusive licenses are not included in the Copyright Act's definition of transfer of copyright ownership, 17 U.S.C. § 101, so PC may be able to argue that the cocktail party exchange resulted in the grant of a nonexclusive license to PC. Courts have held that nonexclusive licenses can be granted in three ways: written, verbally, and implied through conduct. *Effects Associates, Inc. v. Cohen*, 908 F.2d 555 (1990).

PC will first attempt to argue that FP verbally granted a nonexclusive license to PC when she responded to the PC executive's suggestion that they put her photo online by saying, "Sure, whatever you say." This argument will likely fail for several reasons. First, the language itself is very ambiguous. FP did not clearly indicate assent, as she would have if she had said, "Yes, that sounds great, please post my picture online." Rather, her language was dismissive and sarcastic, and almost certainly not meant to be taken at face value. Second, the context—a brief, offhand encounter at a cocktail party—strongly suggests that neither party believed a serious negotiation was taking place. Third, at least the PC executive and possibly also FP were intoxicated, which cuts back against their ability to meaningfully grant legal rights. And finally, FP's response to the situation (and the fact that she did not even remember it had happened) indicates that she was merely trying to blow off a drunk, rather than give consent to use of "Ranch Heroes" online.

PC may also try to argue that FP implied a nonexclusive license through her conduct. A nonexclusive license may be implied through conduct where there is a physical handover of the copyrighted work of authorship, and the circumstances surrounding the handover indicate a grant of use rights as well. *Oddo v. Ries*, 743 F.2d 630 (9th Cir. 1984). Here, there is physical handover because FP gave *Tempo* a copy of "Ranch Heroes," but there is nothing about that handover that suggests she meant to allow the online use. On the contrary, FP explicitly limited that grant to one single use in *Tempo*, and made very clear that she preferred working with *Tempo* because she did not want to have her work go online, and *Tempo* did not have an online edition.

In light of all this, a court would be very unlikely to find that PC's use of "Ranch Heroes" was permitted either by FP's original license in combination with the section 201(c) privilege, or by a later nonexclusive license granted by FP.

PC's online use of "Ranch Heroes" may be a fair use

Even if FP is the author and owner of "Ranch Heroes," and even if there is no argument that she has sanctioned PC's online use of the photograph, PC still may prevail if it can successfully argue that the online version of "Ranch Heroes" amounts to a fair use.

Fair use is a statutory affirmative defense to copyright infringement. Whether a use is fair depends on four non-exclusive factors: the purpose and character of the defendant's use; the nature of the defendant's work; the amount and substantiality of the taking; and the effect of the defendant's use on present and future markets for the plaintiff's work. 17 U.S.C. § 107.

Factor one: the purpose and character of the use

This factor considers two separate issues: the extent to which the use is transformative, *Campbell v. Acuff-Rose Music, Inc.*, 510 U.S. 569, 577 (1994), and the extent to which it is commercial, *Harper & Row, Publishers, Inc. v. Nation Enterprises*, 471 U.S. 539 (1985).

Whether PC's use of "Ranch Heroes" on its website is transformative depends on a comparison of the original purpose of the use in *Tempo* as compared to the photograph's use on the Pulitzer site. The original purpose of the photograph was to document the fires at Blanco Valley, and to highlight the heroism of the workers who saved horses from those fires. Seen from this perspective, the purpose of PC's use was highly transformative, because it was not for the purpose of news reporting (the fires happened long before the site went up, so there was no need to inform anyone), but rather to increase attention to the magazine from the Pulitzer search committee. Adding to this conclusion is that the photograph was transformed in a very physical sense—cropped, shrunk, changed to black-and-white. That PC's use is transformative weighs in its favor and makes it more likely that the online use of "Ranch Heroes" is a fair use.

PC may argue that the original purpose of the photos was not merely to report the news, but also to gain readership and impress possible prize committees, which would make the use on the Pulitzer site much less transformative. This may well have been a secondary or tertiary consideration, but was by no means a primary one, and so likely will not cause this factor to weigh in favor of FP.

PC may argue that its use of "Ranch Heroes" was transformative because it shifted the photograph from an analog to an online medium, but this argument will certainly fail because shifts in medium, without more, are not considered transformative. *UMG Recordings, Inc. v. MP3.com, Inc.*, 92 F. Supp. 2d 349 (S.D.N.Y. 2000).

It is clear that there is some commerciality inherent in PC's use. It has placed "Ranch Heroes" online in order to garner the Pulitzer Prize, journalism's highest honor. Winning this award would have both direct financial benefits (a $10,000 prize) and indirect ones (wider circulation). However, this possibility and its nexus with FP's single photograph is rather remote. Nor is PC's use entirely commercial; it has already extracted commercial value from "Ranch Heroes" by including it in the print version of the magazine, and the website is both free to the public and designed mostly to garner nonmonetary benefits such as fame and prestige. Moreover, courts have recently held that because almost any use can be regarded as commercial in some respect, this factor deserves relatively less weight. *See, e.g., Castle Rock Entertainment v. Carol Publishing Group, Inc.*, 150 F.3d 132 (2d Cir. 1998). The relatively remote commerciality of PC's use likely does not do much to weigh in favor of FP.

Factor two: the nature of the plaintiff's work

This factor looks at two considerations: whether the plaintiff's work is published, and whether it is creative or factual. Published works are somewhat more likely to be subject to a fair use defense than unpublished ones; factual works are more likely to be subject to a fair use defense than creative ones. "Ranch Heroes" was clearly published in *Tempo*, which works in favor of PC and a fair use defense, albeit weakly. PC will also argue that the photo was entirely factual, which also militates in favor of fair use. But although "Ranch Heroes" was clearly a photo of factual events, this does not mean it lacked any creative elements. Photos can possess creativity by virtue of staging, choice of subject matter, and use of equipment to achieve certain effects, all of which would cause "Ranch Heroes" to seem closer to the core of copyright. In light of all this, the second factor does not weigh strongly in favor of either party.

Factor three: The amount and substantiality of the taking

This factor looks at qualitative and quantitative amount taken from plaintiff's work, with an aim of determining the ratio of the taking in relation to plaintiff's work overall and whether that amount of taking was necessary.

PC took nearly all of "Ranch Heroes," except for a section toward the top where the photo was cropped. However, the taking was limited in another sense because the photo was diminished in terms of its overall size (only a few inches square) and colors (the black-and-white format did not capture the richness of the original version). In light of these considerations, the taking was far from total. Moreover, in a qualitative sense the taking failed to take the "heart" (or at least, all of the "heart") of FP's work because by cropping out the clouds, the effect of the smoke in the sky was lost, and FP had identified this as one of the main features distinguishing the photo.

Moreover, the amount taken was justified in light of the purpose of the taking. PC's reason for including "Ranch Heroes" on its website was to impress the Pulitzer committee. In order to do this, it had to include all, or nearly all, of the photo to give a sense of its quality. Courts have held that where a photo was used without permission, but in a smaller form to give some indication of its content, that taking was justified in light of the taking's purpose. *Kelly v. Arriba Soft Corp.*, 280 F.3d 934 (9th Cir. 2002). The modesty of the taking interacts with its purpose to further cause this factor to weigh in favor of PC and fair use.

Factor four: The effect of the defendant's use on present and future markets for the plaintiff's work

This factor considers the impact of the defendant's use on both present and future markets (both primary and secondary) for the plaintiff's work. The impact of PC's use on the primary market for FP's work is negligible. The primary market for a news photograph is immediate, and since the Blanco Valley fires have long since passed, there is virtually no chance that another news outlet will want to acquire the photo to run alongside its coverage.

This does not, however, mean that PC's use has not damaged FP's secondary market—that is, selling licensing rights—for "Ranch Heroes." Because there is always a theoretical market for licensing copyrighted works, the only relevant secondary markets are ones that are present, customary or likely to emerge. *American Geophysical Union v. Texaco, Inc.*, 60 F.3d 913 (2d Cir. 1994). Here, though, there is some evidence that there is a secondary market for prints that has been harmed: Eagle Prints, the company with which FP traditionally works to license prints of her work, has complained that the appearance of "Ranch Heroes" online makes it want to reconsider its relationship with FP.

On the other hand, this argument seems implausible because the kind of photos Eagle Prints sells are high-quality editions one would use for aesthetic enjoyment, hung in a house or an office. By contrast, the version that appeared online could not be used for this purpose since it was low-quality and in black-and-white. Even though it would be theoretically possible for a user to download "Ranch Heroes" from the Pulitzer website and blow it up into a large print, the result would likely be too pixilated to have the same aesthetic appeal as a professionally made print, and in any event would be missing its color as well as the cropped-out area (which, FP indicated, was a major part of the photo's aesthetic appeal). It is also worth considering that some courts would find that the photo's appearance online might have positive effects for FP's reputation, particularly if it earned her or *Tempo* a Pulitzer Prize, and this may overwhelm any marginal negative impact on secondary markets. In light of all this, the effect of PC's online use of "Ranch Heroes" will likely have a negligible effect on FP's market for the work, and this factor weighs in favor of fair use.

Factor analysis

Factors one, three, and four — (one and four likely being the most important factors in this case) — weigh in favor of fair use, while factor two does not weigh very strongly. This indicates that a court would likely consider PC's use to be defensible as a fair one.

* * *

FP will likely be able to show both that she is the author and owner of "Ranch Heroes," and that she did not license its use on PC's website. Despite this, however, PC will likely be able to mount a persuasive fair use defense, and so will likely prevail on this affirmative defense.

Answer to: *The Gift*

Whether *The Gift* is in the public domain depends on when federal copyright in the literary work vested.

If federal copyright in the work vested around the time of its creation, then the work might not be in the public domain in 2017. Whether it vested in 1927, 1928, or 1930, a full copyright term would last 95 years, and would expire in 1922 at the earliest. While 1909 Act terms initially lasted for a maximum of 56 years (28 + 28R), they were extended for 19 years by the 1976 Copyright Act, and then again for 20 years by the Copyright Term Extension Act of 1998, for a total possible coverage of 95 years.

It is not at all clear, though, that a federal copyright that vested around 1927–30 would have a full term. The 1909 Act terms were bifurcated and required renewal in their twenty-eighth year in order to achieve the renewal term that is currently set at 67 years. Here, we do not know whether the owners of the copyright in its twenty-eighth year renewed it; and so if federal copyright vested sometime between 1927–30, it is possible that the work went into the public domain between 1955–58 and has been there ever since.

Ultimately, though, the above analysis is likely beside the point. For the following reasons, it is unlikely that federal copyright in *The Gift* vested near the time of its creation.

I.   Could federal copyright in *The Gift* have vested in 1927?

Vesting of federal copyright under the 1909 Act required general publication with notice or registration of unpublished works with the Copyright Office. Copyright in *The Gift* could not have vested when it was written in 1927, because although there was a valid copyright notice on the work, Sheila did not publish the work during that year. Indeed, she kept *The Gift* entirely secret, neither showing nor giving it to anyone.

II. Could federal copyright in *The Gift* have vested in 1928?

Elise may also argue that copyright in the work vested in 1928, and while this argument is more plausible, it is also certain to fail. Sheila appended proper copyright notice to the single handwritten copy of *The Gift*, but her reading of the story over the radio was not enough to effect general publication. General publication typically entails some distribution of physical copies to the general public, and here while the general public heard *The Gift*, they did not receive copies of the work. Courts have consistently held that performance of a work does not cause publication of the work. *King*; 17 U.S.C § 101 (performance does not cause publication).

III. Did federal copyright in *The Gift* vest in 1930?

Elise may finally argue that placement of the single copy of *The Gift* in the vault in 1930 effected publication, but this argument is also clearly unconvincing. The placement in the vault made the copy of *The Gift* available only to four definitely selected people, and in fact was seen only by two of those people. Placement of the copy in the vault appears to be the very antithesis of publication, since it was a way of keeping the sole copy of *The Gift* secret, rather than introducing copies of it into the public sphere. At the very least, this act would be regarded as one of limited publication, not general publication, and would not have been sufficient to either vest or divest federal copyright.

IV. Did federal copyright in *The Gift* vest as of 1978?

Because federal copyright in *The Gift* did not vest near the time of its publication, and because *The Gift* was not published at any time thereafter, it was clearly an unpublished work subject to state common-law copyright at the time of its creation until the federal 1976 Copyright Act became effective on January 1, 1978. By virtue of this Act, state common-law copyrights such as the one for *The Gift* was subject to were converted to federal terms, and enjoyed the longer of the applicable life-of-the-author-based term (life plus 50 years, ultimately extended to life plus 70 years by the 1998 CTEA) or the minimum applicable term that lasts through either 12/31/2002 or 12/31/2047 in the case of works that were published between 1/1/1978 and 12/31/2002.

V.   What is the duration of the federal copyright in *The Gift*?

  1. Federal terms of previously unpublished works

In light of this, federal copyright in *The Gift* is determined by one of the two minimum terms established by the 1976 Act for common-law copyrights that were converted to federal terms. Sheila died in 1930, so the life-based term of the 1976 Act would have placed the copyright into the public domain as of 2000, which means that even the shorter of the two minimum terms (until 2003) would be preferable to the 1976 Act term. That latter term would last only through 2000, even after the 1998 CTEA extended 1976 Act terms to life of the author plus 70 years. However, if the shorter of the two minimum terms applies to *The Gift*, then the work would be in the public domain as of 2003. So if Elise wants to argue that *The Gift* is protected by federal copyright, she has to successfully argue that the work was published between 1978 and 2003.

Elise can argue that three events during 2000 may have amounted to publication of *The Gift* during this period: her sending an .mp3 copy of *The Gift* to the San Sendero *Times*; her broadcast of *The Gift* over the Internet; and her giving copies of *The Gift* to family members.

  2. Internet broadcast as publication?

The second of these possible arguments for publication is the least substantial: Elise's streaming broadcast of *The Gift* over the Internet. This transmission amounted to a public performance of *The Gift*, but public performance does not, without more, cause publication. 17 U.S.C. § 101 (performance does not cause publication). And since the broadcast did not result in any members of the public obtaining .mp3 version of Elise's reading of *The Gift*, there is no convincing argument that the 2000 Internet broadcast caused publication.

3. Sending to the *Times* as publication?

More plausibly, Elise might argue that by sending the .mp3 version of her reading *The Gift* to the San Sendero *Times* in 2000, she effected the work's publication. This argument is much more plausible than any of the foregoing claims about publication. Elise's sending a digital copy of the work to a large media organization may meet the definition of a publication because it amounts to a broad physical distribution. *See* 17 U.S.C. § 101 (defining "publication" as "the distribution of copies . . . of a work to the public"). But not all distributions are publications; some such acts are only limited publications that do not trigger the implications the Copyright Act typically attaches to publication.

This issue thus requires consideration of the three factors courts typically use to analyze whether a work has been generally published. This test considers three factors: whether the purported publication was to a definitely selected group; whether the purported publication was for a limited purpose; and whether the purported publication was without right of further sale or distribution. *Creative House.*

Definitely selected group. Courts have held that distribution of copies to a definitely selected group, as opposed to members of the general public, weighs against regarding an act as amounting to general publication. Handing out the Oscar statuette to specific actors, for example, was held to be distribution of copies to a definitely selected group. By contrast, distributing copies to the general, undifferentiated public would weigh in favor of regarding that act as one of general publication.

Here, certain features of Elise's distribution of the .mp3 copy appear circumscribed to a definitely selected group. Elise did not send the .mp3 to a large, undifferentiated group whose members she did not know. Rather, she sent the copy to a single, specific newspaper that she was very familiar with, since it was her local paper. As in *Creative House*, this was not a random distribution to the public, but a targeted delivery to one known entity. *Cf. also King* (no publication where distribution was to a specific group of known journalists).

Other features of Elise's distribution of the .mp3, however, seem to weigh against the definiteness of the group. Elise did not specify any particular individual in sending the .mp3 to the San Sendero *Times*. Rather, she sent the .mp3 to the paper via its general-interest email address, info@ sansenderotimes.com, so that anyone who manages that email account could have received the message with the attachment. This seems very different from the targeted distribution at issue in *Creative House*, where every individual who received an Oscar was specifically designated. Indeed, Elise makes very clear that she contemplated that the .mp3 would be shared among the entire *Times* staff, as she indicated in her email asking that it not be shared outside the editorial group. Since the Times consisted of 500 editorial employees at the time the email was sent, the group that Elise contemplated sharing the file with would have been rather large, and she certainly would not have known their individual identities.

This is a hard issue with no clear-cut answer. A strict construction of this rule would say that because Elise did not know the identities of the individuals on the *Times'* 500-person editorial staff, the release was not to a "definitely selected group." A broader construction would say that Elise's efforts to limit the distribution to a specific, clearly defined group would be sufficient, even if she did not know the identity of each individual within the group. *Cf. King* (very unlikely that King knew the identity of every journalist who received the advanced copy of his speech, but still held to be a definitely selected group).

Limited purpose. The distribution of copies for a limited purpose, as opposed to a more diffuse purpose, does not effect publication. Here, the purpose does appear limited, because Elise seems to have sent the San Sendero *Times* the .mp3 copy only to facilitate their writing an article about the forthcoming Internet broadcast of her reading of *The Gift*. This purpose is limited in terms of time and scope. Elise specified that the *Times* may write only a single article, and may only do so for the purpose of reporting on the broadcast (as opposed to other angles related to *The Gift*, such as its history or public perception).

On the other hand, within those constraints, the purpose is not particularly limited, and the purpose itself—publicity—may be construed as actually quite broad. Indeed, the aim of the article that Elise wants the *Times* to write will be to publicize her broadcast, and *The Gift* more generally. Courts have tended to regard distributions with the aim of creating publicity as publications. *E.g., Milton H. Greene Archives* (holding that photos of Marilyn Monroe distributed for publicity purposes were generally published); *see also Creative House* (suggesting that if the Oscar were intended to generally publicize the MPAAS, that would weigh in favor of general publication).

This, too, is a hard and interesting question that will turn on what "purpose" means. Does it refer to the scope of the use, or the goal of the use? Embracing the former standard would weigh against publication; but embracing the latter standard would inveigh in favor of publication.

Without right of further distribution. Where a distribution takes place without the right to further distribute copies, this weighs in favor of publication. The right to further distribute copies can be conferred either explicitly or implicitly. *Cf., e.g., Creative House* (finding implied limitation on further distribution or sale of Oscar statuettes).

Here, there is no language in the email from Elise to the San Sendero *Times*, or anywhere else, explicitly limiting further distribution of the .mp3. There is, however, some language that can be read to impose such limits impliedly, if not explicitly. Elise wrote, "I hope that you will not spread this copy outside the editorial staff of your paper," clearly expressing her desire that the file would be shared only within the *Times* editorial offices. Moreover, Elise expressed how much it would upset her if the file of her reading *The Gift* were widely disseminated, indicating that this would undermine the "mystery" of the work's "magic," and that it would be deeply upsetting to her and her family. Taken together, these statements clearly indicate how much Elise wants the *Times* not to further distribute the .mp3 file of *The Gift*.

On the other hand, all of these statements are phrased in precatory language. That is, they indicate Elise's desire that the .mp3 file not be shared outside the *Times* editorial staff, but they do not express that Elise seeks to actually limit the *Times* staff from doing this. If Elise had wanted to, she could easily have said, "I do not give you permission to use this .mp3 file except for the purpose of writing your article, and I do not authorize you to distribute it outside the *Times* editorial staff." Instead, however, Elise merely used aspirational language like "hope," and illustrated the negative effects distribution would have on her, appearing to urge non-dissemination without requiring it.

Weighing more strongly in favor of finding implied limits on the *Times*' further distribution of the .mp3 file are the circumstances surrounding Elise's sending the file to the *Times*. Her purpose in doing this was clearly only to facilitate their writing an article (see discussion above, discussing limited purpose). This lies in sharp contrast to the publicity photo cases, where the aim of the distribution was to make sure as many eyeballs as possible saw the photos. *E.g., Milton H. Greene Archives* (finding general publication of Marilyn Monroe photos in part because purpose of sending them to publicity agents was to popularize Monroe in the public eye). The purpose in *Greene Archives* and other cases, however, was broadly to facilitate publicity, so the right to further distribute the works could be inferred from the circumstances surrounding their initial distribution. Here, by contrast, the purpose to which the initial distribution of the .mp3 file was intended could have been served without further distribution, so this in combination with the clear indications from Elise that she did not want further distribution (even if she did not clearly preclude that distribution) permit an inference that there was no such right.

Moreover, courts have been very generous in finding implied restrictions on further distribution, especially where, as here, a contrary finding would tend to cause the work to go into the public domain. This judicial tendency likely tips the scales on this factor firmly in favor of Elise.

On balance, a court would likely not find that Elise's sending the .mp3 file of *The Gift* to the *Times* amounted to general publication. The group was reasonably, although not perfectly, well-defined; the purpose was clearly and explicitly limited; and the context of Elise's sending the file allows reasonable inferences that further distribution was not permitted.

4. Gift to relatives as publication?

Regardless of how a judge ruled in terms of whether Elise effected publication of *The Gift* by sending the .mp3 file to the San Sendero *Times* in 2000, it also remains to consider whether Elise effected publication by giving the annotated copy of *The Gift* to her five relatives, including Quentin, that same year.

Definitely selected group. This is an easy issue, and not one that warrants much discussion. The group consists of a very small number, each individual in the group is known to Elise, and the group was very specifically selected. This factor clearly weighs in favor of non-publication.

Limited purpose. Elise's purpose in giving her family members the book seems to have been to commemorate her grandmother's memory, which is pretty clear from the circumstances when the gift was given (family dinner) and Elise's explanation of her aspiration that they be "nice family heirlooms" for Sheila's descendants. This is a very narrow purpose, and more important, one that does not require or entail publication. In fact, one could argue that this purpose is actually inconsistent with publication because Elise's vision of commemorating her grandmother appears to require keeping the copies of *The Gift* within the family, such as by reading it to children or putting it on the mantelpiece.

On the other hand, Elise also used more expansive language in describing her purpose in giving the copies to the relatives, specifically, "you're free to do with them whatever you want," so commemoration may not be the only purpose she had in mind when she gave the copies to the relatives. It could be that she simply meant for there to be no specific purpose beyond giving a sentimental gift to Sheila's other descendants. But this explanation is hard to square with the specific examples she gave to Quentin (read the book to children, put it on your mantelpiece) when he asked what they were supposed to do with the books. On the other hand, these could be taken merely as illustrative (not limitative) examples, and Elise did specifically state that these were not the exclusive purposes to which the gift of *The Gift* was to be put.

Without right of further distribution. There is an argument that Elise used explicit language that gave a right of further distribution when she responded to Quentin's question by saying, "you're free to do with them whatever you want." This is a fairly clear indication that recipients of the gift are not limited in their ability to distribute the copy, and if a court were to credit this language for its plain meaning, that would probably result in a finding that the work has been published.

There are other contextual indicators, though, that this language should not be taken at face value. For one thing, this was not a carefully articulated statement of intent to permit general distribution, but rather a (possibly sharp) rejoinder to what Elise seems to have thought was a foolish or rude question from Quentin. She seems to be saying that she didn't intend any specific actions by the gift's recipients, but this doesn't mean that she was intending that they would re-release the book to the general public. Moreover, Elise's illustrations of what the recipients might do with their copies makes it hard to construe her statement as conferring a general right to distribute further copies. If placing a copy on the mantelpiece is truly illustrative of what Elise imagined recipients would do with their copies of *The Gift*, then it is hard to construe her intent as approving general distribution of the work.

On the other hand, Quentin might respond to this latter point by observing that Elise's motivation in keeping the copies of *The Gift* within the family was to make sure only that Sheila's handwriting remained within the family, which does not preclude distribution of typewritten versions of *The Gift* (such as the very one that Quentin has published). This is a plausible but ultimately not convincing argument, though, since Elise clearly was concerned to keep the content as well as the handwriting of *The Gift* out of the public eye, as evidenced by the intensity with which she endeavored to have her reading of *The Gift* kept under wraps when she streamed it via the Internet in 2000.

Overall, it is unlikely that a court would find *The Gift* was published when Elise gave the copies to five family members. The gift to her family was to a sharply limited group, appears to have been for the relatively defined purpose of commemoration, and was subject to implied, if not explicit, limitations on further distribution. Beyond the factors, this does not seem like the kind of conduct that courts would be likely to regard as a general publication, such as giving out copies of a work to radio stations or publicists for publicity purposes. Even giving MLK's "I Have a Dream" speech to a room of reporters was construed as limited publication, and this clearly seems more limited than that.

VI. Implications

It appears that none of the possible theories on which one might argue that *The Gift* has been published are persuasive, so the work would likely have gone into the public domain at the end of 2002.

This would mean that Quentin was free to publish it, as anyone would have been, in 2010. But there is an interesting twist with respect to Joan's distribution of the work. The version of *The Gift* that Joan distributed was Elise's sound recording, which is arguably a derivative work based on the underlying literary work. Assuming that Elise owns the sound recording, even a thin copyright in it would be enough to state an infringement claim against Joan for distributing verbatim copies of the .mp3 without permission. Thus, even if the underlying literary work were in the public domain, Elise still might be able to recover against Joan for infringement of the derivative work, since Joan reproduced it verbatim by emailing it to her contacts list.

Answer to: The Dude Abides

I. Can Jeff state a successful claim of copyright infringement against DKAG?

    A. Situating the potential lawsuit

Jeff will argue that DKAG should be liable for its unauthorized use of the audiovisual work, *Tea-Vee*, that was originally authored and copyrighted by Maude. Jeff has a plausible argument for copyright infringement of this work to the extent that DKAG is engaging in a public performance of the work without permission of its original author and owner, Maude.

    B. Does Jeff have an enforceable copyright interest in *TeaVee*?

        1. Does Jeff have standing to bring a copyright infringement claim?

Whether there is a valid claim first depends on whether Jeff even has standing to bring a copyright infringement suit in the first place. *TeaVee* was properly registered well before the purported infringement occurred, so registration will create no jurisdictional bar. The standing issue raises two related issues, though: First, did Maude validly transfer to Jeff the right to sue for infringement of *TeaVee*? And second, is Maude's transfer to Jeff of the right to sue for infringement of *TeaVee* enforceable?

            a. Did Maude validly transfer to Jeff the right to sue for infringement of *TeaVee*?

Transfers of copyright (including wholesale assignments as well as exclusive rights) must be in writing and signed by the transferor. § 204(a). The transfer may be reflected in a "note or memorandum of transfer," *id.*, and need not be the "Magna Charta," *Effects Assocs.* Maude's note to Jeff, while highly unorthodox, almost certainly meets the formal requirements for copyright transfer. It is in writing, signed by Maude herself (her reference to her nickname, "Maudie," probably does not undermine this because it clearly identifies her), and describes the subject matter transferred. The note itself is highly unorthodox, written in lipstick on paper, but nothing in section 204(a) suggests that unorthodox style disqualifies a "note or memorandum of transfer." Indeed, the language of section 204(a) was meant to broadly include means of transfer beyond just formal legal documents, hence the expansive "note or memorandum" language.

The content of Maude's note to Jeff may create more difficulty, since it does not clearly transfer an exclusive right. The note may be construed as a "transfer of copyright" because it seems to indicate that Maude has attempted to assign to Jeff an exclusive right, namely the right to bring suit for DKAG's purported infringement of *TeaVee*. The exclusivity of this transfer is clear from Maude's language in the note that she transferred the right "to do whatever you need to do" to "avenge"

DKAG's unauthorized use of *TeaVee* to "you [i.e., Jeff] (and you alone)." The breadth and lack of specificity of the language, though, makes the efficacy of the transfer questionable. Maude could have been clearer, and said, "I transfer to you the exclusive right to enforce the copyright in *TeaVee* on my behalf." Then again, Maude is a layperson and should not be held to the most exacting standard, especially since the policy of the Copyright Act is to encourage transfers, not to disqualify them for formal reasons. This is a hard issue, but a court seeking to enforce the pro-transfer policy of the Copyright Act would likely err in favor of concluding that the transfer was valid. Assuming that this is the case, it remains to consider whether the transfer would even be regarded as enforceable.

b. Is Maude's transfer to Jeff of the right to sue for infringement of *TeaVee* enforceable?

Even if Maude did make a valid transfer of right to sue for infringement of *TeaVee*, it remains unclear whether such a transfer is enforceable. The 1976 Act changed the 1909 Act's indivisibility approach that regarded copyrights as indivisible and capable only of wholesale transfer. § 202. Presently, copyrights may be divided and transferred however an owner wants. And while the Copyright Act limits the ability to sue for infringement to "owners" of copyrights, it defines this term broadly. In order to have standing, a party need only have "any of the exclusive rights" in the work. § 501(a). This section does not require that the "exclusive rights" to which it refers be the exclusive rights in section 106. Thus, one reading of this section is that as long as Maude transferred to Jeff the exclusive right to sue for infringements of *TeaVee*, Jeff has standing.

On the other hand, recent authority suggests a more narrow reading of this statute, one that requires that copyright plaintiffs retain some economic relationship with the work, and precluding parties who have received transfers of the right to sue for infringement (without more) are not enforceable. *Righthaven*. Courts that have articulated this distinction have expressed concern that where only the right to sue for infringement was assigned, the owner of the right to sue would no longer have incentives that were aligned with copyright's constitutional goals of disseminating and encouraging public knowledge, thereby encouraging strike suits and threats of litigation over trivial infringements. *Id.*

Jeff will argue that the plain language of the Copyright Act should prevail, and that he should be able to file suit, because the concern that animated the *Righthaven* court is not present. In contrast to *Righthaven*, the right to sue here was not delegated to enable multiple threats of litigation over trivial uses. Rather, it was assigned in order to enjoin a particular unauthorized use that was of concern to the author of *TeaVee*, to the party seeking to sue, and to aficionados of the genre. The de-linking of the copyright owner's interest and the right to sue is not present in this case (Jeff clearly has a strong stake in the enforcement of the copyright in *TeaVee*), and especially in light of the limited nature of the transfer (and the fact that Jeff seeks only injunctive relief), neither is the concern that Jeff will go around suing lots of trivial infringers to threaten them into lucrative settlements. Indeed, here the interests of the owner and the infringer seem perfectly aligned.

Jeff may further argue that a broad interpretation of the statute, permitting assignment of the right to sue, may actually be a positive development. It allows for interested parties to enforce the interests of owners who choose not to sue, generating more efficiency by taking away from owners the burden of enforcing their copyrights, and allowing delegation of that enforcement to specialists. On this view, *Righthaven* is just wrongly decided, for this reason and also because it is not supported by the plain language of the Copyright Act. If Congress wants to narrow the kinds of exclusive rightsholders who can sue for infringement in federal courts, it remains free to do so. Jeff will argue that this is a job for elected branches, not the courts. Finally, *Righthaven* is just a single case from the District of Colorado, and so not generally binding, and certainly not binding in the (admittedly fictional) District of Sobchak. And while *Righthaven* itself is a District of Colorado case, the Fifth Circuit's decision in *Prather* illustrates that courts are very much split on this issue. Indeed, *Prather* serves as comparatively weightier authority because it is from a higher court.

From a policy perspective, though, permitting assignment of only the right to sue for copyright infringement enables more problematic entities like Righthaven to exist and inflict social harm, even if Jeff himself does not threaten this concern. Finally, denying Jeff the right to sue in this case does not preclude wholesale resolution of the issue. Maude could sue if she wanted to, but she's said she just "doesn't care" that much. If she changes her mind and decides this is a big deal to her, she can always file suit herself.

    2. Did Maude have the right to transfer copyright in *TeaVee*?

        a. Does *TeaVee* possess requisite originality? And is Maude the sole owner of that copyright?

Federal copyright inheres only in original works of authorship fixed in tangible media of expression. § 102(a). That *TeaVee* is fixed is uncontroversial. The work was recorded on a digital video camera in .mp4 format, and then transferred to DVD-ROM. Such digital copies are unambiguously copies within the meaning of the Copyright Act.

Whether *TeaVee* is original is a somewhat harder question, though the answer is still also likely yes. While *TeaVee* merely features a record of someone watching television, this content is not something captured inadvertently with no artistic intentions, as might be the case with a home video of a person watching TV made with a cellphone camera. Rather, the content, as well as the placement of the camera, were inspired by related creative considerations, since Maude told Brandt she wanted it in a place where the viewer could see her face and also discern that she was watching television programs. In addition, the videotape includes a time-counter that indicates where Maude is in her television-watching marathon, a simple but creative touch that adds to the sense of the video being a marathon of TV watching.

Moreover, the amount of originality required to meet the statutory minimum is a "low bar," as the Supreme Court has emphasized in *Feist*. Far less creative video recordings, such as the Zapruder film, have been held sufficiently original to merit copyright protection. *See Time-Life*. In light of this relaxed standard, *TeaVee* has enough creativity (and therefore originality) to cross the low bar that would likely qualify for protection.

What might complicate Jeff's claim, though, is that whatever originality inheres in *TeaVee* inheres in the videotape itself, not in Maude's performance. Performance itself is not copyrightable. Fixations of audiovisual works of live-action events, such as performances or sports games, may be copyrightable—but only insofar as there is some originality in the fixation of the event itself. Here, the idea for and execution of the performance-art piece was Maude's, but the creation of the video recording was almost entirely Brandt's. He placed the camera, did all the technical work associated with the recording, edited the videotape afterward, and (at his own initiative) added the time counter to the final version of *TeaVee*. There is, in other words, a plausible argument that the author of *TeaVee* is *Brandt*, not Maude.

Maude would answer this point by arguing that while she may not have operated the video camera, she was the genesis of the creative ideas fixed in the video that gave it copyright-sufficient creativity. Like Napoleon Sarony, Maude may have no clue how the technical side of making videos works, but she effectively directed *TeaVee*, conceiving of the basic idea, and telling Brandt what to do in order to execute it. Brandt's choice to place the digital video camera behind the television, for example, was at Maude's discretion insofar as she told him that she wanted it placed where she could be seen as watching "awful junk on TV." On this theory, Brandt was just an amanuensis, contributing craftsmanship but no substantial originality to the final product. Maude, after all, registered the work in her own name, and nothing about their interactions suggests that Brandt thought of himself as the co-author of *TeaVee*. And the exhibitions and all other events associated with *TeaVee* appear to regard Maude as the work's sole author. Treehorn Productions appears to have approached Maude and Maude alone in seeking licensing for the work, to take just one example. This suggests that Maude is regarded by outside observers (and thus from an objective perspective) as the work's sole author.

Despite this, there remain flaws in the argument that Maude is the sole author of *TeaVee*. Brandt did not explicitly say anything about his authorship, but as a practical matter he actually did contribute original features of the final work. Maude gave him substantial latitude to place the video camera, and he took the initiative to add the time counter to the video without Maude's approval. It's true that Maude registered the work in her own name, but this gives her only a rebuttable presumption of the validity of her ownership, and is not dispositive. And outside perspectives are also not dispositive of Maude's authorship.

One might also suggest that at the very least, Maude and Brandt are joint authors, since they each contributed to the final work. This claim does well to reflect the extent to which there appear to be multiple authorial contributors to the final version of *TeaVee*. But Brandt may have difficulty making this argument in terms of Maude's (and everyone else's) assumption that she is the sole author. Even individuals who contribute substantial original material to a work of authorship will not be regarded as the work's author if the other contributor(s) did not regard them as co-equal collaborators, but mere helpers. *Aalmuhammed*. But also from the perspective of joint authorship, Maude might also have problems, because she contributed no copyrightable material. She thought of the idea for the film, but the video itself (the only aspect that is copyrightable) was fixed (filmed and edited) entirely by Brandt. (Though her *Sarony* argument that the creativity fixed in the video is hers might overcome this point, since she told Brandt how to create the video in the way she wanted). A joint authorship argument would likely fail, at least for Brandt.

3. Is there infringement?

Easily yes. DKAG is clearly publicly performing *TeaVee* without authorization. This is a public performance despite the DKAG's status as a private entity because the performance itself appears widely available to the public, *Aveco*, and was held at a place open to the public, *see* section 101 (defining "publicly" to include places open to the public). DKAG is showing *TeaVee* for massive profit and has earned $1 million in admission fees, obviating any argument that the performance is immune from liability under section 110(7)'s safe harbor for not-for-profit performances.

4. If there is infringement, does DKAG have an affirmative defense?

If Jeff can bring an infringement suit, and if the copyright in *TeaVee* remains valid, there is no question that DKAG's unauthorized exhibition violates exclusive public performance rights in the work. But DKAG may be able to raise an affirmative defense.

a. First sale

DKAG might raise a first sale defense, but such an argument would certainly fail. While DKAG is the legal owner of the copy of *TeaVee*, the first sale defense entitles DKAG only to engage in public distribution or public display of the work. *See* section 109(a), 109(c). It does not provide any defense to violations of the right of public performance. *See Aveco* (finding liability for unauthorized public performance even where infringer owned copies of work in suit).

b. Fair use

DKAG might also raise a fair use defense, but this defense too would likely lose. The question is whether DKAG's unauthorized, highly profitable public performance (not the content of *TeaVee* itself) counts as fair use.

The first factor strongly undermines DKAG's case for fair use. Their use is entirely commercial and not that transformative. DKAG is simply performing the work in a for-profit art gallery, largely for the purpose of raking in cash. This is an unequivocally commercial use, not just an incidental one. Moreover, DKAG's use is in virtually no way transformative. *TeaVee* was meant to be shown to audiences in an art theater, as it was during its initial exhibition. DKAG is doing just that, except that they're making far more money for the exhibition than SCMA did. This is the same use, both thematically and (though it does not matter as much) in terms of medium. DKAG might be able to pass the laugh test with an argument that they are changing the purpose of *TeaVee* because they are seeking to reach a broader audience than Maude did, by showing the video broadly instead of just for a month. But nothing in the facts substantiates this claim, and courts have defined transformation in terms of the thematic point of the work itself, which is not changed by a possibly slightly different agenda for the use by DKAG. Factor one strongly favors infringement, not fair use.

In terms of the second factor, the work is published (weighing marginally in favor of fair use) but is a thinly copyrighted, basically factual record of an event (weighing marginally against fair use). The second factor is likely a wash.

In terms of the third factor, DKAG used the whole of *TeaVee*. Use of the whole video was not clearly necessary—no one part seems more significant than any other, but one might imagine that you could show bits of it to get the effect. DKAG might respond that the point of *TeaVee* is to show a woman slowly pass out as she watches television, and that in order to make the point they needed to show the entire film in sequential order (though they could have done this in time-lapse, though that might have undermined the point of the film). The third factor does not weigh particularly strongly at all.

The fourth factor raises difficult issues. Maude's position on all her work, including *TeaVee*, is that she will not show or distribute copies to anyone after the initial exhibition. This suggests that Maude had already exhausted her preferred market for her work at the end of the initial showing of *TeaVee* at SCMA. In this sense, DKAG can argue that they did not cause any harm to the "market for or value of" *TeaVee* since there was no market for (or value of) the work. On this theory, Maude lost nothing. Maude's apparent indifference to DKAG's unauthorized performance (telling Jeff, "I don't really care" about their exhibition of the work) seems to support this theory. If Maude had secretly wanted to license *TeaVee* for future performance, she likely would have reacted differently when she learned about DKAG's unauthorized use. Maude appears to be experiencing dignitary, not economic, harm as a result of DKAG's use of *TeaVee*, and this is a harm not reflected in factor four of the fair use analysis. Maude could claim that she lost a theoretical license from DKAG, but this is likely a loser of an argument since markets must be "reasonable, customary, or likely to emerge," *see Texaco*, and Maude has given no indication that she is likely to license her works after their initial performance (nor does she need the money, as she stressed to Jeff).

Will DKAG's fair use defense succeed? It's a hard call. Factors two and three are largely inert, and they are rarely dispositive anyway. Factors one and four are likely diametrically opposed to each other: Factor one favors infringement, while factor four favors fair use. Since these are the two most important factors in any fair use analysis, this makes the fair use defense particularly difficult to resolve. One way to resolve it would be on the basis of policy. It favors fair use to think of this issue in terms of copyright's goal of increasing access to creative production. Maude's decision to keep her work under wraps after its initial exhibition may suit her taste, but it deprives many people of the ability to see her performance art. A finding of fair use in this case would have the effect of making her work more widely available, which is consistent with copyright's goal of enriching the public (as opposed to giving owners maximal control). On the other hand, the fair use defense is supposed to reward creative contributions in order to facilitate creation of work over time. That goal is hardly served here, where DKAG has done nothing to add to, comment on, or critique *TeaVee*, and is just engaging in pure unauthorized performance when it's done nothing to actually enhance or modify the work itself.

Fair use is a hard call. Since transformation tends to be an increasingly dominant factor for courts analyzing fair use, it's probably more likely than not that a court would find DKAG's use not to be fair, but a more market-oriented court could easily go the other way.

5. Are there any enforceable theories other than copyright infringement?

Jeff might also argue that DKAG's unauthorized use of *TeaVee* violates Maude's moral rights in the work. This argument bears initial appeal because the inspiration for the lawsuit appears to be that Jeff wants to redress a moral slight, not to get money from DKAG. This would explain why he is seeking only injunctive relief rather than money damages. Maude, too, appears offended by the unauthorized, largely commercial showing of *TeaVee* at the DKAG.

That said, there is no plausible moral rights argument available to Jeff under VARA. That statute applies only to "works of art," and that term as defined in section 101 does not include audiovisual works like *TeaVee*. See section 101 (defining "works of art" to exclude audiovisual works). A moral rights argument under section 43(a) of the Lanham Act, *cf. Gilliam*, would also likely be unavailing. The one Second Circuit case from the 1970s that held section 43(a) to be a basis for moral rights has never been developed since, and represents an outlier and very weak authority. Moreover, in that case the basis for the moral rights objection was that ABC heavily modified via editing Monty Python's show without telling viewers. Here, by contrast, DKAG showed audiences *TeaVee* in its entirety (though it's hard to imagine any viewers stayed for the entire 63-hour version). And, in any event, Jeff would have a hard time with either theory of moral rights also because moral rights are particular to a work's author, so Maude, not Jeff, would likely be the only party to have an injury that would warrant standing to sue.

II. Treehorn Productions v. DKAG

A. Situating the potential lawsuit

TP will argue that DKAG violated their exclusive right of public performance in their audiovisual works by performing the audio portion of those works without authorization in the context of DKAG's re-exhibition of *TeaVee*.

B. Does TP own a valid copyright?

Ownership of TP's material is not in dispute. TP is the production company that owns the copyrights in the audiovisual works that appear on the Treehorn Network. The real disputed issues are going to be infringement and fair use.

C. Has DKAG infringed TP's copyrights?

The answer to this question is almost certainly yes. DKAG is engaging in an unauthorized public performance of many of TP's copyrighted audiovisual works by publicly performing *TeaVee*, which is shown to any members of the public who pay admission to see it. To the extent that *TeaVee* has audio portions of TP's audiovisual works playing, that is still an unauthorized performance of their work. While *TeaVee* features only the audio portion of TP's works, that is no defense. A partial taking of a work, so long as the work is identifiable, is still infringement. And a *de minimis* argument would also fail. The standard for *de minimis* is that a reasonable viewer would not even recognize the work. *Ringgold*. Here, though, the audio of the TP audiovisual works is "clearly discernible" during *TeaVee*. Nor does it matter that the initial use of TP's works was made by Maude when she did the actual performance. By executing any protectable part of TP's audiovisual works without authorization, DKAG has infringed those copyrights.

1. Are there any affirmative defenses?

DKAG will also argue here that their use of TP's works by performing them publicly in the context of *TeaVee* amounts to fair use. In terms of the first factor, DKAG's use of the shows is somewhat commercial since they are clearly trying to get lots of profit from the showing. But that profit does not really derive from TP's shows. It's really a result of the popularity of *TeaVee*. Then again, *TeaVee* itself used TP's shows to earn its popularity. Certainly the contrast of a performance artist slowly passing out in disgust at the material shown on a conservative, family channel is part of the appeal of *TeaVee*.

Also in terms of the first factor, Maude's use certainly transformed TP's audiovisual works. TP's works were just broadly entertaining shows, but they are used in *TeaVee* as a way to illustrate the emptiness of television itself. It's a classic critique, something that fair use was made for. Here, too, the contrast is helpful—Maude is cynical and harsh, while TP's shows are sunny and light fare. From this perspective, one could even regard Maude as parodying TP's shows since *TeaVee* is a mockery of the material on television, and parody is classically considered fair use. Then again, it's not really a parody because Maude has no negative opinion of TP in particular. She chose the Treehorn Network in particular apparently at random, based on the opinion that all television is terrible. How can Maude be commenting on something she didn't even intend to single out?

The problem with this argument is that the use here is DKAG's showing of TP's works *as part of their showing TeaVee for commercial purposes*. The critical or parodic use is thus Maude's, not DKAG's. It is difficult to think of a reason they should be able to avoid liability when they did not generate the transformative use (though Maude well could have been able to argue that she should have been able to use this argument). In other words, Maude might be able to deploy a fair use defense that presents her use of TP's programming as critical commentary, but it is far less clear that DKAG can also do this, since it does not appear to be sharing Maude's message (or sending any message at all).

In terms of the second factor, TP's works were published, since they are widely screened television programs. This weighs slightly in favor of fair use. It is less clear that the works were purely fictional, since we have little information about them. The second factor may slightly favor fair use, but not enough to tip the balance in either direction.

In terms of the third factor, that only the audio portion of TP's shows appears in *TeaVee* helps DKAG's fair use argument. TP's shows were featured not in their entirety, but only to the extent that their use was necessary to "conjure up" the notion that Maude was watching television. If Maude had featured the entire video portion of the shows as well, this would be a harder argument for DKAG to make. The third factor thus favors fair use.

In terms of the fourth factor, it's a hard call. Certainly TP cannot argue that DKAG's use of its shows in the re-exhibition of *TeaVee* harmed the primary "market for or value of" its works. No one who wants to see the family-oriented, slightly conservative fare offered on the Treehorn Channel is going to pay for admission to DKAG to listen to audio from a random assemblage of those shows. Then again, the mere association between a highly successful exhibition of disparaging performance art and its shows might cause fans of the Treehorn Channel's programming to stay away. They might even (falsely) assume that TP allowed the use, which could send the message that they approve of *TeaVee* and its public exhibition. (Indeed, TP did initially try to negotiate for a license for the work.)

TP does, though, have a decent argument that DKAG harmed the *secondary* market for its work insofar as it did not seek a valid license to publicly perform its shows in the context of *TeaVee*. Such a market clearly exists. TP asked Maude for a license during the first exhibition of the video. They clearly have a pre-set licensing market, and a team of people willing to license. If they were willing to license Maude's use of their programs in the initial exhibition, they would certainly be willing to license them here (though they'd likely want more money since a more purely commercial exhibition is going on). Nor are there any transaction cost problems that make the market untenable, as in the case of photocopying. *Texaco*. Of course, the actual loss to TP appears to be small. TP was willing to license all the programs that appeared in *TeaVee* for a mere $350. This argument does not, though, undermine any claim to fair use. First, the fourth factor does not require that there is a substantial or costly market effect. Second, the amount of the license, while small when applied to SCMA's use, may be larger in the DKAG context because they are a for-profit institution.

DKAG's fair use argument will almost certainly fail. Their use itself (as opposed to Maude's initial use) was not particularly transformative, and they can and should have simply sought a license.

Two other possibly availing defenses would be laches and copyright estoppel. Laches likely fails since there is not a long enough lapse of time. Here, only a couple of years have passed since TP allowed the infringement at the SCMA exhibition to continue without enforcing their copyrights, and laches usually requires a showing that more than a decade has passed since the first nonenforcement of which the plaintiff was aware.

Copyright estoppel is also likely weak as an affirmative defense since there has been no distinct representation that TP will permit any use of their work in *TeaVee*, and certainly not that TP allowed Maude to use their works in her performance art piece. If anything, just the opposite was true: TP objected strenuously to the use of their works in *TeaVee*, but ultimately gave up because Maude put up such resistance and the fee at issue was so modest. Here, by contrast, the amount of value being extracted from TP's works is much greater, and a private for-profit institution like DKAG likely owes a greater licensing fee to owners such as TP for public performance.

Is there a statute of limitations problem? Close, but probably not. The statute of limitations for civil infringement is three years. Maude's initial unauthorized use of TP's works happened in 2009, and the showing at SCMA happened in 2012. Maude's initial use may have been infringing, but TP had no reason to know about it since it was not discernible, so by the discovery rule they likely could not have brought suit until December 2009, when *TeaVee* was widely shown at SCMA. Assuming TP filed suit by the end of November 2012, there would be no civil statute of limitations issue. The issue might be moot for a different reason: TP is suing a different party for a different infringing act that what may have infringed its copyright in 2009. DKAG's infringing act happened only in 2011 at the earliest, and so would not even be close to time-barred.

In all, it is pretty clear that DKAG has infringed TP's copyrights in its audiovisual works. There are no affirmative defenses available to save DKAG from what is a pretty straightforward instance of unauthorized use of TP's work. TP can recover damages (likely including multiple counts of statutory damages since the 63 hours must have covered multiple shows, and TP as a corporate entity likely had registered the copyrights in their works) from and enjoin use of their works by DKAG.

Index